Safe Maneuvering, Efficient Navigation and Intelligent Management for Ships

Safe Maneuvering, Efficient Navigation and Intelligent Management for Ships

Guest Editors

Chunhui Zhou
Yixiong He
Liang Huang

MDPI

Basel • Beijing • Wuhan • Barcelona • Belgrade • Novi Sad • Cluj • Manchester

Guest Editors
Chunhui Zhou
School of Navigation
Wuhan University of Technology
Wuhan
China

Yixiong He
School of Navigation
Wuhan University of Technology
Wuhan
China

Liang Huang
Intelligent Transportation Systems Research Center
Wuhan University of Technology
Wuhan
China

Editorial Office
MDPI AG
Grosspeteranlage 5
4052 Basel, Switzerland

This is a reprint of the Special Issue, published open access by the journal *Journal of Marine Science and Engineering* (ISSN 2077-1312), freely accessible at: https://www.mdpi.com/journal/jmse/special_issues/3793922XBB.

For citation purposes, cite each article independently as indicated on the article page online and as indicated below:

Lastname, A.A.; Lastname, B.B. Article Title. *Journal Name* **Year**, *Volume Number*, Page Range.

ISBN 978-3-7258-7494-1 (Hbk)
ISBN 978-3-7258-7495-8 (PDF)
https://doi.org/10.3390/books978-3-7258-7495-8

Contents

Journal of
*Marine Science
and Engineering*

MDPI

Editorial

Safe Maneuvering, Efficient Navigation and Intelligent Management for Ships

Chunhui Zhou [1,2,3], Yixiong He [1,3] and Liang Huang [2,4,*]

1 School of Navigation, Wuhan University of Technology, Wuhan 430063, China
2 State Key Laboratory of Maritime Technology and Safety, Wuhan University of Technology, Wuhan 430063, China
3 Hubei Key Laboratory of Inland Shipping Technology, Wuhan University of Technology, Wuhan 430063, China
4 Intelligent Transportation Systems Research Center, Wuhan University of Technology, Wuhan 430063, China
* Correspondence: leung.huang@whut.edu.cn

1. Introduction

Maritime transport, serving as the cornerstone of global supply chains, facilitates over 80% of international trade by volume. However, this traditional industry is confronting multifaceted challenges: increasingly congested waterways due to growing maritime traffic elevate the risks of collisions and groundings; stringent environmental regulations from the International Maritime Organization (IMO) impose hard constraints on ship energy efficiency and carbon emissions [1]; and a global shortage of highly skilled seafarers is becoming increasingly apparent. In this context, research on safe ship maneuvering, efficient navigation, and intelligent management is no longer optional but a core driver propelling the shipping industry toward a safe, green, and efficient future. Cutting-edge technologies, exemplified by artificial intelligence (AI), big data analytics, and complex system modeling, are fundamentally reshaping the ship's "perception–decision–action" loop [2]. This shift is transforming ship handling from an experience-dependent art into a science-based paradigm grounded in data and models.

2. An Overview of the Published Articles

Safety remains the top priority in shipping. While traditional safety measures heavily rely on human efforts, intelligent technologies aim to establish a proactive, data-driven safety framework based on human–machine collaboration. Current state-of-the-art research is advancing toward multi-modal information fusion. By integrating data from sources such as radar, computer vision, and AIS, modern intelligent ship systems can achieve all-weather perception beyond the visual horizon, enabling real-time detection and early warning of anomalous behaviors (e.g., deviation from fairways, dangerous approaches) for both their ship and target ships.

In this Special Issue, the study by Zhou et al. (Contribution 1) innovatively constructs an ontology model to identify abnormal ship behavior from a "navigation rule perspective." This approach structurally integrates human nautical knowledge with data, elevating anomaly detection from simple data deviation analysis to a process with semantic interpretability. This paves the way for higher-level situational reasoning and causal analysis by combining knowledge graphs with large models. Chen et al. (Contribution 9) employ Bi-YOLO and OC-SORT algorithms for target ship recognition and tracking. This exemplifies the successful application of edge computing and lightweight AI models in real-time navigation assistance systems, which are crucial for achieving continuous "situation awareness" in autonomous navigation environments. Regarding dynamic and complex risk quantification, Chen et al. (Contribution 4) propose a dynamic calculation method for collision risk in complex navigable waters, where it essentially functions as a real-time decision-support system.

Building on accurate perception, the value of intelligent decision-making lies in prediction and optimization. This Special Issue demonstrates significant progress in ship motion prediction and autonomous control. In the realm of data-driven motion prediction and adaptive control, Guo et al. (Contribution 5) utilize LSTM networks to predict the maneuvering motion of Unmanned Surface Vehicles (USVs), while Wang et al. (Contribution 6) improve the Deep Deterministic Policy Gradient (DDPG) algorithm to optimize the PID controller for USV trajectory tracking. These two studies exemplify the integration of "AI + Control": the former forecasts future states through temporal models, while the latter adaptively adjusts control policies via reinforcement learning to cope with complex sea conditions [3]. This marks a transition in ship control from traditional model-driven methods toward more resilient and self-learning, data-driven approaches.

In multi-agent collaboration and formation control, Tao et al. (Contribution 10) investigate cooperative formation control for multiple ships under time-delay conditions, and Han et al. (Contribution 3) adopt a multi-agent method to simulate ship movements in and out of the port in the Qiongzhou Strait waters. These studies extend intelligence from a single vessel to the coordinated optimization of ship groups. This represents a core characteristic for future intelligent shipping systems—leveraging algorithms like multi-agent reinforcement learning to achieve global optimal utilization of systemic resources such as ports and waterways. Optimizing the sequence of port entries/exits and berthing schedules can effectively reduce port turnaround times, providing a theoretical foundation for alleviating congestion and enhancing efficiency [4].

Intelligent shipping entails not only technological upgrades for individual ships but also the holistic reshaping of the entire maritime transportation system. Several articles in this collection, from a macroscopic systemic perspective, reveal the value of new technologies in enhancing system reliability and assessing external impacts. Han et al. (Contribution 8) apply percolation theory to analyze the reliability of the complex inland waterway transportation network in the Yangtze River. This is a typical big data system modeling approach capable of quantifying the impact of critical node or link failures on the entire network. Liu and Yu (Contributions 7 and 12) empirically analyze the impacts of nearshore and deep-sea offshore wind farm construction on maritime traffic complexity and safety, respectively. Such research fully leverages historical AIS big data, employing data mining and spatial analysis to quantify the interactions between human marine engineering activities and shipping operations. This provides critical decision support for future marine spatial planning and the synergistic development of "shipping-energy" systems.

This Special Issue also addresses emerging and sustainable topics such as polar navigation and alternative fuels. Liu et al. (Contribution 13) and Wang et al. (Contribution 14) investigate the influence of Antarctic sea ice and ship maneuvering in floating ice fields, respectively. These studies combine AI with physical models (e.g., coupled NDEM–MMG modeling) through numerical simulations to explore ship maneuverability in extreme, unstructured environments, accumulating valuable knowledge for the future development of polar routes. Zhou et al. (Contribution 2) analyze pathways for reducing the carbon emissions of ships in the Yangtze River using alternative fuels. Although not directly focused on AI, the findings from this work could serve as constraints embedded into

AI-based fleet energy efficiency management systems, guiding ships to make economically and environmentally sound decisions in areas like route planning and speed optimization.

Funding: This research was funded by the National Natural Science Foundation of China, grant numbers 52171349, 52071249, 52572388, and 42471497, and a research project grant from Shanghai Investigation, Design & Research Institute Co., Ltd. (project No. 2023 FD(83)-002).

Acknowledgments: This paper was edited with the assistance of DeepSeek-V3.2 (accessed 21 October 2025). I have critically assessed and validated any generated feedback. The final version of the paper is my own creation.

Conflicts of Interest: The authors declare no conflicts of interest.

List of Contributions:

1. Zhou, C.; Wen, K.; Zhao, J.; Bian, Z.; Lu, T.; Ko Ko Latt, M.; Wang, C. Ontology-Based Method for Identifying Abnormal Ship Behavior: A Navigation Rule Perspective. *J. Mar. Sci. Eng.* **2024**, *12*, 881. https://doi.org/10.3390/jmse12060881.
2. Zhou, C.; Tang, W.; Ding, Y.; Huang, H.; Xu, H. Analysis of Carbon Emission Reduction Paths for Ships in the Yangtze River: The Perspective of Alternative Fuels. *J. Mar. Sci. Eng.* **2024**, *12*, 947. https://doi.org/10.3390/jmse12060947.
3. Han, D.; Cheng, X.; Chen, H.; Xiao, C.; Wen, Y.; Sui, Z. Simulation Modeling for Ships Entering and Leaving Port in Qiongzhou Strait Waters: A Multi-Agent Information Interaction Method. *J. Mar. Sci. Eng.* **2024**, *12*, 1560. https://doi.org/10.3390/jmse12091560.
4. Chen, Y.; Yu, Q.; Wang, W.; Wu, X. Dynamic Calculation Approach of the Collision Risk in Complex Navigable Water. *J. Mar. Sci. Eng.* **2024**, *12*, 1605. https://doi.org/10.3390/jmse12091605.
5. Guo, R.; Mao, Y.; Xiang, Z.; Hao, L.; Wu, D.; Song, L. Research on LSTM-Based Maneuvering Motion Prediction for USVs. *J. Mar. Sci. Eng.* **2024**, *12*, 1661. https://doi.org/10.3390/jmse12091661.
6. Wang, X.; Yi, H.; Xu, J.; Xu, C.; Song, L. PID Controller Based on Improved DDPG for Trajectory Tracking Control of USV. *J. Mar. Sci. Eng.* **2024**, *12*, 1771. https://doi.org/10.3390/jmse12101771.
7. Liu, J.; Yu, W.; Sui, Z.; Zhou, C. The Impact of Offshore Wind Farm Construction on Maritime Traffic Complexity: An Empirical Analysis of the Yangtze River Estuary. *J. Mar. Sci. Eng.* **2024**, *12*, 2232. https://doi.org/10.3390/jmse12122232.
8. Han, D.; Sui, Z.; Xiao, C.; Wen, Y. Reliability of Inland Water Transportation Complex Network Based on Percolation Theory: An Empirical Analysis in the Yangtze River. *J. Mar. Sci. Eng.* **2024**, *12*, 2361. https://doi.org/10.3390/jmse12122361.
9. Chen, S.; Gao, M.; Shi, P.; Zeng, X.; Zhang, A. Target Ship Recognition and Tracking with Data Fusion Based on Bi-YOLO and OC-SORT Algorithms for Enhancing Ship Navigation Assistance. *J. Mar. Sci. Eng.* **2025**, *13*, 366. https://doi.org/10.3390/jmse13020366.
10. Tao, W.; Tan, J.; Sui, Z.; Wang, L.; Xiong, X. Cooperative Formation Control of Multiple Ships with Time Delay Conditions. *J. Mar. Sci. Eng.* **2025**, *13*, 549. https://doi.org/10.3390/jmse13030549.
11. Chen, J.; Han, Y.; Li, R.; He, Z.; Zhang, Y. Research on the Coupling Dynamics Characteristics of Underwater Multi-Body Separation Considering the Influence of Elastic Constraints. *J. Mar. Sci. Eng.* **2025**, *13*, 627. https://doi.org/10.3390/jmse13040627.
12. Yu, W.; Liu, J.; Yan, P.; Jiang, X. Research on the Impact of Deep Sea Offshore Wind Farms on Maritime Safety. *J. Mar. Sci. Eng.* **2025**, *13*, 699. https://doi.org/10.3390/jmse13040699.
13. Liu, W.; Yan, D.; Peng, Z.; Xie, M.; Sun, Y. Vessel Safety Navigation Under the Influence of Antarctic Sea Ice. *J. Mar. Sci. Eng.* **2025**, *13*, 1267. https://doi.org/10.3390/jmse13071267.
14. Wang, D.; Zou, L.; Zhang, Z.; Chen, X. Numerical Study on Non-Icebreaking Ship Maneuvering in Floating Ice Based on Coupled NDEM–MMG Modeling. *J. Mar. Sci. Eng.* **2025**, *13*, 1578. https://doi.org/10.3390/jmse13081578.

References

1. Halple, P.; Adams, M.; Walker, T. Challenges and opportunities for ports in achieving net-zero emissions in maritime transport. *Transp. Res. Interdiscip. Perspect.* **2025**, *30*, 101379. [CrossRef]
2. Söffker, D.; Bejaoui, A.; Shyshova, O. Progress towards multidimensionally scalable assisted and/or automated ship navigation and control—Part II: Human in the interaction loop. *J. Mar. Eng. Technol.* **2025**, *24*, 294–304. [CrossRef]
3. Lisowski, J. Artificial Intelligence Methods in Safe Ship Control Based on Marine Environment Remote Sensing. *Remote Sens.* **2023**, *15*, 203. [CrossRef]
4. Zheng, H.; Wang, Z.; Duan, S. Integrated optimization of vessel sequencing and bulk carrier berth allocation with shifting in a comprehensive port. *Ocean Eng.* **2025**, *316*, 119891. [CrossRef]

Journal of
Marine Science and Engineering

MDPI

Article

Ontology-Based Method for Identifying Abnormal Ship Behavior: A Navigation Rule Perspective

Chunhui Zhou [1,2], Kunlong Wen [1,2], Junnan Zhao [1,2,*], Ziyuan Bian [1,2], Taotao Lu [1,2], Myo Ko Ko Latt [1,2] and Chengli Wang [3]

[1] School of Navigation, Wuhan University of Technology, Wuhan 430063, China; chunhui@whut.edu.cn (C.Z.); charliewkl@163.com (K.W.); bzy@whut.edu.cn (Z.B.); lutaotao@whut.edu.cn (T.L.); myoko2latt89@gmail.com (M.K.K.L.)
[2] Hubei Key Laboratory of Inland Shipping Technology, Wuhan 430063, China
[3] Zhejiang Scientific Research Institute of Transport, Hangzhou 310039, China; 15868873946@163.com
* Correspondence: junnan@whut.edu.cn

Abstract: Navigation rules are critical for regulating ship behavior, and effective water traffic management requires accurate identification of ships exhibiting abnormal behavior that violates these rules. To address this need, this paper presents an ontology-based method for identifying abnormal ship behavior. First, we analyzed navigation rules (local regulations) to extract key elements. Next, based on this extraction, we built a navigation rule ontology that categorized ship behavior into state behavior (ship behavior at a specific time point) and process behavior (ship behavior in a time interval). We then constructed an abnormal ship behavior ontology, defined using topological relationships and navigation rules. Finally, we constructed inference rules to detect abnormal ship behaviors by using SWRL (Semantic Web Rule Language) and validated the effectiveness of the method with ship instances. The experimental results demonstrate that this method can accurately infer ships' behaviors that deviate from established navigation rules. This research has significant implications for reducing waterborne traffic accidents, improving navigational safety, and safeguarding maritime traffic.

Keywords: navigation rules; abnormal behavior; ontology modeling; SWRL; behavioral inference

1. Introduction

Maritime safety is crucial for the growth of the shipping economy. With the increasing number of vessels, traffic dynamics are becoming increasingly complex, and individual ship behavior is more variable, leading to frequent occurrences of abnormal behavior. Ship anomalies can cause severe consequences, including loss of life, environmental pollution, and property damage, posing significant challenges to maritime traffic regulation and navigational safety. Consequently, conducting research on ship behavior anomaly detection is both necessary and urgent.

With the advancement of maritime monitoring technology, spatial-temporal data on maritime traffic is growing rapidly. A behavior pattern matching model can be constructed to identify abnormal ship behavior by extracting statistical features from historical ship data [1] and analyzing ship behavior patterns [2]. To regulate ship behavior, some waterways have designated fairways and traffic channels, as well as establishing navigation rules such as Traffic Separation Schemes and routing systems. These local navigational rules are particularizations of the International Regulations for Preventing Collisions at Sea (COLREGs), with the goal of adapting to the navigational environments of the local water area while being generally bound by COLREG Rule 10. However, there is currently a lack of effective monitoring methods for detecting ship anomalies that violate navigation rules. Relying solely on manual monitoring (observation and evaluation of vessel behavior by human operators) is insufficient to meet the demands of modern regulatory requirements. Utilizing computational methods to semantically represent navigational rules facilitates the comprehension, interpretation, and effective identification of vessel anomalous behaviors in violation of regulations, thereby significantly enhancing the level of intelligent regulatory oversight.

Ontology, as a computationally recognizable tool [3], compensates for manual monitoring's inadequacies. As a method of knowledge representation, ontology provides a unified semantic framework [4], facilitating systematic modeling and expression of complex navigational rules knowledge, thereby enhancing the understanding of navigational regulations. In maritime regulation, the use of ontology to construct semantic models of navigational rules and vessel behavior enables information sharing and reuse, thereby enhancing the intelligence level of regulatory systems. Ontology enables the effective monitoring and identification of vessel anomalous behaviors by integrating navigational rules and vessel behavior data.

This paper proposes an ontology-based inference method for identifying abnormal ship behavior. The goal is to gain a fundamental understanding and explanation of ship behavior patterns through the analysis and modeling of navigation rules and ship behavior. It allows us to identify abnormal ship behavior that deviates from the rules. This research contributes to a better understanding of abnormal ship behavior and better identification of risk factors, ultimately improving maritime traffic regulation and navigational safety.

The other chapters of this paper are organized as follows: Section 2 reviews some related works; Section 3 introduces the methods for parsing navigation rules and extracting key elements, ontology construction, and ship behavior inference; Section 4 presents the experiments and analysis; Section 5 discusses the method; and Section 6 concludes.

2. Literature Review

2.1. Related Research on the Application of Ontology Technology

Ontology technology, as a formal method of knowledge representation, has been widely applied across diverse domains, including transportation, agriculture, finance, and others.

In the domain of transportation, Yang et al. [5] utilized urban traffic ontology to achieve a unified representation of urban traffic information, as well as to define rules and algebraic operations for semantic fusion at the ontology level, aiming to achieve semantic integrity and consistency in city traffic information. David [6] proposed a transport disruption ontology for modeling events related to travel and transportation that have disruptive impacts on travelers' journeys. It described how to capture traffic accidents and their impacts, as well as outlining the use of ontology rules in an interconnected travel information repository to support intelligent transportation systems. Agarwal et al. [7] utilized knowledge graph-assisted means to ontologize airworthiness rules. Once users created an original design ontology for aircrafts, they could compare it with the airworthiness rule ontology to identify any design vulnerabilities. Bagschik et al. [8] used ontology-based knowledge and modeling and production rule-based knowledge inference to understand the evolutionary dynamics of autonomous transportation systems, focusing on the transition from sparse to dense networks and the gradual increase in network efficiency. Additionally, they designed and implemented a flight safety information ontology that included key components of flight operation information. Mahdi et al. [9] employed the aviation network and methodology based on the Internet Protocol Suite (IPS) to construct a flight information ontology. They used Protege software to conduct the implementation process and reasoning, and they analyzed the system using actual data from Mashhad Airport in Iran.

In other domains, Malik [10] addressed the current lack of agricultural ontology development by proposing a generic method for representing entities and their relationships in an agricultural ontology, achieving the development of domain-specific ontologies in agriculture. Altinok [11] introduced an ontology-driven dialogue manager (OntoDM) to maintain dialogue state and coherence through domain ontologies. This method leverages domain knowledge to track entities of interest, such as products and services, thereby introducing dialogue memory and attention mechanisms, which are particularly applied in the banking and finance domain. Edison [12] constructed ontologies for renal tissue mapping and precision medicine research, facilitating comprehensive mapping of renal molecular, cellular, and anatomical profiles, improving renal data annotation, and redefining renal diseases, thus advancing precision medicine. Ayesha [13] developed an educational ontology detailing various university courses, serving as a guide for students to select future courses according to their needs.

2.2. Related Research on the Application of Ontology Technology in the Maritime Field

Ontology has also been extensively applied in the maritime domain. Song et al. [14], from the perspective of interpretable knowledge modeling, provided a computer-understandable method for behavior modeling. They provided a semantic model (Cognition Modeling and Semantic Reasoning of Ship) for defining ship behavior by combining multi-scale features in cognitive space. Zhong et al. [15] developed an ontological model of ship behavior based on COLREGs, with the goal of assisting machines in comprehending COLREG regulations using knowledge graph technology. The research considers ships as spatiotemporal objects, with behaviors described as variations in object elements at spatiotemporal scales, implemented using the resource description framework (RDF), function mapping, and set expression methods. Wen et al. [16] proposed a semantic model of ship behavior (SMSB), establishing a semantic network grounded in maritime traffic rules and good seamanship. They identified basic ship behavior in various aquatic scenes by constructing ontologies. A semantic model of in-harbor ship behavior based on ontology and the Dynamic Bayesian Network (DBN) was utilized to infer potential ship behavior. Georgios [17] proposed an Ontology-Based Data Access (OBDA) framework for effective maritime surveillance and event management through data access. This framework integrates real-time and historical vessel data to detect complex events and support decision-making. Roy [18] introduced an automatic reasoning concept verification model based on description logics to assist maritime personnel in detecting vessel anomalies and identifying maritime risks. Mirna [19] presented an Ontology-Based International Maritime Law Liability Decision Support System. The system analyzes carrier and shipper liability in cases of cargo loss or damage, utilizing a legal domain ontology called CargO-S to support the design and implementation of chained rules describing liability legal rules. Yu [20] addressed the semantic heterogeneity of heterogeneous data in maritime search and rescue operations through ontology, facilitating knowledge acquisition, sharing, and reuse.

2.3. Related Research on Abnormal Ship Behavior

A large number of scholars have conducted research on the detection of abnormal behavior in ships. According to the type of technology used, this study can be divided into traditional methods and deep learning-based methods. Most traditional methods are designed to detect or recognize specific scenes. Murray [21] utilized the DBSCAN clustering algorithm to cluster ships' trajectories, established a historical trajectory atlas based on the clustering results, and employed the trajectories of normal ships as the standard for judging abnormal behavior. Li [22] proposed a ship behavior anomaly detection method based on trajectory analysis and Dynamic Time Warping (DTW). Abnormal trajectories that deviate from normal behavior are identified by calculating the similarity between trajectories and employing the DTW algorithm for trajectory matching and comparison. Gözde [23] introduced a maritime anomaly behavior detection method based on trajectory pattern analysis. Abnormal trajectories that deviate from normal behavior are identified by extracting features from ship trajectories and applying pattern recognition techniques to predict ship trajectories.

In addition to the traditional methods mentioned above, deep learning-based methods are the mainstream abnormal ship behavior detection methods at present. Singh [24] proposed a framework for anomaly detection based on a multi-class artificial neural network (ANN) to classify intentional and unintentional AIS switch anomalies. Vespe [25] utilized historical AIS data and employed unsupervised learning algorithms, without the need for any specific prior-context descriptions, to identify vessel motion patterns. This facilitated vessel trajectory anomaly detection and enhanced maritime situational awareness by providing vessel traffic characteristics. Yang [26] proposed an abnormal ship behavior recognition method based on LSTM. By manually labeling abnormal ship behavior states and learning from a large amount of ship AIS data, they established an abnormal ship behavior recognition model and trained it on the TensorFlow platform. Liu [27] introduced the attention mechanism into GRU, obtained optimal GRU structural parameters through intelligent algorithms, and utilized the optimized GRU neural network for deeper feature extraction and training of abnormal ship behavior. Zhang [28] utilized trajectory clustering results as a reference model to train the Bidirectional Gated Recurrent Unit (BiGRU) recurrent neural network for real-time ship anomaly detection. The trajectory prediction results of the BiGRU model exhibited minimal error compared to the actual ship trajectories, indicating superior trajectory prediction performance.

Several studies on semantic analysis of abnormal ship behavior have been conducted, but research on detecting and inferring ship anomalies in relation to navigation rules remains relatively limited. This paper proposes an ontology-based inference method for detecting abnormal ship behavior in accordance with navigation rules. First, the key elements of navigation rules are extracted through rule analysis. Next, the navigation rules ontology is constructed, with ship behavior categorized and expressed accordingly. Then, based on the Semantic Web Rule Language (SWRL), inference rules for ship anomalies are developed to enable automated inference of abnormal ship behavior. Finally, experiments are conducted to validate the effectiveness of this anomaly detection approach.

3. Methodology

The framework for inferring abnormal ship behaviors predicated on the ontology of navigational rules is delineated in Figure 1. The methodology for this inference is structured in a four-step process that involves navigation rule analysis and element extraction, as well as the construction of both the navigational rule ontology and the abnormal ship behavior ontology, followed by the formulation of Semantic Web Rule Language (SWRL) inference rules to facilitate the reasoning of abnormal ship behaviors. The process commences with the dissection of textual content pertaining to navigational rules, employing a Latent Dirichlet Allocation (LDA) model to distill key elements from these rules. Subsequently, leveraging these extracted key elements, an ontology of navigational rules is established. Then, the ship behaviors are classified and expressed based on the navigation rules ontology. Ultimately, an ontology for abnormal ship behaviors is constructed, and the SWRL is utilized to devise conditional-action production rule reasoning, enabling the inference of abnormal behaviors in ships.

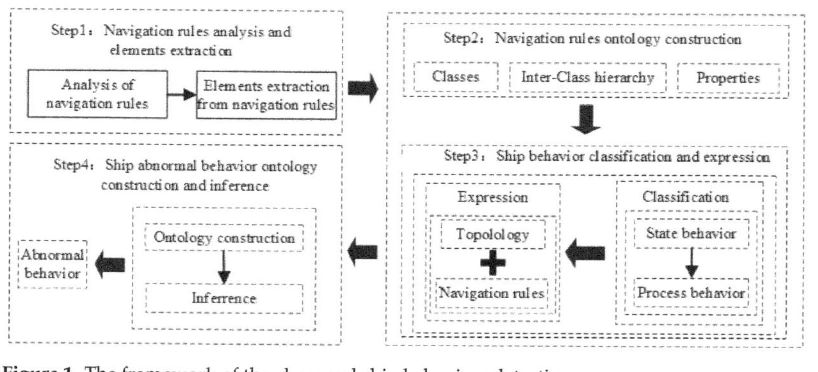

Figure 1. The framework of the abnormal ship behaviors detection.

3.1. Navigation Rule Analysis and Element Extraction

Navigation rules are important guidelines to regulate the behavior of ships, and by parsing the textual content of navigation rules, we can more comprehensively mine the information related to the behavior of ships, so as to extract the elements in the navigation rules.

3.1.1. Analysis of Navigation Rules

In this paper, the regulation of a routing system of the Yangtze River was taken as the research object, and the text content was analyzed to realize the extraction of navigation rules. The regulations consisted of 6 chapters, 33 articles, and 10 annexes covering traffic channel rules, maneuvering rules, berthing rules, and avoidance rules to ensure the safe navigation of ships.

(1) Traffic channel rules

Traffic channel rules were categorized into traffic separation rules and recommended channel rules. Deepwater channels were constructed with upstream and downstream traffic lanes and a separation zone. The traffic separation rules are mainly applicable to large vessels to avoid grounding and other obstacles. The recommended channel rules are largely intended to ensure that smaller vessels can navigate effectively on the recommended routes while also limiting the types of vessels and the speed restrictions.

(2) Maneuvering rules

The maneuvering rules were divided into speed rules, position rules, reporting rules, overtaking rules, large ship navigation rules, small ship navigation rules, high-speed ship navigation rules, special rules, and bridge water area navigation rules.

Speed rules limit the minimum and maximum speeds during maneuvering in the channel. The reporting rules stipulate ships to make position reports at specified positions. Position rules specify the navigational areas for different types of ships. The overtaking rules stipulate the behaviors of the overtaking vessel and the overtaken vessel during the overtaking process. Large ship rules, small ship rules, and high-speed ship rules limit the speed and position of large vessels, small vessels, and high-speed vessels, respectively. The special rules stipulate the navigation requirements for ships in special areas such as precaution areas. The bridge water area rules stipulate the mandatory behavioral norms of ships while passing through this area.

(3) Berthing rules

Berthing rules are categorized into berthing rules for large ships, berthing rules for small ships, and berthing rules for special cases. The berthing rules for large ships require large ships to berth within the limited area declared by a competent authority. Berthing rules for small ships stipulate that small ships should be moored in a specific area. The berthing rules for special cases stipulate for ships to be moored under special conditions.

(4) Avoidance rules

Avoidance rules are divided into general area avoidance rules and special area avoidance rules. The general area avoidance rules stipulate the avoidance requirements for ships navigating on the waterway and recommended channels. Special area avoidance rules provide for the avoidance of ships in special areas such as estuaries, tributaries, and specialized waterways.

According to the text of the navigation rules, a total of 22 rules ($Rule_i = \{rule_1, rule_2 \ldots, rule_{22}\}$) were extracted to establish the different types of rules, as in Table 1; the specific content of each rule is shown in Appendix A.

Table 1. Extractions of navigation rules.

Types of Navigation Rules	Categories	Rules
Traffic channel rules	traffic separation rules	$rule_1$
	recommended channel rules	$rule_2$
Maneuvering rules	speed rules	$rule_3$, $rule_4$
	position rules	$rule_5$, $rule_6$
	reporting rules	$rule_7$, $rule_8$
	overtaking rules	$rule_9$
	large ship rules	$rule_{10}$
	small ship rules	$rule_{11}$
	high-speed ship rules	$rule_{11}$
	special rules	$rule_{12}$
	bridge water area rules	$rule_{13}$, $rule_{14}$, $rule_{15}$, $rule_{16}$, $rule_{17}$
Berthing rules	berthing rules for large ships	$rule_{18}$
	berthing rules for small ships	$rule_{19}$
	berthing rules for special cases	$rule_{20}$
Avoidance rules	general area avoidance rules	$rule_{21}$
	special area avoidance rules	$rule_{22}$

3.1.2. Element Extraction from Navigation Rules

In the study of navigation rules, revealing the underlying themes behind the text helps us to extract the key elements in the rules for a more comprehensive understanding. The LDA (Latent Dirichlet Allocation) model, which treats a document as a combination of multiple themes and describes each theme as a probability distribution of a particular vocabulary word, provides technical support for the extraction of the relevant elements of the navigation rules.

The LDA model treats documents as a combination of multiple topics, representing each topic as a probability distribution over a specific vocabulary. This approach facilitates the understanding and classification of complex navigation rule documents. By employing statistical methods, LDA identifies word patterns within documents and clusters these patterns into distinct topics, effectively revealing the main focus and structure of navigation rules. Additionally, LDA's capability to handle unlabeled data makes it particularly suitable for processing large-scale navigation rule texts, which typically lack predefined labels. This enables the discovery of hidden themes and relationships, thereby supporting the element extraction of navigation rules.

The following are the basic steps of LDA modeling:

(a) Initialize the parameters. Determine the number of topics to be modeled K; determine the number of words in the vocabulary V. The hyperparameters α and β are used to control the sparsity of the topic distribution and the word distribution.
(b) Random assignment of topics. For each vocabulary word in each document, a topic is randomly selected as the initial assignment.
(c) Iterative inference. For each vocabulary word w in each document d, reassign topics; for each topic k, calculate P(topic k | document d) $\times$ P(vocabulary word w | topic k). Reassign topics based on the calculated probabilities.
(d) Statistics on topic and vocabulary distribution. Count the number of occurrences of each topic k in a document and compute the topic distribution P(topic k | document d). Count the number of occurrences of each vocabulary word w in topic k and calculate the vocabulary distribution P(vocabulary word w | topic k).
(e) Repeat steps (c) and (d) until the model converges or reaches a predetermined number of iterations.
(f) Theme analysis and element extraction. After the model has converged, extract the theme distribution of each document, analyze the vocabulary composition of each theme, and find the elements related to them in the navigation rules. At the same

time, according to the needs of ontology construction, manually delete and change the elements in a targeted manner, so as to establish the actual elements.

Based on the elements in the navigation rules in the LDA model, the relevant elements in the navigation rules are mainly the navigation rules (Rules), the (Ships), the (Area), the (Time), the (Trajectory), and the (Behavior), as shown in Table 2.

Table 2. Element extraction.

Types of Elements	Categories	Explanation
Rules	Traffic channel rules	Regulations for traffic routes
	Maneuvering rules	Regulations for ship navigation
	Berthing rules	Regulations for berthing process of ship
	Avoidance rules	Regulations for ship collision avoidance
Ships	Large ship	Length greater than 80 m
	Small ship	Length less and equal than 80 m
	High-speed ship	Speed more than 19 kn
Area	Recommended channel	A route for small ships to navigate
	Deepwater channel	A route for large ships to navigate
	Bridge water area	Water area near the bridge
	Special area	Special precaution area
	Anchorage	Designated position to anchor
Time	Timestamp	At a certain moment
	Time period	A period of time
Trajectory	Trajectory point	Single trajectory point
	Trajectory segment	A line segment connecting multiple trajectory points
Behavior	State behavior	The ship behavior at a certain moment
	Process behavior	The ship behavior in a period of time

3.2. Ontology Construction

In this section, the navigation rule ontology is constructed to convert the navigation rule elements into a structured knowledge base, so as to realize the knowledge sharing of navigation rules. Based on the rule knowledge base, the classification and expression of ship behavior is realized, and then the ontology of abnormal ship behavior is constructed.

3.2.1. Navigation Rule Ontology Construction

This section establishes a navigation rule ontology from the perspective of navigation rule cognition, encompassing the construction of classes and property relationships. Based on the previous analysis of navigation rules and the extraction of relevant elements, three elements—Ships, Rules, and Area—are identified as classes within the navigation rule ontology. Additionally, different navigational rules apply to vessels within various spatial domains. To determine the applicable navigational rules for each Area element, the rules are matched with the Area elements, and the results are stored in the Space_rules class. These four classes are the key to the cognition of navigation rules, as shown in Figure 2; the ontology model of navigation rule cognition, which contains the four elements of navigation rule cognition, can provide a framework to support the cognition of navigation rules.

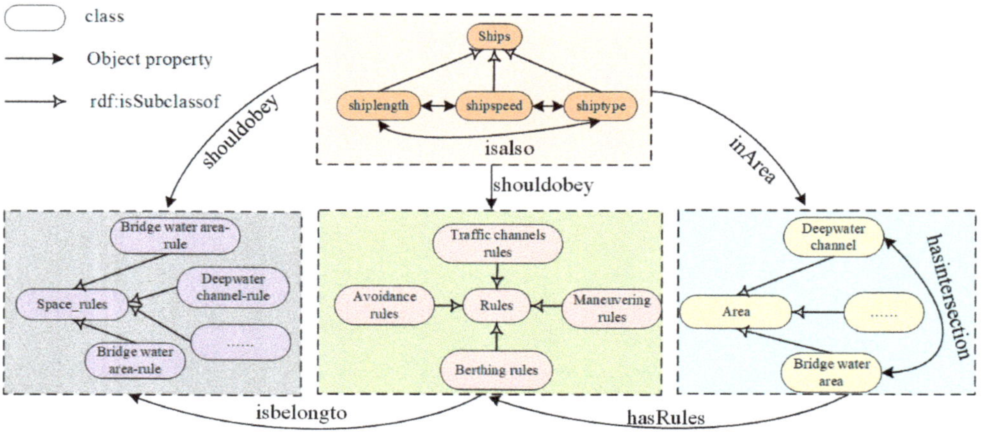

Figure 2. The ontology model for navigation rules.

(1) Class

The Ships class represents ships. A ship is mainly for water transportation and is the basic concept in navigation rules, and the individual ship is represented by MMSI.

The Rules class represents the rules. Rules refer to the navigation regulations that ships navigating in the water should comply with, including traffic channel rules, maneuvering rules, berthing rules, and avoidance rules.

The Area class represents the spatial elements of the waterway. According to the extraction of spatial elements and different navigable waters delineated by the maritime authorities, the fairway is divided into the deepwater channel, recommended channel, anchorage, special area, bridge water area, and other Area elements, each of which contains different subclasses of elements.

The Space_rules class represents the matching of different Area elements with rules.

(2) Object property

According to the relationship between classes, the corresponding relationship properties are established to further improve the expression ability of the navigation rule ontology knowledge, as shown in Table 3.

Table 3. The object properties in navigation rules.

Object Properties	Explanation
hasintersection	The intersection relationship between Area
hasRules, isruleof	The relationship between Area and Rules (inverse of each other)
hasShips, inArea	The relationship between Area and Ships (inverse of each other)
shouldobey	The relationship between Rules and Ships
isbelongto	The relationship between Rules and Space_rules

(3) Data property

Based on the object property between classes alone, it is difficult to accurately express the knowledge of navigation rules, and it is also necessary to define the data property of the concepts. The specific data property settings are shown in Table 4.

Table 4. The data properties in navigation rules.

Data Properties	Explanation
Course	Ship's heading
Lat	Latitude
Length	Ship's length
Lon	Longitude
MMSI	Maritime Mobile Service Identify
Speed	Ship's speed
Type	Ship's type
Width	Ship's width
hasPoint	Point Area element's position
hasLine	Linear Area element's range
hasPolygon	Planar Area element's range
hasName	Area element's name
hasString	Rules' text
hasImportance	The importance of rules

Course, Lat, Length, Lon, MMSI, Speed, Type, and *Width* all represent the data properties of the Ships, which correspond to heading, latitude, longitude, longitude, mobile service identification, speed, ship type, ship width, and other information, respectively.

hasLine, hasPoint, hasPolygon, hasNumber, and *hasName* represent the data properties of the Area elements. *hasPoint* represents the Area element as a point, *hasLine* represents the Area element as a line, *hasPolygon* represents the Area element as a surface, and *hasNumber* is the number of the Area element. *hasName* is the name of the Area element.

hasString and *hasImportance* are the data properties of the Rules. *hasString* indicates that the rule is expressed as a string, and *hasImportance* indicates the importance level of the set rule.

3.2.2. Abnormal Ship Behavior Ontology Construction

The classification and expression of ship behavior is the basis for establishing an ontology of abnormal ship behavior. By classifying and expressing ship behaviors, the scope and characteristics of various ship behaviors can be more clearly understood, so as to effectively determine which behaviors may be abnormal. Accurate behavior classification and expression provide reliable training data and benchmarks for the abnormal ship behavior ontology, which improves its accuracy and efficiency. Therefore, standardized ship behavior classification and expression are essential before the construction of abnormal behavior ontology.

(1) Ship behavior classification

Through the analysis of navigation rules, ship behavior is divided into 2 categories: state behavior and process behavior.

(a) Ship state behavior

Ship state behavior is the state of the ship at any moment. Ship state behavior can be described by the ship's position state, speed state, and heading state. According to whether the ship is moving, the ship state behavior is divided into navigation state behavior and stopping state behavior.

Ship navigation state behavior is the behavior of the ship while navigating in the waters. According to the properties of position, speed, and heading of the ship, the ship navigation state behavior can be divided into different types, as shown in Figure 3.

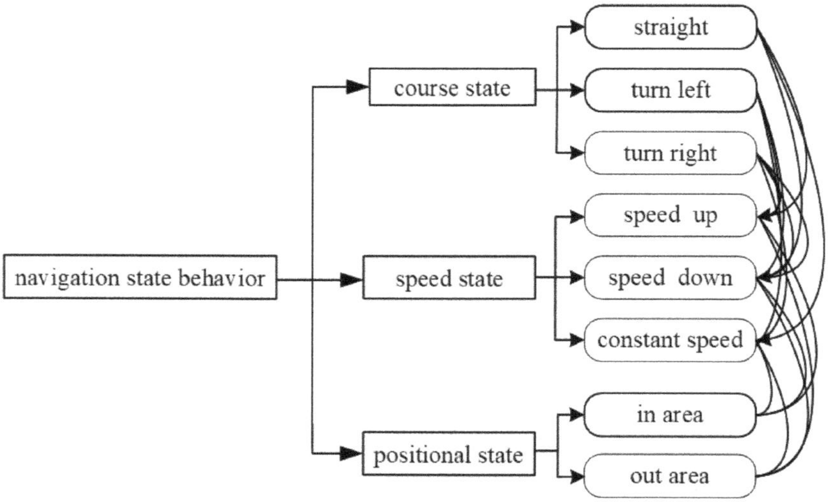

Figure 3. Diagram of ship navigation behavior.

Ship stopping state behavior is the behavior of a ship that remains stationary in the water. Based on the ship's position and speed property, it can be determined whether the ship is anchoring or mooring.

(b) Ship process behavior

Ship process behavior is a series of state behavior combinations of the ship in the process of sailing, maneuvering, and berthing. It is a complex behavioral process demonstrated by a trajectory segment connected with the ship's trajectory points. According to the understanding of the navigation rules in the previous article, the process behavior is divided into four categories: channel area behavior (deepwater channel, recommended channel, special area, bridge water area), wharf area behavior, anchorage behavior, and other general area behavior. Different process behaviors exist in different waters, as shown in Table 5.

Table 5. Classification of ship process behaviors.

Process Behaviors	Categories
channel area behavior	navigation, crossing, entering, leaving
wharf area behavior	berthing, unberthing
anchorage behavior	entering, leaving, anchoring
other general area behavior	turnaround

(2) Ship topology relationships

Ship behavior is related to space and time, and in this study, the DE-9IM model was used to calculate the topological relationship between ship behavior and space. The DE-9IM model [29] was used to describe the topological relationship between entity a and entity b's interior (Interior, I), boundary (Boundary, B), and exterior (Exterior, E), which constitutes an intersection of a 3 × 3 matrix, as in Equation (1):

$$DE9IM(a,b) = \begin{bmatrix} dim(I_a \cap I_b) & dim(I_a \cap B_b) & dim(I_a \cap E_b) \\ dim(B_a \cap I_b) & dim(B_a \cap B_b) & dim(B_a \cap E_b) \\ dim(E_a \cap I_b) & dim(E_a \cap B_b) & dim(E_a \cap E_b) \end{bmatrix} \quad (1)$$

dim refers to the dimension, and DE-9IM computes the intersection between 3 regions of two geometric objects separately to derive the value of *dim*, which is 0 for points, 1 for lines, 2 for faces, and F for the multipoint null set (no intersection).

The topological relationship between ship trajectory elements and spatial elements is mainly manifested as the relationship between point and line, line and line, point and plane, and line and plane, and the set $Tset = \{Tset_1, Tset_2 \ldots, Tset_{12}\}$ of the topological relationship is obtained. The topological relationship of ships in the water space can be represented by one of *Tset*, as shown in Figure 4. The blue point is the ship trajectory point, the blue line is the ship trajectory segment, the black lines are linear Area elements, and the closed planes are planar Area elements.

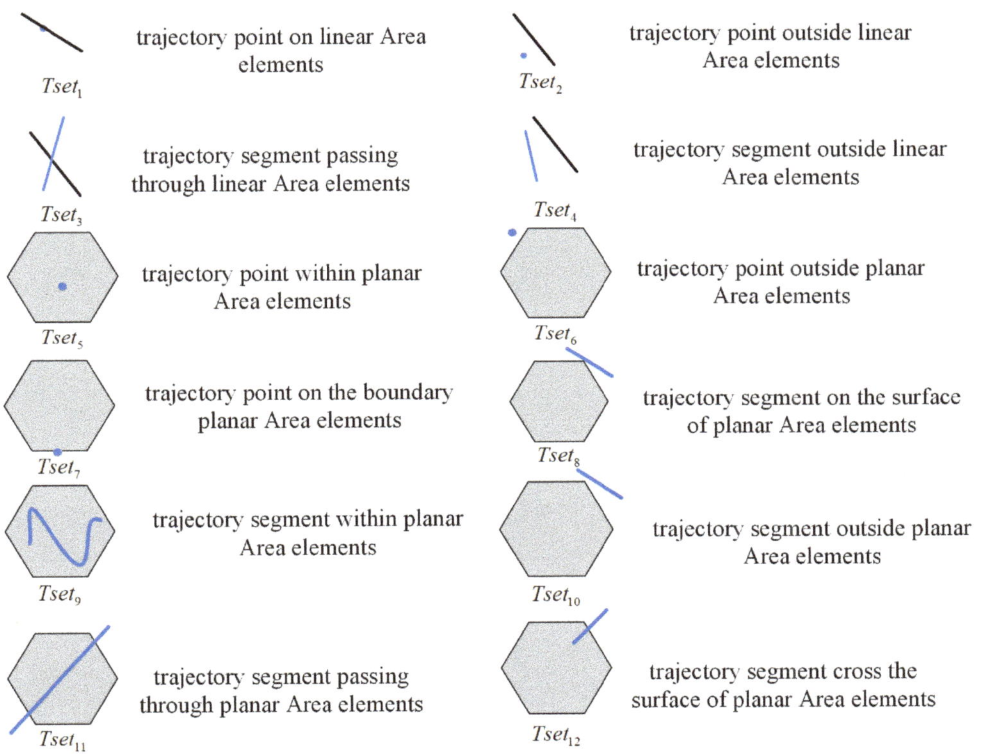

Figure 4. Topological relationship between ship trajectory and Area elements.

(3) Ship behavior expression

Based on the classification of ship behaviors and the calculation of topological relations in the previous section, ship state behaviors and process behaviors are expressed.

(a) Ship state behavior expression

The ship state consists of different parameters which can be expressed by Equation (2):

$$Q_i = \{p_i, t_i, c_i, v_i, a, \varphi\} \quad (2)$$

p_i is the ship's position, t_i is the corresponding time point, c_i is the ship's heading, v_i is the ship's speed, a is the ship's acceleration, and φ is the ship's steering rate.

Combining the states of ship trajectory points and the spatial topological relations, the ship state behavior can be expressed as:

$$state_i = \{Q_i, Tset_j, Rule_k\} \tag{3}$$

Q_i is the ship state, $Tset_j$ is the topological relationship between ship trajectory points and spatial elements, and $Rule_k$ is the rule for matching ship trajectory points.

(b) Ship process behavior expression

On the basis of the expression of ship state behavior, the ship process behavior is expressed by combining the topological relationship between the ship trajectory segment and the spatial elements in the water. The ship process behavior can be expressed as:

$$P = \{(Q_i \ldots Q_{i+n}), Tset_j, Rule_k\} \tag{4}$$

P is a process behavior, $(Q_i \ldots Q_{i+n})$ is a ship trajectory segment, $Tset_j$ is a topological relationship between ship trajectory segments and spatial elements, and $Rule_k$ is a rule for matching ship trajectory segments.

(4) Abnormal ship behavior ontology construction

Abnormal ship behavior usually refers to ship behavior that violates the navigation rules, is inconsistent with normal ship behavior, or has potential risks. Possible abnormalities in ship behavior are divided into 2 categories: state behavior abnormality and process behavior abnormality, as shown in Table 6.

Table 6. Classification of abnormal behavior of ships.

Classification	Categories
State abnormal	large ships with high speed in recommended channel small ships in deepwater channel the speed in the channel is too high the speed in the channel is too low the speed in the bridge water area is too high the speed in the bridge water area is too low
Process abnormal	crossing the bridge water area deviation from the course turnaround in the bridge water area ship going the opposite way from the right direction long time navigating within the separation zone abnormal entering of anchorage area crossing channel with small angle

Based on the 22 navigation rules extracted in the previous section, the existing abnormal ship behaviors were analyzed. Any abnormal ship behavior may violate multiple navigation rules. Additionally, some navigation rules corresponded to ship behaviors that were difficult to quantify, such as maintaining a safe speed. Consequently, after further analysis of each navigation rule, 13 types of abnormal ship behavior were identified, including 6 types of state abnormal behavior and 7 types of process abnormal behavior, as detailed in Table 6.

Among them, the process behavioral abnormality schematic is shown in Figure 5: trajectory 1 is the ship crossing in the bridge area waters, trajectory 2 is the ship deviating from the navigation channel, trajectory 3 is the ship turning around in the bridge area waters, trajectory 4 is the ship going against the flow, trajectory 5 is the ship occupying the separation zone for a long period of time, trajectory 6 is the ship sailing into the anchorage, which is an anchorage abnormality if it accelerates into the anchorage in the process, and trajectory 7 is crossing at a small angle.

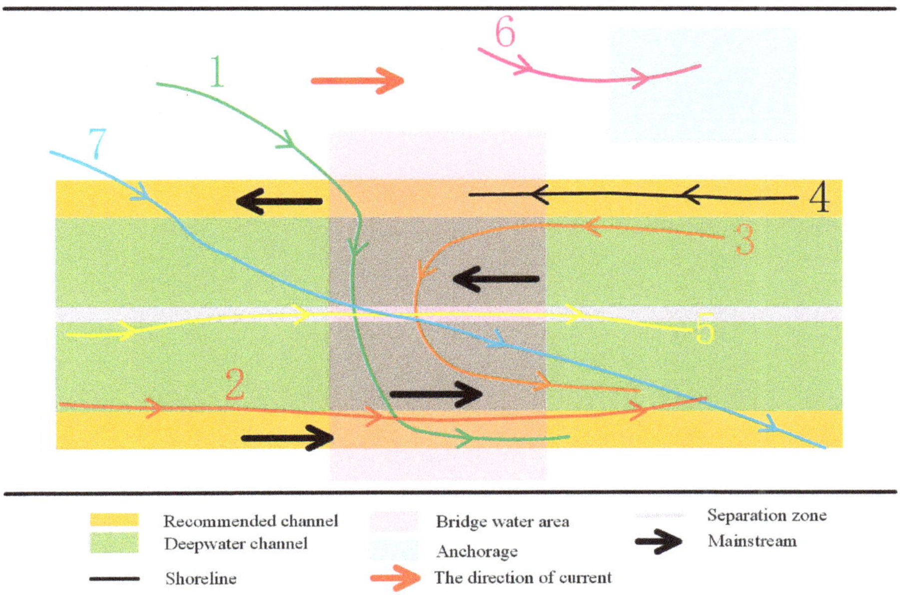

Figure 5. Diagram of abnormal process behavior.

According to the previous classification and expression of abnormal ship behavior, the core classes and the property relationships between the classes in the abnormal ship behavior ontology are shown in Figure 6.

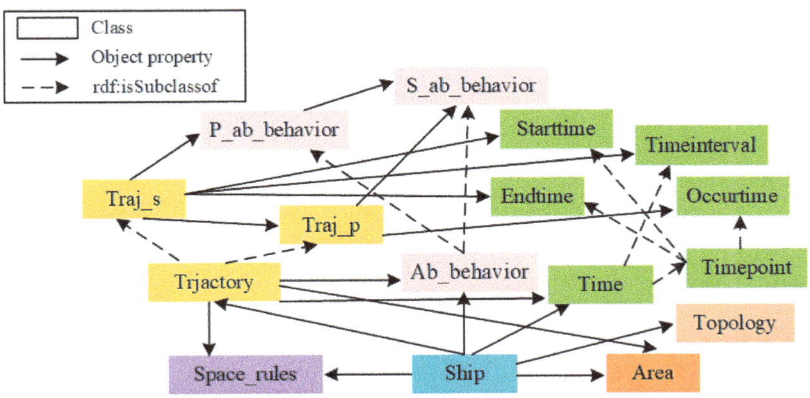

Figure 6. Core classes and interclass relationships in the ontology of abnormal ship behavior.

(a) Classes in the abnormal ship behavior ontology

The Ships, Space_rules, and Area classes involved in the abnormal behavior ontology of ships in this section come from the navigation rules ontology. This section explains the Topology, Time, Trajectory and abnormal behavior (Ab_behavior) classes that are not involved in the navigation rules ontology

Ab_behavior refers to abnormal ship behavior, which is the core class in the abnormal ship behavior ontology. Based on the classification and cognitive results of abnormal ship behavior in the previous section, abnormal ship behavior is divided into two subclasses, which embody the behaviors of the ship trajectory points and ship trajectory segments, respectively, including the class of state behavior abnormality (S_ab_behavior) and the class of process behavior abnormality (P_ab_ behavior). State behavior abnormality can be divided into large ships with high speed in the recommended channel (ab1), non-high speed of ships with dangerous goods in the deepwater channel (ab2), the speed in the channel being too high (ab3), the speed in the channel being too low (ab4), the speed in the bridge water area being too high (ab5), and the speed in the bridge water area being too low (ab6). Process behavior abnormality is divided into crossing the bridge water area (ab7), deviation from the course (ab8), turnaround in the bridge water area (ab9), the ship going the opposite way from the right direction (ab10), spending a long time navigating within the separation zone (ab11), abnormal entering to the anchorage area (ab12), and crossing the channel with a small angle (ab13).

Topology refers to the class of topological relationships, which is a description of the relationship between ship trajectory classes and spatial elements, involving 12 different topological relationships such as $Tset_1$, $Tset_2 \ldots Tset_{12}$. Ship trajectory points and ship trajectory segments have different topological relationships with spatial elements.

Time class refers to the time when abnormal ship behavior occurs and is a key element in the ontology of abnormal ship behavior. According to the characteristics of abnormal ship behavior, time is divided into time points and time intervals.

Trajectory class refers to the trajectory of a ship, which is divided into two subcategories: trajectory points (Traj_p) and trajectory segments (Traj_s).

(b) Object properties

In order to describe the relationship between classes in the abnormal ship behavior ontology and further improve the expressive ability of the ontology knowledge, the object properties of the ontology were established as shown in Table 7.

Table 7. Object properties of abnormal ship behavior ontology.

Object Property	Explanation
haspoint	The relationship between Ships and Traj_p
hasS_ab	The relationship between Ships and S_ab_behavior
hasP_ab	The relationship between Ships and P_ab_behavior
hasRule	The relationship between Ships and Space_rules
hasTraj_s	The relationship between Ships and Traj_s
hasTopo	The topological relationship between Ships and Traj_s
hasTraj_p	The relationship between Traj_s and Traj_p
inArea	The relationship between Ships and Area
hastimepoint	The relationship between Ships and Time point
hastimeinterval	The relationship between Ships and Time interval

Among them, *hastimepoint* contains three sub-properties, *hasOccurtime*, *hasStartime*, and *hasEndtime*, which represent the specific time when the state behavior occurs and the start time and end time of the process behavior, respectively.

(c) Data properties

In order to describe the characteristics of each class of the abnormal ship behavior ontology, the data properties in the abnormal ship behavior ontology were established. The data properties of Ships class, Area class, and Space_rules class in this ontology are consistent with those in the navigation rule ontology. The data property of Time was established for the Time class on this basis, representing the UTC time of Timepoint in the time class, and was stored in the form of a timestamp.

(d) Abnormal ship behavior ontology visualization

After completing the construction of classes and properties of the abnormal ship behavior ontology, it was implemented by using Protégé software. The concepts in the ontology of abnormal ship behavior exist in the form of classes. Based on the interclass relationships in the ontology of abnormal ship behavior, the hierarchical relationships of classes were added to the Protégé software, and visualization was achieved by using the OntoGraf plugin in the software. Figure 7 shows the visualized results of the abnormal ship behavior ontology and its relationships.

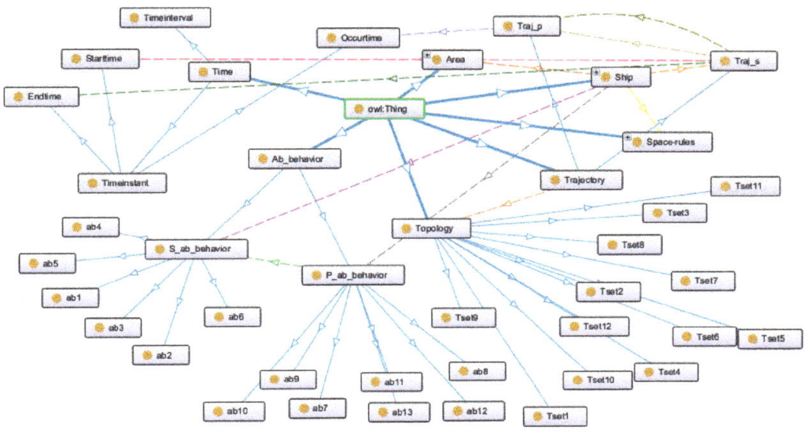

Figure 7. Main classes, attributes, and their relationships in the ontology of abnormal ship behavior.

3.3. Inference Methods for Abnormal Ship Behavior

Abnormal ship behavior inference involves deducing conclusions from established conditions, as illustrated in Figure 8. Once the ship trajectory data are integrated into the ontology, reasoning is applied to the abnormal ship behavior ontology. In this study, we leverage AIS data as a valuable asset for acquiring ship-related information. They furnish vital data, including Maritime Mobile Service Identity (MMSI), timestamp, longitude, latitude, sailing speed, and course of ground (COG), enabling us to utilize inference methods for detecting abnormal ship behavior using pre-processed AIS data.

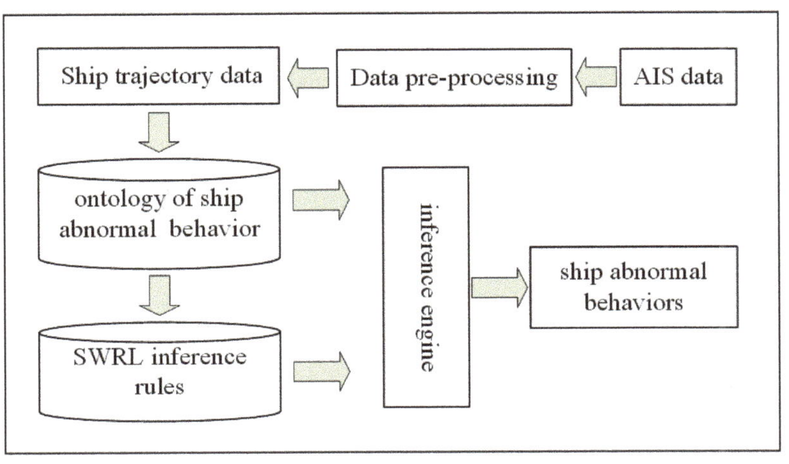

Figure 8. Flowchart of inference method for abnormal behavior of ships.

The inference process comprises ontology reasoning and rule-based reasoning. Ontology reasoning checks the consistency of the abnormal ship behavior ontology to ensure its validity, while rule reasoning applies the formulated SWRL reasoning rules to derive conclusions regarding abnormal ship behavior.

(1) Ontological reasoning

Ontological reasoning refers to the process of acquiring new knowledge by using the definitions of concepts, entities, relationships, and attributes of the ontology, and specific reasoning is divided into satisfiability checking, classification reasoning, and instance reasoning.

Satisfiability checking is a crucial task in ontology reasoning, aimed at ensuring the consistency and validity of the ontology. It involves two aspects: ontology satisfiability checking and concept satisfiability checking. The former checks for contradictions or inconsistencies within the entire ontology, while the latter verifies whether concepts have valid interpretations. As shown in Figure 9a, the intersection of the concepts "Deepwater channel" and "Recommended channel" is Ø, indicating that there is no spatial entity F that can simultaneously belong to both the Deepwater channel and the Recommended channel. If a concept E is an empty set, then the concept is unsatisfiable.

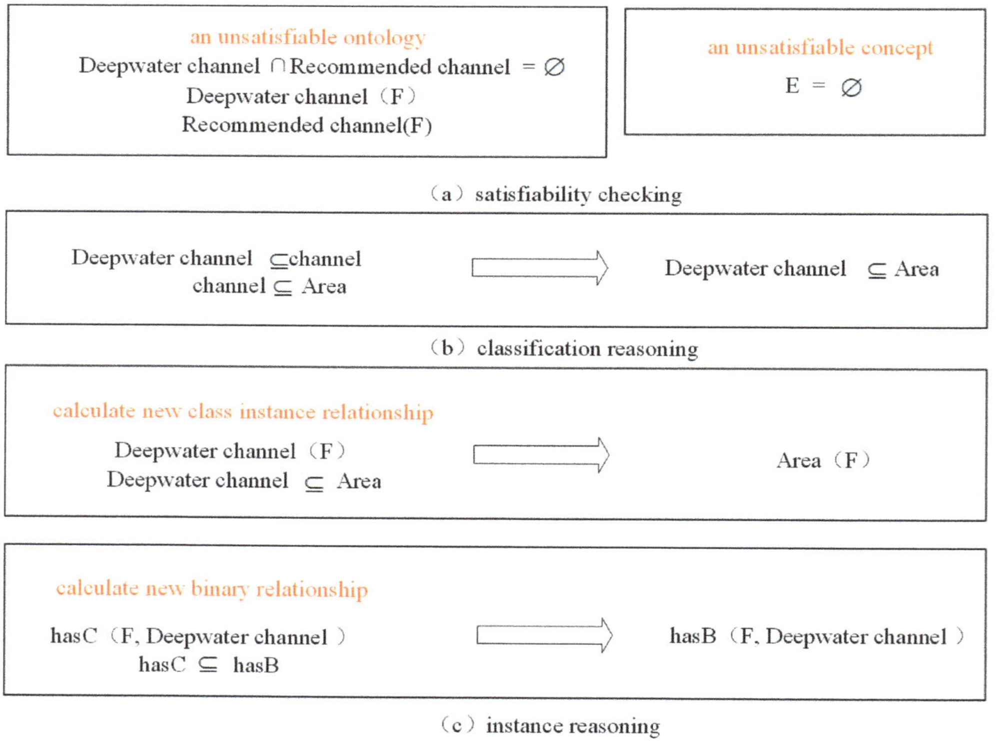

Figure 9. Examples of ontological inference.

Classification reasoning refers to the process of assigning entities or concepts to their appropriate categories. As shown in Figure 9b, if Deepwater channel is a subset of channel, and channel is a subset of Area, then it can be inferred that " Deepwater channel is a subset of Area".

Instance reasoning involves deriving new instances based on known concepts and their relationships. As illustrated in Figure 9c, if it is known that F is a Deepwater channel and it is a subset of Area, then it can be inferred that F is an Area, and a new instance for the Area category is inferred. Additionally, if the relationship between F and Deepwater channel is defined as 'has_C', and 'has_C' is a subclass of 'has_B', it can be inferred that there is a new binary relationship 'has_B' between F and Deepwater channel.

(2) Rule-based reasoning

Rule-based reasoning is primarily implemented through two methods: predicate logic and production rules. However, for many formulas, predicate logic may result in the loss of crucial information during the process of generating clauses, thereby reducing the expressiveness efficiency of those clauses. Hence, the adoption of condition–action production rules, which are easier to articulate, is preferred for reasoning. These rules are formally expressed as "If P Then Q" or "P→Q" [30], wherein if condition P is satisfied, conclusion Q can be inferred. Unlike implication formulas in predicate logic, where P and Q are strictly predicate formulas, in these rules, P and Q can also be symbols outside predicate formulas. In practical applications, P denotes phenomena or facts, while Q represents corresponding conclusions or actions, which facilitates the expression of causal relationships between any two concepts. Rule-based reasoning methods possess a clear logical structure, making them easy to understand and debug. The formalized representation of rules enables intuitive knowledge expression, enhancing system flexibility and adaptability to diverse application scenarios. The independence among rules ensures that adding, deleting, or modifying a specific rule does not directly impact other rules.

The inference rules established in this paper take the form *"if condition_1 ^ condition_2 ^ . . . ^ condition_n, then conclusion"*. The formal representation is as shown in Equation (5), which indicates that there exist three classes, A, B, and C, with a non-empty intersection. If there is a property relationship P1 between an instance "?a" from class A and an instance "?b" from class B, as well as a property relationship P2 between an instance "?b" from class B and an instance "?c" from class C, then it can be inferred that there is a property relationship Q between the instances "?a" and "?c."

$$
\begin{gathered}
\exists\, A, B, C, A^\wedge B^\wedge C = \varnothing \\
if\ A(?a)^\wedge B(?b)\ ^\wedge P1(?a,\ ?b)\ ^\wedge\ C(?c)\ ^\wedge\ P2(?b,\ ?c) \\
then\ Q(?a,\ ?c)
\end{gathered}
\tag{5}
$$

In this paper, SWRL is used to establish corresponding condition–action production rules for anomalous behaviors ab1 to ab13. As an example, the process of formalizing ship behavior rules is illustrated with the anomalous behavior ab1, as follows:

(1) *Ships(?s)^Traj_s(?seg)^Traj_p(?p)^ab1(?Ab1)^haspoint(?s,?p)^Recommended_fairway(?r)^has Topo(?p,?r)^swrlb:equal(?t,"Tset5")^Speed(?p,?a)^Length(?p,?l)^swrlb:greaterThan(?a,"19" ^^xsd:float)^swrlb:greaterThan(?l,"80"^^xsd:float)->hasS_ab(?s,?Ab1)*

(2) *Ships(?s)^Traj_s(?seg)^Traj_p(?p)^rule10(?r10)^Space_rules(?R)^ab1(?Ab1)^hasS_ab(?s,?Ab1)->disobey(?s,?r10)*

In the inference rule (1) described above, a vessel has a trajectory segment, and the segment contains trajectory points. Each trajectory point in the vessel's segment has a topological relationship of type $Tset_5$ with a recommended channel. If the vessel has a length greater than 80 m and a speed exceeding 19 knots, this indicates that a large high-speed vessel is navigating on the recommended channel, suggesting an abnormal state behavior. This leads to the inference that the anomalous behavior is categorized as ab1.

In inference rule (2), the inferred anomalous behavior ab1 is matched with the navigational rules, leading to the deduction that the violated navigational rule is $rule_{10}$.

Since SWRL rules do not inherently possess inference capabilities, an inference engine is required to infer anomalous vessel behaviors. The Pellet inference engine [31] is used to carry out the inference operations, and the resulting OWL ontology files can be further used for knowledge visualization, analysis, or extraction. The inference algorithm process is outlined in Algorithm 1.

Algorithm 1. Pellet reasoning algorithm process.

Input: Set of Concepts C
Output: Concept Tree *T*
Step 1: Initialize by creating a root node x with $L(x) = \varnothing$
Step 2: For each concept C_i in the set C:
    If *Ci* has existential constraints, then
        $L(x) = L(x) \cup \{C_i\}$.
    If $D \in L(x)$ and $\neg D \in L(x)$, then
        mark $\{D, \neg D\}$ as a conflict.
Step 3: For each node x in the tree:
    For each concept C_j with existential constraints in $L(x)$,
    create a new node y,
    set $L(y) = \{C_j\}$,
    add y as a successor to x with an edge $\langle x,y \rangle$.
Step 4: Check whether (x) at each node x contains any conflicts.
    If conflicts are found, prune the branch.
Step 5: The algorithm terminates when all nodes have been expanded without conflicts, or when no further existential constraints can be added.
End.

Suppose that the ontology model for anomalous ship behavior contains information indicating that ship A is navigating on recommended channel C, with its trajectory point B showing that the ship has a length of 90 m and a speed of 20 knots. When examining Ship A's navigational status using the inference rules, an anomalous behavior (ab1) is detected, indicating a violation of $rule_{10}$. The transformation in the ontological inference is illustrated in Figure 10.

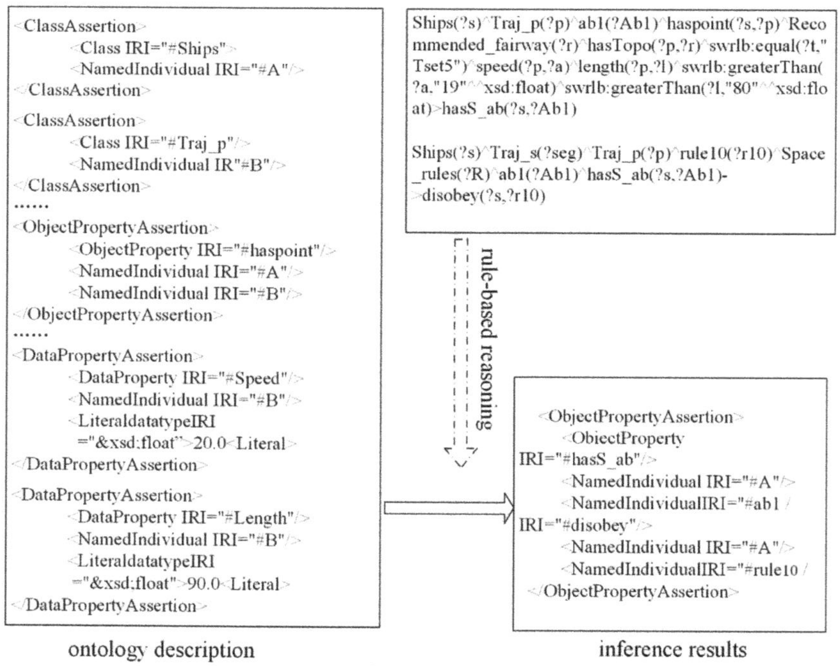

Figure 10. Diagram of anomalous behavior inference expression.

4. Case Study and Results

4.1. Study Area and Dataset

To explore the practicality of the proposed method in this paper, the study area selected was from Red Buoy No. 22 to the mouth of the Yangtze River in the Jiangsu section. Ship AIS trajectories within this area on 6 December 2023 were chosen for conducting experiments on inferring abnormal ship behavior. The original dataset contains seven types of information on ship dynamics and statics, with a total of 877,709 records.

The raw AIS data may present several types of errors, encompassing positional inaccuracies, velocity aberrations, and trajectory deviations. Positional inaccuracies denote instances where vessel data are erroneously marked at incorrect geographical coordinates, potentially including landmasses. Velocity aberrations signify situations where the vessel speed surpasses its maximum allowable navigational limit. Trajectory deviations manifest as discrepancies in ship trajectory points, leading to discernible deviations from neighboring trajectory points. To uphold experimental precision, this research employed a data cleansing strategy to address these irregular data occurrences. Following meticulous data preprocessing, the study retained a dataset comprising 846,675 ship records. AIS data quality dimensions were presented for processing errors of AIS tracks [32]. The ship AIS trajectories in the study area are depicted in Figure 11a.

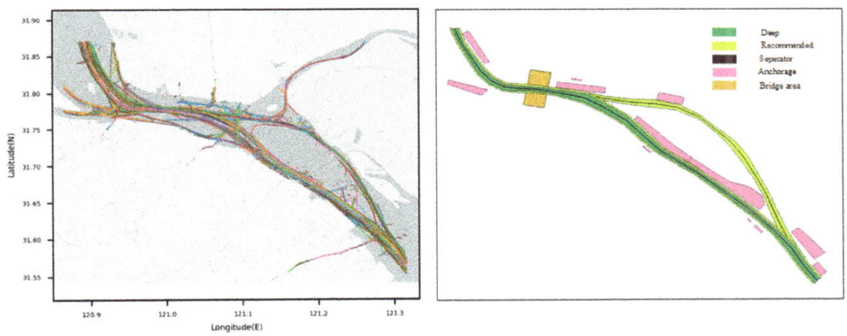

(a) Ship AIS trajectories in the study area (b) Area elements within the study area

Figure 11. Visualizes the study area and experimental data in the research waters.

As shown in Figure 11b, specific Area elements within the study area were delineated, including deepwater channels, recommended channels, separation zones, anchorages, and bridge water areas.

4.2. Results Analysis

Three experiments were designed in this study to validate three types of abnormal behaviors: speed anomalies, turnaround anomalies, and crossing anomalies. For speed anomalies, any speed inconsistent with the prescribed speed in navigation rules within the channel was identified as a speed anomaly. For turnaround anomalies, all turnaround behaviors were first identified, and then turnaround behaviors occurring in bridge areas were inferred as anomalies. For crossing anomalies, all crossing behaviors were initially identified, and then crossing behaviors occurring in bridge areas and those with small crossing angles were inferred as anomalies.

4.2.1. Abnormal Speed Behavior

Navigation rules prescribe speed limits for vessels. Based on the inference results of abnormal ship speed behaviors, the quantities of vessels with excessive and insufficient speeds were counted, respectively. The distribution patterns of these behaviors in bridge areas and channels were analyzed. Furthermore, an analysis of abnormal speed behaviors was conducted for different types of vessels, including cargo ships, tankers, fishing boats, ferries, tugs, law enforcement vessels, and port operation vessels. The specific results are shown in Figure 12, which illustrates (a) the quantity of vessels with excessively low speeds in channels, (b) the quantity of vessels with excessively high speeds in channels, (c) the quantity of vessels with excessively low speeds in bridge water areas, and (d) the quantity of vessels with excessively high speeds in bridge water areas. From the inference results, it can be observed that the number of vessels navigating at excessive speeds in channels was significantly lower than those with low speeds. The majority of vessels with speed abnormalities were cargo ships, and the number of vessels with speed abnormalities in the upstream channel was significantly higher than in the downstream channel. Additionally, the number of vessels traveling at excessive speeds in bridge water areas was higher than in other areas.

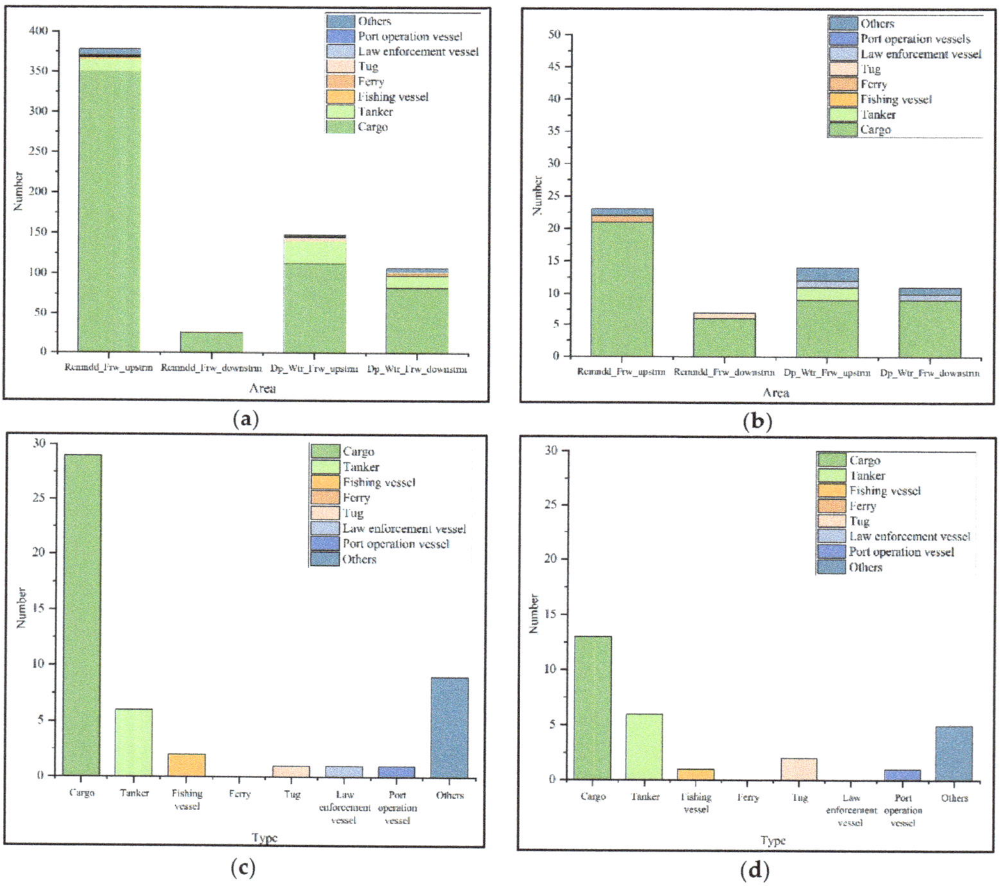

Figure 12. Analysis of inference results for ship speed anomalies. (**a**) Vessels with insufficient speeds in channels; (**b**) vessels with excessive speeds in channels; (**c**) vessels with insufficient speeds in bridge water; (**d**) vessels with excessive speeds in bridge water.

4.2.2. Abnormal Turnaround Behavior

A total of 128 turnaround behaviors were inferred from all the ship behaviors in the study waters, and the regional distribution and time statistics of turnaround behaviors are shown in Table 8.

Table 8. Statistical results for turnaround behavior.

Area	Number	Average Time
bridge water area	1	5 min
channel	29	8 min
near the wharf	41	15 min
near the anchorage	51	10 min

Some of the typical turnaround behaviors are shown in Figure 13. (a) The turnaround trajectory shows that the ship turned around near the waterfront of the pier, with deceleration in the process of approaching the pier, and that the ship might have gone to berth at the pier, which is a normal turnaround behavior. (b) The turnaround trajectory shows that the ship turned around inside the channel near the pier, which is a normal turnaround behavior. (c) The turnaround trajectory shows that the ship navigated from the downward recommended channel and sailed into the upward recommended channel after the turnaround, which is a normal turnaround behavior. (d) The turnaround trajectory in (d) shows that the vessel sailed into the downward recommended channel from the waters outside the channel and sailed into the upward recommended channel after making a U-turn. The vessel was a harbor service vessel, and it may have been a normal turnaround, as it was going to other waters for operation after providing services at other terminals. (e) The turnaround track in (e) shows that the vessel sailed from the inner channel to the outer channel, made a U-turn outside the channel, and sailed into the downward recommended channel. The vessel was a law enforcement vessel, and it may have been an emergency turnaround for the role of law enforcement, which is a normal turnaround behavior. (f) The turnaround trajectory in (f) shows that the vessel was sailing in the bridge water area from the downward recommended channel and sailed into the upward recommended channel after making a turnaround, which is in violation of rule15. This was an abnormal turnaround behavior.

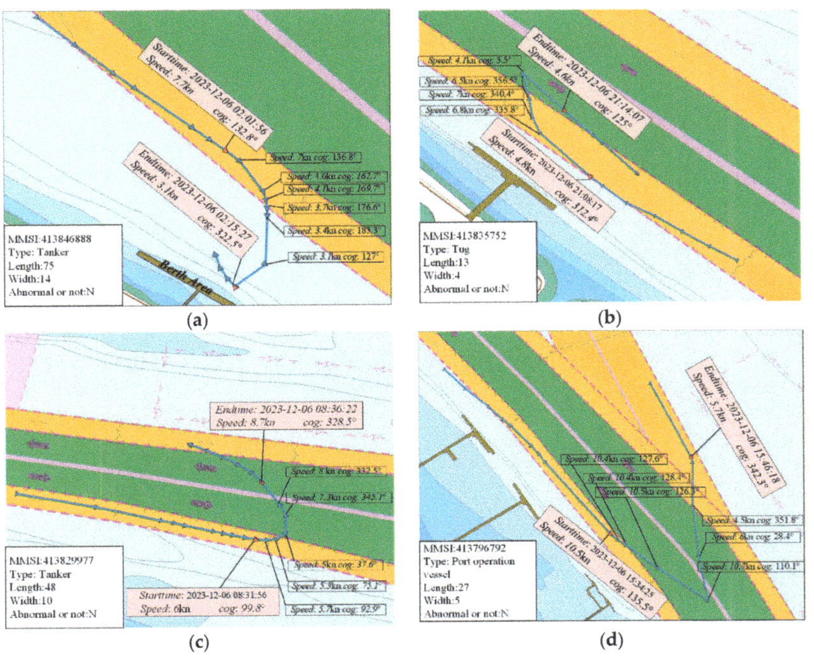

Figure 13. *Cont.*

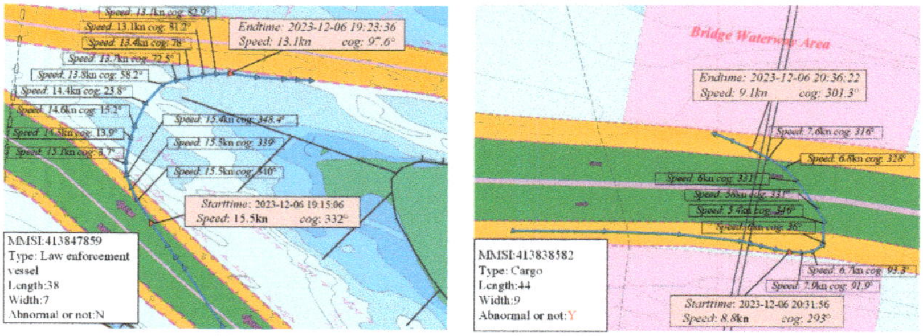

(e) (f)

Figure 13. Partial inference results for turnaround behavior. (**a**) Turnaround trajectory 1; (**b**) turnaround trajectory 2; (**c**) turnaround trajectory 3; (**d**) turnaround trajectory 4; (**e**) turnaround trajectory 5; (**f**) turnaround trajectory 6.

4.2.3. Abnormal Crossing Behavior

To infer abnormal ship crossing behaviors, all ship crossing behaviors were first inferred, resulting in a total of 846 crossing behaviors identified. The spatial distribution and temporal statistics of these crossing behaviors are summarized in Table 9.

Table 9. Statistical results for crossing behavior.

Area	Number	Average Time
crossing in bridge water area	1	7 min
crossing in channel	845	8 min
crossing channel with small angle	0	-

Some of the typical crossing behaviors are shown in Figure 14. Namely, (a) is a ferry sailing back and forth between terminals on both sides of the channel, which is a normal crossing behavior; (b) is a cargo ship crossing the channel from one side of the recommended downstream channel into the other side of the downstream channel near the channel bifurcation, which is a normal behavior; (c) is an oil tanker sailing out of the channel into the recommended upstream channel and then crossing the channel into the recommended downstream channel, which is a normal behavior; (d) is a cargo ship crossing the channel into the anchorage from the upstream deepwater channel, which is a normal crossing; (e) is a cargo ship anchoring in an anchorage and then crossing the channel to berth at a pier in a normal crossing; and (f) is a port service vessel entering the channel from outside the channel and crossing the bridge water area in violation of $rule_{15}$, which is an abnormal crossing.

The experimental results indicate that an abnormal ship behavior inference method based on the ontology of abnormal ship behaviors can accurately infer the existence of abnormal behaviors in ships. This method can accurately identify abnormal ship state behaviors and process behaviors in different scenarios, providing effective technical support for water traffic supervision.

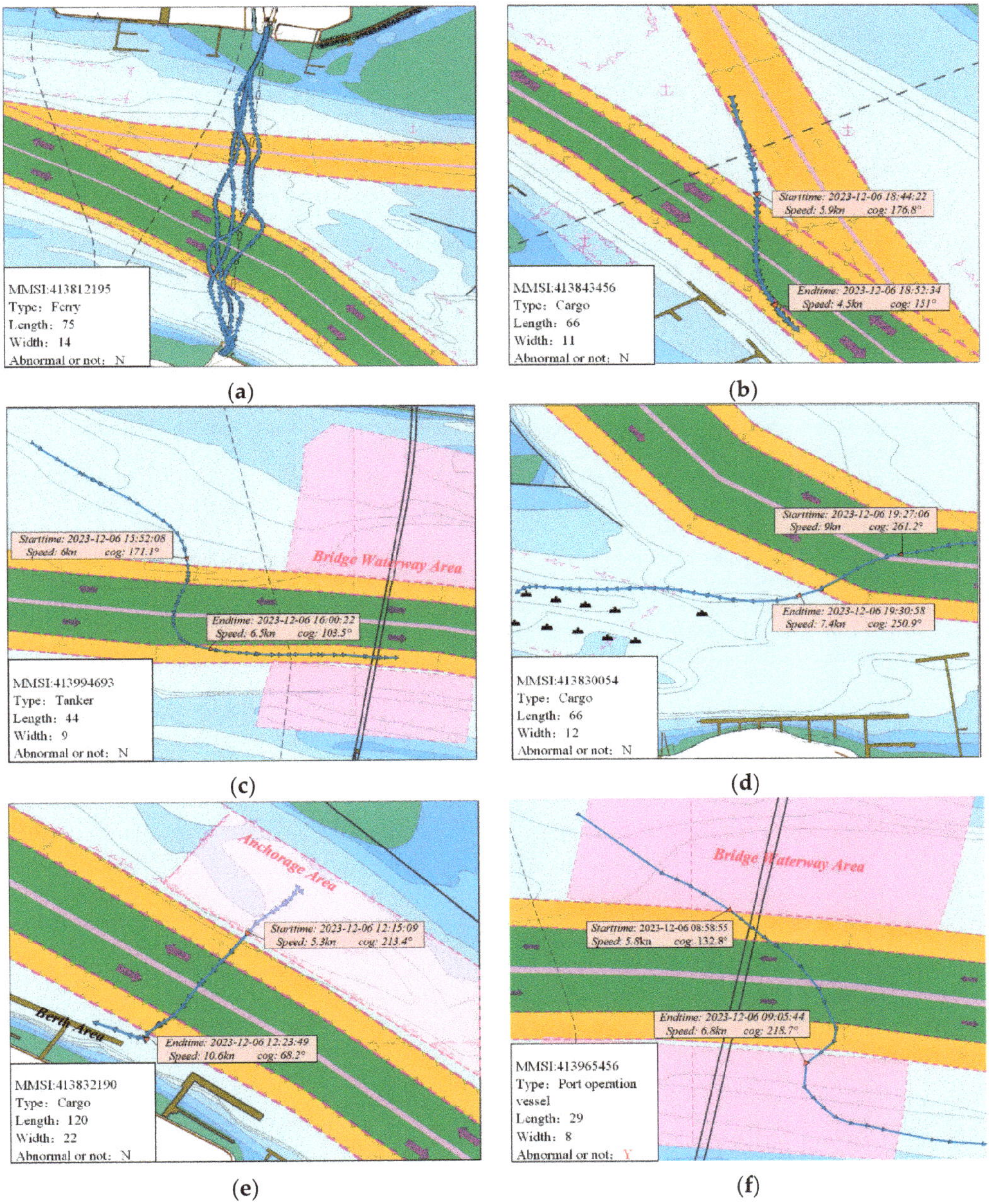

Figure 14. Partial inference results for crossing behavior. (**a**) Crossing trajectory 1; (**b**) crossing trajectory 2; (**c**) crossing trajectory 3; (**d**) crossing trajectory 4; (**e**) crossing trajectory 5; (**f**) crossing trajectory 6.

5. Discussion

Accurately identifying abnormal vessel behavior is crucial for enhancing maritime traffic supervision and navigation safety. There are two primary approaches to identifying abnormal ship behaviors: data-driven and knowledge-driven methods [15]. Data-driven abnormal ship behavior identification methods learn the characteristics of traffic data and predict ship trajectories based on predominant features, thereby identifying "abnormal behaviors" that deviate from these mainstream characteristics. However, these methods lack knowledge about rule-compliant behaviors, making it difficult to determine whether a vessel's behavior adheres to established rules.

Knowledge-driven methods for identifying abnormal ship behaviors leverage behavior inference modeling techniques, including rule-based systems, case-based inference, and ontological inference, to generate identification models. This paper proposes an ontology-based approach for identifying abnormal ship behaviors, achieving accurate identification of vessel behaviors that contravene navigation rules by delving into their intricacies. The advantages of ontology-based inference methods lie primarily in their ability to represent semantic concepts and their relationships in a structured manner, organize and structure knowledge in a clear manner, provide machine-readable representations, and support expressive capabilities for the reasoning process.

Employing the methodology delineated in this study, experiments were carried out within the Jiangsu segment of the Yangtze River, where the abnormal behaviors of ships were systematically identified and analyzed. The results of this study can be applied in the maritime supervision system to achieve accurate identification of abnormal behavior of ships and can automatically match the navigation rules violated by ships. This will effectively reduce the time consumption of manual detection and enhance the intelligence level of maritime supervision.

The semantic expressions of some navigation rules are relatively complex and cover a wide range of abnormal behaviors, which brings challenges to quantitative analysis and inference identification. For example, the safe speed in $rule_3$ is not a fixed value but depends on the specific situation. Such uncertainty makes it difficult for a an inference machine to perform automatic inference and judgement on such rules. Future research endeavors may pivot upon the intricate semantic formulations of navigational rules, employing methodologies such as rule decomposition and knowledge modeling to delve deeper into the analysis of abnormal ship behaviors within complex navigational rules. This pursuit holds promise for extending the applicability of the proposed methodology to maritime domains worldwide, characterized by diverse sets of navigational regulations.

6. Conclusions

Addressing the lack of effective monitoring means for the existing abnormal behaviors of ships violating navigation rules, as it is difficult to meet modern regulatory needs through manual monitoring alone. This paper researched an ontology-based identification method for abnormal behaviors of ships to improve detection efficiency and accuracy. By analyzing the navigation rules, the elements of navigation rules were extracted; according to these, an ontology of navigation rules was established, and the classification and expression of ship behaviors were realized. Then, an ontology of abnormal ship behaviors was established to realize the reasoning of abnormal ship behaviors. The experimental results show that the method can accurately identify the abnormal behavior of ships. The research results of this paper provide a basis for maritime traffic supervision and enhance the level of navigation safety.

Author Contributions: Conceptualization, C.Z.; methodology, K.W., J.Z. and Z.B.; software, Z.B.; validation, C.Z. and K.W.; formal analysis, Z.B., T.L. and M.K.K.L.; investigation, J.Z.; data curation, J.Z.; writing—original draft preparation, K.W. and Z.B.; writing—review and editing, C.Z., K.W., J.Z. and M.K.K.L.; visualization, K.W., J.Z. and T.L.; supervision, C.Z.; project administration, C.Z. and C.W.; funding acquisition, C.Z. All authors have read and agreed to the published version of the manuscript.

Funding: This research was funded by the National Science Foundation of China (grant number 52171349), the Laboratory of Transport Pollution Control and Monitoring Technology (2022JH-F038), and the Key Research Plan of Zhejiang Provincial Department of Science and Technology, China (2021C01010).

Institutional Review Board Statement: No applicable.

Informed Consent Statement: No applicable.

Data Availability Statement: Data is available upon request from the authors.

Acknowledgments: We sincerely thank the editor and reviewers for their kind and helpful comments on this manuscript.

Conflicts of Interest: The authors declare no conflict of interest.

Appendix A. Navigation Rules

(1) Traffic channel rules

rule$_1$: The deepwater channel is mainly for large ships.

rule$_2$: The recommended channel is mainly for small ships.

(2) Maneuvering rules

rule$_3$: Ships should navigate at a safe speed at all times.

rule$_4$: Ships should navigate at speeds between 4kn and 15kn.

rule$_5$: Ships should navigate in specified channel.

rule$_6$: Ships should navigate to the right according to the fairway direction.

rule$_7$: Ships should have a dynamic report when passing a position verification point.

rule$_8$: Ships should report their position when passing a position reporting line.

rule$_9$: Ships should overtake from the port side of the overtaken ship; the overtaken ship should take actions to assist in avoidance.

rule$_{10}$: A large ship with a low speed should navigate along the right edge of the channel and can enter the recommended channel under the condition of ensuring safety.

rule$_{11}$: Small ships carrying dangerous goods at high speed can navigate to the right edge of the deepwater channel.

rule$_{12}$: Ships should obey the special rules in special areas.

rule$_{13}$: Ships should navigate at safe speeds in the bridge water area.

rule$_{14}$: Speed should not exceed 11kn in the bridge water area.

rule$_{15}$: Ships should not stop their engines when bound for navigating, turning, crossing, or passing non-navigable bridge openings in the bridge water area.

rule$_{16}$: Ships should not overtake or navigate side by side when passing through the restricted bridge water area.

rule$_{17}$: When ships approach the docks or berth within the bridge water area, they should avoid normally navigating ships.

(3) Berthing rules

rule$_{18}$: Large ships should be anchored within the anchorage or stopping area.

rule$_{19}$: Small ships should choose anchorage and berthing areas for stopping, excluding sea vessel anchorage and berthing areas. Stopping out of the channel is allowed when it is safe.

rule$_{20}$: In special circumstances, stopping can be performed nearby.

(4) Avoidance rules

rule$_{21}$: Ships that are not navigating in the channel normally should avoid the ships that are navigating in the channel normally.

rule$_{22}$: Ships entering or exiting estuaries, tributaries, or special areas should give way to vessels that are navigating within designated traffic lanes or recommended channels.

References

1. Wang, Y.; Liu, J.; Liu, R.W.; Liu, Y.; Yuan, Z. Data-driven methods for detection of abnormal ship behavior: Progress and trends. *Ocean. Eng.* **2023**, *271*, 113673. [CrossRef]
2. Wen, Y.; Tao, W.; Sui, Z.; Piera, M.A.; Song, R. Dynamic model-based method for the analysis of ship behavior in marine traffic situation. *Ocean. Eng.* **2022**, *257*, 111578. [CrossRef]
3. Breitman, K.K.; Casanova, M.A.; Truszkowski, W. Ontology in computer science. In *Semantic Web: Concepts, Technologies and Applications*; Springer: London, UK, 2007; pp. 17–34.

4. Dou, D.; Wang, H.; Liu, H. Semantic data mining: A survey of ontology-based approaches. In Proceedings of the 2015 IEEE 9th international conference on semantic computing (IEEE ICSC 2015), Anaheim, CA, USA, 7–9 February 2015; IEEE: Piscataway, NJ, USA, 2015; pp. 244–251.
5. Yang, W.D.; Wang, T. The fusion model of intelligent transportation systems based on the urban traffic ontology. *Phys. Procedia* **2012**, *25*, 917–923. [CrossRef]
6. Corsar, D.; Markovic, M.; Edwards, P.; Nelson, J.D. The transport disruption ontology. In Proceedings of the Semantic Web-ISWC 2015: 14th International Semantic Web Conference, Bethlehem, PA, USA, 11–15 October 2015; Proceedings, Part II 14. Springer International Publishing: Cham, Switzerland, 2015; pp. 329–336.
7. Agarwal, A.; Gite, R.; Laddha, S.; Bhattacharyya, P.; Kar, S.; Ekbal, A.; Thind, P.; Zele, R.; Shankar, R. Knowledge Graph—Deep Learning: A Case Study in Question Answering in Aviation Safety Domain. *arXiv* **2022**, arXiv:2205.15952.
8. Bagschik, G.; Menzel, T.; Maurer, M. Ontology based scene creation for the development of automated vehicles. In Proceedings of the 2018 IEEE Intelligent Vehicles Symposium (IV), Changshu, China, 26–30 June 2018; IEEE: Piscataway, NJ, USA, 2018; pp. 1813–1820.
9. Yousefzadeh Aghdam, M.; Kamel Tabbakh, S.R.; Mahdavi Chabok, S.J.; Kheyrabadi, M. Ontology generation for flight safety messages in air traffic management. *J. Big Data* **2021**, *8*, 61. [CrossRef]
10. Malik, N.; Sharan, A.; Hijam, D. Ontology development for agriculture domain. In Proceedings of the 2015 2nd International Conference on Computing for Sustainable Global Development (INDIACom), New Delhi, India, 11–13 March 2015; IEEE: Piscataway, NJ, USA, 2015; pp. 738–742.
11. Altinok, D. An ontology-based dialogue management system for banking and finance dialogue systems. *arXiv* **2018**, arXiv:1804.04838.
12. Ong, E.; Wang, L.L.; Schaub, J.; O'Toole, J.F.; Steck, B.; Rosenberg, A.Z.; Dowd, F.; Hansen, J.; Barisoni, L.; Jain, S.; et al. Modelling kidney disease using ontology: Insights from the Kidney Precision Medicine Project. *Nat. Rev. Nephrol.* **2020**, *16*, 686–696. [CrossRef] [PubMed]
13. Ameen, A.; Khan, K.U.R.; Rani, B.P. Creation of ontology in education domain. In Proceedings of the 2012 IEEE Fourth International Conference on Technology for Education, Hyderabad, India, 18–20 July 2012; IEEE: Piscataway, NJ, USA, 2012; pp. 237–238.
14. Song, R.; Wen, Y.; Huang, L.; Zhang, F.; Zhou, C. Data-driven cognitive modeling and semantic reasoning of ship behavior. In *Maritime Technology and Engineering 5 Volume 1*; CRC Press: Boca Raton, FL, USA, 2021; pp. 269–276.
15. Zhong, S.; Wen, Y.; Huang, Y.; Cheng, X.; Huang, L. Ontological ship behavior modeling based on COLREGs for knowledge reasoning. *J. Mar. Sci. Eng.* **2022**, *10*, 203. [CrossRef]
16. Wen, Y.; Zhang, Y.; Huang, L.; Zhou, C.; Xiao, C.; Zhang, F.; Peng, X.; Zhan, W.; Sui, Z. Semantic modelling of ship behavior in harbor based on ontology and dynamic bayesian network. *ISPRS Int. J. Geo-Inf.* **2019**, *8*, 107. [CrossRef]
17. Santipantakis, G.; Kotis, K.I.; Vouros, G.A. Ontology-based data integration for event recognition in the maritime domain. In Proceedings of the 5th International Conference on Web Intelligence, Mining and Semantics, Larnaca, Cyprus, 13–15 July 2015; pp. 1–11.
18. Roy, J.; Davenport, M. Exploitation of maritime domain ontologies for anomaly detection and threat analysis. In Proceedings of the 2010 International WaterSide Security Conference, Carrara, Italy, 3–5 November 2010; IEEE: Piscataway, NJ, USA, 2010; pp. 1–8.
19. El Ghosh, M.; Abdulrab, H. Ontology-based liability decision support in the international maritime law. In *Legal Knowledge and Information Systems*; IOS Press: Amsterdam, The Netherlands, 2020; pp. 273–276.
20. Weihong, Y. Research on maritime search and rescue decision-making ontology model. In Proceedings of the 2009 International Conference on Environmental Science and Information Application Technology, Wuhan, China, 4–5 July 2009; IEEE: Piscataway, NJ, USA, 2009; Volume 2, pp. 140–142.
21. Murray, B.; Perera, L.P. An AIS-based deep learning framework for regional ship behavior prediction. *Reliab. Eng. Syst. Saf.* **2021**, *215*, 107819. [CrossRef]
22. Li, H.; Liu, J.; Liu, R.W.; Xiong, N.; Wu, K.; Kim, T.H. A dimensionality reduction-based multi-step clustering method for robust vessel trajectory analysis. *Sensors* **2017**, *17*, 1792. [CrossRef] [PubMed]
23. Karataş, G.B.; Karagoz, P.; Ayran, O. Trajectory pattern extraction and anomaly detection for maritime vessels. *Internet Things* **2021**, *16*, 100436. [CrossRef]
24. Singh, S.K.; Heymann, F. Machine learning-assisted anomaly detection in maritime navigation using AIS data. In Proceedings of the 2020 IEEE/ION Position, Location and Navigation Symposium (PLANS), Portland, OR, USA, 20–23 April 2020; IEEE: Piscataway, NJ, USA, 2020; pp. 832–838.
25. Vespe, M.; Visentini, I.; Bryan, K.; Braca, P. Unsupervised learning of maritime traffic patterns for anomaly detection. In Proceedings of the 9th IET Data Fusion & Target Tracking Conference (DF&TT 2012): Algorithms & Applications, London, UK, 16–17 May 2012.
26. Yang, S.; Xinya, P.; Zexuan, D.; Jiansen, Z. An approach to ship behavior prediction based on AIS and RNN optimization model. *Int. J. Transp. Eng. Technol.* **2020**, *6*, 16. [CrossRef]
27. Liu, H.; Liu, Y.; Li, B.; Qi, Z. Ship abnormal behavior detection method based on optimized GRU network. *J. Mar. Sci. Eng.* **2022**, *10*, 249. [CrossRef]
28. Zhang, B.; Hirayama, K.; Ren, H.; Wang, D.; Li, H. Ship anomalous behavior detection using clustering and deep recurrent neural network. *J. Mar. Sci. Eng.* **2023**, *11*, 763. [CrossRef]

29. Romanschek, E.; Clemen, C.; Huhnt, W. A novel robust approach for computing DE-9IM matrices based on space partition and integer coordinates. *ISPRS Int. J. Geo-Inf.* **2021**, *10*, 715. [CrossRef]
30. Wang, Y.; Zhang, Y.; Luo, X. Semantic Query for Engineering Knowledge Graphs Combining Rule Reasoning. *Comput. Sci. Appl.* **2019**, *9*, 993–1002.
31. Mishra, R.B.; Kumar, S. Semantic web reasoners and languages. *Artif. Intell. Rev.* **2011**, *35*, 339–368. [CrossRef]
32. Zhao, L.; Shi, G.; Yang, J. Ship trajectories pre-processing based on AIS data. *J. Navig.* **2018**, *71*, 1210–1230. [CrossRef]

Journal of
Marine Science and Engineering

MDPI

Article

Analysis of Carbon Emission Reduction Paths for Ships in the Yangtze River: The Perspective of Alternative Fuels

Chunhui Zhou [1,2], Wuao Tang [1,2], Yiran Ding [1,3], Hongxun Huang [1,2,*] and Honglei Xu [4]

[1] School of Navigation, Wuhan University of Technology, Wuhan 430063, China; chunhui@whut.edu.cn (C.Z.); 270339@whut.edu.cn (W.T.); dingyr@whut.edu.cn (Y.D.)
[2] Hubei Key Laboratory of Inland Shipping Technology, Wuhan 430063, China
[3] Henan Communications Planning & Design Institute Co., Ltd., Zhengzhou 450003, China
[4] Laboratory of Transport Pollution Control and Monitoring Technology, Beijing 100084, China; xuhl@tpri.org.cn
* Correspondence: huanghx@whut.edu.cn

Abstract: In recent years, carbon emission reduction in the shipping sector has increasingly garnered scholarly attention. This study delves into the pathways for carbon emission reduction in shipping across the Yangtze River, emphasizing fuel alternatives. It initiates by introducing a novel ship carbon emission calculation methodology predicated on voyage data, followed by the development of a predictive model for ship carbon emissions tailored to specific voyages. Then, emission reduction scenarios for various voyage categories are designed and exemplary alternative fuels selected to assess their potential for emission mitigation. Subsequently, scenario analysis is employed to scrutinize the CO_2 emission trajectories under diverse conditions, pinpointing the most efficacious route for carbon emission abatement for inland vessels. Finally, the proposed method is applied to the middle and lower reaches of the Yangtze River. The results indicate that accelerating the adoption of alternative fuels for long-distance cargo ships would greatly accelerate the development of environmentally friendly shipping. Under a scenario prioritizing zero-carbon growth, emissions from inland vessels are anticipated to reach their zenith by 2040. These findings can provide theoretical guidance for emission reductions in inland shipping and effectively promote the green and sustainable development of the shipping sector.

Keywords: ship CO_2 emissions; fuel substitution; carbon emission prediction; scenario analysis; carbon reduction path

1. Introduction

Shipping, serving as the linchpin for global commerce, facilitates 80–90% of the world's cargo transportation, thereby playing an instrumental role in the expeditious advancement of the global economy. Nonetheless, this sector is also a significant source of greenhouse gas (GHG) emissions, positioning it as a pivotal contributor to global warming and climate change [1]. Escalating volumes of maritime transport have led to an incremental rise in the share of carbon dioxide emissions from this sector within the global emission spectrum. The International Maritime Organization (IMO) reported that global maritime GHG emissions amounted to 1.076 billion tons in 2018 [2], with emissions from ships constituting 1.056 billion tons of this total. The IMO has issued warnings indicating that in the absence of efficacious interventions to curb carbon emissions in the maritime sector, we can anticipate a considerable surge in greenhouse gas emissions from this domain in the foreseeable future [3].

In China, carbon emission reduction in inland river shipping has increasingly attracted industry attention. Despite its advantages in capacity and efficiency, inland river shipping faces challenges due to its large carbon emissions and the difficulty of reducing them. The

Yangtze River, known as the "Golden Waterway", is a crucial backbone for the development of the Yangtze River Economic Belt. Whether considering the goals of peak carbon emissions and carbon neutrality, the application of new energy sources, trends in shipping development, or the overall development of the Yangtze River Economic Belt, inland river shipping along the Yangtze River holds an irreplaceable position and role [4]. Therefore, there is an urgent need to study the carbon emission reduction pathways for ships on the Yangtze River trunk line. Thus, the examination of viable pathways for carbon emission reduction in the maritime sector emerges as an essential and pressing endeavor.

To achieve the national dual carbon objectives, various industries are undertaking exploratory research on specific carbon reduction development pathways. In situations where computational resources and sample sizes are limited, the Grey System Theory (GST) model can be effectively utilized to forecast carbon emission trends within particular industries or regions [5]. With the advancement of neural network technology, leveraging neural network models in conjunction with industry-specific development characteristics can significantly enhance the accuracy of energy consumption forecasts in various sectors [6]. An energy structure optimization model can identify critical emission reduction measures and scientifically and rationally plan regional carbon reduction pathways, while comprehensively considering economic development and carbon neutrality objectives [7]. The Long-Range Energy Alternatives Planning System (LEAP) model [8,9], known for its flexible structure, is widely employed at both the national and regional levels to forecast energy demand and carbon emissions through scenario analysis. It can be effectively integrated with traditional econometric analysis models and scenario-based economic analysis models.

In the shipping industry, Zeng et al. [10] utilized scenario analysis to establish four distinct scenarios and applied the LEAP model to predict and analyze the energy consumption and carbon emissions of Yangtze River shipping under various influencing factors. This study provides theoretical recommendations for policy-making. Cao et al. [11] introduced a grey prediction model based on multivariate trend interactions to account for the interplay of carbon emission factors. This model was applied to forecasting CO_2 emissions from Chinese vessels in the maritime sector. Akcan [12] et al. employed a time series analysis model to predict greenhouse gas emissions from different sectors in Turkey. These findings are valuable for organizing and estimating the national greenhouse gas emissions inventory. Yan et al. [13] developed a method for forecasting the carbon footprint of inland waterway vessels, using Yangtze River vessels as a case study. The approach considered alternative fuels and factors associated with cargo growth. This study further examined the life cycle emissions of different alternative fuels. At present, the adoption of low-carbon alternative fuels emerges as an effective strategy to tackle environmental and energy concerns. Notably, liquefied natural gas (LNG), liquefied petroleum gas (LPG), and methanol are among the mature technologies suitable for marine vessels. These alternative fuels represent the primary measures for the shipping industry to realize its medium- to long-term carbon emission reduction goals [14,15].

However, there is a dearth of research on the specific developmental pathways for carbon emission reduction in inland waterway vessels based on fuel substitution. This paper addresses this gap by proposing a method for forecasting the carbon emissions from inland waterway vessels, considering the navigational characteristics of the vessels in the study area. Subsequently, scenario analysis is employed to delineate precise fuel substitution pathways for carbon emission reduction in vessels, aiming to explore the optimal carbon reduction pathways. This research provides theoretical support for policy-making concerning carbon emission reduction in inland waterway vessels.

The rest of the paper is organized as follows. Section 1 reviews the existing research on ship carbon emission reduction measures and carbon emission reduction pathways. Section 2 introduces the detailed methodology. Section 3 presents the case study in the Yangtze River and analysis of the results. Finally, Section 4 summarizes the conclusion.

2. Methods

2.1. Voyage-Based Ship Carbon Emission Calculation Model

Considering the relatively consistent operational range and navigational routes of inland vessels, this study proposed a voyage-based carbon emission accounting framework for inland shipping. Voyages are defined as the process of ships sailing from an origin port to a destination port. Observations of inland vessels' navigational behaviors reveal that these vessels frequently undertake cyclical journeys, either between a port of origin and a destination port or among several ports within a defined timeframe. This study introduces a method for extracting the voyages of inland vessels and categorizes their voyages into three stages. The specific definitions for each stage of a voyage are outlined in Table 1.

Table 1. Division of vessel voyage stages.

Stage Name	Basis of Division
Loading stage	From a vessel's entry into loading port waters to berth waiting, docking, and departure from the dock.
Transit stage	From departure at the loading port to arrival at the unloading port.
Unloading stage	From a vessel's entry into unloading port waters to berth waiting, docking, and departure from the dock.

This study involves retrieving data on the ports located nearest to a ship's furthest trajectory points, thereby determining its port of origin and destination. Utilizing geographical positioning and latitude–longitude information for these ports, voyages are systematically delineated and extracted. The compilation of fundamental port information includes details such as the port's name, geographical coordinates, environmental context, hardware infrastructure, and operational dynamics.

Step 1. Processing single vessel trajectories. Group AIS data by MMSI number, and then sort each group of data by timestamp. Next, calculate the distance between the two farthest points in each vessel's trajectory to determine the nearest ports to these points as the origin and destination ports of the voyage.

Step 2. Classification of voyages. Voyages are divided into two main categories: long-distance and medium–short-distance. Each voyage of a ship is first proposed, and if the voyage includes the starting and ending ports, it is judged as a complete voyage; otherwise, it is an incomplete voyage. For a complete voyage, a voyage with a distance of more than 60 nautical miles (NM) is considered a long-distance voyage, while a voyage with a distance of 60 NM or less is considered a medium–short-distance voyage. Additionally, all incomplete voyages are categorized as long-distance voyages. The threshold of 60 NM for categorizing voyage distances is based on regional ship navigation characteristics and can be adjusted accordingly. The extraction and categorization process for the voyage is shown in Figure 1.

Step 3. Identification of vessel round-trip voyages. Classify vessels based on the total voyage distance S_{total}, calculated from AIS data. The classification method is described by Equation (1).

$$Voyage\ type\ of\ vessel = \begin{cases} Round - trip\ voyage,\ if\ S_{total} > \frac{\pi \cdot D_{max}}{2} \\ One - way\ voyage,\ if\ S_{total} \le \frac{\pi \cdot D_{max}}{2} \end{cases} \quad (1)$$

The carbon emissions across various segments of a ship's journey are meticulously quantified, employing a voyage-based carbon emission accounting framework, delineated as follows:

$$E_T = E_L + E_S + E_U \quad (2)$$

where E_T signifies the aggregate carbon emissions for the voyage, E_L designates the carbon emissions incurred during the ship's loading phase, E_S is indicative of the carbon emissions generated during the navigation phase, and E_U represents the carbon emissions associated with the ship's unloading phase.

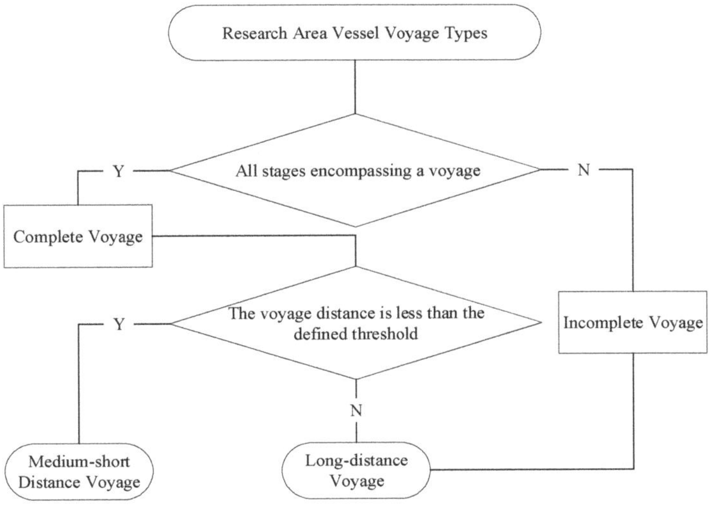

Figure 1. Classification method for vessel voyage types.

In the navigation phase, characterized predominantly by the vessel's sailing condition [16], the carbon emissions associated with this stage, denoted as E_S, are determined through the application of the subsequent formula:

$$E_S = MP \times L_M \times T_M \times EF_{CO_2,M} + AP \times L_A \times T_A \times EF_{CO_2,A} \quad (3)$$

where MP represents the main engine power of the vessel; AP denotes the auxiliary engine power; L_i is the load factor; T_i stands for the operating time; and EF_{CO_2} is the CO_2 emission factor, with M referring to the ship's main engine and A to the auxiliary engine.

Within the loading and unloading stages of a vessel, the operational conditions encompass both sailing and berthing states. The carbon emissions attributable to the vessel's loading phase, denoted as E_L, and those arising during the unloading phase, referred to as E_U, are quantified using Formula (4):

$$\begin{cases} E_L = E_C + E_B \\ E_U = E_C + E_B \end{cases} \quad (4)$$

where E_C signifies the carbon emissions produced during the vessel's navigation state, and E_B indicates the CO_2 emissions incurred when the vessel is in a berthing state. In instances where the vessel undertakes multiple navigation and berthing activities throughout these phases, the CO_2 emissions from all such activities are cumulatively calculated [17]. The carbon emissions attributable to the vessel's navigation state, E_C, and those associated with the berthing state, E_B, are determined using Formula (5).

$$\begin{cases} E_C = MP \times L_{ME} \times T_{M,j} \times EF_{CO_2,M} + AP \times L_A \times T_{A,j} \times EF_{CO_2,A} \\ E_B = AP \times L_{MA} \times T_{A,j} \times EF_{CO_2,A} \end{cases} \quad (5)$$

where i signifies the frequency of various activity states of the vessel within a given voyage phase; $T_{M,j}$ corresponds to the operating time of the main engine during entry i into the navigation state; and $T_{A,j}$ reflects the auxiliary engine's operating time during navigation occurrence i. These metrics can be determined and computed through the analysis of AIS (Automatic Identification System) data.

The calculation formula for the main engine load factor is as follows:

$$L_M = (V/V_{max}) \tag{6}$$

where V represents the ship's speed, and V_{max} denotes the maximum cruising speed of the vessel, with the unit = knots.

Drawing upon pertinent research outcomes from both national and international sources, the load factors for the auxiliary engines of inland vessels have been established, as illustrated in Table 2.

Table 2. Auxiliary machinery load factor.

Vessel Type	Underway	Berthed
Cargo ships	0.17	0.22
Oil tanker	0.13	0.67
Passenger ships	0.45	0.64
Tugboat	0.17	0.22

Data on the main engine power and auxiliary engine power of inland vessels can be obtained from the ship registration database. The auxiliary engine power (*AP*) can be estimated using the following, Formulas (7) and (8).

When the main engine power (*MP*) is less than or equal to 10,000 kW,

$$AP = 0.05MP/0.85 \tag{7}$$

When the main engine power (*MP*) is greater than or equal to 10,000 kW,

$$AP = \frac{0.025MP}{0.85} + 250 \tag{8}$$

The CO_2 emission factor is ascertained by utilizing the reference values provided in Annex 8 of the International Maritime Organization's Marine Environment Protection Committee during its 63rd session, as depicted in Table 3.

Table 3. Vessels' main engine's CO_2 emission factors.

Engine Type	Fuel Consumption Rate (g/kWh)	Emission Factor (g/kWh)	Emission Factor (g/g Fuel)	Emission Factor (g/t)
Main engine	215	670	3.114	3.114
Auxiliary Engine	227	707	3.114	3.114

2.2. A Carbon Emission Prediction Model Based on Fuel Substitution

Using inland shipping as an example, inland waterway vessels generally follow fixed routes, with consistent round-trip distances [13]. This consistency enables the determination of the energy consumption per kilometer for various vessels, thereby simplifying the prediction process. Consequently, by considering variations in alternative fuels and the annual growth rate of cargo transport, a carbon emission prediction model for inland waterway vessels based on fuel substitution is developed. The fuel consumption per kilometer for inland vessels, denoted as FC (kg/km), is determined through Equation (10):

$$FC = EC \times SFC \tag{9}$$

$$EC = E/S_{total} \tag{10}$$

where EC signifies the vessel's energy consumption per kilometer, expressed in kWh/km; and SFC indicates the requisite fuel weight for each unit of energy consumed, quantified in kg/kWh. These specific metrics are established in accordance with the findings from the Fourth Greenhouse Gas Study report released in 2020, as depicted in Table 4. Table 4 includes the specific fuel consumption (*SFC*) of slow-speed diesel engines (SSD), medium-speed diesel engines (MSD), and high-speed diesel engines (HSD), corresponding to heavy fuel oil (HFO), marine diesel oil (MDO), and ethanol.

Table 4. Specific fuel consumption (*SFC*) in units of energy per unit of fuel weight.

Engine Type	Fuel Type	*SFC* (kg Fuel/kWh)
SSD	HFO	175
	MDO	165
	Methanol	350
MSD	HFO	185
	MDO	175
	Methanol	370
HSD	HFO	195
	MDO	185
LBSI	LNG	156

The growth rate of cargo transportation volume is an indicator of economic development and is affected by a combination of economic and demographic factors. Therefore, this study used regression analysis to construct a forecasting model for the growth rate of ship cargo transportation by taking variables such as regional gross domestic product (GDP), retail sales of consumer goods, the per capita disposable income of urban residents, total foreign exports, and population size as predictor variables and the volume of ship cargo transportation as the outcome variable. Given the potential for multicollinearity arising from numerous predictors in regression analysis, the study applies the Least Absolute Shrinkage and Selection Operator (LASSO) algorithm to refine the selection of influential factors. The LASSO algorithm achieves model refinement through the construction of a penalty function, wherein the sum of absolute force coefficients is constrained to be below a fixed threshold. Simultaneously, certain explanatory variables have their coefficients strictly set to zero. Consequently, the LASSO algorithm effectively addresses the issue of multicollinearity and ensures the inclusion of the most significant predictors by imposing a strict zero coefficient on the selected explanatory variable. The optimization formula utilized by the LASSO algorithm is delineated in Equation (11).

$$min_w \|y - Xw\|_2^2 + \alpha \|w\|_1 \tag{11}$$

where w represents the coefficient matrix; α denotes the regularization parameter.

The mathematical regression model is developed to correlate the optimally selected independent variables with cargo volume, as delineated in Equation (12). This facilitates the calculation of the growth rate of the cargo volume for inland vessels. The efficacy of the regression model is subsequently ascertained using an F-test.

$$ln(Y) = \alpha_0 + \alpha_1 ln(X_1) + \varepsilon \tag{12}$$

where Y is the dependent variable; X_1 represents the optimal independent variable; and α and ε are the model coefficients.

Under the assumption that the ratios of the vessel and voyage types remain unchanged, the increase in demand for ship voyages is depicted through the growth rate of the cargo transportation volume. The projected annual voyage count for vessels in the forecasted year is determined by Equation (13):

$$N_i = \begin{cases} (1+r)N_0, i = 1 \\ N_i, i \geq 2 \end{cases} \tag{13}$$

where N_0 represents the annual voyages in the base year; N_1 denotes the annual number of voyages in year i; r is the growth rate of the ship transport volume.

To estimate the regional ship carbon emissions for forecast year i, it is necessary to ascertain the proportions of ships utilizing various alternative fuels as per the designated scenario for that year. The calculation of regional annual carbon emissions, $preEmi_i$, is facilitated using Equation (14), detailed as follows:

$$preEmi_i = \sum\sum k_{ij} \cdot EF_J \cdot FC_j \cdot N_i \cdot L \tag{14}$$

where L represents the distance of a single round-trip voyage for the vessel; N_i denotes the number of voyages in year i; EF_j is the CO_2 emission factor for fuel j, with the specific values determined according to the IMO's GHG4 report, as illustrated in Table 5; k_{ij} indicates the proportion of usage for each alternative fuel in the forecast year; FC_j refers to the per kilometer consumption of fuel j.

Table 5. CO_2 emission factors for different fuels.

Fuel Type	EF_{CO_2} (g CO_2/g Fuel)
HFO	3.114
MDO	3.206
LNG	2.750
Methanol	1.375
H_2	0

2.3. Construction of Ship Carbon Emission Reduction Scenarios Based on Alternative Fuels

In this study, the ships themselves are considered to be the main contributors to emission reductions, mainly cargo ships, tankers, passenger ships, tugboats, and other ship types. LNG fuel, methanol fuel, and hydrogen fuel are used as alternative fuels for the ships. The scenario prediction takes 2021 as the base year for prediction, and the prediction cycle is set to 2050, which is divided into four phases, namely 2021–2025, 2026–2030, 2031–2040, and 2041–2050. With reference to our published policies, different paths are set for each scenario, and each path is coupled with specific emission reduction measures. Since the implementation of emission reduction measures is a gradual process, the total emission reductions generated from the implementation of emission reduction measures during each forecasting stage are averaged for each year.

The scenario design for carbon emission reduction pathways for ships based on fuel substitution requires the design of specific values for parameters such as the ship transportation volume, the proportion of energy-intensive ships, the proportion of LNG-powered ships, the proportion of methanol-powered ships, the proportion of hydrogen-powered ships, and the degree of completeness of supporting facilities. In particular, the proportion of ship types, sizes, and voyage categories are determined based on the information on ship activities in the study area. The baseline scenario (BLS) reflects the carbon emission trends for vessels assuming no new carbon reduction measures are implemented, with all the influencing factors continuing to develop as they currently are. Based on the BLS, pathways for using alternative fuels for different voyage types are established, resulting in four specific fuel substitution development scenarios: a Low-Carbon Scenario (LCS), an Enhanced Low-Carbon Scenario (ELCS), a Zero-Carbon Priority Scenario (ZCPS), and an Enhanced Zero-Carbon Priority Scenario (EZCPS).

In the LCS, adhering to the policy development goals, LNG propulsion technology is initially applied to some existing passenger ships and large cargo ships for long-distance voyages through retrofitting by 2025. From 2026 to 2030, the phase-out and replacement of old, high-energy-consuming, and high-emission vessels leads to a gradual reduction in the proportion of high-energy-consuming ships. Mass production of green smart ships using alternative fuels becomes feasible, resulting in wider application of LNG-powered ships and more comprehensive supporting infrastructure. Between 2031 and 2040, with the benefit of existing fuel-powered ship retirement mechanisms, the proportion of high-energy-consuming ships further decreases. Methanol-powered and hydrogen fuel-cell-powered ships begin to be deployed. LNG and methanol propulsion technologies are employed in long-distance river freight vessels, while hydrogen fuel cell technology is applied in short–medium-distance river passenger ships, tugs, and other types of vessels. By 2041–2050, as alternative fuel technologies mature and supporting infrastructure for new energy and clean energy becomes largely complete, most river freight vessels adopt LNG and methanol propulsion technologies, while river passenger ships, tugs, and other types of vessels for short–medium-distance navigation predominantly use hydrogen fuel cell technology. The development process for the other three alternative ship fuel scenarios is similar to that of the LCS, with differences in the intensity of the ship fuel replacement policies during different time periods.

In different scenarios, the progress of adopting alternative fuels for propulsion type varies by vessel. To achieve the dual carbon targets of the shipping industry, some scenarios will accelerate the adoption of hydrogen-powered fuels. The specific emission reduction pathways for each scenario are outlined in Table 6. The percentages presented in the table indicate the proportion of each voyage type within the respective vessel category.

Table 6. Scenario design for emission reduction through alternative fuels for vessel voyage types.

Scenario		LNG-Powered Ships	Methanol-Powered Ships	Hydrogen-Powered Ships
LCS	2025	50% of passenger ships of 2000 t or larger long-distance cargo ships		
	2030	20% of long-distance cargo ships		
	2040	10% of long-distance cargo ships	40% of medium–short-distance cargo ships	Medium–short-distance passenger ships, tugs, and other ships
	2050	10% of long-distance cargo ships	20% of medium–short-distance cargo ships Long-distance tankers	40% of medium–short-distance cargo ships
ELCS	2025	50% of passenger ships of 2000 t or larger long-distance cargo ships, 40% of medium–short-distance cargo ships		
	2030	20% of long-distance cargo ships	40% of medium–short-distance cargo ships	
	2040	10% of long-distance cargo ships	30% of long-distance cargo ships	Medium–short-distance tankers, passenger ships, tugs, and other vessels
	2050	10% of long-distance cargo ships, 10% of medium–short-distance cargo ships	Long-distance passenger ships, tugs, and other vessels	Long-distance tankers

Table 6. *Cont.*

Scenario		LNG-Powered Ships	Methanol-Powered Ships	Hydrogen-Powered Ships
ZCPS	2025	50% of passenger ships of 2000 t or larger long-distance cargo ships		
	2030	5% of long-distance cargo ships	5% of long-distance cargo ships	40% of medium–short-distance cargo ships, Medium–short-distance tankers, passenger ships, tugs, and other ships
	2040		40% of medium–short-distance cargo ships	40% of long-distance cargo ships, 10% of medium–short-distance passenger ships
	2050		Long-distance passenger ships, tugs, and other ships	Long-distance tankers, 30% of long-distance cargo ships
EZCPS	2025	50% of passenger ships of 2000 t or larger long-distance cargo ships		
	2030	10% of long-distance cargo ships		40% of medium–short-distance cargo ships, Medium–short-distance tankers, passenger ships, tugs, and other ships
	2040		40% of medium–short-distance cargo ships	45% of long-distance cargo ships, 10% of medium–short-distance passenger ships
	2050		Long-distance passenger ships, tugs, and other ships	Long-distance tankers, 40% of long-distance cargo ships

3. Case Study

3.1. Study Area and Data

In this study, the Jiangsu Province section (from Nanjing to Changshu) of the Yangtze River was taken as the case study, as shown in Figure 2. The AIS data for this region are from August to October 2021. The dataset includes over 10 million trajectory points and the sailing trajectories of 14,350 vessels over three months. All the selected vessels are diesel-powered. Regional statistics such as regional GDP and population size over the years, as well as basic data on waterborne cargo transportation volume, are sourced from the Jiangsu Statistical Yearbook.

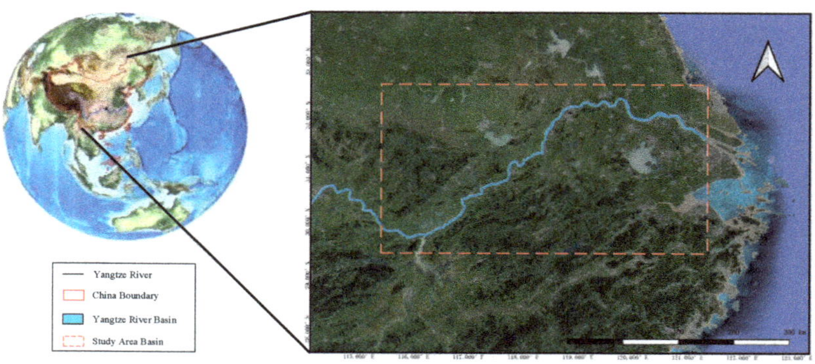

Figure 2. Research area geographic information map.

3.2. Results Analysis

A comprehensive statistical analysis was performed to quantify the contributions to carbon emissions by various ship types in the designated research area, with the findings depicted in Figure 3. The analysis revealed that cargo ships are the predominant source of emissions, constituting 79% of the total. Oil tankers were identified as the next most significant contributors, accounting for 10% of emissions. Additionally, tugboats, passenger ships, and vessels of other classifications were responsible for 5%, 2%, and 4% of emissions, respectively.

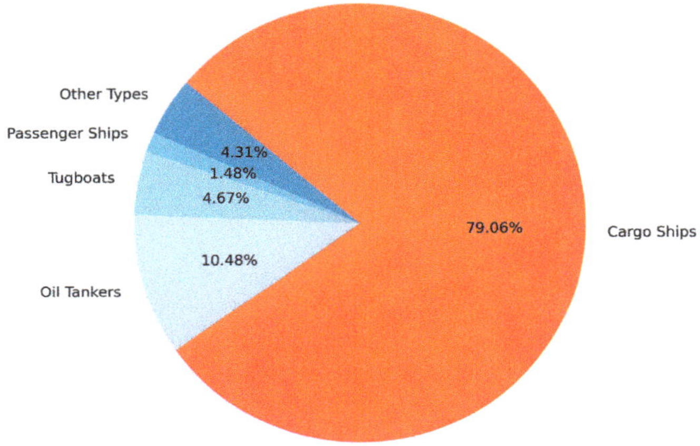

Figure 3. Apportionment of carbon emissions by vessel type.

Following the segmentation of the voyages, the data pertaining to the number of voyages and the cumulative voyage distances across various ship types were compiled, as detailed in Table 7.

Table 7. Activity information on different vessel types in study area.

Vessel Type	Quantity	Voyages	Distance Traveled (NM)
Cargo ships	12,320	28,939	1,443,803
Oil tankers	1037	2481	138,443.5
Tugboats	402	2328	29,670.12
Passenger ships	119	1951	11,829.56
Other types	472	2652	25,2040.7

Employing a voyage classification approach, a detailed statistical analysis was carried out to examine the categorization of voyages for varying vessel types within the specified study area. Cargo ships prominently feature in long-distance voyages, constituting 86.4% of such journeys and approximately 36.5% of the overall vessel count. Notably, there are 2142 vessels exceeding 2000 tons engaged in long-distance travel, making up 40.9% of the long-distance cargo shipping segment. In the context of medium- and short-distance voyages, cargo ships again predominate, representing 85.4% of the vessels in these categories and about 49.4% of the total vessel population. This underscores the significance of cargo ships in the Jiangsu stretch of the Yangtze River as prime candidates for energy source replacement strategies. The prevalence of tankers in long-distance voyages is similar to the level of their participation in medium and short journeys, collectively accounting for 7.2% of the entire fleet. Conversely, passenger ships, tugs, and vessels of other types are primarily involved in medium- and short-range operations. Detailed percentages, the overall voyage shares, and the distribution of voyages across different ship types are depicted in Figure 4.

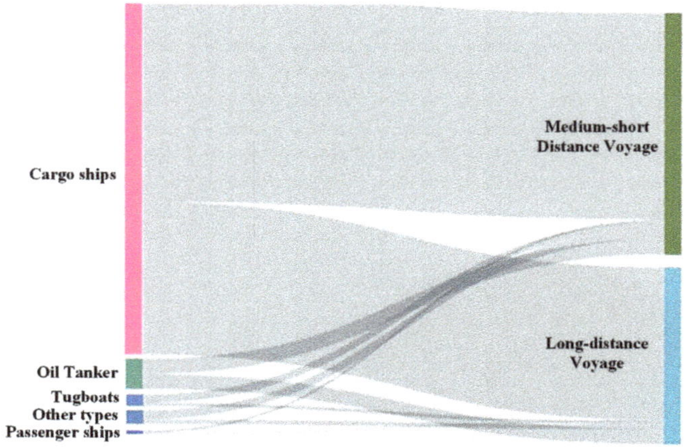

Figure 4. Distribution of voyage types across different vessel categories.

Vessels were systematically classified by type and voyage category, with the CO_2 emissions meticulously calculated for each classification. The outcomes are presented in Table 8. The analysis reveals that cargo ships on long-distance voyages are the predominant source of emissions in this study region, generating 160,881.89 tons of CO_2, equating to 52.86% of the overall emissions. Cargo ships on medium- and short-distance journeys follow, constituting 26.20% of the emissions. Tankers on long-distance routes also play a significant role, contributing 7.10% to the total CO_2 emissions and ranking third in their emission contribution.

Table 8. Carbon emissions of different vessel types in study area (tons).

Vessel Type	Medium–Short-Distance Voyage	Long-Distance Voyage	Total
Cargo ships	79,747.96	160,881.89	240,629.85
Oil tankers	10,284.23	21,608.22	31,892.45
Tugboats	5713.19	8509.35	14,222.54
Passenger ships	2353.26	2155.81	4509.07
Other types	6801.29	6310.30	13,111.59

Employing LASSO regression, an analysis was carried out on Jiangsu Province's annual regional gross domestic product (GDP), population size, and maritime cargo volumes. This analysis pinpointed regional GDP as the optimal independent variable for the regression framework. Subsequent logarithmic regression analysis, facilitated by SPSS 25.0, was utilized to delineate the correlation between maritime cargo volumes and the corresponding yearly GDP. Additionally, the robustness of the regression model was assessed through an F-test, ensuring its statistical validity. The detailed results of this analysis are encapsulated in Table 9.

Table 9. Regression analysis results for ship freight volume and GDP in study area.

Variables	B	SSR	SSE	F
Constants	4.620	2.981	0.129	391.520
Ln(GDP)	0.558			
R^2	0.958			

Jiangsu Province's GDP is anticipated to grow at an annual average rate of approximately 5.5%. By applying the predictive model for ship transportation volume, it is possible to calculate the projected volumes and their corresponding growth rates for pivotal years, as systematically presented in Table 10.

Table 10. Rate of growth of ship transportation volume at different time points.

Year	GDP (100 million CNY/year)	*r* (Freight Growth Rate)
2025	134,249.6249	13%
2030	175,458.8906	31%
2035	229,317.7528	52%
2040	299,709.1317	76%
2045	391,707.8487	105%
2050	511,946.4924	138%

For the study area, different development goals are designed for different scenarios based on the growth rate for the ship transportation volume at key time points in the carbon emission reduction pathway, as well as the corresponding fuel substitution development patterns for vessel voyage types. The development goals for different emission reduction scenarios are referenced from Figure 5.

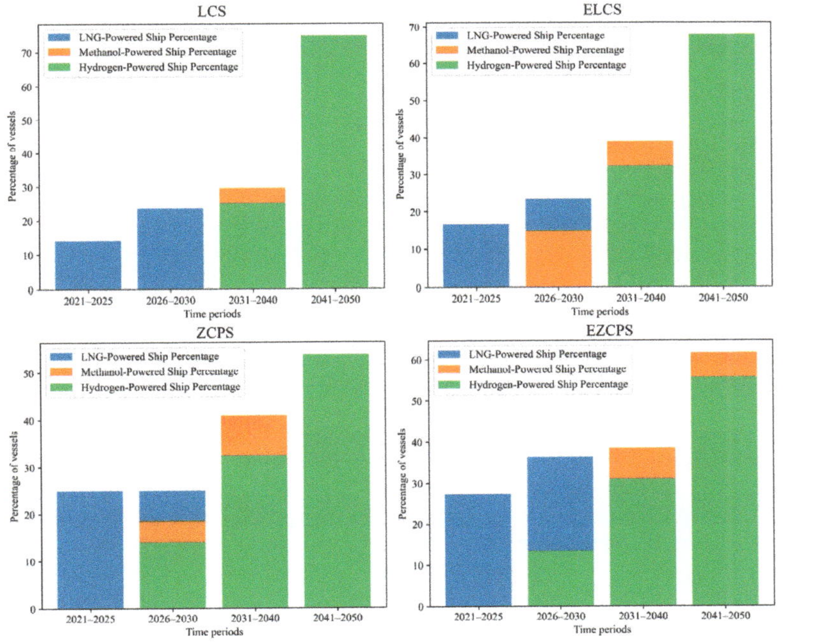

Figure 5. Specific development goals for different emission reduction scenarios.

Figure 6 depicts the temporal evolution in the total CO_2 emissions from vessels in the Jiangsu section of the Yangtze River mainline from 2021 to 2050. In the baseline scenario, the CO_2 emissions from vessels in this region exhibit an annual increase, resulting in a 138% rise by 2050. However, in the intensified zero-carbon scenario, the rapid adoption of zero-carbon fuels replaces diesel, leading the vessels to reach peak carbon emissions by as early as 2025. Subsequently, a substantial reduction in the emission potential emerges from 2039, with the vessel CO_2 emissions in 2050 amounting to merely 43% of those recorded in 2021. It is anticipated that vessel carbon neutrality would be attained by 2060.

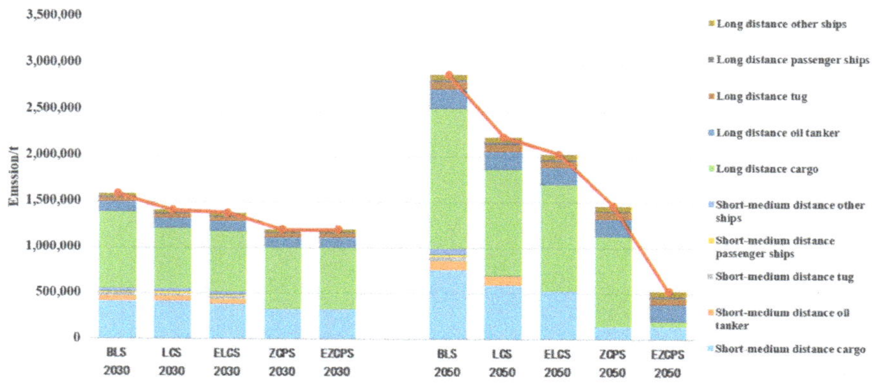

Figure 6. Evolution trends in ship carbon emissions in different development scenarios.

By 2030, across the four optimized scenarios, the proportion of environmentally friendly vessels utilizing alternative fuels in the Jiangsu section of the Yangtze River mainline is estimated to be 25%, 45%, 39%, and 39%, respectively. Except for the low-carbon development scenario, all the scenarios approach approximately 40%. Peak carbon emissions for vessels in the Jiangsu section of the Yangtze River mainline are projected to be reached by 2040 only under the intensified zero-carbon and zero-carbon optimization scenarios. However, in the zero-carbon prioritization scenario, the carbon reduction efficacy of the vessels diminishes between 2040 and 2050, with a decreased reduction capacity. Conversely, in the intensified low-carbon scenario, vessel emission reductions remain robust post-peak emissions, with a significant decline in the vessels' carbon emissions between 2040 and 2050. Carbon neutrality is anticipated to be achieved by 2060. Hence, prioritizing methanol and hydrogen fuels remains imperative for achieving the energy transformation goals for vessels, along with expediting the application of hydrogen fuel to vessels.

In 2050, the CO_2 emissions from vessels in the Jiangsu section of the Yangtze River mainline are projected to decrease by 23.33%, 29.95%, 49.42%, and 81.76% under the four emission reduction scenarios compared to the baseline scenario. The data indicate that prioritizing the development of low-carbon energy sources yields far lower emission reductions compared to prioritizing zero-carbon energy sources. The only distinction between the zero-carbon prioritization scenario and the intensified zero-carbon development scenario is the shift in cargo ships weighing over 2000 tons on long-distance voyages from using LNG fuel to hydrogen fuel, resulting in an increased proportion of zero-carbon fuels in the energy mix. The percentage difference in CO_2 emission reductions between these two scenarios in 2050 is 32.35%. Hence, the results suggest that implementing stricter emission reduction measures for high-emission vessels is crucial to achieving peak carbon emissions.

The short-term and long-term CO_2 emissions from vessels under different scenarios are illustrated in Figure 7. In the short term, prior to 2030, considering the maturity of low-carbon and zero-carbon fuel technologies, along with the level of supporting infrastructure, the emission reduction measures implemented in each scenario are relatively moderate. Consequently, there is no significant decrease in CO_2 emissions under the four emission reduction scenarios by 2030.

Looking at the long term, by 2050, the CO_2 emissions in the low-carbon development scenario and the intensified low-carbon development scenario are notably higher than the levels in 2030. The CO_2 emissions under the zero-carbon prioritization scenario show a slight increase compared to 2030, while under the intensified zero-carbon development scenario, the CO_2 emissions in 2050 significantly decrease compared to those in 2030. In this scenario, it is projected that vessel CO_2 emissions will decrease by 2.3692 million tons compared to the baseline scenario, with cargo ships engaged in long-distance voyages contributing the most to the CO_2 reduction, accounting for 62.36% of the total reduction, with a reduction contribution of 1.4774 million tons.

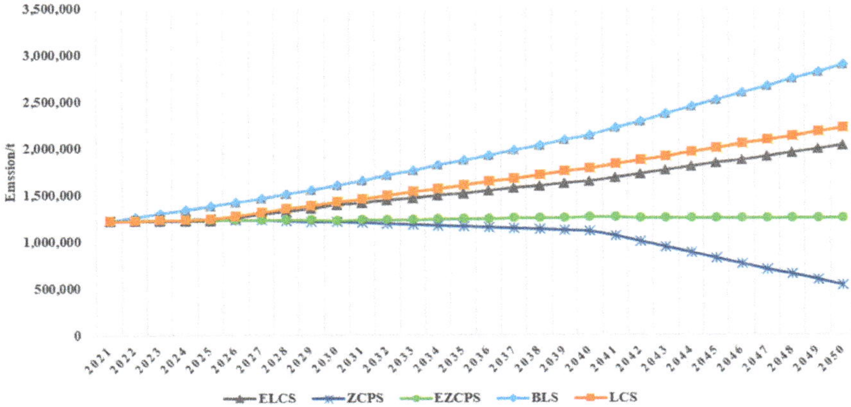

Figure 7. Comparison of long-term and short-term potential for ship carbon emission reductions.

3.3. Discussion and Recommendation

The study of carbon reduction pathways for vessels along the Jiangsu section of the Yangtze River demonstrates that the proposed method effectively identifies specific types of ships with high emission reduction potential, specifically long-distance cargo ships. Moreover, under the ZCPS, the carbon peaking target for the shipping sector can be achieved by 2040. Based on these findings, the following fuel-substitution-based carbon reduction pathway recommendations are proposed.

(1) According to the zero-carbon prioritization model, the following recommendations are proposed for the future adoption of alternative fuels in vessels:
   - Before 2025: Ensure that half of the existing passenger ships and large cargo ships modified for long-distance voyages are equipped with LNG propulsion technology.
   - From 2026 to 2030: Shift the focus of research and development from LNG technology to hydrogen propulsion technology, particularly for LNG-powered cargo ships on long-distance voyages.
   - From 2031 to 2040: Scale up hydrogen-powered vessels, phase out existing LNG-powered ships, and replace them with similar types of hydrogen-powered vessels. Target the replacement of some cargo ships weighing over 2000 deadweight tons engaged in long-distance voyages. Additionally, increase the substitution of diesel-powered vessels with hydrogen-powered vessels. Begin applying methanol propulsion technology to medium- and short-distance cargo ships.
   - From 2041 to 2050: Further reduce the number and proportion of LNG-powered vessels. Scale up methanol-powered vessels and start applying them to long-distance voyages. Hydrogen-powered vessels become the primary type of new energy vessels.

(2) In the middle and lower reaches of the Yangtze River, cargo ships engaged in long-distance voyages continue to be the predominant emitters of high emissions. Implementing more stringent emission reduction measures for these high-emission vessels is crucial to effectively mitigating the overall CO_2 emissions from ships. Therefore, expediting the adoption of hydrogen propulsion technology in large freight vessels and the development of associated infrastructure such as hydrogen refueling stations is

imperative. This will facilitate the prompt deployment of hydrogen-powered vessels for long-distance voyages.

(3) From 2040 onwards, the ZCPS demonstrates a superior carbon reduction performance compared to Scenario 2. By 2050, the ZCPS achieves an additional CO_2 reduction of 716,872 tons compared to the EZCPS, accounting for 32.35% of the total carbon reduction. A comparison of the development pathways reveals that beginning in 2030, the proportion of long-distance cargo ships switching to LNG fuel is 5% lower in the ZCPS than in the EZCPS, while the proportion switching to methanol fuel is 5% higher. These findings suggest that the emission reduction benefits of promoting low-carbon fuels in high-emission ships will increase over time, emphasizing the need to advance the use of low-carbon fuels in high-emission vessels as early as possible.

4. Conclusions

Inland shipping faces a heavy task in carbon emission reduction. To achieve its peak carbon and carbon neutrality goals, proactive measures should be taken in inland navigation to contribute to the overall carbon reduction objectives. This study predicts the CO_2 emissions from ships in the Jiangsu section of the Yangtze River mainline and finds that achieving the carbon reduction goals in shipping is unrealistic under the baseline scenario without any carbon reduction measures. However, under the scenario of strengthened zero-carbon emissions, through measures such as fuel substitution in vessels, it is shown that the peak carbon emissions of ships in the Jiangsu section of the Yangtze River mainline can be achieved by 2025, with regional ship CO_2 emissions reduced to 43% of the baseline level by 2050.

Two shortcomings of this study could be improved in future work. Firstly, when predicting the CO_2 emission trends for ships under different scenarios, the assumption was made that the activity range and routes of the inland ships were relatively fixed. Additionally, only three months of CO_2 emission data from 2021 was used as the input, resulting in some uncertainty in the prediction results. Future research should aim to increase the data scale for historical ship CO_2 emissions to improve the accuracy of the CO_2 emission trend predictions. Secondly, this study only considered three types of alternative fuels. However, other alternative fuels, such as biofuels and ammonia [15], also have significant emission reduction potential. Future studies should consider a wider range of alternative fuels to explore the optimal fuel substitution pathways for decarbonizing shipping.

Author Contributions: Methodology, C.Z. and Y.D.; Resources, Y.D. and H.X.; Writing–original draft, W.T.; Writing–review & editing, H.H. All authors have read and agreed to the published version of the manuscript.

Funding: This work was supported by the National Science Foundation of China (Grant No. 52171349), the Key Research Plan of Zhejiang Provincial Department of Science and Technology, China (Grant No. 2021C01010), and the Laboratory of Transport Pollution Control and Monitoring Technology (Grant No. 2022JH-F038).

Institutional Review Board Statement: Not applicable.

Informed Consent Statement: Not applicable.

Data Availability Statement: Data are contained within the article.

Acknowledgments: We sincerely thank the editor and reviewers for their kind and helpful comments on this manuscript.

Conflicts of Interest: Author Yiran Ding was employed by the company Henan Communications Planning & Design Institute Co., Ltd. The remaining authors declare that the research was conducted in the absence of any commercial or financial relationships that could be construed as a potential conflict of interest.

References

1. Farkas, A.; Degiuli, N.; Martić, I.; Vujanović, M. Greenhouse gas emissions reduction potential by using antifouling coatings in a maritime transport industry. *J. Clean. Prod.* **2021**, *295*, 126428. [CrossRef]
2. Joung, T.-H.; Kang, S.-G.; Lee, J.-K.; Ahn, J. The IMO initial strategy for reducing Greenhouse Gas (GHG) emissions, and its follow-up actions towards 2050. *J. Int. Marit. Saf. Environ. Aff. Shipp.* **2020**, *4*, 1–7. [CrossRef]
3. Xing, H.; Stuart, C.; Spence, S.; Chen, H. Alternative fuel options for low carbon maritime transportation: Pathways to 2050. *J. Clean. Prod.* **2021**, *297*, 126651. [CrossRef]
4. Zhou, C.; Huang, H.; Liu, Z.; Ding, Y.; Xiao, J.; Shu, Y. Identification and analysis of ship carbon emission hotspots based on data field theory: A case study in Wuhan Port. *Ocean Coastal Manag.* **2023**, *235*, 106479. [CrossRef]
5. Chen, L.; Yang, Z.; Chen, B. Decomposition analysis of energy-related industrial CO_2 emissions in China. *Energies* **2013**, *6*, 2319–2337. [CrossRef]
6. Li, Y.; Dai, J.; Zhang, S.; Cui, H. Dynamic prediction and driving factors of carbon emission in Beijing, China, under carbon neutrality targets. *Atmosphere* **2023**, *14*, 798. [CrossRef]
7. Hu, Y.; Chi, Y.; Zhou, W.; Wang, Z.; Yuan, Y.; Li, R. Research on energy structure optimization and carbon emission reduction path in Beijing under the Dual Carbon Target. *Energies* **2022**, *15*, 5954. [CrossRef]
8. Chen, M.; Zhang, C.; Chen, C.; Li, J.; Cui, W. Main pathways of carbon reduction in cities under the target of carbon peaking: A case study of Nanjing, China. *Sustainability* **2023**, *15*, 8917. [CrossRef]
9. Miao, A.-K.; Yuan, Y.; Wu, H.; Ma, X.; Shao, C.-Y. Pathway and Policy for China's Provincial Carbon Emission Peak. *Huan Jing Ke Xue = Huanjing Kexue* **2023**, *44*, 4623–4636. [PubMed]
10. Wu, W.; Zhang, T.; Xie, X.; Huang, Z. Regional low carbon development pathways for the Yangtze River Delta region in China. *Energy Policy* **2021**, *151*, 112172. [CrossRef]
11. Cao, Y.; Yin, K.; Li, X.; Zhai, C. Forecasting CO_2 emissions from Chinese marine fleets using multivariable trend interaction grey model. *Appl. Soft Comput.* **2021**, *104*, 107220. [CrossRef]
12. Akcan, S.; Kuvvetli, Y.; Kocyigit, H. Time series analysis models for estimation of greenhouse gas emitted by different sectors in Turkey. *Hum. Ecol. Risk Assess. Int. J.* **2018**, *24*, 522–533. [CrossRef]
13. Yan, X.; He, Y.; Fan, A. Carbon footprint prediction considering the evolution of alternative fuels and cargo: A case study of Yangtze river ships. *Renew. Sustain. Energy Rev.* **2023**, *173*, 113068. [CrossRef]
14. Brynolf, S.; Fridell, E.; Andersson, K. Environmental assessment of marine fuels: Liquefied natural gas, liquefied biogas, methanol and bio-methanol. *J. Clean. Prod.* **2014**, *74*, 86–95. [CrossRef]
15. Wang, Y.; Cao, Q.; Liu, L.; Wu, Y.; Liu, H.; Gu, Z.; Zhu, C. A review of low and zero carbon fuel technologies: Achieving ship carbon reduction targets. *Sustain. Energy Technol. Assess.* **2022**, *54*, 102762. [CrossRef]
16. Huang, H.; Zhou, C.; Huang, L.; Xiao, C.; Wen, Y.; Li, J.; Lu, Z. Inland ship emission inventory and its impact on air quality over the middle Yangtze River, China. *Sci. Total Environ.* **2022**, *843*, 156770. [CrossRef] [PubMed]
17. Zhou, C.; Ding, Y.; Huang, H.; Huang, L.; Lu, Z.; Wen, Y. Meso-level carbon dioxide emission model based on voyage for inland ships in the Yangtze River. *Sci. Total Environ.* **2022**, *838*, 156271. [CrossRef] [PubMed]

Journal of
Marine Science
and Engineering

MDPI

Article

Simulation Modeling for Ships Entering and Leaving Port in Qiongzhou Strait Waters: A Multi-Agent Information Interaction Method

Dong Han [1,†], Xiaodong Cheng [2,†], Hualong Chen [1,*], Changshi Xiao [1], Yuanqiao Wen [2,3,4] and Zhongyi Sui [5]

1 School of Navigation, Wuhan University of Technology, Wuhan 430070, China; handong@whut.edu.cn (D.H.); cs_xiao@hotmail.com (C.X.)
2 Intelligent Transportation Systems Research Center, Wuhan University of Technology, Wuhan 430070, China; cxd921121@whut.edu.cn (X.C.); yqwen@whut.edu.cn (Y.W.)
3 Sanya Science and Education Innovation Park, Wuhan University of Technology, Sanya 57200, China
4 State Key Laboratory of Maritime Technology and Safety, Wuhan University of Technology, Wuhan 430070, China
5 Department of Logistics and Maritime Studies, The Hong Kong Polytechnic University, Hong Kong 999077, China; zhongyi.sui@polyu.edu.hk
* Correspondence: hualongchen@whut.edu.cn
† These authors contributed equally to this work.

Abstract: Simulation technology has been extensively utilized in the study of ship entry and exit from ports, as well as navigation through waterways. It effectively mirrors the stochastic dynamic changes and interrelationships among various elements within the port system. This paper provides a comparative analysis of the advantages and disadvantages of various modeling methods used in ship navigation simulations. It proposes a simulation modeling approach for ship–port systems based on multi-agent information interaction, which simulates the entire process of ships entering and exiting ports and navigating through complex waterways, achieving a precise and detailed simulation of the entire port entry and exit process in complex waters. Using the Qiongzhou Strait as a case study, the validity and accuracy of the model are verified. The model is employed to quantitatively identify port navigation elements, assess waterway capacity, and evaluate port operational capability. Furthermore, the model enables the analysis of coordination among port channels, berths, and anchorages. Based on simulation results and port development plans, recommendations are provided to enhance port service levels and promote scientific, rational development and efficient operation of ports.

Keywords: port simulation; maritime traffic; multi-agent system; process of ship entering and leaving port; complex waters

1. Introduction

Port economy is a significant driver of national economic development. With increasing global attention to port strategies, port development is advancing toward greater safety, efficiency, and sustainability. Correspondingly, the construction of port channels reflects the operational efficiency and rapid development of the entire port. Therefore, scientifically and rationally planning and designing port channels can enhance ship entry efficiency and stimulate economic growth. Establishing channel facilities that align with the port's throughput capacity is becoming increasingly critical. Consequently, studying the throughput capacity of port channels provides essential decision support and guidance for maximizing the utilization of waterways and berths. The growing size of ships and the increase in port throughput impose higher demands on channel facilities, necessitating adjustments in factors such as channel depth, width, and the number of channels to meet the requirements of port expansion and renovation.

On the other hand, port waters typically exhibit characteristics such as variable meteorological and hydrological conditions, high ship traffic density, frequent cross-encounters, and complex navigation environments, which greatly increase the risk of maritime traffic accidents and congestion. Therefore, it is crucial to develop scientifically and rationally designed traffic organization plans for port ships and to conduct objective quantitative assessments of port ship traffic organization models. These issues are currently pressing and require in-depth research.

Various methodologies are currently employed to investigate the processes associated with ships entering and leaving ports, including empirical analysis, mathematical modeling, system simulation, and multi-method integration, among others. Ports are characterized as discrete stochastic service systems, exhibiting numerous random factors, intricate dynamic interactions, and multi-tiered queuing structures [1]. In contrast to mathematical modeling, which relies on deterministic calculations, simulation technology provides a more accurate representation of the inherent randomness, dynamic changes, and interdependencies among elements within the port navigation and operation system. Given its efficacy in handling systems with significant randomness and complexity, simulation has become an extensively utilized approach in the study of port entry and exit processes.

Maritime traffic simulation generally involves collecting statistical data on waterway traffic activities, analyzing the relationships between various transportation systems, using mathematical models to describe and reproduce their mechanisms, and employing modern computer simulation technology to study their behavior. The simulation modeling of ship entry and exit processes is pivotal in addressing key issues such as port location planning, construction, and operational efficiency. In port location planning, simulation enables a scientific evaluation of the impact of ship navigation on port design. Specifically, the quantitative assessment of site selection for specialized docks—such as LNG terminals and large oil tanker ports—is crucial for effective port planning. For instance, Moran et al. [2] assessed the environmental conditions and port facilities, evaluating port performance through system simulation, applied to the comprehensive planning of Port Blanca. Similarly, Perkovic et al. [3] developed a simulation model for ship navigation and operational systems in coastal ports using agent-based theory, analyzing the impact of LNG ship arrivals on the utilization rates and capacity of bulk cargo berths. Acyut et al. [4] developed a simulation model for Houston's shipping channels, using ship traffic data from two years to design input parameters. They evaluated different channel closure scenarios by analyzing ship waiting times. Xavier et al. [5] researched safety and traffic evaluation metrics for port ship transportation. They constructed a multi-criteria decision-making model and performed simulations based on theoretical models to assess various scenarios. Şirin et al. [6] designed a congestion model for ship navigation in narrow waterways using a heuristic scheduling algorithm. They used metrics such as average arrival time, number of ships passing, and passage time, and conducted experimental validation using the Istanbul Strait navigation pattern. Yang et al. [7] analyzed ship AIS data from the Port of Rotterdam to study the impact of wind, visibility, ocean currents, and ship encounters on ship behavior, including speed, heading, and distance from shore. They highlighted the importance of considering external factors when constructing maritime traffic simulation models for restrictive channels.

This paper models the entire process of ships entering and leaving ports and waterways, including anchorage at the anchorage area, navigation in and out of the waterways, and loading and unloading operations. Through simulation models, it dynamically and comprehensively replicates the entire process of ship navigation in complex water areas. The study includes integrated forecasting and assessment of navigational conditions and operational information within the port system. The objective of the simulation is to optimize the service level and capacity of the port while ensuring navigational safety, thereby achieving intelligent ship management and enhancing the operational efficiency of the port.

The rest of this paper is organized as follows: In Section 2, the advantages and disadvantages and practical scope of the current mainstream simulation methods are analyzed in detail. In Section 3, the simulation model is presented. The simulation model is then verified and applied in Section 4. Finally, Section 5 concludes the paper.

2. Comparison of Mainstream Simulation Methods

System simulation has emerged as a specialized field with the advancement of computer technology since the 1940s. It involves creating a model of an actual system and using this model to test and analyze the real system. Modern system simulation technology and comprehensive simulation systems have become increasingly complex. They are essential tools for analyzing, researching, designing, evaluating, and making decisions in various domains, including traffic systems and power generation systems. The benefits of simulation applications are becoming more significant.

Simulation systems can be categorized based on their models and system characteristics into three main types: continuous systems, discrete-time systems, and discrete-event systems. The primary simulation modeling methods include the Monte Carlo method. Over time, the field has evolved to incorporate techniques such as cellular automata and multi-agent artificial intelligence methods. These approaches have further developed into hybrid models that integrate various simulation techniques.

The Monte Carlo method involves generating random numbers based on the probability distribution of random variables to simulate random processes and address problems with inherent uncertainty. This method has been effectively applied in various maritime contexts. Dąbrowska et al. [8] constructed the semi-Markov model of the change process of hydrometeorological conditions and defined the model parameters. The Monte Carlo simulation program was subsequently created, which can be applied to generate the change process of hydrometeorological conditions and predict the movement of oil spill area. Taking Zhoushan Port in Ningbo, the world's largest port, as an example, Tang et al. [9] put forward two indicators to quantify the energy efficiency of ships powered by land energy when berthing. The installation and connection of OPS in the port area were analyzed. Then, the energy demand of berthed ships was evaluated, and the potential of improving energy efficiency after implementing OPS was evaluated by the Monte Carlo method. He et al. [10] drew lessons from the accident collision risk assessment model in the aviation field and formed a suitable ship domain model according to the characteristics of ship navigation. The Monte Carlo method and the Matlab software (R2024a) were used to study the risk of ships passing through the crossing waterway, and specific countermeasures to control the navigation safety of the crossing waterway were put forward.

Discrete-Event simulation (DES) models track changes in a system only at specific time points, reflecting transitions between states or events. Neagoe et al. [11] established a discrete event simulation model of bulk cargo terminals by using the empirical data collected from weighbridges and truck geographic positioning systems. It was used for scenario analysis of several congestion management measures and evaluation of their sensitivity to increasing terminal throughput. The performance indicators used were truck turnaround time, waiting time, turnaround time reliability, and engine idle emission. Srisurin et al. [12] developed the framework of Discrete-Event Simulation (DES) and applied it to the operation of Ladd Klabunn Inland Container Terminal (LICD), one of the largest dry ports in Southeast Asia, in various operating environments. The DES framework design showed its usefulness in the analysis of LICD, allowing users to include complex operation rules in the model. Hu et al. [13] proposed a simulation-based method to support the operation decision of urban underground logistics systems (ULS) based on subways. Based on the overall concept of the ULS network prototype, this paper expounds on two integration schemes of passenger and cargo transportation in the subway network (collinear separation subway and collinear trailer subway). Petering et al. [13] created a DES model for quay crane terminals, emphasizing algorithms for yard crane dispatching to prevent deadlocks, thus optimizing crane operations. Preston et al. [14] used a discrete-event simulation model to minimize the impact of port road traffic on local communities and the environment. It is especially valuable to determine the future bottlenecks that may be formed in the port due to the expected increase in freight volume and to compare the effectiveness of different intervention measures to address this growth. It was found that flexible space is far more valuable than dedicated space. Xin et al. [15] developed a microcosmic simulation model using AIS data and considering ship acceleration, and deceleration, aimed at analyzing ship behavior under various navigational scenarios. These studies highlight the versatility of DES in modeling and improving efficiency in maritime and port operations.

Cellular automata (CA) models provide a framework for simulating complex systems by dividing space into discrete cells that evolve according to local rules over discrete time steps. These models are particularly useful for analyzing traffic patterns in various environments. Aiming at the safety of LNG ships entering and leaving the port, Liu et al. [16] proposed a port ship traffic research model based on cellular automata. Using Tianjin's LNG receiving station as an example, the ship traffic in Tianjin Port was simulated. Based on the simulation results, the capacity of LNG ships under different special traffic rules and their influence on general shipping traffic flow were obtained. The model provides theoretical support for optimizing the port traffic organization of LNG ships. Małecki et al. [17] developed a CA model for ship traffic in circular and simple cross channels. This model helps assess collision risks and evaluate the capacity of maritime traffic organization. Qi et al. [18] proposed a spatio-temporal discretization method based on the concept of standard ship. By considering safe distances and collision avoidance opportunities, the renewal rules of ship movement were established, in which the maneuverability and maneuverability of the ship were fully considered. The validity of the model was verified by simulating the ship traffic flow in a channel of the Yangtze River. Suo et al. [19] proposed a modeling method based on cellular automata simulation to analyze and evaluate real-time maritime traffic risk in port environments. They designed a CA model to monitor the ship's behavior and the sea channel traffic, combined the cloud model with expert knowledge to improve the modeling method, and finally established a risk assessment model based on fuzzy comprehensive evaluation. Qi et al. [20] introduced a marine traffic model based on CA that accounts for ship acceleration. The model's accuracy was validated by its application to traffic flows in the Dover Strait, Changshan Channel, and Qiongzhou Strait. These CA models enhance our ability to simulate and manage maritime traffic, offering valuable tools for analyzing various scenarios and improving traffic management strategies.

Multi-agent-based modeling and simulation (MABMS) is a powerful approach for simulating complex systems by leveraging autonomous agents that can perceive, react, and interact within their environment. This method is particularly effective for modeling ship traffic flow due to the behavior of ships reflecting human decisions and interactions. Fransen et al. [21] developed an agent-based model to simulate the port navigation service at Rotterdam Port. The model was constructed based on real-world process description and was calibrated and verified using empirical data. It can be used as a tool to analyze the port navigation service chain. He et al. [22] put forward an agent-based comprehensive modeling framework for large-scale multimodal transport simulations, which uses the multi-agent traffic simulation (MATSim) tool kit to solve the ever-changing challenges brought by urbanization and technology-driven human mobility mode transformation. Liu et al. [23] designed a hybrid simulation model, integrating cellular automata and multi-agent methods to analyze traffic efficiency and evaluate different ship organization schemes of these key waterway nodes. Using the Three Gorges-Gezhouba Dam as a case study, four scenarios with different traffic organization schemes, traffic flow, and anchorage capacity were simulated. Xiao et al. [24] proposed a multi-agent simulation model for ship traffic flow on the Yangtze River. The model provided insights into ship interactions, aiding in route planning, bridge design, and traffic management [25]. MABMS offers a nuanced understanding of ship behavior and interactions, making it a valuable tool for improving maritime traffic systems and safety [26].

A comparison of various simulation modeling approaches is presented in Table 1. The comparison of different modeling methods reveals that each research approach has its advantages. However, mathematical models tend to suffer from issues related to accuracy in the simulation of navigation systems. System simulation technology is an effective method for modeling navigation operations systems characterized by multiple variables, randomness, and complexity. Currently, discrete-event modeling and multi-agent modeling are common approaches in channel system simulation. Compared to discrete-event modeling, which provides a linear description of events and lacks detailed simulation, agent-based simulation modeling allows for the interaction of multiple factors and entities, including port resources, ships, navigation rules, and natural conditions. This method is generally applicable to the study of various issues in navigation operation systems.

Table 1. Comparison of mainstream simulation modeling research methods.

Method	Representative Model	Typical Applications	Advantage	Disadvantage
Monte Carlo model	Monte Carlo random simulation method	Generating random traffic flow	The most basic method of ship simulation; the main method to generate ship and navigation path	Normally, it cannot be used alone; It needs to be used in combination with other methods
		Evaluating various maritime traffic conditions		
Discrete-event model	Multi-level queuing system model of channel, anchorage and berth	Analyzing the influence of ship arrival rate on the average waiting time and average waiting length	It can accurately simulate the queuing congestion caused by random factors in the channel, and quantitatively evaluate the throughput capacity and service level of the channel	For the linear description of events, "top-down" gradually calculates along a certain variable, the random dynamic simulation is weak, and the detail simulation is missing
	Simulation model of channel system	Calculating the number of ships service, waiting time and other metrics		
	Simulation model of waterway carrying capacity	Calculating channel capacity and saturation		
Cellular automata	Cellular automata simulation model	Simulation and evaluation of ship traffic flow organization in circular channel and simple cross channel	It is easy to program and calculate high speed by using simple evolution rules to simulate complex nonlinear traffic phenomena, which is more mature in the study of road traffic flow	The influence of ship's navigation on environment is ignored; The distribution randomness is inconsistent, and the simulation accuracy is low
Multi-Agent model	Data-driven, multi-agent maritime traffic model	Simulation of global shipping model	Studying the individual characteristics and behaviors; based on the adaptability and evolution of each agent, it can adapt to emergencies at any time and dynamically adjust its behavior	Complicated calculation, long running time; Immature technology, relatively little programming research
	Traffic simulation model of straight channel	Evaluating the navigation safety of ships at sea, assisting route planning and traffic management		
	Comprehensive simulation model of port ship navigation system	Research on the influence of port service level		
Combination of system simulation and mathematical modeling	Risk assessment model of navigation safety	Calculation of port navigation safety index	Combining the advantages of various simulation modeling methods, the quantitative research effect of a specific problem can be achieved	It is limited to solve only some problems with strong pertinence, and has no universal applicability to navigation problems
	Port traffic flow model based on agent and cellular automata	Calculation of navigation safety and efficiency index		
	Discrete event simulation model of port and waterway	Calculating and evaluating various indexes of waterway carrying capacity and channel service level		

Therefore, this paper proposes a port traffic simulation modeling method based on multi-agent information interaction within the framework of multi-agent simulation modeling. By defining various elements of the port, such as anchorages, berths, and entrance and exit channels, as agents, key information, such as ship speed and position, is exchanged between these agents. The mutual influence among agent states enables a comprehensive simulation of the entire port system. The main contributions of this method include:

(a) Reflecting the entire process of ship entry and exit in complex water areas. For instance, the model can accurately depict the temporal and spatial dimensions of events including ship arrival, anchorage waiting, channel navigation, ship docking, loading and unloading operations, and ship departure. The model provides precision down to the second, offering technical means to study the impact of various events during peak ship arrival periods and off-peak periods.

(b) Quantitatively identifying control factors affecting ship navigation in the area. Based on the simulation of ship navigation operations, the model can quantitatively identify various control elements influencing ship entry and exit in the area, such as hydrometeorological conditions, channel anchorage conditions, and regulatory oversight conditions.

(c) Quantitatively evaluating channel throughput capacity and service level. Port channel throughput capacity is a key indicator of navigational capacity, while the service level of a channel measures the quality of ship operation within that channel. Systematic simulation methods allow for the study of port channel throughput capacity and service levels, which is crucial for improving channel utilization and ensuring port service quality. The calculation methods for coastal port channel throughput capacity can also support relevant regulatory provisions.

(d) Analyzing how regional channels, berths, and anchorages can be properly matched and coordinated. From the perspective of ship entry and exit, resources such as anchorages, channels, and berths are interconnected in both time and space. To enhance the efficiency of port resource utilization, the model explores the establishment of nonlinear relationships between channels, anchorages, and berths based on the simulation of the entire navigation process. This facilitates research into resource allocation and coordination in the management of channels, anchorages, and berths.

3. Model Development

To address the uncertainty, randomness, complexity, and dynamism of traffic flow and navigational environment factors in ship entry and exit processes, this paper proposes a multi-agent information interaction simulation modeling method for the entire ship port entry and exit process. The overall framework of the simulation model is illustrated in Figure 1. The model consists of a main system and a ship navigation system.

Main System: This part deals with the parameter settings related to various aspects of ship entry and exit operations at the port. It also performs the visualization of the simulation, as well as the input, output, and storage of simulation data.

Ship Navigation System: This subsystem is composed of agents for ships, anchorages, channels, and berths. It is responsible for the logical processing of ship behaviors related to port entry and exit.

Both systems interact in real time, with parameters, variables, and logical functions being exchanged and invoked as needed.

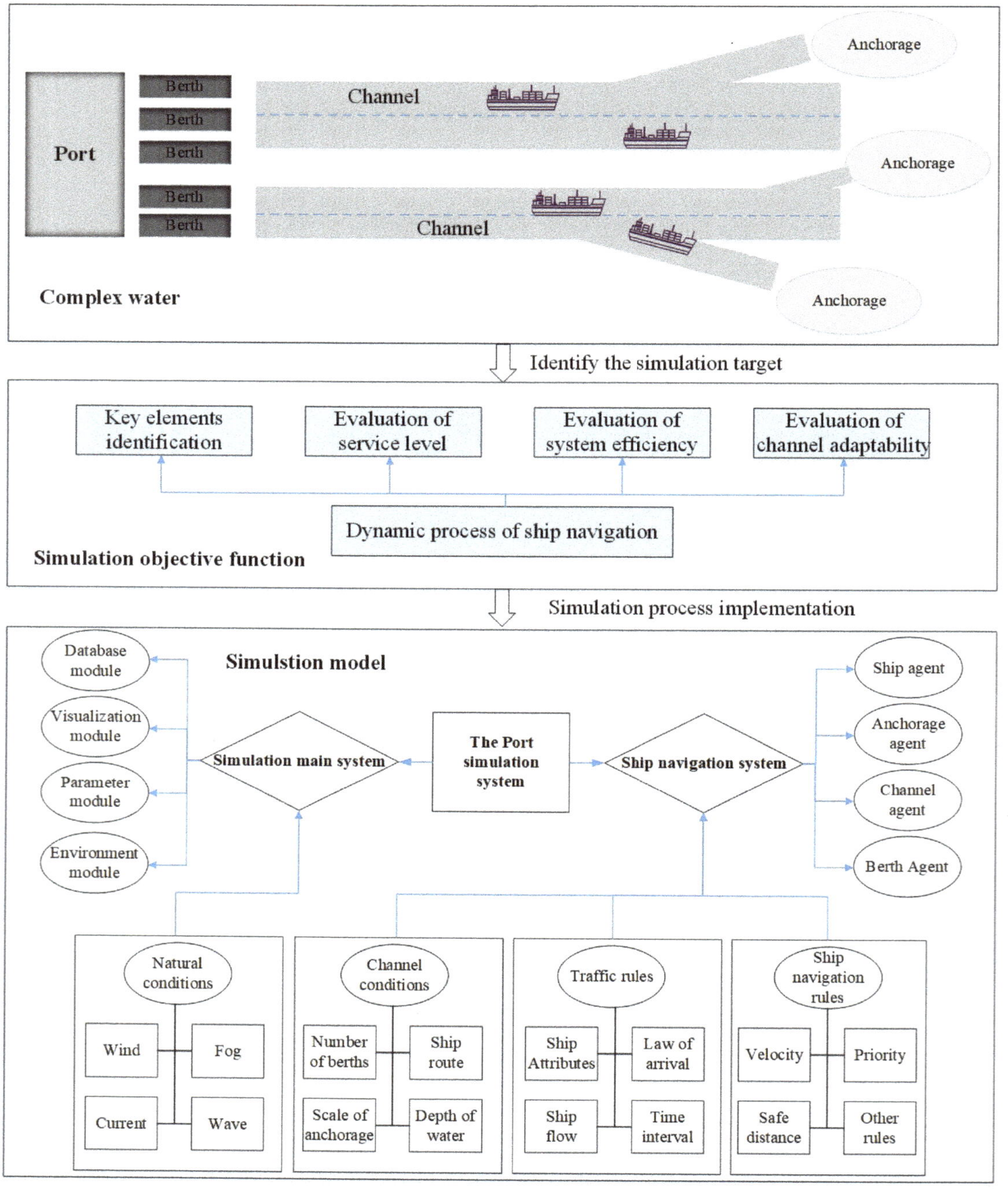

Figure 1. The framework of the simulation model.

3.1. The Simulation Main System

The simulation main system includes modules for parameters, database, visualization, and environment. This section mainly discusses the configuration of the objective functions. In port operations, port capacity and channel service level are particularly significant indicators. Therefore, a multi-objective function can be constructed based on relevant port operation indicators. We can write the multi-objective function as $M(F(m,n),\ G(m,n),\ H(s_1,s_2,\cdots),\cdots)$.

$$F(m,n) = max(\sum_{j=1}^{m}(\sum_{i=1}^{n} t_{ij}));\ t_{ij} \in (0,1) \tag{1}$$

$$G(m,n) = max(\sum_{j=1}^{m}(\sum_{i=1}^{n}(f(i,j) + g(i,j)))) \tag{2}$$

$$f(i,j) = T_{f2ij} - T_{f1ij} \tag{3}$$

$$g(i,j) = T_{g2ij} - T_{g1ij} \tag{4}$$

In Formulas (1)–(4), $F\ (m,n)$ represents the total number of ships entering and leaving the port. m indicates the number of berths, n is the predicted annual number of ships. $t_{ij} = 1$ indicates that the ith ship has finished loading and unloading at the jth berth. $T_{f1ij} = 1$ indicates the time that the ith ship has arrived at the jth berth. $T_{f2ij} = 1$ indicates the time that the ith ship has completed berthing at the jth berth. $T_{g1ij} = 1$ indicates the time that the ith ship has finished loading at the jth berth. $T_{g2ij} = 1$ indicates the time that the ith ship has left the jth berth. $H(s_1,s_2,\cdots)$ expressed as other constraints.

It is essential to emphasize that in the simulation master system, environmental conditions for ports and complex water areas, such as wind, waves, currents, and swells, can be configured. These environmental conditions are crucial within the simulation system. Furthermore, environmental conditions can impact the operability of ships and the availability of navigation channels. Under adverse environmental conditions, port entry and exit channels may be closed, preventing ships from docking at berths. Therefore, the dynamic configuration of wind, waves, currents, and swells is necessary within the simulation system.

Scenarios with varying wind speeds and directions can be set based on weather forecast data to assess their impact on ship navigation into and out of the port. Waves and swells affect ship stability and the safety of port berths. Wave models, such as spectral models, can be employed to generate various sea state conditions and analyze their effects on ships and navigation channels. Currents and tides influence ship maneuverability and port channel accessibility. Flow models, such as two-dimensional or three-dimensional fluid dynamics models, can simulate changes in water flow and assess their impact on port operations. The cumulative effects of environmental conditions may lead to channel closures or restrictions. A comprehensive model incorporating wind, waves, currents, and swells should be used to evaluate the overall impact of the environment on port operations.

Environmental conditions must be updated in real time to reflect actual changes. The simulation system should be capable of receiving and processing the latest environmental data. Feedback regarding environmental impact should be integrated into ship navigation systems and port operation systems to adjust operational strategies and resource allocation. Additionally, visualization modules should display the impact of environmental conditions on port operations, aiding decision-makers in understanding operational scenarios under complex environmental conditions.

3.2. Ship Navigation System

The ship navigation system comprises the Ship agent, Anchorage agent, Channel agent, and Berth agent. It is responsible for determining the logical processes governing ship behavior during the ingress and egress of ports.

Ship agent: Each ship is abstracted as an entity known as the Ship agent. The Ship agent possesses attributes such as type, length, width, draft, speed, time intervals, and loading/unloading times. These attributes can be described using variable ship parameters (type, length, width, draft, time, etc.). The distribution patterns of these attributes are determined through probabilistic statistical methods, which are then used to generate random variables based on these distributions.

Using methods for generating random variables over time intervals, ships can be simulated, and their respective attributes can be produced by other random variables. Once generated, the Ship agent navigates from a starting point along a predefined route. During navigation, it interacts with other agents and makes independent decisions.

The primary function of the Ship agent is to manage all data and operations related to the ship, including its position, speed, heading, load, and other pertinent information. The Ship agent provides real-time status and dynamic information about the ship, enabling other agents to make informed decisions based on these data. For instance, the Ship agent monitors whether the ship is on its planned route and whether it complies with the requirements for port entry and exit.

Anchorage agent: Each anchorage is abstracted as an entity known as the Anchorage agent. The Anchorage agent has attributes such as type, length, width, number of anchorage slots, and status. These attributes can be described using variables like anchorage type, length, width, quantity, and status.

Upon arriving at the port, ships will wait in the anchorage area for berth allocation. After a ship is assigned a berth, it is assessed to ensure that it meets various navigation conditions required for entering the channel. Only when all navigation rules are satisfied can the ship proceed into the channel.

The function of the Anchorage agent is to manage the status and utilization of the anchorage area, including its capacity, the positions of moored ships, and the environmental conditions of the anchorage. It ensures the safety of ships entering the anchorage and coordinates the usage of the anchorage area to optimize ship mooring and waiting times.

Channel agent: The Channel agent represents an abstract model of a waterway, positioned between the Berth agent and the Ship agent, serving as a medium for information exchange. From the role of the Channel agent within the overall model, it is evident that the primary information it needs to obtain includes the navigation status of ships within the channel and the queries submitted by these ships. Given the limited number of ships navigating a single channel at any one time, the volume of data to be processed is relatively small.

In the Channel agent, various parameters need to be established, including safety distances, nighttime navigation rules, ship priority rules, navigation speed regulations, and tide-based rules. Additionally, the Channel agent must consider natural conditions such as day length, wind, fog, ice, currents, waves, and tides. The attributes of the Channel agent can be described using variables related to channel permissions, priorities, speeds, and statuses.

The functions of the Channel agent include managing and monitoring the condition of the waterway, encompassing factors such as channel width, water depth, flow velocity, and other elements that might impact navigation. The Channel agent's role is to assess the channel's navigability and conduct real-time analysis of channel conditions as ships enter and exit the port. The Channel agent takes into account factors like weather, tides, and water currents, and engages in real-time information exchange with ships to ensure safe navigation.

Berth agent: The Berth agent is an abstract representation of berth operations. When a ship arrives at a berth through the port approach channel, loading and unloading operations commence. Upon completion of these operations, the ship will wait at the berth until conditions permit departure. The duration of a ship's stay at a berth varies based on the type and size of the ship, as well as the loading and unloading equipment and capacity. In the context of berth agent functionality, it is necessary to determine the number of berths, the types and sizes of ships that can dock, and the operational status of the berths. Variable berth attributes, such as type, quantity, size, and status, can be employed to describe the characteristics of berth agents.

The primary function of the Berth agent is to manage the allocation and utilization of port berths, including the monitoring of berth availability, reservation status, and the size and facilities of the berths. The role of the Berth agent is to coordinate the scheduling of ship berths, ensuring safe docking and optimizing berth utilization efficiency based on the requirements of the ships and the operational conditions of the port.

The information interaction process among multiple agents is illustrated in Figure 2. When a ship enters the port area, the Ship agent interacts with the Channel agent and Berth agent to determine if it can directly access the entry channel. If direct access to the entry channel is not possible, the Ship agent will interact with the Anchorage agent to determine an anchorage position. Upon receiving the entry command, the Ship agent interacts with both the Channel and Berth agents to confirm the arrival time and berth location. The departure procedure is the reverse of the arrival procedure. Starting from the berth, the Ship agent interacts with the Channel agent to determine the departure time. When the channel conditions are met for departure, the ship will leave the port. When transitioning from one agent to another, the Ship agent must meet the conditions required by the next agent.

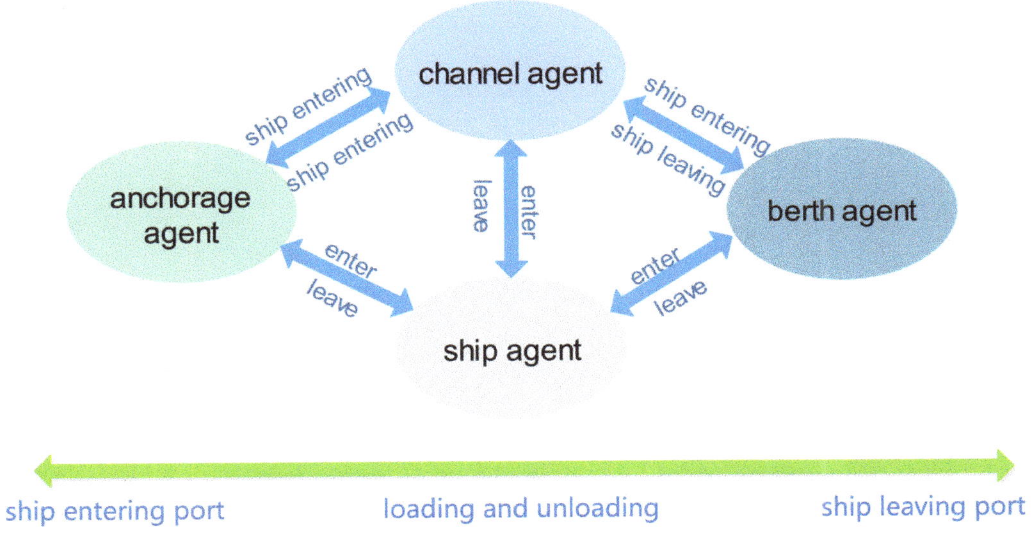

Figure 2. Multi-agent interaction process.

In this system, the Ship agent provides real-time status information on the ship, including its current location and navigation plan. The Channel agent assesses the condition of the current channel and provides information regarding its navigability and environmental conditions. The Anchorage agent decides whether the ship needs to be assigned to an anchorage based on the channel conditions and the ship's requirements. The Berth agent arranges berths based on the availability of port berths and the ship's requirements, providing berth information accordingly. Each agent receives real-time environmental data (e.g., wind speed, wave height, current speed) and updates its status. Additionally, agents adjust their operational strategies based on changes in environmental conditions. For instance, an increase in wind speed may prompt the Channel agent to recommend altering the route or delaying entry. The agents coordinate with each other and share information to facilitate the ship's entry and exit operations.

3.3. Simulation Process

The process of ship navigation and docking has been summarized and simplified. The logical flow of the entire ship entry and exit procedure is illustrated in Figure 3. According to the plan, after ships queue to enter the port, the first step is to determine whether there are available berths. If a berth is available or will soon be available, the ship will proceed to dock based on the type of berth and the order of arriving ships. If no berth is available, the ship will navigate to the anchorage and wait for a berth to become available. Given that the requirements for special ships on the channel may differ from those for standard ships, the next step is to determine whether the ship is a special ship. If it is, it will enter the port according to the specific regulations for special ships. Additionally, before entry, the ship's compliance with other navigation regulations will be assessed.

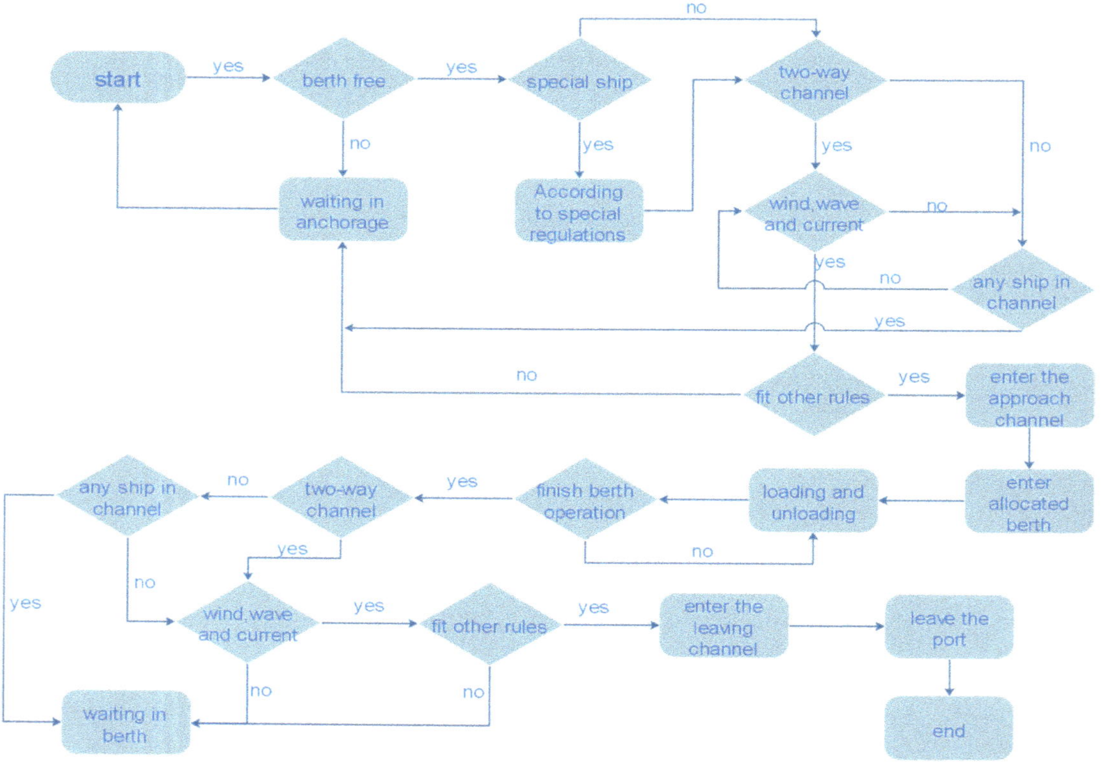

Figure 3. Logical flow of ship entering and leaving port.

The ship will conduct loading and unloading activities at the berth, continuously assessing whether these operations are complete. If not completed, the operations will continue until the loading and unloading tasks are finished. Once completed, the conditions for departure will be evaluated. If the conditions are not met, the ship will remain at the berth until the criteria for departure are satisfied. The assessment method for navigability upon departure is identical to that used for entry.

4. Model Verification and Application

4.1. Traffic Flow Statistics in Qiongzhou Strait

The Qiongzhou Strait, one of China's three major straits, is regarded as the lifeline of Hainan Island. At present, ferry services across the strait constitute the primary mode of transportation for both passengers and cargo between Hainan Island and the mainland. Surveys indicate that over 90% of goods and more than 30% of passengers are transported through the Qiongzhou Strait ferries to and from Hainan Island. Additionally, the Qiongzhou Strait serves as a crucial maritime route between Southeast Asia and western China, underscoring its significant importance. The principal ports and shipping routes of the Qiongzhou Strait are illustrated in Figure 4. Xinhai Port is the largest ferry port on Hainan Island, featuring 18 berths with an annual designed throughput capacity of 2.7 million vehicles and a passenger throughput of 18 million. Furthermore, Xinhai Port operates as a railway ferry terminal with two train berths, handling approximately 600,000 rail cars and 3 million passengers per year.

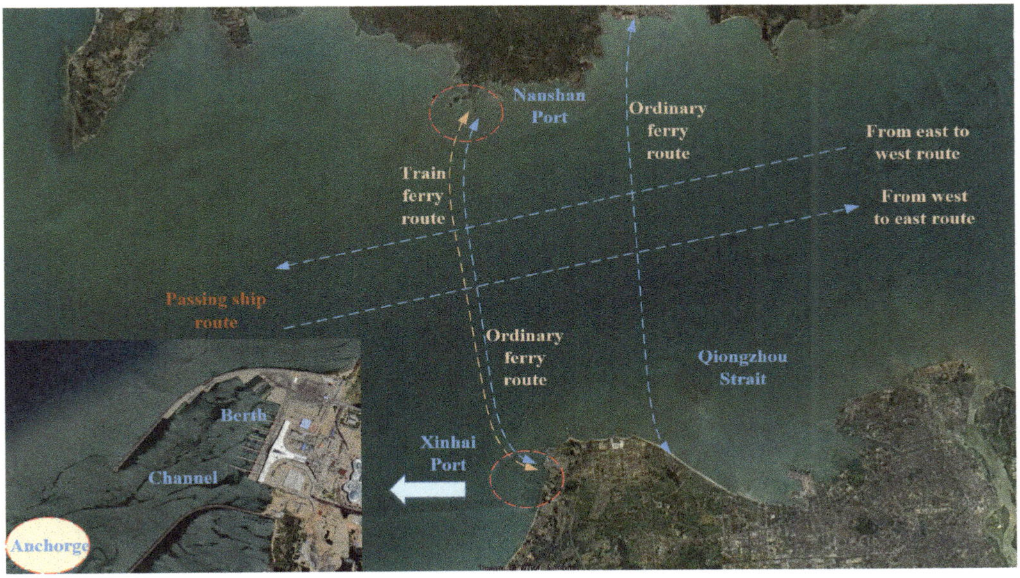

Figure 4. The Layout of Ports and Routes in Qiongzhou Strait.

Currently, maritime authorities have established a set of regulations for ships operating in the Qiongzhou Strait. These regulations encompass speed limits, safety distance constraints, and deep-water navigation routes, all of which are crucial to our modeling efforts. The Qiongzhou Strait is frequently shrouded in fog, with an average of 24 fog days per year. Fog significantly impairs visibility, reducing it to less than one mile, which can lead to disruptions in maritime services. The typhoon season spans from May to November, with September being particularly prominent. Additionally, strong rainfall at any time of day or night further limits visibility. Under these conditions, discrete-event modeling is employed to account for factors such as visibility, wind, currents, and tides, though rain-induced navigational equipment failures are seldom considered.

According to the regulations for ferry transportation in the Qiongzhou Strait, ferries must adhere to a fixed schedule and generally maintain a constant speed of 3–5 knots. At the New Harbor, the access routes for regular ferries are bidirectional, whereas those for rail ferries are unidirectional. The current length of the rail ferry is 188 m, while regular ferries range from 120 to 170 m in length. Based on calculations of ship speed, length, and safety zones, the safety distance in the port area is set at 0.5 nautical miles. Rail ferries operate from 00:00 to 24:00, while regular ferries operate from 05:00 to 23:00.

Ships entering and leaving New Harbor fall into two types: rail ferries and regular ferries. Rail ferries departing from New Harbor have an approximate interval of 90 min per trip, with a minimum departure interval of 115 min and a maximum interval of 130 min. During the off-season (May to November), regular ferries operate at an interval of one per hour, whereas, during the peak season (December to April), they operate at an interval of two per hour. During the off-season, there are 102 regular ferries, and during the peak season, there are 306. In the off-season, there are two departures every two hours with a 0.5 h interval, while in the peak season, there are two departures every 0.5 h with an interval of approximately 5 min between the two.

To comprehensively understand the operational status of traffic flow in the Qiongzhou Strait, we analyzed all AIS data from the Qiongzhou Strait between 2019 and 2022. The traffic flow heatmap, illustrated in Figure 5, clearly delineates the primary navigational routes of the ships. Additionally, we have compiled data on the distribution of ship speeds and inter-ship time intervals for the main routes in the Qiongzhou Strait, which will be used as input parameters for the simulation model.

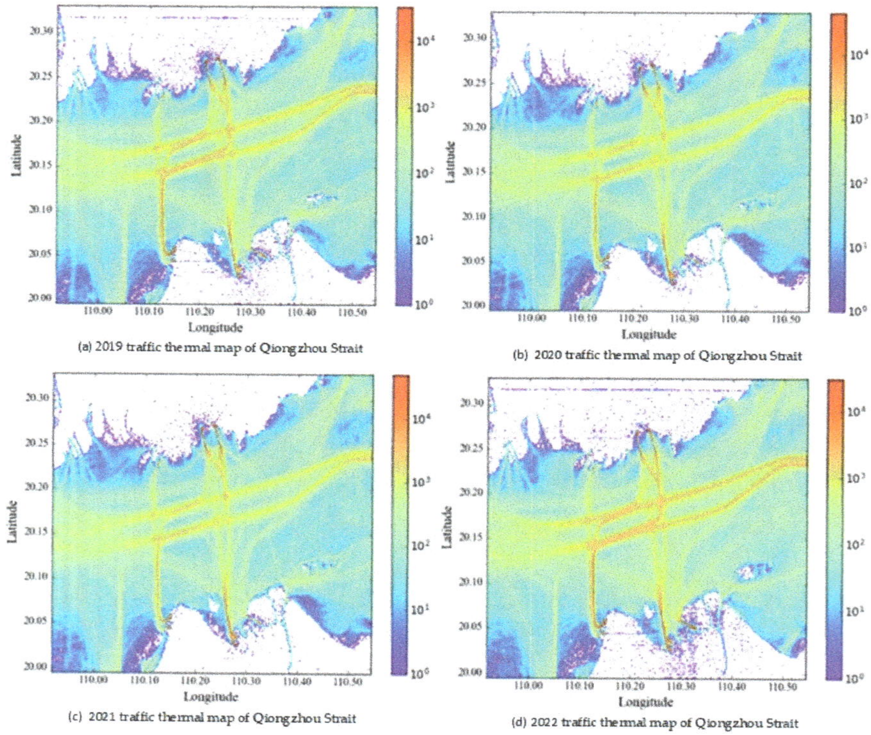

Figure 5. The heatmap of ship traffic flow in Qiongzhou Strait waters from 2019–2022.

The ship speed distribution in Qiongzhou Strait is shown in Table 2. The average speed of ships navigating from east to west within the channel is 12.125 knots, with a minimum speed of 3.9 knots and a maximum speed of 19.8 knots, indicating a substantial range in speed distribution. Conversely, ships traveling from west to east within the channel have an average speed of 9.87 knots, with a minimum speed of 3.2 knots and a maximum speed of 20 knots, also reflecting a significant variation in speed distribution.

Table 2. Distribution of ship speed.

Ship Route	Average Speed	Maximum Speed	Minimum Speed
From east to west	12.1 kn	19.8 kn	3.9 kn
From west to east	9.9 kn	20.0 kn	3.2 kn

The time interval between ship arrivals refers to the time difference between the arrival of consecutive ships at a specific observation line. This time interval is a continuous variable. Statistical analysis of ship intervals in the Qiongzhou Strait from 2019–2022 indicates that the time intervals for ships traveling in both east-to-west and west-to-east directions follow a negative exponential distribution.

If the ship arrival rate conforms to a Poisson distribution, the arrival time intervals will follow a negative exponential distribution. The time intervals for ships on the two main routes are summarized in Table 3. Additionally, the ferry services in the Qiongzhou Strait, including train ferries and conventional ferries, operate on fixed schedules. Therefore, we have also included the ferry schedules as input parameters in the simulation model.

Table 3. Distribution of ship-to-ship time interval.

Type	Minimum Time Interval	Maximum Time Interval	Velocity Distribution Function
From east to west	15 min	106 min	$f(x) = \begin{cases} 6.7191e^{-6.719x} & ,x \geq 0 \\ 0 & ,x < 0 \end{cases}$
From west to east	21 min	98 min	$f(x) = \begin{cases} 3.9416e^{-3.9416x} & ,x \geq 0 \\ 0 & ,x < 0 \end{cases}$

Regarding the berth operations, data from the Qiongzhou Strait ferry operations indicate that the operational time per berth for conventional ferries is 75 min. This includes 20 min for boarding, 20 min for disembarking, 20 min for docking, and 15 min for undocking. In contrast, the operational time per berth for train ferries is 50 min, which comprises 10 min for boarding, 10 min for disembarking, 20 min for docking, and 10 min for undocking. The ferry's navigation speed is 3 knots in the vicinity of the port and 15 knots in open water. There are 4 berths for cargo ferries and 16 berths for conventional ferries.

Based on the traffic flow analysis results, we input the actual traffic operational data into the simulation model. Simultaneously, by incorporating environmental data specific to the Qiongzhou Strait—including wind, wave, and current conditions—we developed the foundational model for the simulation system.

4.2. Application 1: Analysis of the Capacity of Intersecting Waters

According to the basic simulation model established above, we use the simulation model in this section to analyze the ship passing capacity in the intersection waters of ferry routes and passing ship routes in the Qiongzhou Strait.

The confluence zone is formed by the convergence of ferry and east–west-bound ship traffic flows. Ferries and east–west ships sequentially enter the confluence zone, which can be broadly regarded as a service facility, with ferries and east–west ships each constituting a distinct service system. In terms of the confluence zone, both east–west and ferry ships undergo two service processes and two avoidance maneuvers throughout their entry and exit from the confluence area. The overall operational process of ships within the confluence zone can be described as follows:

During the crossing interaction between ferries and ships traveling from west to east, the intentions and situational dynamics of both ferries and east–west ships are assessed. This assessment determines which ships will take the role of the primary ship and which will yield. The yielding ship is required to avoid the primary ship within the confluence zone, where the service facility is defined as the confluence zone itself. The composition of ships traveling from west to east is theoretically infinite. According to channel conditions, a maximum of two ships traveling from west to east can enter the confluence zone simultaneously. The time intervals between ships entering the confluence zone are random, with the distribution and parameters (such as expected values, variances, etc.) of the inter-arrival times being independent of time. The trajectory distribution of east–west ships within the regulated lane system also follows the previously mentioned statistical distribution, with the confluence zone operating under a first-come, first-served rule.

Throughout this process, the number of ships that can be accommodated within the confluence zone is limited due to the requirement for minimum safety distances between ships. Ferry traffic is generated according to a fixed ferry timetable, while east–west ship traffic follows statistical patterns. The confluence zone thus experiences crossing interactions between ferries and east–west ships, with ferry and east–west ships determining avoidance timings based on minimum encounter time and distance principles. Additionally, the avoidance methods and resumption times of yielding ships are assessed. If the resumption time and route fall outside the confluence zone, the avoidance maneuver is deemed unsuccessful, and the yielding ship will be unable to pass through the confluence zone. The maximum throughput capacity of east–west ships through the confluence zone is determined by statistical analysis of the number of east–west ships passing through within 24 h. The simulation diagram is shown in Figure 6.

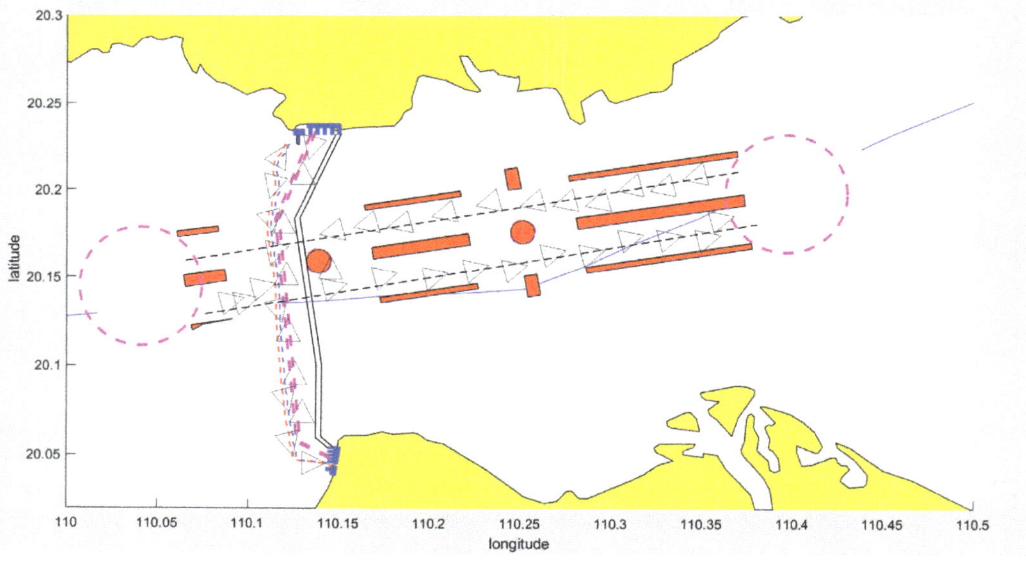

Figure 6. The dynamic simulation process of ships in intersecting waters.

In the simulation, we assume that the short-term ship flow forecast in the east–west direction is 300 ships/day, which is simulated in nine working conditions, that is, the average speed of the east–west ships is 10, 12 and 14 kn, and the minimum safe distance between the east–west ships is 0.5, 1 and 1.5 nm. The simulation results are shown in Table 4.

Table 4. The simulation results of the capacity of intersection waters.

	Safe Distance between Ships = 0.5 nm	Safe Distance between Ships = 1 nm	Safe Distance between Ships = 1.5 nm
Average Speed of passing ships = 10 kn	Train ferry = 19 Ordinary ferry = 72	Train ferry = 15 Ordinary ferry = 68	Train ferry = 14 Ordinary ferry = 59
Average Speed of passing ships = 12 kn	Train ferry = 21 Ordinary ferry = 79	Train ferry = 18 Ordinary ferry = 77	Train ferry = 16 Ordinary ferry = 71
Average Speed of passing ships = 14 kn	Train ferry = 22 Ordinary ferry = 83	Train ferry = 19 Ordinary ferry = 78	Train ferry = 17 Ordinary ferry = 77

Based on the analysis of the aforementioned simulation results, it can be concluded that, given the recent demand for east–west ship traffic at 150 pairs per day, the current traffic organization model is generally adequate to meet the operational requirements. Specifically, the public railway ferries and regional ferries together can handle this demand, with 16 pairs of public railway ferries and 77 pairs of regional ferries operating. At this point, the average sailing speed of east–west ships is 12 knots, and the minimum safety distance is 1 nautical mile.

Furthermore, increasing the sailing speed of east–west ships through the confluence zone significantly enhances the channel's throughput capacity. When the average speed is increased to 14 knots, the throughput capacity is approximately 30% higher compared to a speed of 10 knots. It is important to note that the size of the safety distance between east–west ships directly impacts the throughput capacity of the confluence zone. When the safety distance is set to 0.5 nautical miles, the throughput capacity approximately doubles compared to when the safety distance is set to 1.5 nautical miles. However, setting the safety distance to 0.5 nautical miles reduces the safety margin, thereby increasing the navigational risk.

4.3. Application 2: Analysis of Port and Berth Operation Capacity

Based on the simulation model established in Section 4.1, we evaluated the port operational capacity of the new port in the Qiongzhou Strait to determine its actual operational status. The results of the simulation, as presented in Table 5, indicate the following:

Table 5. The simulation results of the present situation of Xinhai port.

Ship Type	Port Capacity	Current Number	Median Tardiness
Train ferry	57	28	0.20 h
Ordinary ferry	149	72	0.15 h

The analysis of the simulation results shows that, under the current ship traffic conditions, there is no need to establish additional mooring or anchorage areas outside the port zone. The existing port basin capacity is sufficient to meet the demands of incoming and outgoing ships. The utilization rate of port resources for railway ferries and regular ferries is approximately 55%, suggesting that the efficiency of port facilities is relatively moderate with some available capacity.

The number of ships in the inbound channel is 49, while the number in the outbound channel is 51, indicating a generally balanced flow of ships into and out of the port. Berth operations are functioning normally, with no significant incidents of ship congestion observed. Overall, the simulation results demonstrate that the current facilities at the new port are effectively supporting the existing ship traffic, and the port's operational status is stable. There is no need for additional berths or anchorage areas.

The analysis of the simulation results indicates that the throughput capacity of the new port far exceeds the current planned number of ships, ensuring that there will be no delays for ships entering and leaving the port. For conventional ferries, whether during peak or off-peak seasons, the port's capacity remains greater than the number of scheduled sailings. Since the simulation generates ship arrivals based on arrival patterns, the average delay time is attributed to the inherent uncertainty in ship arrivals.

Based on the simulation outcomes, future ship schedules for the new port can be predicted with greater accuracy, enabling better scheduling of ferry services. The current schedule for rail ferries is detailed in Table 6. It is observed that the intervals between train ferry operations are relatively uneven, affecting the port's operational efficiency and average delay times. According to the planning for rail ferries, there is a proposal to increase the daily operation to 24 pairs of train ferries to enhance transport capacity. The simulation results support this decision and validate the feasibility of the proposed plan and its impact on delay times.

Table 6. The current railway ferry operation plan.

Shift Number	Train Ferry Operating Time	Time Interval
1	0:28	-
2	2:26	118 min
3	4:11	105 min
4	5:52	101 min
5	7:36	104 min
6	9:09	93 min
7	10:54	105 min
8	12:37	103 min
9	14:34	117 min
10	16:45	131 min
11	18:18	93 min
12	19:55	97 min
13	21:25	90 min
14	22:50	85 min

Furthermore, the simulation helps identify key navigational factors affecting the port's throughput capacity. In the new port, the critical factors influencing rail ferries are the channel configuration and the number of berths. The rail ferry's inbound channel is unidirectional, leading to mutual interference between inbound and outbound ferries. Additionally, the presence of only two berths for rail ferries significantly restricts the port's throughput capacity. For conventional ferries, key factors include berth operation times and the size of the turning basin, which can be improved through the introduction of new ship types and rational planning of port waters.

In addition, the simulation results can also be applied to guide the port construction and development direction. According to the development plan, a high-speed railway ferry is likely to operate in the Xinhai port; the schedules of a high-speed railway are shown in Tables 7–9, and the simulation results are shown in Figures 7–9.

Table 7. The high-speed railway ferry operation plan (Stage 1).

The Period of Time	Number of High-Speed Railway Ferries	Time Interval
06:00–07:00	4	15 min
07:00–08:00	5	12 min
08:00–09:00	3	20 min
09:00–10:00	3	20 min
10:00–11:00	2	30 min
11:00–12:00	2	30 min

Table 7. *Cont.*

The Period of Time	Number of High-Speed Railway Ferries	Time Interval
12:00–13:00	2	30 min
13:00–14:00	2	30 min
14:00–15:00	2	30 min
15:00–16:00	2	30 min
16:00–17:00	3	20 min
17:00–18:00	3	20 min
18:00–19:00	5	12 min
19:00–20:00	3	20 min
20:00–21:00	2	30 min
21:00–22:00	1	60 min

Table 8. The high-speed railway ferry operation plan (Stage 2).

The Period of Time	Number of High-Speed Railway Ferries	Time Interval
06:00–07:00	4	15 min
07:00–08:00	6	10 min
08:00–09:00	4	15 min
09:00–10:00	3	20 min
10:00–11:00	3	20 min
11:00–12:00	3	20 min
12:00–13:00	3	20 min
13:00–14:00	3	20 min
14:00–15:00	3	20 min
15:00–16:00	4	15 min
16:00–17:00	4	15 min
17:00–18:00	5	12 min
18:00–19:00	6	10 min
19:00–20:00	4	15 min
20:00–21:00	3	20 min
21:00–22:00	2	30 min

Table 9. The high-speed railway ferry operation plan (Stage 3).

The Period of Time	Number of High-Speed Railway Ferries	Time Interval
05:00–06:00	3	20 min
06:00–07:00	5	12 min
07:00–08:00	6	10 min
08:00–09:00	8	7.5 min
09:00–10:00	5	12 min
10:00–11:00	4	15 min
11:00–12:00	4	15 min
12:00–13:00	4	15 min
13:00–14:00	4	15 min
14:00–15:00	4	15 min
15:00–16:00	4	15 min
16:00–17:00	5	12 min
17:00–18:00	6	10 min
18:00–19:00	8	7.5 min
19:00–20:00	6	10 min
20:00–21:00	5	12 min
21:00–22:00	4	15 min

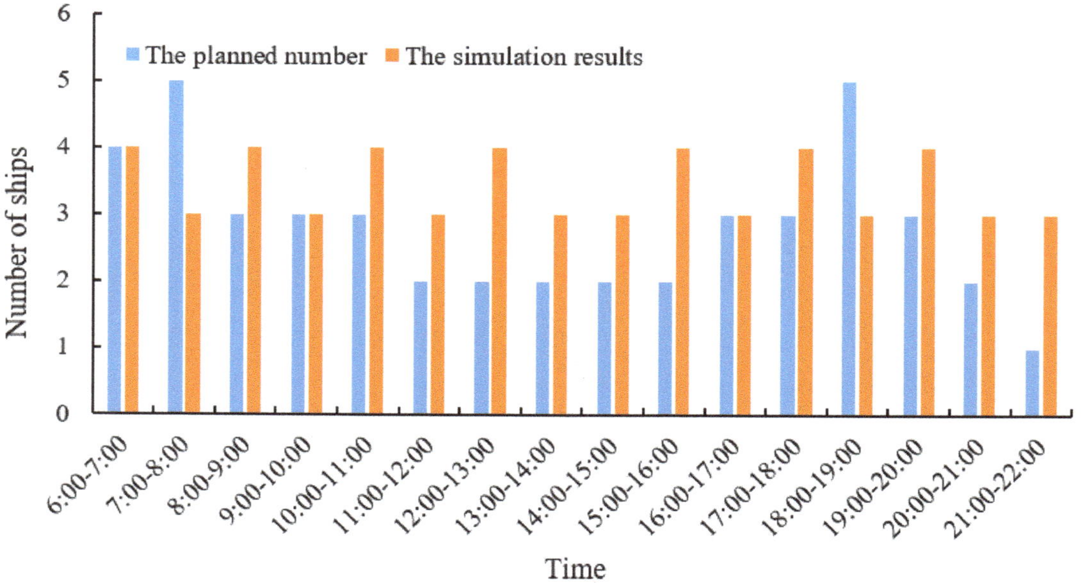

Figure 7. Comparison of the planned number and simulation results for the high-speed railway ferry (Stage 1).

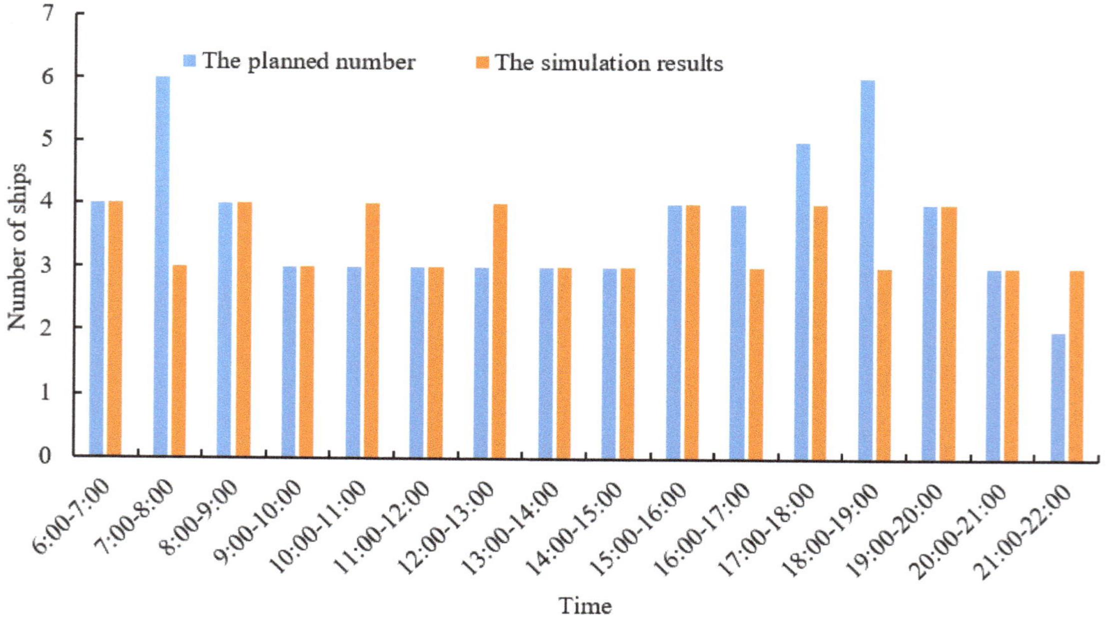

Figure 8. Comparison of the planned number and simulation results for the high-speed railway ferry (Stage 2).

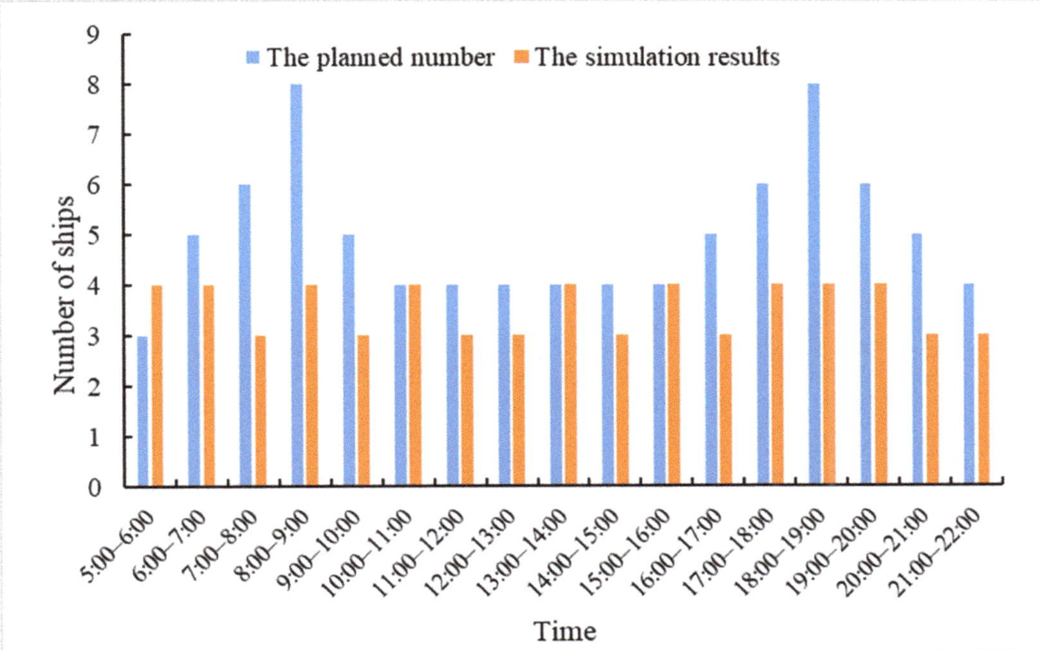

Figure 9. Comparison of the planned number and simulation results for the high-speed railway ferry (Stage 3).

Based on the simulation results, it can be inferred that the port's capacity will reach saturation during the second phase, and once saturation is achieved, the delay rate will increase with the rise in the number of planned ships. To accommodate the transportation demand of the third phase, and given the excess capacity of the conventional ferry berths, we propose converting the existing conventional ferry berths into high-speed rail ferry berths. Utilizing the revised number of berths, the simulation model can be employed to simulate the entire process of ship movement into and out of the port, thereby assessing the overall operational efficiency of the port.

4.4. Discussion

This paper is based on a multi-agent simulation model framework that emphasizes the importance of information exchange among different agents. It establishes a simulation model for the traffic flow in the complex waters of the Qiongzhou Strait, which consists of two main components: first, the simulation of ship traffic flow in the open waters outside the port, and second, the simulation of ship traffic flow in the constrained waters of the port.

The experimental results indicate that by utilizing existing traffic flow statistical data and inputting it into the simulation system, the operational status of ship traffic flow within the water area can be effectively simulated. Depending on the simulation objectives, this model allows for the discussion and analysis of the navigational capacity in areas where ferries and passing ships intersect by providing organizational measures for managing ship traffic flow in these intersection areas and offering effective status analysis data to management authorities. Additionally, the simulation of ship traffic flow in the constrained waters of the port allows for a thorough understanding of the current operational status of the port, facilitates analysis of port operational capacity, and guides port planning and development. It aids in identifying key factors affecting port operations, analyzing constraints on operational capacity, and proposing management and improvement measures.

In this model, key elements involved in ship navigation are defined as agents, which influence each other by changing their states. Compared to existing multi-agent simulation models, the proposed model effectively adjusts the states of multiple agents based on environmental conditions and accurately reflects the changes in ship navigation elements due to environmental variations. By establishing a comprehensive simulation model of the entire ship navigation process, it provides a more thorough analysis of ship traffic flow than single-process simulation models.

During the establishment of the ship traffic flow simulation model, it is crucial to identify simulation parameters that align with actual traffic flow conditions based on existing traffic operational status. In ship traffic flow, AIS data can be used to analyze current traffic flow indicators.

To maintain consistency with real traffic flow conditions, the simulation process needs to be adjusted in real time according to the simulation objectives. In our model, it is convenient to dynamically adjust the simulation based on the states of multiple agents.

5. Conclusions and Prospect

To address the needs of port planning and support decision-making, a port simulation model based on multi-agent information interaction has been developed, considering the current research status and practical requirements. This paper first presents the simulation framework for ship movements into and out of the port. Agents in the simulation model are categorized into Ship agents, Channel agents, Anchorage agents, and Berth agents, based on their types and functions. Next, the paper designs interaction mechanisms for different types of agents. Through information exchange between ship agents and other agents, navigational rules for Ship agents within Anchorage agents, Channel agents, and Berth agents are established. Finally, the proposed simulation model is validated using the example of the new port at the Qiongzhou Strait. Simulation results indicated that the model effectively simulates the entire process of ships entering and exiting the port, and accurately predicted port throughput and average ship delay times. Additionally, based on the simulation results, port planning proposals can be made and validated.

In the future, the proposed multi-agent information interaction port simulation model can be expanded and upgraded to address areas such as multi-source data integration, intelligent scheduling for port water–land coordination, comprehensive planning for port clusters, and joint operations.

Author Contributions: Conceptualization, D.H.; methodology, D.H.; formal analysis, H.C., C.X. and Z.S.; investigation, D.H.; resources, H.C.; data curation, X.C. and Z.S.; writing—original draft, D.H. and X.C.; writing—review & editing, D.H.; supervision, H.C. and C.X.; project administration, Y.W.; funding acquisition, Y.W. All authors have read and agreed to the published version of the manuscript.

Funding: This work is supported by the Research Program of Sanya City through Grant No. 2022KJCX36, the National Natural Science Foundation of China (NSFC) through Grant No. 52072287, and the Zhejiang Provincial Science and Technology Program (Grant No. 2021C01010).

Institutional Review Board Statement: Not applicable.

Informed Consent Statement: Not applicable.

Data Availability Statement: Data are contained within the article.

Acknowledgments: This work is supported by China State Railway Group Co., Ltd. This support is gratefully acknowledged.

Conflicts of Interest: The authors declare no conflict of interest.

References

1. Ham, S.H.; Roh, M.I.; Zhao, L. Integrated method of analysis, visualization, and hardware for ship motion simulation. *J. Comput. Des. Eng.* **2018**, *5*, 285–298. [CrossRef]
2. Moran, V.; Linares, J.; Atienza, R.; Redondo, R.; Iribarren, J.R.; Groenveld, R. Development of the wet infrastructure of the port of the port of Bahia Blanca in Argentina. In Proceedings of the PIANC World Congress, San Francisco, CA, USA, 1–5 June 2014.
3. Perkovic, M.; Gucma, L.; Przywarty, M.; Gucma, M.; Petelin, S.; Vidmar, P. Nautical risk assessment for LNG operations at the Port of Koper. *Stroj. Vestn.-J. Mech. Eng.* **2012**, *58*, 607–613. [CrossRef]
4. Kaneria, A.; Hamidi, M.; Zhu, W.; Craig, B. Traffic simulation of Houston Ship Channel for assessing the impact of waterway closures on ship waiting time. *J. Waterw. Port Coast. Ocean Eng.* **2019**, *145*, 04019014. [CrossRef]
5. Olba, X.B.; Daamen, W.; Vellinga, T.; Hoogendoorn, S.P. Multi-criteria evaluation of ship traffic for port assessment: A case study of the Port of Rotterdam. *Case Stud. Transp. Policy* **2019**, *7*, 871–881. [CrossRef]
6. Özlem, Ş.; Or, İ.; Altan, Y.C. Scheduling and simulation of maritime traffic in congested waterways: An application to the Strait of Istanbul. *J. Navig.* **2021**, *74*, 656–672. [CrossRef]
7. Shu, Y.; Daamen, W.; Ligteringen, H.; Hoogendoorn, S.P. Influence of external conditions and ship encounters on ship behavior in ports and waterways using Automatic Identification System data. *Ocean Eng.* **2017**, *131*, 1–14. [CrossRef]
8. Dąbrowska, E.; Kołowrocki, K. Monte Carlo simulation approach to determination of oil spill domains at port and sea water areas. *TransNav Int. J. Mar. Navig. Saf. Sea Transp.* **2020**, *14*, 59–64. [CrossRef]
9. Tang, D.; Jiang, T.; Xu, C.; Chen, Z.; Yuan, Y.; Zhao, W.; Guerrero, J.M. Assessing the Potential for Energy Efficiency Improvement through Cold Ironing: A Monte Carlo Analysis with Real Port Data. *J. Mar. Sci. Eng.* **2023**, *11*, 1780. [CrossRef]
10. He, Y.; Wan, H.; Tian, W.; Meng, B.; Qin, Z.; Huang, Y. Risk assessment of ship collision in cross-channel based on Monte Carlo method. In Proceedings of the 2021 6th International Conference on Transportation Information and Safety (ICTIS), Wuhan, China, 22–24 October 2021; pp. 306–309.
11. Neagoe, M.; Hvolby, H.H.; Taskhiri, M.S.; Turner, P. Using discrete-event simulation to compare congestion management initiatives at a port terminal. *Simul. Model. Pract. Theory* **2021**, *112*, 102362. [CrossRef]
12. Qu, X.; Meng, Q. Development and applications of a simulation model for ships in the Singapore Straits. *Expert Syst. Appl.* **2012**, *39*, 8430–8438. [CrossRef]
13. Hu, W.; Dong, J.; Yang, K.; Hwang, B.-G.; Ren, R.; Chen, Z. Modeling Real-time operations of Metro-based urban underground logistics system network: A discrete event simulation approach. *Tunn. Undergr. Space Technol.* **2023**, *132*, 104896. [CrossRef]
14. Preston, G.C.; Horne, P.; Scaparra, M.P.; O'hanley, J.R. Masterplanning at the Port of Dover: The use of discrete-event simulation in managing road traffic. *Sustainability* **2020**, *12*, 1067. [CrossRef]
15. Xin, X.; Liu, K.; Yang, X.; Yuan, Z.; Zhang, J. A simulation model for ship navigation in the "Xiazhimen" waterway based on statistical analysis of AIS data. *Ocean Eng.* **2019**, *180*, 279–289. [CrossRef]
16. Liu, J.; Liu, Y.; Qi, L. Modelling liquefied natural gas ship traffic in port based on cellular automaton and multi-agent system. *J. Navig.* **2021**, *74*, 533–548. [CrossRef]
17. Małecki, K. Graph cellular automata with relation-based neighbourhoods of cells for complex systems modelling: A case of traffic simulation. *Symmetry* **2017**, *9*, 322. [CrossRef]
18. Qi, L.; Ji, Y.; Balling, R.; Xu, W. A cellular automaton-based model of ship traffic flow in busy waterways. *J. Navig.* **2021**, *74*, 605–618. [CrossRef]
19. Suo, Y.; Sun, Z.; Claramunt, C.; Yang, S.; Zhang, Z. A dynamic risk appraisal model and its application in VTS based on a cellular automata simulation prediction. *Sensors* **2021**, *21*, 4741. [CrossRef] [PubMed]
20. Qi, L.; Zheng, Z.; Gang, L. Marine traffic model based on cellular automaton: Considering the change of the ship's velocity under the influence of the weather and sea. *Phys. A Stat. Mech. Its Appl.* **2017**, *483*, 480–494. [CrossRef]
21. Fransen, R.W.; Davydenko, I.Y. Empirical agent-based model simulation for the port nautical services: A case study for the Port of Rotterdam. *Marit. Transp. Res.* **2021**, *2*, 100040. [CrossRef]
22. He, B.Y.; Jiang, Q.; Ma, H.; Ma, J. Multi-Agent Multimodal Transportation Simulation for Mega-cities: Application of Los Angeles. *Procedia Comput. Sci.* **2024**, *238*, 736–741. [CrossRef]
23. Vaněk, O.; Jakob, M.; Hrstka, O.; Pěchouček, M. Using multi-agent simulation to improve the security of maritime transit. In *International Workshop on Multi-Agent Systems and Agent-Based Simulation*; Springer: Berlin/Heidelberg, Germany, 2011; pp. 44–58.
24. Xiao, F.; Ligteringen, H.; Van Gulijk, C.; Ale, B. Nautical traffic simulation with multi-agent system for safety. In Proceedings of the 16th International IEEE Conference on Intelligent Transportation Systems (ITSC 2013), The Hague, The Netherlands, 6–9 October 2013; IEEE: Piscataway, NJ, USA, 2013; pp. 1245–1252.
25. Venturini, G.; Iris, Ç.; Kontovas, C.A.; Larsen, A. The multi-port berth allocation problem with speed optimization and emission considerations. *Transp. Res. Part D Transp. Environ.* **2017**, *54*, 142–159. [CrossRef]
26. Szlapczynski, R.; Krata, P.; Szlapczynska, J. Ship domain applied to determining distances for collision avoidance manoeuvres in give-way situations. *Ocean Eng.* **2018**, *165*, 43–54. [CrossRef]

Journal of
Marine Science and Engineering

MDPI

Article

Dynamic Calculation Approach of the Collision Risk in Complex Navigable Water

Yihan Chen [1,*], Qing Yu [2], Weiqiang Wang [3] and Xiaolie Wu [3]

1 School of Data Science and Computing, Xiamen Institute of Technology, Xiamen 361021, China
2 School of Navigation, Jimei University, Xiamen 361021, China; qing.yu@jmu.edu.cn
3 School of Navigation, Wuhan University of Technology, Wuhan 430063, China; weiqiangwang@whut.edu.cn (W.W.); xlwu@whut.edu.cn (X.W.)
* Correspondence: cyh0929@whut.edu.cn; Tel.: +86-18396382676

Abstract: It is vital to analyze ship collision risk for preventing collisions and improving safety at sea. This paper takes Ningbo-Zhoushan Port, a typical complex navigable water, as the research object. Firstly, a probabilistic conflict detection method based on an AIS data-driven dynamic ship domain model is proposed to achieve effective ship conflict detection under uncertain environments. Then, a ship group identification method is proposed, which can extract the ship groups with conflict correlation and space compactness. Finally, according to the characteristics of ship traffic in complex navigable waters, the dynamic calculation of ship collision risk is carried out from individual, regional, and local multi-scale perspectives. The experimental results show that the proposed method can detect the collision risk in a timely, reliable, and effective manner under complex dynamic conditions. As such, they provide valuable insights into ship collision risk prediction and the development of risk mitigation measures.

Keywords: ship navigation safety; risk quantification; complex water; group of ships

1. Introduction

The growing shipping volume leads to higher traffic density and a more complex navigation environment, especially in hot areas such as complex navigable waters. Ship collision and grounding are the most common types of accidents [1]. Such accidents will cause serious economic losses, greatly threaten life safety and the marine environment, and seriously hinder the improvement and development of water transportation efficiency.

Ship navigation safety is the primary issue of global maritime development, and it is the most fundamental prerequisite for improving shipping efficiency, strengthening port operation and management, and ensuring the high-quality development of transportation [2]. Related research shows that the proportion of ship accidents caused by human factors reaches 83%, of which 71% of the human errors are caused by the drivers' inaccurate perception of navigating risks [3]. Accurate, real-time, and dynamic navigation risk perception is an important basis for supervision from the perspective of water navigation management. Especially in the complex navigable waters with high ship density, various types of ships, significant interaction and interference between ships, and great differences in risks in different local waters, more and more attention has been paid to the accurate, real-time, and dynamic calculation of ship navigation risks.

At present, the research on ship navigation risk is mainly carried out along two paths [4]. One is from the perspective of ship navigation and maneuvering. This kind of method usually uses the geometric parameters between the ship and the nearby obstacles to construct risk modeling by carrying out the collision accident frequency and consequence estimation to realize the risk quantification. Second, it is carried out from the perspective of water navigation management, and this kind of method is based on "human–ship–environment management" to identify the risk factors of ship navigation, and construct a cognitive model of domain experts to quantify the risk.

The core port area of Ningbo-Zhoushan Port in was selected as the research water area. It is a unique deep-water port with the highest concentration of ship traffic in the world. There are more than 620 berths here, including about 170 large berths over 10,000 tons and more than 100 ultra-large deep-water berths over 50,000 tons. Restricted geographical area, diverse ship types, dynamic ship movement behavior, and complex navigation environment make ship traffic safety management in this region extremely challenging. Therefore, the waters are typical of complex port waters.

This paper takes complex navigable waters as the research object, conducts relevant research on the dynamic calculation of ship navigation risks, and proposes a ship group division method from the perspective of water navigation management based on the ship conflict probability detection method based on AIS data. It aims to establish a navigation risk quantification model for different local waters that comprehensively considers the spatiotemporal dynamics and uncertainty of ship movement, systematically forms a dynamic calculation theory of ship navigation risk, reduces the regulatory pressure of maritime authorities, and provides a valuable reference for more accurate and timely provision of appropriate control and management strategies based on real conflict situations.

The rest of the study is organized as follows: The second section summarizes the two current paths of studying the risk of ship collision. In the third section, the proposed dynamic calculation method of navigation risk is introduced in detail, including ship conflict probability detection, ship group extraction, and key ship identification. The fourth section gives the application results and performance test of the actual AIS data experiment. The fifth section gives the conclusion.

2. Literature Review

The risk of ship collision has always been a hot topic in the field of ship transportation. Many researchers have devoted themselves to quantifying the probability and risk of ship collision using various methods from different perspectives. This paper summarizes the current research situation at home and abroad based on the two major research paths of ship navigation risk: the navigation risk research based on the perspective of ship steering and the research on ship navigation risk from the perspective of water navigation management. The two research paths are relatively independent. The former is mainly suitable for ship navigation risk calculation in local waters, and its spatial scope is mostly the waters where ships avoid collision, so its scalability is poor. The latter is mostly based on the overall risk level of a specific regional water area, and its spatial scope is relatively wider, and the risk space–time granularity is larger.

2.1. Based on Ship Driving and Maneuvering Perspective

In recent years, the rapid development of various advanced equipment and technologies has improved the ability to collect, store, and process ship trajectory data, providing a rich data source for the detection and analysis of ship collision risks [5,6]. Various definitions and concepts, such as "traffic conflict" [7], "collision candidate" [8], and "near miss" [9], have been used to detect and characterize the collision risk between ships. The relevant risk detection methods can be divided into ship domain-based methods, comprehensive indicator methods, and danger zone-based methods.

Among them, the collision risk detection method based on the ship domain model is one of the most widely used methods at present [10]. The ship domain refers to the area around the ship where other ships or obstacles need to maintain a certain distance. At present, the development of various intelligent technologies and the continuous increase in AIS data sources have promoted the proposal of various ship domain models. These models have different shapes (such as circular [11], polygonal [12], quadruple [13], fuzzy [1], and risk-based [14] ship domains), adopt different theoretical methods (such as based on experience, knowledge, and analysis [15]), and consider different influencing factors (such as ship attributes, crew knowledge and fatigue status, ship maneuverability, traffic conditions, and navigation environment [16]). They perform collision risk assessment and detection based on the intrusion or overlap of ship domains and perform well in quantitatively examining encounter scenarios with collision possibilities and unexpected consequences and in collision warning.

The comprehensive index method usually adopts mathematical expressions or black box models to calculate the collision risk index by integrating relevant factors that characterize the spatiotemporal proximity of ships. Initially, the two most common indicators, namely, the distance to the closest point of approach (DCPA) and the time to the closest point of approach (TCPA), were fused by various technical means (such as binary state (i.e., safe/dangerous), weighted coefficients [17], linear regression [18], and fuzzy theory [19]) to measure the collision risk index (CRI). Subsequently, such methods have been improved and extended by considering more risk-influencing factors (e.g., distance, relative bearing, relative speed, ship maneuverability, and ship domain [20,21]) and adopting advanced fusion techniques (e.g., support vector machine [22], hierarchical analysis method, and Dempster–Shafer evidence theory [23]) to ensure that they are applicable to various complex encounter scenarios. However, most of the methods in such studies follow an assumption that the target ship will maintain its current speed and sail in a straight line in the near future. This assumption often leads to inaccurate or unreliable detection of collision risk, especially when the ship performs certain maneuvers (such as changes in heading or speed) during the encounter. In addition, the interaction between different risk factors makes it difficult for such methods to provide clear meaning and interpretation for the CRI results.

For the hazard area-based methods, they rely on collecting sets of own ship speeds and/or headings that cause a collision risk with the target ship, and if the real-time speed/heading of the own ship falls into these sets, a collision warning is issued. The typical hazard area identification methods include collision threat parameter area (CTPA) [24], projected obstacle area (POA) [25], velocity obstacle (VO) [26], etc., among which VO has been widely used due to its simple implementation and ability to effectively find conflict resolution solutions. Related application examples include combining the ship domain with VO [27], constructing nonlinear VO, probabilistic VO, and generalized VO algorithms by releasing the assumption of the linear motion of ships and considering the maneuverability of ship motion [28], considering the entire ship encounter process when detecting potential collisions [20], and estimating the time-varying collision risk by the percentage of overlapping area between the VO set and the achievable speed set [29]. These studies show that this type of research can detect real collision risks under dynamic traffic conditions and can be applied to various encounter scenarios. However, due to the non-negligible computational cost of mapping the spatiotemporal proximity between ships into velocity space, such methods are difficult to combine with complex danger zone models. Therefore, they are usually combined with some simple risk measurement models, such as constant minimum safety distance and circular ship field, to detect potential collision risks in real time. This leads to the insufficiency of such studies in revealing the differences in the collision risks of ships in different encounter situations.

2.2. From the Perspective of Water Navigation Management

Research on ship navigation risks from the perspective of water navigation management usually quantitatively describes the level of ship navigation risks in a specific navigation water area, which can provide a basis for water navigation management and decision making.

Statistical analysis of historical maritime accidents is one of the basic methods to determine the relationship between collision frequency (and possible accident consequences) and risk factors (such as ship attributes, environmental factors, human behavior, technical failures, and traffic conditions) [30]. Usually, such studies use information such as accident databases and accident investigation reports to support the analysis [31]. Techniques such as correlation analysis, logistic regression, and random process analysis are often used to predict the probability of accidents related to events and environments [32,33] in order to gain a deeper understanding of the conditions under which the probability of ship traffic accidents is higher. However, such studies are highly dependent on historical accident data, which is not always easy to obtain. Especially when studying small sea areas, the frequency of collision accidents is usually very low, which makes it difficult to conduct effective statistical analysis [34]. This problem is particularly prominent when focusing on the relationship between many risk-related factors and collision accidents. Therefore, in order to more clearly understand the formation mechanism of ship collision risk, it is necessary to adopt more data and information sources.

Compared with the statistical analysis of historical accidents, collision risk modeling integrates multiple information sources, such as expert knowledge, historical accident data, and computer simulation results, involving two important components: the frequency/probability of ship collision accidents and the corresponding potential consequences. The application methods of this type of research include Pedersen [35], fault tree [36], Bayesian network [37], and ordered probit model [38]. This type of research can be used to identify important influencing factors causing collision risk, estimate the causal probability of accidents, and analyze the relationship between factors. The relevant research results can help ship regulators understand the frequency and consequences of possible collisions under different traffic situations.

To sum up, almost all the collision risk estimation studies in the current maritime field are deterministic. The deterministic method maps the current state of the ship along a single trajectory to the future, that is, assuming that the future trajectory is fully known in advance. These methods are simple and clear, but ignore the trajectory deviation caused by various uncertainties, which will affect the result of conflict detection. The method adopted in this paper is probabilistic, using the probability density function (PDF) to describe the trajectory of potential uncertainty and calculate the probability of potential conflict. The collision risk under highly uncertain ship trajectories can be predicted more effectively.

In addition, the current research on ship dynamic group detection only focuses on the distance relationship between ships and fails to effectively consider the influence of factors such as the uneven spatial distribution of ships and the geographical characteristics of complex navigable waters. This paper comprehensively considers the risk relationship and spatial distance between ships and divides regional ship traffic into multiple dynamic groups, which helps to reduce the difficulty of understanding ship traffic situation in the whole water area, and further assists in identifying local high-risk/high-density multi-ship encounter scenarios.

3. Methodology: Dynamic Calculation of Navigation Risk

In this section, we systematically describe the dynamic calculation method of ship navigation risk. This method is divided into three interactive steps, each of which is associated with methods of high dependency (see Figure 1). Specifically, this step is achieved using a probabilistic conflict detection framework, which can accurately estimate the conflict criticality in the presence of ship motion dynamics and uncertainty. Secondly, we construct a ship group extraction method based on the conflict interaction between ships and define the ship set of navigation risk interaction. In addition, we realize the discretization of regional water risk assessment. Finally, the key influential ships in the regional traffic situation are identified. The critical supporting techniques in each step are elaborated in the subsequent subsections to demonstrate the logical flow of the methodology.

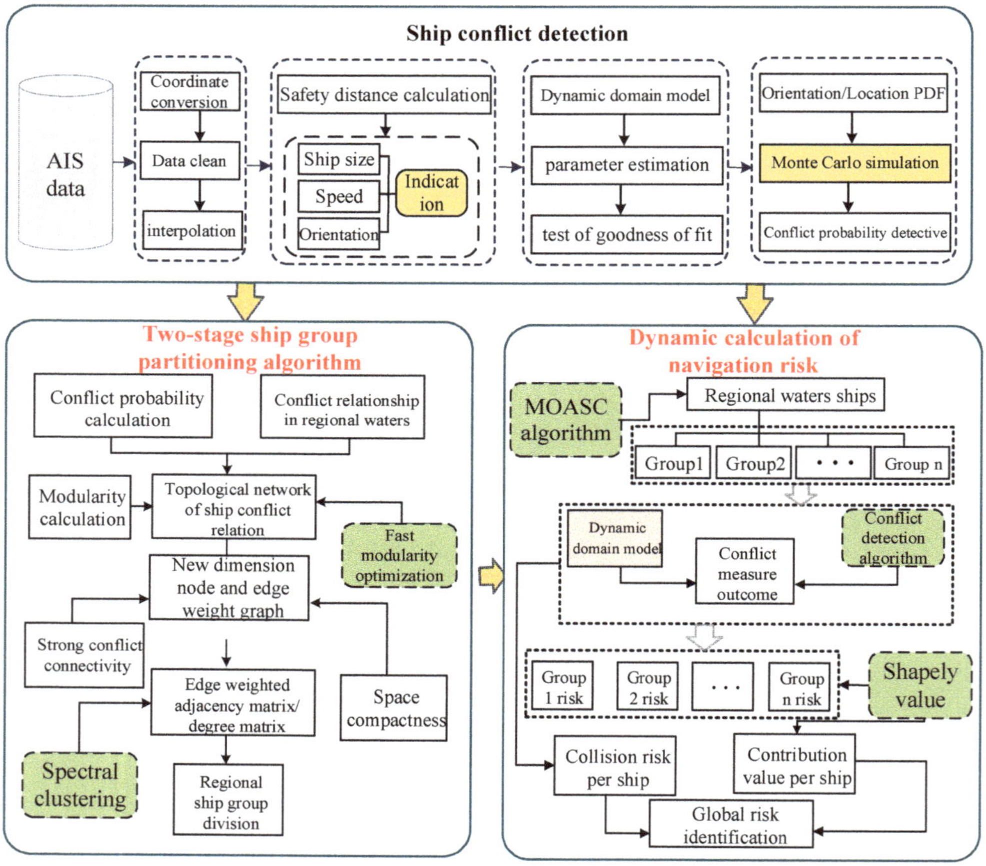

Figure 1. Framework of this paper.

3.1. Probabilistic Conflict Detection

The conflict detection (CD) approach is first developed from a probabilistic risk viewpoint in which the influence of uncertainty related to various sources on the potential conflict is considered. It is designed to quantify the conflict criticality between ship pairs and provide essential functionality for extracting ship groups. The probabilistic CD approach is characterized by a conflict criticality measure and conflict probability estimation.

3.1.1. Conflict Criticality Measure

A conflict occurs when the predicted trajectories of two ships violate the specified separation distance. The paper defines ship conflict based on the *MSD* model [39]. The method of conflict identification is shown in Figure 2. If the sum of the *MSD* of the two ships and the distance between the two ships within the prediction time satisfy Formula (1), then ship *A* and ship *B* are considered to be in a conflict state:

$$D(t) \leq MSD_A(t) + MSD_B(t), \quad (1)$$

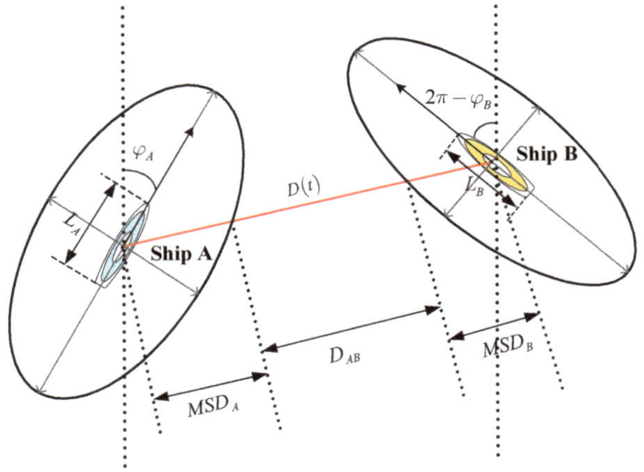

Figure 2. Ship conflict illustration.

Where *D(t)* is the distance between the two ships, $MSD_A(t)$ and $MSD_B(t)$ represent the distances between the ship centers and their dynamic domain boundaries, respectively. Because we focus on identifying ship conflicts with ship motion uncertainty, inequality (1) is a probabilistic issue.

Given that the PDF for the unsafe separation (i.e., $(D(t) \leq MSD_A(t) + MSD_B(t)))$ between the two ships at time t is denoted as $f_{\gamma L(t)}$, the instantaneous occurrence probability of a conflict is expressed as Formula (2):

$$PC(t) = \Pr(L(t) \leq 0) = \int_{-\infty}^{0} f_{L(t)}(\rho)d\rho, \quad (2)$$

where *L(t)* equals $(D(t) - MSD_A(t) - MSD_B(t))$.

The maximum conflict probability within the predicted range is used to measure the severity of the conflict as shown in Formula (3):

$$P_{con}(\tau) := \max_{t\in[0,T]} PC(t), \quad (3)$$

3.1.2. Conflict Probability Estimation

The probabilistic CD is based on the prediction of ship trajectories with uncertainty. Therefore, considering the ship motion model with uncertain mode of ship heading and ship position, we use the Monte Carlo simulation algorithm which can accurately calculate the conflict probability to extend CD to the probability framework.

The initial position of the two ships is determined, but the ship is affected by many uncertain factors, such as the pilot's maneuver and intention, wind and waves, mechanical failure, and so on. Considering the fluctuation of the ship's trajectory, the equation of the ship's motion is expressed as Formulas (4) and (5):

$$\dot{X}_O = (x_O, y_O) + W_O = (V_O \sin\varphi_O, V_O \cos\varphi_O) + W_O, \quad (4)$$

$$\dot{X}_T = (x_T, y_T) + W_T = (V_T \sin \varphi_T, V_T \cos \varphi_T) + W_T, \tag{5}$$

Among them, φ_O and φ_T are the heading angles of X_O and X_T, respectively. $W_O \sim \Psi(0, \mathcal{Q}_O)$ and $W_T \sim \Psi(0, \mathcal{Q}_T)$ are the errors of the ship's predicted position. $\mathcal{Q}_O$ and $\mathcal{Q}_T$ are the error covariance matrixes related to trajectory uncertainty.

The probability of ship conflict depends on the relative motion between ships. The distance between ships at any time, that is, the relative position, can be expressed as Formula (6):

$$D(t) = \sqrt{A \cdot t^2 + B \cdot t + C}, \tag{6}$$

Among the top Formulas (7)–(9):

$$A = (V_{xO} - V_{xT})^2 + (V_{yO} - V_{yT})^2, \tag{7}$$

$$B = 2[(x_O - x_T)(V_{xO} - V_{xT}) + (y_O - y_T)(V_{yO} - V_{yT})], \tag{8}$$

$$C = (x_O - x_T)^2 + (y_O - y_T)^2, \tag{9}$$

The dynamic domain boundary between ships has a significant influence on the severity of the conflict. The Formulas (10) and (11) are used to calculate the dynamic domain boundary distance of the ship in all directions at a certain time.

$$MSD_{\mathrm{A}}(t) = \left(1.19539 \cdot L_A \cdot V_A(t)^{0.33618} \cdot \left(1.866 - 0.61874 \cdot \sin\left(\frac{2.32601 - Q_{BA}(t)}{1.59485} \cdot \pi\right)\right)\right), \tag{10}$$

$$MSD_{\mathrm{A}}(t) = \left(1.19539 \cdot L_A \cdot V_A(t)^{0.33618} \cdot \left(1.866 - 0.61874 \cdot \sin\left(\frac{2.32601 - Q_{BA}(t)}{1.59485} \cdot \pi\right)\right)\right), \tag{11}$$

where $V_A(t), V_B(t)$ are the predicted speeds of ships A and B at t time, respectively, and are assumed to be zero-mean Gaussian distribution. $Q_{BA}(t)$ and $Q_{AB}(t)$ represent the predicted relative position of the target ship relative to the own ship at time t.

Under the influence of various uncertain factors, the ship's course will change (affecting the relative orientation between ships), thereby affecting the MSD. The uncertainty component of the course prediction is taken into account and is described as Formula (12):

$$\varphi^T(t) = \varphi(t) + \varepsilon(t), \tag{12}$$

$\varepsilon(t)$ represents the course prediction error component of the ship at time t.

In [40], the uncertainty distribution PDF of the ship's course and position extracted based on the AIS data drive is used as the assumption of the uncertainty component of this article. It uses Kernel Density Estimation (KDE), a non-parametric estimation method, to identify the uncertain components of the PDF of a data set via the Formula (13):

$$g(x) = \frac{1}{k'} \sum_{i=1}^{k'} \phi_h(x - x_i) = \frac{1}{k'h} \sum_{i=1}^{k'} \phi_h\left(\frac{x - x_i}{h}\right), \tag{13}$$

Among them, ϕ_h is the kernel function with bandwidth h that satisfies $\phi_h(x)>0$ and $\int_R \phi_h(x)dx = 1$, and K' represents the number of elements in the data set within the bandwidth h.

Note that $D(t) \leq MSD_A(t) + MSD_B(t)$ in the inequality $D(t)$ and MSD are functions of the position and heading prediction error components. Therefore, whether the equation is established as a probabilistic event, its occurrence probability needs to be determined by a probability-based calculation method.

Conflict probability calculation is an important part of probabilistic conflict detection in a practical environment. In this paper, Monte Carlo simulation is used to solve the problem. For Monte Carlo simulation, in the sampling iteration loop, N groups of random variable samples are generated according to the probability density function of the given random variable, and then each group of samples is inserted into the conflict quantization model to obtain a deterministic solution of whether there is a conflict. Further, an approximate result estimate can be obtained by using the set of all the sample deterministic solutions. That is the probability of conflict. The N value in the sampling iteration loop determines the accuracy of the approximate solution.

In general, in a limited time range, the collision probability of encountering ships tends to show a peak at some time periods and is relatively small in other time periods. Given that only the maximum conflict probability in the predicted time range needs to be accurately estimated, the time points with a high conflict probability can be roughly extracted before a large number of iterations are performed. Based on this principle, a two-stage Monte Carlo simulation algorithm is constructed to estimate the conflict severity effectively. At the same time, in order to determine how many iterations (N) are sufficient to guarantee the desired estimation accuracy, the Hoefffing inequality [40] is adopted to describe the relationship between N and approximation accuracy, as shown in Formula (14):

$$N \geq \frac{\log(2/\delta)(b-a)^2}{2\varepsilon^2}, \tag{14}$$

where ε represents the accuracy, $1-\delta$ represents the confidence, and a and b represent the lower and upper limits of the estimate. This inequality shows that for a finite number of iterations N, Monte Carlo simulation can ensure that the accuracy reaches ε with a confidence of $1-\delta$. In this study, the prediction accuracy was designed to be 1% in order to provide accurate conflict warning for practical applications. It takes a total of 15,000 iterations with a confidence of 1–2 $\times$ 10^{-3} to achieve this accuracy. Algorithm 1 provides a detailed pseudo-code for a two-stage Monte Carlo simulation algorithm.

Algorithm 1: MC simulation algorithm

Input: Probability density function of random variable at different time,
Sampling frequency, Forecast time frame T
Output: P_{con}
1: Function $f\left(\dot{V}_O, \dot{V}_T, \dot{\varphi}_O, \dot{\varphi}_T, L, log_O, lat_O, log_T, lat_T\right)$ Return $L(t)$
2: $hits \leftarrow 0$
3: $N \leftarrow 15,000$
//The moment with high probability of conflict is extracted from ship A
4: For $t = 1, 2, \cdots, T$ do
5: Generate a random sample vector of position/course for each ship
6: For $i \leftarrow 1$ to N do
7: $\quad \dot{V}_O \sim V_O + N(0, \sigma_O)$
8: $\quad \dot{V}_T \sim V_T + N(0, \sigma_T)$
9: Call function f to calculate based on random sample vector $L(t)$
10: $\quad$ if $L(t) \leq 0$ then
11: $\quad\quad hits = hits + 1$
12: $\quad$ End if
13: $PC(t) = hits/N$
14: End for
15: $P_{con} = \max\{PC(t)\}, t \in T$

3.2. Ship Group Extraction

The framework for grouping regional ships is shown in Figure 3. First, the method proposed in Section 3.1 is used to detect conflicts between the ships in the core port area of Ningbo-Zhoushan Port. Secondly, a ship topology network is generated based on the conflict relationship between the ships. Then, coupled fast modularity optimization and spectral clustering (FMOASC) algorithms are used to group the regional ships.

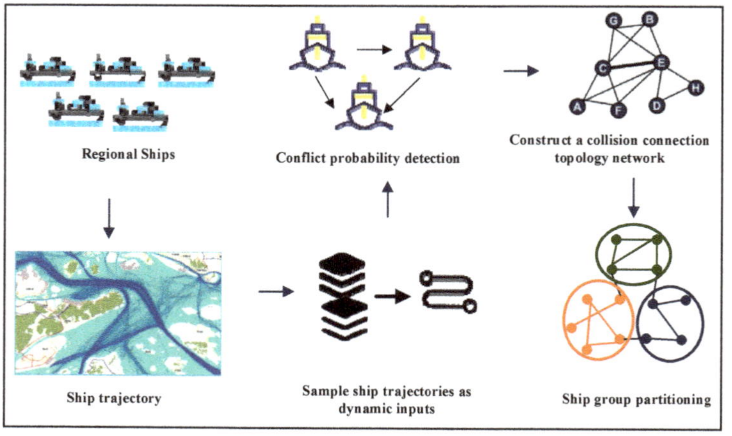

Figure 3. Ship group division framework.

The implementation of FMOASC includes the following three steps: solving the optimal modularity, constructing the new dimension information graph of node and edge relationship, and extracting the features of Laplacian matrix and clustering, as shown in Figure 4:

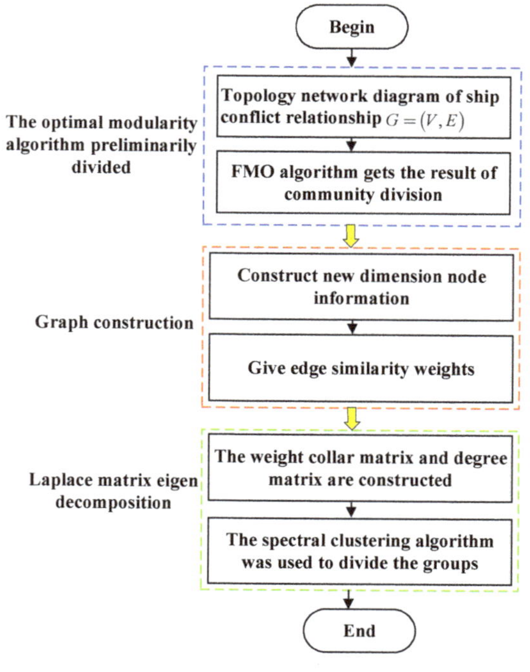

Figure 4. FMOASC algorithm.

3.2.1. Preliminary Group Partition Based on FMO Algorithm

One of the principles of regional ship grouping is to find the ship combination with a strong conflict connection within the group and a relatively weak connection between different groups of ships. Based on the conflict connection relationship between the ships, the FMO algorithm is used to divide the regional ships into sub-communities. The preliminary division of the ship group is more concerned with the conflict connection between the ships, so grouping across spatial distances may occur.

Modularity is a strength index to measure the division of a network into sub-communities, which can be used to evaluate the division of communities. The calculation method of modularity is as shown in Formula (15):

$$Modularty = \frac{1}{2m}\sum_{i,j}\left[w_{ij} - \frac{k_i k_j}{2m}\right]\delta(c_i, c_j), \tag{15}$$

where w_{ij} represents the edge weight between nodes V_i and V_j, k_i is the sum of the edge weights attached to node V_i, C_i represents the community to which node V_i is divided, $2m$ is the sum of the edge weights in the network, and $\delta(u, v)$ is defined as a simple incremental function as Formula (16):

$$\delta(u, v) = \begin{cases} 1, u = v \\ 0, u \neq v \end{cases}, \tag{16}$$

In the regional ship undirected weighted graph $G = (V, E)$, taking the ship as the node, $V = \{v_1, v_2, \cdots, v_n\}$ as the node set, and $v_i \in V, i = 1, 2, \cdots, n$ as the ship node, the ship with conflict relationship is connected, $E = \{e_1, e_2, \cdots, e_m\}$ is the edge set, $e_{ij} = (v_{j1}, v_{j2})$, $e_i \in E, j = 1, 2, \cdots, m$ is the conflict relation edge, and the weight is the conflict probability value.

FMO can find the highly modular division of the network in a short time and show a complete hierarchical community structure. It is a bottom-up greedy optimization algorithm based on modularity maximization. Starting from each node as a community, the algorithm merges the neighboring communities in turn, calculates the modularity change ΔM, and continuously merges the communities along the direction of the maximum increase in modularity M until the result of community division corresponding to the maximum modularity M is obtained. The iterative process is shown in Figure 5.

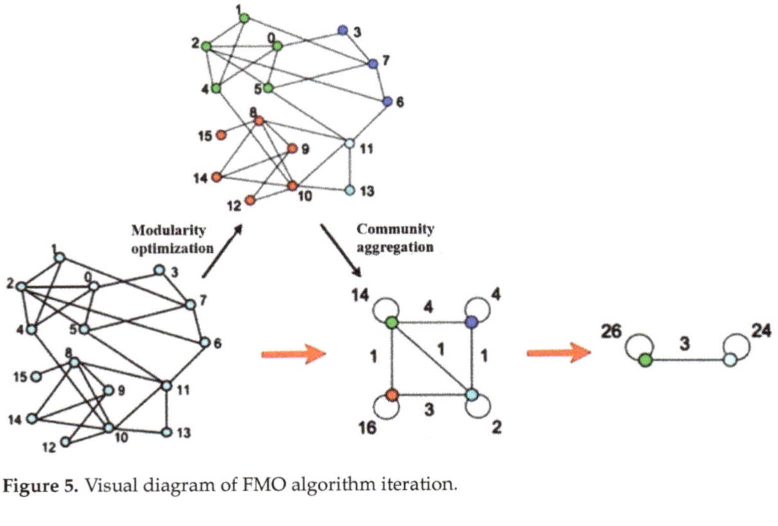

Figure 5. Visual diagram of FMO algorithm iteration.

The modularity gain ΔM gained by moving the orphaned nodes to the community can be calculated by the following Formula (17):

$$\Delta M = \left[\frac{\Sigma_{in} + k_{i,in}}{2m} - \left(\frac{\Sigma_{tot} + k_i}{2m}\right)^2\right] - \left[\frac{\Sigma_{in}}{2m} - \left(\frac{\Sigma_{tot}}{2m}\right)^2 - \left(\frac{k_i}{2m}\right)^2\right], \tag{17}$$

Among them, Σ_{in} is the sum of the weights of the connected edges in the community C, Σ_{tot} is the sum of the weights of the connections associated with the node in C, k_i is the sum of the weights of the connections associated with the node i, $k_{i,in}$ is the sum of the weights of the connected edges from the node i to the nodes in C, and m is the sum of the weights of all the connection relations in the network. When a node i is removed from its community, expressions are used to evaluate the change in modularity.

Through the preliminary division of regional ships through the FMO algorithm, sub-communities based on the conflict connection relationships between ship nodes can be obtained. It is the basis for the subsequent optimal division using the SC algorithm, and the basis for constructing new dimensional information on the connection relationships between ships.

3.2.2. Optimal Group Partition Based on Spectral Clustering

Based on the preliminary grouping results of FMO, combined with the goal of conflict connectivity and spatial compactness, a new dimension of information is constructed to represent the edge weight between ship nodes. The function representation of the edge weight between ships is constructed according to the probability of conflict between ships and the spatial distance. The new dimension information graph is represented as $G' = (V', E')$, where $V' = \{v_1, v_2, \cdots, v_n\}$ is the node set, $v_x \in V', x = 1, 2, \cdots, n$ is the node, $E' = \{e'_1, e'_2, \cdots, e'_z\}$ is the edge set, and $e'_y = (v_{y1}, v_{y2}), e'_y \in E', v_{y1} \neq v_{y2}, y = 1, 2, \cdots, z$ is the edge of the graph.

In the second stage of group division, the grouping results obtained by the FMO algorithm need to be fine-tuned. The more important goal of this stage is to consider the influence of ship spatial distance on the basis of conflict relations. Therefore, it is necessary to weaken the influence of conflict connections between ships and obtain spatially compact grouping results. Based on the influence of weakening the conflict connection relationship, the distance between ships $dist'$, the collision probability p_{ij} between ships, and the preliminary division group label $label_{vi}$ are obtained, and the similarity feature vector $D_{ev} = (dist', p_{ij}, label_{vi})$ is proposed, where $label_{vi}$ is the group tag obtained based on the FMO algorithm. The calculation of $dist'$ is as shown in Formula (18):

$$dist'_{ij} = f(x) = \begin{cases} 0, p_{ij} \geq 0.5 \\ dist_{ij} * (1 - p_{ij}), 0.1 \leq p_{ij} < 0.5, \\ dist_{ij}, p_{ij} < 0.1 \end{cases} \tag{18}$$

Next, standardize each feature vector, that is, $z_i = (t_i - \mu)/\sigma$.

Among them, z_i represents the standardized eigenvalues corresponding to each eigenvector; t_i and μ are the eigenvalues and the average values of eigenvalues corresponding to each eigenvector, respectively; and σ is the standard deviation of the corresponding eigenvalues of all the eigenvectors. The Euclidean distance corresponding to the normalized feature vector between all the nodes is $d_{ij} = \|D_{evi} - D_{evj}\|$, and the edge weight is $w_{ij} = \exp(-d_{ij}/std(d_{ij}))$, where $std(d_{ij})$ is the standard deviation of d_{ij}.

Through the feature extraction and decomposition of the Laplacian matrix L (the calculation formula is $L = D - W$. W is the adjacency matrix which represents the adjacency relationship between nodes. D is the degree matrix, and the concept of degree indicates how many edges of a node are connected to it) and K-means clustering, the optimal division result of ship group is obtained.

3.2.3. Group Quantity Adjustment Indicator

Using the FMOASC algorithm to divide the ship groups can obtain schemes with different numbers of groups. In order to select the ship group division scheme with excellent performance in terms of modularity and the number of noise points, an index I for the comprehensive evaluation of these two important considerations is introduced. The modularity and the number of noise points of each grouping scheme are used as the evaluation parameters, and the weighted normalization formula is used for calculation, as shown in Formulas (19)–(21):

$$I = w_m r'_m - w_c r'_c, \tag{19}$$

$$r'_m = \frac{r_m - r_m^{\min}}{r_m^{\max} - r_m^{\min}}, \tag{20}$$

$$r'_c = \frac{r_c^{\max} - r_c}{r_c^{\max} - r_c^{\min}}, \tag{21}$$

Among them, r_m and r_c are the modularity and the number of noise points corresponding to the ship grouping scheme, respectively; r'_m and r'_c are the modularity and the number of noise points after normalization, respectively; and w_m,w_c are the weights corresponding to the modularity and the number of noise points, respectively.

By comparing the indicators under different grouping schemes, the number of ship groups is selected, and a balanced result in terms of modularity and the number of noise points is obtained.

3.3. *Dynamic Calculation of Ship Navigation Risk*

In order to identify the navigation risks of ships in different local waters and regions in complex navigable waters, explore the evolution law of ship navigation risks, and assist maritime regulatory authorities in tracking potential high-risk ships and grasping local high-risk waters, this section carries out the following work based on the ship conflict probability detection and the extraction of ship groups from the perspective of water navigation management: first, the problem of ship navigation risk assessment is described, and the framework of global risk assessment is explained; secondly, the Shapley value method based on the cooperative game is introduced to identify the contribution of each ship in a multi-ship encounter situation; and finally, the navigation risks of single ships, different local waters, and regions are quantified, and the navigation risks of the research waters are visualized using data visualization technology. This will help maritime regulatory authorities to have a more comprehensive understanding of real-time collision risks, effectively grasp the risks and traffic complexity of different local waters and regions, and thus have a deeper understanding of ship navigation risks, providing guidance for the formulation of risk mitigation measures.

3.3.1. Risk Assessment Framework

The ship navigation risk system is composed of a set of all the ships sailing in the research waters at a certain time, as shown in Figure 6. For example, if there are n ships in the system, the system can be represented by a graph $G(t) = \{S, E(t)\}$, where S is a set of ships, represented as $\{S : s_1, s_2, s_3 \ldots, s_n\}$, and the elements in the set are each ship, where the edge set is $E(t) \subset S \times S$, which represents the conflict relationship between the ships, and the edge weight is the conflict probability value between the ships. The conflict probability of ship s_i and ship s_j at time t is represented by $p_{ij}(t)$ only when there is a conflict between s_i and s_j at time t, $(s_i, s_j) \in E(t)$, that is, when and only when $p_{ij}(t) \neq 0$, $(s_i, s_j) \in E(t)$.

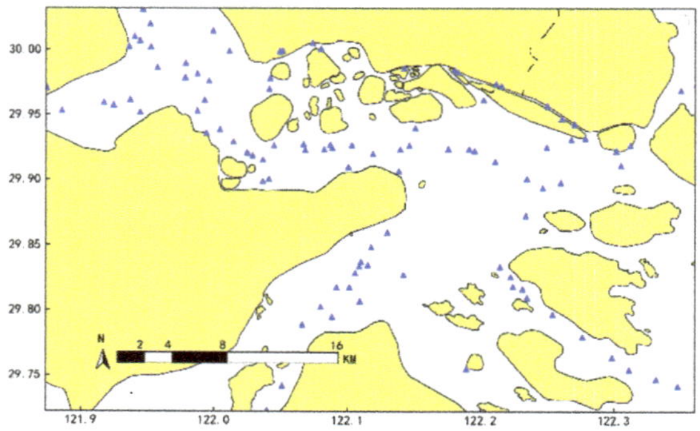

Figure 6. Ship system diagram.

Figure 7a,b are the spatial position distribution and conflict connection relationship diagrams of ships at a certain moment. Combining Figure 7a,b, we can see that at a certain moment, there is no connection between the ships that are far away or even close but have a tendency to move away from each other. Therefore, the ship system graph is not connected but is divided into several subgraphs. Assume $G_i(t) = \{S_i, E_i(t)\}(i = 1, 2, 3, \cdots, m)$ is a connected subgraph of $G(t)$, a subgraph (that is, a ship group divided according to the FMOASC algorithm) is a subset (subsystem) of the ship system, and m is the number of subsystems. The relationship between the ship navigation risk system and subsystems in the study waters is $G(t) = G_1(t) \cup G_2(t) \cup \cdots \cup G_m(t)$. For any two subgraphs $G_i(t)$ and $G_j(t)$, there exists $S_i \cap S_j = \varnothing$.

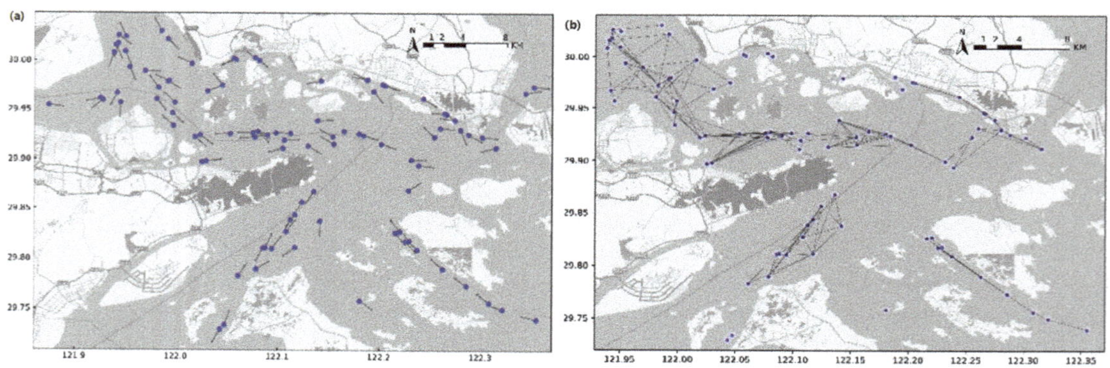

Figure 7. Ship position distribution and conflict connection diagram: (**a**) spatial position distribution and heading; (**b**) ship conflict connection.

The collision risk of the kth (represents the KTH ship subsystem in a ship system, where k is a positive integer) subsystem $G_i(t)$ is represented by $p_k(t)$. For any pair of ships with a non-zero collision probability, the risk of the subsystem in which they are located will be affected by the collision probability between them, which in turn affects the system risk of the regional ship composition. This paper will model $p_k(t)$ as the function of $p_{ij}(t) \neq 0$, that is $p_k(t) = f_k(p_{ij}(t), \cdots, p_{ul}(t))$, where $(s_i, s_j) \in E_k(t)$ and $p_{ij}(t) \neq 0$.

3.3.2. Global Risk Assessment

The process of evaluating global collision risk is shown in Figure 8:

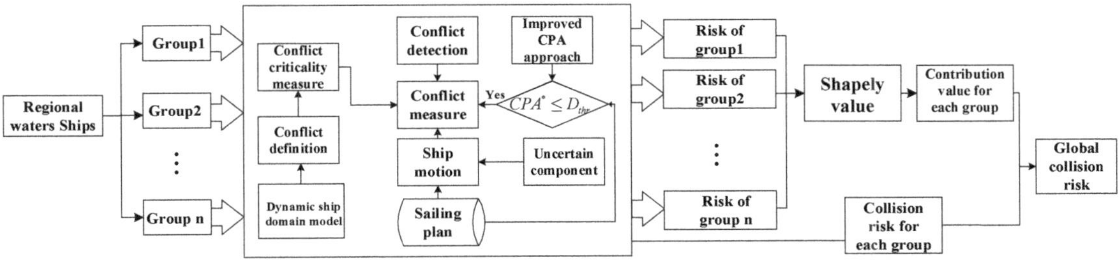

Figure 8. Global collision risk assessment process. (where, CPA* represents the nearest encounter point calculated in the case of turning point considered in this paper).

It is assumed that the global collision risk of a multi-ship encounter is composed of the collision risk of each ship in the situation. However, due to the different encounter types and collision avoidance maneuvers between different ships, the contribution of each ship to the global collision risk will also be different. Based on the above assumptions, the global collision risk (GCR) of a multi-ship encounter can be expressed by the following Formula (22):

$$GCR = \sum_{i=1}^{n} CR_i \times C_i, \tag{22}$$

Among them, CR_i and C_i refer to the collision risk and contribution of the ship i in the multi-ship encounter scenario, respectively.

In order to evaluate the global collision risk in multi-ship encounters, it is necessary to first determine the collision risk of each ship in the encounter and its contribution. For complex navigable waters with high ship density, a large number of ships will be in the same waters at the same time. The calculation of the global collision risk needs to traverse all the ships in the waters at the same time. Therefore, the calculation complexity is very large. In order to simplify the calculation, this paper adopts the ship group division method from the perspective of the water navigation management proposed in Section 3.2, divides the ships in the study waters into different ship groups, and then identifies the collision risk of each ship based on the ship conflict probability detection method proposed in Section 3.1. Subsequently, the Shapley value method in the cooperative game (to be introduced in the next subsection) is used to determine the contribution of each ship. The collision risk within the ship group is calculated according to Formula (22). On this basis, all the collision risks of the different ship groups are integrated through Formula (23) to obtain the Regional Collision Risk (RCR).

$$RCR = \sum_{j=1}^{m} GCR_j \times C_j, \tag{23}$$

Among them, GCR_j is the collision risk of each group, and C_j is the contribution of each ship group.

3.3.3. Local/Regional Navigation Risk Quantification

The scope of the ship navigation risk events discussed is aimed at two or more ships; that is, at least two ships are the system objects of the ship navigation risk events. The navigation status of the ship can be obtained based on AIS data, and the probability of conflict between ships can be obtained using the ship conflict probability detection method proposed in Section 3.1. This degree of conflict is a measure of the severity of the conflict from the perspective of each ship. The forms of local and regional system risks are characterized by $p_k(t) = f_k(p_{ij}(t), \cdots, p_{ul}(t))$ and $F(t) = f(p_k(t), \cdots, p_m(t))$, respectively.

3.3.4. Contribution Determination

The Shapley value method was proposed by Shapley L.S. in 1953 to solve the problem of the conflicts caused by the distribution of benefits among multiple participants in the process of cooperation. It is a solution method in the field of cooperative games. The Shapley value method represents the contribution of each participant to the entire group. A major advantage of applying the Shapley value is that the benefits are distributed according to the marginal contribution rate of the members to the combination. This solves the problem of benefit distribution because the method distributes the cooperation amount by estimating the contribution of each participant. This method is used to calculate the contribution of each ship to the navigation risk in multi-ship encounters. The general form of the Shapley value is as shown in Formula (24):

$$S_i[A] = \sum_{T \subseteq N, i \in T} \frac{(t-1)!(n-t)!}{n!}[A(T) - A(T - \{i\})], \tag{24}$$

Among them, i refers to the participants in the game, T refers to the combination consisting of participants i, t refers to the number of participants in the combination T, n refers to the number of participants in the entire group, $A(T)$ refers to the amount generated by the combination T, $A(T - \{i\})$ refers to the amount generated by the combination before the participants i join T, and $S_i[A]$ refers to the Shapley value corresponding to the participants i.

When applying the Shapley value method, the multi-ship encounter is regarded as a cooperative game, each ship in the encounter scenario is regarded as a game subject, and its collision risk is regarded as the game amount. Ships can form different combinations through permutations and combinations. According to Formula (23), when calculating the Shapley value of each ship, it is first necessary to find the risk $A(T)$ of each combination. The number of combinations is the sum of all the permutations of the encountering ships, expressed as Formula (25):

$$A\{1, 2, \cdots n\} = \sum_{i=1}^{n} CR_{i|1,2,\cdots,n}, \tag{25}$$

Among them, $CR_{i|1,2,\cdots,n}$ refers to the collision risk of the ship i in an n-ship encounter. Each ship's contribution is calculated as follows:

1. Find out all the ship combinations by arranging them.
2. For each combination, the combined risk value is calculated by summing the risk of each ship according to Formula (24).
3. Calculate the Shapley value of each ship according to Equation (23).
4. Normalize the Shapley value to obtain the contribution degree of each ship to the global collision risk.

In addition to the vessels with a high risk of collision, VTS supervisors also need to focus on the vessels with a high Shapley value, which is essential for the control and management of global collision risk because the reduction in the collision risk of ships with a high Shapley value is conducive to the mitigation of global collision risk.

4. Applications and Case Study Results

In this section, we apply and evaluate the performance of the proposed dynamic calculation method for ship navigation risk. Section 4.1 presents the case study and the relevant AIS data. Section 4.2 presents the experimental results of ship probabilistic conflict detection. Section 4.3 presents the experimental analysis of the ship grouping method. Section 4.4 quantifies and statistically analyzes the navigation risk in different local waters.

4.1. Study Area and Data Description

Ningbo-Zhoushan Port was selected as the experimental research area to test the dynamic calculation method of ship navigation risk proposed in this paper. In terms of cargo throughput, the port is the largest port in the world with high traffic density, limited navigable waters, and complex spatiotemporal uncertainty in ship movement. Therefore, the port is a representative of complex waters. AIS data for one month were collected from the port. The region for evaluation is bounded between the longitudes 122°06 E–122°16 E and latitudes 29°49 N–29°57 N (see Figure 9). Since ships such as fishing vessels, pilot boats, and tugboats often coexist to perform tasks and may not comply with conventional maritime safety rules, the experimental analysis used AIS data from general commercial ships including cargo ships and tankers. Although AIS provides a powerful and easily accessible data source for maritime traffic research, the collected data often have problems such as missing data or incorrect position and speed information due to various technical failures. Therefore, the AIS data preprocessing module is crucial to improve data quality. This study adopts a systematic preprocessing procedure to clean the data; in this way, we can remove possible noise and reconstruct clean and reliable trajectory data for the experimental analysis. In other words, this data-cleaning process is a prerequisite for real-time analysis.

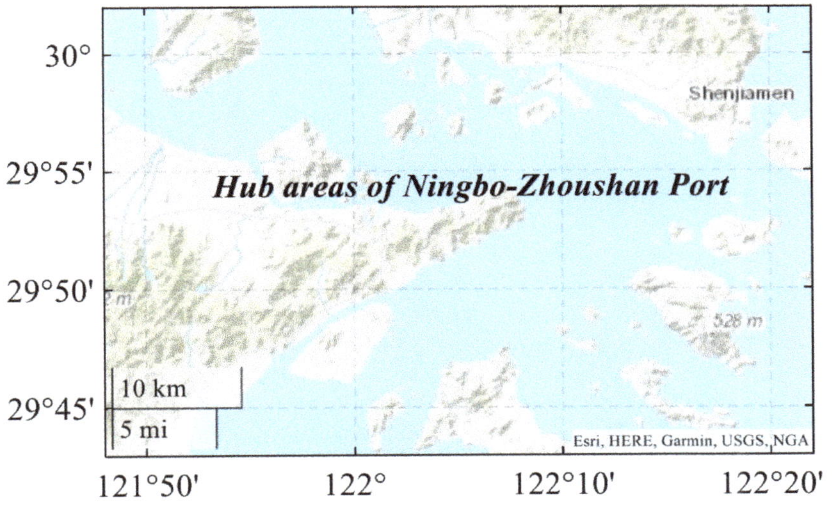

Figure 9. Ningbo-Zhoushan Port, China.

4.2. Conflict Probability Detection Based on Ship Encounter Scenarios

To test the performance of the proposed approach under the condition that the encountering ships have changeable spatiotemporal motion behaviors, a ship-pair encounter scenario derived from the historical data is presented (see Figure 10). The lines in Figure 10 are the trajectories of the ship pair involved in the encounter, where "x" marks the ships' starting locations and "△" are their final locations. It can be seen that one ship basically sails linearly, while another one has a turning behavior during the encounter. The data of the ships at corresponding times are input into the conflict probability calculation model to obtain the ship conflict analysis diagram, as shown in Figure 10b.

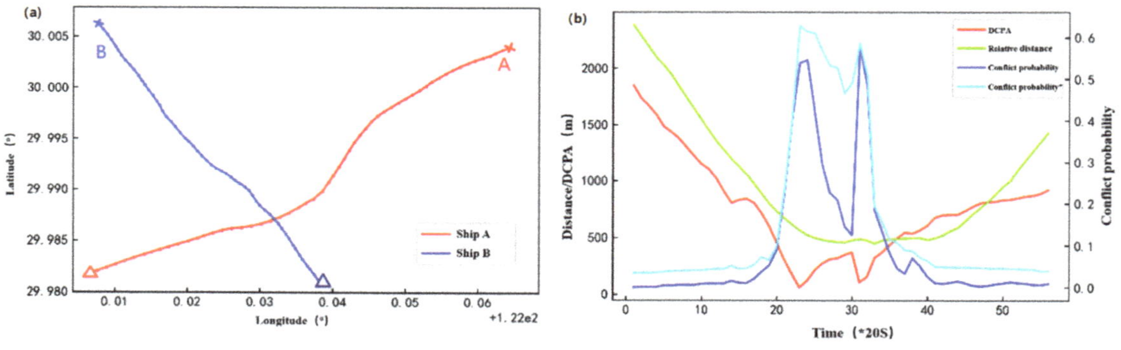

Figure 10. Ship collision probability detection: (**a**) ship trajectory; (**b**) DCPA/relative distance and conflict probability.

Figure 10b shows the change in the conflict probability with and without considering the turning point in the encounter scenario (where the conflict probability * curve is the conflict probability detection result obtained based on the method proposed in this paper). Due to the turning behavior of ship A, DCPA has two troughs during the encounter. Figure 10b shows that without considering the turning point, the conflict probability value fluctuates greatly with the change in DCPA, which may confuse the marine navigator when identifying the collision risk. Obviously, conflict identification without considering the turning point becomes invalid in this encounter scenario. This is because DCPA assumes that the ship sails linearly without changing its heading and speed. Therefore, traditional collision risk assessment methods based on DCPA may provide false alarms, hindering their application in highly dynamic traffic environments.

In addition, it can be noted from Figure 10b that due to the turning behavior, the traditional risk detection method will fluctuate due to the decrease in DCPA even when ships tend to move away from each other, while the method proposed in this paper can detect risks stably. When two ships are approaching, the probability of conflict increases and reaches a high level because of the potential conflict caused by the uncertainty inherent in the space–time movement of ships. Therefore, the proposed collision detection method can detect potential conflicts in advance by considering the dynamic and uncertain characteristics of ship motion, so as to provide accurate and timely collision warning.

In order to further verify the effectiveness of the proposed conflict probability detection method in multi-ship encounter scenarios, a three-ship encounter scenario extracted from real AIS data was selected for the experiment. The ship navigation trajectory is shown in Figure 11a. This paper measures the distance between multiple ships using the average ship spacing, as shown in Formula (26):

$$D_{aver} = \sum_{i=1,j=1}^{n} D_{ij}/n(n-1), \tag{26}$$

where D_{ij} is the distance between ship i and ship j. The change in conflict probability and average distance over time in the multi-ship encounter scenario is shown in Figure 11b. The red curve is the total P_{con} value of ship A and the other two ships in the multi-ship encounter scenario, and the blue curve and orange curve represent the conflict probability values $P_{con}AB$ and $P_{con}AC$ of ship A and ship B and ship A and ship C, respectively. The dotted line is the sum. It can be observed that the total value P_{con} is higher than that of any single target ship. This finding is consistent with the general understanding of collision risk; that is, ships participating in multi-ship encounters usually face greater risks than two-ship encounters. It can be seen from Figure 11b that the average distance between the ships is negatively correlated with the conflict probability. In addition, by comparing the red curve and the black dotted line, it is found that the total value P_{con} of ship A with ship B and ship C is not the sum of it and each target ship. Therefore, the proposed conflict probability detection method can not only detect the conflict probability of the ship when multiple ships encounter, but also provide the probability of the occurrence of multi-ship conflicts.

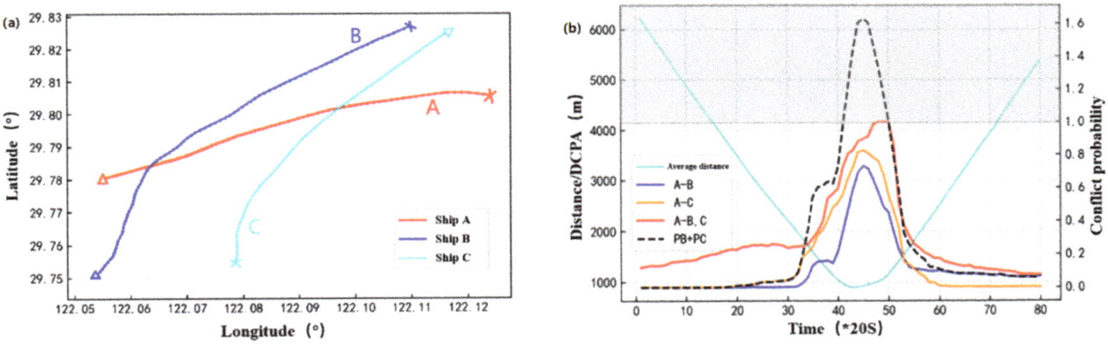

Figure 11. Multi-ship collision probability detection: (**a**) ship trajectory; (**b**) DCPA/relative distance and conflict probability.

The conflict probability provides a criticality measure that can be used to distinguish between the conflicts that can be ignored (below the conflict probability detection standard threshold) and the conflicts that need to be avoided (above the conflict detection standard threshold). In addition, the conflict probability can also be used to determine the priority of conflict resolution.

4.3. Ship Grouping Experiment

The ships in the research waters at a certain moment (as shown in Figure 12) were grouped using the FMO, SC, and FMOASC algorithms, and a comparative experiment was conducted using modularity and the number of noise points as grouping indicators. FMOASC was used as the experimental group, and FMO and SC were used as the control group. The results are shown in Figure 13.

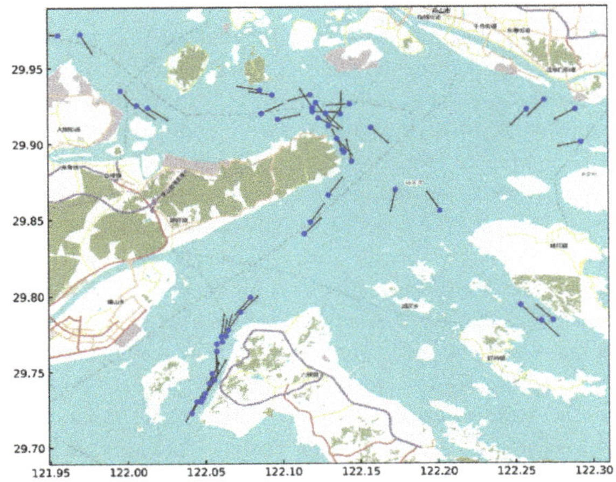

Figure 12. Spatial distribution of ships at a certain time.

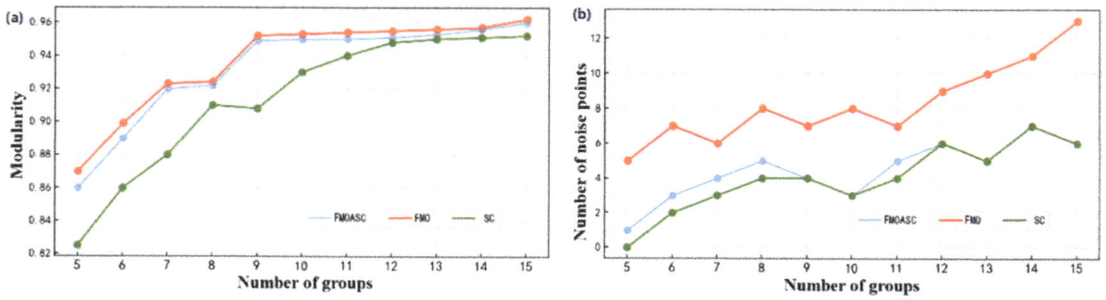

Figure 13. Comparison of experimental results: (**a**) modularity; (**b**) number of noise points.

As can be seen from Figure 13a, in terms of the modularity index, the results of the FMO and SC algorithms are quite different, especially when the number of groups is small. Overall, the modularity of SC is also lower than that of FMO. The FMOASC algorithm proposed in this paper combines the advantages of both the FMO and SC algorithms, so the modularity of the FMOASC algorithm can be maintained at a high level. From the curve corresponding to the FMOASC algorithm, it can be seen that since the algorithm comprehensively considers the topological connection relationship and spatial characteristics of ship conflicts, as the number of groups decreases, the modularity of the FMOASC algorithm decreases significantly slower than that of the SC algorithm, indicating that the loss value of the modularity of the algorithm will not be large when the number of groups is small. The modularity value of FMOASC becomes closer and closer to that of FMO as the number of groups increases until it almost completely overlaps. Therefore, the modularity of the grouping results obtained by the FMOASC algorithm proposed in this paper is high, which can achieve the effect of division with close connections within the group and sparse connections between groups.

It can be seen from Figure 13b that the number of noise points of the SC algorithm is significantly lower than that of the FMO, while the number of noise points obtained by the FMOASC algorithm proposed in this paper is very close to that of the SC algorithm. As the number of groups increases, especially when the number of groups is 10 or more, the noise point number curves of FMOASC and SC almost overlap, so the number of noise points obtained by FMOASC is small. FMOASC combines the FMO and SC algorithms to divide the ship groups. The algorithm integrates the advantages of the two algorithms, which can not only maintain a high modularity, but also minimize the number of noise points, and has a balanced performance in modularity and the number of noise points.

Figure 14 shows the comprehensive evaluation index values of the different grouping schemes when the ships in the study area (shown in Figure 9) are divided into ship groups using the FMOASC algorithm. By analyzing Figure 14, it can be found that the highest comprehensive evaluation value ($I = 0.5828$) is the division scheme with 10 ship groups, so this division scheme is adopted. The ship group division results obtained by the three algorithms are shown in Figure 15.

Figure 15a shows the position distribution and heading of ships in the research waters at a certain moment. The ellipses in Figure 15b–d represent different groups. As can be seen from Figure 15b, Group 4 spans the spatial distance. This is because FMO only considers the conflict relationship between ships and does not consider the spatial position of ships. Considering only the current conflict relationship has another disadvantage. Some ships do not have a conflict relationship currently, but they have a tendency to approach each other and should be put in one group for comprehensive consideration. The advantage is that the FMO algorithm can divide ships that are close in spatial distance but have a tendency to move away from each other (no conflict relationship) into different groups.

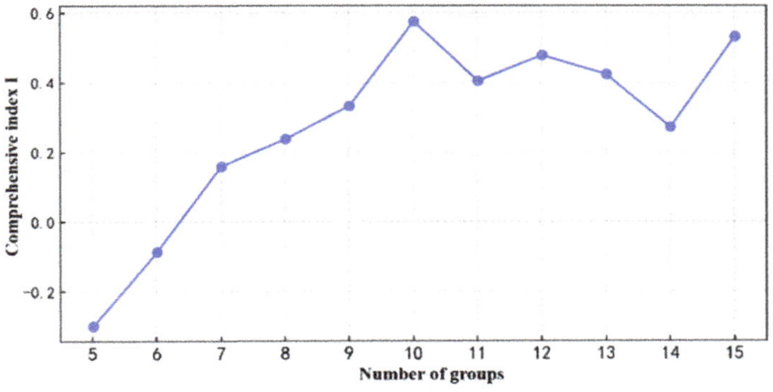

Figure 14. Ship group division comprehensive evaluation index.

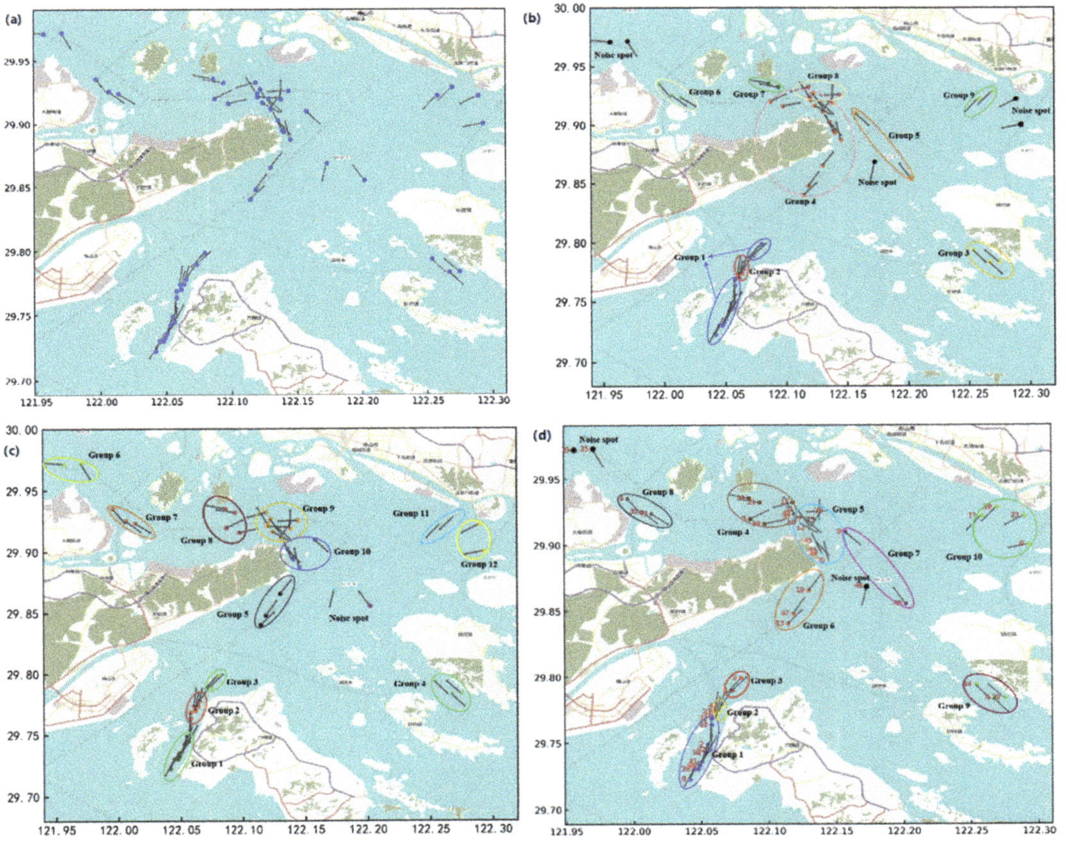

Figure 15. Results of ship group division based on three algorithms: (**a**) spatial distribution of ships; (**b**) FMO algorithm group partitioning; (**c**) SC algorithm group partitioning; (**d**) FMOASC algorithm group partitioning.

By observing the results of the SC algorithm, we can find two types of situations that do not meet the principles of group division proposed in this paper. The first type: the distance between ships is close but they are already in a state of leaving each other and do not pose a risk. The SC algorithm will classify such ships into a group. It is not meaningful to manage such ships as a group. The second type: there is a conflict relationship between ships, but the ships that are far apart at the moment are not classified into a group. Such ships should be classified into a group for management so as to timely discover the risks of ship navigation. These two types of divisions occur because the SC algorithm only uses the spatial distance between ships as the edge weight and constructs a similarity matrix to divide ships into groups. The FMOASC algorithm proposed in this paper divides ship groups by comprehensively considering the conflict connection relationship and spatial position between ships. On the basis of considering the conflict connection relationship, the spatial position of the ship is considered so that a more ideal group division result can be obtained from the perspective of water navigation management.

4.4. Quantifying Risks in Different Local Waters

Using 7,680,496 AIS data from the study area for one month, conflict data were calculated. The conflict distribution visualization diagram for each hour is shown in Figure 16. The numbers under each sub-figure in the figure represent 24 time periods, such as "1" which represents the conflict distribution during the 00:00–01:00 time period. As shown in Figure 16(1–4), the number of ship conflicts during the 00:00–04:00 time period is relatively small; in Figure 16(5–15), the conflict distribution area is wider and is roughly distributed in the Fudu Waterway, Luotou Waterway, and Xiazhimen Channel. Among them, the frequency of ship conflicts in the Luotou Waterway and Xiazhimen Channel is higher. The reason for the higher frequency of conflicts in the Luotou Waterway is that ship traffic from other directions converges in this water area, increasing the frequency of multiple ship encounters. In addition, ship turning due to terrain geometric constraints in this water area may also be one of the reasons for this result. In fact, the Luotou Waterway is an official warning area issued by the Ningbo-Zhoushan VTS Center, which to some extent verifies the effectiveness of the conflict probability detection method proposed in this paper in identifying high collision risk areas. The Xiazhimen Channel is the main channel for large ships to enter and leave the port, but the navigation width is narrow, so it becomes one of the areas with high collision risk. One possible reason for the high frequency of ship conflicts in the Fudu Waterway is that the traffic width in this water area is narrow, resulting in a reduction in the minimum passing distance between encountering ships, and so, many high-severity conflicts occur. The degree and distribution range of ship conflicts are expanding in the time period of 20:00–24:00, which may be due to the increase in the number of ship conflicts caused by the reduced visibility at night.

The distribution of ship conflicts during the day and at night is explored; that is, the ship conflicts in the time periods of 06:00–18:00 and 18:00–06:00 are counted, and two conflict distribution images are generated every 10 days, as shown in Figure 17, where "Daytime" in the sub-image represents the conflict distribution in the time period of 06:00–18:00, and "Night" represents the conflict distribution image in the time period of 18:00–06:00. As can be seen from the figure, the degree of conflict is more severe during the day than at night, the number of conflicts is larger, and the high-risk areas are concentrated in the waters of the intersection of the Luotou Waterway and Zhitouyang, Fodu Waterway, Xiazhimen Channel, and the southern part of Damao Island. Among them, the waters south of Damao Island are the main roads connecting the port hub with offshore ship traffic. It is the area with the highest ship traffic density and the highest frequency of ship encounters in the port; the intersection of the Luotou Waterway and Zhitouyang waters, and the intersection of the Xiazhimen Channel and Zhitouyang waters are both navigation warning areas officially established by the maritime department, which verifies the accuracy and effectiveness of this article's conflict research at the micro-time and space scale.

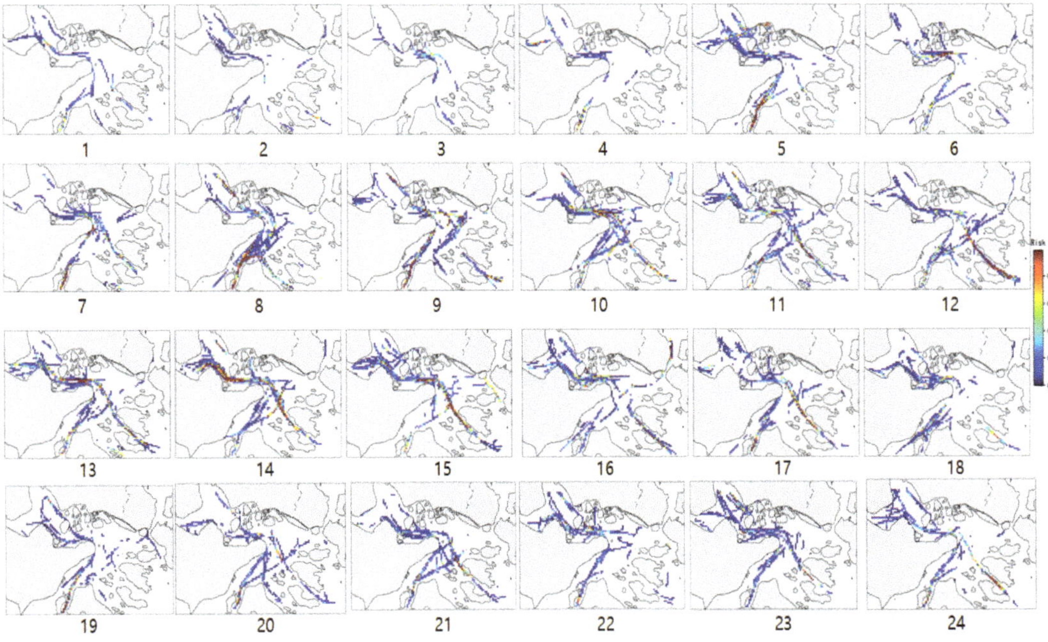

Figure 16. Hourly conflict distribution visualization.

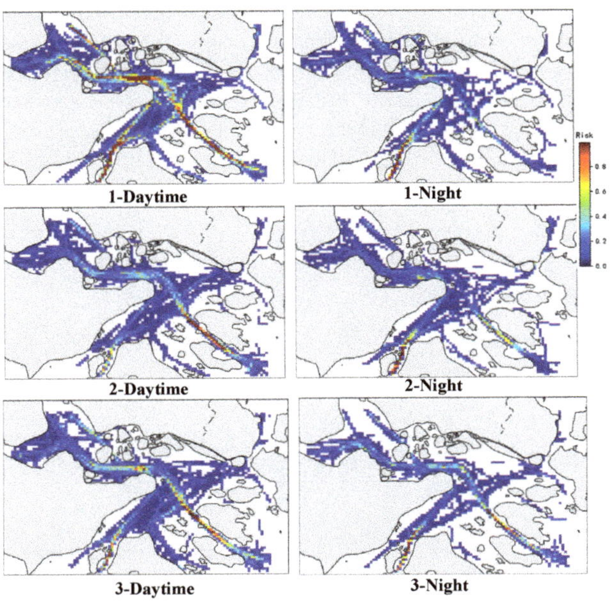

Figure 17. Visualization of conflict distribution every 12 h.

Figure 18 shows the characteristics of the distribution of the hourly conflict probability values in the study waters. It can be observed that the median conflict probability fluctuates slightly over time. In the 11:00–15:00 time period, the median of conflicts between ships is larger than that in the other time periods. The possible reason is that the ship traffic volume in this time period is large and the possibility of dangerous encounters between ships is high. The maximum conflict probability is basically maintained at 1, which means that ship encounters with high conflict severity will occur at every time period. VTS centers can use indicators such as the median and maximum values to more comprehensively understand the real-time collision risks and traffic complexity in the region, thereby improving their ability to deal with dangerous encounters caused by high traffic intensity.

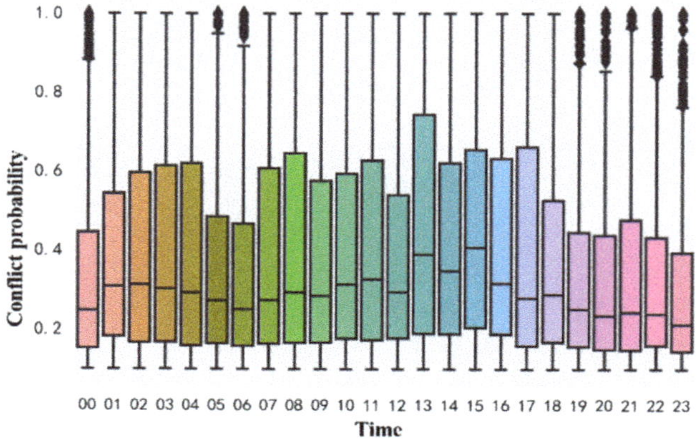

Figure 18. Time distribution of conflict.

Figure 19 shows the number of conflicts per hour in the study waters. It can be seen that ship conflicts occur more frequently in the time periods of 05:00, 07:00–11:00, and 13:00–17:00, which is consistent with the actual traffic conditions in the study waters, because the ship traffic density is higher during the day. Based on the identification results of the conflict distribution in time and space, marine navigators and maritime departments can have a deeper understanding of when and where to enhance situational awareness during the navigation process of ships, providing a valuable reference for traffic regulatory departments to formulate and implement appropriate regulatory strategies.

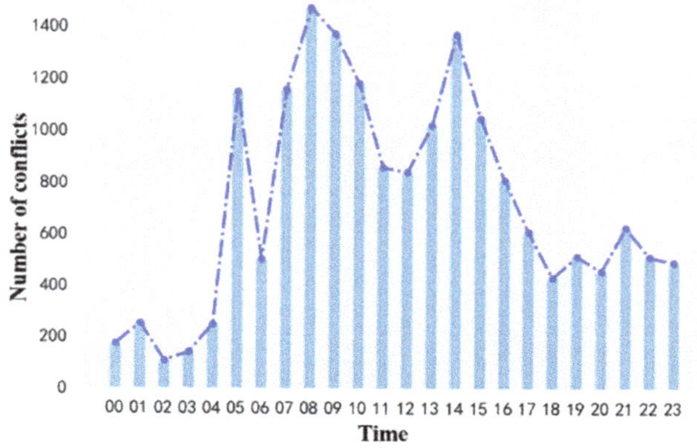

Figure 19. Time distribution of the number of conflicts.

The distribution of conflict severity and the corresponding cumulative probability distribution are shown in Figure 20. It can be seen from the figure that the severity of most conflicts is below 0.2, which indicates that the probability of a ship being involved in a higher conflict is much lower than the probability of it being involved in a minor conflict. In order to further demonstrate the characteristics of the detected conflicts, Figure 21 shows the number of different conflict types among the different ship types. It can be seen that the number of crossing encounter conflict types is the largest, followed by overtaking, and then head-on. Compared with overtaking and head-on conflicts, the proportion of conflicts in crossing encounter scenarios is higher mainly because the relatively large angle range is classified as crossing encounters. In addition, the number of conflicts between cargo ships in the three encounter scenarios is much higher than that of the other ships, which may be due to the large number of cargo ships in the study waters and the frequent encounters.

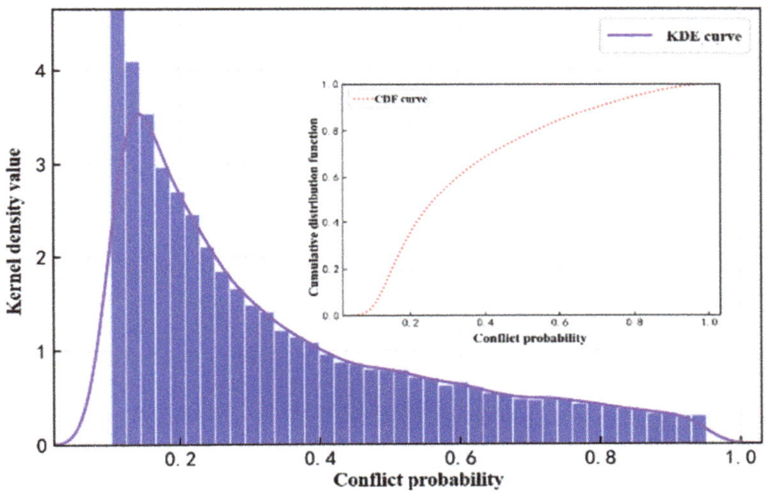

Figure 20. Conflict severity and CDF.

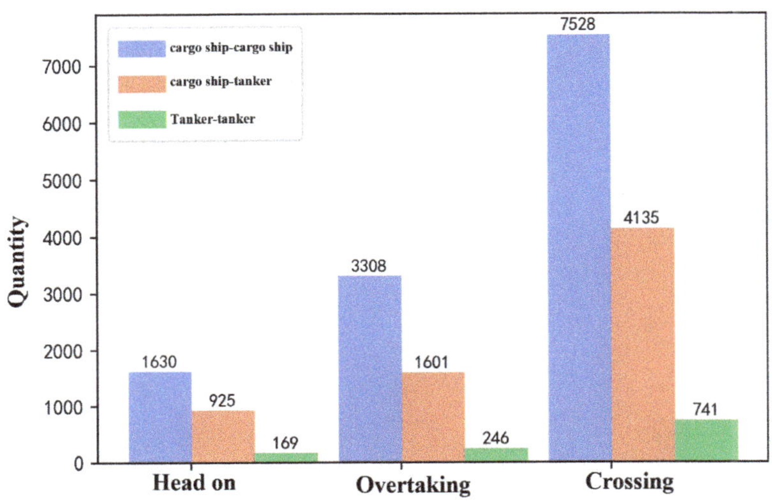

Figure 21. Number of conflicts between ship types.

In order to verify the effectiveness and feasibility of the global risk assessment method proposed in this paper, the complexity of maritime traffic is introduced as a collision risk indicator for evaluation. The complexity of maritime traffic is used to indicate the degree of traffic conditions, including the degree of congestion and risk. Although the traffic complexity model is not a traditional risk assessment model, it can reflect the instantaneous collision risk to a certain extent. Generally speaking, the higher the traffic complexity, the higher the collision risk, because when the traffic situation becomes complicated, the difficulty of avoiding collision increases. In addition, compared with simple indicators such as traffic density and ship distance, it can more fully reflect the risk of ship collision. Therefore, this paper uses traffic complexity as an indicator of the effectiveness of the global risk assessment framework.

The definition of the maritime traffic complexity model includes two parts: the traffic density factor and the traffic conflict factor. The traffic density factor is described by the relative distance between ships, and the traffic conflict factor is described by the length, speed, and relative orientation of the ship. The traffic complexity is expressed as Formulas (27) and (28):

$$Com(D_{ij}, V_{ij}, \theta_{ij}) = Den_{ij}(D_{ij}) + Pconf_{ij}(D_{ij}, V_{ij}, \theta_{ij}), \tag{27}$$

$$Com(i) = \frac{1}{N} \sum_{i \neq j, j=1}^{N} Com_{ij}(D_{ij}, V_{ij}, \theta_{ij}), \tag{28}$$

Among them, Com_{ij}, Den_{ij}, and $Pconf_{ij}$ are the traffic complexity, traffic density complexity, and traffic conflict complexity of the ship i and ship j, respectively. $D_{ij}, V_{ij}, \theta_{ij}$ are the relative distance, relative speed, and relative orientation between the ship i and ship j, respectively; $Com(i)$ is the traffic complexity of the ship i, which is the average of the sum of all the complexities involving ship i.

According to the ship group extraction algorithm proposed in this paper, the ships in the study waters at a certain time are divided into 10 ship groups, as shown in Figure 22. The contribution value of each ship in each ship group obtained by the Shapley value method in the cooperative game is shown in Figure 23. The collision risk and traffic complexity of each ship group are shown in Figure 24.

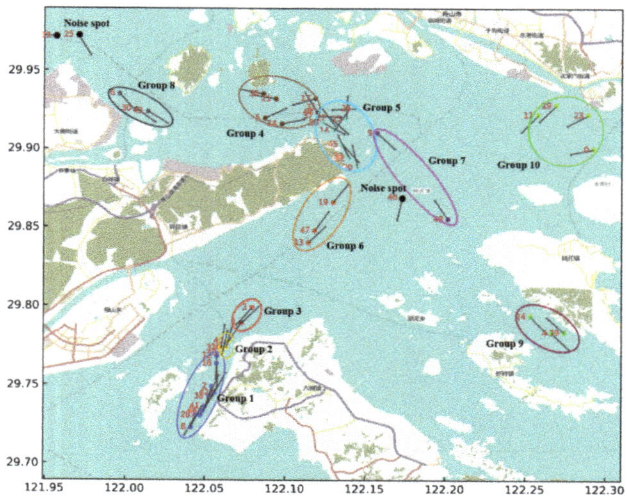

Figure 22. Results of ship group division.

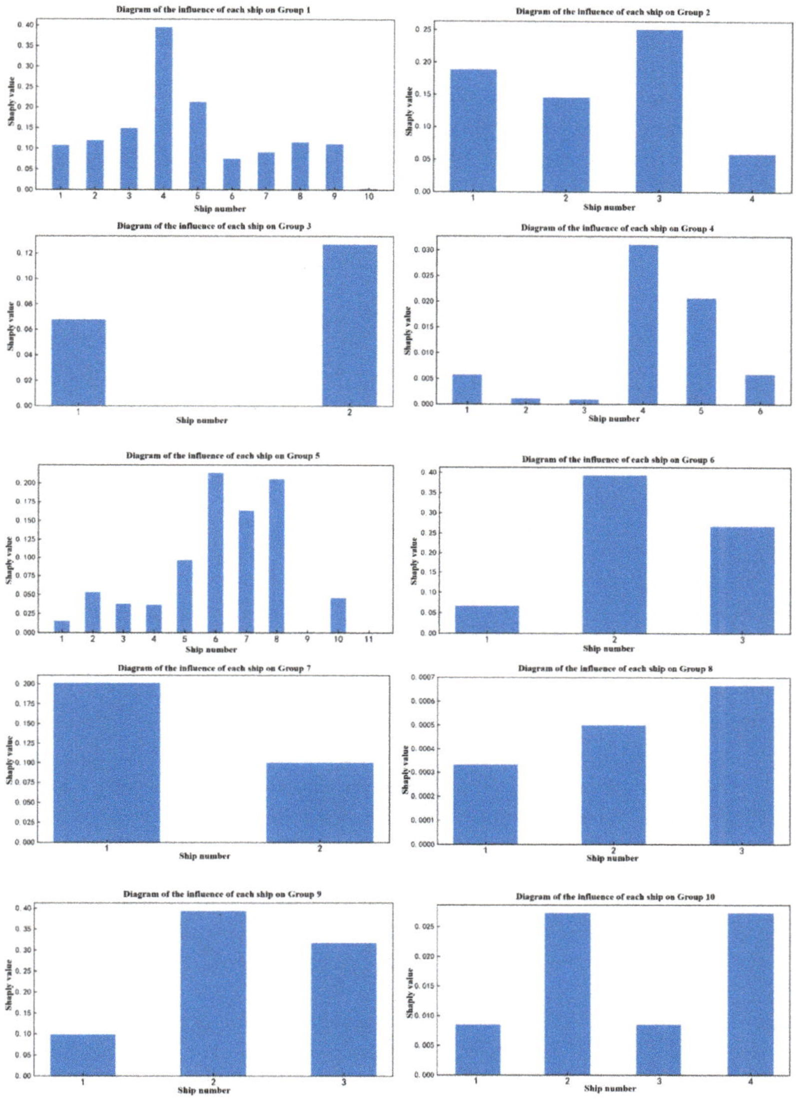

Figure 23. The contribution of each ship in each group.

It can be seen from Figure 24 that the group with the highest collision risk is Group 1, which reaches 0.5058. It can be seen that the ship traffic density in Group 1 is large, there are many ship conflicts, and the narrow channel width leads to a reduced passing distance between the ships, resulting in a high risk within the group; Group 7 has the lowest collision risk of 0.09, and the distance between the ships in the group is relatively large, resulting in a conflict of lower severity; and the collision risk in Group 3 is significantly greater than that in Group 7. This is because the distance between the ships in Group 3 is much smaller than that in Group 7. When approaching each other, the distance is negatively correlated with the collision risk. Therefore, the collision risk calculated according to this framework is consistent with the actual traffic conditions in the study waters. In addition, it can be seen from Figure 24 that the traffic complexity curve and collision risk curve of each group have the same change trend. In order to quantitatively analyze the correlation between the change trend in collision risk and traffic complexity of the 10 ship groups, a Pearson correlation analysis was performed. The analysis results show that at a confidence level of 99%, the change trend in collision risk of the 10 ship groups is strongly correlated with the change trend in traffic complexity, with a correlation coefficient of 0.923 and a *p*-value of less than 0.001. Therefore, it can be proved that the collision risk of different ship groups in the waters calculated according to the proposed framework is effective.

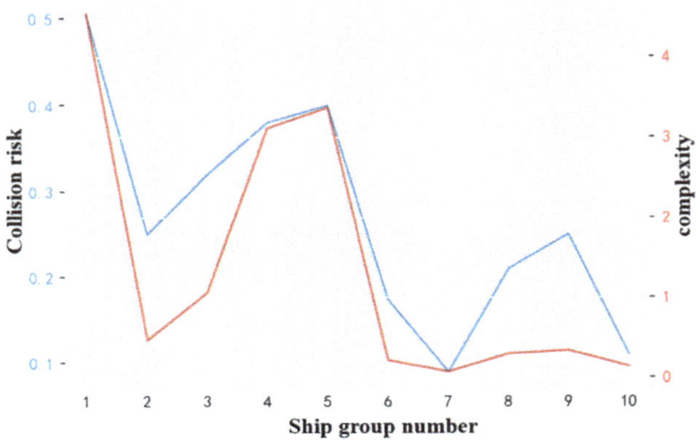

Figure 24. Collision risk and traffic complexity for each group.

5. Conclusions

The main contributions of this paper are summarized as follows:

(1) Aiming at the effective perception of ship collision risk in the dynamic navigation scene of complex navigable waters, we propose a novel calculation method for conflict probability. This method can detect the probability of ship conflict in a complex dynamic environment in a timely and accurate manner, and provide valuable information for the quantification of ship collision risks and safety supervision from the perspective of water navigation management.

(2) In order to realize the fast and accurate grouping of ships in complex navigable waters and facilitate the safety supervision of different local waters, we propose a two-stage algorithm of ship group division based on fast modularity optimization and spectral clustering algorithm. It is convenient for maritime regulatory authorities to more comprehensively and clearly grasp the internal connection and attributes between ships involved in decision making, which helps regulatory personnel to effectively capture high-risk traffic clusters, better understand the risk status of different local waters, and provide targeted supervision and management plans to improve ship traffic safety and efficiency.

(3) Based on the ship conflict detection method and the ship group extraction from the perspective of water navigation management, the regional ships are detected for conflict probability and contribution identification, and the risks of different local waters and regions are quantified.

Despite the advantages mentioned above, the proposed approach still exposes some limitations. This study needs to be further improved from the following aspects:

The ship trajectory prediction method needs to be developed. Therefore, one of the future research directions is to combine trajectory data mining methods to build a hybrid trajectory prediction model to support conflict probability estimation with both cooperative and non-cooperative ships.

The method emphasizes the estimation of the probability of conflict occurrence. However, since the potential consequences are not explicitly considered in the probability of conflict, a comprehensive assessment of navigational risk may not be sufficient. In fact, once a collision occurs, there are a large number of possible accident scenarios with different probabilities and consequences. Therefore, an improved model that takes into account both the probability of occurrence and the consequences can help shipowners and maritime safety authorities better understand the actual risk level of traffic conditions.

In the future, the space–time evolution trend in ship groups can be analyzed to help understand the process of their formation, development, contraction, merger, decomposition, and disappearance. An in-depth study of these evolutionary laws can provide a basis for the risk prediction of local dynamic groups in the future, thus providing a prerequisite for issuing early collision warnings and responding to risk management.

Author Contributions: Conceptualization, Y.C. and Q.Y.; methodology, Y.C.; software, W.W.; validation, W.W., X.W. and Y.C.; formal analysis, Y.C.; investigation, Q.Y.; resources, Q.Y.; data curation, Q.Y.; writing—original draft preparation, Y.C.; writing—review and editing, Y.C.; visualization, Y.C.; supervision, X.W.; project administration, Q.Y.; funding acquisition, Q.Y. All authors have read and agreed to the published version of the manuscript.

Funding: This research was funded by the National Natural Science Foundation of China (Grant No. 52201412), China. This research was supported by the university-level Young and Middle-aged Research Fund of Xiamen Institute of Technology (No. KYT2023001).

Institutional Review Board Statement: Not applicable.

Informed Consent Statement: Not applicable.

Data Availability Statement: The data in this paper are from the course group of the author.

Conflicts of Interest: The authors declare no conflicts of interest.

References

1. Goerlandt, F.; Montewka, J. Maritime Transportation Risk Analysis: Review and Analysis in Light of Some Foundational Issues. *Reliab. Eng. Syst. Saf.* **2015**, *138*, 115–134. [CrossRef]
2. Liu, Z.; Li, Y.; Zhang, Z.; Yu, W.; Han, B.; Du, Y. Spatial Modeling and Analysis Approach for Ship-Encounters Dynamic Spatial–Temporal Domain. *Ocean Eng.* **2023**, *278*, 114373. [CrossRef]
3. Yim, J.-B.; Kim, D.-S.; Park, D.-J. Modeling Perceived Collision Risk in Vessel Encounter Situations. *Ocean Eng.* **2018**, *166*, 64–75. [CrossRef]
4. Chen, P.; Huang, Y.; Mou, J.; van Gelder, P.H.A.J.M. Probabilistic Risk Analysis for Ship-Ship Collision: State-of-the-Art. *Saf. Sci.* **2019**, *117*, 108–122. [CrossRef]
5. Zhao, Y.; Suo, Y.; Xian, B. Ship Encounter Scenario and Maneuvering Behavior Mining Based on AIS Data. In *International Conference on Wireless Communications, Networking and Applications*; Springer Nature Singapore: Singapore, 2022; pp. 58–65.
6. Liu, J.; Zhang, J.; Yang, Z.; Wan, C.; Zhang, M. A Novel Data-Driven Method of Ship Collision Risk Evolution Evaluation during Real Encounter Situations. *Reliab. Eng. Syst. Saf.* **2024**, *249*, 110228. [CrossRef]
7. Lei, P.-R. Mining Maritime Traffic Conflict Trajectories from a Massive AIS Data. *Knowl. Inf. Syst.* **2020**, *62*, 259–285. [CrossRef]
8. Chen, P.; Huang, Y.; Mou, J.; van Gelder, P.H.A.J.M. Ship Collision Candidate Detection Method: A Velocity Obstacle Approach. *Ocean Eng.* **2018**, *170*, 186–198. [CrossRef]
9. Zhang, W.; Goerlandt, F.; Kujala, P.; Wang, Y. An Advanced Method for Detecting Possible near Miss Ship Collisions from AIS Data. *Ocean Eng.* **2016**, *124*, 141–156. [CrossRef]
10. Kundakçı, B.; Nas, S.; Gucma, L. Prediction of Ship Domain on Coastal Waters by Using AIS Data. *Ocean Eng.* **2023**, *273*, 113921. [CrossRef]
11. Fujii, Y.; Tanaka, K. Traffic Capacity. *J. Navig.* **1971**, *24*, 543–552. [CrossRef]
12. Wang, Y.; Chin, H.-C. An Empirically-Calibrated Ship Domain as a Safety Criterion for Navigation in Confined Waters. *J. Navig.* **2016**, *69*, 257–276. [CrossRef]
13. Wang, N. A Novel Analytical Framework for Dynamic Quaternion Ship Domains. *J. Navig.* **2013**, *66*, 265–281. [CrossRef]

14. Zhang, L.; Meng, Q. Probabilistic Ship Domain with Applications to Ship Collision Risk Assessment. *Ocean Eng.* **2019**, *186*, 106130. [CrossRef]
15. Szłapczyński, R.; Niksa-Rynkiewicz, T. A Framework of A Ship Domain-Based Near-Miss Detection Method Using Mamdani Neuro-Fuzzy Classification. *Pol. Marit. Res.* **2018**, *25*, 14–21. [CrossRef]
16. Dinh, G.H.; Im, N. The Combination of Analytical and Statistical Method to Define Polygonal Ship Domain and Reflect Human Experiences in Estimating Dangerous Area. *Int. J. e-Navig. Marit. Econ.* **2016**, *4*, 97–108. [CrossRef]
17. Zhen, R.; Riveiro, M.; Jin, Y. A Novel Analytic Framework of Real-Time Multi-Vessel Collision Risk Assessment for Maritime Traffic Surveillance. *Ocean Eng.* **2017**, *145*, 492–501. [CrossRef]
18. Chin, H.C.; Debnath, A.K. Modeling Perceived Collision Risk in Port Water Navigation. *Saf. Sci.* **2009**, *47*, 1410–1416. [CrossRef]
19. Wang, N.; Yuen, K.F.; Yuan, J.; Li, D. Ship Collision Risk Assessment: A Multi-Criteria Decision-Making Framework Based on Dempster–Shafer Evidence Theory. *Appl. Soft Comput.* **2024**, *162*, 111823. [CrossRef]
20. Zhang, M.; Montewka, J.; Manderbacka, T.; Kujala, P.; Hirdaris, S. A Big Data Analytics Method for the Evaluation of Ship—Ship Collision Risk Reflecting Hydrometeorological Conditions. *Reliab. Eng. Syst. Saf.* **2021**, *213*, 107674. [CrossRef]
21. Gil, M.; Montewka, J.; Krata, P.; Hinz, T.; Hirdaris, S. Determination of the Dynamic Critical Maneuvering Area in an Encounter between Two Vessels: Operation with Negligible Environmental Disruption. *Ocean Eng.* **2020**, *213*, 107709. [CrossRef]
22. Gang, L.; Wang, Y.; Sun, Y.; Zhou, L.; Zhang, M. Estimation of Vessel Collision Risk Index Based on Support Vector Machine. *Adv. Mech. Eng.* **2016**, *8*, 168781401667125. [CrossRef]
23. Li, B.; Pang, F.-W. An Approach of Vessel Collision Risk Assessment Based on the D–S Evidence Theory. *Ocean Eng.* **2013**, *74*, 16–21. [CrossRef]
24. Lenart, A.S. Analysis of Collision Threat Parameters and Criteria. *J. Navig.* **2015**, *68*, 887–896. [CrossRef]
25. Larson, J.; Bruch, M.; Ebken, J. Autonomous Navigation and Obstacle Avoidance for Unmanned Surface Vehicles. In *Unmanned systems technology VIII*; Gerhart, G.R., Shoemaker, C.M., Gage, D.W., Eds.; SPIE: San Diego, CA, USA, 2006; p. 623007.
26. Huang, Y.; van Gelder, P.H.A.J.M.; Wen, Y. Velocity Obstacle Algorithms for Collision Prevention at Sea. *Ocean Eng.* **2018**, *151*, 308–321. [CrossRef]
27. Szlapczynski, R.; Szlapczynska, J. A Target Information Display for Visualizing Collision Avoidance Maneuvers in Various Visibility Conditions. *J. Navig.* **2015**, *68*, 1041–1055. [CrossRef]
28. Huang, Y.; Chen, L.; van Gelder, P.H.A.J.M. Generalized Velocity Obstacle Algorithm for Preventing Ship Collisions at Sea. *Ocean Eng.* **2019**, *173*, 142–156. [CrossRef]
29. Huang, Y.; van Gelder, P.H.A.J.M. Time-Varying Risk Measurement for Ship Collision Prevention. *Risk Anal.* **2020**, *40*, 24–42. [CrossRef]
30. Idiri, B.; Napoli, A. The Automatic Identification System of Maritime Accident Risk Using Rule-Based Reasoning. In Proceedings of the 2012 7th International Conference on System of Systems Engineering (SoSE), Genova, Italy, 16–19 July 2012; IEEE: Piscataway, NJ, USA, 2012; pp. 125–130.
31. Hänninen, M. Bayesian Networks for Maritime Traffic Accident Prevention: Benefits and Challenges. *Accid. Anal. Prev.* **2014**, *73*, 305–312. [CrossRef]
32. Kujala, P.; Hänninen, M.; Arola, T.; Ylitalo, J. Analysis of the Marine Traffic Safety in the Gulf of Finland. *Reliab. Eng. Syst. Saf.* **2009**, *94*, 1349–1357. [CrossRef]
33. Bye, R.J.; Aalberg, A.L. Maritime Navigation Accidents and Risk Indicators: An Exploratory Statistical Analysis Using AIS Data and Accident Reports. *Reliab. Eng. Syst. Saf.* **2018**, *176*, 174–186. [CrossRef]
34. Du, L.; Goerlandt, F.; Kujala, P. Review and Analysis of Methods for Assessing Maritime Waterway Risk Based on Non-Accident Critical Events Detected from AIS Data. *Reliab. Eng. Syst. Saf.* **2020**, *200*, 106933. [CrossRef]
35. Terndrup Pedersen, P. Collision and Grounding Mechanics. *Proc. WEMT* **1995**, *95*, 125–157.
36. Martins, M.R.; Maturana, M.C. Application of Bayesian Belief Networks to the Human Reliability Analysis of an Oil Tanker Operation Focusing on Collision Accidents. *Reliab. Eng. Syst. Saf.* **2013**, *110*, 89–109. [CrossRef]
37. Fan, S.; Blanco-Davis, E.; Yang, Z.; Zhang, J.; Yan, X. Incorporation of Human Factors into Maritime Accident Analysis Using a Data-Driven Bayesian Network. *Reliab. Eng. Syst. Saf.* **2020**, *203*, 107070. [CrossRef]
38. Weng, J.; Li, G.; Chai, T.; Yang, D. Evaluation of Two-Ship Collision Severity Using Ordered Probit Approaches. *J. Navig.* **2018**, *71*, 822–836. [CrossRef]
39. Chen, Y.; Liu, K.; Xin, X.; Miao, P.; Zhang, M. Ship collision probability detection method based on AIS data. *Chin. Nav.* **2022**, *45*, 15–22.
40. Xin, X.; Liu, K.; Yang, Z.; Zhang, J.; Wu, X. A Probabilistic Risk Approach for the Collision Detection of Multi-Ships under Spatiotemporal Movement Uncertainty. *Reliab. Eng. Syst. Saf.* **2021**, *215*, 107772. [CrossRef]

Journal of
*Marine Science
and Engineering*

MDPI

Article

Research on LSTM-Based Maneuvering Motion Prediction for USVs

Rong Guo [1,2], Yunsheng Mao [1,2], Zuquan Xiang [1,2], Le Hao [1,2], Dingkun Wu [3] and Lifei Song [1,2,*]

[1] Key Laboratory of High Performance Ship Technology, Wuhan University of Technology, Ministry of Education, Wuhan 430070, China
[2] School of Naval Architecture, Ocean and Energy Power Engineering, Wuhan University of Technology, Wuhan 430070, China
[3] College of Mechanical and Electrical Engineering, Beijing University of Chemical Technology, Beijing 100029, China
* Correspondence: songlifei@whut.edu.cn

Abstract: Maneuvering motion prediction is central to the control and operation of ships, and the application of machine learning algorithms in this field is increasingly prevalent. However, challenges such as extensive training time, complex parameter tuning processes, and heavy reliance on mathematical models pose substantial obstacles to their application. To address these challenges, this paper proposes an LSTM-based modeling algorithm. First, a maneuvering motion model based on a real USV model was constructed, and typical operating conditions were simulated to obtain data. The Ornstein–Uhlenbeck process and the Hidden Markov Model were applied to the simulation data to generate noise and random data loss, respectively, thereby constructing a sample set that reflects real experiment characteristics. The sample data were then pre-processed for training, employing the MaxAbsScaler strategy for data normalization, Kalman filtering and RRF for data smoothing and noise reduction, and Lagrange interpolation for data resampling to enhance the robustness of the training data. Subsequently, based on the USV maneuvering motion model, an LSTM-based black-box motion prediction model was established. An in-depth comparative analysis and discussion of the model's network structure and parameters were conducted, followed by the training of the ship maneuvering motion model using the optimized LSTM model. Generalization tests were then performed on a generalization set under Zigzag and turning conditions to validate the accuracy and generalization performance of the prediction model.

Keywords: unmanned surface vehicle; maneuvering motion model; black-box model; machine learning; long short-term memory network

1. Introduction

Unmanned Surface Vehicles (USVs) have found extensive applications in hydrographic surveying, maritime weather forecasting, coastal port security, and marine environmental monitoring [1]. Reliable maneuverability is fundamental to USV intelligence, as many control algorithms depend on accurate motion prediction, which necessitates a precise understanding of the USV's motion prediction model. However, the nonlinear and time-varying dynamics of USVs pose significant challenges for model parameter identification and the design of model-based control algorithms [2].

Currently, two primary methods are employed for ship maneuvering modeling. The first is mechanistic modeling, which utilizes either classical Newtonian mechanics or the Lagrange method, combined with fluid dynamics, to establish mathematical models that describe the ship's dynamic behavior. The main mechanistic models used for ship maneuvering prediction include the Abkowitz model [3], the Maneuvering Modeling Group (MMG) model [4], and the Nomoto model [5]. The Abkowitz model focuses on the influence of hydrodynamic forces and moments in the ship's maneuvering equations, while the MMG model decomposes the hydrodynamic forces into components acting on the hull, propeller, and rudder, considering their interactions. The Nomoto model, which describes the ship's posture and motion response using a set of differential equations, is valued for its simplicity and ease of understanding, although it has limitations in precision [6]. Zou Zaojian applied Support Vector Machines (SVMs) to identify hydrodynamic derivatives and moments within the Abkowitz model, enhancing the accuracy of ship maneuvering predictions [7]. However, Xu developed an optimal truncated LS-SVM method [5,8], validated through self-propelled experiments [9], though their study did not address scale effects. Pandey described a three-degree-of-freedom (3DoF) MMG mathematical model for the Wave Adaptive Modular Vessel (WAM-V) [10], using a combination of captive model testing and system identification to calculate maneuvering derivatives, with the MMG model simulations demonstrating good performance in turning characteristics. Nonetheless, issues like ocean disturbances remain unresolved. Luo W. et al. [11] utilized a two-layer feedforward neural network to identify the maneuverability indices and linear hydrodynamic derivatives within the linear MMG model, demonstrating the stability of the estimated parameters. However, the study involved significant simplifications of the MMG model, and the accuracy of parameter identification remains to be improved. Carrillo S. et al. [12] conducted ship motion modeling based on the Nomoto maneuvering model and used the least squares method to identify the KT parameters.

The second modeling approach is black-box modeling. This method measures the input and output data of a maneuvering ship, and establishes a model that describes the input-output characteristics during ship maneuvering through appropriate processing and computation. Notably, this approach does not require detailed descriptions of the dynamic characteristics of the maneuvering process. In the identification work using white-box models, the task primarily involves identifying coefficients or parameters within a predetermined model, thus making the accuracy of identification dependent on the limitations of the mathematical model [13]. Using fixed, linear, and time-invariant mathematical models for ship maneuvering makes it challenging to generalize predictions, as these models fail to capture the complex nonlinear characteristics of ship motions. When the mathematical model is highly complex, the number of parameters to be identified becomes excessive, relying heavily on a large volume of high-quality sample data. It becomes difficult to obtain accurate model parameters in the presence of disturbances or irregular sample data [14]. Additionally, the precision of hydrodynamic parameter calculations for the hull, propeller, and rudder significantly affects the accuracy of motion predictions. Moreover, factors such as design and manufacturing errors, equipment wear during operation, the maneuvering environment, and variations in ship loading can all contribute to inaccuracies in the ship's motion model throughout a ship's lifecycle. These inaccuracies limit the effectiveness of using white-box models for motion prediction. However, employing white-box models can aid in improving the original mathematical models. Bonci et al. [15] improved the fully nonlinear Abkowitz model by identifying the USV model through CFD free-running simulations. This work utilized high-precision CFD data to eliminate the typical characteristic noise present in outdoor tank experiment data.

Over the past decade, numerous machine learning methods have demonstrated remarkable performance in the field of system identification [16], including Support Vector Regression (SVR) [17], Least Squares Support Vector Machines (LSSVM) [18], and Wavelet Neural Networks (WNN) [16]. Zou Zaojian [19] proposed a black-box modeling method based on BP neural networks for the 3-DOF ship maneuvering model, validating the potential of network-based models as control models or state observers in the domain of ship motion control. This method utilized a fully connected neural network to establish a black-box model of 3-DOF ship maneuvering, requiring only three maneuvering operations to identify and validate the model. However, the study did not account for environmental disturbances in the black-box model. Additionally, a black-box offline modeling method for ship maneuvering was proposed using Multi-Output ν Support Vector Regression (MO-ν-SVR), which optimized the computational efficiency and operability of traditional SVR models. Nevertheless, the research did not consider external disturbances that might influence the dynamic characteristics of the ship. Liu et al. [20], based on free-sailing experiments with the KVLCC2 ship model and a multi-degree-of-freedom Wave Energy Converter (WEC), proposed three identification frameworks: parametric grey-box modeling, non-parametric grey-box modeling, and Bayesian regression-based black-box modeling. They summarized the prerequisites for using these frameworks and demonstrated that the black-box model constructed through Bayesian regression exhibited stronger generalization ability in the loss function compared to SVM and ANN, due to the incorporation of prior knowledge. However, the wave energy training set used in the study was based on regular waves, which limits its generalizability.

In conclusion, the development of ship maneuverability prediction is characterized by diverse modeling approaches, data-driven methodologies, and an emphasis on model accuracy and generalization capabilities. Simultaneously, experimental methods and data validation techniques are continually being refined. As technology advances, research into ship maneuverability will become more in-depth and sophisticated, providing more reliable theoretical support for ship design and operation. Intelligent algorithms also hold significant promise in this field; however, challenges such as extensive training time, complex parameter tuning processes, and heavy reliance on mathematical models pose substantial obstacles to their application. To address these challenges, this paper proposes a Long Short-Term Memory Network (LSTM)-based modeling algorithm for USV maneuvering. By learning from historical USV motion data, the model developed in this study captures the maneuvering characteristics of the USV through machine learning. The subsequent sections of this paper are organized as follows: In Section 2, a maneuvering motion model based on a real USV model was constructed to obtain sample data. The sample data were then pre-processed for training. In Section 3, an LSTM-based black-box motion prediction model was established. In Section 4, an in-depth comparative analysis and discussion of the model's network structure and parameters were conducted, followed by the training of the ship maneuvering motion model using the optimized LSTM model.

2. Sample Data Set Construction and Data Processing

2.1. The Maneuvering Motion Model of USV

The 3-DOF MMG motion model of the USV is described as follows:

$$\begin{cases} \dot{x} = ucos\varphi - vsin\varphi \\ \dot{y} = usin\varphi + vcos\varphi \\ \dot{\varphi} = r \\ \dot{u} = \frac{1}{m+m_x}\left[(m+m_y)rv + X_H + X_P + X_R\right] \\ \dot{v} = \frac{1}{m+m_y}\left[-(m+m_x)rv + Y_H + Y_P + Y_R\right] \\ \dot{r} = \frac{1}{I_{zz}+J_{zz}}(N_H + N_P + N_R) \end{cases} \tag{1}$$

where x and y are the coordinates of the USV in the geodetic coordinate system, u is the longitudinal velocity, v is the lateral velocity, r represents the rate of angular, φ is the angle of the heading, m_x is the additional longitudinal mass, m_y is the additional transverse mass, and I_{zz} is the inertia moment of yaw. J_{zz} is the additional moment of inertia in yaw. X, Y, and N represent hydrodynamic forces and moments, while the subscripts H, P, and R represent the hull, propeller, and rudder, respectively.

The approximate model for calculating X_{calm}, Y_{calm}, N_{calm} was established using the MMG model:

$$\begin{cases} X_{calm} = X_H + X_P + X_R \\ Y_{calm} = Y_H + Y_R \\ N_{calm} = N_H + N_R \end{cases} \tag{2}$$

The force acting on the hull is approximate to the hydrodynamic derivative X_H, Y_H, N_H, and can be expressed as

$$\begin{cases} X_H = X_0 + X_u\Delta u + X_{uu}(\Delta u)^2 + X_{uuu}(\Delta u)^3 + X_{vv}v^2 + X_{rr}r^2 + X_{vr}vr \\ Y_H = Y_v v + Y_{vvv}v^3 + Y_{\dot{v}}\dot{v} + Y_r r + Y_{rrr}r^3 + Y_{\dot{r}}\dot{r} + Y_{vrr}vr^2 + Y_{vvr}v^2 r \\ N_H = N_v v + N_{vvv}v^3 + N_{\dot{v}}\dot{v} + N_r r + N_{rrr}r^3 + N_{\dot{r}}\dot{r} + N_{vrr}vr^2 + N_{vvr}v^2 r \end{cases} \quad (3)$$

where $\Delta u = u - u_0$ is the speed difference of the ship relative to the initial ship speed, and $-X_0$ is the resistance when the speed of ship is u_0. The model of the USV used in this study is depicted in Figure 1. The parameters of the USV can be found in reference [18].

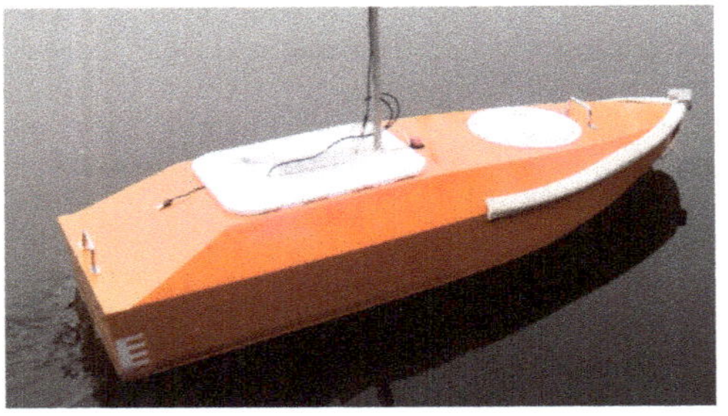

Figure 1. Model of the USV.

2.2. Sample Data Acquisition

According to Equation (1), simulations of zigzag and turning maneuvers were conducted for the USV under both still water and wave conditions, with a time step of 0.1 s. These simulations covered rudder angles ranging from 10° to 35°, ensuring the availability of the motion data necessary for subsequent maneuverability predictions. In the simulations, the wave conditions were characterized by a wavelength of 5 m and a wave height of 0.3 m. The conditions of simulation are listed in Table 1.

Table 1. Conditions of simulations.

Scenarios	Conditions
No Wave	10°/10° Zigzag
	15°/15° Zigzag
	20°/20° Zigzag
	25° Turning
	30° Turning
	35° Turning
Wave	10°/10° Zigzag
	15°/15° Zigzag
	20°/20° Zigzag
	25° Turning
	30° Turning
	35° Turning

Due to the inherent noise present in ship trials, noise errors primarily arise from sensor inaccuracies related to angles, positioning, and other measurements. The UWB positioning system may also experience data loss and inaccuracies due to interference from scatterers, water surface, and ferromagnetic materials. Additionally, wireless signals may encounter indeterminate additional delays when penetrating obstacles. Consequently, noise was added to the simulation data, and a portion of the data points were randomly discarded to simulate the errors, high-frequency disturbances, and data acquisition losses typically encountered in ship trials.

By combining the Ornstein–Uhlenbeck (OU) process for noise and the Hidden Markov Model (HMM) for data loss, the ith final simulated data $x_i^{(simu)}$ is expressed as

$$x_i^{(simu)}, y_i^{(simu)} = \begin{cases} x_i^{(noisy)}, y_i^{(noisy)} & if\ the\ HMM\ is\ in\ state\ S_1 \\ NULL & if\ the\ HMM\ is\ in\ state\ S_2 \end{cases} \tag{4}$$

where $x_i^{(simu)}, y_i^{(simu)}$ is the data added with OU noise. Take x as an example:

$$x_i^{(noisy)} = x_i^{(ideal)} + x_i^{(OU)} \tag{5}$$

where $x_i^{(ideal)}$ is the data from the conditions form simulation shown in Table 1, and $x_i^{(OU)}$ represents OU noise. OU noise is a time-correlated stochastic process initially used to describe Brownian motion in physics. In RL, it is employed to generate smooth and orderly noise sequences that aid in exploring the action space. The mathematical expression for the OU process is

$$dx_i = \theta(\mu - x_i)dt + \sigma dW_i \tag{6}$$

where $x_i^{(OU)}$ is the ith value of the noise at time t. θ is the parameter controlling the speed of noise regression to the mean. μ is the long-term mean of the noise. σ is the intensity of noise fluctuations. dW_i is the standard Brownian motion.

At each time step, the noise is updated according to the following OU process:

$$x_{i+1} = x_i + \theta(\mu - x_i)\Delta t + \sigma\sqrt{\Delta t}\mathcal{N}(0,1) \tag{7}$$

where $\mathcal{N}(0,1)$ is a normal distribution with mean 0 and variance 1. When executing the strategy, the generated OU noise is added to the actions derived from the deterministic strategy.

S_1 and S_2 in Formula (4) are two states in the HMM, which is employed to represent the states of data transmission, where the states represent whether the data is successfully received or lost. HMM is used for modeling systems that have unobservable states with observable outcomes. S_1 indicates that the data is successfully transmitted, and S_2 indicates that the data is lost. The transition probabilities between these states are given by the matrix P:

$$P = \begin{pmatrix} P_{11} & P_{12} \\ P_{21} & P_{22} \end{pmatrix} \tag{8}$$

where P_{ij} represents the probability of transitioning from state S_i to state S_j.

2.3. Sample Data Processing

In the USV motion data samples obtained, the different elements of the input vector should hold equal importance; however, differing scales among these elements can influence how regression algorithms assess their significance. Therefore, before model training, the input vectors were normalized using the following:

$$\begin{aligned} X^{(formal)} &= X^{(simu)}./\max(|X^{(simu)}|) \\ Y^{(formal)} &= Y^{(simu)}./\max(|Y^{(simu)}|) \end{aligned} \tag{9}$$

where $X^{(formal)}$ denotes the normalized input matrix, and $Y^{(formal)}$ denotes the normalized output matrix. $X^{(formal)}$={$x_i^{(formal)}|i = 1,2,...N$}. For simplification of the equations, x will be used to represent $x^{(formal)}$ in subsequent discussions, and the same applies to the simplification of $y^{(formal)}$.

Disregarding factors such as speed fluctuations during ship trials allows the ship model's motion to be approximated as a discrete linear dynamic system. A Kalman filter was employed for preliminary filtering of the system:

$$x_i = A \times x_{i-1} + B \times u_i + \omega_{i-1} \tag{10}$$

$$z_i = H \times x_i + v_i \tag{11}$$

where x_i represents the system state matrix, z_i is the observed state matrix, A is the state transition matrix, B is the control input matrix, H is the observation matrix, ω is the process noise, and v is the measurement noise. Both ω and v are assumed to follow Gaussian white noise distributions with covariances Q and R, respectively. The parameters are $Q = \sigma_Q^2 \times \begin{bmatrix} q & 0 \\ 0 & q \end{bmatrix}$, $q = \begin{bmatrix} \frac{1}{4}\Delta t^4 & \frac{1}{2}\Delta t^3 \\ \frac{1}{2}\Delta t^3 & \Delta t^2 \end{bmatrix}$; $R = \begin{bmatrix} \sigma_R^2 & 0 \\ 0 & \sigma_R^2 \end{bmatrix}$ where $\sigma_Q = 1$, $\sigma_R = 20$, with Δt representing the data sampling interval.

Subsequently, Lagrange polynomial interpolation was applied to reconstruct missing data points in the case of lost ship motion data samples in discrete signals. For each known data point, a corresponding Lagrange basis polynomial was constructed:

$$l_i(t) = \prod_{\substack{j=1 \\ j \neq i}}^{n} \frac{t - t_j}{t_i - t_j} \tag{12}$$

The Lagrange interpolation polynomial was then obtained by summing the weighted basis functions:

$$L(t) = \sum_{i=1}^{n} x(t_i) l_i(t) \tag{13}$$

Finally, substituting $t = t_m$ into the interpolation polynomial $L(t)$ provides the estimated value of $x(t_m)$:

$$x(t_m) = \sum_{i=1}^{n} x(t_i) l_i(t_m) \tag{14}$$

where $l_i(t_m)$ is the value of the i-th basis polynomial where $t = t_m$.

To ensure the robustness of the sample data, a radial reach filter (RRF) was applied for further processing of the filtered data. The first step involves forward filtering to obtain the initial filtered signal, which is then reversed in the time domain. The reversed signal undergoes a second filtering process, and, finally, the output is reversed again in the time domain to obtain a radial reach filtered signal. This signal has zero phase distortion, and its amplitude-frequency characteristics are corrected by the square of the filter's amplitude-frequency response.

Let z represent the frequency domain, where $z = e^{jw}$. The process can be expressed by the following equations:

$$\left.\begin{aligned} Y_1(e^{jw}) &= X(e^{jw})H(e^{jw}) \\ Y_2(e^{jw}) &= e^{-jw(N-1)}Y_1(e^{-jw}) \\ Y_3(e^{jw}) &= Y_2(e^{jw})H(e^{jw}) \\ Y(e^{jw}) &= e^{-jw(N-1)}Y_3(e^{-jw}) \end{aligned}\right\} \tag{15}$$

where $X(e^{jw})$ is the input, $Y(e^{jw})$ is the output, $H(e^{jw})$ is the impulse response sequence, and $Y_i(i = 1, 2, 3)$ represents the intermediate response. The RRF effectively eliminates phase distortion, providing an accurate representation of data trends. However, it requires the "time-reversal" of the signal sequence, which implies that it cannot be used for real-time data processing. Therefore, this method is only suitable for offline data processing, where the complete experimental data is collected first, followed by filtering and comparison with simulation tests.

The dataset was split into a 9:1 ratio for the training set and test set, with the test set used for the final evaluation of the model's overall generalization performance to ensure robust performance on unseen data. To prevent overfitting, a portion of the training data was extracted to form a validation set, which was used for preliminary evaluation and hyperparameter tuning of the model. During training, the validation set performance was monitored to determine whether training should be halted. This study employed the K-fold cross-validation method.

3. LSTM-Based USV Motion Black-Box Prediction Model

The velocities u, v and angular velocity r in Equation (1) were discretized using the Euler difference method, leading to the iterative equations that predict the motion from time step k to k + 1, as represented by Equations (16) through (18):

$$u(k+1) = u(k) \quad + \tfrac{h}{m+m_x}\Big[X_u u(k) - 2u_0 X_{uu} u(k) + 3X_{uuu} u_0^2 u(k) \\ + X_{uu} u^2(k) - 3X_{uuu} u^2(k) u_0 + X_{uuu} u^3(k) + X_{vv} v^2(k) \\ + X_{rr} r^2(k) + X_{vr} v(k) r(k) + (m + m_y) v(k) r(k) - X_{uuu} u_0^3 \\ + X_{uu} u_0^2 - X_u u_0 + X_0 + X_P + X_R\Big] \tag{16}$$

$$v(k+1) = v(k) \quad + \tfrac{h}{m+m_y-Y_{\dot{v}}}\Big[Y_v v(k) + Y_{vvv} v^3(k) + Y_r r(k) \\ - \tfrac{Y_{\dot{r}}}{m+m_y-Y_{\dot{v}}} r(k) + Y_{rrr} r^3(k) - (m + m_x) v(k) r(k) \\ + Y_{vrr} v(k) r^2(k) + Y_{vvr} v^2(k) r(k) + Y_R\Big] \\ + \tfrac{Y_{\dot{r}}}{m+m_y-Y_{\dot{v}}} r(k+1) \tag{17}$$

$$r(k+1) = r(k) \quad + \tfrac{h}{I_{zz}+J_{zz}-N_{\dot{r}}}\Big(N_v v(k) - \tfrac{N_{\dot{v}}}{I_{zz}+J_{zz}-N_{\dot{r}}} v(k) + N_{vvv} v^3(k) \\ + N_r r(k) + N_{rrr} r^3(k) + N_{vrr} v(k) r^2(k) + N_{vvr} v^2(k) r(k) \\ + N_R\Big) + \tfrac{N_{\dot{v}}}{I_{zz}+J_{zz}-N_{\dot{r}}} v(k+1) \tag{18}$$

From these equations, the following black-box prediction model was developed:

$$\begin{cases} u(k+1) = \rho_1(u(k), v(k), r(k), \delta(k)) \\ v(k+1) = \rho_2(u(k), v(k), r(k), \delta(k)) \\ r(k+1) = \rho_3(u(k), v(k), r(k), \delta(k)) \end{cases} \tag{19}$$

where $\rho(\cdot)$ represents a nonlinear vector function describing the nonlinear relationship between the input and output of samples. $\boldsymbol{x}$ denotes the input matrix composed of input vectors $\boldsymbol{x}_i$, $\boldsymbol{x} = [\boldsymbol{x}_1, \cdots \boldsymbol{x}_i, \cdots, \boldsymbol{x}_N]^T$; $\boldsymbol{x}_i = [u_i, v_i, r_i, \delta_i]$, with the superscript T indicating matrix transposition; $\boldsymbol{y}$ represents the output matrix composed of output vectors $\boldsymbol{y}_i$, $\boldsymbol{y}_i = [\boldsymbol{u}_i, \boldsymbol{v}_i, \boldsymbol{r}_i]$. The index i corresponds to the i-th data point, with i ranging from 1 to N, where N is the number of sample points in the sample set S, and t_i is the corresponding time.

This black-box model reveals the nonlinear mapping relationship between the ship's motion variables and the rudder angle. The system's inputs are represented by the vector $\{u(k), v(k), r(k), \delta(k)\}$, corresponding to the outputs $\{u(k+1), v(k+1), r(k+1)\}$. Therefore, the input and output vectors for the black-box modeling can be expressed as

$$\begin{cases} input : [u(k), v(k), r(k), \delta(k)] \\ output : [u(k+1), v(k+1), r(k+1)] \end{cases} \tag{20}$$

A schematic of the machine learning-based black-box modeling and motion prediction process is presented in Figure 2. At each step, the input vector $[u(k), v(k), r(k), \delta(k)]$ is fed into the LSTM, and the corresponding output in LSTM represents the USV motion output vector y_t.

LSTM is a variant of Recurrent Neural Networks (RNNs), specifically designed to address the issues of vanishing and exploding gradients encountered in traditional RNNs when dealing with long sequences. The primary characteristic of LSTM is its ability to capture and retain long-term dependencies, enabling effective learning and memory of information when processing long sequence data. The LSTM architecture comprises input gates, forget gates, output gates, and memory cells, which control the flow of information and allow the LSTM model to selectively retain or discard previous information. This design enables LSTM to capture long-term dependencies more effectively when processing long sequences, thereby improving model performance. Each LSTM unit in the continuous sequence shares the same parameters, with inputs and outputs corresponding to adjacent time steps in the time series. At time step t, the network's input is X_t, the memory cell is C_t, and the output is the hidden state h_t.

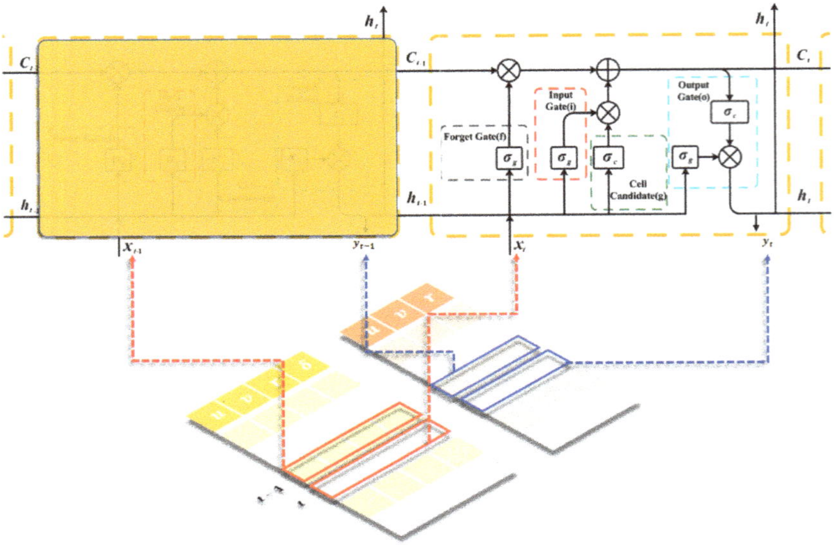

Figure 2. USV motion prediction model based on LSTM.

The core of LSTM lies in the forget gate, which determines which parts of the previous memory should be retained and which should be discarded, enabling autonomous learning without external intervention. The forget gate takes the current input X_t and the previous hidden state h_{t-1} as inputs, and outputs a decay coefficient f_t (ranging from 0 to 1) that represents the proportion of information retained. The calculation of the forget gate is given by Equation (21):

$$f_t = \text{sigmoid}\left(W_f \cdot [h_{t-1}, X_t] + b_f\right) \tag{21}$$

where h_{t-1} is the hidden state of the previous LSTM unit, X_t is the current input, and W_f and b_f are used for the linear transformation before the sigmoid function is applied. The input gate determines how much new information should be added to the memory cell C_t. The input gate takes the current input X_t and the previous hidden state h_{t-1} as inputs, and outputs the memory decay coefficient i_t and the learned memory content $\tilde{C}_t$. The memory decay coefficient i_t calculated by the sigmoid layer and the memory content $\tilde{C}_t$, generated by the tanh layer, are given by Equations (22) and (23), respectively:

$$i_t = \text{sigmoid}(W_i \cdot [h_{t-1}, X_t] + b_i) \tag{22}$$

$$\tilde{C}_t = \tanh(W_c \cdot [h_{t-1}, X_t] + b_c) \tag{23}$$

The memory cell C_t of LSTM is updated using the outputs of the forget gate and the input gate, as shown in Equation (24):

$$C_t = f_t \times C_{t-1} + i_t \times \tilde{C}_t \tag{24}$$

Finally, the hidden state h_t of the LSTM unit is determined based on the memory cell C_t. First, the sigmoid layer determines which memory cells C_t will be activated for output, represented by o_t. Then, the memory cell C_t is processed by the tanh function to obtain a value between −1 and 1, which is multiplied by the output of the sigmoid gate to obtain the final output h_t. The calculations for o_t and the final output h_t are shown in Equations (25) and (26):

$$o_t = \text{sigmoid}(W_O \cdot [h_{t-1}, X_t] + b_O) \tag{25}$$

$$h_t = o_t \times \tanh(C_t) \tag{26}$$

The outputs C_t and h_t at time t are used as inputs for the next time step. In a multi-layer stacked LSTM model, the output sequence from the previous layer is used as input for the next layer. The output of the last layer, specifically the hidden state h_t at the final time step, represents the predicted USV motion state.

During the model training process, the difference between the predicted values and the actual values is analyzed to facilitate self-learning based on predefined rules. The model optimizes itself by adjusting internal parameters to achieve the best performance. The model is updated with the goal of minimizing the prediction error. Since this model update involves a non-convex optimization problem, it is challenging to reliably search for the global optimal solution using gradient descent. To enhance the global search capability of gradient descent, the Adam optimization algorithm is employed. Adam combines the concepts of momentum and RMSprop, taking into account both first-order and second-order moment estimates of the gradients, thereby improving the effectiveness of gradient descent in non-convex optimization problems. The root mean square error (RMSE) and correlation coefficient (CC) are used to comprehensively evaluate the prediction accuracy of the model. RMSE is used to compare the differences between predicted and actual observed values, with smaller differences indicating better predictive performance. CC measures the strength and direction of the linear relationship between the predicted and actual observed values. When the CC between the model's predicted data and the actual data approaches 1, it indicates a high degree of consistency between the predicted and actual data, resulting in improved predictive performance.

To validate the generalization of the LSTM-based black-box model, the trained model is used to predict the generalization set, and the predicted values are compared with the expected values. Since the trained model already possesses motion prediction capabilities, only the initial ship state $[\mathrm{u}(0), \mathrm{v}(0), \mathrm{r}(0)]$ and control input ($\delta(i)$) during the maneuver are required during the entire prediction process. Generalization performance assessment focuses on the RMSE and CC of the longitudinal speed u, lateral speed v, and yaw rate r within the dataset.

4. Analysis on Network Structure and Simulation

LSTM is employed to model the 3-DOF ship motion black-box model in both still water and wave environments, followed by a comparative analysis of the maneuverability prediction results based on different machine learning methods. Compared to LSSVM and SVR, the structure of LSTM is more complex and time-consuming; its parameters include the number of network layers, the number of neurons, the degree of regularization, learning rate, batch size, and the number of training epochs. Currently, there is no general method to directly determine the optimal network structure using optimization algorithms; these parameters are typically manually set based on experience and experimentation to determine the best combination. To evaluate the performance of the trained models under different parameter settings, the generalization ability was tested using data from the 20°/20° zigzag maneuvering test.

4.1. Discussion of Network Structure

To explore the impact of different neural network structures on model performance, various parameter combinations were tested, including the number of LSTM layers (ranging from one to five), the number of neurons (ranging from 16 to 128), and regularization methods (none, dropout), as well as regularization parameters.

(1) Impact of Network Structure on Prediction Accuracy:

The training settings were as follows: the Adam method was used for learning rate adjustment, with an initial learning rate set to 0.001; the window width (timesteps) was set to 3; the maximum number of LSTM iterations (epochs) was set to 100; and the batch size was set to 64. The impact of different network structures on performance is illustrated in Figure 3. The meaning of the parameters on the X-axis in Figures 3–6 is shown in Table 2.

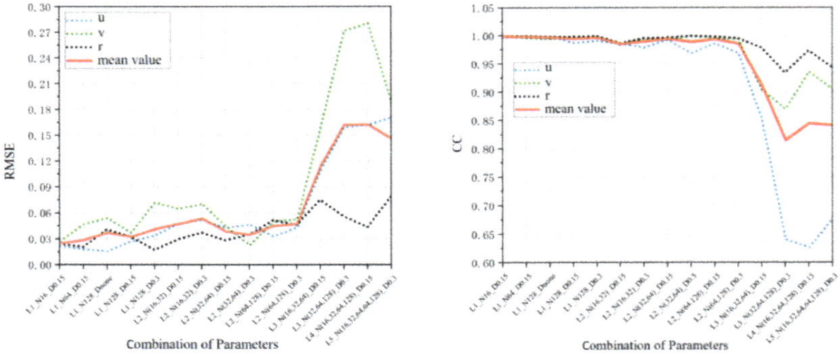

(**a**) RMSE (**b**) CC

Figure 3. Impact of Network Structure on Prediction (the mean represents the average value of the corresponding parameter).

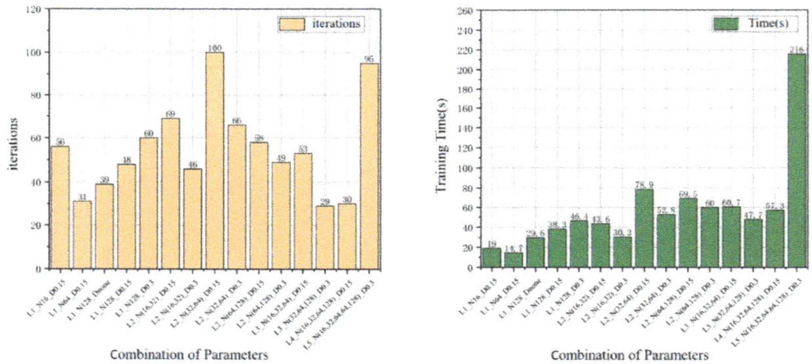

(**a**) Iterations (**b**) Training Time(s)

Figure 4. Impact of Network Structure on Training Time.

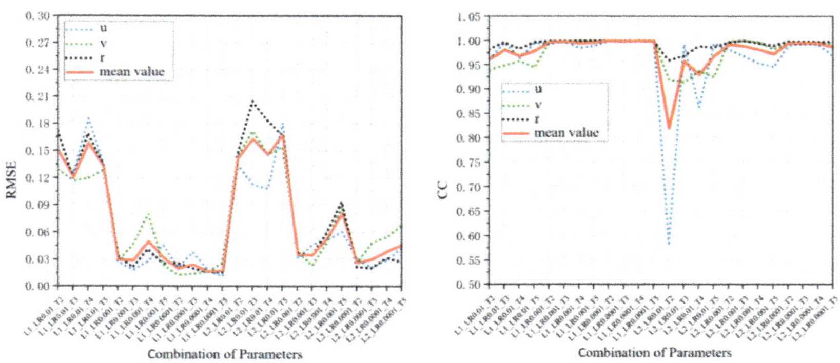

(**a**) RMSE (**b**) CC

Figure 5. Impact of Training Settings on Prediction Performance.

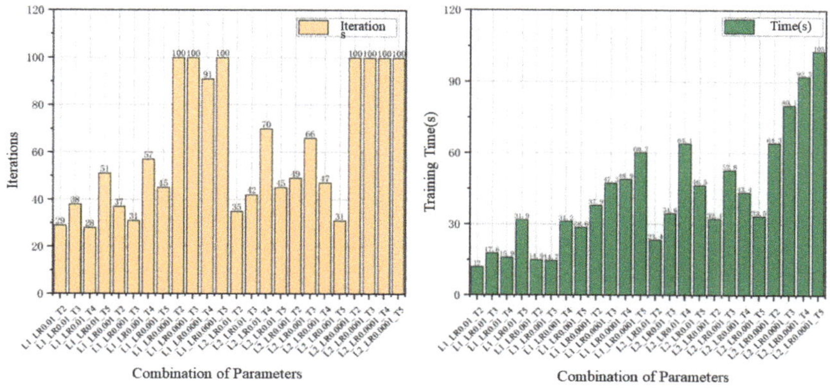

(**a**) Iterations (**b**) Training Time(s)

Figure 6. Impact of training parameters on Training Time.

Table 2. The meaning of the parameters on the X-axis in Figures 3–6.

Parameters on the X-Axis	Meaning
L	the number of LSTM layers
N	the number of neurons per layer
D	the dropout regularization rate
LR	the initial learning rate
T	the window function width

(1) Impact of the Number of LSTM Layers: As shown in the figure, with an increase in the number of LSTM layers, RMSE and CC generally exhibit a deteriorating trend. This indicates that while increasing the complexity of the network can improve the prediction accuracy to some extent, excessive complexity may lead to overfitting, resulting in a decline in prediction accuracy.

(2) Number of Neurons: With an increase in the number of neurons, RMSE and CC fluctuate, but are less significant than the impact of the number of LSTM layers. For example, when there is one layer, increasing the number of neurons from 16 to 128 causes the RMSE mean to rise from 0.0246 to 0.0370 and the CC mean to drop from 0.998 to 0.996; when there are two layers, increasing the number of neurons causes the RMSE mean to fluctuate slightly around 0.04 and the CC mean to fluctuate slightly around 0.98. Therefore, increasing the number of neurons does not significantly improve prediction accuracy, indicating that, for this training problem, merely increasing the number of neurons and thus the network's complexity and flexibility does not enhance prediction accuracy.

(3) Regularization Method: For a single-layer network with 128 neurons, the prediction performance is best when the dropout rate is 0.15—with an RMSE mean of 0.0322 and a CC value of 0.9944—outperforming the unregularized case (RMSE mean of 0.0370 and CC value of 0.9965). However, when the dropout rate is increased to 0.3, performance declines, with an RMSE mean of 0.0412 and a CC value of 0.9962. For a two-layer network with a configuration of 32 and 64 neurons, performance is worse, with a dropout rate of 0.15, an RMSE mean of 0.03859, and a CC value of 0.99394, compared to an RMSE mean of 0.0349 and a CC value of 0.98897 when the dropout rate is 0.3. Increasing the LSTM network layers increases complexity, and moderately increasing the dropout rate can prevent excessive reliance on specific input data, thereby enhancing the model's robustness.

Using dropout as a regularization method effectively prevents model overfitting and improves generalization ability. Conversely, a lack of regularization may lead to overfitting and reduced generalization ability. The choice of regularization parameters depends on the model's complexity; for complex networks, moderately increasing the dropout rate can enhance network robustness.

(2) Impact of Network Structure on Iterations

The iterations play a critical role in training. If the number of epochs is too small, the model may be undertrained, failing to capture the complex structures and long-term dependencies in the sequence, leading to underfitting. Conversely, if the number of epochs is too large, it may result in overfitting, where the model overemphasizes the details of the training data but performs poorly on unseen data. EarlyStopping can be used to monitor performance on the validation set and automatically determine the appropriate number of iterations. Therefore, in this study, the batch size was set to 100, the maximum number of epochs was set to 100, and EarlyStopping was used to prevent overfitting.

The number of LSTM network layers, the number of neurons, and the regularization parameters also influenced the training duration of the neural network. The training times for different neural network structures are shown in Figure 4.

(1) LSTM Network Layers:

As the number of LSTM layers increased, the number of epochs exhibited oscillations around 50. Overall, increasing the complexity and flexibility of the network helped better capture the characteristics of the 3-DOF model, thereby reducing training time. However, as the network became too large, the computational load increased sharply, leading to no significant improvement in prediction accuracy, while the training time became excessively long. Different parameter combinations led to varying learning abilities, resulting in oscillatory effects.

(2) Number of Neurons:

As the number of neurons increased, the iterations and training time showed an upward trend but still exhibited oscillations. This is because an increase in the number of neurons leads to an increase in the number of network parameters, thereby increasing computational load and memory consumption.

(3) Regularization Parameters:

In a single-layer network structure, increasing the dropout rate led to a gradual increase in the number of iterations and training time. However, in all two-layer network structures, increasing the dropout rate led to a decrease in the number of iterations and training time. Regularization parameters primarily affect the generalization ability and overfitting of the network, rather than its complexity and computational load. Increasing the dropout rate significantly impacts the simple structure of a single-layer network, reducing network robustness and increasing training time. For complex networks, increasing the regularization parameters may affect convergence speed and iteration count, indirectly influencing training time.

Comprehensive analysis revealed that, for this training set, the LSTM network was most effective when configured with 1–2 layers. The number of neurons and regularization did not significantly affect accuracy.

4.2. Discussion of Training Settings

Once the neural network structure is determined, the prediction accuracy is significantly influenced by the training settings. The following discussion covers several aspects of network training settings, including learning rate adjustment for the LSTM network (initial learning rate), training batch size, and window function width.

The following discussion covers the impact of different initial learning rates and window function widths on the two network configurations, as Figure 5 shows.

(1) Learning Rate:

In both single-layer and double-layer networks, the worst performance was observed when the initial learning rate was set to 0.01. As the learning rate gradually decreased to 0.0001, network performance improved, reaching its best state with LR = 0.0001, demonstrating excellent prediction performance and strong correlation. Setting the initial learning rate too high can lead to rapid convergence, missing the optimal solution, or even causing unstable training.

(2) Window Function Width:

When LR = 0.0001, the prediction accuracy of the single-layer network remained stable across different window function widths, maintaining excellent prediction accuracy. The best performance was achieved at T = 4, with RMSE reduced to 0.01649 and CC increased to 0.99931. Conversely, in the double-layer network, when LR = 0.001 or 0.0001, prediction accuracy was negatively correlated with the window function width, with RMSE increasing and CC decreasing. Increasing the window width in the LSTM double-layer network may lead to long-term dependency loss and gradient vanishing, reducing prediction accuracy. In contrast, the single-layer network was less affected, being simpler in structure with fewer parameters, making it easier to train and optimize.

To compare the appropriate window function width for the single-layer network, the training time for different window function widths can be observed in Figure 6.

Comparative analysis reveals that the model configuration with a total network layer count of 6, an LSTM network layer count of 1, 64 neurons, and a dropout regularization rate of 0.15—trained using a 5-fold cross-validation with a batch size of 32, an Adam optimizer with a learning rate of 0.0001, and a window function width of 2—exhibited the best performance in terms of RMSE and CC. The resulting RMSE was close to zero and the CC was close to 1, indicating that this model possesses excellent learning and generalization capabilities, making it highly suitable for subsequent ship maneuverability prediction tasks. Figure 7 shows the network parameters and structure of the optimized LSTM model.

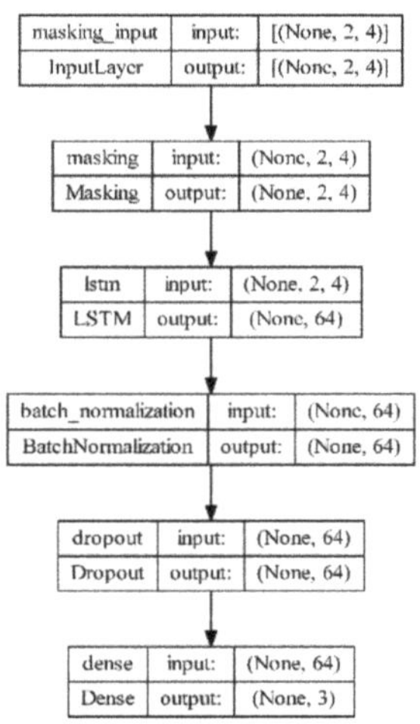

Figure 7. The network parameters and structure of the optimized LSTM model.

4.3. Comparing Simulations

Based on the optimized LSTM structure, the motion prediction model was trained using sample data. The trained LSTM model was then applied to the validation set under wave conditions, comparing simulations based on the MMG model with those based on the LSTM black-box model. The validation set included both a 20°/20° zigzag test (as shown in Figure 8) and a 35° turning test (as shown in Figure 9), representing two of the most distinct maneuvering scenarios for USVs, neither of which were present in the training or testing datasets, ensuring the accuracy of generalization validation.

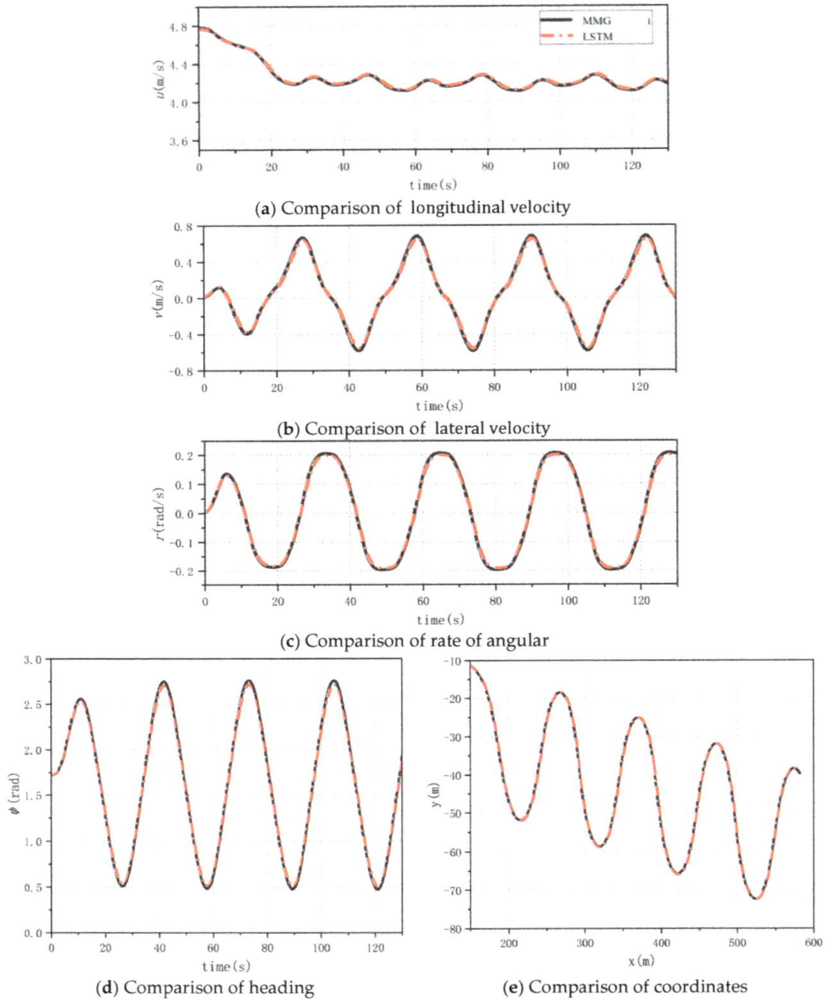

(**a**) Comparison of longitudinal velocity
(**b**) Comparison of lateral velocity
(**c**) Comparison of rate of angular
(**d**) Comparison of heading
(**e**) Comparison of coordinates

Figure 8. Comparison of motion prediction results for the 20°/20° zigzag test under wave conditions.

The comparison of simulations under wave disturbances for the two validation sets reveals that the predictions from the LSTM black-box model closely match the simulation results from the MMG model. This indicates that the black-box model constructed using the LSTM network demonstrates excellent learning and generalization capabilities. Despite the presence of complex noise distribution in the sample data and the loss of some data, the data preprocessing steps effectively repaired these deficiencies. Then, the LSTM neural network structure learned information from this data, with the forget gate playing a crucial role in filtering out disturbances in the sample data, thereby retaining essential information in the neural network that provides valuable insights for the model.

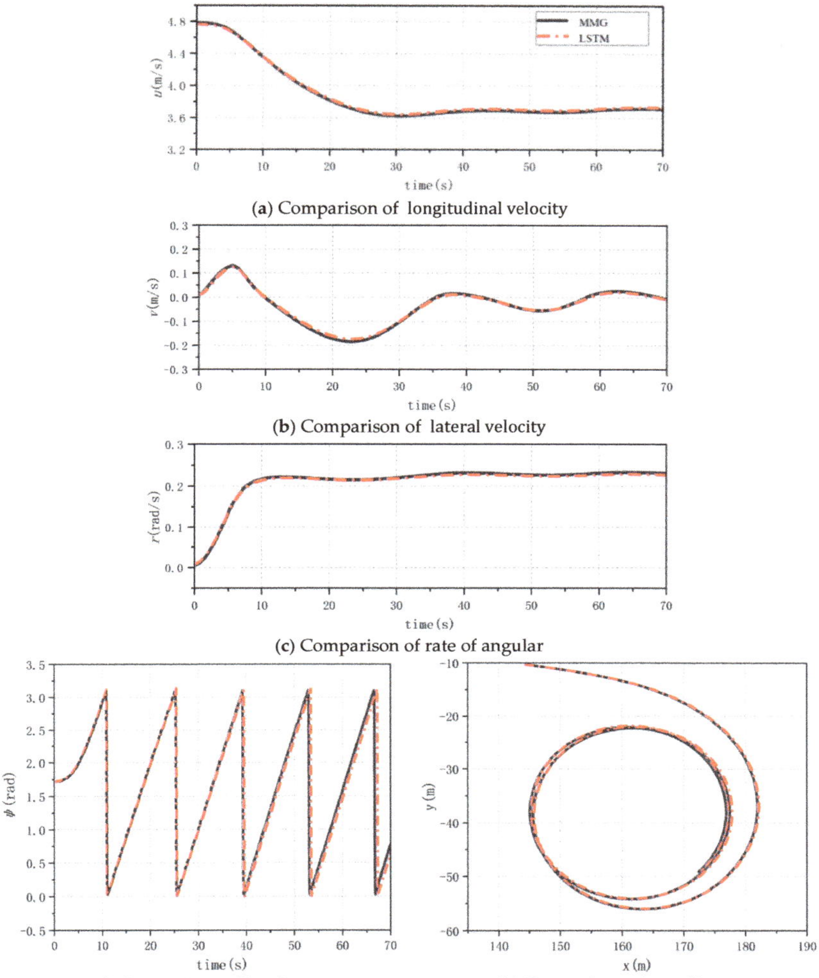

(**a**) Comparison of longitudinal velocity

(**b**) Comparison of lateral velocity

(**c**) Comparison of rate of angular

(**d**) Comparison of heading

(**e**) Comparison of coordinates

Figure 9. Comparison of motion prediction results for the 35° turning test under wave conditions.

5. Conclusions

There is a logical challenge in applying simulation data to USV motion model identification, as the simulated data is often overly perfect, lacking noise and sampling loss issues. This results in machine learning algorithms easily capturing the features of the sample set but producing models with poor generalization, making them difficult to apply to other scenarios or in real-world situations. In response to this challenge, this paper addresses the identification of USV motion prediction models by developing an offline prediction model using machine learning methods. A simulation data processing method based on OU noise and the HMM is proposed, which brings the sample data closer to experimental data, which is characterized by random noise and random data loss. Subsequently, a sample data preprocessing strategy that includes MaxAbsScaler normalization, Kalman filtering and RRF smoothing, and Lagrange interpolation is proposed. This preprocessing allows the sample data to be effectively used in subsequent machine learning training. Following this, a 3-DOF black-box prediction model for USV maneuvering based on LSTM networks is established. The research then conduct a thorough comparative study of the LSTM-based black-box prediction model across three aspects: prediction accuracy, computational speed, and the complexity of parameter tuning. Based on the comparison results, an optimized selection strategy is proposed and proceeded with model training. Finally, the trained black-box model is applied to two validation datasets under different operating conditions, demonstrating the effectiveness and robustness of the proposed method. The findings of this research can be utilized in actual USV operations, where real-time navigation data can be used to train the USV maneuvering prediction model. This model can then be employed in model-based control systems, such as Model Predictive Control (MPC), to achieve stable USV navigation in complex environments. In this study, the focus was on offline modeling and prediction of USV maneuvering data. Future research should emphasize the utilization of real-time data for rapid, online, real-time training.

Author Contributions: Data curation, R.G., Y.M. and Z.X.; funding acquisition, Y.M. and Z.X.; methodology, L.S.; software, L.H.; visualization, L.H. and D.W.; writing—original draft, L.H.; writing—review & editing, L.S. and R.G. All authors have read and agreed to the published version of the manuscript.

Funding: This research was funded by the National Natural Science Foundation of China, grant numbers 51809203.

Institutional Review Board Statement: Not applicable.

Informed Consent Statement: Not applicable.

Data Availability Statement: The original contributions presented in the study are included in the article, further inquiries can be directed to the corresponding author.

Conflicts of Interest: The authors declare no conflicts of interest.

Abbreviations

USVs	Unmanned Surface Vehicles
MMG	Maneuvering Modeling Group
SVM	Support Vector Machines
3DoF	Three-Degree-of-Freedom
WAM-V	Wave Adaptive Modular Vessel
CFD	Computational Fluid Dynamics
SVR	Support Vector Regression
LSSVM	Least Squares Support Vector Machines
WNN	Wavelet Neural Networks
BP	Back Propagation
WEC	Wave Energy Converter
LSTM	Long Short-Term Memory Network
OU	Ornstein–Uhlenbeck
HMM	Hidden Markov Model
RNN	Recurrent Neural Network
RMSE	Root Mean Square Error
CC	Correlation Coefficient

References

1. Wang, S. Research on development status and combat applications of USVs in worldwide. *Command. Syst.* **2019**, *44*, 11–15.
2. Yuan, X.Y. Hierarchical model identification method for unmanned surface vehicle. *J. Shanghai Univ. (Nat. Sci.)* **2020**, *26*, 896–908.
3. Abkowitz, M.A. Measurement of hydrodynamic characteristics from ship maneuvering trials by system identification. *Trans. Soc. Nav. Archit. Mar. Eng.* **1980**, *88*, 283–318.
4. Liu, Y.; Zou, L.; Zou, Z.; Guo, H.P. Predictions of ship maneuverability based on virtual captive model tests. *Eng. Appl. Comput. Fluid Mech.* **2018**, *12*, 334–353. [CrossRef]
5. Xu, H.; Soares, C.G. Hydrodynamic coefficient estimation for ship manoeuvring in shallow water using an optimal truncated LS-SVM. *Ocean Eng.* **2019**, *191*, 106488. [CrossRef]

6. He, H.; Wang, Z.; Zou, Z.; Liu, Y. System Identification Based on Completely Connected Neural Networks for Black-Box Modeling of Ship Maneuvers. In *Advances in Guidance, Navigation and Control*; Lecture Notes in Electrical Engineering; Springer: Singapore, 2022; Volume 644. [CrossRef]
7. Zhang, X.; Zou, Z. Identification of models of ship manoeuvring motion using Support Vector Regression and Particle Swarm Optimization. *J. Ship Mech.* **2016**, *20*, 1427–1432. [CrossRef]
8. Xu, H.; Hinostroza, M.A.; Wang, Z.; Guedes Soares, C. Experimental investigation of shallow water effect on vessel steering model using system identification method. *Ocean Eng.* **2020**, *199*, 106940. [CrossRef]
9. Xu, H.; Hassani, V.; Soares, C.G. Uncertainty analysis of the hydrodynamic coefficients estimation of a nonlinear manoeu-vring model based on planar motion mechanism tests. *Ocean Eng.* **2019**, *173*, 450–459. [CrossRef]
10. Pandey, J.; Hasegawa, K. Study on turning manoeuvre of catamaran surface vessel with a combined experimental and simulation method. *IFAC-PapersOnLine* **2016**, *49*, 446–451. [CrossRef]
11. Luo, W.; Zhang, Z. Modeling of ship maneuvering motion using neural networks. *J. Mar. Sci. Appl.* **2016**, *15*, 426–432. [CrossRef]
12. Carrillo, S.; Contreras, J. Obtaining first and second order nomoto models of a fluvial support patrol using identification techniques. *Ship Sci. Technol.* **2018**, *11*, 19–28. [CrossRef]
13. Liu, C.D.; Zhang, H.; Han, Y.; Shi, C. Black-box modeling and prediction of ship maneuverability based on Least Square Support Vector Machine. *J. Ship Mech.* **2013**, *17*, 872–877. [CrossRef]
14. Xu, F.; Chen, Q.; Zhou, Z. Modeling of Underwater Vehicles' Maneuvering Motion by Using Integral Sample Structure for Identification. *J. Ship Mech.* **2014**, 211–220.
15. Bonci, M.; Viviani, M.; Broglia, R.; Dubbioso, G. Method for estimating parameters of practical ship manoeuvring models based on the combination of RANSE computations and System Identification. *Appl. Ocean Res.* **2015**, *52*, 274–294. [CrossRef]
16. Gupta, P.; Rasheed, A.; Steen, S. Ship performance monitoring using machine-learning. *Ocean Eng.* **2022**, *254*, 111094. [CrossRef]
17. Zhang, Y.Y.; Wang, Z.H.; Zou, Z.J. Black-box modeling of ship maneuvering motion based on multi-output nu-support vector regression with random excitation signal. *Ocean Eng.* **2022**, *257*, 111279. [CrossRef]
18. Song, L.; Hao, L.; Tao, H.; Xu, C.; Guo, R.; Li, Y.; Yao, J. Research on Black-Box Modeling Prediction of USV Maneuvering Based on SSA-WLS-SVM. *J. Mar. Sci. Eng.* **2023**, *11*, 324. [CrossRef]
19. He, H.; Zou, Z. Black-Box Modeling of Ship Maneuvering Motion Using System Identification Method Based on BP Neural Network. In Proceedings of the ASME 2020 39th International Conference on Ocean, Offshore and Arctic Engineering, Virtual, Online, 3–7 August 2020; Volume 6B: Ocean Engineering. [CrossRef]
20. Liu, Y.; Xue, Y.; Huang, S.; Xue, G.; Jing, Q. Dynamic Model Identification of Ships and Wave Energy Converters Based on Semi-Conjugate Linear Regression and Noisy Input Gaussian Process. *J. Mar. Sci. Eng.* **2021**, *9*, 194. [CrossRef]

Journal of
Marine Science and Engineering

MDPI

Article

PID Controller Based on Improved DDPG for Trajectory Tracking Control of USV

Xing Wang [1,2], Hong Yi [1,3], Jia Xu [2], Chuanyi Xu [4] and Lifei Song [4,*]

1 School of Ocean and Civil Engineering, Shanghai Jiao Tong University, Shanghai 200240, China; wangxing786235493@163.com (X.W.); yihong@mail.sjtu.edu.cn (H.Y.)
2 China Ship Development and Design Center, Wuhan 430064, China; jiaxu_china@163.com
3 Key Laboratory of Marine Intelligent Equipment and System, Shanghai Jiao Tong University, Ministry of Education, Shanghai 200240, China
4 Key Laboratory of High Performance Ship Technology, Wuhan University of Technology, Ministry of Education, Wuhan 430070, China; xcyzm@foxmail.com
* Correspondence: songlifei@whut.edu.cn

Abstract: When navigating dynamic ocean environments characterized by significant wave and wind disturbances, USVs encounter time-varying external interferences and underactuated limitations. This results in reduced navigational stability and increased difficulty in trajectory tracking. Controllers based on deterministic models or non-adaptive control parameters often fail to achieve the desired performance. To enhance the adaptability of USV motion controllers, this paper proposes a trajectory tracking control algorithm that calculates PID control parameters using an improved Deep Deterministic Policy Gradient (DDPG) algorithm. Firstly, the maneuvering motion model and parameters for USVs are introduced, along with the guidance law for path tracking and the PID control algorithm. Secondly, a detailed explanation of the proposed method is provided, including the state, action, and reward settings for training the Reinforcement Learning (RL) model. Thirdly, the simulations of various algorithms, including the proposed controller, are presented and analyzed for comparison, demonstrating the superiority of the proposed algorithm. Finally, a maneuvering experiment under wave conditions was conducted in a marine tank using the proposed algorithm, proving its feasibility and effectiveness. This research contributes to the intelligent navigation of USVs in real ocean environments and facilitates the execution of subsequent specific tasks.

Keywords: unmanned surface vehicles; PID controller; reinforcement learning; DDPG

1. Introduction

Unmanned surface vehicles (USVs), also known as Autonomous Surface Vessels (ASVs), are capable of autonomous navigation and operations. They are often deployed in complex and harsh oceanic environments, which necessitate robust autonomous navigation capabilities. This autonomous navigation serves as the foundation for subsequent tasks such as collision avoidance, automatic docking, target tracking, and formation control. Among these capabilities, autonomous trajectory tracking is a critical aspect that highlights the USV's navigational proficiency. When navigating dynamic ocean environments with significant wave and wind disturbances, USVs face time-varying external interferences and limitations due to their underactuated nature, leading to reduced navigational stability and increased difficulty in trajectory tracking. Over the years, researchers have relentlessly explored the trajectory tracking control mechanisms of USVs under wave and wind conditions.

Do K. D. [1] investigated the trajectory tracking control of USVs in the presence of wind and wave disturbances using the Serret–Frenet frame. An adaptive robust trajectory tracking controller for underactuated USVs was developed by designing nonlinear observers for the lateral velocity and yaw rate based on nonlinear backstepping and the Lyapunov stability theory [2].

Sun [3] designed an exponentially stable trajectory tracking controller for USVs based on the dynamic surface control theory. Aguiar A. P. [4] researched trajectory tracking control for USVs using switching control techniques, while Fahimi F. [5] proposed a robust sliding mode trajectory tracking control method. Harmouche M. [6] addressed the lack of speed measurement feedback in the trajectory tracking of USVs by proposing a control method based on observer technology and backstepping. Katayama H. [7] introduced a straight-line trajectory tracking control method for underactuated vessels with semi-global uniform asymptotic stability, utilizing nonlinear sampled-data control theory, state feedback, output feedback control techniques, and observer technology [8,9]. However, the aforementioned methods, including optimal control, feedback linearization, and backstepping, require precise modeling to achieve high control accuracy [10]. The motion model of a USV is affected by variables such as speed and load, making precise modeling challenging. Moreover, disturbances from wind, waves, and currents during navigation complicate the path-following control of USVs. Therefore, in real oceanic environments, control algorithms based on deterministic models or those with non-adaptive control parameters often fail to achieve the desired control performance.

The PID control algorithm remains dominant in ship autopilot systems because of its simplicity and reliability. However, when USVs experience substantial time-varying disturbances, the effectiveness of fixed-parameter PID algorithms is not satisfactory. Researchers have sought to enhance the effectiveness through improving the adaptability of PID parameters [11]. Most efforts are focused on combining PID with other theories such as fuzzy control and neural networks to achieve the adaptive tuning of PID parameters.

Adaptive PID controllers adjust PID parameters dynamically during the process of tracking a desired heading, significantly enhancing the algorithm's dynamic response. However, due to model uncertainties and external disturbances, a discrepancy between the estimated and actual system outputs often exists. Hu Zhiqiang [12] proposed an online self-optimizing PID heading control algorithm, which facilitates the online adjustment of control parameters and exhibits robust performance and interference resistance.

Genetic algorithms (GAs), known for their stable global optimization capabilities, are frequently used for parameter tuning in various USV path controllers. Liu [13] has demonstrated the use of GA for the online tuning of PID parameters to implement adaptive PID control. However, these controllers face challenges such as prolonged parameter optimization times, which can impact the real-time applicability on actual vessels. Designing crossover and mutation operators within the optimization process can shorten the optimization time and enhance the algorithm's real-time performance [14].

Fuzzy logic control translates expert knowledge into fuzzy rules; it can effectively address the impacts of model uncertainties and random disturbances on USV path-following control. In practical applications, fuzzy logic is often used for the parameter tuning of PID controllers and sliding mode controllers due to its rapid response and real-time performance [15,16]. Liu [15] has established fuzzy rules according to path point errors, heading errors, and error differentials to improve control smoothness. However, the accuracy of fuzzy controllers mainly depends on the complexity of the fuzzy rules, which is generally constructed based on expert knowledge and dynamic models, so complex rules may lead to computational challenges [17].

Peng Yan [18] researched the challenges faced by USV systems, such as large inertia, long time delays, nonlinearity, difficulty in precise modeling, and susceptibility to external disturbances like waves. The study revealed that traditional PID control often fails to achieve satisfactory trajectory tracking performance. Consequently, a PID cascade controller based on generalized predictive control (GPC-PID) was designed to separately control the heading and steering motions of USVs, providing enhanced resistance to external disturbances. Additionally, radial basis function (RBF) neural networks can approximate model uncertainties and external disturbances affecting PID parameters, thus improving the robustness and interference resistance of the controller. RBF neural networks are frequently employed to model the impact of internal and external disturbances on PID parameters.

Reinforcement Learning (RL) has been extensively applied in control systems [19]. Its capability to operate without precise mathematical models and its self-learning abilities make it particularly effective in addressing challenges related to model uncertainties and unknown disturbances in USV trajectory tracking control [20,21]. Neural networks were utilized within sliding mode controllers to tune controller parameters, with RL employed to evaluate the tuning efficacy [22]. This approach enabled the self-learning of neural network parameters, addressing the low model accuracy requirement of sliding mode control while mitigating its chattering issue.

Sun [3] explored trajectory tracking control for underactuated USVs under unknown disturbances using neural network control technologies. Another study [23] employed Q-learning for PID parameter tuning, demonstrating that this controller can effectively resist external disturbances and facilitate the motion control of mobile robots through experiments. Bertaska [24] developed a multi-mode switching controller using Q-learning, which intelligently switches controllers based on the environment and the operational state of the USV, enhancing control performance across different conditions.

Magalhaes [25] proposed a RL control method based on Q-learning that mimics fish swimming motions to control the fins and tail of an unmanned underwater vehicle (UUV) for trajectory tracking. Bian [26] employed neural network controllers for ship trajectory tracking control; however, such learning methods require the pre-acquisition of reliable ship navigation sample data. Deep Q Networks (DQNs), which incorporate experience replay and fixed Q-targets, significantly enhance the stability and expressiveness of complex RL problems [27]. However, DQNs remain constrained to discrete action or state spaces based on Q-learning, making them challenging to apply to the continuous control problem of USV motion under dynamic wave conditions, where low control precision can lead to chattering.

Wu [28] modeled the trajectory tracking problem as a Markov Decision Process (MDP) based on the maneuvering characteristics and control requirements of ships. The DDPG algorithm was used as the controller, and offline learning methods were applied for controller training. Simulation tests showed promising results, although the simulation environment lacked environmental disturbances. Woo [29] introduced a trajectory tracking controller based on Deep Reinforcement Learning (DRL), allowing USVs to learn navigation experiences during voyages. In repetitive trajectory tracking simulations, the control strategy was trained to enable adaptive interaction with the environment, achieving trajectory following. However, this method directly employed DRL as the control strategy rather than adaptive parameter matching, which lacks the mature performance of classical control algorithms. Additionally, it did not leverage the dynamic performance of USVs within the controller, but treated it as a black box, which demands high-quality training data. Without comprehensive training data, the control performance may not meet expectations.

The analysis above highlights several key issues in the current trajectory tracking control methods for USVs: Firstly, many existing algorithms fail to consider the impact of time-varying environmental disturbances. Secondly, when employing machine learning algorithms for training USV motion controllers, acquiring sample data poses significant challenges, and the quality of these training samples greatly influences the performance of machine learning-based controllers. Thirdly, when using RL algorithms such as Q-learning for controller training, these approaches typically use a black box method to compensate for time-varying and difficult-to-quantify environmental disturbances. However, the motion and control models established by these methods are based on discrete mathematical models with low precision. Fourthly, directly using RL as a controller, rather than for adaptive parameter tuning, fails to leverage the superior performance of classical control algorithms and relies entirely on black box processes, which preclude the utilization of USV dynamics within the controller.

To address these challenges, this paper proposes a trajectory tracking control algorithm for USVs that calculates PID control parameters based on an improved Deep Deterministic Policy Gradient (DDPG) algorithm. By integrating RL algorithms with classical control theory, this approach aims to enhance the adaptability of USV motion controllers. The subsequent sections of this paper are organized as follows: Section 2 introduces the maneuvering motion model and parameters for USVs, the guidance law for path tracking, and the PID control algorithm employed. Section 3 provides a detailed explanation of the proposed method for calculating PID parameters based on the improved DDPG algorithm and outlines the state, action, and reward settings for training the RL model. Section 4 presents the simulation results of various algorithms, demonstrating the superiority of the algorithm proposed in this study. In Section 5, maneuvering experiment in wave conditions was conducted in a marine tank using the proposed algorithm, proving its feasibility and effectiveness.

2. The Maneuvering Motion Model of USV and Path-Following Controller for USV

2.1. The Maneuvering Motion Model of USV

The 3-DOF Maneuvering Modeling Group (MMG) motion model of the USV is described as follows [30]:

$$\begin{cases} \dot{x} = ucos\varphi - vsin\varphi \\ \dot{y} = usin\varphi + vcos\varphi \\ \dot{\varphi} = r \\ \dot{u} = \frac{1}{m+m_x}\left[(m+m_y)rv + X_H + X_P + X_R\right] \\ \dot{v} = \frac{1}{m+m_y}\left[-(m+m_x)rv + Y_H + Y_P + Y_R\right] \\ \dot{r} = \frac{1}{I_{zz}+J_{zz}}(N_H + N_P + N_R) \end{cases} \quad (1)$$

where X, Y, and N represent hydrodynamic forces and moments, while the subscripts H, P, and R represent the hull, propeller, and rudder, respectively. x and y are the coordinates of the USV in the geodetic coordinate system, φ is the angle of the bow, u represents the longitudinal velocity of the USV in the local coordinate system, v is the lateral velocity, and r denotes the angular velocity in the local coordinate system. m_x is the additional longitudinal mass, m_y is the additional transverse mass, and I_{zz} is the inertia moment of yaw. J_{zz} is the additional moment of inertia in yaw.

The model for calculating X_{calm}, Y_{calm}, N_{calm} was established using the MMG model.

$$\begin{cases} X_{calm} = X_H + X_P + X_R \\ Y_{calm} = Y_H + Y_R \\ N_{calm} = N_H + N_R \end{cases} \quad (2)$$

The force acting on the hull is approximate to the hydrodynamic derivative, X_H, Y_H, N_H, and can be expressed as

$$\begin{cases} X_H = X_0 + X_u\Delta u + X_{uu}(\Delta u)^2 + X_{uuu}(\Delta u)^3 + X_{vv}v^2 + X_{rr}r^2 + X_{vr}vr \\ Y_H = Y_v v + Y_{vvv}v^3 + Y_{\dot{v}}\dot{v} + Y_r r + Y_{rrr}r^3 + Y_{\dot{r}}\dot{r} + Y_{vrr}vr^2 + Y_{vvr}v^2 r \\ N_H = N_v v + N_{vvv}v^3 + N_{\dot{v}}\dot{v} + N_r r + N_{rrr}r^3 + N_{\dot{r}}\dot{r} + N_{vrr}vr^2 + N_{vvr}v^2 r \end{cases} \quad (3)$$

where $\Delta u = u - u_0$ is the speed difference of the ship relative to the initial ship speed and $-X_0$ is the resistance when the speed of ship is u_0. The geometric and physical models of the USV used in this study are depicted in Figure 1. Table 1 illustrates parameters of the USV.

Using Computational Fluid Dynamics (CFD) and regression analysis, the hydrodynamic derivatives for static water maneuvering have been obtained, as shown in Table 2.

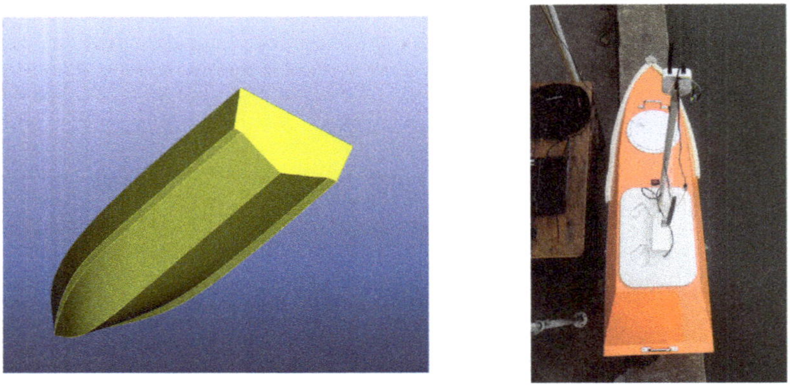

(**a**) 3D model (**b**) Entity model

Figure 1. Model of the USV.

Table 1. Parameters of the USV.

Part	Items	Definition	Value
Hull	$L_{pp}[\text{m}]$	Length between Perpendiculars	1.5
	$B[\text{m}]$	Breadth of Waterline	0.444
	$d[\text{m}]$	Depth	0.107
	C_B	Block Coefficient	0.395
	$x_G[\text{m}]$	X-position of Gravity Center relative to Midship	−0.12
	$z_G[\text{m}]$	Z-position of Gravity Center relative to Baseline	−0.3
	$I_z\left[\text{kg}\cdot\text{m}^2\right]$	Gyration about Z-axis	3.947
	$I_x\left[\text{kg}\cdot\text{m}^2\right]$	Gyration about X-axis	0.35
Propeller	D_p [m]	Diameter	0.029
	Z_P	Number of Blades	5
Rudder	A_R $[\text{m}^2]$	Longitudinal Projection Area	0.001675
	H_R [m]	Rudder Height	0.05

Table 2. Hydrodynamic derivatives.

Hydrodynamic Derivative	Value
X'_0	−0.0026
X'_u	−0.000700
$X'_{\dot{u}}$	−0.000238
X'_{uu}	0.002500
X'_{uuu}	−0.001800
X'_{vv}	0.002744
X'_{rr}	−0.002807
X'_{vr}	0.01247
Y'_v	−0.01471
$Y'_{\dot{v}}$	−0.007049
Y'_{vvv}	0.112200
N'_v	−0.006399
N'_{vvv}	−0.006952
Y'_r	0.003013
$Y'_{\dot{r}}$	−0.000777
Y'_{rrr}	−0.000467
N'_r	−0.001708
$N'_{\dot{v}}$	−0.000283
$N'_{\dot{r}}$	−0.000419
N'_{rrr}	−0.000261
Y'_{vvr}	−0.005687
Y'_{vrr}	−0.013020
N'_{vvr}	−0.015600
N'_{vrr}	−0.001047

The hydrodynamic interaction coefficients between the ship, propeller, and rudder are presented in Table 3.

Table 3. Ship–propeller–rudder hydrodynamic interaction coefficients.

Interaction Coefficients	Definition	Value
α_H	Rudder Force Correction Factor	0.5
t_p	Thrust Reduction Coefficient	0.01
w_{p0}	Wake Fraction Coefficient	0.01
ε		0.52
κ	Propeller–Rudder Interaction Coefficient	0.23
t_R		0.15
γ	Speed Coefficient	1.55
K_T	Open Water Propeller Thrust Coefficient	$0.5932 - 0.1971\mathrm{J_p} - 0.0481\mathrm{J_p^2}$

These hydrodynamic coefficients are used to account for the interactions between the ship, propeller, and rudder when calculating maneuvering forces.

2.2. The LOS Guidance Rule and PID Controller

The LOS strategy aims to guide the USV to track a virtual target along the desired trajectory, minimizing the position and heading deviations between the USV's actual location and the target, ultimately ensuring the USV reaches the intended path. The trajectory tracking strategy using LOS is illustrated in Figure 2.

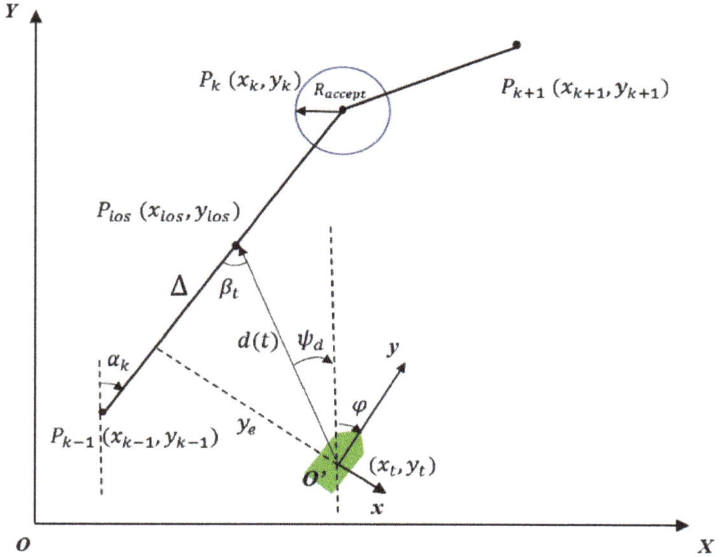

Figure 2. LOS guidance strategy.

In Figure 2, XOY denotes the global coordinate system, $xO'y$ denotes the local coordinate system, and the USV's position is denoted as P, with heading angle φ, longitudinal velocity u, lateral velocity v, and yaw rate r. The target trajectory is segmented into several approximate straight-line segments, with the current segment being tracked lying between points $\mathrm{P_{k-1}}$ and $\mathrm{P_k}$. The lateral tracking error is denoted as y_e, the lookahead distance as Δ, and the desired heading angle as ψ_d. During the curve tracking process, the sub-target along the trajectory needs to be switched. The switch occurs from $\mathrm{P_{k-1}}$ to $\mathrm{P_k}$ when $\overrightarrow{\mathrm{P_{k-1}P}}\cdot\overrightarrow{\mathrm{P_{k-1}P_k}} < 0$.

The PID controller is a linear regulator that compares the desired heading angle $\psi_d(k)$ with the actual heading angle $\varphi(k)$ to form the heading angle deviation $e(k)$:

$$e(k) = \psi_d(k) - \varphi(k) \tag{4}$$

The desired rudder angle can be expressed as Equation (5):

$$\delta(k) = K_p e(k) + K_i \sum_{i=0}^{k} e(i)dt - K_d(e(k) - e(k-1))/dt \tag{5}$$

Considering the integral saturation condition of the PID controller, the PD parameters are adjusted to ensure the USV quickly tend to the desired track and keep the USV navigating within the error range. Therefore, Equation (5) can also be expressed as Equation (6):

$$\delta = K_p e + K_d(e - e') \tag{6}$$

where e' is the error at the previous moment. The neural network is performed to produce the appropriate PD parameters.

3. PID Parameter Calculating Model Based on an Improved DDPG Algorithm

3.1. Algorithm Description

The tracking control process of USVs is a time-sequential decision-making problem characterized by MDPs. Thus, a USV can be regarded as an agent, with its motion control expressed in the form of $\{s, A, P(s'|s,\ a),\ R\}$. Herein, the details are as follows:

a. $P(s'|s,a)$ is the state transition matrix and refers to the probability of transitioning to the next state s' after applying action a in the current state s.
b. *s*, the state set encompasses all states and exhibits the Markov property; that is, future states depend only on the current state and are independent of past states.
c. *A*, the action set, comprises all possible actions that the agent can select. State transitions depend not only on the environment but also on the agent's ability to guide state transitions by selecting different actions.
d. *R*, the reward function, maps states and actions to rewards, reflecting preferences for different states.

Executing actions transitions the system from an initial state to a terminal state, forming a trajectory τ, represented as

$$\tau = (s_0, a_0, s_1, a_1, \ldots s_t, a_t) \tag{7}$$

where s_0 is the initial state, s_t is the terminal state, and a_i is the action chosen at time step i.

The aim is to maximize the cumulative reward $R(\tau)$ along the trajectory, expressed as

$$R(\tau) = \sum_{t=0}^{T} \gamma^t r_t \tag{8}$$

where T is the terminal time, r_t is the reward at time t, and γ is the discount factor, with values ranging between 0 and 1.

To maximize the cumulative reward $R(\tau)$, the policy π must be continuously optimized. The policy π maps states s to actions a, and the agent chooses actions based on the observed state according to the policy. The strategy that maximizes the cumulative reward is called the optimal policy, denoted as π^*.

$$\pi^* = \text{argmax}_\pi E_{\tau\sim\pi}[R(\tau)] \tag{9}$$

where E is the expectation, $\tau \sim \pi$ is the trajectory τ based on policy π.

The goal of RL is to find the optimal policy π^*.

$$Q^*(s,a) = \max_\pi(E_{\tau\sim\pi}[R(\tau)|s_t = s, a_t = a]) \tag{10}$$

$Q^*(s,a)$ denotes the optimal action value function, can be used to provide the best action, and can be recursively expressed based on the Bellman equation:

$$Q^*(s,a) = E_{s'\sim P}\left[r(s,a,s') + max_{a'}\left[\gamma Q^*(s',a')\right]\right] \tag{11}$$

where $s' \sim P$ denotes the next state derived from the environment transition probability P, and a' represents the subsequent action obtained from the policy π.

$$a^*(s) = \text{argmax}_a Q^*(s,a) \tag{12}$$

$a^*(s)$, the best actions, can be recursively expressed by the Bellman equation.

In policy-based methods, the policy is denoted as π_θ, where θ represents a set of parameters constituting the policy. The goal is to maximize the expected return $J(\pi_\theta) = E_{\tau\sim\pi_\theta}[R(\tau)]$, and gradient ascent is employed to update the parameters θ and optimize the policy.

$$\theta_{k+1} = \theta_k + \alpha\nabla J(\pi_\theta)|_{\theta_k} \tag{13}$$

where $\nabla J(\pi_\theta)$ is the policy gradient.

The improved DDPG algorithm in this study utilizes an Actor–Critic architecture, comprising four networks, detailed as follows:

(1) Current Actor Network

The input to the current Actor is the state space s, and the output is the action a. In this study, the state space is defined as

$$s = \left[u, v, r, \varphi, e_{psi}, y_e, d, \alpha_k, \dot{d}, \dot{e_{psi}}\right] \tag{14}$$

where u and v are the longitudinal and lateral velocities, r is the yaw rate, φ is the heading angle, e_{psi} is the lateral deviation from the target trajectory, d is the rudder angle, and α_k is the inclination angle of the target trajectory. The action a is defined as

$$a = \left[k_p, k_d\right] \tag{15}$$

The objective of updating the Actor is to maximize the Q-value evaluated by the current Critic network. Thus, the gradient of the Actor is updated via backpropagation through the Critic's gradient.

The Actor network architecture, as shown in Figure 3, consists of an input layer, two hidden layers, and an output layer. The input layer has a dimension of 10, the two hidden layers contain 400 and 300 neurons, and the output layer has a dimension of 2. To extract features effectively, and also to prevent gradient saturation and vanishing problems, ReLU is used in the hidden layers and Tanh is used in the output layer.

Figure 4 illustrated the relationship between the Actor network and USV motion controller. During training in the simulation system, the Actor outputs actions based on the input state through its neural network. These actions, representing PID control parameters, are utilized for USV motion control. The control deviation of the USV is used as input to obtain the USV control output variables, such as steering actions in heading control. Consequently, the USV executes steering actions, which are resolved through the rudder force model in the simulation environment, resulting in the USV's subsequent motion posture.

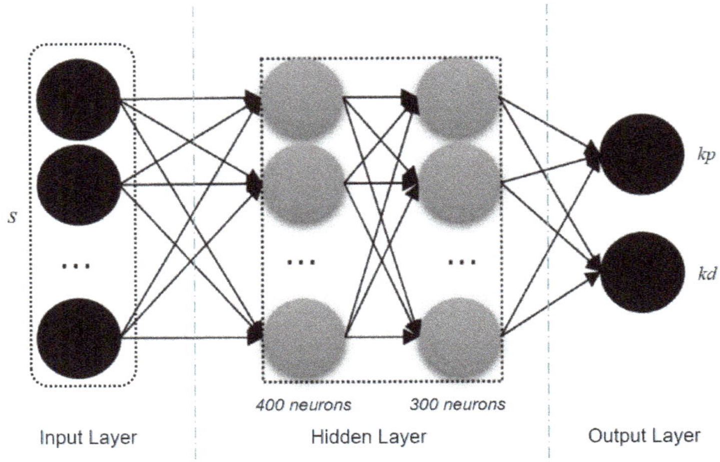

Figure 3. The Actor network.

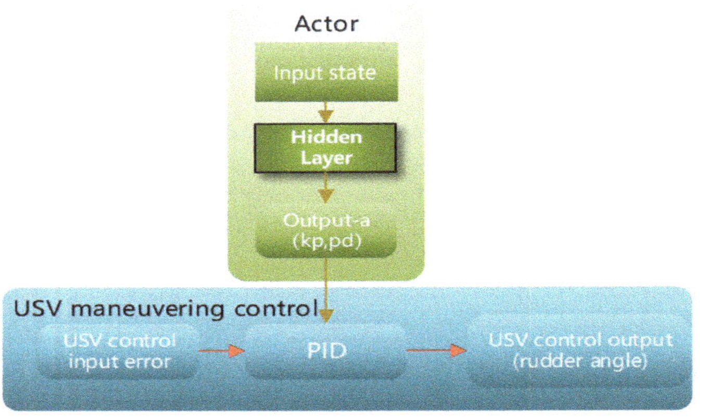

Figure 4. Relationship between the Actor network and USV motion controller.

(2) Target Actor Network

The Target Actor network generates target actions a', which are fed into the Target Critic network. The structure of the Target Actor mirror that of the current Actor network. Its weights are obtained via soft updates from the current Actor's weights using Polyak averaging:

$$\theta_{target} \leftarrow \tau\theta_{current} + (1-\tau)\theta_{target} \quad (16)$$

where θ_{target} represents the target network parameters, $\theta_{current}$ is the current network parameters, and τ is a small coefficient. The arrow symbol used here is used to update θ_{target}. This slow update process maintains the stability and relative independence of the target network, facilitating smoother changes that enhance algorithm stability and convergence.

(3) Current Critic network

The current Critic network evaluates the value of action a in state s. Training the current Critic network requires target values, which are computed using the Target Critic and Target Actor networks. The current Critic is a feedforward neural network; its structure is depicted in Figure 5. The input is a concatenation of the environmental state s and action a, outputting the state-action value $Q(s,a)$. The hidden layers contain 400 and 300 neurons, and the output layer dimension is 1, representing the state-action value.

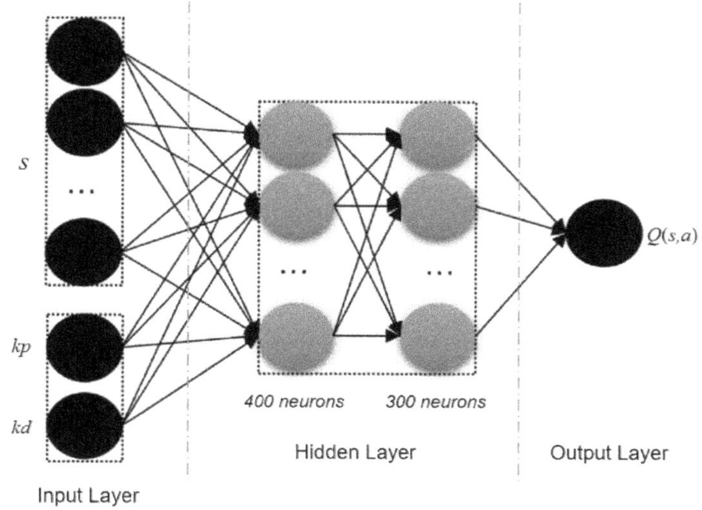

Figure 5. Critic network.

(4) Target Value Network (Target Critic)

The Target Critic network calculates the target Q-value $Q'(s,a)$ and, combined with the actual reward r, computes the TD error, which is used to update the weights of the current Critic network. The structure of the Target Critic network mirrors that of the current Critic but is used for target updates. Its weights are also obtained through soft updates from the current Critic's weights. The input consists of the environmental state s and action a', and the output is the state-action value $Q'(s,a)$.

3.2. Ornstein–Uhlenbeck (OU) Noise

OU noise is a time-correlated stochastic process initially used to describe Brownian motion in physics. In RL, it is employed to generate smooth and orderly noise sequences that aid in exploring the action space. The mathematical expression for the OU process is

$$dx_t = \theta(\mu - x_t)dt + \sigma dW_t \tag{17}$$

where x_t is the value of the noise at time t, θ is the parameter controlling the speed of noise regression to the mean, μ is the long-term mean of the noise, σ is the intensity of noise fluctuations, and dW_t is the standard Brownian motion.

At each time step, the noise is updated according to the following OU process:

$$x_{t+1} = x_t + \theta(\mu - x_t)\Delta t + \sigma\sqrt{\Delta t}\mathcal{N}(0,1) \tag{18}$$

where $\mathcal{N}(0,1)$ is a normal distribution with mean 0 and variance 1. When executing the strategy, the generated OU noise is added to the actions derived from the deterministic strategy.

3.3. Binary Experience Pool Based on Adaptive Batching

To address the slow training speed of the DDPG algorithm, the experience pool is divided into a success experience pool and a failure experience pool. To eliminate correlations between data, an adaptive batch size function is designed, where B experiences are sampled from each of the success and failure pools. New experience is gained from the environment (including the current state, action taken, reward received, next state, and termination status), and it is added to the buffer. During each current network training session, a random batch of experiences is sampled from the buffer, effectively breaking the temporal correlation between experiences and ensuring that training data are more independently and identically distributed.

$$\sigma = 1 + \frac{n_e}{n_{max}} \tag{19}$$

$$B = \lfloor \sigma n \rfloor \tag{20}$$

In this context, n_e represents the number of training iterations, and n_{max} denotes the total number of training iterations set.

The overall algorithmic process is as follows:

1. The Actor generates a set of actions, to which OU noise is added.
2. The agent obtains the next state based on the current action and inputs it into the reward function. The data from (s_t, a_t, r, s_{t+1}) is categorized into the successful experience pool or the failed experience pool based on success or failure.
3. A sample of n experiences is drawn from the experience pool, and both s_t and s_{t+1} are input into the Actor network, while (s_t, a_t, r, s_{t+1}) are fed into the Critic network, where iterative updates are performed.
4. The Target Actor network receives s_t and s_{t+1}; inputs action a and random noise into the agent, which interacts with the environment to obtain the next action a_{t+1}; and outputs it to the Target Critic network. The action values Q are then received to update the network.
5. The Target Critic network receives s_{t+1} and a_{t+1} and calculates the Q-values. These values are then combined with the rewards to compute the labels used for iterative network updates. See Figure 6.

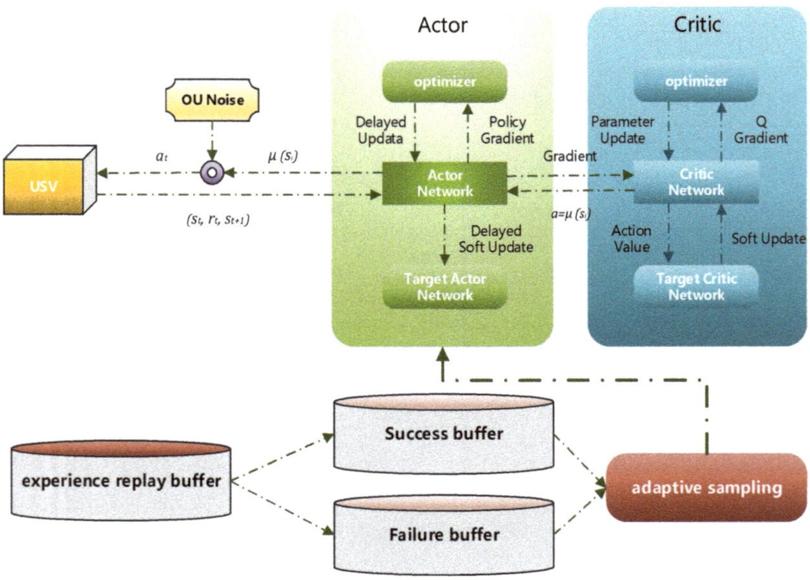

Figure 6. The flowchart of the improved DDPG.

3.4. Reward Definition and Analysis

Based on the maneuvering characteristics of USVs and the features of path tracking control, the reward function is defined as follows:

$$r_{psi} = \begin{cases} 0, & e_{psi} \leq 0.1 \\ -e_{psi} - 0.1e_{psi\_last}, & e_{psi} > 0.1 \end{cases} \tag{21}$$

$$r_{y_e} = \begin{cases} 0, & y_e \leq 0.1 \\ -0.1, & y_e > 0.1 \end{cases} \tag{22}$$

$$r = r_{y_e} + r_{psi} \tag{23}$$

The reward function comprehensively considers both the lateral deviation and heading angle deviation in trajectory tracking, with the expectation that both deviations remain minimal. According to the reward setting, if the heading angle deviation is less than 0.1, the reward is 0. Conversely, if the heading angle deviation exceeds 0.1, a negative reward is generated, with the magnitude of the negative reward positively correlated with the consecutive heading angle deviations. This design aims to use RL to reduce the heading angle deviation. For lateral deviation, the requirement is to keep it within 1 m. Within this range, the lateral deviation reward is 0, but if it exceeds 1 m, a negative reward of −0.1 is applied, aiming to reduce lateral deviation through RL.

Below is an analysis of typical scenarios based on this reward setting (see Figure 7):

(a) $y_e > 1$ [m], $e_{psi} > 0.1$ [rad]: As illustrated in the scenario, both the lateral and heading angle deviations receive significant negative rewards (on the order of −0.1). During training, actions receiving nearly 0 rewards will be emphasized, guiding the USV to alter its heading angle toward the LOS target point and reduce lateral error. According to the reward setting, the priority between altering the motion direction toward the LOS target point and approaching the tracking trajectory to reduce lateral deviation is dynamically adjusted.

(b) $y_e > 1$ [m], $e_{psi} < 0.1$ [rad]: In this scenario, the lateral deviation receives a significant negative reward (on the order of −0.1), while the negative reward for heading angle deviation is minor (close to 0). During training, actions with nearly 0 rewards are reinforced, guiding the USV to approach the tracking trajectory to reduce lateral error without excessively adjusting the heading angle, which could lead to increased lateral deviation and negative rewards for heading angle deviation. According to the reward setting, the priority between turning toward the LOS target point and approaching the tracking trajectory is dynamically adjusted.

(c) $y_e < 1$ [m], $e_{psi} > 0.1$ [rad]: Here, the lateral deviation receives a minor negative reward (close to 0), while the heading angle deviation incurs a significant negative reward (on the order of −0.1). During training, actions yielding nearly 0 rewards are emphasized, guiding the USV to adjust its heading angle toward the LOS target to reduce the heading angle deviation. However, due to the inertia of USV motion and the narrow 1 m reward boundary for lateral deviation, if the heading angle deviation is substantial, the USV might overshoot the 1 m boundary during adjustment, resulting in oscillation around the tracking trajectory. To avoid this, the USV should not have excessive heading angle deviation when entering this scenario.

(d) $y_e < 1$ [m], $e_{psi} < 0.1$ [rad]: In this case, both lateral and heading angle deviations receive minor negative rewards (close to 0). The USV's trajectory tracking control tends to stabilize, meeting the tracking requirements and maintaining this condition despite wave disturbances. However, if the USV enters this scenario and maintains stability, there may exist a steady-state lateral error of less than 1 m. With 0 rewards for both lateral and heading angle deviations, this steady-state error might not be corrected. This issue can be addressed by dynamically changing the LOS target point, but this requires a longer training time.

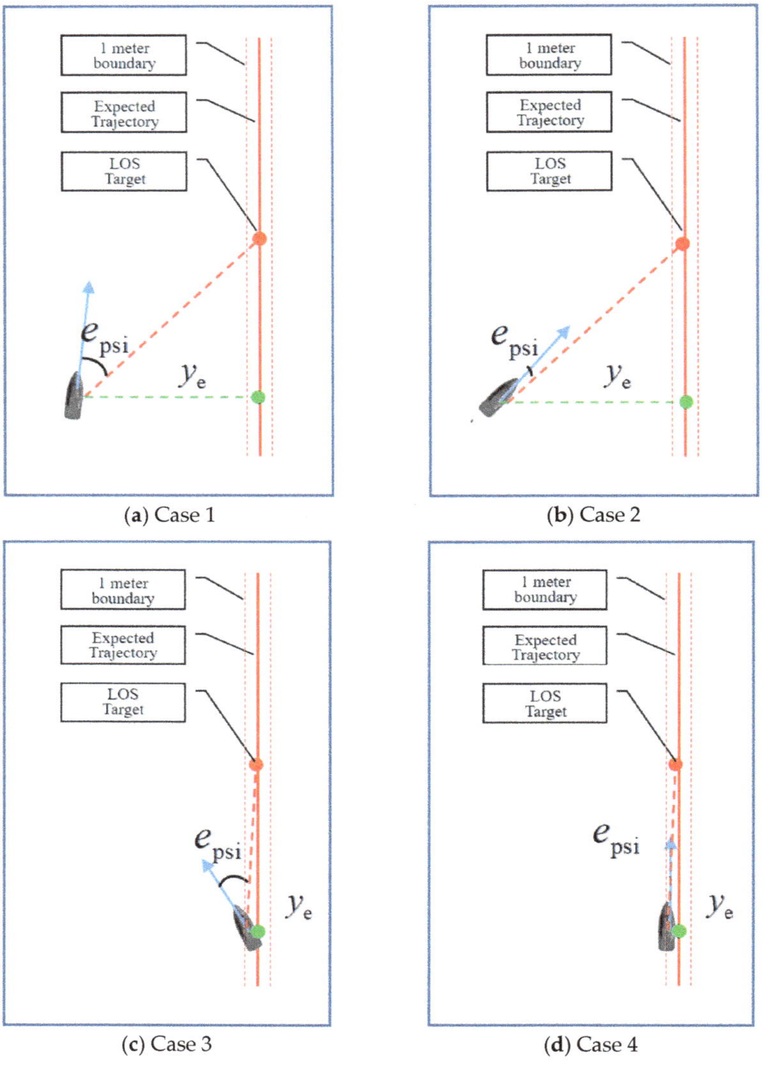

Figure 7. Typical scenarios based on this reward setting.

4. Simulation Results and Analysis

To validate the effectiveness of the proposed improved DDPG-based PID control algorithm for USV trajectory tracking, this study conducts a comprehensive comparison with both an adaptive PID control algorithm and a standard DDPG-based PID control algorithm. The hardware used for model training includes a desktop computer equipped with an Intel Core i5-12700 CPU (Intel, Santa Clara, CA, USA) and 8 GB of RAM. The software environment consists of the Windows 11 operating system, TensorFlow version 2.1.19 (GPU), and Python version 3.9.1. During the adaptive navigation control, the RL parameter tuner was trained for a total of 1500 steps per episode, with a sampling time of 0.1 s. The desired trajectory was set as a straight line parallel to the *y*-axis, and a total of 2000 episodes were trained. Each episode terminated either upon reaching the specified number of training steps or upon arriving at the designated end point on the straight line.

The simulation environment was designed to include scenarios with wave disturbances. To assess the system's stability and resilience against external disturbances, a transverse force of $\left[-0.2\times10^3, 0.2\times10^3\right]$ [N] and a turning moment of $\left[-0.2\times10^3, 0.2\times10^3\right]$ [N·m] were introduced as perturbations. This is modeled as $f(x) = 0.2U(t)$, where $U(t)$ represents an independent random variable at each time point, following a uniformly distributed random function $U(t) \sim f\_u(-1,1)$, with $f\_u()$ denoting the random distribution. The applied transverse disturbance force is depicted in Figure 8, while the turning disturbance moment is illustrated in Figure 9.

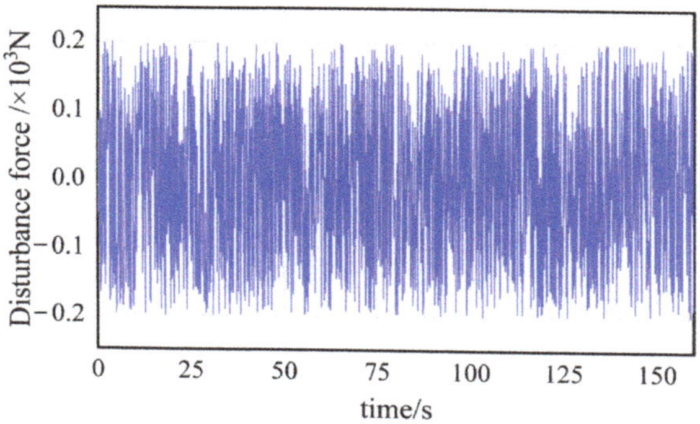

Figure 8. Transverse disturbing force.

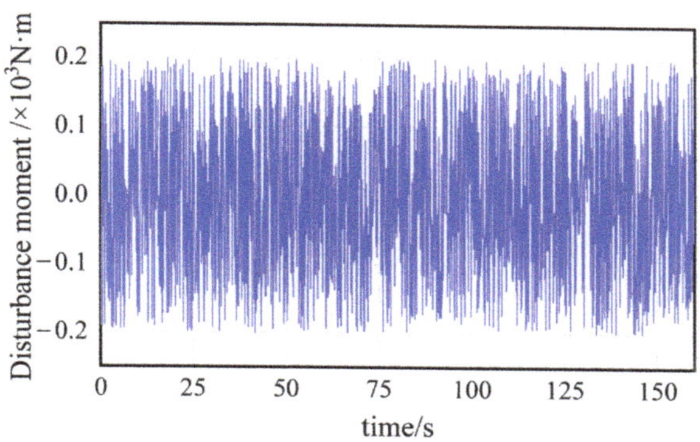

Figure 9. Turning disturbing moment.

4.1. Comparative Analysis of Zigzag Trajectory Tracking

Figure 10 presents the results of Zigzag trajectory tracking under wave disturbance using adaptive PID algorithms, PID parameters calculated by the DDPG algorithm, and PID parameters determined by the improved DDPG algorithm. The trajectory path points are set as polylines between the coordinates (0, 0), (45, 45), (85, 5), and (125, 45). The figures indicate that, due to disturbances, all three algorithms exhibit significant overshoot in the initial stage. However, the USV is eventually able to adjust to the desired trajectory. During target point transitions, each algorithm demonstrates effective control performance, with lateral deviation errors fluctuating within acceptable limits and heading angle deviations rapidly diminishing until stabilization; the rudder angle changes are also smooth. Notably, both RL algorithms outperform the adaptive PID controller in managing lateral deviations and heading tracking. Moreover, the method employing PID parameters calculated using the improved DDPG algorithm results in a smoother desired heading angle, indicating superior tracking performance. Its steering curve is also more stable. See also Table 4.

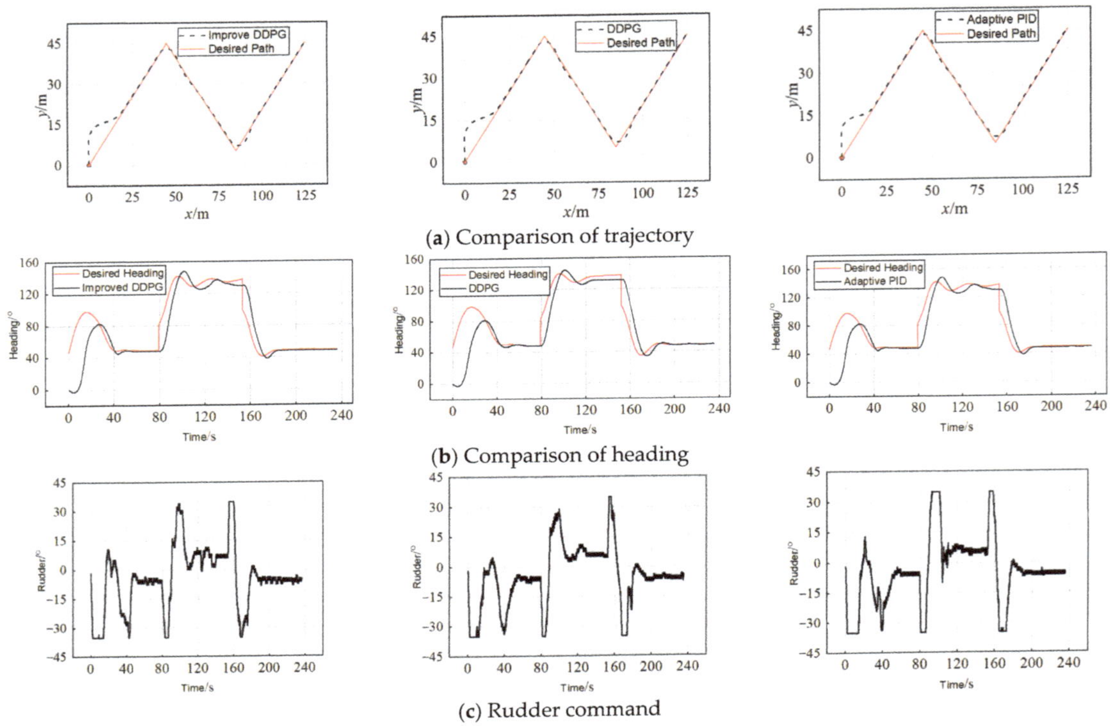

Figure 10. Comparison of Zigzag tracking with PID parameter adjustment using different algorithms under disturbance of wave.

Table 4. Comparison of Zigzag trajectory tracking metrics.

Controller	Stable Mean Lateral Error/m	Relative Cross-Track Error	Mean Heading Angle Tracking Deviation/°
Improved DDPG and PID	0.109	0.245	3.601
DDPG and PID	0.388	0.874	3.952
Adaptive PID	0.985	2.218	6.584

4.2. Comparative Analysis of Curved Trajectory Tracking

Figure 11 illustrates the comparison of tracking a circular trajectory with a radius of 10 m under sea state 4 with a 90 degree wave, using the three different aforementioned algorithms for PID parameter calculating. It is evident that the USV can quickly adjust to the desired trajectory, demonstrating effective control performance. The lateral deviation errors fluctuate within acceptable limits, and the heading angle deviations rapidly decrease and stabilize. The changes in rudder angle are also smooth. Both RL algorithms outperform the adaptive PID controller in managing lateral deviation and heading tracking. When using the adaptive PID controller and the controller based on DDPG-calculated PID parameters, significant initial mistakes can lead to difficulties in quickly eliminating errors. Combined with the inertia of the USV and wave disturbances, this can result in oscillations. In contrast, the improved DDPG algorithm for PID control dynamically adjusts control parameters according to the trend in tracking error changes, reducing oscillations near the trajectory and achieving better control performance. The resulting desired heading angle and steering curve are smoother, indicating that this controller is highly adaptable and robust, providing superior tracking performance. See also Table 5.

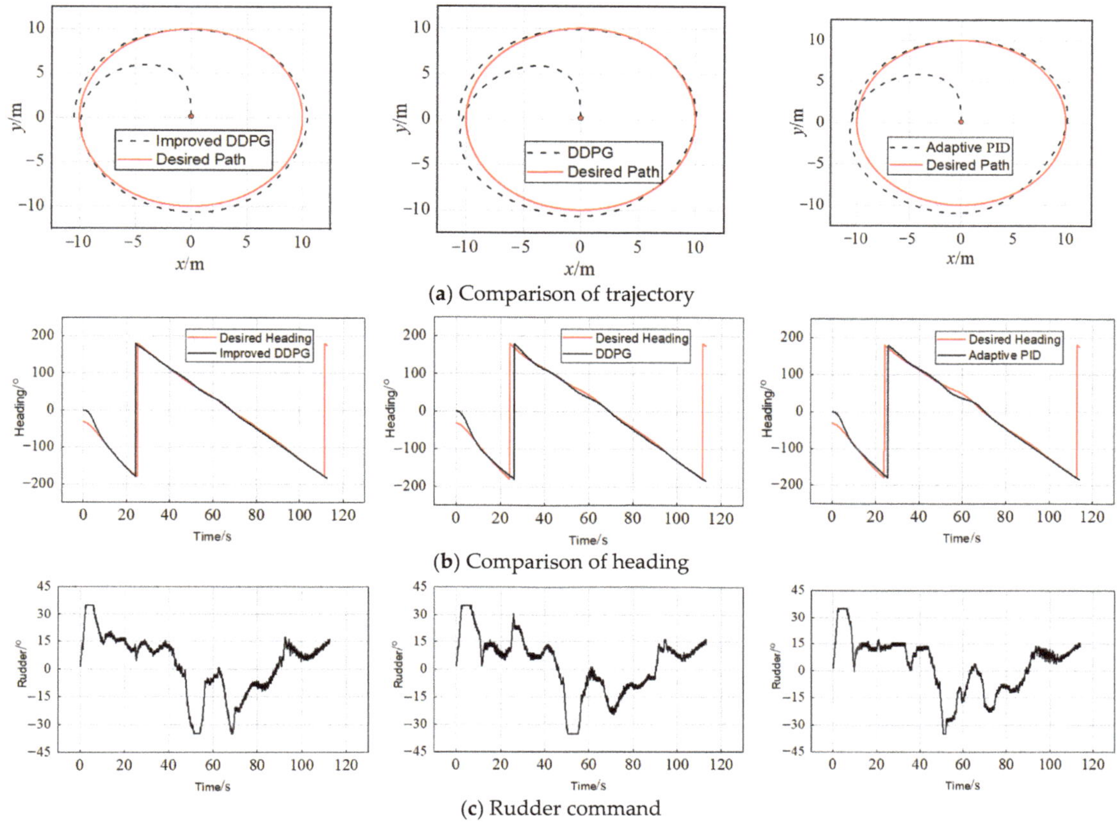

Figure 11. Comparison of circle trajectory tracking with PID parameter adjustment using different algorithms under wave disturbance.

Table 5. Comparison of circle trajectory tracking metrics.

Controller	Stable Mean Lateral Error [m]	Relative Cross-Track Error	Mean Heading Angle Tracking Deviation [deg]
Improved DDPG and PID	0.402	0.905	1.98
DDPG and PID	0.568	1.279	2.56
Adaptive PID	0.652	1.468	2.98

5. Experimental Results and Analysis

It is challenging to conduct curve tracking experiments due to the wave maker located in the ship towing tank, which has a limited width. Therefore, this study conducted Zigzag trajectory tracking control experiments under wave conditions only. The positioning equipment used was an indoor UWB system, and the USV was equipped with a gyroscope for heading, a servo motor for propeller adjustment, and a rudder servo for steering. The main control board was an STM32, facilitating wireless serial communication with the host computer. The host computer sent commands to the model ship, and the USV transmitted real-time sensor data back to the host for display. Simultaneously, the host computer performed control calculations based on the collected data, utilizing the proposed improved DDPG algorithm for calculating PID parameters.

The experiment involved six irregular trajectory points. Initially, the propeller speed was adjusted in still water to achieve a USV speed of 0.8 [m/s], corresponding to a Froude number of 0.21. The USV's heading was adjusted based on its real-time position relative to the first target point of the trajectory. Once the wave-making machine established a stable waveform with the desired amplitude and wavelength, intelligent control was activated on the host computer. The USV dynamically adjusted its rudder angle according to the algorithm, ensuring movement along the trajectory points. The aforementioned method was used to measure and record the motion data of the USV. The experimental process is depicted in Figure 12, and the six trajectory points along with the USV's motion trajectory are shown in Figure 13.

Figure 12. Path tracking control experiment of USV in waves.

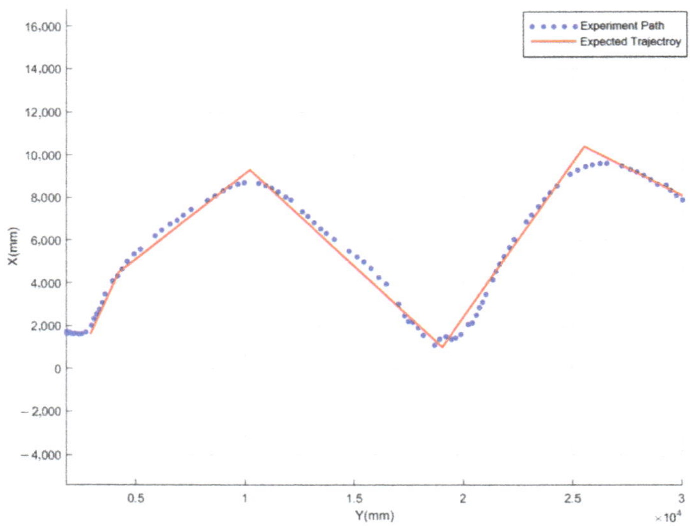

Figure 13. Motion trajectory of USV path tracking control in waves.

The experiment demonstrated that, despite wave disturbances, the USV effectively tracked all trajectory points with a smooth path, achieving a maximum trajectory error of approximately 200 [mm]. This error is small and is primarily attributed to deviations in trajectory point acquisition caused by the UWB positioning accuracy and the resulting control deviations. Under the current hardware conditions and operating modes, the positioning accuracy was optimized using filtering techniques; however, it is still affected by equipment precision, UWB positioning methods, and electromagnetic interference from water waves and metal tracks in the tank. Despite these challenges, the experiment and error analysis indicate that the intelligent matching technique for control parameters based on the proposed method achieves an excellent control accuracy under existing conditions.

Figure 14 illustrates the real-time feedback of the rudder angle and the measured heading angle during the experiment. The changes in heading reveal five major trend adjustments required for path tracking, corresponding to the five segments in the actual trajectory. The heading changes were smooth, with a maximum rudder angle of 50 degrees at sharp turns along the target trajectory. The adaptive control yielded favorable results.

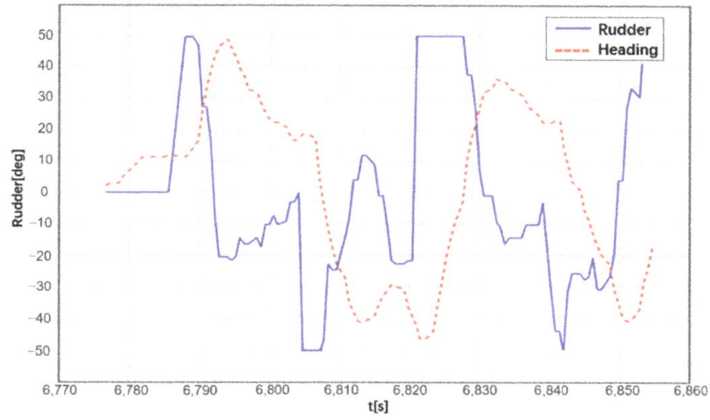

Figure 14. Rudder angle and heading angle curves in USV path tracking control experiment in waves.

6. Conclusions

In this study, we present a novel algorithm that integrates DDPG with a PID controller to achieve path following in the presence of complex conditions, particularly wave interference. The algorithm begins by leveraging a 3-DOF MMG maneuvering motion model, which serves as the foundation for subsequent DDPG training. CFD simulations and regression analysis are employed to extract hydrodynamic derivatives and interaction coefficients necessary for precise motion prediction. We further detail the LOS guidance strategy, which directs the USV to follow a virtual target along the desired trajectory, with PID parameters adjusted dynamically via the DDPG framework.

The design of both the Actor and Critic networks is carefully structured, and to address the issue of slow training speeds in DDPG, we implement a dual-experience pool, separating the successful and failed experiences. Additionally, an adaptive batch size function is introduced to minimize data correlations, further enhancing the training efficiency. The reward function is rigorously formulated to account for both the lateral deviation and heading angle deviation, and its effectiveness is thoroughly examined under various operating conditions.

Simulations and experimental trials involving path following in Zigzag and turning maneuvers, conducted under wave disturbance, demonstrate the algorithm's robust performance. The USV maintained superior tracking accuracy, even under continuously varying wave directions, highlighting the algorithm's strong generalization capabilities and robustness.

Two key practical insights emerge from this work: First, the desired trajectory must align with the USV's maneuvering limits. Trajectory points that exceed the USV's steering capabilities, especially under full rudder conditions, will render the target trajectory unattainable in the presence of external disturbances. This not only compromises tracking performance but also hinders the Reinforcement Learning process. Second, while improving tracking accuracy, setting excessively small thresholds for error in the reward function can lead to instability in the neural network. Lowering the static error threshold makes successful experiences more difficult to achieve, thereby slowing the agent's learning rate and significantly increasing the training time.

Author Contributions: Data curation, C.X.; funding acquisition, J.X. and L.S.; methodology, L.S.; software, C.X. and H.Y.; visualization, C.X.; writing—original draft, C.X. and X.W.; writing—review and editing, X.W. and L.S. All authors have read and agreed to the published version of the manuscript.

Funding: This research was funded by the National Natural Science Foundation of China, grant numbers 51809203.

Institutional Review Board Statement: Not applicable.

Informed Consent Statement: Not applicable.

Data Availability Statement: The original contributions presented in the study are included in the article, further inquiries can be directed to the corresponding author.

Conflicts of Interest: The authors declare no conflicts of interest.

Nomenclature

USV	Unmanned Surface Vehicles
DDPG	Deep Deterministic Policy Gradient
PID	Proportion Integration Differentiation
RL	Reinforcement Learning
ASVs	Autonomous Surface Vessels
Gas	Genetic Algorithms
GPC-PID	PID cascade controller based on Generalized Predictive Control
RBF	Radial Basis Function
UUV	Unmanned Underwater Vehicle
DQN	Deep Q Networks
MDP	Markov Decision Process
DRL	CFD: Computational Fluid Dynamics
MMG	Maneuvering Modeling Group
OU	Ornstein–Uhlenbeck
LOS	Line Of Sight

References

1. Do, K.D. Practical control of underactuated ships. *Ocean Eng.* **2010**, *37*, 1111–1119. [CrossRef]
2. Wei, L.; Hui, Y. Super-Twisting Sliding Mode Control for the Trajectory Tracking of Underactuated USVs with Disturbances. *J. Mar. Sci. Eng.* **2023**, *11*, 636. [CrossRef]
3. Sun, J.; Wang, N.; Meng, J.E.; Liu, Y. Extreme learning control of surface vehicles with unknown dynamics and disturbances. *Neurocomputing* **2015**, *167*, 535–542. [CrossRef]
4. Aguiar, A.P.; Hespanha, J.P. Trajectory-tracking and path-following of underactuated autonomous vehicles with parametric modeling uncertainty. *IEEE Trans. Autom. Control* **2007**, *52*, 1362–1379. [CrossRef]
5. Fahimi, F.; Van Kleeck, C. Alternative trajectory-tracking control approach for marine surface vessels with experimental verification. *Robotica* **2013**, *31*, 25–33. [CrossRef]
6. Harmouche, M.; Laghrouche, S.; Chitour, Y. Global tracking for underactuated ships with bounded feedback controllers. *Int. J. Control* **2014**, *87*, 2035–2043. [CrossRef]
7. Katayama, H.; Aoki, H. Straight-line trajectory tracking control for sampled-data underactuated ships. *IEEE Trans. Control Syst. Technol.* **2014**, *22*, 1638–1645.
8. Awad, N.; Lasheen, A.; Elnaggar, M.; Kamel, A. Model predictive control with fuzzy logic switching for path tracking of autonomous vehicles. *ISA Trans.* **2022**, *129*, 193–205. [CrossRef]
9. Chen, H.; Tang, G.; Wang, S.; Guo, W.; Huang, H. Adaptive fixed-time backstepping control for three-dimensional trajectory tracking of underactuated autonomous underwater vehicles. *Ocean Eng.* **2023**, *275*, 114109. [CrossRef]

10. Li, Z.F.; Lei, K. Robust Fixed-Time Fault-Tolerant Control for USV with Prescribed Tracking Performance. *J. Mar. Sci. Eng.* **2024**, *12*, 799. [CrossRef]
11. Zhao, B.; Zhang, X.; Liang, C.; Han, X. An improved model predictive control for path-following of USV based on global course constraint and event-triggered mechanism. *IEEE Access* **2021**, *9*, 79725–79734. [CrossRef]
12. Hu, Z.; Zhou, H. The course control based on an on-line self-adjusted PID control algorithm for unmanned surface vehicles. *Robot* **2013**, *35*, 263–268. [CrossRef]
13. Liu, S.; Fang, L.; Ge, Y.M.; Fu, H.X. GA-PID adaptive control research for ship course-keeping system. *J. Syst. Simul.* **2007**, *19*, 3783–3786.
14. Ouyang, Z.; Yu, W. PID Control with Improved Genetic Algorithm for Ship Steering. *Navig. China* **2017**, *40*, 13–16.
15. Liu, S.; Xing, B.; Zhu, W. A fusion fuzzy PID controller with real-time implementation on a ship course control system. In Proceedings of the 2015 23th Mediterranean Conference on Control and Automation, Torremolinos, Spain, 16–19 June 2015.
16. Fan, Y.; Li, C.; Wang, G.; Guo, C.; Zhao, Y. Design and validation of course tracking controller for unmanned surface vehicle. *J. Dalian Marit. Univ.* **2017**, *43*, 1–7.
17. Sharma, A.; Zheng, Q.; Noel, M.M. Active disturbance rejection control for cargo ship steering. In Proceedings of the American Control Conference, Chicago, IL, USA, 1–3 July 2015; pp. 3956–3961.
18. Peng, Y.; Wu, W. USV Tracking Control Based on Cascade GPC-PID. *Control Eng. China* **2014**, *21*, 245–248.
19. Huang, H.; Gong, M.; Zhuang, Y.; Sharma, S.; Xu, D. A new guidance law for trajectory tracking of an underactuated unmanned surface vehicle with parameter perturbations. *Ocean Eng.* **2019**, *175*, 217–222. [CrossRef]
20. Wang, N.; Gao, Y.; Yang, C.; Zhang, X. Reinforcement learning-based finite-time tracking control of an unknown unmanned surface vehicle with input constraints. *Neurocomputing* **2022**, *484*, 26–37. [CrossRef]
21. Wu, C.; Yu, W.; Li, G.; Liao, W. Deep reinforcement learning with dynamic window approach based collision avoidance path planning for maritime autonomous surface ships. *Ocean Eng.* **2023**, *284*, 115208. [CrossRef]
22. Wang, R.; Shen, Z. Fuzzy adaptive iterative sliding mode control for sail-assisted ship trajectory tracking. In Proceedings of the 2017 4th International Conference on Information, Cybernetics and Computational Social Systems(ICCSS), Dalian, China, 24–26 July 2017.
23. Yang, X.; Yan, X.; Liu, W.; Ye, H.; Du, Z.; Zhong, W. An improved stanley guidance law for large curvature path following of unmanned surface vehicle. *Ocean Eng.* **2022**, *266*, 112809. [CrossRef]
24. Bertaska, I.R.; Von, E. Experimental evaluation of supervisory switching control for unmanned surface vehicles. *IEEE J. Ocean Eng.* **2018**, *44*, 7–28. [CrossRef]
25. Magalhães, J.; Damas, B.; Lobo, V. Reinforcement learning: The application to autonomous biomimetic underwater vehicles control. *IOP Conf. Ser. Earth Environ. Sci.* **2018**, *172*, 12–19. [CrossRef]
26. Bian, X.Q. Adaptive Neural Network Control System of Path Following for AUVs. In Proceedings of the 2012 Proceedings of IEEE Southeastcon, Orlando, FL, USA, 15–18 March 2012.
27. Xiaofei, Y.; Yilun, S.; Wei, L.; Hui, Y.; Weibo, Z.; Zhengrong, X. Global path planning algorithm based on double DQN for multi-tasks amphibious unmanned surface vehicle. *Ocean Eng.* **2022**, *266*, 112809. [CrossRef]
28. Wu, C.; Yu, W. Deep reinforcement learning with intrinsic curiosity module based trajectory tracking control for USV. *Ocean Eng.* **2024**, *308*, 118342. [CrossRef]
29. Woo, J.; Yu, C.; Kim, N. Deep reinforcement learning based controller for path following of an unmanned surface vehicle. *Ocean Eng.* **2019**, *183*, 155–166. [CrossRef]
30. Song, L.; Xu, C.; Hao, L.; Yao, J.; Guo, R. Research on PID Parameter Tuning and Optimization Based on SAC-Auto for USV Path Following. *J. Mar. Sci. Eng.* **2022**, *10*, 1847. [CrossRef]

Journal of
Marine Science and Engineering

MDPI

Article

The Impact of Offshore Wind Farm Construction on Maritime Traffic Complexity: An Empirical Analysis of the Yangtze River Estuary

Jian Liu [1], Wenbo Yu [1], Zhongyi Sui [2,*] and Chunhui Zhou [3]

1 Shanghai Investigation, Design & Research Institute Co., Ltd., Shanghai 200335, China; liujian@sidri.com (J.L.); ywb1225@126.com (W.Y.)
2 Department of Logistics and Maritime Studies, Faculty of Business, The Hong Kong Polytechnic University, Hong Kong 999077, China
3 School of Navigation, Wuhan University of Technology, Wuhan 430063, China; chunhui@whut.edu.cn
* Correspondence: zhongyi.sui@polyu.edu.hk; Tel.: +86-18696118075

Abstract: The rapid growth of offshore wind farms (OWFs) as renewable energy sources has heightened concerns about maritime traffic safety and management in high-density traffic zones. These areas, characterized by complex interactions among diverse ship types and spatial constraints, require advanced situational awareness to prevent collisions and ensure efficient operations. Traditional maritime traffic systems often lack the granularity to assess the multifaceted risks around OWFs. Existing research has explored local traffic patterns and collision risks but lacks comprehensive frameworks for evaluating traffic complexity at both micro and macro levels. This study proposes a new complexity assessment model tailored to OWF areas, integrating micro-level ship interactions and macro-level traffic flow conditions to capture a holistic view of traffic dynamics. Using extensive historical AIS data from the Yangtze River Estuary, the model evaluates the impact of the proposed OWF on existing traffic complexity. The results demonstrate that OWFs increase navigational complexity, particularly in route congestion, course adjustments, and encounter rates between ships. Different ship types and sizes were also found to experience varying levels of impact, with larger ships and tankers facing greater challenges. By providing a quantitative framework for assessing traffic complexity, this research advances the field's ability to understand and manage the risks associated with OWFs. The findings offer actionable insights for maritime authorities and OWF operators, supporting more effective traffic management strategies that prioritize safety and operational efficiency in high-density maritime areas.

Keywords: traffic management; situation awareness; offshore wind farm; maritime traffic complexity

1. Introduction

With the rapid expansion of offshore wind farms (OWFs) as critical sources of renewable energy, ensuring their safe and efficient operation has become a key concern [1,2]. OWFs are typically located in high-traffic maritime areas, where a diverse range of commercial ships, fishing boats, and recreational vessels coexist. This dynamic environment introduces significant challenges for maritime operators and OWF managers, especially in maintaining situational awareness (SA) to prevent collisions and operational disruptions. Effective situational awareness, which involves real-time perception of the surrounding environment, understanding of traffic dynamics, and projection of future risks, is essential for decision-making in these areas [3–5].

Maritime traffic complexity around OWFs is influenced by various factors, including different ship types, unpredictable weather, and spatial constraints imposed by OWFs [6,7]. Traditional maritime traffic management systems typically rely on radar and Automatic Identification System (AIS) data to track ship positions and movements [8,9]. However, these systems often fall short in addressing the unique complexities and risks of operations near OWFs [10]. Furthermore, the coexistence of OWF structures and dense maritime traffic necessitates advanced methods for risk assessment and management. Previous research has made progress in studying maritime safety and traffic flow near OWFs, but most studies focus primarily on local traffic patterns or collision risks. They often lack a broader, systemic perspective needed to measure traffic complexity at both micro and macro levels. The absence of a comprehensive framework capturing nuanced interactions between ships and OWFs across scales—from individual ship behaviors to broader traffic flow dynamics—has limited tools for accurately assessing traffic complexity in OWF areas. This gap limits predictive accuracy in understanding and mitigating risks posed by traffic complexity, especially under different environmental conditions and operational scenarios.

To address this gap, a novel maritime traffic complexity model is proposed to improve situational awareness in OWF areas. This model integrates micro-level interactions—both among ships and between ships and OWFs—and macro-level traffic conditions, providing a comprehensive understanding of traffic complexity. This system-level approach captures interactions among ship movements across scales and OWF spatial constraints, enabling more accurate risk assessments locally and globally.

This study focuses on the waters near the Yangtze River Estuary, where an OWF is planned. This region is characterized by high maritime traffic density and diverse ship types. In this area, ships navigate frequently, and the OWF's construction could significantly impact existing shipping lanes and ship passages. By analyzing and comparing extensive historical traffic data, this research aims to assess how the construction of the offshore OWF will affect traffic complexity in these waters and ensure safe ship passage after the OWF's construction. The findings will offer valuable data and support decision-making for maritime traffic management authorities and OWF operators, aiding in route optimization, traffic safety, and operational efficiency. This will help reduce ship collision risks while supporting sustainable development in the Yangtze River Estuary and the promotion of green energy.

The remainder of this paper is structured as follows: Section 2 reviews relevant research on maritime traffic safety in OWF areas. Section 3 outlines the proposed model and methodology. Section 4 presents the findings from actual maritime traffic data, and Section 5 discusses the findings and offers suggestions for future research.

2. Literature Review

Research consistently emphasizes that the presence of OWFs introduces additional risks for maritime traffic, primarily due to restricted navigable space and the close proximity of ships to wind turbines. Studies utilize fault tree analysis and statistical models to evaluate these risks, highlighting that ship collisions with turbines are more likely in high-traffic areas, particularly where adverse weather conditions exacerbate navigational difficulties [11–13]. AIS data are frequently used to monitor real-time ship movements and assess collision hotspots, offering predictive insights into areas where risks are heightened [14,15]. The combination of restricted sea room, weather impacts, and diverse ship types contributes to increased collision probabilities [16].

The spatial constraints imposed by OWFs significantly alter existing traffic flow, leading to rerouting and increased congestion in maritime areas. Studies indicate that OWFs reduce available navigable space, creating congestion points that heighten collision risks [17,18]. Changes affect not only commercial shipping routes but also fishing and recreational traffic, resulting in denser, more complex traffic environments [19,20]. Simulations and traffic models predict how OWFs impact ship behavior, suggesting that traffic densities and potential conflicts will increase, especially in regions with complex navigational patterns [21,22]. Additionally, the interaction between ship sizes and maneuverability in restricted areas complicates traffic dynamics [23].

Several studies focus on the increased navigational complexity in areas surrounding OWFs, which are often located in high-density maritime zones. Poor visibility, environmental conditions such as strong tides or high winds, and the complexity of ship encounters contribute to higher accident probabilities [24–26]. Research indicates that traditional maritime navigational aids may not suffice in these environments, necessitating enhanced navigational systems and increased deployment of surveillance technologies such as radar and real-time monitoring systems to reduce collision risks [27,28]. Additionally, inadequate marking of wind turbines and insufficient separation distances between OWFs and major shipping routes are identified as primary concerns affecting safe navigation [29,30].

To address safety concerns, advanced technologies like machine learning and enhanced Vessel Traffic Service (VTS) systems are increasingly being integrated into maritime safety strategies around OWFs. Machine learning models can process large datasets, such as AIS data, to predict ship behavior and identify potential conflict zones, enabling more proactive decision-making [31–33]. Enhanced VTS systems, which provide real-time data on ship positions and environmental conditions, are critical in managing traffic complexity near OWFs [34,35]. Regulatory measures, such as establishing exclusion zones and rerouting traffic, are recommended to reduce navigational hazards. Implementing these measures can significantly improve maritime safety, reduce congestion, and prevent accidents [36–39].

Despite the growing body of the literature examining maritime traffic safety in relation to OWFs, significant research gaps remain, particularly concerning the quantification of traffic complexity in these environments. While existing studies have largely focused on the risks of ship collisions and the implications of traffic flow changes due to the construction of OWFs, there is limited investigation into how these factors interact over time and the extent of their cumulative impacts on traffic complexity.

(i) Most prior research has primarily dealt with qualitative assessments of safety and risk management, often using anecdotal evidence or case studies without providing a comprehensive framework to quantitatively measure traffic complexity in OWF areas. The proposed research aims to fill this gap by developing specific metrics and models to quantify the complexity of maritime traffic in relation to OWFs before and after their construction.
(ii) While some studies have addressed the changes in navigational patterns and collision risks in areas surrounding OWFs, few have conducted thorough comparative analyses of traffic complexity levels before and after the establishment of OWFs. Most existing studies focus on local traffic patterns or immediate impacts, lacking a longitudinal perspective that could provide insights into how traffic dynamics evolve over time.
(iii) Although some studies have explored analytics in maritime safety, the integration of these technologies specifically to measure and analyze traffic complexity in the context of OWFs is under-researched. The proposed research could leverage these technologies to create models that assess how traffic complexity changes in relation to ship behaviors in OWF areas.

The complexity assessment method proposed in this paper for OWF areas and the contributions of this work are threefold:

(i) Unlike most previous studies that focus on qualitative assessments, this method develops specific quantitative metrics using actual data, allowing for an accurate measurement of traffic complexity in OWF areas. This advantage makes the research findings more scientific and objective, contributing to policy formulation and risk management.
(ii) This paper conducts a systematic comparative analysis of the impact of traffic complexity before and after the construction of OWFs, filling the gaps in the existing literature on this topic. Through comparison, it clearly reveals the specific effects of OWF construction on maritime traffic dynamics, providing strong empirical support.
(iii) In assessing traffic complexity, this paper comprehensively considers the interactions among ships as well as the interactions between ships and OWFs. This holistic approach will help to gain a deeper understanding of the collective influence of various

factors on traffic complexity, thereby enhancing the evaluation and management of operational risks.

The method presented in this paper not only addresses the shortcomings of current research but also offers new ideas and tools for future traffic safety management in OWF area, promoting further research and practice in this field.

3. Method

3.1. Research Area

The research area is the Yangtze River Estuary, one of the busiest maritime traffic corridors globally, marked by a high shipping density and complex traffic dynamics. The Yangtze River Estuary links the Yangtze River Basin with the East China Sea and serves as a critical intersection of China's inland waterways and international shipping routes. A diverse range of ships navigate these waters, including cargo ships, container ships, fishing boats, and passenger ships. The region also contains dense networks of shipping lanes, anchorages, and frequent fishing activities, further intensifying maritime traffic complexity. A plan to construct an OWF near the Yangtze River Estuary is currently part of China's green energy strategy. The Yangtze River Estuary has abundant wind resources, making it suitable for OWF development. According to the Shanghai 2024 offshore wind power project competitive allocation work plan (https://fgw.sh.gov.cn/fgw_ny/20240320/b12c958e447240989804e75351945baf.html, accessed on 3 December 2024), the proposed OWF areas are shown in Figure 1. However, the presence of OWF facilities and the resulting navigation route adjustments are expected to significantly impact local traffic complexity. Therefore, selecting the Yangtze River Estuary as the study area will effectively reflect the potential impact of OWF construction on traffic within a highly complex maritime environment.

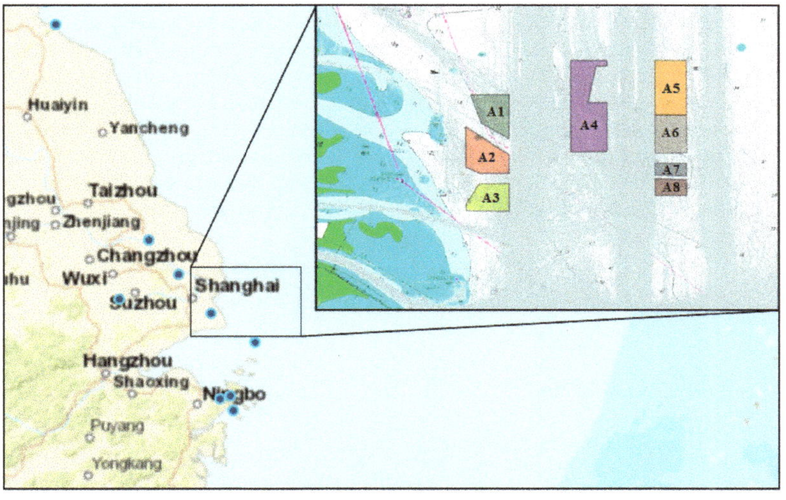

Figure 1. Research area and the proposed OWF areas.

To conduct a comprehensive analysis of traffic complexity, historical ship AIS data from the research area were used to validate the proposed method's effectiveness. The AIS data include latitude, longitude, speed, course, and ship type, offering detailed trajectories of ship movements in the area and reflecting traffic conditions before the OWF's construction. According to the SOLAS, all cargo ships above 300 tons engaged in international navigation, all cargo ships above 500 tons engaged in domestic navigation, and all passenger ships must be equipped with AIS equipment. AIS data are received in a series of messages at irregular time intervals, and errors are inevitable during data collection, transmission, and reception. Therefore, the data must undergo cleaning and interpolation to reduce the impact of errors. Additionally, since AIS data are sent at different times randomly, interpolation is needed to process the data.

First, the AIS data were cleaned by removing data with abnormal ship positions, speeds, and courses in the experimental dataset. After cleaning and filtering the AIS data, a linear interpolation algorithm with a 2 s interval was applied. Table 1 shows a sample of the preprocessed AIS data. Using this AIS data, this study developed a traffic complexity evaluation model to analyze the dynamic relationships among ships and between ships and the OWF. This study quantified the baseline traffic complexity before the OWF's construction by calculating complexity factors and then compared it with post-construction data to evaluate the impacts on navigational safety and traffic flow.

Table 1. Portion of preprocessed AIS data.

MMSI	Latitude	Longitude	Speed	Course
413342350	122.7509°	31.4386°	11.6 kn	169.9°
413361840	122.8218°	31.3933°	10 kn	4.5°
413702570	122.8139°	31.3952°	9.8 kn	355.9°
413705420	122.7197°	31.4539°	6.0 kn	166.2°
413275370	122.8043°	31.4577°	13.1 kn	17.6°
...	...	...	...	...
413256860	122.7545°	31.4473°	6.8 kn	170.4°

3.2. *Complexity Measurement for Ship–Ship Relationship*

3.2.1. Dynamic Traffic Density Factor

Traffic density is often used to evaluate the characteristics of waterway traffic flow. However, traditional methods fail to fully capture the spatial distribution and aggregation of ships. To achieve a more accurate analysis of traffic flow, the concept of dynamic density was introduced. This concept not only considers the number of ships but also incorporates their distribution and movement within a specific area, providing a better reflection of the dynamic changes in waterway traffic [40,41]. Suppose there are n ships in the area and that their positions can be expressed as: $\{(x_i, y_i)|i \in n\}$. In this section, the positions of ships are obtained by converting the latitude and longitude into Gauss coordinates, with the units in meters. The central position of these n ships can then be calculated as:

$$\vec{P} = \begin{bmatrix} \overline{X} \\ \overline{Y} \end{bmatrix} = \begin{bmatrix} \frac{1}{n}\sum_{i=1}^{n} x_i \\ \frac{1}{n}\sum_{i=1}^{n} y_i \end{bmatrix} \tag{1}$$

The distance from ship i to $\vec{P}$ is:

$$s_i = \sqrt{(x_i - \overline{X})^2 + (y_i - \overline{Y})^2} \tag{2}$$

Therefore, an exponential function can be constructed to reflect the nonlinear relationship between ship aggregation and complexity.

$$C_{den}^{i} = e^{-\lambda s_i} \tag{3}$$

where λ represents the weight of the distance. As the distance decreases, the complexity increases nonlinearly.

The λ reflects the sensitivity of maritime supervision to changes in the distance between ships. A greater distance weight indicates a higher sensitivity to the variation in ship-to-ship distance, emphasizing the impact of the distance on the dynamic density.

Suppose there is only one ship in a given region; the dynamic density at that moment is 1. When another ship gradually enters the region from a distant location, the change in the dynamic density is minimal and can almost be ignored. Therefore, under such circumstances, the dynamic density of the region remains largely unchanged, leading to the following conclusion:

$$C_{den}^{1} \approx C_{den}^{2} = 2 \bullet e^{-\lambda \bullet \frac{D_{\max}}{2}} = 1 \tag{4}$$

where $D_{\max}$ represents the distance beyond which the interaction between the two ships becomes insignificant.

For ships that are 50 m or longer, Rule 22 of the COLREGs specifies that the masthead light must be visible from a minimum distance of 6 nautical miles. Consequently, the distance $D_{\max}$ is generally assumed to be 6 nm in this research. Therefore, it can be calculated that $\lambda = 0.231$.

3.2.2. Ship Approaching Factor

When analyzing the approach trends of a pair of ships, both their positional proximity and the rate of change in that proximity are taken into account. To represent the positional proximity between ships, elliptical distance is utilized. The Ed_{ij} between ship i and ship j can be expressed as:

$$Ed_{ij} = \sqrt{\frac{(x_i - x_j)^2}{a_i^2} + \frac{(y_i - y_j)^2}{b_i^2}} \tag{5}$$

In this context, a_i and b_i denote the major and minor semi-axes of the elliptical ship domain, respectively. This paper employs the Fujii ship domain model, a well-established framework that has been extensively validated since its inception. Within the Fujii ship domain model, the ship's domain is represented as an ellipse, making it ideal for measuring the elliptical distance between ships and calculating their approach factor. Here, a represents the major semi-axis of ship i's domain, while b signifies the minor semi-axis. Given that inland waterways are typically narrow, a_i is set to $2L$ and b_i is set to $0.8L$, where L is the length of the ship [42]. The coordinates of the ship are denoted as (x, y). When the condition $Ed_{ij} < 1$ is met, one ship j's domain is encroached upon by ship i.

The rate of change in the positional proximity indicates how quickly two ships are closing the distance between them, which can be expressed as:

$$k_{ij}(t) = \frac{Ed_{ij}(t) - Ed_{ij}(t-1)}{Ed_{ij}(t-1)} \tag{6}$$

where k_{ij} represents the change rate of positional proximity between the pair of ships. If $k_{ij} < 1$, the ships are approaching each other. If $k_{ij} > 1$, the two ships are moving apart, with their relative distance continuously increasing. If k_{ij} equals 1, it indicates that both ships are sailing in parallel at the same speed.

Then, the approach factor between ship i and ship j can be formulated as:

$$C_{ap}^{ij} = \begin{cases} \left(\frac{1}{Ed_{ij}}\right)^{1+k_{ij}}, & E_{ij} \geq 1 \\ \left(\frac{1}{Ed_{ij}}\right)^{1-k_{ij}}, & E_{ij} < 1 \end{cases} \tag{7}$$

where C_{ap}^{ij} represents the ship approaching factor between ship i and ship j. As Ed_{ij} decreases, C_{ap}^{ij} increases, reaching a value of one or more when the ships are in conflict. A positive C_{ap}^{ij} indicates that the ships are moving apart, resulting in lower complexity. Conversely, a negative C_{ap}^{ij} signifies that the ships are closing in on each other, leading to higher complexity. In conclusion, this equation effectively models the complexity of the interaction between ships.

3.3. Complexity Measurement for Ship–OWF Relationship

After the construction of the OWF is completed, the existing maritime traffic flow will be significantly impacted. The navigation patterns of ships in the OWF area will be changed, and adjustments to their routes may be required to avoid the wind turbines, thereby increasing the complexity of navigation. To address this, a measurement was developed to describe the complexity relationship between ships and the OWF area.

The complexity relationship between ships and the OWF area takes into account the dynamic behavior of ships as they approach the boundaries of the OWF area, with the complexity of navigation being increased as the ships move closer to the boundary. This is because, near the OWF, navigation guidelines must be followed by the ship, and collisions with other ships and interference with the wind turbines must be avoided. As the distance between the ship and the OWF boundary decreases, the potential navigation risks and constraints are increased, leading to a rise in the overall navigational complexity.

The space proximity between ship i and the OWF o's boundary, denoted as D_{io}, is calculated as follows:

$$D_{io} = \begin{cases} \alpha e^{-|d_{io}-D_s|/D_s} & d_{io} > D_s \\ 1 & d_{io} \leq D_s \end{cases} \tag{8}$$

where d_{io} is defined as the distance between ship i and the OWF o's boundary, and D_s is the safety distance from the OWF o's boundary. According to current regulations in China, the safety distance for OWF areas is set at 2 nautical miles.

α is an adjustment parameter representing the relative motion between the ship and the OWF area. If the ship is approaching the OWF area, the complexity between them is considered; otherwise, it is not. As shown in Figure 2, the area with the red-bordered box is the area generating complexity with ship i, while the area with the black dashed border can be disregarded. The calculation method for α is as follows:

$$\alpha = \begin{cases} 0, & \dfrac{\vec{v}\cdot\vec{b}}{|\vec{v}|\cdot|\vec{b}|} \leq 0 \\ 1, & \dfrac{\vec{v}\cdot\vec{b}}{|\vec{v}|\cdot|\vec{b}|} > 0 \end{cases} \tag{9}$$

where $\vec{v}$ is the motion direction vector of the ship. $\vec{b}$ is the direction vector from the ship to the OWF o's boundary (the normal vector of the nearest boundary). When $\frac{\vec{v}\cdot\vec{b}}{|\vec{v}|\cdot|\vec{b}|} > 0$, it indicates that the ship is moving toward the boundary (approaching the OWF). When $\frac{\vec{v}\cdot\vec{b}}{|\vec{v}|\cdot|\vec{b}|} < 0$, it indicates that the point is moving away from the boundary (leaving the OWF). When $\frac{\vec{v}\cdot\vec{b}}{|\vec{v}|\cdot|\vec{b}|} = 0$, it indicates that the point is moving parallel to the boundary.

The changing rate as the ship approaches the OWF o's boundary is then calculated as follows:

$$V_{io}(t) = \frac{d_{io}(t) - d_{io}(t-1)}{d_{io}(t-1)} \tag{10}$$

Based on the spatial proximity and the approaching rate between ship i and OWF o's boundary, the complexity between them is calculated as follows:

$$C_{owf}^{io} = {D_{io}}^{1-V_{io}} \tag{11}$$

It can be seen that the range of C_{owf}^{io} is from 0 to 1. As the distance between ship i and OWF o's boundary decreases, the corresponding complexity gradually increases.

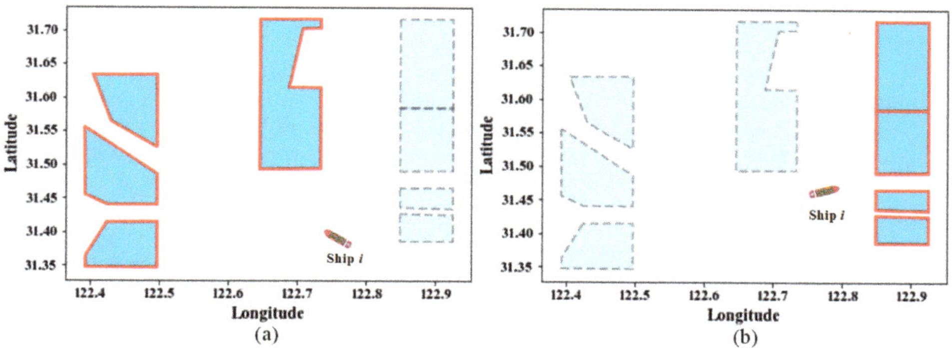

Figure 2. The relationship between ship and OWF area. (**a**) The relationship between ship i and A1–A4. (**b**) The relationship between ship i and A5–A6.

3.4. Global Complexity Evaluation

Due to the high traffic density, multi-ship encounters have become common in OWF areas. The complexity of these multi-ship encounters is greater and more serious than that of single ship-pair encounters, making it necessary to assess the overall complexity [43,44]. Given that there are n ships in the OWF area, the dynamic traffic density C_{den} for the n ships is calculated as:

$$C_{den} = \sum_{i=1}^{n} C_{den}^{i} = \sum_{i=1}^{n} e^{-0.231 s_i} \tag{12}$$

The ship approaching factor C_{ap} for the n ships is calculated as:

$$C_{ap} = \sum_{i=1}^{n} \sum_{\substack{j=1 \\ j \neq i}}^{n} C_{ap}^{ij} \tag{13}$$

The total amount of complexity between n ships and m OWF areas is calculated as:

$$C_{owf} = \sum_{i=1}^{n} \sum_{o=1}^{m} C_{owf}^{io} \tag{14}$$

The Min–Max standardization method is applied to normalize each indicator's value, allowing for a comprehensive consideration of the three factors. If a factor's value is represented as x, the standardized value x' is given by:

$$x' = \frac{x - x_{\min}}{x_{\max} - x_{\min}} \tag{15}$$

The maximum and minimum values of the factors are determined through the analysis of extensive historical data. Once the three factors have been standardized, the overall complexity is calculated as follows:

$$|C| = w_1 C'_{den} + w_2 C'_{ap} + w_3 C'_{owf} \tag{16}$$

where C'_{den}, C'_{ap}, and C'_{owf} are the standardized values of the three factors, and their corresponding weights are also represented as w_1, w_2, and w_3, respectively.

4. Results and Analysis

4.1. Comparative Analysis Before and After OWF Construction

AIS data from 31 July 2023, between 00:00 and 24:00, were selected for model validation. The three factors were assigned the same weight, each being 1/3. As shown in Figure 3, the red line reflects the trafneededfic complexity in the proposed OWF area, and the blue line reflects the traffic complexity without the OWF area. The change in the number of ships is shown in Figure 4.

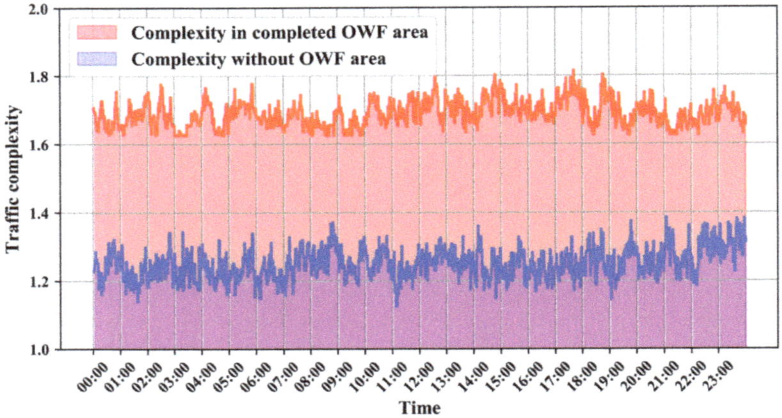

Figure 3. Comparison of traffic complexity before and after OWF construction.

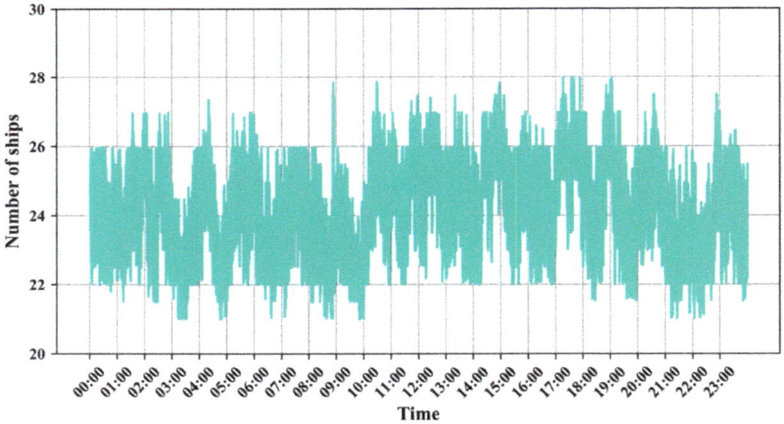

Figure 4. The change in the number of ships.

In the absence of the OWF's construction, the complexity of maritime traffic in this area is primarily influenced by density and proximity factors. Specifically, the density factor reflects the distribution of ships within the area and the overall traffic volume—the higher the ship density, the more complex the navigation environment. The proximity factor, on the other hand, indicates the distance and relative closeness between ships—the closer the ships are to each other, the higher the potential collision risk and, consequently, the complexity. In this context, traffic complexity is mainly driven by route congestion and ships' evasive maneuvers in high-density waters.

Overall, the navigational complexity shows a gradual upward trend, suggesting that over time, the relative movements of ships in the monitored area have become more complex, possibly due to an increase in the number of ships or dynamic changes in their movements. Frequent peaks and troughs in the graph reflect sudden changes in ship movements. This may relate to instantaneous traffic congestion, ships approaching or departing from the OWF area, or maneuvers such as turning, slowing down, or accelerating. For instance, when the relative distance between ships decreases, their speed changes dramatically, or their direction shifts, navigational complexity may spike, creating peaks. At certain points, complexity values sharply rise and quickly drop; this "spike" may result from a sudden decrease in ship distance or a group of ships approaching a specific area. These abrupt changes typically reflect high-density clustering or rapid turning of ships, causing a significant increase in navigational complexity over a short period. Although navigational complexity fluctuates, there is a slow upward trend, suggesting that ship activities in the area are becoming more frequent.

The changes in complexity after the completion of the OWF construction are illustrated by the red line in Figure 3. Overall, the red line is significantly higher than the blue line, clearly indicating that the presence of the OWF area indeed increases the complexity of navigation. The shaded area between the red and blue lines represents the additional complexity induced by the construction of the OWF. This phenomenon is not only visually represented in the graph but also reflects the navigation challenges faced by ships under different circumstances. As can be seen from Figure 3, the impact of the OWF on navigation is not static; rather, it fluctuates over time and with varying traffic levels. This variability may be closely related to factors such as navigation conditions, weather conditions, ship traffic, and the operational status of the OWF. The size of the shaded area not only reflects the degree of complexity increase but also poses new demands for navigation management. For instance, during periods of heightened complexity, there may be a need for additional monitoring or guiding measures in the shipping lanes to reduce the risk of ship collisions. This means that during high-complexity periods, relevant management departments should consider increasing maritime patrols, enhancing AIS monitoring, and other measures to ensure navigational safety.

After the construction of the OWF, ships will frequently need to adjust their courses to avoid the OWF area, especially when the farm occupies traditional shipping routes. This not only results in changes to navigation routes but may also increase the travel time and fuel consumption of ships. Additionally, due to changes in ship speeds and narrower navigation channels, the safe distances between ships are reduced, further complicating operations and increasing the complexity of travel paths. This complexity not only poses challenges for crew decision-making but may also lead to decreased navigation efficiency. Therefore, these dynamic changes require shipping companies and relevant management agencies to adopt more comprehensive traffic management strategies to ensure the safety and efficiency of maritime operations. Navigational management systems need to continuously adapt to these changes in complexity, adjusting navigation planning and management measures in a timely manner. At the same time, ship operators should enhance their understanding of OWF areas and improve their ability to respond to complex navigational environments, ensuring that they can safely and efficiently complete their navigation tasks even after the construction of the OWF.

4.2. Traffic Complexity Analysis in Different OWF Areas

This study focuses on the impact of OWF construction on ship navigation. Therefore, this section provides a detailed analysis of traffic complexity within each proposed OWF area, based on the complexity assessment method outlined in Section 3.3. It is important to note that the complexity between ships and the OWF is not normalized in this section. The aim is to quantify and compare the navigation complexity characteristics of different OWF areas, revealing the potential impact of OWF construction on traffic safety in surrounding waters. Through such complexity analysis, not only can a scientific basis for OWF site selection be provided, but it can also inform the development of relevant navigation safety management measures. Figure 5 shows the changes in traffic complexity across different OWF areas from 00:00 to 24:00 on 31 July 2023.

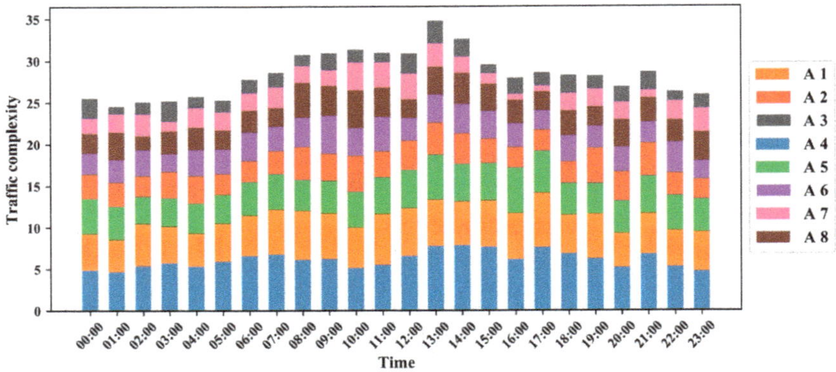

Figure 5. Complexity between different OWF areas and ships.

Further, data from July 2023 were selected to analyze the complexity between ships and the proposed OWF areas. The contribution of each proposed OWF area to the complexity of the research area is shown in Figure 6.

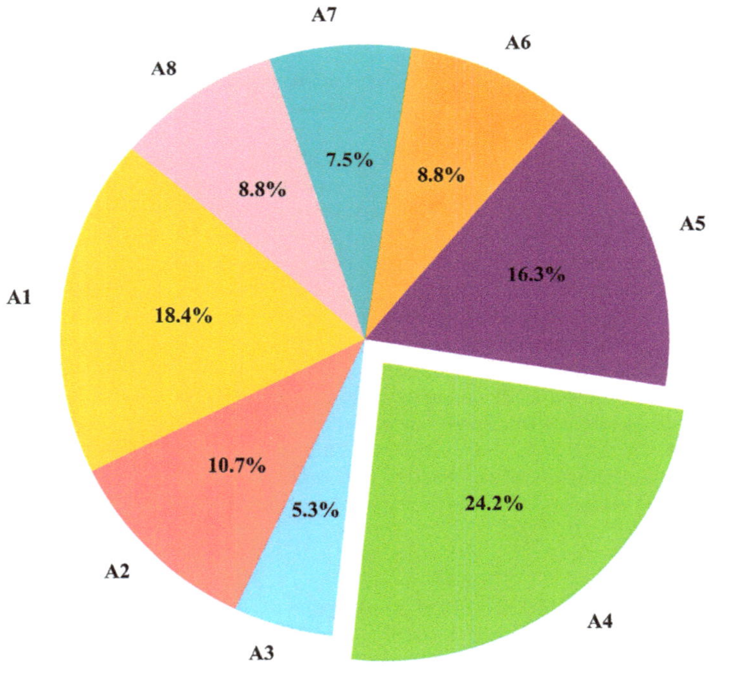

Figure 6. Contribution of different OWF areas to traffic complexity.

Based on the above analysis, it is evident that A4 contributes the most to the complexity of the research area. Since the proposed A4 occupies the habitual shipping routes, ships must adjust their courses, which may lead to an increase in crossing points and, consequently, a higher likelihood of collisions. This risk is particularly significant in low-visibility or adverse weather conditions, where ships have less reaction time, increasing safety risks. Once the OWF is completed, ships will need to navigate around the OWF area, potentially causing delays in travel time and increasing the risk of crew fatigue, especially in emergencies. In unexpected situations (such as mechanical failures or changes in weather), ships may struggle to find safe routes for evasion, raising the probability of accidents.

Adjustments in shipping routes may lead to a significant increase in traffic flow on certain pathways. For example, ships may opt for longer or busier routes, thereby affecting the overall traffic pattern. If multiple ships choose to detour via the same alternative route, it may result in congestion on that route, increasing the chances of delays and accidents. This situation can become more complex during peak times, where the concentration of ships may exacerbate the issue. The traffic load on alternative routes may exceed their designed capacity, leading to reduced navigation efficiency and potential safety hazards. Monitoring and managing these routes are essential to ensure smooth traffic flow. Over time, changes in ship traffic flow can impact the environment, economy, and regional development. Therefore, ongoing monitoring and assessment of traffic flow changes are crucial for formulating long-term management policies.

4.3. Contribution of Ship Types to Complexity Between Ship and Proposed OWF Area

The Yangtze River Estuary is an important shipping channel with very heavy traffic. It is not only a major domestic cargo transportation hub but also a key node in international shipping. The area hosts a diverse range of ship types, including cargo ships, tankers, container ships, and bulk carriers. Ships of different types and sizes exhibit significant variations in navigation behavior. For example, container ships typically sail at higher speeds and are suited for long-distance transport, while tankers require more safety distance to prevent accidents. Furthermore, due to the high concentration of industries near the Yangtze River Estuary, frequent ship traffic creates a complex traffic environment in the waters. This diversity of ship movements not only increases the complexity of navigation but also heightens the risk of collisions. In adverse weather conditions or low-visibility conditions, the responsiveness of various ships is limited, potentially leading to safety hazards. Therefore, understanding the complexity between different types of ships and proposed OWF areas is crucial for improving navigation safety and developing appropriate traffic management measures.

Figure 7 illustrates the distribution of ship types within the research area. Dry cargo ships are the most common type, making up 51.1% of the total traffic in the area, indicating a high volume of dry cargo transportation. Bulk carriers and multipurpose ships each account for over 12%, specifically 12.5% and 12.3%, respectively. This suggests a significant presence of ships capable of carrying various cargo types. Container ships and tankers represent 9.2% and 8.5% of the total, respectively, reflecting the area's importance for both containerized and liquid bulk cargo. A small proportion of ships, such as bulk cement carriers (1.2%) and salvage ships (0.9%), show the specialized nature of some traffic within the region. The remaining ship types each constitute less than 1% of the total, including liquefied gas carriers (0.6%), ro-ro ships (0.5%), and government and service ships (each below 0.5%). Other types, such as chemical tankers, workboats, dredgers, and tugboats, each account for a minor portion. The diverse range of ship types suggests a complex maritime environment, likely contributing to traffic complexity and navigation challenges, especially in areas where routes overlap. Specialized ships (such as chemical tankers and ro-ro ships) add unique risks and requirements for navigation, which could impact traffic safety and efficiency.

The complexity generated by the top-five-ranked ship types in the proposed OWF area was analyzed, as shown in Figure 8. When analyzing the traffic complexity between different types of ships and proposed OWF areas, the ships' navigation characteristics, sailing speed, and their interaction with the proposed OWF area need to be considered. The impact of different ship types on traffic complexity can vary significantly. In analyzing the traffic complexity between these ship types and the proposed OWF area, the navigational behavior and potential impact of each ship type on the proposed OWF area should be taken into account.

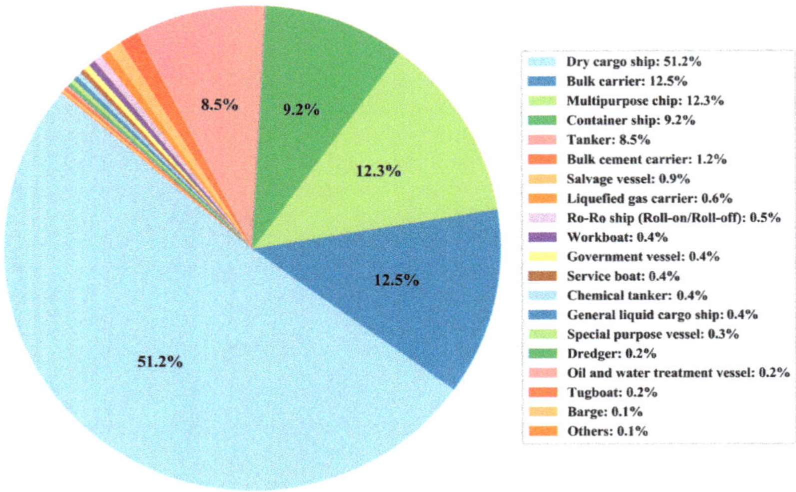

Figure 7. Distribution of ship types in the research area.

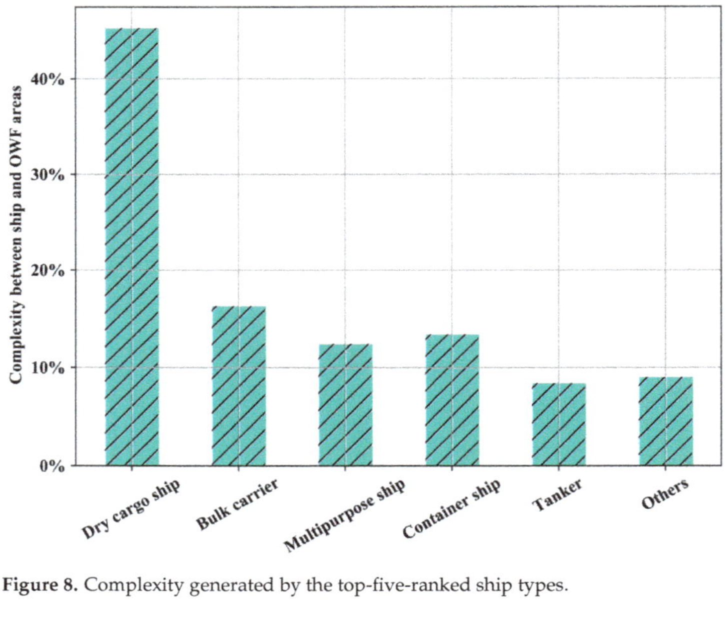

Figure 8. Complexity generated by the top-five-ranked ship types.

Dry cargo ships are the primary ship type in this region and have the greatest impact on the traffic complexity around the proposed OWF. This type of ship usually carries a large amount of cargo and has poor maneuverability, especially in narrow waters or areas that require frequent turns. When navigating near the OWF, if dry cargo ships need to adjust their course to avoid the proposed OWF, complexity may increase, particularly in areas with a high traffic density or intersecting routes. Due to their high inertia, dry cargo ships are slow to react in sudden situations, raising the likelihood of accidents near the proposed OWF. Bulk carriers, which account for a significant proportion of ships in the research area (approximately 12.5%), typically transport large volumes of bulk cargo and have limited maneuverability due to their heavy loads. When the proposed OWF blocks their usual route, bulk carriers need to take detours, which can increase traffic pressure in overlapping routes and thus raise navigational complexity. Multipurpose ships, which have flexible cargo capabilities and often carry diverse cargo types, have a maneuverability between that of bulk carriers and container ships. Given their relatively high navigational flexibility, multipurpose ships have a lower impact on the proposed OWF area, although route adjustments may still be necessary during periods of high traffic, contributing to an increase in complexity. Container ships generally travel at high speeds and have stringent requirements for navigational conditions, needing to pass through with minimal safe distance. The construction of the OWF may force container ships to adjust their routes or even slow down to detour, potentially causing route-crossing risks and, particularly during peak times, traffic bottlenecks. Tankers usually transport flammable, explosive liquid cargo, which demands high safety standards. They have limited maneuverability and travel at slower speeds, necessitating a larger safety buffer when near the OWF, which may increase navigational complexity for other ships. Other smaller specialized ships (such as LPG carriers, chemical carriers, barges, etc.) make up a smaller percentage of the traffic but require high safety standards, especially chemical and LPG carriers, which need stringent risk controls. When these ships adjust their routes due to OWF obstructions, they may contribute to traffic congestion, particularly in high-traffic areas, and their hazardous cargo introduces additional risk factors.

5. Discussion

With the construction of OWFs occupying parts of existing routes, ships need to adjust their courses to avoid the OWFs, significantly impacting the traditional route layout. These adjustments may result in longer travel paths, increased travel times, and higher fuel consumption. This is especially problematic in high-density-traffic areas, where such changes exacerbate congestion and elevate collision risks. The complexities brought about by route reconfiguration particularly affect large, low-maneuverability ships such as tankers and cargo ships, whereas smaller and more agile vessels are comparatively less impacted. This finding highlights that different ship types experience varying levels of complexity within OWF areas, with larger ships often requiring greater safety distances and navigation space, which, in turn, increases navigational complexity. Additionally, OWF construction introduces certain interferences with the navigation equipment of surrounding vessels. OWF structures can create obstacles on radar, potentially compromising the accurate detection of surrounding ships' positions and distances and thereby reducing situational awareness. This interference becomes more pronounced in low-visibility or adverse weather conditions, where ships approaching OWF areas may encounter navigation errors, heightening collision risks. Thus, more effective navigational assistance systems are required to address the limitations of traditional equipment within OWF areas.

In response to these challenges, several optimization recommendations are proposed. First, layered route planning specifically for OWF areas should be implemented to alleviate congestion resulting from route adjustments, particularly by providing more suitable navigable paths for large, low-maneuverability vessels. Second, it is recommended that OWF managers and maritime authorities collaboratively promote route optimization efforts, integrating real-time AIS data and big data analysis techniques to dynamically adjust for ship types and traffic flow. Early warnings for high-complexity periods can facilitate timely adjustments to travel routes or speeds, mitigating risks during peak traffic. Future OWF planning should avoid major shipping lanes or high-density traffic areas whenever possible and fully consider the navigational needs of different ship types to minimize the impact on existing route systems. Finally, relevant management authorities should continuously monitor and assess navigational risks in OWF areas, increasing surveillance and support measures during high-complexity and high-risk periods to ensure vessel safety.

6. Conclusions

This study developed a novel maritime traffic complexity model specifically for OWF areas, addressing a critical gap in current maritime safety research. The findings show that the proposed OWF significantly increases navigational complexity in high-density traffic areas, as evidenced by increased route congestion, changes in navigation patterns, and higher encounter rates among ships. The Yangtze River Estuary, a region characterized by dense and diverse traffic, provided an ideal environment for evaluating these dynamics. By comparing traffic complexity before and after the OWF's construction, this research offers strong empirical support for the anticipated navigational challenges in the proposed OWF areas.

This study not only provides a practical framework for assessing and managing maritime traffic complexity in the proposed OWF areas but also emphasizes the necessity of proactive policies and technological upgrades in these increasingly congested waters. However, the maritime traffic system is extremely complex, especially in OWF areas. Research on the complexity of maritime traffic in these areas is still in its early stages, and to accurately describe the traffic dynamics in OWF areas, a more comprehensive understanding of the composition and characteristics of the traffic system in these waters is needed. Future research could further enhance this model by incorporating real-time data and environmental variables to improve predictive accuracy. There are several issues with the proposed method that require further in-depth exploration and supplementation. AIS data were used in this study, but the potential incompleteness of the AIS data may still introduce some uncertainty. In future work, more reliable data sources will be incorporated, and data collection methods will be continuously improved to further enhance the accuracy and completeness of the data. Although a complexity model for maritime traffic in OWF areas was proposed in this research, human factors were not considered. Since most accidents are caused by human factors, future research could focus on obtaining real-time behavioral data related to the Officer on Watch (OOW) through relevant sensors, such as electroencephalogram (EEG) data and eye movement data, to study traffic situation complexity. While this study considered the relationship between ships and OWFs, it did not take into account the impact of ship type and maneuverability on complexity. In practical navigation, ship type is a very important factor. For example, oil tankers, LNG carriers, and passenger ships should receive more attention than other cargo ships when navigating in OWF areas. Therefore, future research should consider this factor. This study lays a solid foundation for developing more robust traffic management practices, ultimately supporting the safe and sustainable development of OWFs in critical maritime corridors.

Author Contributions: Conceptualization, J.L. and W.Y.; methodology, J.L. and Z.S.; software, J.L. and W.Y.; validation, Z.S. and C.Z.; formal analysis, J.L.; investigation, W.Y.; resources, J.L. and C.Z.; data curation, J.L., W.Y. and C.Z.; writing—original draft preparation, J.L.; writing—review and editing, Z.S. and C.Z.; visualization, J.L. and W.Y.; supervision, Z.S. and C.Z.; project administration, C.Z.; funding acquisition, C.Z. All authors have read and agreed to the published version of the manuscript.

Funding: This work was supported by a research project grant from Shanghai Investigation, Design & Research Institute Co., Ltd. (project No. 2023 FD(83)-002) and the National Natural Science Foundation of China (NSFC) through Grant No. 52171349.

Institutional Review Board Statement: Not applicable.

Informed Consent Statement: Not applicable.

Data Availability Statement: Dataset available on request from the authors.

Conflicts of Interest: Author Jian Liu and Wenbo Yu were employed by the company Shanghai Investigation, Design & Research Institute Co., Ltd. The remaining authors declare that the research was conducted in the absence of any commercial or financial relationships that could be construed as a potential conflict of interest.

References

1. Perveen, R.; Kishor, N.; Mohanty, S.R. Off-shore wind farm development: Present status and challenges. *Renew. Sustain. Energy Rev.* **2014**, *29*, 780–792. [CrossRef]
2. Mehdi, R.A.; Baldauf, M.; Deeb, H. A dynamic risk assessment method to address safety of navigation concerns around offshore renewable energy installations. *Proc. Inst. Mech. Eng. M-J. Eng.* **2020**, *234*, 231–244. [CrossRef]
3. Neshenko, N.; Nader, C.; Bou-Harb, E.; Furht, B. A survey of methods supporting cyber situational awareness in the context of smart cities. *J. Big Data* **2020**, *7*, 1–41. [CrossRef]
4. Sui, Z.; Huang, Y.; Wen, Y.; Zhou, C.; Huang, X. Marine traffic profile for enhancing situational awareness based on complex network theory. *Ocean Eng.* **2021**, *241*, 110049. [CrossRef]
5. Sui, Z.; Wen, Y.; Huang, Y.; Zhou, C.; Du, L.; Piera, M.A. Node importance evaluation in marine traffic situation complex network for intelligent maritime supervision. *Ocean Eng.* **2022**, *247*, 110742. [CrossRef]
6. Premalatha, M.; Abbasi, T.; Abbasi, S.A. Wind energy: Increasing deployment, rising environmental concerns. *Renew. Sustain. Energy Rev.* **2014**, *31*, 270–288.
7. Vetters, J.; Thomassen, G.; Van Passel, S. Sailing through end-of-life challenges: A comprehensive review for offshore wind. *Renew. Sustain. Energy Rev.* **2024**, *199*, 114486. [CrossRef]
8. Martelli, M.; Virdis, A.; Gotta, A.; Cassarà, P.; Di Summa, M. An outlook on the future marine traffic management system for autonomous ships. *IEEE Access* **2021**, *9*, 157316–157328. [CrossRef]
9. Ribeiro, C.V.; Paes, A.; de Oliveira, D. AIS-based maritime anomaly traffic detection: A review. *Expert Syst. Appl.* **2023**, *231*, 120561. [CrossRef]
10. Lin, M.S.M.; Lu, B.S. Risk assessment and management in the offshore wind power industry: A focus on component handling operations in ports. *Saf. Sci.* **2023**, *167*, 106286. [CrossRef]
11. Yan, Z.; Xiao, Y.; Cheng, L.; He, R.; Ruan, X.; Zhou, X.; Zhou, X.; Li, M.; Bin, R. Exploring AIS data for intelligent maritime routes extraction. *Appl. Ocean Res.* **2020**, *101*, 102271. [CrossRef]
12. Tsai, Y.M.; Lin, C.Y. Investigation on improving strategies for navigation safety in the offshore wind farm in Taiwan Strait. *J. Mar. Sci. Eng.* **2021**, *9*, 1448. [CrossRef]
13. Cao, W.; Wang, X.; Li, J.; Zhang, Z.; Cao, Y.; Feng, Y. A novel integrated method for heterogeneity analysis of marine accidents involving different ship types. *Ocean Eng.* **2024**, *312*, 119295. [CrossRef]
14. Yu, Q.; Liu, K.; Chang, C.H.; Yang, Z. Realising advanced risk assessment of vessel traffic flows near offshore wind farms. *Reliab. Eng. Syst. Saf.* **2020**, *203*, 107086. [CrossRef]
15. Feng, H.; Grifoll, M.; Yang, Z.; Zheng, P. Collision risk assessment for ships' routeing waters: An information entropy approach with Automatic Identification System (AIS) data. *Ocean Coast. Manag.* **2022**, *224*, 106184. [CrossRef]
16. Xue, H.; Qian, K. Ship collision avoidance based on brain storm optimization near offshore wind farm. *Ocean Eng.* **2023**, *268*, 113433. [CrossRef]
17. Allal, A.; Sahnoun, M.H.; Adjoudj, R.; Benslimane, S.M.; Mazar, M. Multi-agent based simulation-optimization of maintenance routing in offshore wind farms. *Comput. Ind. Eng.* **2021**, *157*, 107342. [CrossRef]
18. Rawson, A.; Brito, M. Assessing the validity of navigation risk assessments: A study of offshore wind farms in the UK. *Ocean Coast. Manag.* **2022**, *219*, 106078. [CrossRef]
19. Serra-Sogas, N.; O'Hara, P.D.; Pearce, K.; Smallshaw, L.; Canessa, R. Using aerial surveys to fill gaps in AIS vessel traffic data to inform threat assessments, vessel management and planning. *Mar. Policy* **2021**, *133*, 104765. [CrossRef]
20. Hou, G.; Xu, K.; Lian, J. A review on recent risk assessment methodologies of offshore wind turbine foundations. *Ocean Eng.* **2022**, *264*, 112469. [CrossRef]
21. Ladeira, I.; Márquez, L.; Echeverry, S.; Le Sourne, H.; Rigo, P. Review of methods to assess the structural response of offshore wind turbines subjected to ship impacts. *Ships Offshore Struct.* **2023**, *18*, 755–774. [CrossRef]
22. Vilela, R.; Burger, C.; Diederichs, A.; Bachl, F.E.; Szostek, L.; Freund, A.; Braasch, A.; Bellebaum, J.; Beckers, B.; Piper, W.; et al. Use of an INLA latent gaussian modeling approach to assess bird population changes due to the development of offshore wind farms. *Front. Mar. Sci.* **2021**, *8*, 701332. [CrossRef]
23. Gucma, S.; Gralak, R.; Przywarty, M.; Ślączka, W. Maximum safe parameters of outbound loaded vessels for wind turbine installation. *Appl. Sci.* **2022**, *12*, 3868. [CrossRef]
24. Kim, S.J.; Seo, J.K.; Ma, K.Y.; Park, J.S. Methodology for collision-frequency analysis of wind-turbine installation vessels. *Ships Offshore Struct.* **2021**, *16*, 423–439. [CrossRef]
25. Gao, H.; Xie, C.; Liu, K.; Chen, S.; Zhou, L.; Liu, Z.; Wang, R. Modeling of safe distance between ship routes and offshore wind farm based on tolerable collision probability. *IEEE Access* **2022**, *10*, 71777–71790. [CrossRef]
26. Lan, H.; Ma, X.; Qiao, W.; Deng, W. Determining the critical risk factors for predicting the severity of ship collision accidents using a data-driven approach. *Reliab. Eng. Syst. Saf.* **2023**, *230*, 108934. [CrossRef]
27. Ren, Z.; Verma, A.S.; Li, Y.; Teuwen, J.J.; Jiang, Z. Offshore wind turbine operations and maintenance: A state-of-the-art review. *Renew. Sustain. Energy Rev.* **2021**, *144*, 110886. [CrossRef]
28. Zhang, K.; Pakrashi, V.; Murphy, J.; Hao, G. Inspection of Floating Offshore Wind Turbines Using Multi-Rotor Unmanned Aerial Vehicles: Literature Review and Trends. *Sensors* **2024**, *24*, 911. [CrossRef]

29. Marcjan, K.; Kotkowska, D. Identification of Navigational Risks Associated with Wind Farms. *Eur. Res. Stud. J.* **2023**, *26*, 595–611. [CrossRef]
30. Alphan, H. Modelling potential visibility of wind turbines: A geospatial approach for planning and impact mitigation. *Renew. Sustain. Energy Rev.* **2021**, *152*, 111675. [CrossRef]
31. Huang, I.L.; Lee, M.C.; Nieh, C.Y.; Huang, J.C. Ship classification based on ais data and machine learning methods. *Electronics* **2023**, *13*, 98. [CrossRef]
32. Yan, K.; Wang, Y.; Wang, W.; Qiao, C.; Chen, B.; Jia, L. A system-theory and complex network-fused approach to analyze vessel–wind turbine allisions in offshore wind farm waters. *J. Mar. Sci. Eng.* **2023**, *11*, 1306. [CrossRef]
33. Wang, S.; Zou, Y.; Wang, X. An intelligent decision-making approach for multi-ship traffic conflict mitigation from the perspective of maritime surveillance. *J. Mar. Sci. Eng.* **2024**, *12*, 1719. [CrossRef]
34. Liu, X.; Hu, Y.; Ji, H.; Zhang, M.; Yu, Q. A deep learning method for ship detection and traffic monitoring in an offshore wind farm area. *J. Mar. Sci. Eng.* **2023**, *11*, 1259. [CrossRef]
35. Machado, J.T.M.; de Andrés, M. Implications of offshore wind energy developments in coastal and maritime tourism and recreation areas: An analytical overview. *Environ. Impact Assess.* **2023**, *99*, 106999. [CrossRef]
36. Shafiee, M.; Zhou, Z.; Mei, L.; Dinmohammadi, F.; Karama, J.; Flynn, D. Unmanned aerial drones for inspection of offshore wind turbines: A mission-critical failure analysis. *Robotics* **2021**, *10*, 26. [CrossRef]
37. Moreno, F.C.; Gonzalez, J.R.; Muro, J.S.; Maza, J.G. Relationship between human factors and a safe performance of vessel traffic service operators: A systematic qualitative-based review in maritime safety. *Saf. Sci.* **2022**, *155*, 105892. [CrossRef]
38. Santos, P.; Santos, M.; Trslic, P.; Weir, A.; Dooly, G.; Omerdic, E.; Toal, D. Developments in Underwater Robot Capabilities for Offshore Wind. In Proceedings of the OCEANS 2023-Limerick, Limerick, Ireland, 5–8 June 2023; pp. 1–5.
39. Garcia-Teruel, A.; Rinaldi, G.; Thies, P.R.; Johanning, L.; Jeffrey, H. Life cycle assessment of floating offshore wind farms: An evaluation of operation and maintenance. *Appl. Energy* **2022**, *307*, 118067. [CrossRef]
40. Ducruet, C. The geography of maritime networks: A critical review. *J. Transp. Geogr.* **2020**, *88*, 102824. [CrossRef]
41. Sui, Z.; Wen, Y.; Huang, Y.; Zhou, C.; Xiao, C.; Chen, H. Empirical analysis of complex network for marine traffic situation. *Ocean Eng.* **2020**, *214*, 107848. [CrossRef]
42. Fujii, Y.; Tanaka, K. Traffic capacity. *J. Navig.* **1971**, *24*, 543–552. [CrossRef]
43. Mon, D.; Cheng, C.; Lin, J. Evaluating weapon system using fuzzy analytic hierarchy process based on entropy weight. *Fuzzy Sets Syst.* **1994**, *62*, 127–134. [CrossRef]
44. Tian, W.; Zhu, M.; Han, P.; Li, G.; Zhang, H. Pairwise ship encounter identification and classification for knowledge extraction. *Ocean Eng.* **2024**, *294*, 116752. [CrossRef]

Journal of
Marine Science and Engineering

MDPI

Article

Reliability of Inland Water Transportation Complex Network Based on Percolation Theory: An Empirical Analysis in the Yangtze River

Dong Han [1], Zhongyi Sui [2,*], Changshi Xiao [1] and Yuanqiao Wen [3,4,5]

1 School of Navigation, Wuhan University of Technology, Wuhan 430063, China; handong@whut.edu.cn (D.H.); cs_xiao@hotmail.com (C.X.)
2 Department of Logistics and Maritime Studies, Faculty of Business, The Hong Kong Polytechnic University, Hong Kong 999077, China
3 State Key Laboratory of Maritime Technology and Safety, Wuhan University of Technology, Wuhan 430063, China; yqwen@whut.edu.cn
4 Intelligent Transportation Systems Research Center, Wuhan University of Technology, Wuhan 430063, China
5 Sanya Science and Education Innovation Park, Wuhan University of Technology, Sanya 572000, China
* Correspondence: zhongyi.sui@polyu.edu.hk

Abstract: Inland water transportation is regarded as a crucial component of global trade, yet its reliability has been increasingly challenged by uncertainties such as extreme weather, port congestion, and geopolitical tensions. Although substantial research has focused on the structural characteristics of inland water transportation networks, the dynamic responses of these networks to disruptions remain insufficiently explored. This gap in understanding is critical for enhancing the resilience of global transportation systems as trade volumes grow and risks intensify. In this study, percolation theory was applied to evaluate the reliability of the Yangtze River transportation network. Ship voyage data from 2019 were used to construct a complex network model, and simulations of node removal were performed to identify key vulnerabilities within the network. The results showed that the failure of specific nodes significantly impacts the network's connectivity, suggesting which nodes should be prioritized for protection. This research offers a dynamic framework for the assessment of inland water transportation network reliability and provides new insights that could guide policy decisions to improve the resilience of critical waterway systems. By identifying potential points of failure, this study contributes to the development of a more robust global trade infrastructure.

Keywords: traffic management; inland water transportation complex network; Yangtze river; reliability

1. Introduction

Inland water transportation, a vital element of global trade, significantly impacts both the efficiency and stability of the global economy. The complex shipping network connecting major ports ensures the continuous flow of goods and services [1,2]. As globalization intensifies, the reliability of inland water transportation networks has attracted increasing attention from academia and industry alike [3,4]. Multiple uncertainties, including weather conditions, port congestion, piracy, and geopolitical tensions, present significant challenges to the robustness and resilience of inland water transportation networks [5].

Prior studies have thoroughly examined the structural characteristics of inland water transportation networks and their effects on network reliability. Research grounded in complex network theory has been particularly prominent. Scholars have analyzed the topological structures of shipping networks to identify critical nodes and key routes essential for network stability. Ducruet studied global shipping networks, highlighting the importance of port connectivity as critical nodes for overall network stability [6]. Kaluza et al. demonstrated the critical role of shipping routes in the global transportation system through their study of maritime routes [7]. However, despite offering in-depth analyses of static network characteristics, the dynamic responses of networks to random failures or malicious attacks remain insufficiently explored. To fill these gaps, researchers have begun incorporating more dynamic and sophisticated analytical approaches. Recently, risk assessment and disaster management models have been increasingly applied to maritime transport networks to more accurately assess the impacts of potential risks on network reliability. Pant et al. developed a risk model to evaluate threats to port connectivity posed by natural disasters, such as earthquakes [8]. These studies highlight the significant impact of natural disasters and extreme events on the reliability of maritime transport networks. Nevertheless, despite advances in risk assessment, these models still rely heavily on historical data and pre-existing assumptions, limiting their ability to uncover the underlying mechanisms and response patterns of networks during sudden events. Percolation theory, a fundamental tool in network science, provides a fresh perspective for examining the connectivity and robustness of complex networks under various disruption scenarios. By simulating the progressive failure of nodes or links, percolation theory reveals network behavior and critical thresholds under random or targeted attacks [9]. Although widely applied in transportation, energy, and communication networks, its application to maritime transport networks remains underexplored. Several studies have attempted to apply percolation theory to the analysis of maritime networks [10–13]. Sohn investigated the effects of key node failures on the connectivity of the Korean shipping network [14]. However, these studies primarily focus on individual countries or regions and lack a comprehensive analysis of global or large-scale shipping networks.

This study aims to perform a systematic empirical analysis of the Yangtze River transportation network's reliability using percolation theory. The Yangtze River, one of the busiest inland waterways globally, plays a critical role in China's economic development and has significant implications for global trade flows. Through detailed network structure analysis, this study demonstrates how connectivity shifts under different percolation scenarios and identifies key vulnerabilities and resilience factors. Additionally, this research explores potential links between incidents and environmental changes, offering scientific insights for the design and management of inland water transportation networks. This study extends the application of percolation theory to inland water transportation and provides novel insights and methods to enhance the safety and efficiency of global shipping systems.

This study addresses a gap in the resilience analysis of the Inland Water Transportation Complex Network (IWTCN) using percolation theory. While previous studies have used percolation theory to examine the robustness of transportation networks, most have focused on single network structures or the impact of specific nodes. The novelty of our approach lies in its comprehensive analysis of network resilience, which not only considers the overall network structure but also explores the load-bearing capacity of key nodes and their influence on failure propagation. This integrated approach provides a more thorough evaluation of network performance under multiple failure scenarios, especially in complex cases involving multiple node failures. Additionally, the research differentiates itself from previous works by incorporating geographical distribution and dynamic factors. This provides a more nuanced perspective on inland water transportation network resilience, enabling us to assess the network's vulnerability in real-world scenarios, such as when multiple nodes are affected simultaneously.

The structure of the paper is as follows: Section 2 reviews previous research in the field. Section 3 presents the methodology and data used in this study. Section 4 discusses the findings related to the characteristics of inland water transportation in the Yangtze River. Finally, Section 5 provides the conclusions.

2. Literature Review

Transportation networks are generally regarded as complex systems comprising nodes (e.g., ports, airports, rail stations) and edges (e.g., roads, railways, maritime routes) that form diverse structures. These networks frequently exhibit small-world and scale-free characteristics. In small-world networks, most nodes are connected by relatively short paths, ensuring high connectivity efficiency throughout the system. On the other hand, scale-free networks indicate that a few nodes (hubs) possess numerous connections, which are crucial for the overall performance of the network [15–18]. Although these properties provide some redundancy, the failure of critical hubs can lead to cascading failures [19–21].

When analyzing transportation systems, network models primarily focus on node centrality, clustering coefficients, and path efficiency to identify weak links and optimize designs, thereby enhancing system robustness [22,23]. Barrat et al. examined the architecture of complex weighted networks, emphasizing the dynamic behavior of transportation systems under varying traffic intensities and network densities [24]. Further studies used these models to analyze maritime flows and network diversity, stressing the significance of dynamic structures in transportation networks [25]. In temporal networks, nodes and edges are time-dependent, adding an extra layer of complexity. Holme and Saramäki examined how temporal factors influence network stability and reliability, particularly in relation to traffic flow changes and performance under different conditions [26].

Reliability analysis of transportation networks focuses on assessing system performance during node or edge failures. Many studies examine the robustness of transportation networks under both random failures and targeted attacks. Albert et al. studied the fault tolerance of complex networks, revealing that scale-free networks (common in transportation systems) are highly resistant to random failures but very susceptible to targeted hub attacks [10]. This weakness is particularly evident in maritime networks, where a small number of critical ports handle most traffic flows. To enhance reliability, game theory methods have been used to simulate transportation systems during failure conditions. Bell introduced a game theory framework to assess network performance under uncertainty and optimize route selection [27]. Sun analyzed the robustness of transportation networks under interference, showing that even minor disruptions to key nodes can cause cascading failures, reducing overall system efficiency [28]. Additionally, vulnerability assessments provide crucial insights for identifying potential risks in transportation systems and help develop mitigation strategies.

Percolation theory is an essential tool for analyzing network connectivity changes when nodes or edges fail. Initially designed to study fluid flow in porous media, percolation theory has since been applied to network theory to understand connectivity and functionality in large-scale systems, such as transportation networks. Callaway et al. were the first to apply percolation theory to complex networks, demonstrating that critical node failures can collapse network connectivity. In transportation networks, percolation models simulate disruptions such as accidents, natural disasters, or targeted attacks [11]. Cohen et al. applied percolation theory to study internet robustness and compared it to failure patterns in transportation systems [29]. Some researchers extended this theory to scale-free networks, demonstrating that when hub nodes fail, the network fragments and becomes inefficient [30,31]. In transportation systems, the percolation threshold is a critical measure for evaluating network breakdown points. Newman and Pastor-Satorras used percolation theory to simulate epidemic spread, a model that is also applicable to analyzing failure propagation in transportation systems. These models offer valuable tools for planners to identify critical thresholds and strengthen infrastructure to prevent catastrophic failures [32,33].

Despite significant theoretical advancements, there are still several limitations in practical applications. First, most complex network and percolation theory models assume a static network topology, while real-world transportation networks are dynamic in both time and space. This assumption neglects the effects of traffic flow, seasonal variations, climate, and political factors on transportation system performance [26,34]. Consequently, these models offer limited predictive and guiding power under dynamic conditions. Additionally, although complex network theory effectively explains topological features, it often lacks adequate physical explanations for node failure triggers like natural disasters or equipment malfunctions [10,35]. Current research tends to emphasize network structural characteristics, paying less attention to control and monitoring mechanisms in real-world traffic management. Another limitation is that applying percolation theory to transportation networks is often based on theoretical assumptions and lacks adequate validation using real-world data. Many studies on percolation models focus on the global impact of node failures, with insufficient consideration of improving local system reliability through targeted measures [29,36]. Such studies may fail to fully capture the unique characteristics of specific regions when applied to particular areas.

To better understand the key findings and methods from these studies, we have summarized the most relevant research in Table 1. This table presents a comparative overview of the major studies that have shaped our understanding of transportation network reliability, including their focus areas, key findings, methods used, and the primary insights gained from each. The studies discussed in the table highlight the different approaches and methodologies applied to the study of transportation networks, offering a clearer view of the field's development.

Table 1. Summary of key studies in transportation network reliability.

Research Topic	Milestones	Method/Model	Key Insights
Dynamic behavior of complex weighted networks	Emphasized the impact of varying traffic intensities and network densities on transportation systems	Dynamic behavior analysis	Highlighted the importance of dynamic structures in transportation networks
Fault tolerance in complex networks	Scale-free networks are resistant to random failures but vulnerable to targeted hub attacks	Fault tolerance analysis	Found that scale-free networks are prone to targeted attacks on critical hubs
Application of percolation theory	Demonstrated that critical node failures cause network connectivity collapse	Percolation model	Showed that percolation theory is effective in simulating disruptions in transportation systems
Temporal networks stability	Temporal factors significantly influence network stability and reliability	Time-dependent network models	Analyzed how traffic flow changes affect network performance over time
Percolation theory and network robustness	Compared failure patterns in transportation and internet systems using percolation theory	Percolation theory application	Found that failure patterns in transportation networks are similar to those in internet systems
Robustness of transportation networks under interference	Minor disruptions to key nodes can cause cascading failures and decrease efficiency	Simulation of system interference	Revealed that even small disruptions can lead to large-scale system inefficiencies

This study focuses on the reliability of the Yangtze River shipping network through an empirical analysis grounded in percolation theory. Despite the growing body of research on network reliability, much of the existing literature on inland water transportation networks has either examined isolated network structures or focused solely on specific nodes without considering the overall resilience of the entire system. While percolation theory has been applied to study transportation network robustness, there is a significant gap in understanding how key nodes' load-bearing capacities and their role in failure propagation affect overall network resilience, especially in complex and large-scale maritime networks. This study fills that gap by integrating the analysis of both network structure and dynamic load-bearing capacities to assess resilience under multiple failure scenarios.

The motivation for focusing on the Yangtze River shipping network stems from its critical role in China's inland transportation system. As one of the world's busiest and most vital inland waterway routes, the Yangtze River network serves as a key artery for both domestic and international trade. The disruptions in this network can have severe economic and logistical consequences, which makes it an ideal case study for understanding the resilience of large-scale inland water transportation networks. By using real data from this network, this study aims to provide a detailed empirical validation of the Yangtze River network's connectivity and robustness.

The findings from this research are particularly relevant not only for the Yangtze River but also for other maritime and inland waterways. The insights into network resilience, failure thresholds, and load-bearing capacities can be generalized to similar large-scale transportation systems, including key maritime networks in other regions. This study offers a methodology that can be applied to assess resilience across different geographical regions, thus providing actionable insights for enhancing the robustness of maritime transportation systems worldwide.

3. Method

3.1. Dataset

The Yangtze River, often referred to as the golden waterway, is the largest river flowing through both eastern and western China, serving as a crucial route for travel and commercial trade. The study area in this research focuses on the stretch of the Yangtze River from Sichuan to Anhui, as shown in Figure 1. This region is an important part of the Yangtze River Economic Belt, covering several economically developed provinces. It has high shipping traffic and a complex waterway transportation network, and it is representative, making it well-suited to reflect the characteristics of transportation in the upper and middle reaches of the Yangtze River. The transportation network in the Jiangsu section is closely connected to inland water transportation, with distinct characteristics of seaports. However, this study focuses on inland waterway transportation networks. To maintain the study's focus and consistency, only regions closely related to inland shipping were selected for analysis. Therefore, the Jiangsu section was excluded from the study due to its specific maritime attributes.

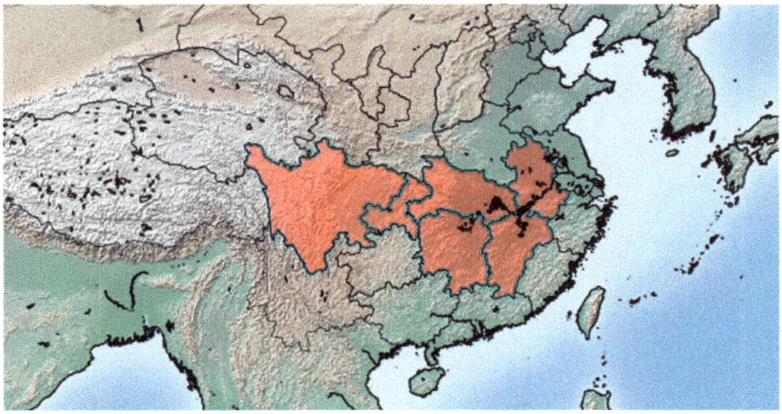

Figure 1. Research area in this study.

In recent years, ship voyage data have emerged as a crucial resource for analyzing navigation patterns. The dataset employed in this study consists of ship voyage information. Under current maritime regulations, ships are required to submit detailed voyage records, including the vessel's name, type, the maritime authority at the point of departure, time of departure, the maritime authority at the destination, time of arrival, number of crew members, and other relevant information. This research focuses on ship voyage data from the Yangtze River for the year 2019, with vessels operating solely within port areas excluded from consideration. The data used in this research were supplied by the Changjiang River Administration of Navigational Affairs, which operates under the Ministry of Transport of China. A sample of these data can be found in Table 2.

Table 2. Some of the data used in this study.

Ship Name	Ship Type	MD of Departure	Departure Time	MD of Destination	Arrival Time	Number of Crew Members
Xiaoganhongda2668	Bulk ship	Maanshan MD	2019/1/31 19:20	Huangshi MD	2019/2/7 16:26	7
Yishigong5	Oil tanker	Sanxia Baqu MD	2019/1/31 19:52	Chongqing Fuling MD	2019/2/5 9:03	10
Minda	LNG ship	Anqinggangqu MD	2019/1/31 20:30	Wuhan Yangluo MD	2019/2/2 14:00	12
Yushenzhou10	Bulk Ship	Yichanggangqu MD	2019/1/31 23:00	Chongqing Wanzhou MD	2019/2/8 7:40	10
...	...	...	...	...	...	...

3.2. Modelling IWTCN and Topological Properties

The theory of complex networks has found extensive applications in transportation research, especially in maritime systems. In maritime transport, global networks typically model shipping routes as edges and ports as nodes, which is in line with complex network theory. While these networks are commonly used to analyze global systems, the IWTCN was specifically designed to explore the unique characteristics of the Yangtze River transport system.

In order to construct the IWTCN model, the maritime departments (MD) of the ships' origin and destination points in the dataset were determined. Each MD in the study area was mapped as a node, with routes between MDs defining the edges. As a result, the network consists of 63 MDs and their corresponding connections. Details of the MDs are provided in Table 3. The IWTCN model for the Yangtze River comprises 63 nodes and 3110 edges. Notably, the network has no isolated nodes, indicating that all variables in the spatial correlation network are interconnected.

Table 3. MDs and abbreviation.

No.	MD	No.	MD	No.	MD	No.	MD
1	Cuiping (CP)	17	Yunyang (YY)	33	Huarong (HR)	49	Jiujiang Xingang (JJXG)
2	Nanxi (NAX)	18	Fengjie (FG)	34	Linxiang (LX)	50	Hukou (HK)
3	Jiangan (JG)	19	Wushan (WS)	35	Xintan (XT)	51	Pengze (PZ)
4	Naxi (NX)	20	Badong (BD)	36	Xianning (XN)	52	Huayang (HY)
5	Jiangyang (JY)	21	Guizhou (GZ)	37	Jinkou (JK)	53	Dongliu (DL)
6	Hejiang (HJ)	22	Baqu (BQ)	38	Zhuankou (ZK)	54	AnqingGangqu (AQGQ)
7	Yongchuan (YC)	23	Gezhouba (GZB)	39	Wuhan Gangqu (WHGQ)	55	Niutoushan (NTS)
8	Jiangjin (JJ)	24	Yidu (YD)	40	Qingshan (QS)	56	Congyang (CY)
9	Banan (BN)	25	Zhijiang (ZJ)	41	Yangluo (YL)	57	Chizhou (CZ)
10	Chaotianmen (CTM)	26	Gongan (GA)	42	Erzhou (EZ)	58	Tongling (TL)
11	Changshu (CS)	27	Shashi (SS)	43	Huanggang (HG)	59	Digang (DG)
12	Fuling (FL)	28	Jiangling (JAL)	44	Huangshi Gangqu (HSGQ)	60	Yuxikou (YXK)

Table 3. *Cont.*

No.	MD	No.	MD	No.	MD	No.	MD
13	Fengdu (FD)	29	Shishou (SIS)	45	Jinchun (JC)	61	Wuhu Gangqu (WUHGQ)
14	Zhongxian (ZX)	30	Jianli (JL)	46	Fuchi (FC)	62	Cihu (CH)
15	Shizhu (SZ)	31	Honghu (HH)	47	Wuxue (WX)	63	Maanshan (MAS)
16	Wanzhou (WZ)	32	Chenglingji (CLJ)	48	Jiujiang Gangqu (JJGQ)		

Several variables commonly used in complex network analysis, including cumulative degree distribution, vertex strength, average path length, clustering coefficient, and betweenness centrality, are chosen to examine the overall structure of the IWTCN. The IWTCN can be represented by an adjacency matrix $A(N \times N)$, where $a_{ij} = 1$ signifies that MDs i and j form an OD pair. Otherwise, $a_{ij} = 0$. Additionally, N represents the total count of nodes in the IWTCN.

(1) Cumulative degree distribution (CDD).

The degree of node i, indicating the number of edges it connects to, can be determined using the following formula:

$$k_i = \sum_{j=0}^{N} a_{ij} \quad (1)$$

One common way to quantify a node's connectivity within a network is by using the concept of degree. In the analysis network, higher-degree nodes provide easier access to more MDs. In the IWTCN, the CDD represents the probability of randomly selecting a node with a degree of at least k, and it is calculated as follows:

$$P(k) = \sum_{k\prime=k}^{\infty} p(k\prime) \quad (2)$$

The CDD plays a key role in identifying various network behaviors in actual transportation systems, such as the spread of traffic flow and the robustness of the network.

(2) Vertex strength (VS).

The total of a node's edge weights is known as its VS. The average VS is defined as follows.

$$S_i = \sum_{j \in N_i} w_{ij} \quad (3)$$

$$\overline{S} = \frac{1}{N}\sum_{i=1}^{N} S_i \quad (4)$$

where $\overline{S}$ is the average VS of a network, S_i is the vertex strength of node i, w_{ij} is the weight of the edge between node i and node j, N_i is the set of adjacent points of node i.

(3) Average path length (APL).

The formula below is applied to calculate the APL, representing the mean of the shortest number of edges between any randomly selected pair of nodes in the IWTCN.

$$L = \frac{1}{\frac{1}{2}N(N-1)}\sum_{i \geq j} d_{ij} \quad (5)$$

where d_{ij} is the fewest number of edges that connect nodes i to j.

(4) Clustering coefficient (CC).

The CC quantifies how many nodes in a graph are inclined to form clusters. In real-world networks, nodes often form closely connected groups with a higher density of links. The CC is defined by the following equation:

$$C_i = \frac{E_i}{C_{k_i}^2} \tag{6}$$

where C_i denotes the local CC of node i, E_i indicates the number of realized connections among the neighbors of node i, while $C_{k_i}^2$ refers to the total number of potential connections among those neighbors.

(5) Betweenness centrality (BC).

BC quantifies how much a node influences the shortest paths between all node pairs and is frequently used to illustrate transitivity within transportation networks. A higher value of B_i indicates a more important role for transfer MD i. The betweenness of node i is determined by the fraction of shortest paths that pass through it:

$$B_i = \sum\nolimits_{s \neq i \neq t} \frac{n_{st}^i}{g_{st}} \tag{7}$$

where g_{st} indicates the total number of shortest paths from s to node t, and n_{st} refers to the count of those shortest paths in g_{st} that pass through node i.

3.3. Percolation Model on Complex Network

Percolation theory is one of the simplest models explaining systemic phase transition phenomena, describing the transition process between locally connected states and globally connected states within a system [37]. Many real-life problems can be explained by percolation theory, such as the minimum proportion of nodes that need to be removed to cause system collapse, the minimum proportion of trees that need to be cut down to prevent the spread of forest fires, and the minimum population size that needs to be vaccinated to prevent the widespread transmission of diseases [38–40].

(1) Determination of percolation threshold.

In the percolation process, the critical value p_c at which the network undergoes a phase transition is obtained by computing the variation in the size G of the largest connected cluster and the size SG of the second largest connected cluster with respect to the node (or edge) occupancy rate p. When p is less than p_c, the size G of the largest connected cluster is relatively small, indicating the absence of a connected cluster containing the majority of nodes in the network. Conversely, when p exceeds p_c, the size G of the largest connected cluster is comparable to the size of the network's nodes. For transportation networks, at this point, traffic flow can reach the majority of nodes in the network. According to percolation theory, in practical applications, the occupancy rate p at which the size SG of the second largest connected cluster reaches its peak is considered the percolation threshold. The calculation process of p_c is as follows:

Step 1: Initialize a network with N nodes and corresponding edges.

Step 2: Gradually increase the occupancy rate p, activating nodes or edges randomly.

Step 3: For each p, calculate the sizes G (largest connected cluster) and SG (second-largest connected cluster).

Step 4: Plot the relationship between p and G or SG. The p value at which SG reaches its maximum is taken as the percolation threshold p_c.

(2) Relative size of the giant cluster $p_\infty(p)$.

The order parameter $p_\infty(p)$ is defined as shown in Equation 8, where p_G represents the relative size of the largest connected cluster G. Before the network reaches the percolation threshold, there is no giant cluster present in the network, and the value of $p_\infty(p)$ is 0. After the network reaches the percolation threshold, the order parameter $p_\infty(p)$ represents the proportion of nodes in the largest connected cluster to all nodes in the network, and this value increases continuously as the node occupancy rate p increases. The relative size of the giant cluster is often considered an important indicator when describing the percolation process of the network.

$$p_\infty(p) = \begin{cases} 0, & p < p_c \\ p_G, & p \geq p_c \end{cases} \tag{8}$$

(3) Size distribution of finite connected clusters.

At the percolation threshold p_c, besides the giant cluster (i.e., the largest connected cluster), the network also contains several relatively small connected clusters. By statistically analyzing the sizes of these connected clusters, it is observed that their distribution follows a power-law distribution. The formula is as follows:

$$n_s \sim s^{-a} \tag{9}$$

where n_s represents the number of clusters containing s nodes, and a represents the Zipf exponent.

3.4. Reliability Indicators of IWTCN Based on Percolation

The reliability of the transportation system, as defined in this study, is derived from reliability theory. It is characterized by the system's ability to transport people or goods from one designated location to another within the time estimated by travelers, even when internal or external disruptions are encountered. Fragility is measured by the structural robustness of the network when facing such disturbances. A structural reliability metric for transportation networks is introduced through the application of the percolation process at the critical point of percolation. The focus is placed on interpreting the significance of the "giant component" and "critical point" within the percolation parameters. In a transportation network, a connected sub-cluster, referred to as the "giant component", is understood as the representation of ports within this sub-cluster being connected through transportation routes. The existence of a giant component is taken to indicate that a majority of MD within the network are interconnected, signifying that the network's connectivity and accessibility are robust.

In this section, the process of node removal within the network is treated as a percolation process, with the structural robustness of the network under internal and external disturbances being assessed from the perspective of fragility. The network's structural reliability metric is proposed at the percolation critical point based on the proportion of nodes removed. Initially, the sequence of node removal is selected, as different sequences are expected to have varying impacts on the network's reliability. Following each node removal, the size of the largest connected component G and the second-largest connected component SG within the network are calculated, with the variations in the sizes of these two components being tracked as the proportion of removed nodes p increases. The percolation critical point is then identified by analyzing the changes in the component sizes and the node removal proportion at this critical point p_c is defined as the structural reliability metric for the transportation network. When p is equal to 0, no nodes have been removed, resulting in the network being in a fully connected state, where the size of the largest connected component G corresponds to the total number of nodes. As p increases, nodes and certain subcomponents are progressively separated from the largest connected component, leading to a decrease in the size of G and an increase in the size of SG. The node removal proportion p at which SG reaches its maximum is identified as the critical node removal proportion p_c, which is subsequently defined as the structural reliability metric for the transportation network.

According to percolation theory, the critical node removal proportion p_c is understood to represent the critical point at which a transportation network transitions from global to local connectivity. When the node removal proportion is below p_c, the network is considered to maintain global connectivity, allowing most MDs within the network to establish connections via transportation routes. However, when the node removal proportion exceeds p_c, the transport of people or goods becomes restricted to local regions, and routes are no longer able to traverse the entire network. Consequently, the critical node removal proportion p_c is proposed as a structural reliability metric for the transportation network, reflecting its capacity to withstand internal and external disruptions. A smaller p_c suggests that the network is likely to become paralyzed following the removal of relatively few nodes, indicating weaker structural resilience to such attacks and, therefore, lower reliability. In contrast, a larger p_c implies that the network structure is able to maintain global connectivity even after the removal of a significant number of nodes, demonstrating greater resilience and higher reliability.

4. Results

4.1. Analysis of Topological Characteristics of IWTCN

The structure of the IWTCN in the Yangtze River is shown in Figure 2. Table 4 presents the fundamental topological characteristics of IWTCN. The average in-degree of IWTCN is approximately 45.07. The top five MDs with the highest in-degree are Chaotianmen (67), Shashi (66), Yidu (66), Chenglingji (66), and Fuling (64). The average out-degree of IWTCN is 46.04. The five MDs with the highest out-degrees are Fuling (65), Chaotianmen (64), Shashi (64), Yidu (64), and Wanzhou (62). The out-degree reflects the traffic volume managed by each MD. The network has a diameter of 3, with an average shortest path length of 1.34. Furthermore, the average clustering coefficient of the network is 0.796. Due to its short path lengths and high clustering, the IWTCN can be classified as a small-world network.

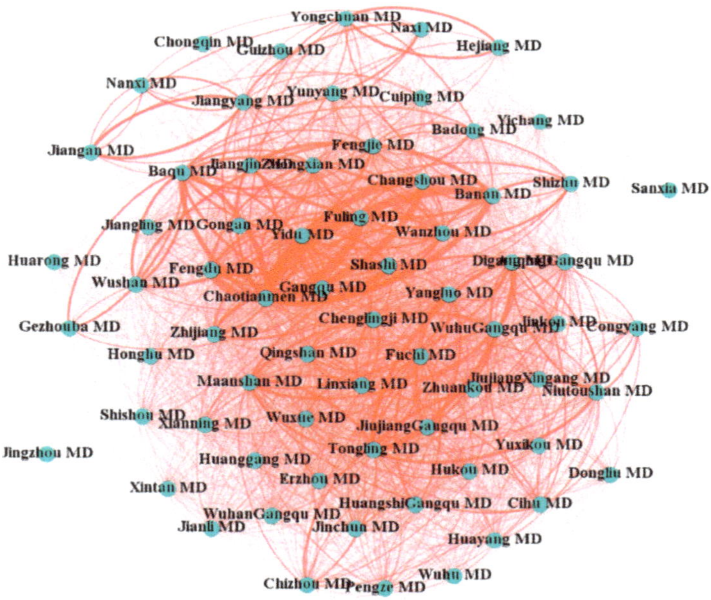

Figure 2. The structure of the IWTCN in the Yangtze River.

Table 4. Basic network parameters of IWTCN.

Nodes	Edges	Average In-Degree	Average Out-Degree	Average Path Length	Diameter	Average Cluster Coefficient
63	3110	45.07	46.04	1.34	3	0.796

Figure 3 illustrates the distributions of various topological features.

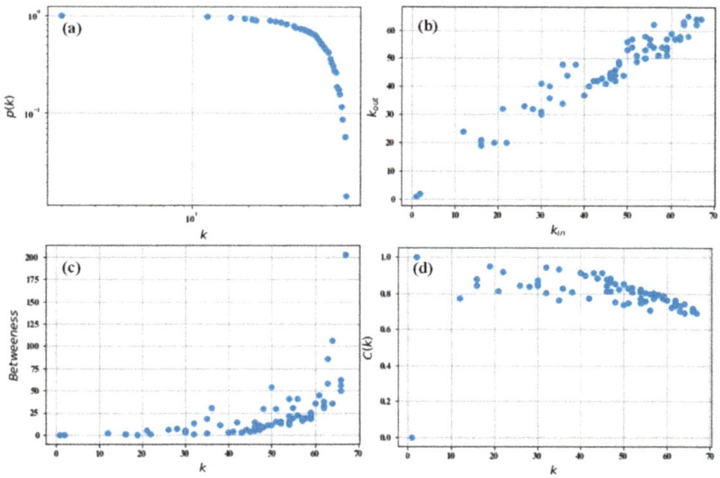

Figure 3. (**a**) The cumulative degree distribution of IWTCN. (**b**) The correlation between k_{in} and k_{out} of IWTCN. (**c**) The betweenness-degree correlation of IWTCN. (**d**) The clustering-degree correlation of IWTCN.

The degree distribution reveals the structure of the IWTCN and its relevance in network analysis. As depicted in Figure 3a, IWTCN follows a power-law degree distribution. In the directed IWTCN, the cumulative in-degree distribution, $p(k_{in})$, and cumulative out-degree distribution, $p(k_{out})$, closely align with the distribution $p(k)$ observed in the undirected network. The relationship between in-degree (k_{in}) and out-degree (k_{out}) is shown in Figure 3b. The strong correlation between k_{in} and k_{out} suggests that IWTCN is a symmetrical network, implying that if a shipping route exists from MD j to MD i, there is a high likelihood of a route in the opposite direction as well. To assess the importance of nodes in the transitivity of the IWTCN, the correlation between degree and betweenness centrality was examined. As shown in Figure 3c, nodes with higher degrees tend to handle more transfer operations. The relationship between node degree and clustering coefficient is presented in Figure 3d. It can be observed that while high-degree MDs are densely connected, several low-degree MDs remain sparsely connected. This results in higher clustering coefficients for the low-degree nodes.

Overall, the topological analysis indicates that IWTCN is a small-world network, distinguished by a power-law degree distribution and a superlinear correlation between betweenness and degree.

4.2. Percolation Process on IWTCN for Reliability Analysis

The structural reliability metric was applied to assess the IWTCN. Three types of percolation processes were analyzed: random node deletion, degree-based node deletion, and betweenness centrality-based node deletion.

Random deletion refers to the process where each node has an equal probability (1/63) of being removed from the network. Intentional deletion involves two scenarios: removing nodes in descending order of either degree centrality or betweenness centrality. Figure 4 illustrates the changes in the size of the G and the SG as the number of removed nodes increases across three scenarios: random deletion, degree centrality-based deletion, and betweenness centrality-based deletion.

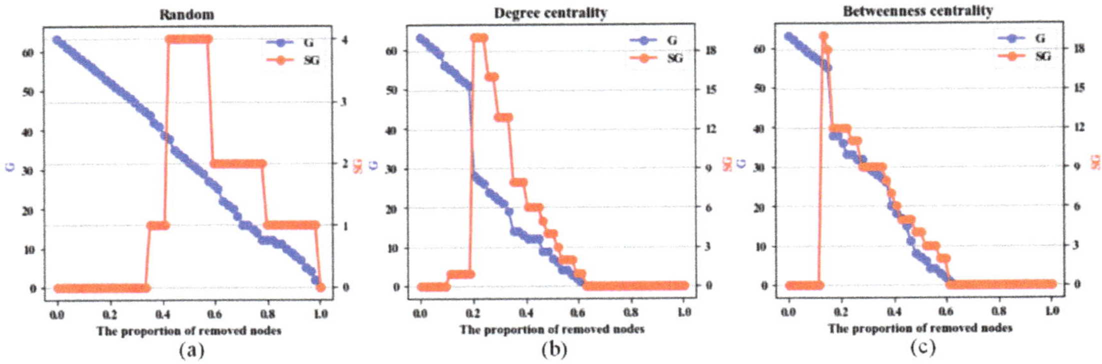

Figure 4. The percolation process of IWTCN under three strategies. (**a**) Random node deletion. (**b**) Degree-based node deletion. (**c**) Betweenness centrality-based node deletion.

A comparison of Figure 4a–c reveals that the decline in G is more gradual during random deletion compared to intentional deletion. When 18 nodes (approximately 28% of the total) are removed, G in the random deletion scenario remains at 45, suggesting that global connectivity is preserved. However, in the intentional deletion scenarios, G is reduced to 23 and 29, respectively, both falling to less than half of the total number of nodes. At this stage, the network is reduced to local connectivity, significantly impairing its functionality.

These results imply that under random deletion, the decline in G is primarily caused by node removal, leading to the nodes' separation from the largest connected component. Conversely, under intentional deletion, the removal of high-centrality nodes causes specific subcomponents to detach from the largest connected component, accelerating network fragmentation.

4.3. Identification of Critical Nodes During Percolation Process

The percolation process indicates that the IWTCN has relatively low reliability when subjected to deliberate attacks. The failure of a few local nodes can disrupt the entire network's connectivity, halting the transportation of goods and hindering normal system operations. The network loses global connectivity when 21% of nodes are removed based on degree centrality and 17% based on betweenness centrality. These local nodes should be regarded as key nodes in the transportation system and prioritized for protection. In actual operations, when a node fails, goods are often rerouted to nearby nodes, which may cause those nodes to fail due to insufficient capacity. Therefore, once key nodes are identified, their influence scope should be determined, and proactive measures should be implemented to prevent further failure spread.

First, key nodes are identified, particularly those removed during global connectivity loss from two types of deliberate attacks. Further analysis shows that under betweenness centrality-based removal, the critical nodes that fail are Chaotianmen (CTM), Wuhan Gangqu (WHGQ), Tongling (TL), Maanshan (MAS), and Shashi (SS). When removing based on degree centrality, the critical nodes that fail are Chaotianmen (CTM), Tongling (TL), Wuhan Gangqu (WHGQ), Digang (DG), and Maanshan (MAS). Next, the influence scope of a key node is determined by observing the increase in betweenness of remaining nodes after its failure. The change in a node's betweenness reflects its structural impact, and this metric is widely used across various fields. The five nodes with the largest variation in betweenness after a key node fails are considered its influence scope. The results are presented in Table 5, Figures 5 and 6.

Table 5. Critical nodes and their impacts.

MG	Ranking of the Betweenness Centrality Variations in Node				
	No. 1	No. 2	No. 3	No. 4	No. 5
Chaotianmen (CTM)	Baqu (BQ)	Chaotianmen (CTM)	Baqu (BQ)	Chaotianmen (CTM)	Baqu (BQ)
Wuhan Gangqu (WHGQ)	Chaotianmen (CTM)	Wuhan Gangqu (WHGQ)	Chaotianmen (CTM)	Wuhan Gangqu (WHGQ)	Chaotianmen (CTM)
Tongling (TL)	Maanshan (MAS)	Tongling (TL)	Maanshan (MAS)	Tongling (TL)	Maanshan (MAS)
Digang (DG)	Maanshan (MAS)	Digang (DG)	Maanshan (MAS)	Digang (DG)	Maanshan (MAS)
Maanshan (MAS)	Digang (DG)	Maanshan (MAS)	Digang (DG)	Maanshan (MAS)	Digang (DG)
Shashi (SS)	Wuhan Gangqu (WHGQ)	Shashi (SS)	Wuhan Gangqu (WHGQ)	Shashi (SS)	Wuhan Gangqu (WHGQ)

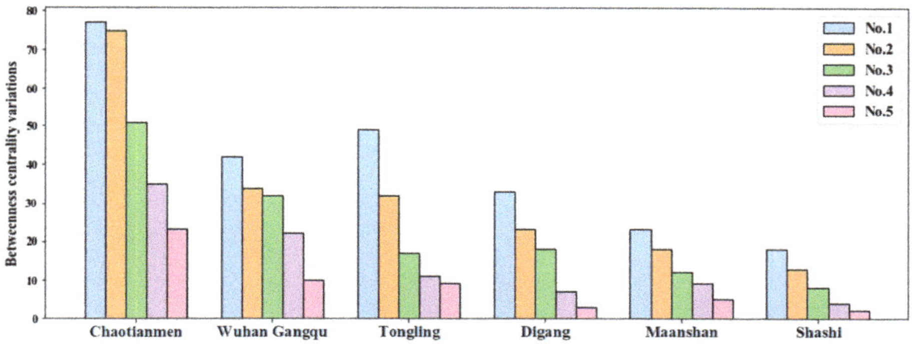

Figure 5. Impact degree of key nodes based on betweenness centrality variation.

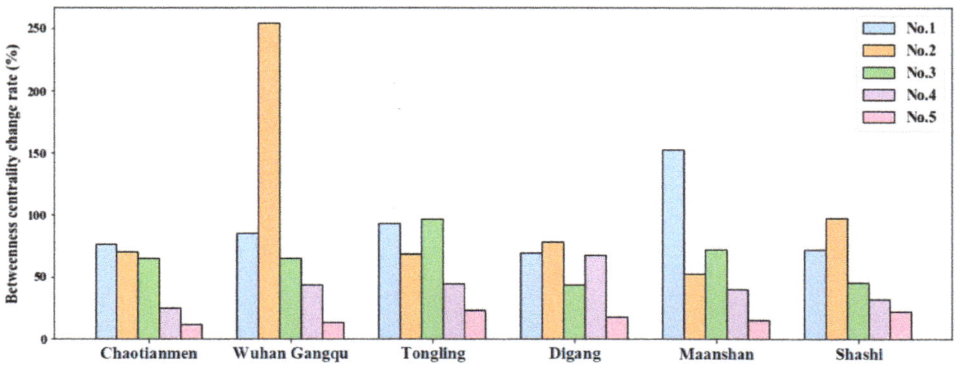

Figure 6. Impact degree of key nodes based on betweenness centrality change rate.

Figure 5 illustrates the degree of impact based on betweenness incremental values, which quantify the influence of port failures on the overall transportation network. The results show that the impact degrees of various key port failures differ significantly according to their betweenness incremental values. For instance, Chaotianmen's (CTM) failure has the greatest impact, with betweenness incremental values exceeding 20 for five ports within its influence range. As a crucial hub, Wuhan Gangqu's (WHGQ) failure also causes a substantial disruption to the network, particularly in the middle and upper reaches of the Yangtze River. This concentration of impact can be attributed to the geographical distribution constraints of these key ports, where failures at strategic locations can ripple through the entire network, severely affecting regional transport and economic activities.

In the context of the current transportation challenges, this finding is particularly relevant as it underscores the vulnerability of key hubs in critical river networks like the Yangtze. For example, the impact of Chaotianmen's (CTM) failure demonstrates a situation where a seemingly isolated incident could affect a broad section of the transport system, potentially leading to cascading failures across the region. This highlights the need for enhanced risk management strategies and targeted infrastructure improvements in such key nodes to ensure system resilience.

However, Figure 6 reveals that the changes in betweenness incremental rates differ significantly from those in betweenness incremental values. The betweenness incremental rate is a more nuanced metric, as it accounts for the load-bearing capacity of the nodes. Specifically, it reflects how much additional load a node can handle before its failure leads to widespread disruption. For a given betweenness incremental value, a higher betweenness incremental rate indicates a greater capacity required to absorb additional load. For example, following Wuhan Gangqu's (WHGQ) failure, the betweenness incremental values of Chaotianmen (CTM) and Chenglingji (CLJ) are similar, suggesting that both are similarly impacted in terms of the overall flow of goods and services. However, Chaotianmen's (CTM) betweenness incremental rate is 85%, while Yidu (YD)'s exceeds 254%. This discrepancy indicates that Yidu (YD), despite having a similar betweenness incremental value, has a much lower capacity to handle the additional traffic load caused by Wuhan Gangqu's (WHGQ) failure. Therefore, Yidu (YD) must be better prepared to mitigate the consequences of Wuhan Gangqu's (WHGQ) failure, including reinforcing its infrastructure and optimizing traffic management to prevent further fault propagation across the network.

These findings directly relate to the practical problem of ensuring robust and resilient transportation networks, particularly in regions with critical hubs like the Yangtze River. The research demonstrates the importance of not only identifying key nodes with high betweenness but also evaluating their load-bearing capacity to better allocate resources for infrastructure improvement. Specifically, high-betweenness nodes with low incremental rates, such as Yidu (YD), should be prioritized for reinforcement to avoid cascading failures in the event of neighboring node failures. This insight has important implications for disaster preparedness, infrastructure planning, and network optimization in real-world transportation systems. Moreover, these findings highlight the importance of proactive measures to protect critical nodes. In real-world maritime operations, when a critical node fails, rerouting traffic to nearby nodes may lead to their overload, causing additional failures. Therefore, identifying key nodes and understanding their influence on the network's structure allows for better decision-making in infrastructure planning and disaster response, ensuring the resilience and sustainability of transportation systems.

5. Conclusions

This study used percolation theory to assess the reliability and robustness of the IWTCN in the Yangtze River. Key vulnerabilities affecting network connectivity under different node removal scenarios were identified through an in-depth analysis of the structural characteristics of this complex network. Certain nodes, especially those with high degree and betweenness centrality, were found to play a critical role in maintaining global connectivity. The importance of protecting strategic nodes to prevent cascading network failures was emphasized. This research provides valuable insights into improving waterborne transportation systems, particularly by enhancing the resilience of critical waterway infrastructures. Simulations of targeted disruptions and random failures showed that the IWTCN in the Yangtze River has low reliability under deliberate attacks, especially when high-centrality nodes are compromised. These findings can guide future traffic management strategies, particularly in optimizing emergency response systems and mitigating potential disruptions caused by natural disasters, accidents, or malicious actions. This research provides theoretical support for emergency response while ensuring smooth waterway operations.

This study provides important decision-making support for maritime policymakers. The findings highlight the vulnerabilities of critical ports and transportation hubs, particularly those with high betweenness centrality. Policymakers should focus on these nodes' vulnerabilities and implement targeted protective measures to prevent global network disruptions caused by node failures. Additionally, as global trade evolves and climate change introduces uncertainty, policymakers can use the framework provided in this study to assess and strengthen the resilience of key maritime routes and ports, ensuring that connectivity in the transportation network remains intact during extreme weather events, port congestion, or unforeseen incidents. For port authorities and network operators, the study emphasizes the necessity of strengthening the protection of key nodes in infrastructure planning and daily operations. Ports and major transport hubs, given their central role in the transportation network, should be prioritized for infrastructure reinforcement and risk management. By implementing real-time monitoring and emergency response systems, port authorities can respond more effectively to potential failures and mitigate the economic and social impacts of transportation disruptions. The study also indicates that dynamic simulations based on percolation theory can help operators develop more flexible emergency plans, particularly when facing extreme weather or sudden transportation disruptions, enhancing their response capabilities.

The percolation theory model used in this study can also help assess the resilience of other river systems in the face of node failures. For example, river systems like the Amazon, Rhine, and Mississippi are key trade and regional logistics channels, similar to the Yangtze River. By applying similar analyses to these rivers, we can reveal their vulnerabilities during peak transportation periods or when facing natural disasters, providing valuable insights for their management and protection. The results show that maintaining key nodes in these river systems—particularly transportation hubs, ports, and river junctions—can significantly enhance network stability and prevent transportation disruptions from causing major economic impacts. This study is not limited to analyzing a single region's network but provides a framework that can be extended to global maritime networks. As a critical infrastructure supporting international trade, the connectivity of global maritime networks directly affects the global economy. The study indicates that by identifying and protecting key nodes in the global maritime network, the overall system's resilience can be improved, reducing the impact of natural disasters, accidents, or malicious actions on global shipping. To address the rapid changes in global trade, policymakers should use this study's framework to assess the vulnerabilities of major global shipping lanes and ports and formulate more forward-looking maritime policies to enhance the resilience of the maritime transportation system.

As intelligent and automated technologies are gradually implemented in waterway management, this study's results can also serve as a theoretical foundation for optimizing intelligent transportation systems. Real-time data analysis combined with network optimization allows dynamic adjustments to shipping schedules, improving transport efficiency and reducing environmental and economic losses. By identifying high-risk nodes, future intelligent shipping systems can automatically reroute or divert, ensuring the smooth operation of IWTCN even under high loads or sudden incidents.

While this study provides valuable insights into the reliability and resilience of transportation networks, there are several limitations to consider. (i) Many of the models used in this study assume a static network topology. However, transportation networks are dynamic and subject to changes over time due to factors such as seasonality, political conditions, and infrastructure changes. These dynamic elements are not fully captured in this analysis, which may affect the study's applicability to systems that experience frequent changes in traffic flow or network structure. (ii) The study primarily focuses on networks like the Yangtze River system. While the findings are valuable for this context, their applicability to other geographical regions with different network configurations, infrastructures, or socio-political contexts may be limited. Further studies should explore how the conclusions can be extended to other transportation systems, both inland and maritime. (iii) The study assumes that node failures are binary (i.e., nodes either fail or remain operational) and does not account for more complex scenarios, such as partial failures or gradual degradation of performance. More advanced failure models could offer a more realistic representation of how transportation networks operate under stress. (iv) While the study examines the impact of node failures based on static conditions, it does not fully incorporate temporal factors, such as traffic flow changes over time or the influence of seasonal disruptions. Temporal variations in traffic, economic conditions, and environmental factors are important to consider, as they can significantly influence the resilience of the network. Despite these limitations, the study provides a foundation for understanding the robustness of transportation networks and offers a framework for future research aimed at improving network resilience and disaster preparedness.

Author Contributions: Conceptualization, D.H. and Z.S.; methodology, D.H. and Z.S.; software, D.H.; validation, Z.S. and Y.W.; formal analysis, Z.S.; investigation, D.H.; resources, C.X. and D.H.; data curation, Y.W.; writing—original draft preparation, D.H.; writing—review and editing, Z.S. and C.X.; visualization, D.H.; supervision, Z.S. and C.X.; project administration, Y.W.; funding acquisition, Y.W. All authors have read and agreed to the published version of the manuscript.

Funding: This work is supported by the National Natural Science Foundation of China (NSFC) through Grant No. 52072287 and the Research Program of Sanya City through Grant No. 2022KICX36.

Institutional Review Board Statement: Not applicable.

Informed Consent Statement: Not applicable.

Data Availability Statement: Dataset available on request from the authors.

Conflicts of Interest: The authors declare no conflicts of interest.

References

1. Fu, S.; Zhang, D.; Wang, Y.; Yan, X.P.; Zio, E. Framework for quantitative resilience analysis of maritime transportation system from risk perspectives: A case study of a ship stuck in ice in Arctic waters. In Proceedings of the 26th European Safety an Reliability Conference, ESREL, Glasgow, Scotland, 25–29 September 2016; 69, p. 359.
2. Liu, J.; Bai, J.; Luo, Y. Security in IoT-Enabled Digital Twins of Maritime Transportation Systems. *IEEE Trans. Intell. Transp.* **202** *24*, 2359–2367. [CrossRef]
3. Montewka, J.; Ehlers, S.; Goerlandt, F.; Hinz, T.; Tabri, K. A framework for risk assessment for maritime transportation systems— case study for open sea collisions involving RoPax vessels. *Reliab. Eng. Syst. Saf.* **2014**, *124*, 142–157. [CrossRef]
4. Sui, Z.; Wen, Y.; Huang, Y.; Zhou, C.; Xiao, C.; Chen, H. Empirical analysis of complex network for marine traffic situation. *Ocea Eng.* **2020**, *214*, 107848. [CrossRef]
5. Wang, P.; Zhu, Y. Resilience and vulnerability analysis of maritime networks under critical disruptions. *Reliab. Eng. Syst. Sa* **2022**, *168*, 106657.
6. Ducruet, C.; Lugo, I. Structure and dynamics of transportation networks: Models, methods and applications. *J. Transp. Geog* **2013**, *30*, 77–87. [CrossRef]
7. Kaluza, P.; Kölzsch, A.; Gastner, M.T.; Blasius, B. The complex network of global cargo ship movements. *J. R. Soc. Interface* **2010**, 1093–1103. [CrossRef] [PubMed]
8. Pant, R.; Hall, J.W.; Blainey, S.P. Vulnerability assessment framework for interdependent critical infrastructures: Case-study f Great Britain's rail network. *Eur. J. Transp. Infrast.* **2015**, *15*, 35–53. [CrossRef]
9. Kim, M.; Radicchi, F. Shortest-path percolation on random networks. *Phys. Rev. Lett.* **2024**, *133*, 047402. [CrossRef] [PubMed]
10. Albert, R.; Jeong, H.; Barabási, A.L. Error and attack tolerance of complex networks. *Nature* **2000**, *406*, 378–382. [CrossRef]
11. Callaway, D.S.; Newman, M.E.J.; Strogatz, S.H.; Watts, D.J. Network robustness and fragility: Percolation on random graph *Phys. Rev. Lett.* **2000**, *85*, 5468–5471. [CrossRef] [PubMed]
12. Sui, Z.; Wen, Y.; Huang, Y.; Zhou, C.; Du, L.; Piera, M.A. Node importance evaluation in marine traffic situation complex netwo for intelligent maritime supervision. *Ocean Eng.* **2022**, *247*, 110742. [CrossRef]
13. Stamos, I. Transportation networks in the face of climate change adaptation: A review of centrality measures. *Future Transp.* **202** *3*, 878–900. [CrossRef]
14. Sohn, J. Evaluating the robustness of the South Korean maritime transport network: A percolation approach. *J. Transp. Geog* **2016**, *51*, 147–157.

15. Barabási, A.L.; Albert, R. Emergence of scaling in random networks. *Science* **1999**, *286*, 509–512. [CrossRef] [PubMed]
16. Sui, Z.; Huang, Y.; Wen, Y.; Zhou, C.; Huang, X. Marine traffic profile for enhancing situational awareness based on complex network theory. *Ocean Eng.* **2021**, *241*, 110049. [CrossRef]
17. Ding, Y.; Pan, R.; Zhang, Y.; Zhang, B. A matrix completion bootstrap method for estimating scale-free network degree distribution. *Knowl. Based Syst.* **2023**, *277*, 110803. [CrossRef]
18. Wang, P.; Ling, G.; Zhao, P.; Pan, W.; Ge, M.F. Identification of important nodes in multi-layer hypergraphs based on fuzzy gravity model and node centrality distribution characteristics. *Chaos Soliton. Fract.* **2024**, *188*, 115503. [CrossRef]
19. Newman, M.E.J. The structure and function of complex networks. *SIAM Rev.* **2003**, *45*, 167–256. [CrossRef]
20. Ma, X.; Zhou, H.; Li, Z. On the resilience of modern power systems: A complex network perspective. *Renew. Sust. Energ. Rev.* **2021**, *152*, 111646. [CrossRef]
21. Zhou, J.; Coit, D.W.; Felder, F.A.; Tsianikas, S. Combined optimization of system reliability improvement and resilience with mixed cascading failures in dependent network systems. *Reliab. Eng. Syst. Saf.* **2023**, *237*, 109376. [CrossRef]
22. Boccaletti, S.; Latora, V.; Moreno, Y.; Chavez, M.; Hwang, D.U. Complex networks: Structure and dynamics. *Phys. Rep.* **2006**, *424*, 175–308. [CrossRef]
23. Duan, J.; Li, D.; Huang, H.J. Reliability of the traffic network against cascading failures with individuals acting independently or collectively. *Transport. Res. C-Emer.* **2023**, *147*, 104017. [CrossRef]
24. Barrat, A.; Barthelemy, M.; Pastor-Satorras, R.; Vespignani, A. The architecture of complex weighted networks. *Proc. Natl. Acad. Sci. USA* **2004**, *101*, 3747–3752. [CrossRef]
25. Ducruet, C. Network diversity and maritime flows. *J. Transp. Geogr.* **2013**, *30*, 77–88. [CrossRef]
26. Holme, P.; Saramäki, J. Temporal networks. *Phys. Rep.* **2012**, *519*, 97–125. [CrossRef]
27. Bell, M.G.H. A game theory approach to measuring the performance reliability of transport networks. *Transport. Res. B–Meth.* **2000**, *34*, 533–545. [CrossRef]
28. Sun, G. Robustness analysis of an urban public traffic network based on a multi-subnet composite complex network model. *Entropy* **2023**, *25*, 1377. [CrossRef] [PubMed]
29. Cohen, R.; Erez, K.; Ben-Avraham, D.; Havlin, S. Resilience of the internet to random breakdowns. *Phys. Rev. Lett.* **2000**, *85*, 4626–4629. [CrossRef]
30. Albert, R.; Barabási, A.L. Statistical mechanics of complex networks. *Rev. Mod. Phys.* **2002**, *74*, 47–97. [CrossRef]
31. Dorogovtsev, S.N.; Mendes, J.F.F. Critical phenomena in complex networks. *Rev. Mod. Phys.* **2008**, *80*, 1275–1335. [CrossRef]
32. Newman, M.E.J. Spread of epidemic disease on networks. *Phys. Rev. E* **2002**, *66*, 016128. [CrossRef] [PubMed]
33. Pastor-Satorras, R.; Vespignani, A. Epidemic dynamics in finite size scale-free networks. *Phys. Rev. E* **2001**, *65*, 036104. [CrossRef]
34. Nassar, R.F.; Ghisolfi, V.; Annema, J.A.; van Binsbergen, A.; Tavasszy, L.A. A system dynamics model for analyzing modal shift policies towards decarbonization in freight transportation. *Res. Transp. Bus. Manag.* **2023**, *48*, 100966. [CrossRef]
35. Tang, L.; Han, Y.; Zalhaf, A.S.; Zhou, S.; Yang, P.; Wang, C.; Huang, T. Resilience enhancement of active distribution networks under extreme disaster scenarios: A comprehensive overview of fault location strategies. *Renew. Sust. Energ. Rev.* **2024**, *189*, 113898. [CrossRef]
36. Wandelt, S.; Xu, Y.; Sun, X. Measuring node importance in air transportation systems: On the quality of complex network estimations. *Reliab. Eng. Syst. Saf.* **2023**, *240*, 109596. [CrossRef]
37. Hnatič, M.; Honkonen, J.; Lučivjanský, T.; Mižišin, L. Universality Classes of Percolation Processes: Renormalization Group Approach. *Symmetry* **2023**, *15*, 1696. [CrossRef]
38. Tanaka, F. Comparative Study on the Models of Thermoreversible Gelation. *Int. J. Mol. Sci.* **2022**, *23*, 10325. [CrossRef] [PubMed]
39. Hamedmoghadam, H.; Zheng, N.; Li, D.; Vu, H.L. Percolation-based dynamic perimeter control for mitigating congestion propagation in urban road networks. *Transport. Res. C-Emer.* **2022**, *145*, 103922. [CrossRef]
40. Bai, X.; Ma, Z.; Zhou, Y. Data-driven static and dynamic resilience assessment of the global liner shipping network. *Transpor. Res. E–Log.* **2023**, *170*, 103016. [CrossRef]

Journal of
Marine Science
and Engineering

MDPI

Article

Target Ship Recognition and Tracking with Data Fusion Based on Bi-YOLO and OC-SORT Algorithms for Enhancing Ship Navigation Assistance

Shuai Chen, Miao Gao *, Peiru Shi, Xi Zeng and Anmin Zhang

School of Marine Science and Technology, Tianjin University, Tianjin 300072, China; 2022227022@tju.edu.cn (S.C.)
* Correspondence: gaomiao@tju.edu.cn

Abstract: With the ever-increasing volume of maritime traffic, the risks of ship navigation are becoming more significant, making the use of advanced multi-source perception strategies and AI technologies indispensable for obtaining information about ship navigation status. In this paper, first, the ship tracking system was optimized using the Bi-YOLO network based on the C2f_BiFormer module and the OC-SORT algorithms. Second, to extract the visual trajectory of the target ship without a reference object, an absolute position estimation method based on binocular stereo vision attitude information was proposed. Then, a perception data fusion framework based on ship spatio-temporal trajectory features (ST-TF) was proposed to match GPS-based ship information with corresponding visual target information. Finally, AR technology was integrated to fuse multi-source perceptual information into the real-world navigation view. Experimental results demonstrate that the proposed method achieves a mAP0.5:0.95 of 79.6% under challenging scenarios such as low resolution, noise interference, and low-light conditions. Moreover, in the presence of the nonlinear motion of the own ship, the average relative position error of target ship visual measurements is maintained below 8%, achieving accurate absolute position estimation without reference objects. Compared to existing navigation assistance, the AR-based navigation assistance system, which utilizes ship ST-TF-based perception data fusion mechanism, enhances ship traffic situational awareness and provides reliable decision-making support to further ensure the safety of ship navigation.

Keywords: data fusion; marine autonomous surface ships; ship traffic safety; ship recognition and tracking; machine vision; AR navigation assistance

1. Introduction

With the rapid development of the shipping industry, the increasing number of ships and the complexity of maritime traffic situations have highlighted the issue of navigation safety. In 2021, the European Maritime Safety Agency published the "Annual Overview of Marine Casualties and Incidents [1]", which reported 15,481 maritime incidents between 2014 and 2020. The data indicates that approximately 53.5% of the investigated incidents were caused by improper human manipulation. In this context, Maritime Autonomous Surface Ships (MASSs) have emerged as the times require, utilizing advanced technologies such as the Internet of Things, big data, artificial intelligence, etc., to swiftly respond to maritime industry needs with little to no human intervention. The Maritime Safety Committee's (MSC) 100th session [2] formally defines MASSs from a legislative perspective as ships that can operate autonomously to varying degrees without human interaction, offering advantages such as low costs, low risks, and easy maintenance, thus garnering widespread attention from scholars around the world [3]. To promote the development of MASS technology, Rolls-Royce has proposed the vision of "smart ships", emphasizing the application of AR and data fusion technologies, which are believed to bring revolutionary progress to ship navigation systems. In line with this trend, AR technology has gradually become a key means to enhance the safety and operational efficiency of ships. Several companies and research institutions have made significant progress in integrating AR technology with the maritime sector. Specifically, the ClearCruise AR yacht navigation system, developed by the UK-based Raymarine company, captures the forward view in real time using high-definition cameras. It combines onboard sensor data and utilizes AR technology to overlay virtual information, providing decision support to the operator [4]. The HiNAS 2.0 navigation system, developed by the South Korean company Avikus, integrates AR technology. It has been successfully applied to the transoceanic navigation of the LNG ship "Prism Courage", significantly improving the safety and operational efficiency of autonomous ship navigation [5]. Although research on AR-assisted navigation systems in the maritime field is still in its early stages, its potential has been widely recognized. Researchers Laera et al. [6], in their study of 11 AR maritime solutions, pointed out that AR technology holds significant research value in maritime applications and is expected to further optimize ship navigation, situational awareness, and decision support functions, thereby having a profound impact on the safety and efficiency of the shipping industry.

Currently, mainstream ship navigation assistance systems mainly focus on visual scenarios. These systems fuse real-time perceived environmental information with heterogeneous data, such as the Automatic Identification System (AIS) [7,8], and present key navigation information in a visual format. However, these systems have shortcomings in terms of insufficient perception means, insufficient accuracy, real-time performance, single mutual communication information, and high demands on the operator's ability to interpret and understand the information, which make it difficult to meet the requirements of efficient navigation assistance in complex waterways. Therefore, many scholars have actively pursued strategies for integrating multiple perception methods, such as radar, sonar, Synthetic Aperture Radar (SAR), remote sensing, cameras, etc. [9–12], in order to comprehensively and accurately acquire information about the navigation environment. However, an effective and intelligent data fusion mechanism has not yet been proposed in the existing research, and at the same time, the method of expressing and understanding the sensing information is more demanding for the crew. Specifically, for the perception of ship target positions, existing research predominantly focuses on methods utilizing shore-based fixed-view cameras to project AIS position coordinates onto image coordinates for matching and fusion. However, this approach fails to address the issue of matching and fusion for ships with a deactivated AIS, as their specific position coordinates cannot be obtained [13]. Furthermore, current multi-source perception data fusion methods primarily concentrate on the relationship between target image positions and AIS positions at a single moment [14], neglecting the long-term trajectory characteristics of ships. Consequently, in busy waters with high ship density or when AIS signals are subject to interference, ensuring high-quality association and fusion of perception data becomes challenging. Additionally, the expression and interpretation methods of perceived information in existing navigation assistance systems impose high cognitive demands on crew members [15], potentially leading to decision-making errors. To address these challenges, in this study, a perception data fusion framework based on ship spatio-temporal trajectory features (ST-TF) was proposed. This framework was designed for application in ship AR navigation assistance systems, offering a more reliable and efficient solution for navigation and surveillance in complex waterways.

The main contributions of this paper are summarized as follows:

- Fusion Location Ship (FLShip) dataset: The FLShip dataset has been constructed based on data collected from six self-developed MASSs, which includes stereo and monocular image sequences, as well as high-frequency attitude and GPS data from the MASSs. A variety of navigational scenarios and environmental conditions are encompassed by the dataset, providing essential support for ship target detection, multi-source information fusion, and autonomous navigation research.
- Optimization of ship tracking system: To improve the detection performance of small targets while reducing the model's parameter count, a Bi-YOLO network based on BiFomer has been proposed, achieving more efficient and accurate ship identification. In response to complex navigational environments, the more powerful OC-SORT algorithm has been incorporated to ensure stable tracking of targets. The superiority of this method has been validated through comparative experiments with several advanced detection and tracking algorithms.
- Ship target absolute position estimation: In order to realize the position estimation of the target ship in the state of no reference, a visual localization model based on binocular imaging was constructed. By fusing the attitude information from a binocular camera, absolute position estimation of maritime targets at the moving end of a ship is successfully realized.
- Perception data fusion based on ship ST-TF: To effectively integrate information from multiple perception sources, a novel perception data fusion method based on ship ST-TF was proposed. This approach employs a dynamic time warping (DTW) algorithm to align multi-source perception data, achieving spatio-temporal synchronization between different sensory inputs, while aiming to ensure the accuracy and reliability of the fused perception information.

The rest of the paper is organized as follows. Section 2 begins with a review of state-of-the-art research on ship perception methods, visual target detection and tracking, and multi-sensor data fusion. In Section 3, the proposed perception data fusion framework based on ship ST-TF is described in detail. Then, in Section 4, field experiments are conducted to evaluate and validate the system performance to demonstrate the effectiveness of our framework. Finally, Section 5 summarizes the main contributions of this paper and discusses future perspectives. The organization of the sections is shown in Figure 1.

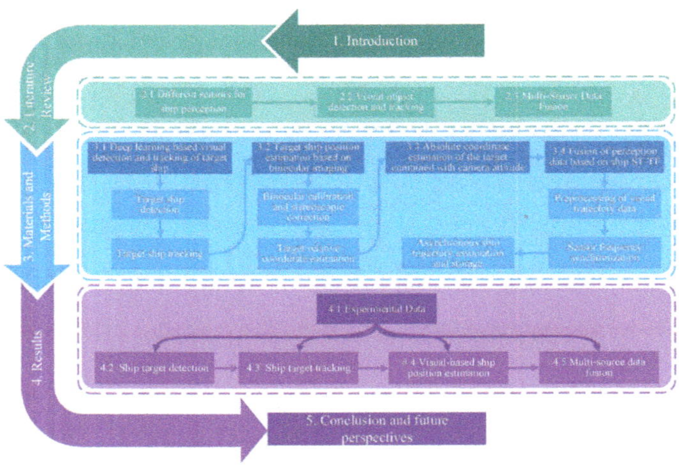

Figure 1. Organization diagram of the sections of this paper.

2. Literature Review

This section focuses on recent research related to our work, namely ship perception methods, visual target detection and tracking, and multi-sensor data fusion.

2.1. Different Sensors for Ship Perception

Currently, ship perception methods are mainly divided into two categories: active perception and passive perception. Active perception methods include mariner radar, sonar, SAR, etc., while passive perception methods include optical remote sensing, cameras, AISs, etc.

Various maritime perception methods have their own advantages and limitations. Mariner radar is virtually unaffected by visibility, lighting, and noise but it is expensive, has blind spots, and may experience reduced detection accuracy in the presence of sea clutter. In contrast, sonar performs well in detecting, positioning, and tracking underwater targets [16]. However, sonar images often suffer from poor quality, low contrast, and low resolution, requiring additional image enhancement processing for target identification and localization. Simultaneously, SAR systems have unique advantages in ship detection [17]. However, when dealing with both stationary and moving targets, SAR systems may exhibit image distortion and blurring [18], which makes the extraction of target behavior information more complicated. Optical remote sensing technology has garnered significant attention in recent years, especially in target identification and situational awareness [19]. However, remote sensing images are influenced by factors such as noise, seasonal climate, and light intensity, making them unable to work reliably in all weather conditions. In comparison to other sensors, cameras, as passive sensors similar to the human eye, operate by capturing information about the color, contours, and textures of objects. Cameras are widely used in areas such as driverless and target recognition [20]. Additionally, cameras can be used to measure the distance to the target and determine the direction and position of the target. Due to their advantages of high-precision measurement and not revealing the position of the detection system, cameras have demonstrated high application value in many fields [21]. AIS data contains a wealth of information to ensure the safety of maritime navigation. It is widely used in ship behavior analysis, route planning, and collision avoidance decision-making research [22,23].

Table 1 presents the characteristics of the primary ship perception methods. From this, we can conclude that relying solely on a single sensor has significant limitations. It fails to provide sufficient accuracy and completeness in capturing ship navigation dynamic data. In contrast, a multi-source data fusion framework leverages the strengths of multiple sensors, enabling a more comprehensive and precise perception of the navigation environment. This approach is particularly well suited for diverse and complex application scenarios.

Table 1. Comparison of different sensor perception methods.

Perception Methods			Target Recognitior Rate	Spatial Resolu-tion	Perception Range	Robustness	Real-Time Perfor-mance	Data Fusion Compati-bility	Power Con-sumption	Cost
ACTIVE	Radar	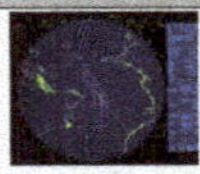	High	Medium	Large	High	High	Medium	Medium	High
	Sonar		Medium	Medium	Medium	Medium	Medium	Medium	Medium	Low
	SAR		Medium	Low	Medium	High	High	High	Low	Medium
	Remote Sensing		Medium	Medium	Medium	Medium	High	High	Low	Medium
PASSIVE	Camera		High	High	Small	Low	Low	Low	High	High
	AIS	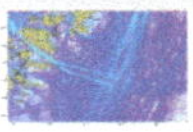	High	Low	Large	High	Low	Low	Medium	High

2.2. Visual Object Detection and Tracking

With the continuous advancement of computer vision technology, visual detection and tracking methods based on deep learning have been widely applied in the field of ship detection and tracking, owing to their outstanding performance. The use of neural networks as the basis of algorithms has become a mainstream trend for classification and detection tasks, and such algorithms are divided into two main routes. The first comprises two-stage algorithms based on region recommendation, including R-CNN [24], Fast R-CNN [25], and Faster R-CNN [26]. This route essentially inherits the idea of traditional detection algorithms, where regions that may contain targets are first screened, followed by feature extraction and classification. The second route comprises end-to-end one-stage algorithms, such as the YOLO series [27–30] and SSD [31]. These algorithms directly transform the bounding box location problem into a regression problem, thus reducing computational complexity and enabling the network to detect targets with a lightweight architecture. Specifically, D. Zhang et al. used the Mask R-CNN algorithm and Faster R-CNN algorithm, respectively, to construct ship target feature extraction and a recognition model, and compared the accuracy and performance of these two algorithms in target detection and classification by classifying warships and civilian ships [32]. Aiming at the problem of traditional shipboard radar having difficulty performing the task of detecting near-small ships, Chen, Z et al. proposed a small-ship detection method based on an improved GAN and CNN, and the experimental results show that their method significantly improved the detection effect of small ships [33]. To address the challenges of missed detection and misidentification in ship target detection within SAR images under complex scenes, Chen, Z. et al. proposed a CSD-YOLO model based on YOLOv7. This model was validated on the SSDD and HRSID datasets, demonstrating significant improvements over Faster R-CNN, FCOS, YOLOv3, YOLOv5s, and YOLOv7 algorithms, with marked enhancements in multi-scale ship target feature extraction [34]. To address the challenges of low-visibility weather scenarios, Liu et al. developed an enhanced Convolutional Neural Network (CNN) to improve ship detection under different weather conditions, and experimental results under different monitoring conditions showed that their method outperforms SSD, Faster R-CNN, YOLOv2, and YOLOv3 in terms of detection accuracy [35].

In recent years, scholars have explored the application of visual detection and tracking technology for information mining in maritime videos. Zheng et al. applied binocular stereo vision technology to the recognition and estimation of the depth of inland waterway ships and used the MobileNetV1 network as the feature extraction module of the YOLOv4 model for ship detection, greatly reducing the amount of computation while ensuring accuracy. In addition, a sub-pixel-level feature point detection and matching algorithm was used for depth estimation, which enriched the ship's perception of the navigation environment [36]. Zhou et al. proposed a deep learning-based framework for extracting ship speeds in haze environments, used the YOLOv5 detector and Deep SORT tracker to detect and track the ship, and estimated the ship speed by calculating the mapping relationship between image space and real space, which provided important value for guaranteeing the safety of ship navigation [37].

2.3. Multi-Sensor Data Fusion

To obtain more accurate and consistent ship motion perception data, multi-source data fusion methods have become a focus of attention in the academic community [38,39]. Maritime radars, AISs, and cameras are the most widely used sensors in maritime transportation systems, each possessing distinct advantages and limitations. Therefore, effectively integrating data from these sensors to enhance ship detection and tracking accuracy has become a key research focus.

In previous studies, scholars have made a lot of effort in the fusion of maritime radars, AISs, and video surveillance cameras. For example, to improve the accuracy of AIS visual target association, Ding et al. proposed a three-step calibration method that projects image coordinates onto geographic coordinates [14]. By employing the Hungarian algorithm, they identified the optimal matches, effectively integrating AIS data with ship trajectories. Gülsoylu et al. introduced an image–AIS data fusion approach for fixed and periodically panning cameras [40]. This method utilizes the YOLOv5 model for ship detection, applies homography transformation for coordinate conversion, and assigns AIS messages to the nearest bounding box in the image using k-dimensional tree-based nearest neighbor search. The accuracy of the fusion framework was further validated. To improve ship tracking efficiency, Chen et al. integrated the AIS with maritime video surveillance. They adjusted the camera's attitude and focus based on AIS-reported positions to achieve stable tracking of specific ships [41]. Although this method performs well in single-target scenarios, it faces significant limitations in multi-ship scenarios and cannot achieve efficient multi-target tracking. Additionally, maritime radar images often contain false echoes, and AIS data transmission may experience loss, leading to uncertainties in estimating ship speed and heading. To address this issue, Xu et al. proposed a method that integrates radar sequence images with AIS data for estimating ship speed and heading [42]. This method was applied in the Yangtze River Basin, effectively reducing the uncertainty in ship speed and heading estimation. To improve waterway traffic monitoring in inland waterways, Lu et al. proposed a framework for ship identification through the fusion of visual detection and AIS data [43]. This method estimates the distance from the camera and the azimuth relative to the camera of the identified ship target based on the bounding box size in the shore-based monocular camera image and the ship length in the AIS data. However, this approach is only applicable for the distance estimation of ships with a side-facing orientation to the camera. Moreover, due to the effects of marine background, occlusion, and weather conditions, the bounding box size often varies, further impacting the accuracy of the estimation. For the fusion of ship trajectories, Qu et al.

proposed a vision-based framework for fusing ship and AIS trajectories [13] that uses the YOLOX detector and optimized Deep SORT tracker to extract ship image trajectories, preprocesses AIS data, and projects AIS coordinates to the image coordinate system. The Hungarian algorithm then associates AIS and visual data for intelligent maritime traffic monitoring in inland waterways. However, this method does not fully consider the limited computing resources of onboard devices, and the use of original YOLOX may result in slower inference speed. Zhang et al. proposed a method for matching AIS and video data by combining region division and an improved Kalman filter [44]. The method utilizes an enhanced LSTM network for accurate trajectory prediction of AIS data and applies a single-stage object detection model to analyze video data collected from buoys. This approach enables fast and efficient data fusion, significantly improving the accuracy and flexibility of channel detection.

The aforementioned studies indicate that, despite significant research focused on fusing multiple data sources for ship target perception, two unresolved issues remain. First, existing studies often fail to fully consider the limitations of onboard computational resources, leading to bottlenecks in inference speed, which affect system real-time performance and efficiency. Second, most research focuses on fusion perception methods for shore-based or fixed-angle cameras, while less attention is given to the challenges posed by onboard cameras in real-world navigation environments, such as the effects of fog interference and AIS data instability. Therefore, from the perspective of practical ship applications, optimizing the inference speed of perception models and the data fusion mechanism to improve the accuracy and usability of multi-source perception methods is an urgent problem that needs to be addressed.

3. Materials and Methods

This section provides a detailed description of the perceptual data fusion framework based on ship ST-TF, as shown in Figure 2. The framework includes ship detection and tracking, ship trajectory extraction based on binocular vision, and multi-source spatio-temporal data fusion. For the video data captured by the shipboard camera, the Bi-YOLO network is first used for ship target detection, and to address the ship occlusion problem in complex navigation environments, the more powerful OC-SORT algorithm is introduced to achieve stable target tracking. In the visual trajectory extraction stage, a visual localization model is constructed based on the principle of binocular imaging. This model is then integrated with the attitude information of the camera, enabling the shipborne terminal to perform absolute position estimation of ship targets. Subsequently, in the multi-source spatio-temporal data fusion, the visual trajectory is pre-processed to suppress the measurement noise, and then the DTW algorithm is used to match the visual trajectory with the GPS trajectory and align the spatio-temporal data points. After the trajectory matching, the data storage area is redesigned to jointly store the navigation information of the host ship and the target ship, thus improving the efficiency of the trajectory association. Finally, based on the results of multi-source perception data fusion, a ship AR navigation assistance system is developed, which improves the overall navigation experience of ship driving and enhances safety in the maritime field.

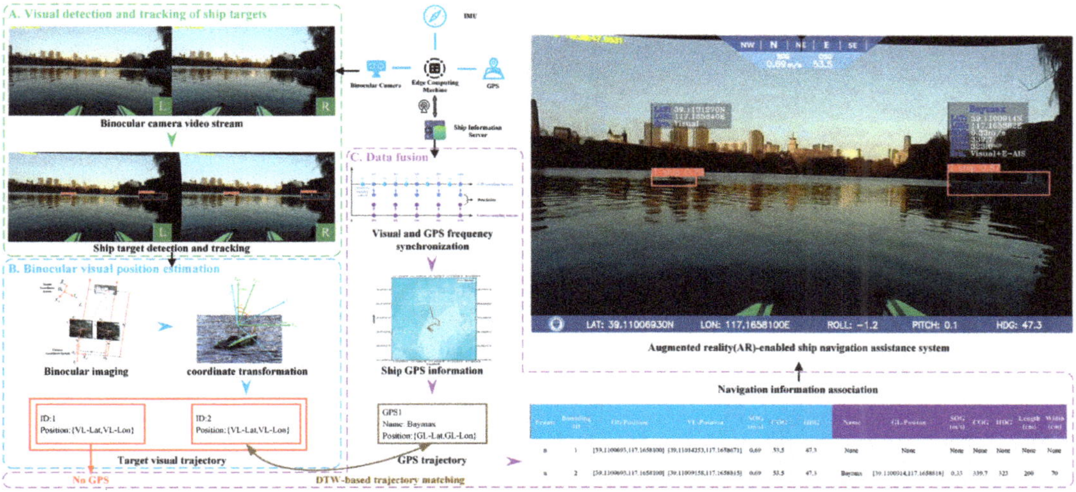

Figure 2. A perception data fusion framework based on ship ST-TF for ship AR navigation assistance.

3.1. Deep Learning-Based Visual Detection and Tracking of Target Ship

3.1.1. Target Ship Detection

YOLO (You Only Look Once) is a single-stage deep learning object detection algorithm. It has revolutionized real-time object detection by combining region proposals and classification into a unified neural network, significantly reducing computation time. Its unique design has made it highly popular in the deep learning community, offering superior accuracy and faster detection speeds compared to other object detection algorithms. The strength of YOLO is that it is not only limited to the original task, that is, the detection of 80 categories defined by the MS-COCO dataset, but also widely used in various detection fields, becoming the backbone model or benchmark for many tasks. YOLO11, the latest iteration of this series [45], represents the state-of-the-art in object detection technology, providing a solid and cutting-edge technical foundation for our research. In this study, the accuracy of ship target identification plays a crucial role in the final data fusion results. However, limited computational resources on the shipborne edge devices constrain this process. Furthermore, existing ship target detection models primarily focus on medium- to large-sized targets, and their performance for small targets is suboptimal. This makes them unsuitable for scenarios in open waters or nighttime navigation, where small, inconspicuous targets may be present. To enhance the detection of small targets while reducing the model's parameter count, a Bi-YOLO network has been proposed. This network incorporates the C2f_BiFormer module, which combines convolutional operations with the BiFormer block [46] into the backbone layer of YOLOv11, achieving more efficient and accurate ship identification. The structure of the Bi-YOLO network is shown in Figure 3.

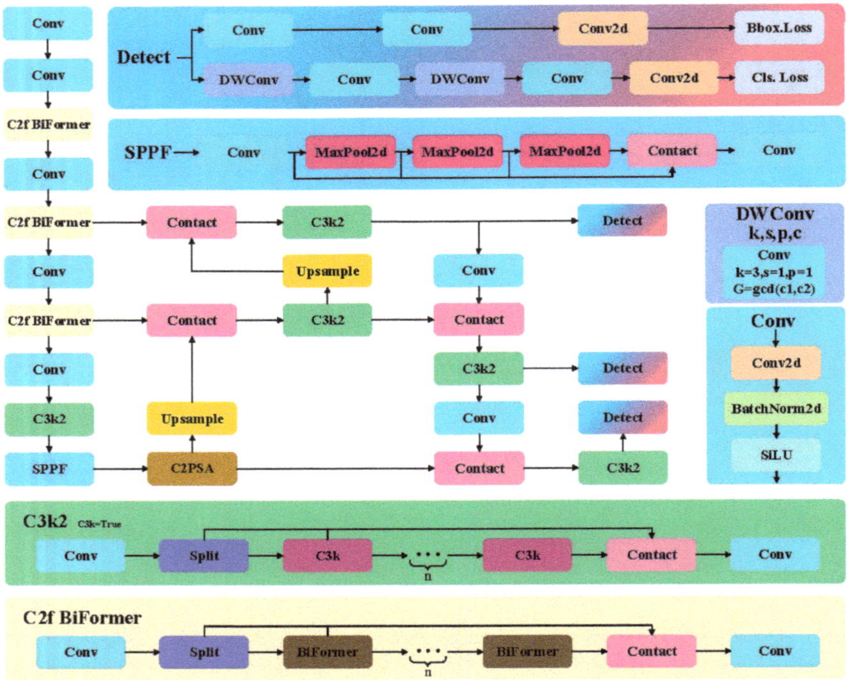

Figure 3. The structure of the Bi-YOLO network.

In YOLO11 network, the backbone utilizes Conv and C3k2 modules for downsampling, this can lead to the loss of contextual features to some extent, thereby reducing the resolution of the feature maps and losing important contextual information. The introduction of the C2f_BiFormer module helps mitigate the loss of small target information during downsampling, enabling the model to focus more on task-relevant information when processing inputs. This module employs a dual-level routing attention strategy to enhance feature representation through two key mechanisms: routing between regions via a directed graph, which helps the model focus on specific areas of the image; and token-to-token attention, which further refines the model's attention to these regions.

BiFormer block: The overall architecture of the BiFormer block is shown in Figure 4a. The BiFormer block is a transformer-based vision network architecture composed of several submodules, including deep convolution, layer normalization, Bi-Level Routing Attention (BRA), and MLP. The plus sign indicates the merging of two feature vectors. The submodules are executed sequentially to optimize the input features within each BiFormer block. The process begins with a 3×3 depthwise convolution, which slightly encodes positional information. Then, the BRA module is combined with a two-layer MLP with an expansion rate of e, further optimizing the features by capturing and modeling relationships across positions.

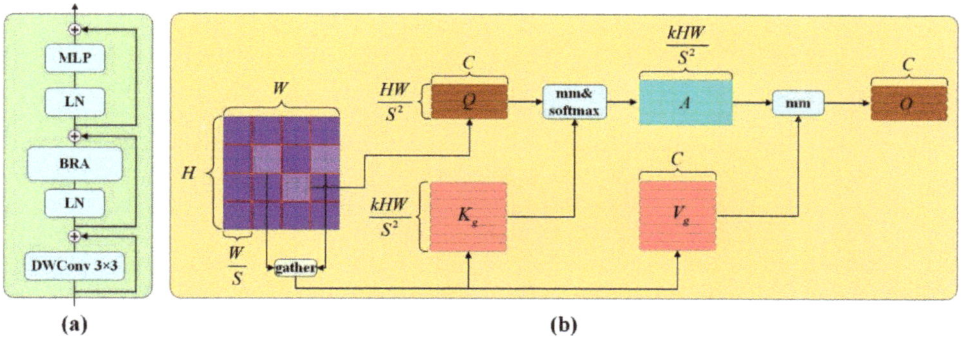

Figure 4. (**a**) Details of a BiFormer block; (**b**) Structure of the BRA.

BRA module: The operating principle of the BRA module is shown in Figure 4b. BRA is an advanced attention mechanism that employs a bi-level routing strategy to achieve dynamic, query-aware sparsity. The main steps of BRA include the following:

a. Region partition and input projection: Given a 2D input feature map $X \in \mathbb{R}^{H \times W \times C}$, where H is the height, W is the width, and C is the number of channels. We divide it into S×S nonoverlapping regions, such that each region contains $\frac{HW}{S^2}$ feature vectors. This is achieved by reshaping X into $X_r \in \mathbb{R}^{S^2 \times \frac{HW}{S^2} \times C}$. We then derive the query Q, key K, and value tensor $V \in \mathbb{R}^{S^2 \times \frac{HW}{S^2} \times C}$, using linear projections.

$$X_r \in reshape(X, S^2, \frac{HW}{S^2}, C) \quad (1)$$

$$Q = X_r W_q, K = X_r W_k, V = X_r W_v \quad (2)$$

where W_q, W_k, and W_v represent the learnable weight matrices.

b. Region-to-region routing with a directed graph: We then find the attending relationship by constructing a directed graph. Specifically, we first compute region-level queries and keys by applying an average to Q and K within each region, resulting in Q_r and $K_r \in \mathbb{R}^{S^2 \times C}$. Subsequently, we derive the adjacency matrix $A_r \in \mathbb{R}^{S^2 \times S^2}$ for the region-to-region affinity map by performing matrix multiplication between Q_r and the transposed K_r:

$$Q_r = mean(Q, 1), K_r = mean(K, 1) \quad (3)$$

$$A_r = Q_r K_r^T \quad (4)$$

The values in the adjacent matrix, A_r, quantify the semantic relationships between pairs of regions. The core step that we perform next is to prune the affinity graph by keeping only top-k connections for each region. To achieve this, we construct a routing index matrix, $I_r \in \mathbb{N}^{S^2 \times k}$, using a row-wise top-$k$ selection operation:

$$I_r = topIndex(A_r) \quad (5)$$

c. Token-to-token attention: Finally, token-to-token attention is performed within the specified regions. Each query token selectively attends to the query and context pairs corresponding to the defined routing areas. The attention function is then applied to these refined feature pairs to generate the final output. This process is expressed as follows:

$$K_g = \text{gather}(K, I_r), V_g = \text{gather}(V, I_r) \quad (6)$$

$$O = Atttention(Q, K_g, V_g) + LCE(V) \tag{7}$$

In this, K_g, V_g are the gathered key and value tensor, $Attention(\cdot)$ represents the attention function, and $LCE(\cdot)$ denotes the term that enhances local context, parameterized through deep convolution. The BiFormer block significantly reduces computational complexity by adopting a BRA strategy. Under a proper region partition factor S, its complexity is $O(S^2 \cdot k \cdot d)$. In contrast, the traditional global attention mechanism has a complexity of $O((HW)^2)$, while the axial attention mechanism has a complexity of $O((HW)^{\frac{3}{2}})$. This sparse computation strategy not only improves computational efficiency but also effectively reduces interference from irrelevant regions, thereby enhancing the robustness and accuracy of the model in handling small target detection tasks on the water surface.

3.1.2. Target Ship Tracking

Traditional motion-based tracking algorithms often use Kalman filters to predict the motion of the target. However, when the target exhibits nonlinear motion or encounters occlusion, long-term linear estimates may become highly inaccurate, leading to tracking failures. To address this problem, an Observation-Centric SORT (OC-SORT) [47] is used as the main tracking algorithm in this paper. Ship targets are tracked in real-time independently within the left and right images.

OC-SORT introduces three modules, namely Observation-Centric Online Smoothing (OOS), Observation-Centric Momentum (OCM), and Observation-Centric Recovery (OCR) to cope with the errors caused by target occlusion and nonlinear motion. Among them, Observation-Centric Re-Update (ORU) is proposed to reduce the cumulative error when an object is untracked and re-associated after a certain period of time, e.g., when the last observation before untracking is denoted as z_{t_1}, the observation that triggered the re-association is denoted as z_{t_2}, and the virtual trajectory $T_{virtual}$ is denoted as

$$\hat{z} = T_{virtual}(z_{t_1}, z_{t_2}, t), t_1 < t < t_2 \tag{8}$$

When the lost trajectory is re-associated along the virtual trajectory, OOS alternates between the prediction and update stages, backchecking the parameters of the Kalman filter back and forth, to prevent the accumulation of errors due to occlusion or missed detections. When constructing the association cost matrix, most multi-object tracking methods typically rely on two key points: motion features and appearance features. However, OC-SORT introduces OCM into the association cost during the tracking process, by incorporating the directional consistency of the trajectories into the association cost matrix. The association cost matrix can be represented as follows:

$$C(\hat{X}, Z) = C_{\text{IoU}}(\hat{X}, Z) + \lambda C_v(\mathcal{Z}, Z) \tag{9}$$

where $(\hat{X}, Z)$ is the set of estimated states and observations for the tracked object, λ is the weight factor, $\mathcal{Z}$ includes the observed trajectories of all existing tracks, C_{IoU} calculates the Intersection over Union (IOU), and C_v calculates the consistency of the orientation of the trajectory and the orientation of the historical and new observations of the trajectory.

Finally, after completing the association stage based on the predictions from the Kalman filter, OC-SORT applies OCR techniques to attempt to correlate the observations of mismatched trajectories with mismatched observations. This strategy helps reduce the generation of new trajectories, thereby enhancing the overall accuracy of multi-object tracking.

3.2. Target Ship Position Estimation Based on Binocular Imaging

3.2.1. Binocular Calibration and Stereoscopic Correction

Camera calibration is a prerequisite for stereo vision, where the imaging model typically assumes that the camera has no distortion under ideal conditions and describes the imaging process using a linear model. However, in practical applications, lens errors can cause distortion, affecting the imaging position of the images. Perspective, radial, and tangential distortion are the main types of distortion, with radial and tangential distortion having a significant impact on imaging. It has been shown that camera calibration [48] is an effective way to solve the camera lens distortion problem. Through the calibration process, we can obtain the parameters of the camera such as the distortion coefficients, rotation matrix, and translation vectors, which can be used as important input data for the next stereo correction. As the camera will be affected by the optical lens and its own process, the imaging process is prone to distortion, resulting in the left and right images not achieving coplanar and line alignment and requiring stereoscopic correction through left and right camera image plane reprojection, so that it is coplanar and aligned, so as to improve the accuracy of stereoscopic vision. Figure 5 shows a comparison of the effects before and after calibration and stereo rectification of our onboard stereo camera.

Figure 5. (**a**) to (**b**) illustrate the Driving-Leaves binocular camera before and after calibration and stereo rectification, and (**c**) to (**d**) illustrate the Baymax binocular camera before and after calibration and stereo rectification.

3.2.2. Target Relative Coordinate Estimation Based on Binocular Imaging

Under ideal conditions, the camera imaging model is assumed to be a central projection linear model. Based on the pinhole imaging model, visual target relative positioning can be achieved. In this process, we need to consider the world coordinate system $O_W - X_w Y_w Z_w$ (which represents the reference coordinate system for the camera and object position), the camera coordinate system $O_C - X_C Y_C Z_C$ (with the camera optical center as the origin and the optical axis direction as the Z-axis), the image coordinate system $o_i - x_i y_i$ (corresponding to the camera coordinate system with the origin at the intersection of the image plane and the optical axis of the camera), and the pixel coordinate system $o_P - u_i v_i$ (a two-dimensional plane with the origin at the top-left corner of the first pixel). These four coordinate systems are interrelated, forming the transformation process from the world coordinate system to the pixel coordinate system, providing the foundation for achieving visual target localization. The relationships among the four coordinate systems and the binocular imaging process are illustrated in Figure 6.

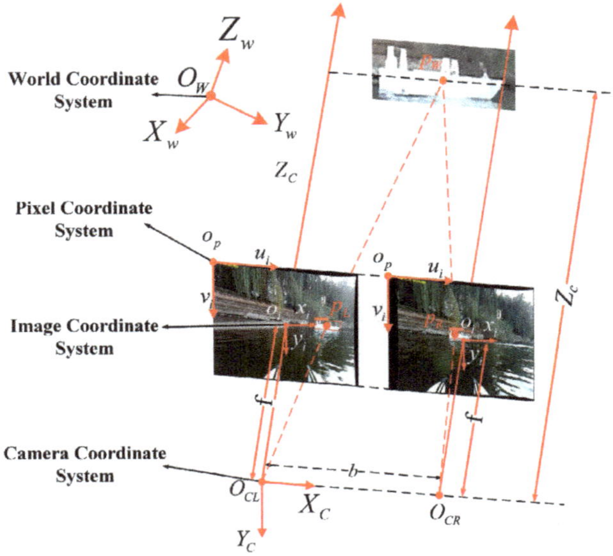

Figure 6. Conceptual diagram of the binocular imaging process.

According to the pinhole imaging principle, the transformation relationship between the pixel coordinate system and the world coordinate system is as follows:

$$Z_c \begin{bmatrix} u \\ v \\ 1 \end{bmatrix} = \begin{bmatrix} f_x & 0 & c_x \\ 0 & f_y & c_y \\ 0 & 0 & 1 \end{bmatrix} \begin{bmatrix} R & T \end{bmatrix} \begin{bmatrix} X_w \\ Y_w \\ Z_w \\ 1 \end{bmatrix} \tag{10}$$

where $\begin{bmatrix} f_x & 0 & c_x \\ 0 & f_y & c_y \\ 0 & 0 & 1 \end{bmatrix}$ is the intrinsic parameter matrix of the camera, which is obtained from the camera calibration above. R and T are the rotation matrix and translation vector, respectively.

Based on the binocular imaging principle (Figure 6) and the similarity of triangle proportions, we can derive the following:

$$Z_c = \frac{fb}{X_L - X_R} = \frac{fb}{(u_L - u_R)d_x} = \frac{bf_x}{u_L - u_R} \tag{11}$$

Here, X_L and X_R represent the physical dimensions corresponding to the target's u_L and u_R in the pixel coordinate system. d_x denotes the physical size of each pixel on the horizontal axis. b is the baseline of the binocular camera system.

Assume that the origin of the world coordinate system is the optical center of the left-eye camera. To transform from the camera coordinate system to the world coordinate system, a counterclockwise rotation around the X_c axis of the camera coordinate system by an angle $\alpha = 90°$ (viewed from the positive direction of the X_c axis towards the negative direction, rotating counterclockwise) is required. The transformation of the coordinate system can be expressed as follows:

$$Z_c \begin{bmatrix} u \\ v \\ 1 \end{bmatrix} = \begin{bmatrix} f_x & 0 & c_x \\ 0 & f_y & c_y \\ 0 & 0 & 1 \end{bmatrix} \begin{bmatrix} X_w \\ -Z_w \\ Y_w \end{bmatrix} \tag{12}$$

(X_w, Y_w, Z_w) are the relative coordinates of the target ship relative to the world coordinate system with the optical center of the left-eye camera as the origin.

3.3. Absolute Coordinate Estimation of the Target Combined with Camera Attitude

The following study will provide a detailed description of the coordinate transformation process based on camera attitude. Through a multi-step transformation, the relative coordinates obtained from stereo vision (i.e., coordinates in the carrier coordinate system) will be converted to determine the precise position of the target on Earth. First, the relative coordinates of the target ship are converted to the east—north—up (ENU) coordinate by using the camera attitude information to accurately extract the target's position information relative to the carrier. Subsequently, through further coordinate mapping, it is converted to the Earth-centered, Earth-fixed (ECEF) coordinate, and finally, the conversion to the World Geodetic System 1984 (WGS-84) coordinate system is realized, i.e., the latitude and longitude coordinates of the target are obtained, and each coordinate system is shown in Figure 7. This conversion process can extract the accurate latitude and longitude coordinates of the target on the Earth's surface, which is the basis for realizing the global positioning of the target location. This part will introduce this conversion process in detail.

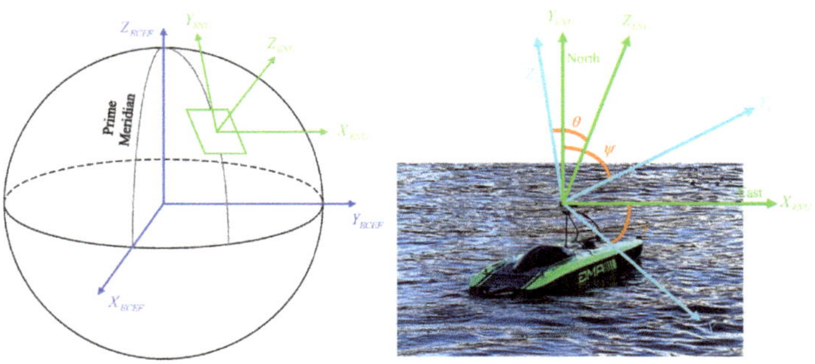

Figure 7. Illustration of coordinate system conversion.

Specifically, the transformation from the carrier coordinate system (i.e., the world coordinate system assumed in the previous text) to the ENU coordinate system is accomplished through the camera's attitude angles. The ENU coordinate system is a local coordinate system centered at the position of the camera, with the X_{ENU}-axis pointing east, the Y_{ENU}-axis pointing north, and the Z_{ENU}-axis pointing up. When there is an attitude angle of the shipboard camera, it is necessary to rotate the point $P_w(X_w, Y_w, Z_w)$ under the carrier coordinate system around the Y_w axis by the roll angle γ, around the X_w axis by the pitch angle θ, and around the Z_w axis by the yaw angle $-\psi$, in order to obtain the point $P_{ENU}(X_{ENU}, Y_{ENU}, Z_{ENU})$ under the ENU coordinate system. The transformation from the carrier coordinate system to the ENU coordinate system can be expressed as follows:

$$R_{CN} = \begin{bmatrix} \cos\psi\cos\gamma + \sin\psi\sin\theta\sin\gamma & \sin\psi\cos\theta & \cos\psi\sin\gamma - \sin\psi\sin\theta\cos\gamma \\ -\sin\psi\cos\gamma + \cos\psi\sin\theta\sin\gamma & \cos\psi\cos\theta & -\sin\psi\sin\gamma - \cos\psi\sin\theta\cos\gamma \\ -\cos\theta\sin\gamma & \sin\theta & \cos\theta\cos\gamma \end{bmatrix} \tag{13}$$

$$\begin{bmatrix} X_{ENU} \\ Y_{ENU} \\ Z_{ENU} \end{bmatrix} = R_{CN} \begin{bmatrix} X_w \\ Y_w \\ Z_w \end{bmatrix} \tag{14}$$

Here, R_{CN} represents the rotation matrix for transforming from the carrier coordinate system to the ENU coordinate system.

The ECEF coordinate system has its origin at the center of the Earth, represented by mutually orthogonal X, Y, and Z axes. The transformation relationship between point $P_{ENU}(X_{ENU}, Y_{ENU}, Z_{ENU})$ in the ENU coordinate system and point $P_{ECEF}(X_{ECEF}, Y_{ECEF}, Z_{ECEF})$ in the ECEF coordinate system involves the real-time latitude (lat) and longitude coordinates (lon) of the ship itself, as well as the coordinates of the ship's position in the ECEF coordinate system denoted as $(L_{ECEF}, L_{ECEF}, L_{ECEF})$. The transformation relation is as follows:

$$\begin{bmatrix} X_{ECEF} \\ Y_{ECEF} \\ Z_{ECEF} \end{bmatrix} = \begin{bmatrix} -\sin(lon) & -\cos(lon)\sin(lat) & \cos(lon)\cos(lat) \\ \cos(lon) & -\sin(lon)\sin(lat) & \sin(lon)\cos(lat) \\ 0 & \cos(lat) & \sin(lat) \end{bmatrix} \begin{bmatrix} X_{ENU} \\ Y_{ENU} \\ Z_{ENU} \end{bmatrix} + \begin{bmatrix} L_{ECEF} \\ L_{ECEF} \\ L_{ECEF} \end{bmatrix} \tag{15}$$

Finally, the WGS-84 coordinate system is used to express the position of a point on Earth in terms of geodetic latitude B, geodetic longitude L, and geodetic height H. The conversion process between point $P_{ECEF}(X_{ECEF}, Y_{ECEF}, Z_{ECEF})$ in the ECEF coordinate system and point $P_G(B, L, H)$ in the WGS-84 coordinate system can be obtained through iterative calculations. The conversion relationship here is the following:

$$\begin{cases} L = \arctan\frac{Y_{ECEF}}{X_{ECEF}} \\ B = \arctan\frac{Z+Ne^2\sin B}{\sqrt{X_{ECEF}^2+Y_{ECEF}^2}} \\ H = \frac{Z_{ECEF}}{\sin B} - N(1-e^2) \end{cases} \tag{16}$$

In the equation, N represents the radius of curvature in prime vertical, e is the first eccentricity of the reference ellipsoid, and B is the iterative quantity. Initially, the geodetic latitude B is computed based on the initial latitude B_1. Subsequently, B is updated iteratively until the convergence condition is met, resulting in the desired latitude and longitude coordinates. These steps will provide us with accurate positional information for the target on the Earth.

$$B_1 = \arctan\frac{Z}{\sqrt{X^2+Y^2}} \tag{17}$$

3.4. Fusion of Perception Data Based on Ship ST-TF

3.4.1. Preprocessing of Visual Trajectory Data

Due to factors such as ship navigation, camera shake, errors in bounding box size during manual annotation, and interference from the horizontal plane background, there may be small positional discrepancies between the detected bounding box size and the actual outline of the target ship. This can lead to incorrect estimation of the image coordinates for tracking the target ship, which subsequently affects the accuracy of visual localization estimates. To address these challenges effectively, we employ Kalman filtering to preprocess the position coordinates of the visual estimates, ensuring a smoother and more reliable trajectory. Kalman filtering is able to effectively suppress noise in measurements and processes, and better adapt to changes in the actual system, thereby improving the accuracy and stability of position estimation.

3.4.2. Visual Localization Frequency Synchronized with Target Ship GPS Frequency

When performing visual perceptual localization and GPS information fusion, it is critical to ensure that camera and GPS outputs are acquired at the same time to avoid significant errors in the information fusion results. Typically, the time for each sensor is independent, and the sampling frequencies vary. In this experiment, the target ship's GPS operates at frequencies of 5 Hz and 10 Hz, while the camera's operating frequency is set to 5 fps, meaning that it captures 5 frames per second with a 200 ms interval between each frame, which is the same as the GPS working frequency of the host ship. Here, we use the lower frequency camera sensor as a reference and apply systematic sampling to the 10 Hz GPS data to ensure synchronization between the world coordinates calculated by the camera and the GPS coordinates. This frequency synchronization strategy helps effectively integrate information from different sensors, enhancing the accuracy of visual perception localization and GPS information fusion. The frequency synchronization process is shown in Figure 8.

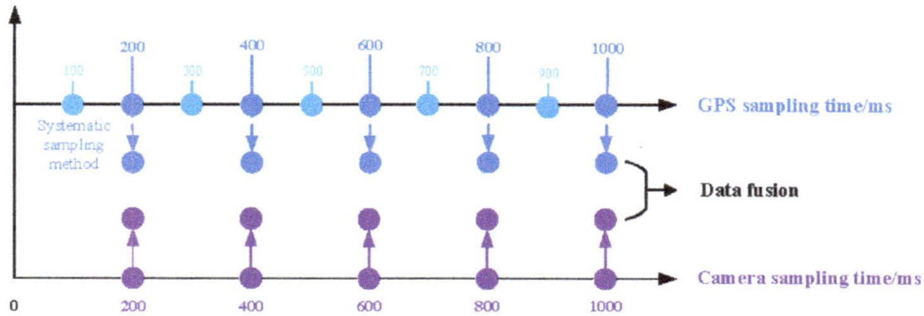

Figure 8. Synchronization process of different sensor frequencies.

3.4.3. Asynchronous Nonlinear Ship Trajectory Association and Storage Based on the DTW Algorithm

The core of data fusion is the matching association between visual and GPS trajectories. This section addresses the limitation of using cosine distance, which focuses solely on the directional information of vectors without accounting for positional differences between trajectory points. Therefore, Euclidean distance is employed as the similarity measure to globally assess vector similarity. The data sources used for matching in this study consist of two parts: First, high-frequency dynamic and static information uploaded to the server by the edge computing device of the experimental ship, referred to as the enhanced AIS (E-AIS). This information is collected through multi-sensors (e.g., GPS, IMU) with a high update frequency, making it suitable for the experimental environment. Second, visual positioning data of the target ship is computed in real time by the edge computing device onboard the ship. It is important to note that there are significant differences between E-AISs and traditional onboard AIS systems. While traditional AIS devices provide both static and dynamic information about the ship, their transmission frequency is irregular, and data loss may occur during communication, leading to delays or missing updates. Furthermore, visual positioning may be affected by ship occlusion in certain scenarios, resulting in trajectory loss and exhibiting nonlinear characteristics. To address these challenges, this study employs a Euclidean distance-based DTW algorithm for matching and aligning GPS data from the E-AIS or traditional AIS with the visual positioning data of the target ship, thereby achieving precise alignment and integration of trajectory points.

The DTW algorithm is a method for measuring trajectory similarity. It can be employed to compare the similarity between two nonlinear time series of varying lengths and to achieve optimal alignment between them [49]. Let the coordinate sequence of visual estimates be denoted as $n(n = 1, \ldots, N)$, while the edge computing device retrieves the historical GPS trajectory sequence $m(m = 1, \ldots, M)$ of surrounding ships by querying the ship information database. In practical applications, in order to reduce the computational burden, the edge computing device only retrieves the trajectory information of ships within the monitoring area of the host ship for the past 5 min. When Euclidean distance is used to measure similarity, a smaller distance indicates a higher similarity between two sequences. The formula for calculating similarity is as follows:

$$\begin{cases} DTW(n,m) = d(n,m) \ ,n = 1\&m = 1 \\ DTW(n,m) = d(n,m) + \min\{DTW(n-1,m), DTW(n,m-1), DTW(n-1,m-1)\}, n = 1,2,\cdots,N\&m = 1,2,\cdots,M \end{cases} \quad (18)$$

$DTW(n,m)$ is calculated as the sum of the Euclidean distance $d(n,m)$ between current elements and the cumulative distance to the nearest element that can be reached. $DTW(N,M)$ serves as the result of the similarity measurement between two sequences. When the similarity measurement result between two trajectories falls below a preset similarity threshold, the visual-based ship trajectory and the GPS-based ship trajectory are directly associated, and data points are aligned. Figure 9 illustrates the asynchronous nonlinear ship trajectory sequence association using the DTW algorithm.

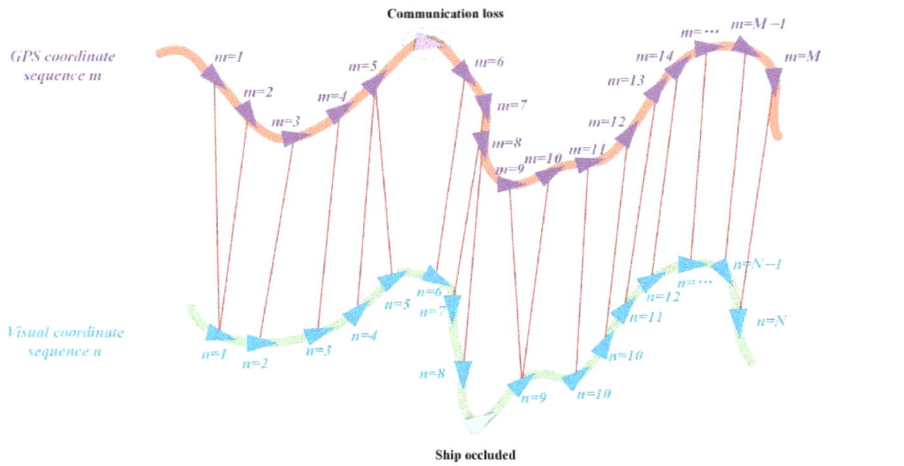

Figure 9. Asynchronous nonlinear ship trajectory sequence association based on the DTW algorithm.

Referring to the fusion data storage design in [13], we have redefined the method for storing correlated data based on our experimental approach. Specifically, after applying the DTW algorithm, the associated results are used to retrieve the target ship's static information (IMO, Name, Length, Breadth—note that the IMO number is a virtual number, as the experimental ship is a self-developed small MASS without an official IMO number, used solely for experimental purposes) and dynamic information (Time, SOG, COG, HDG) from the E-AIS database. These data are then integrated with the dynamic and static information of the experimental ship for joint storage. This combined storage approach aims to support AR-based ship navigation systems with multi-source data, as shown in Figure 10. The blue table represents the navigation information of the own ship and the estimated visual position of the target ship, while the purple table represents the correlated navigation information of the target ship. To enhance the efficiency of trajectory association, similarity measurements are conducted every 5 min for trajectories already associated in the data storage area. During this period, the system retains the association status of these trajectories by default and refrains from performing similarity measurements with other trajectories.

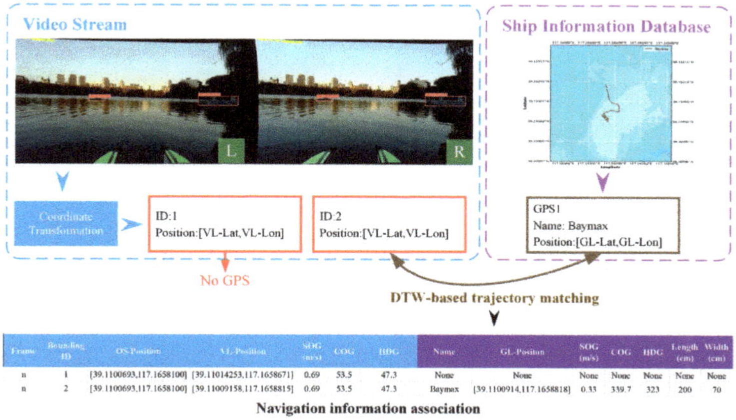

Figure 10. Asynchronous ship trajectory association and joint data storage method.

4. Results

In this section, we conducted extensive experiments on ship target detection, tracking, and fusion localization to evaluate the proposed methods and validate their practicality. The experiments were conducted on the Ubuntu 20.04 operating system and Python version 3.8.10. The hardware configuration included an NVIDIA RTX 2080Ti GPU (manufactured by NVIDIA Corporation, Santa Clara, California, USA), Intel(R) Xeon(R) Platinum 8255C CPU (manufactured by Intel Corporation, Santa Clara, California, USA). The model framework was based on PyTorch 2.0.0.

4.1. Experimental Data

In this section, a benchmark dataset (FLShip) was constructed for ship target detection, tracking, and fused localization. Compared to existing open-source maritime datasets, FLShip introduces multidimensional innovations in its design. It not only includes continuous stereo and monocular image frames captured from a first-person perspective during navigation but also introduces high-frequency E-AIS information corresponding closely to the image data of both target and own MASSs for the first time. This feature significantly enhances the dataset's applicability in supporting multi-source information fusion research for MASSs, providing crucial data support for research in maritime target detection, multi-sensor data fusion, and autonomous navigation. The experiments utilized seven MASSs developed by Tianjin University as test subjects. The E-AIS data from the MASSs, including attitude and GPS information, are obtained by subscribing to the /mavros/imu/data topic for attitude data and the /mavros/global_position/global topic for positional data via the ROS system. These data are uploaded in real time to a server via 4G networks (which can be replaced by satellite communication as needed), ensuring efficient data transmission and storage. Figure 11 and Table 2 provide additional details about the MASSs used in this experiment, including their ID, length, breadth, equipped equipment, and levels of autonomy navigation. Among them, the edge computing devices equipped on the experimental ship include Raspberry Pi 4B (manufactured by Raspberry Pi Foundation, Cambridge, UK), Jetson Orin Nano Developer Kit, and Jetson Nano (manufactured by NVIDIA Corporation, Santa Clara, California, USA).

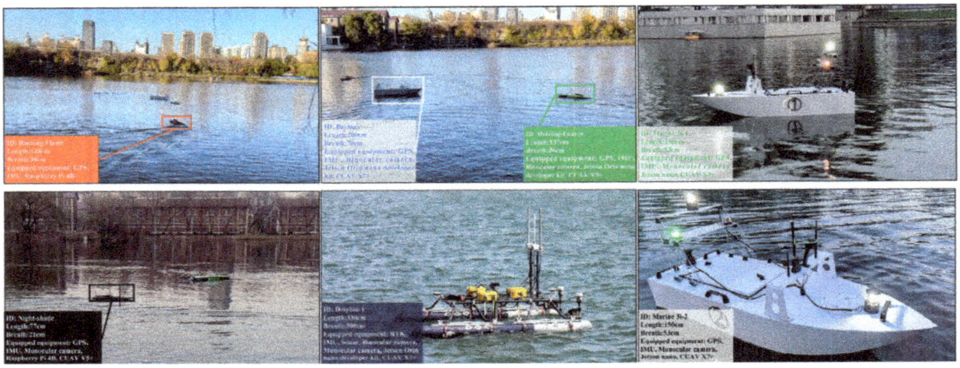

Figure 11. The MASSs used in the experimental process.

Table 2. Details of the MASS.

ID	Equipped Equipment					Autonomy Level
	GPS	IMU	Camera	Edge Computing Box	Controller	
Roaring-Flame	☑	☑	⊠	Raspberry Pi 4B	Manual	Remote Control
Driving-Leaves	☑	☑	Binocular	Jetson Orin nano developer kit	CUAV V5+	Programmed Control
Baymax	☑	☑	Binocular	Jetson Orin nano developer kit	CUAV X7+	Programmed Control
Night-shade	☑	☑	Monocular	Raspberry Pi 4B	CUAV V5+	Programmed Control
Marine 3i-1	☑	☑	Monocular	Jetson nano	CUAV X7+	Programmed Control
Marine 3i-2	☑	☑	Monocular	Jetson nano	CUAV X7+	Programmed Control
Dolphin-1	☑	☑	Monocular and Binocular	Jetson Orin nano developer kit	CUAV X7+	Programmed Control

To validate the effectiveness of the proposed method, seven scenes with varying resolutions, noise levels, and visibility conditions were extracted from the dataset for ship target detection, tracking, and fused localization experiments, as illustrated in Figure 12. Table 3 presents additional details about the FLShip dataset, including the number of ships (NOS), the number of ships with E-AISs (NOE), the frequency of ship E-AISs (FOE), video quality, video frame rate, video resolution, and the average speed of the host ship.

Table 3. Detailed information of the FLShip dataset.

Video	NOS	NOE	FOE	Video Quality	Video Frame Rate	Video Resolution (px)	Speed (m/s)
Scene-1	2	2	5&10	Good	5	2560 × 720	0.65
Scene-2	3	2	5	Good	5	2560 × 720	0.42
Scene-3	2	2	5	Good	5	2560 × 720	0.11
Scene-4	2	2	1&5	Poor (Medium noise)	25	640 × 480	0.53
Scene-5	4	3	5	Poor (Fog and waves)	30	1920 × 1080	2.1
Scene-6	3	3	5	Fair (Cool color tone and low light)	5	4416 × 1242	0.41
Scene-7	3	3	5	Poor (Minimal light and high contrast)	5	4416 × 1242	0.15

Figure 12. The data samples from the FLShip dataset.

4.2. Ship Target Detection Experiment

To evaluate the performance of the Bi-YOLO algorithm in complex scenarios, we conducted comparative experiments on the FLShip dataset using various benchmark algorithms. These included Deformable-DETR [50], RTMdet [51], YOLOv7 [52], YOLOv8s, and the original YOLO11s. Evaluation metrics included mAP@0.5, mAP@0.5:0.95, GFLOPs, Params, and model size.

The mAP is a comprehensive evaluation metric for object detection system performance, allowing for reliable comparison between different algorithms or models across various datasets. mAP@0.5 operates by calculating the average precision (AP) for all images in the first class when the IoU threshold is set to 0.5, and then repeating the process for the remaining classes. The average of these AP values gives the mAP score. mAP@0.5:0.95 is an extension of mAP, which calculates multiple AP values within the IoU range from 0.5 to 0.95 (with a step size of 0.05) and averages them. Specifically, mAP@0.5:0.95 provides a more comprehensive assessment of model performance across varying strictness conditions by considering multiple IoU thresholds. Compared to the single mAP@0.5, mAP@0.5:0.95 demands that the model maintain high detection accuracy at higher IoU thresholds, thus better reflecting the model's robustness and accuracy in complex scenarios. In addition to precision metrics, the computational efficiency of the model is an important factor in assessing its practical value. GFLOPs reflect the computational complexity of the model, while Params directly determine the model's storage and memory usage. In practical applications, especially on resource-constrained edge computing devices, achieving lower GFLOPs and Params is crucial for improving deployment efficiency.

This study conducted object detection model training based on the FLShip dataset. The dataset comprises 6286 images of MASSs captured in both inland and maritime environments. To enhance the model's generalization capability and reduce the risk of overfitting, data augmentation techniques, including random brightness adjustment (±30%) and Gaussian noise injection (σ = 0.05), were applied to improve the model's adaptability in complex environments. The dataset was split into training, validation, and test sets at a ratio of 76:16:8 to ensure sufficient training data. This experiment did not use external datasets for validation, focusing instead on the unique characteristics of the FLShip dataset. This dataset is highly representative of real-world application scenarios, containing a rich variety of MASS target information along with complementary E-AIS data, making the experimental results more practically valuable. As shown in Figure 13, we analyzed the performance of Bi-YOLO and mainstream detection models during training by examining the mAP@0.5 metric change curve. The experimental results demonstrate that, in the early stages of training, Bi-YOLO exhibited a performance improvement trend similar to YOLO11s and YOLOv8s, significantly outperforming YOLOv7, Deformable-DETR, and RTMdet-l. As training progressed, Bi-YOLO's detection performance gradually surpassed that of other algorithms, with a 0.4% mAP advantage over YOLO11s and a gap of more than 3.4% compared to traditional architectures like Deformable-DETR. Overall, Bi-YOLO not only showed a faster convergence speed during training but also demonstrated stronger competitiveness in final detection performance, confirming its advantages in object detection tasks.

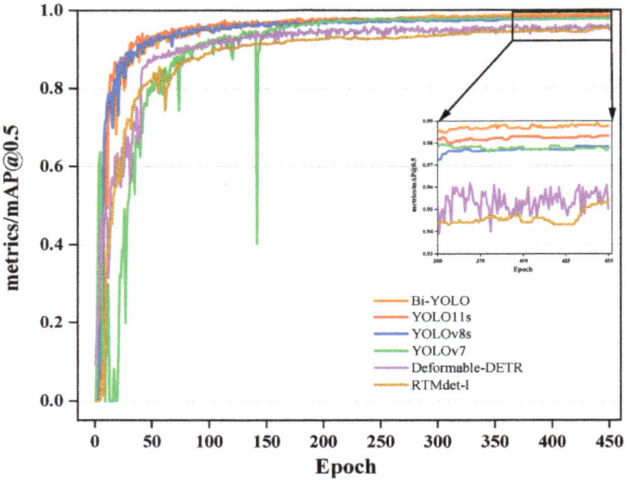

Figure 13. Training mAP@0.5 curves for Bi-YOLO and various object detection algorithms.

To further demonstrate the effectiveness of the proposed method, we compared the Bi-YOLO model with YOLO11s, YOLOv8s, YOLOv7, Deformable-DETR, and RTMdet on the FLShip validation set. The experimental results are shown in Table 4. As observed, Bi-YOLO outperforms the other models in both mAP@0.5 and mAP@0.5:0.95 metrics, achieving 98.7% in mAP@0.5 and 79.6% in mAP@0.5:0.95, with improvements of 0.4 and 0.5 percentage points over YOLO11s, respectively, demonstrating the model's comprehensive capability in target detection under various conditions. As shown in Figure 14, we present a comparison of the detection performance between YOLO11s and Bi-YOLO on the same set of images. In Figure 14c, YOLO11s missed detection because the target ship was far away and the light was dim, which caused the ship to be confused with the background; in Figure 14b,d, YOLO11s also failed to detect the target due to fog interference and the ship being far away. Bi-YOLO showed excellent robustness and adaptability when dealing with complex environments, especially in the detection of small targets at long distances in inland waters and in the sea environment due to interference caused by fog and waves. Bi-YOLO can still accurately identify all targets in these complex environments. This advantage is mainly attributed to the introduced C2f_BiFormer module, which enhances feature representation and fine-grained target feature extraction, enabling the model to perform more stably in detecting small, long-range targets, ensuring precise target capture even in complex, low-visibility scenarios.

Table 4. Evaluation results of ship detection algorithms on the FLShip validation set.

Models	Evaluation Metrics				
	mAP@0.5/% (↑)	mAP@0.5:0.95/% (↑)	Model Size/MB (↓)	Params/106 (↓)	GFLOPs (↓)
Bi-YOLO (ours)	98.7	79.6	17.4	8.9	19.4
YOLO11s	98.3	79.1	19.2	9.413187	21.3
YOLOv8s	97.8	78.3	21.3	11.135987	28.6
YOLOv7	97.7	75.5	71.3	36.479926	103.2
Deformable-DETR	95	61.3	646.5	40.099	123
RTMdet-l	95.3	74.3	825.1	52.255	79.951

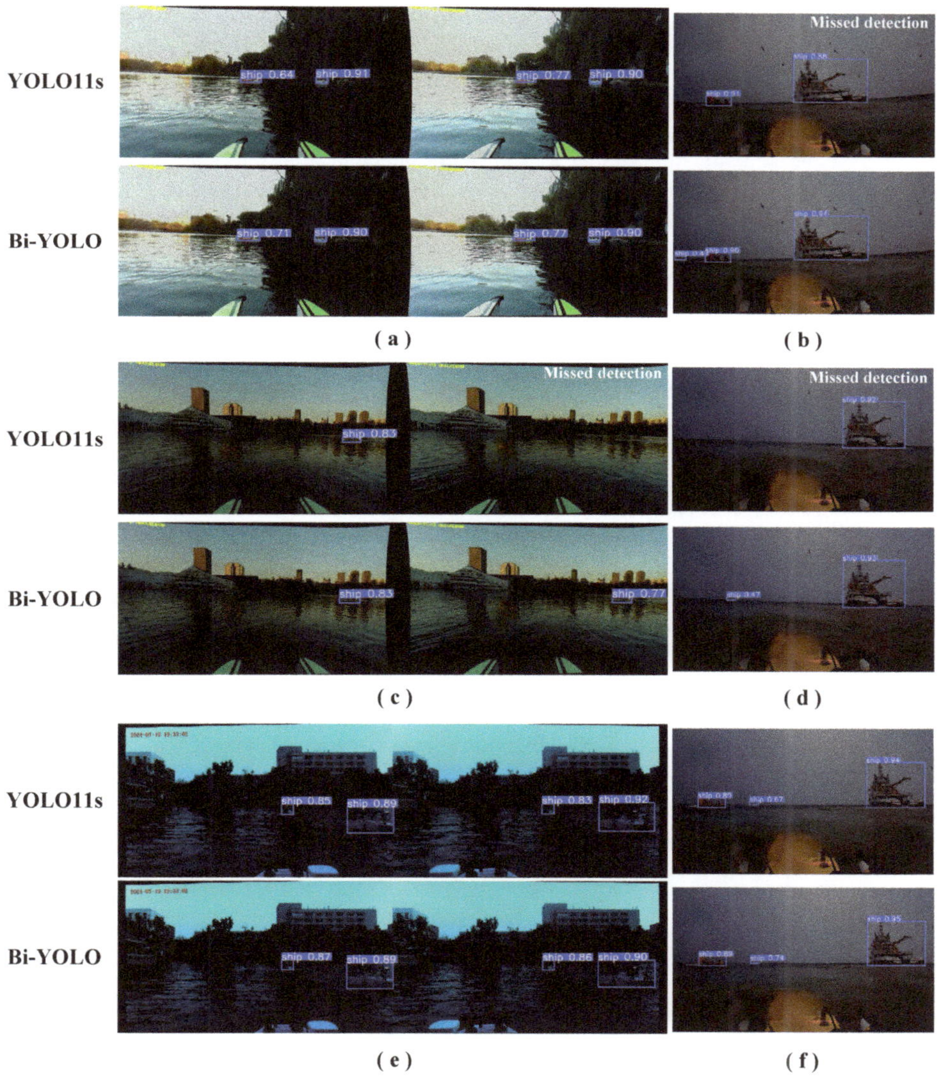

Figure 14. (a–f) respectively show the comparison of detection effects between YOLO11s and Bi-YOLO.

Compared to the classic Deformable-DETR and RTMdet-l, Bi-YOLO has demonstrated significant improvements in detection capabilities in complex scenarios. For instance, the mAP@0.5:0.95 metric improved by 18.3 percentage points over Deformable-DETR. This improvement is particularly important because mAP@0.5:0.95 better reflects the model's precision in locating small targets under high IoU conditions. Despite Bi-YOLO's excellent performance across multiple accuracy metrics, model complexity and real-time performance remain key considerations in practical applications, especially in embedded hardware environments. In the experiments, Bi-YOLO achieved 19.4 GFLOPs, with 8.9 M parameters and a model size of 17.4 MB, reaching an FPS of 120. Compared to the latest YOLO11s, Bi-YOLO achieves significant optimizations in model size, number of parameters, and computational complexity. Specifically, the model size of Bi-YOLO is reduced by 9.3%, the number of parameters is decreased by 5.4%, and the computational complexity is lowered by 8.9%. These optimizations enhance Bi-YOLO's application potential, making it particularly suitable for environments with limited computing resources.

4.3. Ship Target Tracking Experiment

In the ship target tracking experiments, to validate the tracking performance of the algorithm used in this study under complex scenarios, six scenes with varying resolutions, noise levels, brightness, and contrast were selected from the FLShip dataset for extensive tracking experiments.

Four state-of-the-art trackers, i.e., StrongSORT [53], OC-SORT, Byte Track [54], and BOT-SORT [55], are selected for the comparative tracking experiments in this paper. The performance of the trackers is evaluated using metrics such as Multi-Object Tracking Accuracy (MOTA), Identification F1 (IDF1), and Identity Switches (IDs). Additionally, we evaluated the speed of the tracker in terms of frames per second (FPS). Although the runtime may vary significantly with different hardware, the specific details are shown in Table 5. MOTA is calculated based on false positives (FPs), false negatives (FNs), and identity switches (IDs), emphasizing detection performance. In contrast, IDF1 better measures the consistency of ID matching, and IDs measure the performance of the multi-object tracking model in handling target identity switches. An upward arrow $\uparrow$ indicates that a higher value of the metric corresponds to better performance, while a downward arrow $\downarrow$ indicates that a lower value of the metric corresponds to better performance.

From Table 5, it can be observed that, under the same detector, OC-SORT demonstrates higher localization accuracy and tracking performance across different scenarios and complex environments. Compared to StrongSORT, ByteTrack, and BOT-SORT, OC-SORT maintains MOTA and IDF1 scores above 90%, even in conditions of severe noise interference or insufficient lighting, accompanied by faster inference speeds, allowing it to perform real-time perception updates at a higher frame rate. This implies that OC-SORT can handle input images more frequently and provide real-time and accurate target tracking information, thus providing reliable perception and decision support for subsequent applications.

Table 5. Multi-ship tracking evaluation results in six scenarios.

Video	Detector	Tracker	Evaluation Metrics			
			MOTA/% (↑)	IDF1/% (↑)	IDs (↓)	FPS/Hz (↑)
Scene-1	Bi-YOLO	StrongSORT	90.4	95.7	0	31
		OC-SORT (ours)	96.3	98	0	65
		ByteTrack	88.6	93.7	0	78
		BOT-SORT	94.1	97.3	0	18
Scene-2	Bi-YOLO	StrongSORT	89.7	94.1	1	26
		OC-SORT (ours)	93.3	96.4	0	57
		ByteTrack	91.8	95.9	0	75
		BOT-SORT	90.9	94.9	0	15
Scene-3	Bi-YOLO	StrongSORT	93.7	95.1	0	29
		OC-SORT (ours)	97.7	98.5	0	41
		ByteTrack	92.5	95.4	0	74
		BOT-SORT	96.2	96.3	0	14
Scene-4	Bi-YOLO	StrongSORT	95	95.5	1	36
		OC-SORT (ours)	93.8	97.2	0	78
		ByteTrack	93.6	96.7	0	86
		BOT-SORT	94.7	94.2	2	28
Scene-5	Bi-YOLO	StrongSORT	90.8	93.7	0	24
		OC-SORT (ours)	92.7	91.8	0	55
		ByteTrack	88.5	86.4	0	66
		BOT-SORT	88	89.9	4	10
Scene-6	Bi-YOLO	StrongSORT	87.3	93.2	1	27
		OC-SORT (ours)	90.6	96.2	0	52
		ByteTrack	85.1	91.5	0	67
		BOT-SORT	86.7	89.3	6	12

Figures 15–17 present the tracking results of four different trackers in Scene-2, Scene-4 with noise interference, and Scene-6 with low lighting conditions. It can be observed that the StrongSORT and BOT-SORT trackers experience multiple ID switches in Scene-2, Scene-4, and Scene-6. Additionally, ByteTrack exhibits lower IOU at several time points (e.g., T1 and T3 in Scene-4, and T4 in Scene-6), resulting in relatively lower bounding box localization accuracy. Comparative experiments show that OC-SORT achieves more stable tracking of the target ship while ensuring real-time performance, striking a good balance between real-time processing and stability. The combination of the Bi-YOLO detector and the OC-SORT tracker used in this study maintains high accuracy and stability in multi-ship tracking tasks, providing a solid foundation for precise and stable target localization in subsequent experiments.

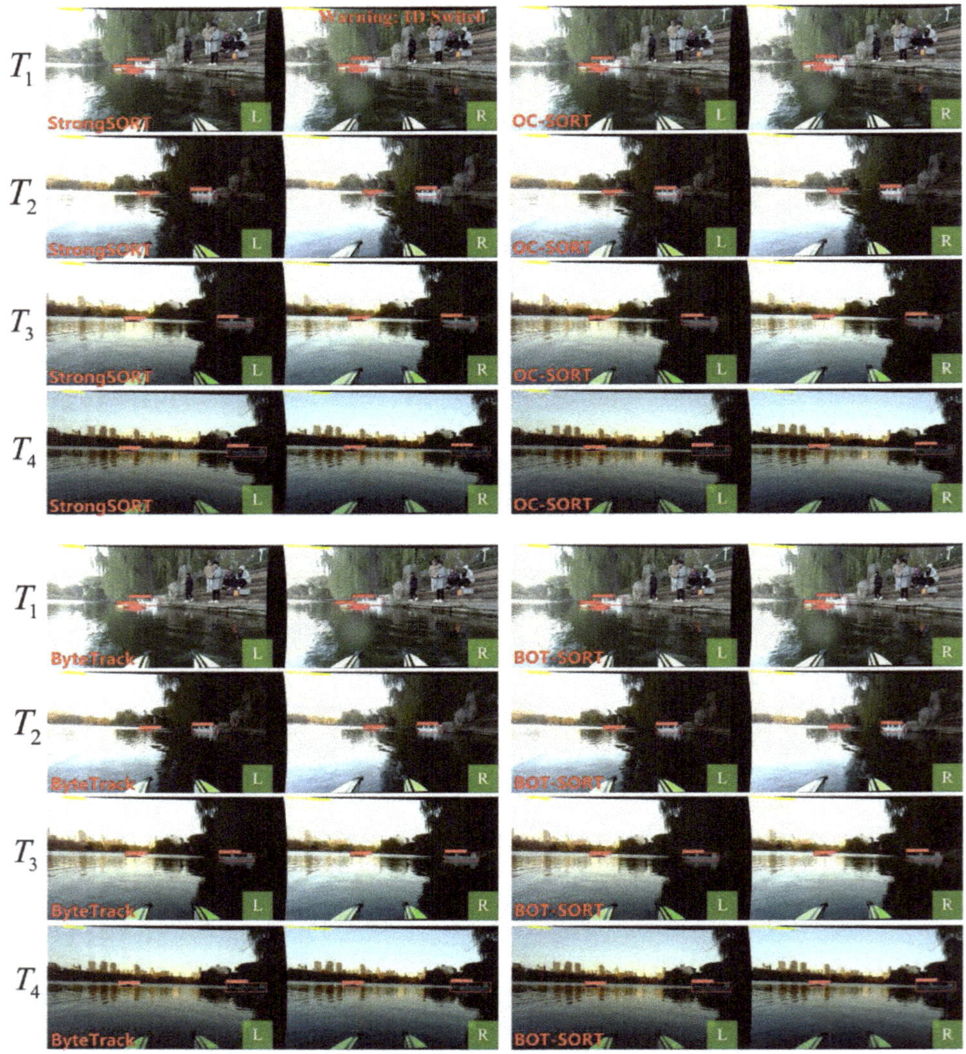

Figure 15. Tracking performance comparison of four state-of-the-art object trackers in Scene-2.

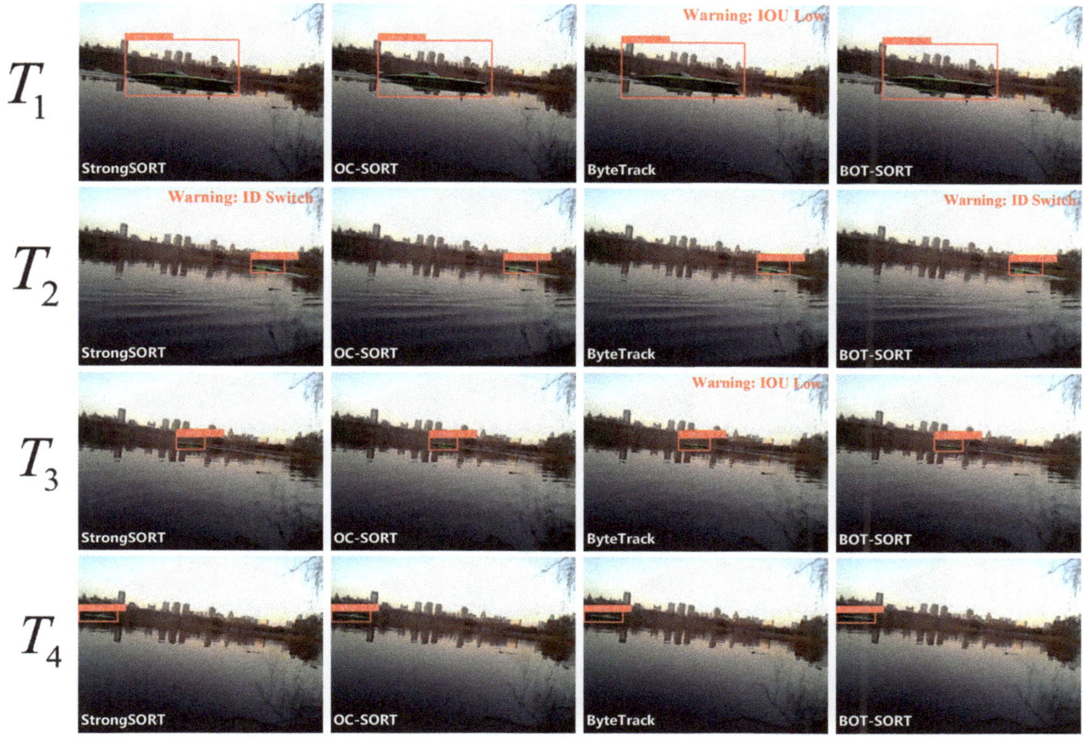

Figure 16. Tracking performance comparison of four state-of-the-art object trackers in Scene-4.

4.4. Visual-Based Ship Position Estimation Experiment

To validate the accuracy of the ship position estimation method in this study, we also recorded the real-time position and attitude data of the host ship and the target ship in real time during the video data collection and then uploaded them to the server for storage. The actual GPS data uploaded by the target ship serves as a ground truth for comparison. To facilitate the comparison between the real value of longitude and latitude and the measured value extracted by vision, systematic sampling is performed according to the GPS frequency of the target ship to ensure that the collected position information can be matched frame by frame. To verify the robustness and accuracy of the position estimation method, this paper selects videos recorded in different navigation states for position estimation experiments. In addition, the mean absolute error (MAE), mean square error (MSE), mean absolute percentage error (MAPE), and mean relative position error (MRPE) are also introduced in the experiment to comprehensively evaluate the position estimation method proposed in this paper.

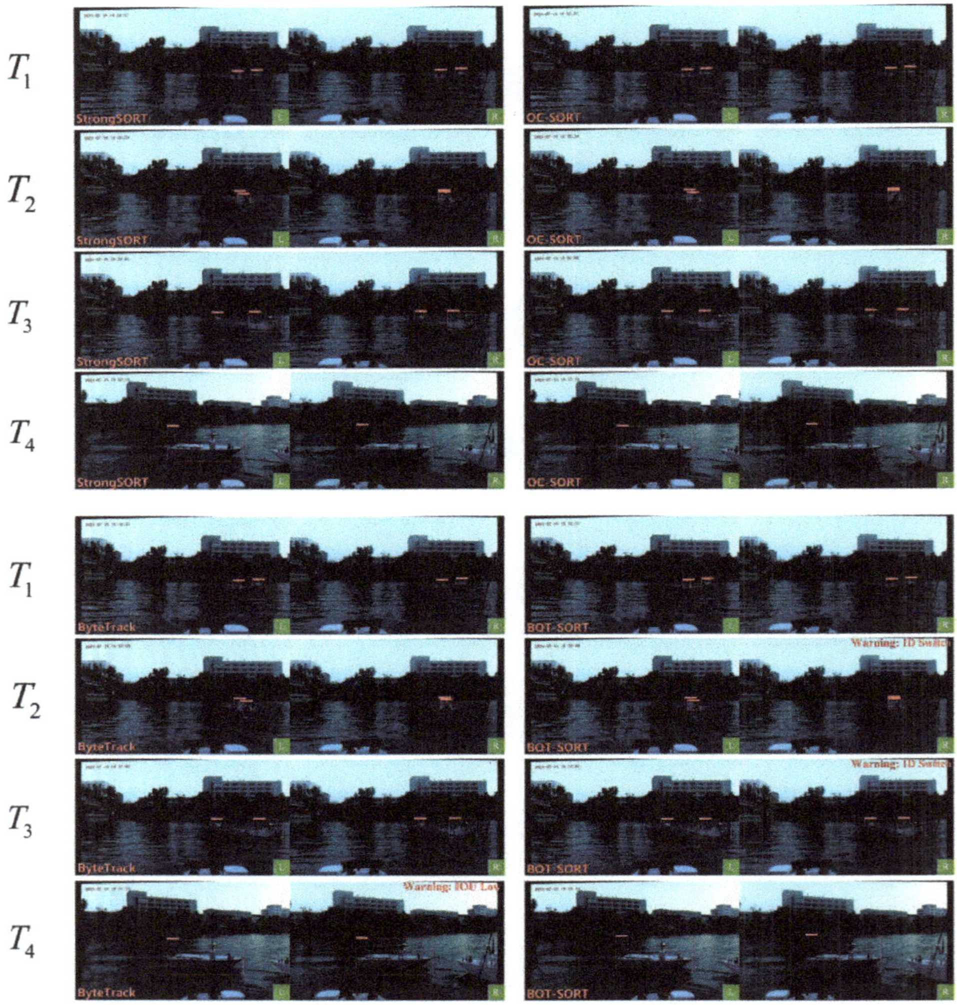

Figure 17. Tracking performance comparison of four state-of-the-art object trackers in Scene-6.

Figures 18–20 present the results of multi-target visual position extraction and comparison across various scenes. The purple trajectories represent the estimated positions of the target ship obtained using our framework through stereo images, while the blue trajectories indicate the actual GPS data of the target ship (i.e., its ground truth positions). The pink trajectories correspond to the GPS data of our own ship, which approximately represents the camera's position. Table 6 presents the MAE, MSE, MAPE, and MRPE values for visual latitude and longitude estimates across different scenes compared to the true values. In Scene-1, the own ship performed reverse motion and large-angle turning maneuvers. These movements caused significant vibrations and sensor noise, which notably impacted the accuracy of visual position estimation. Consequently, this scenario imposed higher precision requirements on the sensors. Under these conditions, the MRPE in Scene-1 was higher than that in Scene-2. Additionally, since stereo vision-based localization relies on disparity, the resolution of depth information decreases with increasing target distance as the disparity angle diminishes. This limitation resulted in lower position estimation accuracy in Scene-3 compared to other scenarios. Nevertheless, our framework demonstrated strong robustness in Scene-3, achieving an MAE of $5.6403 \times 10^{-6\circ}$ and MSE of $4.0986 \times 10^{-11\circ}$ and keeping the MRPE within 8.76%. These results indicate that the proposed framework can achieve high-precision target position estimation even in complex scenarios, providing stable and reliable trajectory features for subsequent multi-source data association.

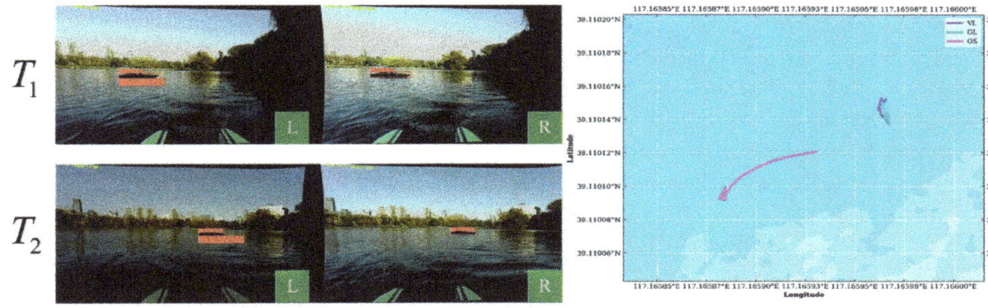

Figure 18. The visual position estimation results of the 'Roaring-Flame' MASS in Scene-1.

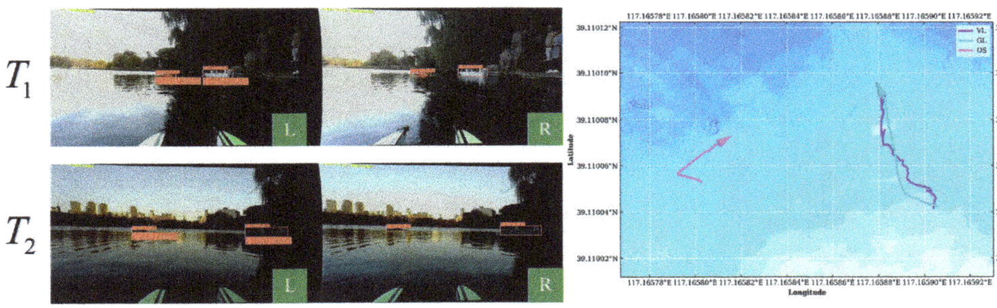

Figure 19. The visual position estimation result of the 'Baymax' MASS in scene-2.

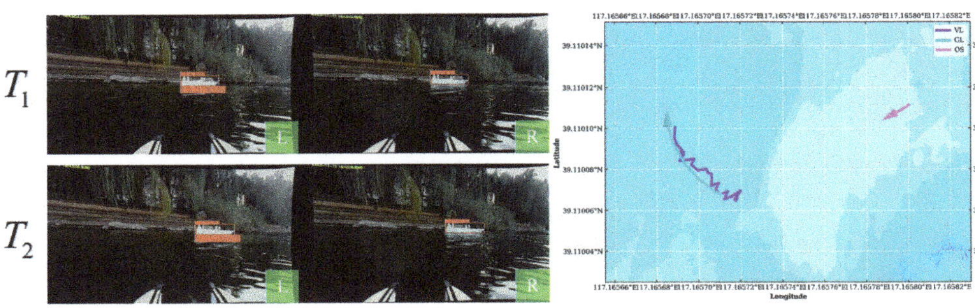

Figure 20. The visual position estimation results of the 'Baymax' MASS in Scene-3.

Table 6. The MAE, MSE, MAPE, and MRPE values for target ship position estimates in multiple scenes.

Video	Feature	MAE (°)	MSE (°)	MAPE (%)	MRPE (%)
Scene-1	Coordinates	1.68×10^{-6}	4.25×10^{-12}	3.37×10^{-8}	4.44
Scene-2	Coordinates	2.39×10^{-6}	8.16×10^{-12}	3.91×10^{-8}	4.4
Scene-3	Coordinates	5.64×10^{-6}	4.1×10^{-11}	8.2×10^{-8}	8.76

4.5. Multi-Source Data Fusion Experiment

In this section, we aim to verify the effectiveness of the proposed multi-source data fusion method. Specifically, we utilize a Euclidean distance-based DTW algorithm to associate the visual trajectory of the target ship (generated by fusing data from a camera, GPS, and IMU) with the GPS trajectory in the E-AIS database. The dynamic and static information of both the own ship and the target ship is then jointly stored. Considering the crew's sailing habits and information needs, we constructed a simple, intuitive, and easy-to-understand human–computer interface, and constructed the AR navigation assistance results in the left camera image, so that the crews can understand the ship's navigation status more comprehensively and intuitively and improve the efficiency of acquiring and understanding the navigation information. Figure 21 visually demonstrates the AR navigation assistance results for the ship based on the perceptual data fusion framework.

Figure 21. The AR navigation assistance effects of ships constructed at different timestamps in multiple scenes.

In Figure 21, the results of AR navigation assistance provide comprehensive information about the tracked ships, including static details (IMO, Name, Length, Breadth) and dynamic information (Lat, Lon, SOG, COG, HDG), as well as navigation information for the host ship (Lat, Lon, SOG, COG, HDG, etc.). The ship data fusion method proposed in this paper successfully and accurately matches the visual and GPS trajectories. The dynamic information is updated in real time with the movement of the ship, allowing the ship AR navigation system to more accurately reflect the current status. The navigation assistance system helps the crew to improve the efficiency of information acquisition and understanding during navigation and also provides the crew with richer navigation assistance information, so as to improve the overall navigation experience.

The unique feature of the perceptual data fusion method based on ship ST-TF is that it can respond to possible emergencies such as communication or other equipment failures by displaying the visual latitude and longitude coordinates (as shown by the left ship in Scene 2 of Figure 21) without being associated with the GPS trajectory. Even in these emergencies, the system is still able to provide basic location information to the crew, providing critical data support for emergency response, search, and rescue operations. In addition, for ships not associated with a GPS track, displaying their visual latitude and longitude coordinates can effectively monitor and identify illegal ship operations. In terms of maritime surveillance, this feature can make up for the defects of communication equipment not configured according to regulations or maliciously shut down, and enhance the maritime surveillance capability, thereby strengthening the security of the entire maritime field.

5. Conclusions and Future Perspectives

In this paper, a perceptual data fusion framework based on ship ST-TF was proposed for ship AR navigation assistance systems to ensure navigation safety and enhance maritime surveillance efficiency. The main contributions of this paper are as follows. First, the ship tracking system was optimized by introducing the Bi-YOLO network, which incorporates the C2f_BiFormer module to enhance the detection performance of small targets while reducing model parameters. Additionally, the more robust OC-SORT algorithm was integrated to achieve real-time and stable tracking of moving ship targets. Second, a visual localization model of maritime targets based on binocular imaging was constructed, and the absolute position estimation of maritime targets in the absence of a reference was achieved by fusing the attitude information of the camera. Subsequently, a perceptual data fusion method based on ship ST-TF was proposed. This method temporally and spatially fused the visual trajectory with the GPS trajectory from the E-AIS database. It also further integrated other dynamic and static information. Finally, a ship AR navigation assistance system was developed in conjunction with the proposed multi-source fusion perception framework. Comprehensive experiments on multi-scene MASS tracking, visual position estimation, and multi-source data fusion were conducted on the newly developed FLShip dataset to validate the robustness and effectiveness of the proposed perceptual data fusion framework based on ship ST-TF. The results of comparative experiments with various advanced object detection and tracking algorithms demonstrate that even in low-resolution, noisy, and low-brightness scenes, the framework achieves a mAP@0.5 of 98.7% in multi-ship detection while maintaining a MOTA between 90% and 98%, all while reducing the model's parameter count. The framework successfully extracted reliable visual trajectories of target ships and validated the accuracy of visual position estimation across multiple scenes, ensuring the accurate association between visual detection and E-AISs. The ship AR navigation assistance system based on the multi-source fusion perception framework proposed in this paper is able to enhance the ability of MASS traffic situational awareness, provide more comprehensive and intuitive navigation information for the crew, make it easier to cope with the challenges of complex waterways and ensure the safety of ship navigation. In addition, in the case of equipment failure or illegal operation of the target ship, the navigation assistance system is still able to provide critical dynamic data support for tasks such as emergency response, search and rescue, and maritime surveillance by presenting the visual latitude and longitude coordinates of the target, thus enhancing the safety level of the entire maritime field.

Although the proposed framework performs well in scenarios with noise, wave interference, and low visibility, vision-based perception strategies remain constrained by imaging conditions. Additionally, with the integration of multi-sensor perception systems, optimizing real-time performance and ensuring compatibility with existing ship navigation systems are critical prerequisites for practical deployment. To address these challenges, future research will focus on the following directions to enhance system robustness and adaptability, thereby ensuring effectiveness and reliability in real-world applications:

- Multi-sensor fusion technology: In-depth research on the fusion mechanisms of multi-source sensors, such as cameras, radars, and AISs, will be conducted. Dynamic sensor weight adjustment based on the navigation environment will provide more accurate ship motion information, further strengthening situational awareness in the era of MASS autonomous navigation and offering advanced and reliable solutions for maritime navigation.
- MASS self-organizing networks and data sharing: Research will focus on meeting the shared needs of MASS autonomous navigation and the construction of maritime spatial information. A highly efficient MASS self-organizing network architecture will be established to enable real-time sharing and collaborative processing of perception data, supporting comprehensive, multi-angle maritime environment awareness and laying the foundation for building smarter, more collaborative maritime traffic systems.
- Overcoming deployment and implementation challenges: Through model compression and hardware acceleration technologies, the computational demands will be reduced, and inference efficiency will be improved to ensure real-time performance on low-power embedded platforms. At the same time, efforts will be made to resolve compatibility issues between perception models and existing ship automation systems, navigation software, and international maritime regulations. The development of open interfaces compliant with IMO standards will facilitate seamless integration of technology with existing navigation systems, ensuring the alignment of performance, regulatory compliance, and safety, thus promoting stable and reliable deployment.

Author Contributions: S.C.: Conceptualization, Formal analysis, Investigation, Methodology, Validation, Visualization, Writing—original draft, Writing—review and editing. M.G.: Conceptualization, Data curation, Funding acquisition, Methodology, Writing—review and editing. P.S.: Visualization, Validation, Formal analysis. X.Z.: Data curation, Writing—review and editing, Visualization, Formal analysis. A.Z.: Supervision, Funding acquisition, Data curation. All authors have read and agreed to the published version of the manuscript.

Funding: This project was supported partially by the National Natural Science Foundation of China (52201414), Young Elite Scientists Sponsorship Program of the China Institute of Navigation (No. YESSCIN2023002), National R&D Program of China (2022YFC3006000, 2022YFB3207400), Natural Science Foundation of Tianjin (22JCQNJC00290) and Fundamental Research Funds for the Central Public Welfare Research Institutes (TKS20240305) and Tianjin Transportation Technology Development Plan Project (2023-47).

Institutional Review Board Statement: Not applicable.

Informed Consent Statement: Not applicable.

Data Availability Statement: Data are contained within the article.

Conflicts of Interest: The authors declare no conflicts of interest.

References

1. European Maritime Safety Agency Annual Overview of Marine Casualties and Incidents. Available online: https://www.emsa.europa.eu/newsroom/latest-news/item/4266-annual-overview-of-marine-casualties-and-incidents-2020.html (accessed on 13 June 2024).
2. Maritime Safety Committee. *Report of the Maritime Safety Committee on Its One Hundredth Session*; IMO: London, UK, 2019.
3. Kretschmann, L.; Burmeister, H.-C.; Jahn, C. Analyzing the Economic Benefit of Unmanned Autonomous Ships: An Exploratory Cost-Comparison Between an Autonomous and a Conventional Bulk Carrier. *Res. Transp. Bus. Manag.* **2017**, *25*, 76–86. [CrossRef]
4. Teledyne FLIR. Available online: https://www.flir.cn/marine/navigation/ (accessed on 15 November 2024).
5. HD Hyundai's Avikus Successfully Conducts the World's First Transoceanic Voyage of a Large Merchant Ship Relying on Autonomous Navigation Technologies. Available online: https://avikus.ai/en-us/press/hd-hyundais-avikus-recognized-for-innovation-at-ces-for-second-consecutive-year-1-0-0-0-1 (accessed on 5 January 2025).
6. Laera, F.; Fiorentino, M.; Evangelista, A.; Boccaccio, A.; Manghisi, V.M.; Gabbard, J.; Gattullo, M.; Uva, A.E.; Foglia, M.M. Augmented Reality for Maritime Navigation Data Visualisation: A Systematic Review, Issues and Perspectives. *J. Navig.* **2021**, *74*, 1073–1090. [CrossRef]
7. Clunie, T.; DeFilippo, M.; Sacarny, M.; Robinette, P. Development of a Perception System for an Autonomous Surface Vehicle Using Monocular Camera, LIDAR, and Marine RADAR. In Proceedings of the 2021 IEEE International Conference on Robotics and Automation (ICRA), Xi'an, China, 30 May 2021; pp. 14112–14119.
8. Liu, R.W.; Guo, Y.; Nie, J.; Hu, Q.; Xiong, Z.; Yu, H.; Guizani, M. Intelligent Edge-Enabled Efficient Multi-Source Data Fusion for Autonomous Surface Vehicles in Maritime Internet of Things. *IEEE Trans. Green Commun. Netw.* **2022**, *6*, 1574–1587. [CrossRef]
9. Huo, G.; Wu, Z.; Li, J. Underwater Object Classification in Sidescan Sonar Images Using Deep Transfer Learning and Semisynthetic Training Data. *IEEE Access* **2020**, *8*, 47407–47418. [CrossRef]
10. Wei, S.; Zeng, X.; Qu, Q.; Wang, M.; Su, H.; Shi, J. HRSID: A High-Resolution SAR Images Dataset for Ship Detection and Instance Segmentation. *IEEE Access* **2020**, *8*, 120234–120254. [CrossRef]
11. Liu, Z.; Yuan, L.; Weng, L.; Yang, Y. A High Resolution Optical Satellite Image Dataset for Ship Recognition and Some New Baselines. In Proceedings of the 6th International Conference on Pattern Recognition Applications and Methods, Porto, Portugal, 24–26 February 2017; SCITEPRESS—Science and Technology Publications: Porto, Portugal, 2017; pp. 324–331.
12. Prasad, D.K.; Rajan, D.; Rachmawati, L.; Rajabally, E.; Quek, C. Video Processing From Electro-Optical Sensors for Object Detection and Tracking in a Maritime Environment: A Survey. *IEEE Trans. Intell. Transport. Syst.* **2017**, *18*, 1993–2016. [CrossRef]
13. Qu, J.; Liu, R.W.; Guo, Y.; Lu, Y.; Su, J.; Li, P. Improving Maritime Traffic Surveillance in Inland Waterways Using the Robust Fusion of AIS and Visual Data. *Ocean Eng.* **2023**, *275*, 114198. [CrossRef]
14. Ding, H.; Weng, J. A Robust Assessment of Inland Waterway Collision Risk Based on AIS and Visual Data Fusion. *Ocean Eng.* **2024**, *307*, 118242. [CrossRef]
15. Singh, A.; Zhou, J.; Lin, C.-T.; Lal, S.; Eidels, A.; Jiang, X.; Brown, S. Enhancing Marine Navigation Performance Using the Head-Up Interface. In Proceedings of the 2024 IEEE International Conference on Systems, Man, and Cybernetics (SMC), Kuching, Malaysia,, 6–10 October 2024; pp. 496–502.
16. Wang, X.; Jiao, J.; Yin, J.; Zhao, W.; Han, X.; Sun, B. Underwater Sonar Image Classification Using Adaptive Weights Convolutional Neural Network. *Appl. Acoust.* **2019**, *146*, 145–154. [CrossRef]
17. Zhang, X.; Huo, C.; Xu, N.; Jiang, H.; Cao, Y.; Ni, L.; Pan, C. Multitask Learning for Ship Detection From Synthetic Aperture Radar Images. *IEEE J. Sel. Top. Appl. Earth Obs. Remote Sens.* **2021**, *14*, 8048–8062. [CrossRef]
18. Skolnik, M.I. (Ed.) *Radar Handbook*, 3rd ed.; McGraw-Hill Education: New York, NY, USA, 2008; ISBN 978-0-07-148547-0.
19. Zhang, S.; Wu, R.; Xu, K.; Wang, J.; Sun, W. R-CNN-Based Ship Detection from High Resolution Remote Sensing Imagery. *Remote Sens.* **2019**, *11*, 631. [CrossRef]
20. Jin, H.-S.; Cho, H.; Jiafeng, H.; Lee, J.-H.; Kim, M.-J.; Jeong, S.-K.; Ji, D.-H.; Joo, K.; Jung, D.; Choi, H.-S. Hovering Control of UUV through Underwater Object Detection Based on Deep Learning. *Ocean Eng.* **2022**, *253*, 111321. [CrossRef]
21. Zhang, Y.; Li, Q.-Z.; Zang, F.-N. Ship Detection for Visual Maritime Surveillance from Non-Stationary Platforms. *Ocean Eng.* **2017**, *141*, 53–63. [CrossRef]
22. Gao, M.; Shi, G.-Y. Ship-Handling Behavior Pattern Recognition Using AIS Sub-Trajectory Clustering Analysis Based on the T-SNE and Spectral Clustering Algorithms. *Ocean Eng.* **2020**, *205*, 106919. [CrossRef]
23. Zhao, J.; Yan, Z.; Zhou, Z.; Chen, X.; Wu, B.; Wang, S. A Ship Trajectory Prediction Method Based on GAT and LSTM. *Ocean Eng.* **2023**, *289*, 116159. [CrossRef]
24. Girshick, R.; Donahue, J.; Darrell, T.; Malik, J. Rich Feature Hierarchies for Accurate Object Detection and Semantic Segmentation. In Proceedings of the 2014 IEEE Conference on Computer Vision and Pattern Recognition, Columbus, OH, USA, 23–28 June 2014; IEEE: New York, NY, USA, 2014; pp. 580–587.
25. Girshick, R. Fast R-CNN. In Proceedings of the 2015 IEEE International Conference on Computer Vision (ICCV), Santiago, Chile, 7–13 December 2015; IEEE: New York, NY, USA, 2015; pp. 1440–1448.

26. Ren, S.; He, K.; Girshick, R.; Sun, J. Faster R-CNN: Towards Real-Time Object Detection with Region Proposal Networks. *IEEE Trans. Pattern Anal. Mach. Intell.* **2017**, 39, 1137–1149. [CrossRef] [PubMed]
27. Redmon, J.; Divvala, S.; Girshick, R.; Farhadi, A. You Only Look Once: Unified, Real-Time Object Detection. In Proceedings of th 2016 IEEE Conference on Computer Vision and Pattern Recognition (CVPR), Las Vegas, NV, USA, 27–30 June 2016; IEEE: New York, NY, USA, 2016; pp. 779–788.
28. Redmon, J.; Farhadi, A. YOLO9000: Better, Faster, Stronger. In Proceedings of the 2017 IEEE Conference on Computer Vision an Pattern Recognition (CVPR), Honolulu, HI, USA, 21–26 July 2017; IEEE: New York, NY, USA, 2017; pp. 6517–6525.
29. Redmon, J.; Farhadi, A. YOLOv3: An Incremental Improvement. In *Computer Vision and Pattern Recognition*; Springe Berlin/Heidelberg, Germany, 2018.
30. Bochkovskiy, A.; Wang, C.-Y.; Liao, H.-Y.M. YOLOv4: Optimal Speed and Accuracy of Object Detection. *arXiv* **202** arXiv:2004.10934.
31. Liu, W.; Anguelov, D.; Erhan, D.; Szegedy, C.; Reed, S.; Fu, C.-Y.; Berg, A.C. SSD: Single Shot MultiBox Detector. In *Compute Vision—ECCV 2016*; Lecture Notes in Computer Science; Leibe, B., Matas, J., Sebe, N., Welling, M., Eds.; Springer Internationa Publishing: Cham, Switzerland, 2016; Volume 9905, pp. 21–37. ISBN 978-3-319-46447-3.
32. Zhang, D.; Zhan, J.; Tan, L.; Gao, Y.; Župan, R. Comparison of Two Deep Learning Methods for Ship Target Recognition wit Optical Remotely Sensed Data. *Neural Comput. Applic.* **2021**, 33, 4639–4649. [CrossRef]
33. Chen, Z.; Chen, D.; Zhang, Y.; Cheng, X.; Zhang, M.; Wu, C. Deep Learning for Autonomous Ship-Oriented Small Ship Detectio *Saf. Sci.* **2020**, 130, 104812. [CrossRef]
34. Chen, Z.; Liu, C.; Filaretov, V.; Yukhimets, D. Multi-Scale Ship Detection Algorithm Based on YOLOv7 for Complex Scene SA Images. *Remote Sens.* **2023**, 15, 2071. [CrossRef]
35. Liu, R.W.; Yuan, W.; Chen, X.; Lu, Y. An Enhanced CNN-Enabled Learning Method for Promoting Ship Detection in Maritim Surveillance System. *Ocean Eng.* **2021**, 235, 109435. [CrossRef]
36. Zheng, Y.; Liu, P.; Qian, L.; Qin, S.; Liu, X.; Ma, Y.; Cheng, G. Recognition and Depth Estimation of Ships Based on Binocula Stereo Vision. *J. Mar. Sci. Eng.* **2022**, 10, 1153. [CrossRef]
37. Zhou, Z.; Zhao, J.; Chen, X.; Chen, Y. A Ship Tracking and Speed Extraction Framework in Hazy Weather Based on Deep Learnir *J. Mar. Sci. Eng.* **2023**, 11, 1353. [CrossRef]
38. Chi Ming, W.; Yanan, L.; Lanxi, M.; Jiuhu, C.; Zhong, L.; Sunxin, S.; Yuanchao, Z.; Qianying, C.; Yugui, C.; Xiaoxue, D.; et Intelligent Marine Area Supervision Based on AIS and Radar Fusion. *Ocean Eng.* **2023**, 285, 115373. [CrossRef]
39. Wu, Y.; Chu, X.; Deng, L.; Lei, J.; He, W.; Królczyk, G.; Li, Z. A New Multi-Sensor Fusion Approach for Integrated Ship Moti Perception in Inland Waterways. *Measurement* **2022**, 200, 111630. [CrossRef]
40. Gülsoylu, E.; Koch, P.; Yildiz, M.; Constapel, M.; Kelm, A.P. Image and AIS Data Fusion Technique for Maritime Computer Visio Applications. In Proceedings of the IEEE/CVF Winter Conference on Applications of Computer Vision (WACV) Worksho Waikoloa, HI, USA, 3–8 January 2024; pp. 859–868.
41. Chen, J.; Hu, Q.; Zhao, R.; Guojun, P.; Yang, C. Tracking a Vessel by Combining Video and AIS Reports. In Proceedings of t Second International Conference on Future Generation Communication and Networking, Hainan, China, 13–15 December 20 IEEE: New York, NY, USA, 2008; Volume 2, pp. 374–378.
42. Xu, X.; Wu, B.; Teixeira, Â.P.; Yan, X.; Soares, C.G. Integration of Radar Sequential Images and AIS for Ship Speed and Headi Estimation Under Uncertainty. *IEEE Trans. Intell. Transport. Syst.* **2024**, 25, 5688–5702. [CrossRef]
43. Lu, Y.; Ma, H.; Smart, E.; Vuksanovic, B.; Chiverton, J.; Prabhu, S.R.; Glaister, M.; Dunston, E.; Hancock, C. Fusion of Camera-Bas Vessel Detection and Ais for Maritime Surveillance. In Proceedings of the 2021 26th International Conference on Automation a Computing (ICAC), Portsmouth, UK, 2–4 September 2021; IEEE: New York, NY, USA, 2021; pp. 1–6.
44. Zhang, R.; Zhao, C.; Liang, Y.; Hu, J.; Pan, M. Edge-Based Dynamic Spatiotemporal Data Fusion on Smart Buoys for Intellige Surveillance of Inland Waterways. *J. Mar. Sci. Eng.* **2025**, 13, 220. [CrossRef]
45. Jocher, G.; Chaurasia, A.; Qiu, J. Ultralytics YOLO 2024. Available online: https://github.com/ultralytics/ultralytics (access on 28 November 2024).
46. Zhu, L.; Wang, X.; Ke, Z.; Zhang, W.; Lau, R. BiFormer: Vision Transformer with Bi-Level Routing Attention. In Proceedings the IEEE/CVF Conference on Computer Vision and Pattern Recognition, Vancouver, BC, Canada, 17–24 June 2023.
47. Cao, J.; Pang, J.; Weng, X.; Khirodkar, R.; Kitani, K. Observation-Centric Sort: Rethinking Sort for Robust Multi-Object Tracki In Proceedings of the IEEE/CVF Conference on Computer Vision and Pattern Recognition, Vancouver, BC, Canada, 17–24 Ju 2023; pp. 9686–9696.
48. Song, L.; Wu, W.; Guo, J.; Li, X. Survey on Camera Calibration Technique. In Proceedings of the 2013 5th International Conferer on Intelligent Human-Machine Systems and Cybernetics, Hangzhou, China, 26–27 August 2013; IEEE: New York, NY, USA, 20 pp. 389–392.
49. Toohey, K.; Duckham, M. Trajectory Similarity Measures. *Sigspatial Spec.* **2015**, 7, 43–50. [CrossRef]

50. Zhu, X.; Su, W.; Lu, L.; Li, B.; Wang, X.; Dai, J. Deformable DETR: Deformable Transformers for End-to-End Object Detection. *arXiv* **2020**, arXiv:2010.04159.
51. Lyu, C.; Zhang, W.; Huang, H.; Zhou, Y.; Wang, Y.; Liu, Y.; Zhang, S.; Chen, K. RTMDet: An Empirical Study of Designing Real-Time Object Detectors. *arXiv* **2022**, arXiv:2212.07784.
52. Wang, C.-Y.; Bochkovskiy, A.; Liao, H.-Y.M. YOLOv7: Trainable Bag-of-Freebies Sets New State-of-the-Art for Real-Time Object Detectors. In Proceedings of the IEEE/CVF Conference on Computer Vision and Pattern Recognition, New Orleans, LA, USA, 18–24 June 2022.
53. Du, Y.; Zhao, Z.; Song, Y.; Zhao, Y.; Su, F.; Gong, T.; Meng, H. Strongsort: Make Deepsort Great Again. *IEEE Trans. Multimed.* **2023**, *25*, 8725–8737. [CrossRef]
54. Zhang, Y.; Sun, P.; Jiang, Y.; Yu, D.; Weng, F.; Yuan, Z.; Luo, P.; Liu, W.; Wang, X. Bytetrack: Multi-Object Tracking by Associating Every Detection Box. In Proceedings of the European Conference on Computer Vision, Tel Aviv, Israel, 23–27 October 2022; Springer: Berlin/Heidelberg, Germany, 2022; pp. 1–21.
55. Aharon, N.; Orfaig, R.; Bobrovsky, B.-Z. BoT-SORT: Robust Associations Multi-Pedestrian Tracking. *arXiv* **2022**, arXiv:2206.14651. [CrossRef]

Journal of
Marine Science and Engineering

MDPI

Article

Cooperative Formation Control of Multiple Ships with Time Delay Conditions

Wei Tao [1,2], Jian Tan [3], Zhongyi Sui [4,*], Lizheng Wang [5] and Xin Xiong [2,6]

1 School of Mathematics and Computer Science, Wuhan Polytechnic University, Wuhan 430048, China; taowei@whpu.edu.cn
2 State Key Laboratory of Maritime Technology and Safety, Wuhan University of Technology, Wuhan 430063, China
3 Faculty of Civil Engineering and Geosciences, Delft University of Technology, Stevinweg, 1, 2628 CN Delft, The Netherlands; j.tan-2@tudelft.nl
4 Department of Logistics and Maritime Studies, Faculty of Business, The Hong Kong Polytechnic University, Hong Kong 999077, China
5 Shenzhen Maritime Safety Administration, Shenzhen 518000, China
* Correspondence: zhongyi.sui@polyu.edu.hk

Abstract: The cooperative control of multiple autonomous surface vehicles (ASVs) is a critical area of research due to its significant applications in maritime operations, such as search and rescue and environmental monitoring. However, challenges such as communication delays and dynamic topologies often hinder stable cooperative control in practical scenarios. This study addresses these challenges by developing a formation control method based on consensus theory, focusing on both formation control and time delay. First, a simplified ASV characteristic model is established, and a basic consensus control algorithm is designed and analyzed for stability, considering different communication topologies. Then, to handle delays, the formation control method is extended, and the stability of the revised algorithm is rigorously proven using the Lyapunov function. Simulation results demonstrate that the proposed control strategy effectively maintains formations, even in the presence of communication delays. In the end, comparative simulations are carried out to demonstrate the effectiveness and robustness of the proposed controller. Simulation results demonstrate that the proposed control strategy effectively maintains formations, even in the presence of communication delays, with a convergence time of approximately 100 s and a formation error stabilizing at around 7 m. This research lays a foundation for more reliable cooperative control systems for ships, with potential applications in a variety of maritime and autonomous systems.

Keywords: autonomous surface vehicles; cooperative control; communication topologies; time delay; consensus theory

1. Introduction

The collaboration of vessels in waterway transportation systems offers many benefits. First, it can enhance the safety of waterway transport through communication between vessels. Such communication provides additional information, such as data about objects that sensors cannot detect and the intentions of other vessels. This information helps vessel operators collaborate and take effective actions [1]. Second, collaboration can improve transportation efficiency [2]. For example, vessels can coordinate their navigation plans to avoid congestion at ports and locks [3]. Additionally, by integrating route planning with infrastructure scheduling, vessels can adjust their speeds to reach their destinations on time, optimizing the use of infrastructure resources [4]. Finally, collaboration allows a group of vessels to perform tasks more effectively, such as search and rescue, ocean sampling, and hydrographic surveys [5]. Therefore, optimizing waterway transport performance requires not only the automation of individual vessels but also collaboration between them.

Given the advantages of vessel cooperation, recent years have seen increasing research on various cooperative methods [6,7]. For cooperative methods, communication is the premise of formation control. However, communication delays are inevitable in reality. Delays in communication among formation members may lead to inaccuracies in the status of the ship and even lead to invalidation of the whole operation. Thus, communication delays are crucial in ship formation control.

Cooperative control of multiple autonomous surface vehicles has become a crucial area of research due to its potential to revolutionize various maritime applications, including search-and-rescue operations, environmental monitoring, and autonomous transportation [8]. These applications benefit from the cooperative capabilities of multiple ships, leading to enhanced efficiency, safety, and adaptability in dynamic maritime environments. However, the practical implementation of cooperative control for ships is often hindered by challenges such as communication delays, which significantly impact the stability and performance of cooperative behaviors, especially in real-time operations.

This study addresses the challenges of formation control by proposing a novel strategy based on consensus theory. The core methodology involves the design and analysis of a simplified autonomous surface vehicle model, in which a basic consensus algorithm is employed to ensure the stability of formation control under varying communication topologies. Building on this approach, this study also accounts for communication delays, a common issue in practical scenarios, and adapts the formation control method accordingly. The stability of the revised control algorithm is rigorously validated using Lyapunov's stability theory, providing a solid theoretical foundation for its reliability. Our contributions are as follows:

(1) Development of a consensus-based formation control algorithm capable of handling various communication topologies, ensuring stability in dynamic environments.
(2) Extension of the control strategy to accommodate communication delays, with rigorous proof of its stability through Lyapunov's stability theory.

This article is organized as follows. In Section 1, the introduction presents the importance of cooperative control for ships and outlines the research objectives and contributions of this study. Section 2 defines the core challenges of communication delays and dynamic topologies in multi-ASV coordination and formulates the problem to be addressed. Section 3 discusses the development of a consensus-based formation control strategy for ships, designed to handle communication delays and dynamic topologies. The proposed formation control strategy is verified through simulations in Section 4. Section 5 summarizes the findings and discusses the implications and potential future research directions.

2. Literature Review

Formation control in multi-agent systems, especially for autonomous surface vehicles (ASVs), is crucial for tasks like navigation and coordination in dynamic environments. Several key approaches have shaped the field, focusing on decentralized control and stability. Jadbabaie et al. introduced the nearest neighbor rules for agent coordination, enabling decentralized consensus and stable formations without a central controller [9]. Chung et al. highlighted the challenges of aerial swarm coordination, underscoring the need for adaptive strategies in complex environments [10]. Bunic and Bogdan's potential-function-based approach ensures formation stability and collision avoidance in 3D space [11]. Chang et al. also contributed with algorithms for collision avoidance, vital for maintaining safe formations in high-density environments [12]. Do's local potential functions allow for dynamic position adjustments while avoiding obstacles [13]. Anh et al. advanced this by combining rotational and repulsive forces for better obstacle avoidance and formation stability [14]. Optimization-based methods, such as those explored by Piet et al., offer valuable extensions by improving formation efficiency in constrained environments [15].

In recent years, several studies have further expanded the field. For instance, a study on multi-agent systems under external communication disturbances developed new control strategies for formation stability in the presence of unreliable communication [16]. Another work focused on formation control in directed topologies, providing a comprehensive framework for the stability of multi-agent systems [17]. Research on uncertain multi-agent systems addressed formation control under nonlinear constraints, integrating control barrier functions to ensure both safety and stability [18]. A recent paper also explored collision avoidance in multi-agent systems using consensus mechanisms, demonstrating effective formation control and collision avoidance in multi-agent systems [19]. Additionally, a study on discrete-time linear multi-agent systems proposed a control method based on stress matrices, addressing formation stability in both static and dynamic leader scenarios [20]. Another significant contribution is from a neural-network-based approach, which handles uncertainty in nonlinear multi-agent systems, enhancing cooperative formation control [21]. These studies provide the foundation for robust formation control methods. Our work extends these principles by developing a consensus-based algorithm that addresses the unique challenges of communication delays and dynamic topologies in ASV formations.

Many studies have focused on addressing the formation control problem in the presence of communication delays in ASVs, AUVs (Autonomous Underwater Vehicles), and UAVs (Unmanned Aerial Vehicles). Broadly, the existing approaches can be categorized into three main types: data-driven, observer-based, and event-triggered methods, as outlined in Table 1.

Table 1. Literature review.

Research Article	Type of Vehicles			Number of Vehicles				Communication Constraints		Method
	ASV	AUV	UAV	3	4	5	6	Time-Delay	Packet Dropouts	
[22]	•			•				•	•	Auto-regressive model
[23]	•			•				•		Proportional–integral (PI) predictive control
[24]	•				•			•		RBF neural networks
[25]	•						•	•		Rational approximation, based on the Hermite–Feje'r tangential interpolation condition
[26]	•						•	•		Luenberger observer
[27]	•				•			•		Radial basis function (RBF) neural networks, event-triggered
[28]	•						•	•		Consensus theory, adaptive control
[29]		•				•		•		Consensus theory
[30]		•				•		•	•	Consensus theory
[31]		•				•		•		Robust control, observer
[32]			•	•				•		Consensus theory
[33]			•		•			•	•	Consensus theory

The • represents the objects (including the values of aircraft type, quantity, and communication constraints) studied in the paper.

Data-driven approaches primarily aim to develop models that predict communication latency or the states of multi-agent systems at each time step based on historical communication data. Common techniques in this category include auto-regressive models [22], PID control [23], emerging artificial intelligence models [24], and function approximation [25]. These methods are heavily dependent on historical data but can be computationally expensive and are prone to overfitting, especially when large datasets are required for model development.

Observer-based methods involve designing state observers or estimators to estimate the states of neighboring agents in the system. Notable observer models include high-gain observers [26], predictive state observers [27], and Luenberger observers [28]. Despite their strengths, these methods are often challenged by issues related to parameter selection and tuning, and they tend to be sensitive to external disturbances or noise.

Event-triggered methods adjust the communication topology dynamically when communication delays or bandwidth usage exceed predefined thresholds. These strategies often depend on measurable control variables such as rudder angles [29] or the current system state. Event-triggered mechanisms are frequently combined with other approaches, such as neural networks (NNs) [30], to reduce the communication burden among formation members. In addition to the methods mentioned above, consensus-based formation control algorithms have successfully addressed the delay problem due their convenient design [31].

Problems involving consensus-based formation control whilst considering delay have been applied and validated on various intelligent transportation platforms, including underwater [32–34] and air vehicles [35,36], though their application in the maritime field remains relatively limited.

On the other hand, current research classifies formation control methods into three primary categories based on formation structure [37]. The leader–follower approach designates one vessel as the leader, which follows a desired trajectory, while the followers adjust their positions relative to the leader using predefined offsets. The behavioral approach assigns different weights to various desired behaviors, such as clustering and formation maintenance, to guide the control process [38]. The virtual structure approach treats the entire formation as a single virtual entity, with the motion of individual vessels governed by the movement of this virtual structure. Formation control focuses on guiding a group of vessels to achieve a specific geometric configuration and follow a predefined path [39]. The majority of research in vessel formation control adopts one of three primary strategies: the leader–follower framework [40], the behavioral approach, or the virtual structure method. These approaches consider vessel-specific characteristics and environmental disturbances, ensuring adaptability to varying operational conditions [41–43].

Despite the extensive research on these methods, several critical gaps remain in the literature. Firstly, most existing methods either ignore or only partially account for the impact of communication delays on the stability of multi-agent systems. In maritime applications, where delays are often caused by long communication distances or limited bandwidth, effective compensation for delays is essential to maintaining system stability. Secondly, many studies assume a static communication topology, but in practice, the topology of communication links can change dynamically due to the motion of agents. Methods that can adapt to changing communication topologies while maintaining stable formation control are still lacking.

3. Problem Statement and Formulation

This section addresses the key challenges and formulations necessary for the cooperative control of autonomous surface vehicles in a formation.

3.1. Formation Matrix Description for Ship Formation

In designing formation control strategies, a matrix capable of describing the ASV formation structure is required. This matrix enables ships positioned at different locations and with varying initial states to converge with the desired formation through control strategies, ensuring that their states become consistent. In real-world scenarios, the formation structure of ships is determined based on the tasks to be executed. Selecting an appropriate formation structure contributes to improved formation stability and enhanced cooperative capabilities.

The formation description method, as shown in Figure 1, directly projects the desired relative distances between the ships and the virtual center of the formation onto the coordinate axes. In this figure, we present a method for describing the formation of autonomous surface vehicles (ASVs) in a two-dimensional plane. The desired relative distances between the ASVs and the virtual center of the formation are projected onto the coordinate axes, simplifying the geometric relationships between the vehicles. Specifically, the virtual center serves as the reference point, and the relative positions of the ships are described in terms of their distance from this center. This approach allows for a straightforward representation of the formation, making it easier to design and implement control strategies. The cooperative variables, including position, velocity, and orientation angle, are key to achieving consensus in the formation control algorithm. These variables are synchronized among the ships to maintain the desired formation and ensure stability. This approach uses the direction coordinate system to represent these projections more straightforwardly. In Figure 1, p_c represents the virtual center of the formation and serves as the reference point for other vehicles. $p_i = [x_i, y_i]^T$ denotes the spatial coordinates of ASV i. $p_{iF} = [x_{iF}, y_{iF}]^T$ represents the desired relative position between ASV i and the virtual center of the formation. In the context of formation control strategies, the information that needs to achieve consensus is referred to as cooperative variables. For example, if the desired outcome is for all ships in the formation to align their orientation angles, then the orientation angle becomes a cooperative variable.

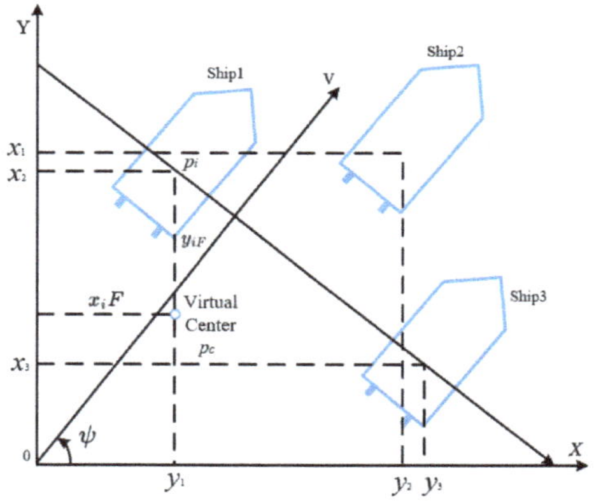

Figure 1. Formation description under coordinate axis decomposition.

The two-dimensional spatial coordinates of ships are first selected as cooperative variables. The control goal is to ensure that each ASV achieves the desired distance from a reference point, expressed as:

$$\|p_{ic} - p_c\| \to 0 \tag{1}$$

where $p_{ic} = p_i - p_{iF}$. To preserve the formation, it is also necessary to ensure that the velocities and orientation angles of all ships remain consistent. These requirements are expressed as:

$$\|v_i - v_j\| \to 0, \|\psi_i - \psi_j\| \to 0 \tag{2}$$

where v_i and ψ_i denote the linear velocity and angle of ASV i, respectively. To design an effective formation control strategy, it is essential to ensure that each ASV accurately obtains and converges to these cooperative variables, which include position, velocity, and orientation angle.

3.2. Construction of Communication Topology Models

To model and control twin-propulsion ships, graph theory is utilized to establish a communication topology structure that connects individual ships, thereby forming a coordinated formation system. The following discusses the use of mathematical graph theory to describe the information exchange relationships between ships within a group.

In graph theory, graphs are divided into directed graphs and undirected graphs. A directed graph is represented as $G = (v_n, \varepsilon_n)$, where $v_n = \{1, 2, \ldots, n\}$ is the set of nodes (representing the ships). $\varepsilon_n = v_n \times v_n$ is the set of edges (representing communication links between nodes). An edge $(i, j) \in \varepsilon$ indicates that node j is a neighboring node of node i.

In most practical formation scenarios, directed graphs are typically used to represent the communication topology. In a directed graph, multiple nodes capable of transferring information can be connected, forming a directed path. For instance, in a directed path, information can flow from node 1 to node 4 sequentially.

Some specific communication topology structures in graph theory have significant implications for formation control of ships. During the design process, these structures are often referred to or adapted to optimize the communication topology for the formation system. By leveraging insights from graph theory, the design of robust communication structures enables efficient coordination and control of ASV formations. For a directed graph (v_n, ε_n), the adjacency matrix $A_n = [a_{ij}] \in R^{n\times n}$ is defined as follows: for any edge $(i,j) \in \varepsilon_n$, node i can receive information from node j, and $a_{ij} > 0$.

For a directed weighted graph with n n nodes, the in-degree of a certain node is defined as $d_{ii} = \sum a_{ij}$ The in-degree matrix is then $D = \text{diag}\{d_{ii}\}$.

The Laplacian matrix $L_n = [l_{ij}] \in R^{n\times n}$ is defined as:

$$l_{ij} = \begin{cases} -a_{ij},\ i \neq j \\ \sum_{i\neq j} a_{ij},\ i = j \end{cases} \tag{3}$$

Equivalently, $L_n = [l_{ij}] \in R^{n\times n}$, $L_n = D - A_n$, where $D = [d_{ij}] \in R^{n\times n}$. By the properties of the matrix, for any $(i,j) \notin \varepsilon_n$, $l_{ij} = -a_{ij} = 0$, the Laplacian matrix L_n satisfies the following:

$$l_{ij} \leq 0, i \neq j,\ \sum_{j=1} l_{ij} = 0,\ i = 1, 2, \cdots n \tag{4}$$

The Laplacian matrix of a directed graph is asymmetric; it satisfies the property of having a simple zero eigenvalue. For the communication topology shown in Figure 2, using graph theory, we model the communication network between the ships, with nodes representing the ships and edges representing communication links. A directed graph is used to depict the flow of information, ensuring that each ship can receive and transmit data to its neighboring ships. The structure of this communication network is critical for maintaining stable formation control, as it determines how the ships share information with each other. The corresponding matrix representation is as follows:

$$A = \begin{bmatrix} 0 & 1 & 0 & 0 & 0 & 0 \\ 1 & 0 & 0 & 0 & 0 & 0 \\ 1 & 0 & 0 & 0 & 0 & 0 \\ 0 & 1 & 1 & 0 & 0 & 0 \\ 0 & 0 & 1 & 0 & 0 & 1 \\ 0 & 0 & 0 & 1 & 1 & 0 \end{bmatrix}, D = \begin{bmatrix} 1 & 0 & 0 & 0 & 0 & 0 \\ 0 & 1 & 0 & 0 & 0 & 0 \\ 0 & 0 & 1 & 0 & 0 & 0 \\ 0 & 0 & 0 & 2 & 0 & 0 \\ 0 & 0 & 0 & 0 & 2 & 0 \\ 0 & 0 & 0 & 0 & 0 & 2 \end{bmatrix}, L = \begin{bmatrix} 1 & -1 & 0 & 0 & 0 & 0 \\ -1 & 0 & 0 & 0 & 0 & 0 \\ -1 & 0 & 1 & 0 & 0 & 0 \\ 0 & -1 & -1 & 2 & 0 & 0 \\ 0 & 0 & -1 & 0 & 2 & 1 \\ 0 & 0 & 0 & -1 & -1 & 2 \end{bmatrix}$$

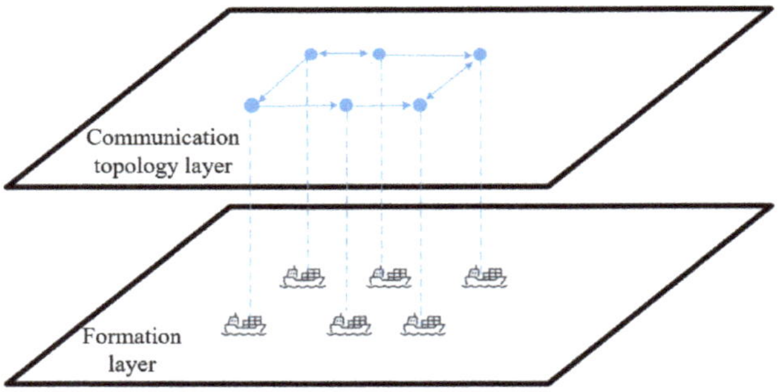

Figure 2. Communication topology network of ship formations.

3.3. Dynamic Model

Assuming that the formation consists of multiple ships, according to the literature [44], the kinematic model of the ith $(i = 1, 2, \cdots N)$ ASV can be represented as:

$$\dot{\eta}_i = R(\varphi_i)\boldsymbol{v_i} \tag{5}$$

where $\eta_i = \begin{bmatrix} x_i & y_i & \varphi_i \end{bmatrix}^T$ is the position and heading vector of the ASV, x_i is the longitudinal position of the ASV, y_i is the lateral position of the ASV, φ_i is the heading angle of the ASV, $\boldsymbol{v}_i = \begin{bmatrix} u_i & v_i & r_i \end{bmatrix}^T$ is the velocity vector of the ASV, and $R(\varphi_i)$ is the standard rotation matrix of the ASV, defined as:

$$R(\varphi_i) = \begin{bmatrix} \cos(\varphi_i) & -\sin(\varphi_i) & 0 \\ \sin(\varphi_i) & \cos(\varphi_i) & 0 \\ 0 & 0 & 1 \end{bmatrix} \tag{6}$$

The research object of this study is a two-propeller-driven unmanned surface vehicle. This type of ASV is equipped with two independently operating propellers, which are controlled by DC motors. The heading angle of the ASV is adjusted by the speed difference between the left and right propellers.

To better analyze the cooperative control problem of ASV formations, a simplified dynamics model was constructed based on a single ASV. A global coordinate system XOY is established in a two-dimensional plane, as shown in Figure 3. A structural diagram of the two-propeller-driven ASV is provided to facilitate the analysis of its dynamics model. According to the literature [45], the nonlinear dynamics model of the ith ASV can be expressed via a characteristic modeling approach.

Firstly, the relationship between motor commands and thrust on the vessel can be described as a nonlinear equation:

$$T_{\text{thrust}} = f_{\text{thrust}}(C_{\text{conmand}}) \tag{7}$$

where T_{thrust} is the motor's thrust force, C_{command} is the thrust command to the motor, and f_{thrust} is a nonlinear function between thrust force and thrust command. We obtain the model employed for building the characteristic model from Equation (5):

$$X(k+1) = f_1(k)X(k) + f_2(k)X(k-1) + g_0(k)u_i(k) \tag{8}$$

$$X(k) = [\psi(k), u(k)] \tag{9}$$

$$u_i(k) = \left[C_{\text{part-command}} \cdot C_{\text{stbd-command}}\right]^T \tag{10}$$

$$f_1(k) = \begin{bmatrix} f_{11}(k) & 0 \\ 0 & f_{22}(k) \end{bmatrix} f_2(k) = \begin{bmatrix} f_{12}(k) & 0 \\ 0 & f_{21}(k) \end{bmatrix} \tag{11}$$

$$g_0(k) = \begin{bmatrix} g_{11}(k) & g_{12}(k) \\ g_{13}(k) & g_{14}(k) \end{bmatrix} \tag{12}$$

where $\psi(k)$ is the heading angle of the ASV, $X(k)$ is the vector that consists of the heading and surge speed, $u_i(k)$ is the linear speed in surge direction, $u_i(k)$ is the control vector, and the parameters $f_1(k)$, $f_2(k)$, $g_0(k)$ are the time-varying characteristic parameters.

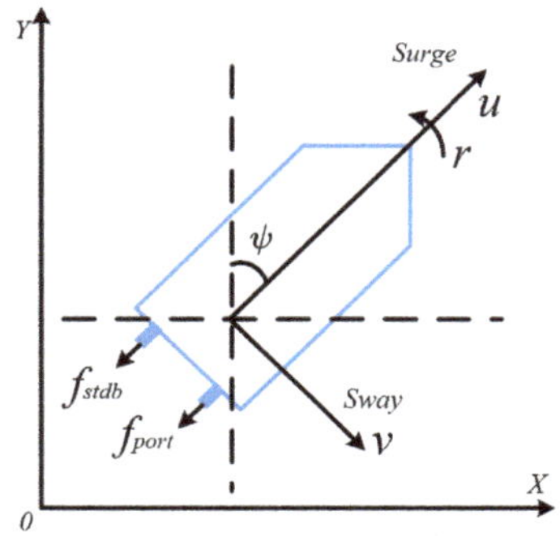

Figure 3. Kinematics of dual-propulsion ship.

4. Cooperative Formation Control Strategies for Autonomous Surface Vehicles

Formation control refers to enabling a group of ships, initially at different positions and states, to form a specific formation structure that allows for mutual communication and cooperation based on predefined rules. These rules represent cooperative control strategies for the formation. This study focuses on studying the capabilities of multi-ASV systems in formation generation, maintenance, etc. Based on consensus theory, cooperative formation control strategies are designed for conditions with time delays.

4.1. Cooperative Formation Control Strategy

Before designing cooperative formation control strategies, the stability of consensus under the communication topology is analyzed, and a fundamental consensus-based cooperative control strategy is presented.

4.1.1. Stability Analysis of Consensus Control Strategy

The formation of an ASV group is influenced by the communication topology within the formation. Therefore, it is essential to analyze the stability of the designed control strategies. For the formation communication topology, Ren proposed the consensus conditions for Lagrangian dynamics under a fixed communication topology.

Lemma 1. *For entities with autonomous decision-making and execution capabilities, their state information equations can be represented using a double-integrator dynamic system, also known as a second-order system. The equations are as follows:*

$$\dot{p}_{\mathrm{i}} = q_{\mathrm{i}},\ \dot{q}_{\mathrm{i}} = u_i \tag{13}$$

where p_i *represents the state information of the i-th ASV,* q_i *corresponds to the derivative of the state information, representing the velocity, and* u_i *is the control input for the i-th ASV. For motion systems that can be expressed using Equation (13), a consensus algorithm can be applied during formation control. The consensus algorithm is given as:*

$$u_i = -\sum\nolimits_j^n a_{ij}\left[(p_i - p_j) + \alpha(q_i - q_j)\right] \tag{14}$$

where α *is a positive scalar, representing the gain coefficient for the derivative changes between two moving entities.*

Further, when directly considering higher-order multi-intelligent systems, the state equations can be represented as:

$$\begin{cases} \dot{x}_i^{(0)} = x_i^{(1)} \\ \vdots \\ \dot{x}_i^{(l-1)} = u_i \end{cases} \tag{15}$$

where $x_i^l \in R^m$ represents the state variable of information, x_i^l represents the l-th order derivative of x_i, $x_i^{(0)}$ is the original state variable, and u_i is the control input. For the aforementioned higher-order system, a consensus algorithm for higher-order systems can be designed based on the second-order consensus algorithm referenced in the literature. The algorithm is as follows:

$$u_i = -\sum\nolimits_{j \in N_i} a_{ij}\left[\sum\nolimits_{k=0}^{l-1} \alpha_k\left(x_i^{(k)} - x_j^k\right)\right] \tag{16}$$

where $\alpha_k \in N$, $\alpha_k \neq 0$ represent the weights of the state variables, when $x_i^{(k)} \to x_j^k$ indicates that the k-th derivatives of the state variables of agents i and j approach each other as time progresses. The multi-agent system achieves asymptotic stability when the states across agents converge.

Properly setting the state variable weights, α_k, is a critical step in designing the consensus algorithm. To address this, the following theorem is provided.

Lemma 2. *In a multi-agent system with a minimum spanning tree, if the weights of the state variables* α_k *ensure that the system is Hurwitz-stable, the information of all agents can achieve consensus stability.*

To prove this, control Algorithm (16) is substituted into the system Equation (17). This yields:

$$\begin{cases} \dot{x}_i^{(0)} = x_i^{(1)} \\ \dot{x}_i^{(1)} = x_i^{(2)} \\ \vdots \\ \dot{x}_i^{(l-1)} = -\sum_{j \in N_i} a_{ij}\left[\sum_{k=0}^{l-1} \alpha_k\left(x_i^{(k)} - x_j^k\right)\right] \end{cases} \tag{17}$$

where $x_i = \left[x_i^{(0)}, x_i^{(1)}, \cdots, x_i^{(l-1)}\right]^T$. To represent the system in state-space form, let $y_i = x_i$. The state-space matrix equation for the multi-agent system can be expressed as follows:

$$\begin{cases} \dot{x}_i = A' x_i + B^l u_i \\ y_i = C' x_i + D' u_i \end{cases} \tag{18}$$

If u_i is represented in matrix form, it can be expressed as follows:

$$u_i = \begin{bmatrix} -\sum_{j=1}^{n} l_{11}\left(x_i^{(0)} - x_j^{(0)}\right) \\ -\sum_{j=1}^{n} l_{22}\left(x_i^{(1)} - x_j^{(1)}\right) \\ \vdots \\ -\sum_{j=1}^{n} l_{ll}\left(x_i^{(l-1)} - x_j^{(l-1)}\right) \end{bmatrix} \tag{19}$$

In this case, $l_{11}, l_{22}, \cdots, l_n$, refer to the diagonal elements of the Laplacian matrix L, which are defined based on the communication topology. According to the definition of the Laplacian matrix:

$$A' = \begin{bmatrix} 0 & 1 & 0 & \cdots & 0 \\ 0 & 0 & 1 & \cdots & 0 \\ \vdots & \vdots & \vdots & \ddots & \vdots \\ 0 & 0 & 0 & \cdots & 1 \\ 0 & 0 & 0 & \cdots & 0 \end{bmatrix}_{l \times l}, \quad B^l = \begin{bmatrix} 0 & 0 & 0 & \cdots & 0 \\ 0 & 0 & 0 & \cdots & 0 \\ \vdots & \vdots & \vdots & \ddots & \vdots \\ 0 & 0 & 0 & \cdots & 0 \\ \alpha_0 & \alpha_1 & \alpha_2 & \cdots & \alpha_{l-1} \end{bmatrix}_{l \times l} \tag{20}$$

For a high-order system, with C^l as the l-order identity matrix and D^l as the zero matrix, the stability analysis of the closed-loop system can be conducted. According to modern control theory, the open-loop transfer function of the system can be derived as follows:

$$G^l(s) = C^l\left(sI - A^l\right)B^l \tag{21}$$

After simplification, the matrix form of the open-loop transfer function for the high-order system can be expressed as:

$$G^l(s) = \begin{bmatrix} \frac{\alpha_0}{s^l} & \frac{\alpha_1}{s^l} & \cdots & \frac{\alpha_{l-1}}{s^l} \\ \frac{\alpha_0}{s^{l-1}} & \frac{\alpha_1}{s^{l-1}} & \cdots & \frac{\alpha_{l-1}}{s^{l-1}} \\ \vdots & \vdots & \ddots & \vdots \\ \frac{\alpha_0}{s} & \frac{\alpha_1}{s} & \cdots & \frac{\alpha_{l-1}}{s} \end{bmatrix} \tag{22}$$

The closed-loop transfer function matrix $\phi^L(s)$ for the system satisfies the following form:

$$\phi^L(s) = G^l(s)\left(I_l + G^l(s)\right)^{-1} \tag{23}$$

The characteristic polynomial of the closed-loop transfer function, which determines the eigenvalues of the system, satisfies the following relationship:

$$\det\left(\phi^l(s)\right) = \det\left(I_l + G^l(s)\right) \cdot \det\left(sI_l - A^l\right) \tag{24}$$

To compute the characteristic polynomial for the closed-loop system, we derive the determinants $\det\left(I_l + G^l(s)\right)$ and $\det\left(sI_l - A^l\right)$ as follows:

$$I_l + G^l(s) = \begin{bmatrix} 1+\frac{\alpha_0}{s^l} & \frac{\alpha_1}{s^l} & \cdots & \frac{\alpha_{l-1}}{s^l} \\ \frac{\alpha_0}{s^{l-1}} & 1+\frac{\alpha_1}{s^{l-1}} & \cdots & \frac{\alpha_{l-1}}{s^{l-1}} \\ \vdots & \vdots & \ddots & \vdots \\ \frac{\alpha_0}{s} & \frac{\alpha_1}{s} & \cdots & 1+\frac{\alpha_{l-1}}{s} \end{bmatrix}_{l\times l} \tag{25}$$

By performing elementary row and column operations on Equation (25), we obtain:

$$I_l + G^l(s) = \begin{bmatrix} 1+\frac{\alpha_0}{s^l}+\cdots+\frac{\alpha_{l-1}}{s} & \frac{\alpha_1}{s^l} & \frac{\alpha_2}{s^l} & \cdots & \frac{\alpha_{l-1}}{s^l} \\ -s & 1 & 0 & \cdots & 0 \\ 0 & -s & 1 & \cdots & 0 \\ \vdots & \vdots & \vdots & \ddots & \vdots \\ 0 & 0 & \cdots & -s & 1 \end{bmatrix}_{l\times l} \tag{26}$$

Expanding along the first column yields:

$$\det\left(I_l + G^l(s)\right) = 1 + \frac{\alpha_0}{s^l} + \frac{\alpha_1}{s^{l-1}} \cdots + \frac{\alpha_{l-1}}{s} \tag{27}$$

$$\det(sI_l - A') = \begin{bmatrix} s & -1 & 0 & \cdots & 0 \\ 0 & s & -1 & \cdots & 0 \\ \vdots & & \ddots & & \vdots \\ 0 & 0 & \cdots & s & -1 \\ 0 & 0 & \cdots & 0 & s \end{bmatrix}_{|x|} = s^l \tag{28}$$

The closed-loop characteristic polynomial is expressed as:

$$\begin{aligned} \det(\phi'(s)) &= \det\left(I_l + G^l(s)\right) \cdot det(sI_l - A') \\ &= \left(1 + \frac{\alpha_0}{s^l} + \frac{\alpha_1}{s^{l-1}} \cdots + \frac{\alpha_{l-1}}{s}\right) \cdot s^l \end{aligned} \tag{29}$$

According to the polynomial stability theorem, the necessary and sufficient condition for the asymptotic stability of the closed-loop system is that all closed-loop poles (roots of the polynomial) lie in the left-half plane of the complex domain. Based on the Routh–Hurwitz criterion, the system is stable if $\alpha_0, \alpha_1, \cdots, \alpha_{l-1}$ form a Hurwitz polynomial. If $\alpha_0, \alpha_1, \cdots, \alpha_{l-1}$ satisfy the Hurwitz condition, the control strategy introduced in this section ensures that the state information of all system orders achieves consensus stability.

The subsequent cooperative formation control strategy and encirclement control strategy for unmanned surface vehicles, as discussed in later sections of this paper, are designed based on the principles in Equation (16).

4.1.2. State Control for Cooperative Motion

In the study of cooperative motion for multiple autonomous surface vehicles, state control is a critical factor that cannot be overlooked. The designed cooperative control strategy must ensure the convergence of state information for the ships to have practical significance. As discussed in the mathematical modeling section in Section 2, the heading angle and velocity are the two most important state variables, as they directly affect the motion trajectory of ships. Therefore, this study prioritizes the control of these two state variables.

Heading control is crucial for the state control of ships. The designed formation control strategy must ensure that the heading angles of all individual ships converge to a common value when the formation stabilizes. The simplified formula for the change in heading angle is expressed as:

$$\dot{\psi}_i = \frac{1}{\tau_\psi}(\psi_i^c - \psi_i) \tag{30}$$

where ψ_i is the current heading angle of ASV i, ψ_i^c is the desired heading angle generated by the formation control strategy, and τ_ψ is the time constant for heading adjustment.

The next stage heading angle of an ASV is calculated based on its current heading angle ψ_i and the control command ψ_i^c. The control command ψ_i^c is generated by the formation control strategy and integrates the heading angles of all ships in the formation at the same time, producing a control adjustment specific to ASV i.

As illustrated in Figure 4, consider three ships with initial heading angles $\psi_1 > \psi_2 > \psi_3$ through internal communication within the formation and adjustment based on the neighboring ships' heading angles; the heading angles are gradually aligned, ultimately achieving $\psi_1 = \psi_2 = \psi_3$. During the adjustment process, the following constraint must be satisfied: $|\Delta\psi_i| < \pi$.

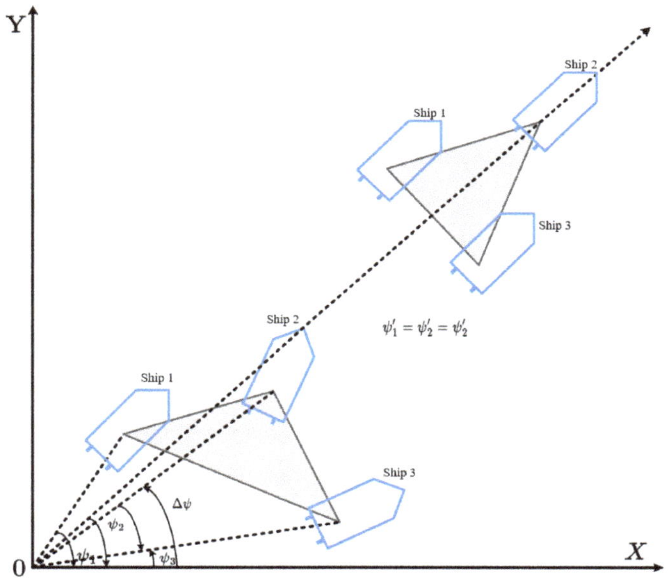

Figure 4. Schematic diagram of multi-ship formation direction adjustment.

This ensures smooth convergence and avoids abrupt or excessive heading changes, facilitating stable and cooperative formation behavior. The consensus control strategy for the heading angle is given by:

$$\begin{cases} \psi_i^c = \psi_i + \frac{1}{1+n_i} u_i \\ u_i = -\sum_{j=1}^{n} a_{ij}(\psi_i - \psi_j) \end{cases} \tag{31}$$

where n_i is the number of ships connected to ASV i in the communication topology, a_{ij} is the weight of the adjacency matrix in the communication topology, and u_i is the cooperative control term for the heading angle of ASV i. Traditional methods use Equation (31) for heading control. However, this approach cannot guarantee that the ships reach the desired heading angle, meaning it cannot determine the final attitude. This paper proposes an improved control strategy based on consensus theory to ensure convergence of the ships' heading angles. The improved method is as follows:

$$\begin{cases} \psi_i^c = \psi_i + \frac{1}{1+n_i} u_i \\ u_i = -b_i(\psi_i - \psi^q) - \sum_{j=1}^{n} a_{ij}(\psi_i - \psi_j) \end{cases} \tag{32}$$

where u_i is the cooperative control term, composed of two parts, and b_i is the coefficient of the desired tracking term. The velocity variation formula for the formation can be simplified as:

$$\dot{v}_i = \frac{1}{\tau_v}(v_i^c - v_i) \tag{33}$$

The consistency control strategy for speed convergence to the expected value is as follows:

$$\begin{cases} v_i^c = v_i + \frac{1}{1+n_i} u_i \\ u_i = -c_i(v_i - v^q) - \sum_{j=1}^{n} a_{ij}(v_i - v_j) \end{cases} \tag{34}$$

Then, the characteristic model-based intelligent adaptive control of ψ and ψ can be designed based on our research [1], with the controllers involved achieving tracking control of the desired ship state.

4.1.3. Cooperative Formation Control Strategy Based on Consensus Theory

In addition to ensuring that the heading angles and velocities of all ships converge, formation control must also ensure that the positions of all ships form a specific formation. Therefore, under the condition of a communication topology, a cooperative formation control strategy is designed based on consensus theory to enable ships to autonomously form a given formation. Since ships operate in a two-dimensional space, the design of the cooperative formation control strategy only needs to consider the North and East directions.

When the ships have not completed the formation task, the desired spacing between vehicles in the final formation must be obtained from the communication topology structure. For ASV i, the completion of the formation task must satisfy the following conditions, as shown in Equation (35):

$$\begin{aligned} (x_i' - x_{iF}') - \left(x_j' - x_{jF}'\right) = 0 \\ (y_i' - y_{iF}') - \left(y_j' - y_{jF}'\right) = 0 \end{aligned} \tag{35}$$

Simplifying these equations yields:

$$\begin{aligned} x_i' - x_j' - x_{ij}'^q = 0 \\ y_i' - y_j' - y_{ij}'^q = 0 \end{aligned} \tag{36}$$

where $x_{ij}'^q, y_{ij}'^q$ represent the desired spacing between ASV i and its neighboring ASV j in the communication topology.

Assume the current position of ASV i is p; to achieve the formation, ASV i adjusts its heading angle and velocity to reach position pi'. The velocity components in the X- and Y-axes are given as:

$$v_i'^x = v_i \cos \Delta\psi_i \tag{37}$$

$$v_i'^y = v_i \sin \Delta\psi_i \tag{38}$$

During the process of forming the predetermined formation, the heading angle and velocity—two critical state variables—are continuously changing. The cooperative formation control strategy based on consensus theory is expressed as:

$$v_i^c = v_i - \sum_{j=1}^{n} a_{ij}\left[\tau_r(v_i - v_j) + k_i^{vch}\left(x_i' - x_j' - x_{ij}'^q\right)\right] \tag{39}$$

$$\psi_i^c = \psi_i - \sum_{j=1}^{n} a_{ij}\left[\frac{1}{1+n_i}(\psi_i - \psi_j) + k_i^{\psi ch}\left(y_i' - y_j' - y_{ij}'^q\right)\right] \tag{40}$$

where $k_i^{vch}, k_i^{\psi ch}$ represent the variable gains that measure the influence of the desired formation spacing on the control commands. Their values become 0 when the formation is achieved.

Using Equations (39) and (40), ships with different initial positions and states can form a specified formation, and their heading angles and velocities will converge to a consistent state. During the actual motion of ASV formations, specific motion directions and speeds are assigned based on different task requirements, and different control strategies are adopted accordingly. The following three improved algorithms are proposed:

$$v_i^c = v_i - \sum_{j=1}^{n} a_{ij}\left[\tau_v(v_i - v_j) + k_i^{vch}\left(x_i' - x_j' - x_{ij}'^q\right)\right] \tag{41}$$

$$\psi_i^c = \psi_i - b_i^{ch}(\psi_i - \psi^q) - \sum_{j=1}^{n} a_{ij}\left[\frac{1}{1+n_i}(\psi_i - \psi_j) + k_i^{\psi ch}\left(y_i' - y_j' - y_{ij}'^q\right)\right] \tag{42}$$

By using Equations (40)–(42), the direction of convergence of the formation can be made to reach ψ^q:

$$v_i^c = v_i - c_i^{ch}(v_i - v^q) - \sum_{j=1}^{n} a_{ij}\left[\tau_v(v_i - v_j) + k_i^{vch}\left(x_i' - x_j' - x_{ij}'^q\right)\right] \tag{43}$$

$$\psi_i^c = \psi_i - \sum_{j=1}^{n} a_{ij}\left[\frac{1}{1+n_i}(\psi_i - \psi_j) + k_i^{\psi ch}\left(y_i' - y_j' - y_{ij}'^q\right)\right] \tag{44}$$

By using Equations (43) and (44), the convergence speed of the formation can be set to v^q:

$$v_i^c = v_i - c_i^{ch}(v_i - v^q) - \sum_{j=1}^{n} a_{ij}\left[\tau_v(v_i - v_j) + k_i^{vch}\left(x_i' - x_j' - x_{ij}'^q\right)\right] \tag{45}$$

$$\psi_i^c = \psi_i - b_i^{ch}(\psi_i - \psi^q) - \sum_{j=1}^{n} a_{ij}\left[\frac{1}{1+n_i}(\psi_i - \psi_j) + k_i^{\psi ch}\left(y_i' - y_j' - y_{ij}'^q\right)\right] \tag{46}$$

By constructing a reasonable communication topology within the ASV group and combining the algorithms described in Equations (43) and (44) through (45) and (46), the ASV cluster can effectively achieve the desired formation in a two-dimensional plane. These algorithms ensure that the heading angle, velocity, and relative positions between ships converge to the specified formation parameters, enabling efficient and robust cooperative formation control.

4.1.4. Formation Maintenance and Transformation of ASV Formations

During the execution of tasks by an ASV formation, the formation system may adapt to different tasks by adjusting its heading angles and velocities. Sometimes, only one state variable is adjusted, while at other times, both heading angles and velocities are changed simultaneously. Therefore, it is essential to ensure that the ASV formation can perform autonomous cooperative motion under any circumstance.

The previous section identified that factors influencing computational burden include the complexity of the algorithm and the number of variables. Considering that during ASV formation movement, there are scenarios where only one state variable (heading angle or velocity) needs to change, while in others, both must change simultaneously, different formation control strategies should be adopted accordingly. The following introduces two cases.

During the task execution process, when the task point's position changes or an obstacle appears in the path ahead, the formation control strategy described in Equations (41) and (42) can be used to reset the heading angle of the ASV formation.

When performing target tracking tasks, where the target's position and state continuously change, the ASV formation needs to utilize the formation control strategy described in Equations (45) and (46). This enables the ships to adjust their heading angles and velocities in real-time based on the target's position and state information. By employing the strategies provided above, ASV formations can effectively complete various tasks. Part of these formation control strategies will be validated in the simulation section.

4.2. *Cooperative Control Strategies for Formations Under Delay*

During the motion of an ASV formation, individual ships must exchange information with others to understand their motion states. However, in practical formation experiments, issues such as communication delay, noise, and packet loss are unavoidable. Therefore, delays must be considered in the design and implementation of formation control strategies.

4.2.1. Sources of Communication Delays

Communication delay is the time required for a signal to travel from one agent to another. It depends on the communication medium and the physical distance between the agents. Longer distances or slower communication mediums result in longer transmission times. The communication diagram and controller diagram of an unmanned ship are shown in Figure 5.

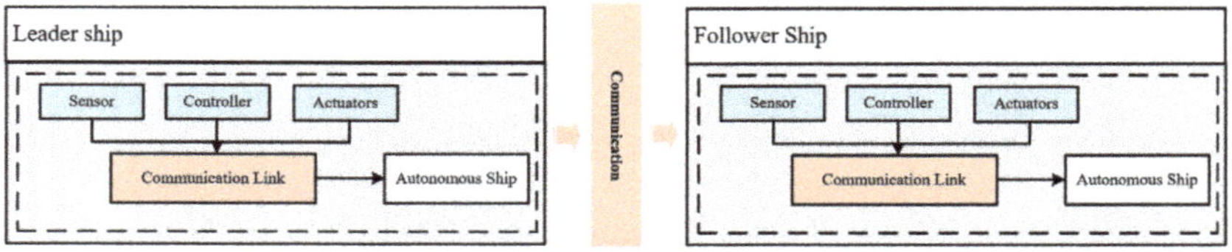

Figure 5. Communication diagram and controller diagram of unmanned ships.

Communication delays can severely impact the performance of formation control algorithms. The key challenges caused by delays include lag in feedback and instability in the formation. When agents rely on outdated information from neighbors, it can result in decisions based on inaccurate positions or velocities, leading to inefficient coordination and delayed responses in formation adjustments. In some cases, long delays can prevent the system from achieving consensus, causing the formation to oscillate or fail to reach a stable state.

The stability of the delay-based consensus formation cooperative control strategy was demonstrated in the previous section. Therefore, it is crucial to study the communication topology structure of ASV formations under delay conditions. The delay communication topology structure increases the number of undirected paths between nodes, reducing the dependence on single sources of information. The structure is shown in Figure 6.

The internal communication topology of ships plays a crucial role in ensuring formation control. Forming a directed spanning tree is a necessary condition for achieving convergence and consensus in the formation. The main advantage of the delay communication model is that while building upon the strong connectivity structure, it increases the feedback among ships, thereby reducing communication delays during the formation process.

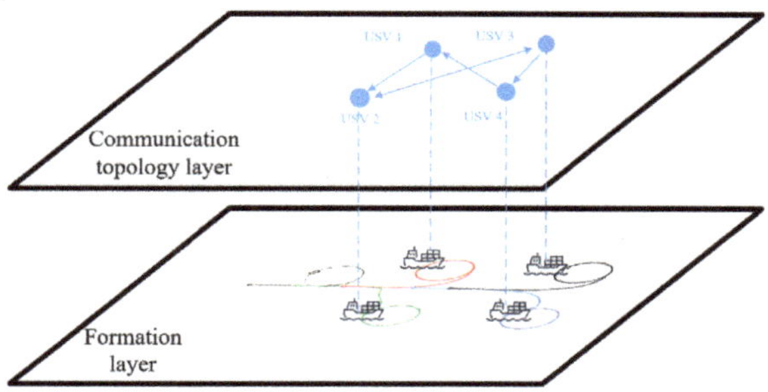

Figure 6. Communication network structure considering delay.

Additionally, this topology provides some level of protection for individual ships. For example, if there are differences in the construction costs of various ships, the communication topology architecture can leverage these differences through weight coefficients to influence the formation. Higher-cost ships, often with better communication capabilities, act as primary nodes, and other ships adjust their formation direction relative to these primary nodes.

For addressing the delay issue in ASV formations, adopting the delay communication model offers significant advantages. It ensures formation convergence, enhances feedback, and optimizes the communication structure by prioritizing critical nodes. This approach reduces the maximum directed path threshold, making the formation more robust and efficient.

4.2.2. Control Strategies for Delayed Formations Based on Consensus Theory

Communication delays within an ASV formation mean that the state of an ASV at the next time step is influenced not only by its current state but also by the previous states of other ships. Thus, the control strategy for delayed formations must account for providing control inputs to the ships. Ensuring the stability of the cooperative control strategy under delay conditions. To address the negative effects of communication delays, we developed a consensus mechanism within the control algorithm.

By considering the synchronous coupling method, it is possible to achieve state synchronization among the formation ships. This method is applied to the cooperative control strategy by using the delayed state of the previous time step to construct the control input for the current time step.

The control components for the ASV formation in the X- and Y-plane dimensions are given as:

$$\begin{cases} u_i^x = -\eta_1 \sum_{j\in N_i} \left[x_i(t-\tau) - x_j(t-\tau) - d_{ij}^x\right] - \eta_2 \sum_{j\in N_i} \left[v_i^x(t) - v_j^x(t)\right] + \eta_2 b_i \left[v_o(t) - v_i^x(t)\right] \\ u_i^y = -\eta_1 \sum_{j\in N_i} \left[y_i(t-\tau) - y_j(t-\tau) - d_{ij}^y\right] - \eta_2 \sum_{j\in N_i} \left[v_i^y(t) - v_j^y(t)\right] + \eta_2 b_i \left[v_o(t) - v_i^y(t)\right] \end{cases} \tag{47}$$

To combine the control components in the X- and Y-directions, the velocity and heading angle control commands for formation ships are derived based on the ASV kinematic model:

$$v_i^c = v_i + \tau_v \left(u_i^x \cos\psi_i + u_i^y \sin\psi_i\right) \tag{48}$$

$$\psi_i^c = \psi_i + \frac{\tau_\psi}{v} \left(u_i^y \cos\psi_i - u_i^x \sin\psi_i\right) \tag{49}$$

Further, the precise control commands with added desired convergence values are given as:

$$v_i^c = v_i - c_i(v_i - v^q) + \tau_v \left(u_i^x \cos\psi_i + u_i^y \sin\psi_i\right) \tag{50}$$

$$\psi_i^c = \psi_i - b_i(\psi_i - \psi^q) + \frac{\tau_\psi}{v}\left(u_i^y \cos\psi_i - u_i^x \sin\psi_i\right) \tag{51}$$

The above strategy enables the effective cooperative control of multi-ASV formations under delayed conditions. By combining kinematic modeling with precise control adjustments for the velocity and heading angle, the strategy ensures the formation can achieve the desired configuration while compensating for communication delays.

The following block diagrams shown in Figure 7 illustrate the steps involved in the proposed consensus-based formation control strategy. The diagrams show the flow of information through the system, from the initial measurement of the relative positions, velocities, and headings of the ASVs to the computation of control inputs. The diagrams also demonstrate how the communication topology and time delays are incorporated into the control process to adjust the control inputs accordingly.

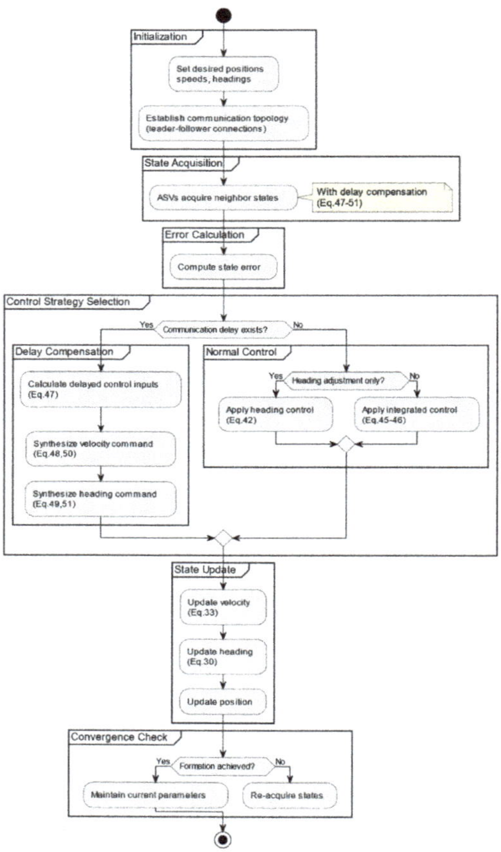

Figure 7. Block diagrams of proposed control strategies.

4.2.3. Stability Proof of Cooperative Control Strategies Under Delay

In this subsection, we prove the stability of the cooperative control strategy under delay conditions for ASV formations, as designed in the previous section. Assume the state information of ASV i is represented by $p_i = [x_i, y_i]^T$, $q_i = \left[v_i^x, v_i^y\right]^T$ For the ASV formation construct $p = [p_1, p_2, \cdots p_n]^T$, the formation system is modeled using a double-integrator dynamic system based on the motion characteristics of ASV formations. By substituting the control inputs derived from the delayed formation control strategy into the system equations, we obtain:

$$\begin{cases} \dot{p}(t) = q(t) \\ \dot{q}(t) = -\eta_1[Lp(t-\tau) - \mathrm{diag}(AR_1)] - \eta_2(L+B)[q(t) - v_o(t) \otimes I_n] \end{cases} \tag{52}$$

where A is the adjacency matrix, $R_1 = [\mathrm{r}_{ij}]$ is the desired formation spacing matrix $r_{ij} = \left[r_{ij}^x, r_{ij}^y\right]^T$ represents the desired spacing in the x- and y-directions, and $I_n = [1, \cdots, 1]^T$ is identity vector.

Let $Lp(t-\tau) - \mathrm{diag}(AR_1) = \overline{p}(t)$, $q(t) - v_o(t) \otimes I_n = \overline{q}(t)$; the system then transforms to:

$$\begin{cases} \dot{\overline{p}}(t) = l\overline{q}(t) \\ \dot{q}(t) = -\eta_1 \overline{p}(t-\tau) - \eta_2(L+B)\overline{q}(t) \end{cases} \tag{53}$$

Further, define $[\overline{p}(t), \overline{q}(t)] = w(t)$, and the system becomes:

$$\dot{w}(t) = \begin{bmatrix} 0 & L \\ 0 & -\eta_2(B+L) \end{bmatrix} w(t) + \begin{bmatrix} 0 & 0 \\ -\eta_1 I_n & 0 \end{bmatrix} w(t-\tau) \tag{54}$$

To analyze stability, we construct a Lyapunov–Krasovskii function as follows:

$$V(t) = w^T(t)Pw(t) + \int_{t-\tau}^{t} w(s)Qw(s)ds + \int_{-f}^{0}\int_{t+\theta}^{t} \dot{w}^T(s)R\dot{w}(s)d\theta ds \tag{55}$$

Taking the derivative of $V(t)$ gives:

$$\begin{aligned} \dot{V}(t) = 2w^T(t)P\dot{w}(t) + w^T(t)Qw(t) - w^T(t-\tau)Qw(t-\tau) \\ +\tau\dot{w}^T(t)R\dot{w}(t) - \textstyle\int_{t-\tau}^{t} \dot{w}^T(s)R\dot{w}(s)ds \end{aligned} \tag{56}$$

Then, we obtain:

$$\dot{w}(t) = Ew(t) + Fw(t-\tau) \tag{57}$$

We can obtain the following:

$$2w^T(t)P\dot{w}(t) = 2w^T(t)P(Ew(t) + Fw(t-\tau)) \tag{58}$$

For any $x, y \in R^n$ and positive definite matrix $M \in R^{n\times n}$, the following can be obtained:

$$2x^Ty \le x^TM^{-1}x + y^TMy \tag{59}$$

For Equation (59), there are:

$$\begin{aligned} 2w^T(t)PFw(t-\tau) &= 2w^T(t)PF\left[w(t) - \textstyle\int_{t-\tau}^{t} \dot{w}(s)ds\right] \\ &= 2w^T(t)PFw(t) - 2w^T(t)PF\textstyle\int_{t-\tau}^{t} \dot{w}(s)ds \\ &\le 2w^T(t)PFw(t) + \tau w^T(t)PFR^{-1}F^TPw(T) + \textstyle\int_{t-r}^{t} \dot{w}^T(s)R\dot{w}(s)ds \end{aligned} \tag{60}$$

Furthermore, for the integral terms within Equation (61), there are:

$$\begin{aligned} &\textstyle\int_{1-t}^{t} \dot{w}^T(s)R\dot{w}(s)ds = \tau[Ew(t) + Fw(t-\tau)]^TR[Ew(t) + Fw(t-\tau)] \\ &= \tau w^T(t)E^{\tau}REw(t) + \tau w^T(t-\tau)F^{\tau}REw(t) + \\ &\tau w^T(t)E^TRFw(t-\tau) + \tau w^T(t-\tau)F^TREw(t-\tau) \end{aligned} \tag{61}$$

Furthermore, Equation (57) can be converted into:

$$\begin{aligned}&\dot{V}(t) \leq 2w^T(t)PFw(t) + \tau w^T(t)PFR^{-1}F^TPw(t) + w^T(t)Qw(t)\\&-w^T(t-\tau)Qw(t-\tau) + \tau w^T(t)E^TREw(t) + \tau w^T(t-\tau)F^TREw(t)\\&+\tau w^T(t)E^TRFw(t-\tau) + \tau w(t-\tau)F^TREw(t-\tau)\end{aligned} \tag{62}$$

Further, extracting the variables from Equation (63) gives:

$$N = (E+F)^TP + P(E+F) + \tau E^TRE + \tau PFR^{-1}F^TP + Q \tag{63}$$

where

$$\begin{aligned}\dot{V}(t) &\leq \begin{bmatrix} w(t) \\ w(t-\tau) \end{bmatrix}^T \begin{bmatrix} N & \tau E^TRF \\ & \tau F^TRF - Q \end{bmatrix} \begin{bmatrix} w(t) \\ w(t-\tau) \end{bmatrix}\\ &\leq \begin{bmatrix} w(t) \\ w(t-\tau) \end{bmatrix}^T M \begin{bmatrix} w(t) \\ w(t-\tau) \end{bmatrix}\end{aligned} \tag{64}$$

According to the Schur complement lemma, for a given symmetric matrix $X \in R^{n\times n}$, it can be partitioned as follows:

$$X = \begin{bmatrix} x_{11} & x_{12} \\ x_{21} & x_{22} \end{bmatrix} \tag{65}$$

where $x_{11} \in R^{m\times m}, x_{22} \in R^{(n-m)\times(n-m)}, x_{12} = x_{21}^T, x_{21} \in R^{(n-m)\times m}, x_{12} \in R^{m\times(n-m)}$.

Then, $X < 0$ if and only if either of the following conditions are satisfied: $x_{11} < 0$, $x_{22} - x_{21}x_{11}^{-1}x_{12} < 0$ or $x_{22} < 0$, $x_{11} - x_{12}x_{22}^{-1}x_{21} < 0$.

Define $N_1 = (E+F)^TP + P(E+F) + \tau E^TRE + Q$. For the matrix M in Equation (65), we have:

$$M = \begin{bmatrix} N_1 & PF & \tau E^{\tau}RF \\ * & -\frac{R}{\tau} & 0 \\ * & * & \tau F^{\tau}RF - Q \end{bmatrix} \tag{66}$$

Using the Schur complement lemma, $M < 0$ can be determined by ensuring the conditions of the lemma are satisfied. Once $M < 0$ is confirmed, Equation (66) yields $\dot{V}(t) < 0$.

Based on the Lyapunov stability theorem, $\dot{V}(t) < 0$ ensures that the formation control strategy under delay conditions stabilizes the formation. This means that applying the proposed delay-based cooperative control strategy enables the ASV formation to maintain stability and achieve the desired formation even under communication delay conditions. Thus, for formations with a directed spanning tree communication topology and positive definite symmetric matrices satisfying Equation (66), the consensus-based formation control strategy designed in this study ensures that the ASV cluster can complete formation tasks in the presence of communication delays.

5. Simulation Verification of Multi-ASV Cooperative Formation Control Strategy

This section validates the designed cooperative formation control strategy through simulations. In this study, three experiments were conducted to design and validate the consistency-theory-based formation control under the delay of the formation.

5.1. Parameter Selection

The model we used in the simulation experiments was obtained by parameter identification based on a real twin-propulsion ship and real experimental data. Figure 8 shows the real twin-propulsion ASV used in our simulation. This ASV was predeveloped by us (as described in [44]) and a simulation model based on the feature model was built for it. This ASV is equipped with two 24 V thrust motors with a maximum thrust of 55 N. The length, width, and distance of the vessel from the propulsion motors are about 1.7, 0.75, and 0.5 m, respectively.

Based on the above unmanned ship model, three sets of experiments were carried out in this thesis to verify the effectiveness of the formation cooperative control algorithm based on the consistency theory, the cooperative control strategy under the formation time delay, and the comparison of the cooperative control under different control parameters, respectively. For the experiments conducted in this study, the simulation was performed using MATLAB 2023 a for modeling the system dynamics, control algorithm development, and simulation of the formation control strategy. MATLAB 2023 a provided a robust platform for implementing the control laws and performing the necessary computations. Additionally, to simulate real-time communication between the ASVs, we utilized the Robot Operating System 1(ROS 1). ROS 1 facilitated the integration of various system components, including communication between the ASVs and the simulation environment. It also allowed for the simulation of sensor data exchange and actuator control in real time, ensuring a more realistic representation of the cooperative behavior and interactions between the ASVs.

Figure 8. The twin-propulsion ASV used for modeling in simulation experiments.

In Case I, the cooperative formation control algorithm based on consensus theory, as designed in the previous section, was applied. The parameter values in the control algorithm were set as $k_i^{wh} = k_i^{zch} = 1.1/t, k_i^{ych} = \sqrt{\frac{1.1}{t}}, \eta = 1.2$. The formation was set to achieve a square formation, with the velocity maintained at 1.5 m/s and the heading angle changing dynamically to enable circular motion. The corresponding formation matrix is as follows:

$$K^x = \begin{bmatrix} 0 & 75 & 0 & 75 \\ -75 & 0 & 0 & -75 \\ -75 & 0 & 0 & -75 \\ 0 & 75 & 75 & 0 \end{bmatrix}, K^y = \begin{bmatrix} 0 & 0 & 59 & 59 \\ 0 & 0 & 59 & 59 \\ -59 & -59 & 0 & 0 \\ -59 & -59 & 0 & 0 \end{bmatrix}$$

To demonstrate the excellence of designed method for formation control, other algorithms were used to compare with the method in this paper. In the longitudinal direction, two good formation control methods [41–43] were selected.

In Case II, the algorithm coefficients were set as $\eta_1 = 0.73, \eta_2 = 1.02, b_i = 0.8$. The desired formation was a diamond shape, with a desired heading angle of $\pi/4$. The initial position of ASV 1 was [36, −5], the horizontal velocity was 0.8, and the angle of direction was 0.59 rad. The initial position of ASV 2 was [20, 8], the horizontal velocity was 2.8, and the angle of direction was 0.38 rad. The initial position of ASV 3 was [7, −2], the horizontal velocity was 3.8, and the angle of direction was 1.22 rad. The initial position of ASV 4 was [23, −8], the horizontal velocity was 1.8, and the angle of direction was 0.89 rad. The transmission delay caused by data exchange was approximately 220 ms. Considering the high volume of data communication among the four ships, the simulation assumed a random communication delay ranging from 0.7 s to 1.2 s. The communication topology structure is shown in Figure 6. The cooperative control strategy based on consensus theory under delay conditions was applied to control the state variables of the ships within the formation.

In Case III, the experimental trajectory was parameterized as $x_R = t, y_R = 20 \cdot \sin(0.05t)$. The control method and control parameters of the second group of experiments were adopted, and the control parameters were set as the first group, while the second group of control parameters was set, and the controller under the second group of control parameters was set as the control group to explore the effect of the change in the control parameters on the experimental results. The first set of parameters was set as $\eta_1 = 0.73, \eta_2 = 1.02, b_i = 0.8$, and the second set of parameters was set as $\eta_1 = 0.93, \eta_2 = 1.42, b_i = 0.8$. The initial position of the leader was $[-45, -5, 0]$. The initial position of the first follower was $[-53, -13, 0]$, and the relative position of its formation was $[-5, -5]$. The initial position of the second follower was $[-53, -2, 0]$, and the relative position of its formation was $[-5, 5]$. The desired speed in the experimental setup was 1.2 m/s. The main parameter settings are shown in Table 2.

Table 2. Main parameter settings.

Parameter	Value		
	Case 1	Case 2	Case 3
η	1	0.73, 1.02	1st 0.73, 1.02; 2nd 0.93, 1.42.
initial position of ASV 1	[19, 0]	[36, −5]	[−53, −13, 0]
initial position of ASV 2	[8, 0]	[20, 8]	[−5, −5]
initial position of ASV 3	[0, 0]	[7, −2]	[−53, −2, 0]
initial position of ASV 4	[32, 0]	[23, −8]	[−5, 5]

5.2. Results and Analysis

The results of our simulations and the analysis of these results are presented in this section. The simulations were designed to test the effectiveness of the cooperative formation control strategy, especially under conditions involving time delays. The experiments were conducted in three cases, each testing different aspects of the control strategy.

5.2.1. Case I: Circular Cooperative Formation Control

In this experiment, the ships were tasked with forming a square formation while maintaining circular motion. The formation was achieved successfully, as shown in the trajectory results (Figure 9). The results confirm that the proposed consensus-based cooperative formation control strategy effectively guided the ships to their target positions. The virtual ship in Figure 8 served as an idealized reference to evaluate the performance of the actual ASVs in the formation. It was not a physical entity but rather a computational model that represented the perfect trajectory and positioning of the ASVs in the formation, assuming no errors or delays. The inclusion of the virtual ship allowed for a clear comparison between the ideal and real behaviors of the ASVs, helping to highlight the deviations caused by factors such as communication delays, velocity constraints, and heading adjustments.

By comparing the actual ASVs with the virtual ship, we can assess how well the formation control algorithm performed and whether the ASVs maintained the desired formation under realistic conditions. For the formation trajectory, as shown in Figure 9a, the four ships, starting from different initial positions, utilized the proposed control strategy to eventually form a square formation while maintaining circular motion. Although the trajectories intersected in space, ships passed through the same points at different times, preventing collisions. The coordinate system used in Figure 9 is a standard Cartesian coordinate system (X, Y), which allows for a clear representation of the relative positions and movements of the ships. The "ground truth" was defined as the reference system from which these coordinates were derived, ensuring that all position data presented in the figure are based on a consistent frame of reference.

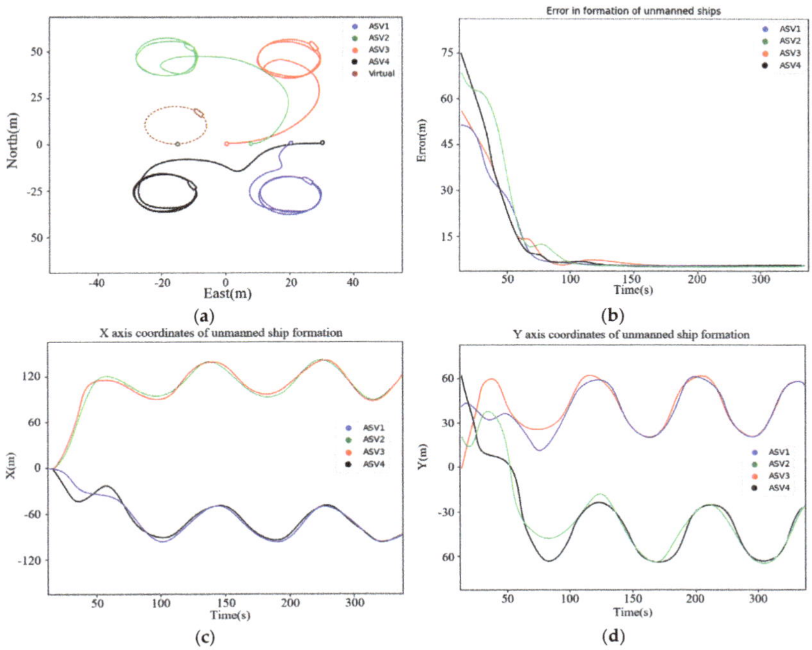

Figure 9. Results of the experiment. (**a**) Results of formation trajectory; (**b**) results of error; (**c**) results of X direction; (**d**) results of Y direction.

From Figure 9c,d, it can be observed that the final positions of ASV1 and ASV2 converged to the same state in the Y direction, while maintaining the given formation spacing in the X direction. Similarly, ASV2 and ASV4 converged to the same state in the X direction, while maintaining the given formation spacing in the Y direction. This demonstrates that, within a finite time, the four ships with different initial positions and states successfully formed a formation. In our study, the formation error stabilized at approximately 7 m after 100 s of operation. In contrast, previous methods, such as those proposed by [41–43], resulted in formation errors of 11 m, 10 m, and 13 m, respectively, under similar conditions. This shows that our approach achieved a more accurate formation with less deviation. Our method converged to the desired formation in about 100 s. Refs. [41,42] achieved convergence in 120 s, while [43] reported a convergence time of 150 s. The shorter convergence time of our approach suggests better efficiency in forming the desired configuration. Table 3 presents the results of the comparison of the average trajectory tracking error values between the control method used in this paper and the comparison method. As can be seen from the table, the method proposed in this paper had smaller tracking errors.

In conclusion, the consensus-based cooperative formation control strategy designed in the previous sections enables ships with different initial states and positions to effectively form a predetermined formation and achieve circular motion.

Table 3. Comparison of mean trajectory tracking errors for the heterogeneous MSV system.

Error	Proposed	DEFSMFC	NONNS	NOETC
ea(m)	7.605	10.895	10.0975	13.3825
*e*Asv1(m)	9.73	11.91	11.39	13.51
*e*Asv2 (m)	8.60	10.63	17.6	14.38
*e*Asv3 (m)	5.31	9.81	10.31	10.73
*e*Asv4 (m)	6.78	11.23	1.090	14.91

5.2.2. Case II: Cooperative Control Strategy Under Delays

This experiment was conducted to evaluate the control strategy under communication delays. The ships were tasked with forming a diamond-shaped formation.

The results of the formation trajectory, shown in Figure 10a, indicate that despite the delays, the ships successfully formed the diamond-shaped formation.

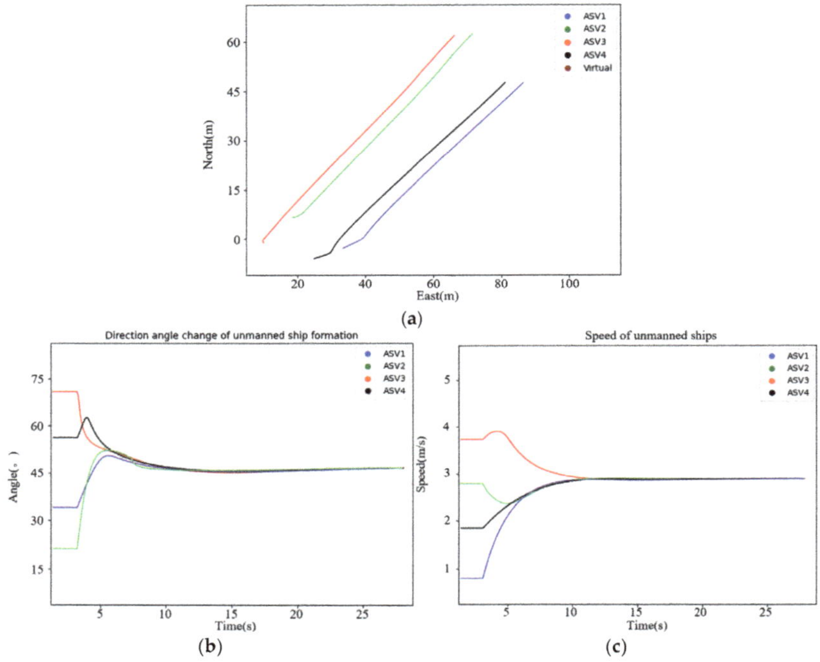

Figure 10. Results of cooperative control strategy under delays. (**a**) Results of formation trajectory; (**b**) results of heading angle; (**c**) experimental results of speed.

The responses of the heading angle and speed of each ship in the first thirty seconds are presented in Figure 10b,c. The results demonstrate that the delay-based cooperative control strategy enabled the ships to converge in both heading angle and speed. The system remained stable despite the communication delays.

A significant feature of this experiment is that the control strategy could adapt to delays, allowing the ships to achieve consensus in a reasonable time. The 220 ms delay was handled effectively, demonstrating the robustness of the control strategy under real-world conditions. In our simulations, the 220 ms delay was considered acceptable because our method adapted to this delay through the adaptive control strategy and ensured that the system remained stable. The results from our simulations, which show minimal formation errors and stable control under this delay, are provided to substantiate this claim. Our experiment was conducted under ideal conditions in an obstacle-free environment, and with a fixed 220 ms delay, the algorithm of our proposed new framework was effective. The strategy also effectively tracked the desired heading angle and velocity. However, due to the presence of delays and the fact that the control inputs for the next time step depend on the states from the previous time step, the convergence time for heading angle and velocity increased.

5.2.3. Case III: Sinusoidal Cooperative Formation Control

In this case, the cooperative formation control was tested under sinusoidal trajectory conditions. The goal was to evaluate how well the formation control could handle parameter changes. The effectiveness of the control effect under different parameter setting scenarios was analyzed using the sinusoidal trajectory as an example. Among them, Figure 11a shows the experimental results of the control method under different parameter setting scenarios, i.e., the effectiveness of ASV formation control under delays. The experimental results show that the first set of parameter settings had a better smoothing effect on the reference trajectory generation of the follower, while the smoothed desired trajectory affected the control effect of ASV formation. Combined with Figure 11b, it can be concluded that the desired trajectory smoothing process could effectively improve the convergence speed of the ASV formation. Figure 11c demonstrates the variation in the bow angle and speed of the following ship with different controllers. The experimental results demonstrate that the method proposed in this paper can effectively realize ship formation control and can handle the time delay disturbance.

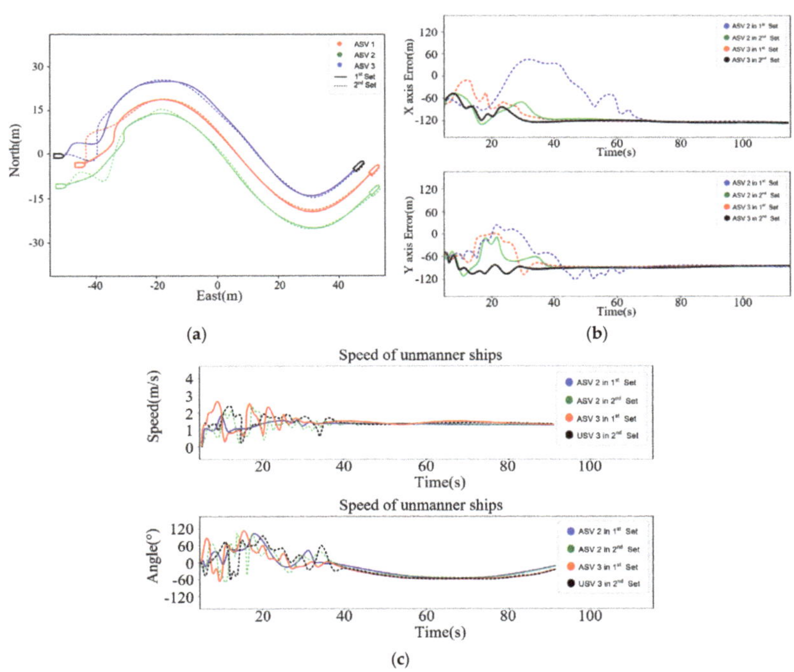

Figure 11. Results of cooperative control strategy under different parameters. (**a**) Results of formation trajectory; (**b**) experimental results of error; (**c**) experimental results of heading angle and speed.

6. Conclusions

This paper mainly studied the cooperative control strategy of ASV formations. Firstly, a separate state control strategy was designed based on the kinematic model of ships, which can control the speed and direction angle of ships within the formation to converge. Secondly, based on consistency theory, a control strategy for multiple ASV formations in ideal environments was designed, effectively enabling multiple ships to form and maintain a certain formation. Then, in response to the time delay problem that occurs during the formation of ships, a multi-ASV formation cooperative control strategy based on consistency theory under time delay conditions was designed, and the convergence and stability of the control strategy were proven using Lyapunov's theorem. Finally, simulation verification was conducted on the proposed ASV formation cooperative control strategy. As a direction for future research, we plan to explore the interaction between autonomous vessels and human-operated vessels, particularly in cases where human operators deviate from expected behaviors or regulations. In addition, we will focus on incorporating additional environmental factors, such as ocean currents, and expanding the application scenarios of this method under different tasks.

Author Contributions: Conceptualization, W.T., X.X. and Z.S.; methodology, W.T., X.X. and Z.S.; software, W.T.; validation, Z.S. and L.W.; formal analysis, Z.S.; investigation, W.T.; resources, J.T. and W.T.; data curation, L.W.; writing—original draft preparation, W.T. and X.X.; writing—review and editing, Z.S. and J.T.; visualization, W.T.; supervision, Z.S. and J.T.; project administration, L.W.; funding acquisition, L.W. All authors have read and agreed to the published version of the manuscript.

Funding: This work is supported by the Young Talents Project of the Science Research Program of Hubei Provincial Department of Education through grant no.2023Q20231606.

Institutional Review Board Statement: Not applicable.

Informed Consent Statement: Not applicable.

Data Availability Statement: Dataset available on request from the authors.

Conflicts of Interest: The authors declare no conflicts of interest.

Abbreviations

Main Symbol	Definition/Description
p_i	Spatial coordinates of ASV i
p_{iF}	The desired relative position between ASV *i* and the virtual center of the formation
η_i	The position and heading vector of the ASV
v_i	The velocity vector of the ASV
φ_i	The heading angle of the ASV
$\boldsymbol{R}(\varphi_i)$	The standard rotation matrix of the ASV
p_i	The state information of the *i*-th ASV
u_i	The control input for the *i*-th ASV
x_i^l	The state variable of information which is the *l*-th order derivative of *xi*
α_k	The weights of the state variables
$G^l(s)$	The open-loop transfer function matrix of the system
$\phi^L(s)$	The closed-loop transfer function matrix of the system
$k_i^{vch}, k_i^{\psi ch}$	Variable gains that measure the influence of the desired formation spacing on the control commands

References

1. Wen, Y.; Tao, W.; Sui, Z.; Piera, M.A.; Song, R. Dynamic model-based method for the analysis of ship behavior in marine traffi[c] situation. *Ocean Eng.* **2022**, *257*, 111578. [CrossRef]
2. Du, B.; Xie, W.; Zhang, W.; Chen, H. A target tracking guidance for unmanned surface vehicles in the presence of obstacles. *IEE[E] Trans. Intell. Transp. Syst.* **2023**, *25*, 4102–4115. [CrossRef]
3. Zhang, M.; Du, L.; Wen, Y.; Guo, L.; Wu, B. Optimization of ship transport capacity structure for traffic congestion alleviation o[n] inland waterways. *Ocean Eng.* **2024**, *311*, 118841. [CrossRef]

4. Granado, I.; Hernando, L.; Galparsoro, I.; Gabiña, G.; Groba, C.; Prellezo, R.; Fernandes, J.A. Towards a framework for fishing route optimization decision support systems: Review of the state-of-the-art and challenges. *J. Clean. Prod.* **2021**, *320*, 128661. [CrossRef]
5. Bae, I.; Hong, J. Survey on the developments of unmanned marine vehicles: Intelligence and cooperation. *Sensors* **2023**, *23*, 4643. [CrossRef]
6. Li, J.; Zhang, G.; Zhang, W.; Zhang, X. Robust control for cooperative path following of marine surface-air vehicles with a constrained inter-vehicles communication. *Ocean Eng.* **2024**, *308*, 118240. [CrossRef]
7. Tao, W.; Zhu, M.; Chen, S.; Cheng, X.; Wen, Y.; Zhang, W.; Negenborn, R.R.; Pang, Y. Coordination and optimization control framework for vessels platooning in inland waterborne transportation system. *IEEE Trans. Intell. Transp. Syst.* **2023**, *24*, 15667–15686. [CrossRef]
8. Peng, Z.; Wang, J.; Wang, D.; Han, Q.-L. An overview of recent advances in coordinated control of multiple autonomous surface vehicles. *IEEE Trans. Ind. Inform.* **2020**, *17*, 732–745. [CrossRef]
9. Jadbabaie, A.; Lin, J.; Morse, A. Coordination of Groups of Mobile Autonomous Agents Using Nearest Neighbor Rules. *IEEE Trans. Autom. Control* **2003**, *48*, 988–1001. [CrossRef]
10. Chung, S.J.; Paranjape, A.A.; Dames, P.; Shen, S.; Kumar, V. A Survey on Aerial Swarm Robotics. *IEEE Trans. Robot.* **2018**, *34*, 837–855. [CrossRef]
11. Bunic, M.; Bogdan, S. Potential Function Based Multi-Agent Formation Control in 3D Space. *IFAC Proc. Vol.* **2012**, *45*, 682–689. [CrossRef]
12. Chang, D.; Shadden, S.; Marsden, J.; Olfati-Saber, R. Collision Avoidance for Multiple Agent Systems. In Proceedings of the 42nd IEEE International Conference on Decision and Control, Maui, HI, USA, 9–12 December 2003.
13. Do, K. Formation Control of Mobile Agents Using Local Potential Functions. In Proceedings of the 2006 American Control Conference, Minneapolis, MN, USA, 14–16 June 2006.
14. Anh, D.; La, H.; Nguyen, T.; Horn, J. Formation Control for Autonomous Robots with Collision and Obstacle Avoidance Using a Rotational and Repulsive Force–Based Approach. *Int. J. Adv. Robot. Syst.* **2019**, *16*, 172988141984789.
15. Piet, B.; Ablak, M.; Strub, G.; Changey, S.; Petit, N. Experiments of High-Level Formation Flight of a Medium-Scaled Swarm of Micro UAVs in a Confined Environment with Obstacles. In Proceedings of the 2025 AIAA SciTech, Orlando, FL, USA, 6–10 January 2025.
16. Abbasi, M.; Marquez, H.J. Dynamic Event-Triggered Formation Control of Multi-Agent Systems With Non-Uniform Time-Varying Communication Delays. *IEEE Trans. Autom. Sci. Eng.* 2024; *early access*.
17. Lodhi, Z.A.; Zhang, K. Formation Control of Multi-agent Systems Over Directed Topologies: A Sliding Mode Control Approach With Prescribed-time Convergence. *Int. J. Control Autom. Syst.* **2024**, *22*, 3177–3190. [CrossRef]
18. Cao, X.; Li, K.; Li, Y. Robust adaptive formation control for nonlinear multi-agent systems with range constraints. *Nonlinear Dyn.* **2024**, *112*, 1917–1929. [CrossRef]
19. Epp, M.; Molinari, F.; Raisch, J. Exploiting Over-The-Air Consensus for Collision Avoidance and Formation Control in Multi-Agent Systems. *arXiv* **2024**, arXiv:2403.14386.
20. Onuoha, O.; Kurawa, S.; Tang, Z.; Dong, Y. Discrete-time stress matrix-based formation control of general linear multi-agent systems. *arXiv* **2024**, arXiv:2401.05083.
21. Moeurn, S.K. Distributed Cooperative Formation Control of Nonlinear Multi-Agent System (UGV) Using Neural Network. *arXiv* **2024**, arXiv:2403.13473.
22. Liu, G.-P. Predictive control of networked nonlinear multiagent systems with communication constraints. *IEEE Trans. Syst. Man Cybern. Syst.* **2020**, *50*, 4447–4457. [CrossRef]
23. Zhang, D.-W.; Liu, G.-P.; Cao, L. Proportional integral predictive control of high order fully actuated networked multiagent systems with communication delays. *IEEE Trans. Syst. Man Cybern. Syst.* **2023**, *53*, 801–812. [CrossRef]
24. Psillakis, H.E. Adaptive NN cooperative control of unknown nonlinear multiagent systems with communication delays. *IEEE Access* **2021**, *51*, 5311–5321. [CrossRef]
25. Qi, T.; Lu, R.; Chen, J. Consensus of continuous-time multiagent systems via delayed output feedback: Delay versus connectivity. *IEEE Trans. Autom. Control* **2021**, *66*, 1329–1336. [CrossRef]
26. Pang, Z.H.; Luo, W.C.; Liu, G.P.; Han, Q.L. Observer-based incremental predictive control of networked multi-agent systems with random delays and packet dropouts. *IEEE Trans. Circ. Syst. II Express Briefs* **2021**, *68*, 426–430. [CrossRef]
27. Liu, G.P. Coordinated control of networked multiagent systems via distributed cloud computing using multistep state predictors. *IEEE Trans. Cybern.* **2022**, *52*, 810–820. [CrossRef] [PubMed]
28. Su, H.; Chen, J.; Chen, X.; He, H. Adaptive observer-based output regulation of multiagent systems with communication constraints. *IEEE Trans. Cybern.* **2021**, *51*, 5259–5268. [CrossRef]
29. Zhang, C.; Zhang, G.; Zhang, X. DVSL guidance-based composite neural path following control for underactuated cable-laying vessels using event-triggered inputs. *Ocean Eng.* **2021**, *238*, 109713. [CrossRef]

30. Chen, C.; Zou, W.; Xiang, Z. Event-triggered connectivity-preserving formation control of heterogeneous multiple USVs. *IEEE Trans. Syst. Man Cybern. Syst.* **2024**, *54*, 7746–7755. [CrossRef]
31. Chen, Y.; Guo, X.; Luo, G.; Liu, G. A formation control method for AUV group under communication delay. *Front. Bioeng. Biotechnol.* **2022**, *10*, 848641. [CrossRef]
32. Li, J.; Du, J.; Li, Y.; Xu, G. Distributed robust prescribed performance 3-D time-varying formation control of underactuated AUVs under input saturations and communication delays. *IEEE J. Ocean. Eng.* **2023**, *48*, 649–662. [CrossRef]
33. Li, J.; Tian, Z.; Zhang, H. Discrete-time AUV formation control with leader-following consensus under time-varying delays. *Ocean Eng.* **2023**, *286*, 115678. [CrossRef]
34. Sadeghzadeh-Nokhodberiz, N.; Meskin, N. Consensus-based distributed formation control of multi-quadcopter systems: Barrier Lyapunov function approach. *IEEE Access* **2023**, *11*, 142916–142930. [CrossRef]
35. Du, Z.; Qu, X.; Shi, J.; Lu, J. Formation control of fixed-wing UAVs with communication delay. *ISA Trans.* **2024**, *146*, 154–16 [CrossRef] [PubMed]
36. Liu, Y.; Bucknall, R. A survey of formation control and motion planning of multiple unmanned vehicles. *Robotica* **2018**, *36*, 1019–1047. [CrossRef]
37. Cui, Z.; Guan, W.; Zhang, X. ASV formation navigation decision-making through hybrid deep reinforcement learning using self-attention mechanism. *Expert Syst. Appl.* **2024**, *256*, 124906. [CrossRef]
38. Liu, H.; Weng, P.; Tian, X.; Mai, Q. Distributed adaptive fixed-time formation control for UAV-ASV heterogeneous multi-agent systems. *Ocean Eng.* **2023**, *267*, 113240. [CrossRef]
39. Lee, J.H.; Jeong, S.K.; Ji, D.H.; Park, H.Y.; Kim, D.Y.; Choo, K.B.; Jung, D.W.; Kim, M.J.; Oh, M.H.; Choi, H.S. Unmanned surface vehicle using a leader–follower swarm control algorithm. *Appl. Sci.* **2023**, *13*, 3120. [CrossRef]
40. Tan, G.; Zhuang, J.; Zou, J.; Wan, L. Coordination control for multiple autonomous surface vehicles using hybrid behavior-based method. *Ocean Eng.* **2021**, *232*, 109147. [CrossRef]
41. Wang, S.; Zhu, M.; Wen, Y.; Sun, W.; Zhang, W.; Lei, T. Formation tracking control for networked heterogeneous MSV systems with actuator faults: A distributed optimal event-triggered fixed-time sliding mode fault-tolerant control approach. *Ocean Eng.* **2024**, *313*, 119370. [CrossRef]
42. Chen, B.; Hu, J.; Zhao, Y.; Ghosh, B.K. Finite-time observer based tracking control of uncertain heterogeneous underwater vehicles using adaptive sliding mode approach. *Neurocomputing* **2022**, *481*, 322–332. [CrossRef]
43. Meng, C.; Zhang, W.; Du, X. Finite-time extended state observer based collision-free leaderless formation control of multiple AUVs via event-triggered control. *Ocean Eng.* **2023**, *268*, 113605. [CrossRef]
44. Fossen, T.I. *Guidance and Control of Ocean Vehicles*; Wiley: Hoboken, NJ, USA, 1999.
45. Wen, Y.; Tao, W.; Zhu, M.; Zhou, J.; Xiao, C. Characteristic model-based path following controller design for the unmanned surface vessel. *Appl. Ocean Res.* **2020**, *101*, 102293. [CrossRef]

Journal of
Marine Science and Engineering

MDPI

Article

Research on the Coupling Dynamics Characteristics of Underwater Multi-Body Separation Considering the Influence of Elastic Constraints

Jiahui Chen [1], Yanhua Han [2,*], Ruofan Li [2], Zhenmin He [1] and Yong Zhang [2]

[1] China Ship Scientific Research Center, Wuxi 214082, China; kaiwaichen@163.com (J.C.); tt1124859356@163.com (Z.H.)
[2] College of Astronautics, Nanjing University of Aeronautics and Astronautics, Nanjing 210016, China; liruofan1@nuaa.edu.cn (R.L.); yongzhang@nuaa.edu.cn (Y.Z.)
* Correspondence: hanyanhua@nuaa.edu.cn

Abstract: Based on the Newton–Euler method, a multi-body coupling dynamics model of the separation process of underwater vehicles is established. The conditions of contact and detachment between the sub-vehicle and each group of elastic gaskets are analyzed in detail, and the elastic gasket constraint model is established to simulate the elastic contact and detachment process. Based on the Computational Fluid Dynamics (CFD) method, the hydrodynamic data of vehicles under different cases is calculated. In this context, a relatively accurate hydrodynamic database is established, where the hydrodynamic of the Unmanned Underwater Vehicle (UUV) is obtained through fitting, while those of the sub-vehicles are calculated using online interpolation. These provide conditions for realizing Fluid–Structure Interaction (FSI) calculation. Utilizing the FSI simulation method in the multi-body separation process, the separation dynamics of the multi-vehicle under the influence of elastic constraint parameters are analyzed. The simulation results show that the pitching attitude angles of the UUV and sub-vehicle in the separation process are negatively correlated with the change of elastic constraint stiffness, and the load is positively correlated with it, which are in opposite optimization directions. When the total stiffness of the elastic gaskets remains constant, changes in the number of elastic gaskets have a minimal impact on the UUV and sub-vehicle motion state during separation, but significantly affects the load fluctuations on the sub-vehicle, leading to structural vibration issues. The analysis method established in this paper is capable of quickly assessing the safety of underwater vehicle separation for different elastic gasket schemes, thereby facilitating the optimization of parameters.

Keywords: multi-body separation; elastic constraints; Newton–Euler method; structural load

1. Introduction

An Unmanned Underwater Vehicle (UUV) is capable of carrying various devices to perform specific tasks in extreme and dangerous environments, effectively replacing humans for underwater operations, and has therefore experienced rapid development. In the civilian field, UUV is widely used, including underwater surveys, marine resource development, underwater engineering construction and maintenance, as well as underwater search and rescue, which greatly improves the feasibility of underwater operations. In the military field, UUV is also used for anti-torpedo and underwater reconnaissance, providing critical intelligence and then enhancing strategic decision-making capabilities [1–4]. Under specific operating conditions, the sub-vehicle needs to be separated from the UUV to enable it to independently perform and complete assigned tasks. Therefore, it is necessary to study the dynamic characteristics of underwater vehicles in the separation process to improve their safety [5].

Firstly, this study investigated the coupling dynamics of a multi-vehicle system during the separation process. The ideas and methods for dynamics modeling of the multi-body separation process provided in the following literature served as a reference for dynamics modeling in this paper.

Han et al. [6,7] studied the two-body coupling dynamics between the carrier aircraft and the rocket during the launch process under the influence of gravity. In Ref. [6], the force conditions acting on the rocket and the degree of freedom of motion of the whole multi-body system were studied, and the launch process was segmented into five distinct stages. Utilizing the Newton–Euler approach, the coupling dynamics equations were formulated for the air launch and the carrier aircraft rocket without a launch tube. Subsequently, numerical simulations were carried out to explore the motion characteristics of the system throughout the launch process. In Ref. [7], the air-launch process was categorized into two distinct scenarios: one where the aircraft carries the rocket during flight, and the other where the rocket exits the launch tube propelled by gravity. Ultimately, the dynamics model of the launch process was established based on the Newton–Euler method, which described the motion characteristics of the multi-body system in the launch process. In the research by Wang et al. [8], the motion equations and missile launch dynamics equations for a vehicle-mounted missile system were formulated using a multi-body system analysis approach based on transfer matrix techniques and launch dynamics theory. In this study, the research object was modeled separately, and the models of each subsystem were then organically combined to obtain the whole system dynamics model. Finally, through numerical simulations, the motion characteristics of the entire launch process of the vehicle-mounted missile system were analyzed, and the correctness of the modeling was verified. In the research by Zhang et al. [9], the hydrodynamic parameters of the missile were determined by integrating experimental data with system identification methods. The study then focused on analyzing the change in the wake flow generated by the missile and constructed a mathematical model to describe the interaction forces between successive launch missiles. Using this model, the researchers were able to forecast the flight paths and orientation variations of missiles under different launch scenarios, providing a solid theoretical basis for refining launch strategies. This study initially investigated the coupling dynamics interactions between the UUV and sub-vehicle during their separation. Previous research (Refs. [6–9]) had focused on the motion coupling relationships during the separation process of multi-body systems and developed a comprehensive multi-body dynamics coupling model to describe these interactions. This has certain reference significance for this study.

Refs. [10–12] studied the effects of different factors on underwater projectile launches. Weiland et al. [10] investigated the effects of the relative velocity between the submarine and the horizontal flow, as well as the launch depth, on projectile launching, providing valuable reference conclusions for the initial conditions of projectile launching. Shang et al. [11] derived the dynamics model for the underwater vertical ejection of projectiles, examining how lateral flow affects their motion characteristics. It was pointed out that the projectiles were subjected to significant lateral impact during the launch process, and attention should be paid to their vibration problem. Wang et al. [12] explored the flight path characteristics of projectiles during the separation process from submarines via numerical simulation. They examined how different water flow conditions influence the motion of projectiles and determined that water velocity is a key factor in dictating the success of projectile separation. Refs. [13–15] were dedicated to studying the mechanical environment and fluid dynamics characteristics of missiles or underwater vehicles during underwater launch. Tan et al. [13] examined the mechanical conditions of submarines when separating projectiles horizontally, developed a ballistic dynamics model and studied the emergency countermeasures for submarines in case of projectile ignition failure. In the research conducted by Cheng et al. [14], a coupled mathematical model involving both air and water dynamics during the underwater missile launch process was established, and the interaction between air and water flow was simulated through numerical methods. The experimental results are helpful for optimizing the design of underwater launch systems. Zhang et al. [15] utilized a multi-phase flow model and dynamic grid technology to conduct 3D numerical simulations of the initial launch phase of submarine-launched missiles under cold ejection conditions. The research focused on analyzing the fluid dynamics characteristics and the formation and evolution of tail bubbles during this phase. The findings offer a crucial foundation for the development and enhancement of the performance of submarine-launched missiles. Wang et al. [16] explored how installation parameters affect the secure release of mission payloads from autonomous underwater vehicles (AUVs). The trajectory and attitude changes of the mission payload and AUV after separation were analyzed at different cruising speeds and separation depths. Li et al. [17] conducted a comprehensive analysis of the fluid dynamics and structural response of launch tubes during the underwater launch process using fluid–structure coupling numerical simulation techniques. Their study revealed that significant pressure fluctuations within the launch tube occur during the dominant cavitation period. Additionally, they found that both lateral flow velocity and launch depth have a substantial impact on the performance and structural integrity of the launch tube. These findings offer critical insights and guidance for the design optimization of launch tubes in underwater launch systems. Lv et al. [18] constructed a simulation model for the submarine vertical missile launch process, based on the submarine's spatial motion equations. Utilizing numerical simulation results, they assessed the influence of uncertain factors on both the missile launch process and the submarine's stability control. This research provides valuable insights into how these factors affect the overall launch dynamics and control mechanisms of submarines during missile ejection. Brito et al. [19,20] developed a numerical simulation tool based on the coupling of Smoothed Particle Hydrodynamics (SPH) and multi-body dynamics to investigate the FSI of an Oscillating Wave Surge Converter (OWSC) and a Wave Energy Hyperbaric Converter (WEHC) under complex mechanical constraints. These studies validated the model's accuracy under nonlinear wave conditions, offering valuable reference in hydrodynamics and FSI modeling. The literature above focuses on studying the effects of underwater separation processes [21] under different working conditions on the platform, payload, launch tube and flow field, providing important references for the constraint setting and simulation condition setting in the launch tube in this paper.

In Ref. [5], the dynamics equations for the underwater separation of a multi-vehicle system under the rigid constraint of the launch tube are derived. Additionally, the impacts of various factors—such as mass ratio and separation depth—on the separation process between the UUV and the sub-vehicle are examined. Building upon the research of Ref. [5], this paper further examines the influence of elastic constraints between the launch tube and the sub-vehicle on the motion and mechanical properties of the multi-vehicle system. To enhance the realism of the simulation of the contact and separation process between the UUV and the sub-vehicle, several sets of elastic gaskets are installed within the launch tube. On this foundation, the coupling dynamics of the multi-vehicle separation process are investigated, and numerical simulations are conducted under a range of typical operating conditions.

The innovation of this paper lies in developing a complete two-rigid-body coupled dynamics model of UUV and sub-vehicle, considering the elastic gaskets in the launch tube.

The analysis method established in this paper is capable of quickly assessing the safety of underwater vehicle separation for different elastic gasket schemes, thereby facilitating the optimization of parameters.

2. Multi-Vehicle Coupling Dynamics Modeling

2.1. Multi-Vehicle Model and Coordinate Definition

The multi-vehicle system mentioned in this paper includes UUV and a sub-vehicle. A vertical launch tube is installed inside the UUV, which contains multiple sets of elastic gaskets, in order to restrain and buffer the sub-vehicle.

The following coordinate systems are established to describe the motion state of multiple vehicles: inertial coordinate system A($o_A x_A y_A$), UUV Body-fixed coordinate system B($o_B x_B y_B$), launch tube coordinate system C($o_C x_C y_C$) and sub-vehicle Body-fixed coordinate system D($o_D x_D y_D$). All motion is reduced into a two-dimensional plane. The position and orientation definitions of all coordinate systems are shown in Figure 1. o_B and o_D are the centroids of the UUV and sub-vehicle, respectively.

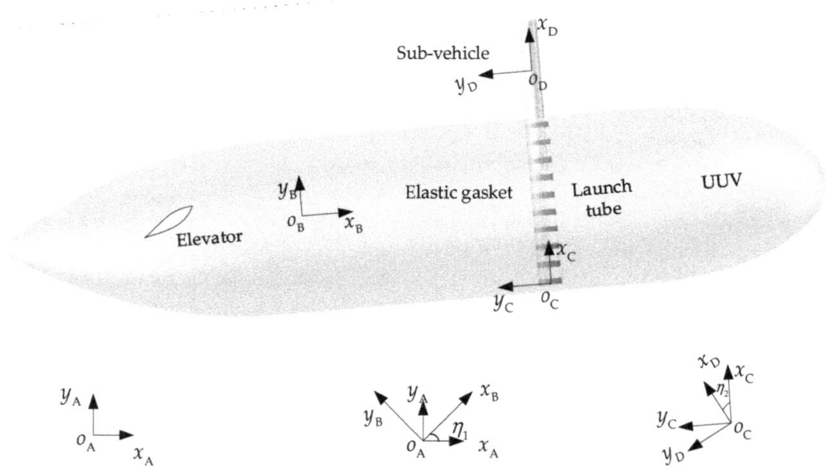

Figure 1. Schematic diagram of the multi-vehicle system.

This paper also focuses on pitching motion. The pitch angle of the UUV relative to the A coordinate system is denoted as η_1, while the pitch angle of the sub-vehicle relative to the launch tube is denoted as η_2.

The model parameters of the multi-vehicle system, as well as the meanings of the subscript and superscript symbols in the formulas are shown in Table 1.

Table 1. Model parameters of the multi-vehicle system and the meaning of the subscript.

Model Parameters	Meanings	Superscript and Subscript	Meanings
m_u	Mass of UUV	A, B, C, D	Corresponding coordinate system
m_s	Mass of sub-vehicle	u, s, la	UUV, sub-vehicle, launch tube
J_u	Pitch moment of inertia of UUV	w	Water
J_s	Pitch moment of inertia of sub-vehicle	sb	The bottom center of sub-vehicle
R_{la}	Radius of launch tube	en	Engine of UUV
R_s	Radius of sub-vehicle	e	Elastic gasket
ρ	Water density		

The transformation relations of vectors in different coordinate systems mentioned in this paper are as follows.

$$\{v_{\mathrm{A}} = T_{\mathrm{AB}}v_{\mathrm{B}},\ v_{\mathrm{B}} = T_{\mathrm{BC}}v_{\mathrm{C}},\ v_{\mathrm{C}} = T_{\mathrm{CD}}v_{\mathrm{D}} \tag{1}$$

where

$$\left\{ T_{\mathrm{AB}} = \begin{pmatrix} \cos\eta_1 & -\sin\eta_1 \\ \sin\eta_1 & \cos\eta_1 \end{pmatrix}, T_{\mathrm{BC}} = \begin{pmatrix} 0 & -1 \\ 1 & 0 \end{pmatrix}, T_{\mathrm{CD}} = \begin{pmatrix} \cos\eta_2 & -\sin\eta_2 \\ \sin\eta_2 & \cos\eta_2 \end{pmatrix} \right. \tag{2}$$

The calculation method of absolute derivative is shown in Equation (3).

$$\frac{\mathrm{d}\vec{v}_{\mathrm{B}}}{\mathrm{d}t} = \left(\dot{v}_x^{\mathrm{B}}, \dot{v}_y^{\mathrm{B}}\right)_{\mathrm{B}}^{\mathrm{T}} + \omega_{\mathrm{B}}^{\times} \cdot \left(v_x^{\mathrm{B}}, v_y^{\mathrm{B}}\right)_{\mathrm{B}}^{\mathrm{T}} \tag{3}$$

where

$$\omega_{\mathrm{B}}^{\times} = T_{\mathrm{AB}}{}^{\mathrm{T}}\dot{T}_{\mathrm{AB}} = \begin{pmatrix} 0 & -\dot{\eta}_1 \\ \dot{\eta}_1 & 0 \end{pmatrix} \tag{4}$$

Equations (1)–(4) will be repeatedly used in the subsequent derivation process.

2.2. Kinematic Analysis

In this section, the kinematics of UUV and sub-vehicle are given, including position, velocity, acceleration vector and moment of momentum in different coordinate systems.

The absolute position vector of the UUV's centroid is defined by Equation (5). In this paper, absolute vectors refer to those defined relative to the origin of the inertial coordinate system A. Unless otherwise stated, vectors associated with the UUV and sub-vehicle are defined relative to their respective centroids.

$$\vec{r}_{\mathrm{u}} = \left(x_{\mathrm{u}}^{\mathrm{A}}, y_{\mathrm{u}}^{\mathrm{A}}\right)_{\mathrm{A}}^{\mathrm{T}} \tag{5}$$

Compute the first- and second-time derivatives of Equation (5) to determine the absolute velocity and acceleration of the UUV, respectively. Subsequently, transform these quantities into the B coordinate system using Equation (1). This yields Equations (6) and (7).

$$\vec{v}_{\mathrm{u}} = \begin{pmatrix} \dot{x}_{\mathrm{u}}^{\mathrm{A}} \cos\eta_1 + \dot{y}_{\mathrm{u}}^{\mathrm{A}} \sin\eta_1 \\ -\dot{x}_{\mathrm{u}}^{\mathrm{A}} \sin\eta_1 + \dot{y}_{\mathrm{u}}^{\mathrm{A}} \cos\eta_1 \end{pmatrix}_{\mathrm{B}} \tag{6}$$

$$\vec{a}_{\mathrm{u}} = \begin{pmatrix} \ddot{x}_{\mathrm{u}}^{\mathrm{A}} \cos\eta_1 + \ddot{y}_{\mathrm{u}}^{\mathrm{A}} \sin\eta_1 \\ -\ddot{x}_{\mathrm{u}}^{\mathrm{A}} \sin\eta_1 + \ddot{y}_{\mathrm{u}}^{\mathrm{A}} \cos\eta_1 \end{pmatrix}_{\mathrm{B}} \tag{7}$$

The position vector $\vec{r}_{\mathrm{la}}^{\,\mathrm{u}}$ of the launch tube bottom center (o_{C}) relative to the UUV is given by Equation (8), with its components in the B coordinate system being known parameters.

$$\vec{r}_{\mathrm{la}}^{\,\mathrm{u}} = \left(x_{\mathrm{la}}^{\mathrm{u,B}}, y_{\mathrm{la}}^{\mathrm{u,B}}\right)_{\mathrm{B}}^{\mathrm{T}} \tag{8}$$

The position vector of the sub-vehicle centroid relative to the bottom center of the launch tube is given by Equation (9).

$$\vec{r}_{\mathrm{s}}^{\,\mathrm{la}} = \left(x_{\mathrm{s}}^{\mathrm{la,C}}, y_{\mathrm{s}}^{\mathrm{la,C}}\right)_{\mathrm{C}}^{\mathrm{T}} \tag{9}$$

By transforming Equation (9) into the B system and substituting it into formula $\vec{r}_{\mathrm{s}}^{\mathrm{u}} = \vec{r}_{\mathrm{la}}^{\mathrm{u}} + \vec{r}_{\mathrm{s}}^{\mathrm{la}}$, the position vector $\vec{r}_{\mathrm{s}}^{\mathrm{u}}$ of the sub-vehicle relative to UUV can be obtained. Use Equation (3) to calculate the time derivative of this vector $\vec{r}_{\mathrm{s}}^{\mathrm{u}}$. The projection component expression of the relative velocity vector $\vec{v}_{\mathrm{s}}^{\mathrm{u}}$ between the sub-vehicle and UUV in the B coordinate system can be derived. By substituting vectors $\vec{v}_{\mathrm{u}}$ and $\vec{v}_{\mathrm{s}}^{\mathrm{u}}$ into formula $\vec{v}_{\mathrm{s}} = \vec{v}_{\mathrm{u}} + \vec{v}_{\mathrm{s}}^{\mathrm{u}}$, the absolute velocity vector of the sub-vehicle can be determined:

$$\vec{v}_{\mathrm{s}} = \begin{bmatrix} \dot{x}_{\mathrm{u}}^{\mathrm{A}} \cos\eta_1 + \dot{y}_{\mathrm{u}}^{\mathrm{A}} \sin\eta_1 - \dot{\eta}_1 (y_{\mathrm{la}}^{\mathrm{u,B}} + x_{\mathrm{s}}^{\mathrm{la,C}}) - \dot{y}_{\mathrm{s}}^{\mathrm{la,C}} \\ -\dot{x}_{\mathrm{u}}^{\mathrm{A}} \sin\eta_1 + \dot{y}_{\mathrm{u}}^{\mathrm{A}} \cos\eta_1 + \dot{\eta}_1 (x_{\mathrm{la}}^{\mathrm{u,B}} - y_{\mathrm{s}}^{\mathrm{la,C}}) + \dot{x}_{\mathrm{s}}^{\mathrm{la,C}} \end{bmatrix}_{\mathrm{B}} \tag{10}$$

Using Equation (3), compute the time derivative of the velocity vector $\vec{v}_{\mathrm{s}}$ to determine the absolute acceleration of the sub-vehicle.

$$\vec{a}_{\mathrm{s}} = \begin{bmatrix} \ddot{x}_{\mathrm{u}}^{\mathrm{A}} \cos\eta_1 + \ddot{y}_{\mathrm{u}}^{\mathrm{A}} \sin\eta_1 - \ddot{\eta}_1 (y_{\mathrm{la}}^{\mathrm{u,B}} + x_{\mathrm{s}}^{\mathrm{la,C}}) - \ddot{y}_{\mathrm{s}}^{\mathrm{la,C}} - \dot{\eta}_1^{\,2} (x_{\mathrm{la}}^{\mathrm{u,B}} - y_{\mathrm{s}}^{\mathrm{la,C}}) - 2\dot{\eta}_1 \dot{x}_{\mathrm{s}}^{\mathrm{la,C}} \\ -\ddot{x}_{\mathrm{u}}^{\mathrm{A}} \sin\eta_1 + \ddot{y}_{\mathrm{u}}^{\mathrm{A}} \cos\eta_1 + \ddot{\eta}_1 (x_{\mathrm{la}}^{\mathrm{u,B}} - y_{\mathrm{s}}^{\mathrm{la,C}}) + \ddot{x}_{\mathrm{s}}^{\mathrm{la,C}} - \dot{\eta}_1^{\,2} (y_{\mathrm{la}}^{\mathrm{u,B}} + x_{\mathrm{s}}^{\mathrm{la,C}}) - 2\dot{\eta}_1 \dot{y}_{\mathrm{s}}^{\mathrm{la,C}} \end{bmatrix}_{\mathrm{B}} \tag{11}$$

The moments of momentum of UUV and sub-vehicle relative to their respective centroids are given below.

$$\vec{h}_{\mathrm{u}} = \vec{b}_3 J_{\mathrm{u}} \dot{\eta}_1 \tag{12}$$

$$\vec{h}_{\mathrm{s}} = \vec{b}_3 J_{\mathrm{s}} (\dot{\eta}_1 + \dot{\eta}_2) \tag{13}$$

where $\vec{b}_3$ is the outward unit vector perpendicular to the longitudinal plane of the multi-vehicle system.

2.3. Force and Moment Analysis

The forces acting on the UUV and sub-vehicle are presented in this section, including hydraulic force, launch thrust, engine driving force, elastic constraints (elastic force) and reaction force, among others.

The hydraulic force and moment acting on the UUV are defined in the B coordinate system, as given by Equation (14).

$$\left\{ \vec{F}_{\mathrm{u}}^{\mathrm{w}} = (F_{\mathrm{u},x}^{\mathrm{w,B}}, F_{\mathrm{u},y}^{\mathrm{w,B}})_{\mathrm{B}}^{\mathrm{T}},\ \vec{M}_{\mathrm{u}}^{\mathrm{w}} = \vec{b}_3 M_{\mathrm{u}}^{\mathrm{w}} \right. \tag{14}$$

The engine driving force $\vec{F}_{\mathrm{u}}^{\mathrm{en}}$ exerted on the UUV is assumed to act along its body-fixed longitudinal axis, with a magnitude of T. The pitch moment provided by the elevator is denoted as $\vec{M}_{\mathrm{u}}^{\delta_{\mathrm{e}}}$.

$$\left\{ \vec{F}_{\mathrm{u}}^{\mathrm{en}} = (T, 0)_{\mathrm{B}}^{\mathrm{T}},\ \vec{M}_{\mathrm{u}}^{\delta_{\mathrm{e}}} = \vec{b}_3 M_{\mathrm{u}}^{\delta_{\mathrm{e}}} \right. \tag{15}$$

Similarly, the hydraulic force and moment acting on the sub-vehicle are defined in the B coordinate system, as given by Equation (16).

$$\left\{ \vec{F}_{\mathrm{s}}^{\mathrm{w}} = (F_{\mathrm{s},x}^{\mathrm{w,B}}, F_{\mathrm{s},y}^{\mathrm{w,B}})_{\mathrm{B}}^{\mathrm{T}},\ \vec{M}_{\mathrm{s}}^{\mathrm{w}} = \vec{b}_3 M_{\mathrm{s}}^{\mathrm{w}} \right. \tag{16}$$

The following is an analysis of the internal forces between the UUV and the sub-vehicle, including launch thrust and elastic constraint (elastic force). In this section, the moment centers under consideration are the centroids of the UUV and sub-vehicle.

The launch thrust $\vec{f}$ is experienced by the sub-vehicle along the longitudinal axis of its body, with a magnitude of f.

$$\vec{f} = (f, 0)_D^T \tag{17}$$

Assuming that the launch thrust acts at the bottom center of the sub-vehicle, the distance from its centroid to this bottom center is denoted as l_{s1}, while the distance from the centroid to its head is denoted as l_{s2}.

The position vector of the sub-vehicle bottom center relative to UUV is given by Equation (18).

$$\vec{r}^{\,u}_{sb} = \begin{pmatrix} x^{u,B}_{la} - y^{la,C}_{s} + l_{s1}\sin\eta_2 \\ y^{u,B}_{la} + x^{la,C}_{s} - l_{s1}\cos\eta_2 \end{pmatrix}_B \tag{18}$$

The reaction moment exerted by this launch thrust on the UUV is given by Equation (19).

$$\vec{M}^{f}_{u} = \vec{r}^{\,u}_{sb} \times (-\vec{f}) = -\vec{b}_3 f (x^{u,B}_{la}\cos\eta_2 + y^{u,B}_{la}\sin\eta_2 + x^{la,C}_{s}\sin\eta_2 - y^{la,C}_{s}\cos\eta_2) \tag{19}$$

Next, the force and the moment of the elastic gasket installed in the launch tube on the sub-vehicle will be analyzed, as well as the reaction force and moment on the UUV.

The elastic gasket configuration inside the launch tube is shown in Figure 2, whose serial number is denoted by $\mathrm{L}_i, \mathrm{R}_j (i, j = 1 \sim n)$.

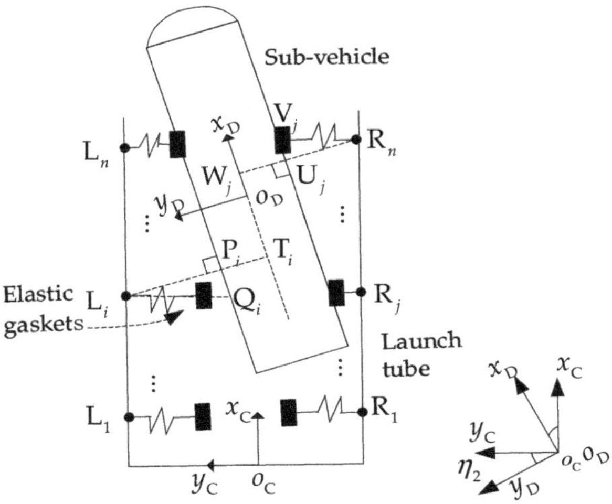

Figure 2. Elastic gaskets configuration diagram inside the launch tube.

The axial position of the elastic gaskets can be expressed as $x^{la,C}_1, x^{la,C}_2, \ldots, x^{la,C}_n$ in the C coordinate system. Assuming that n pairs of elastic gaskets are evenly distributed with a distance of Δl, the Equation (20) can be obtained.

$$x^{la,C}_i = x^{la,C}_1 + (i-1)\Delta l (i = 1 \sim n) \tag{20}$$

The position vectors of $\mathrm{L}_i, \mathrm{R}_j (i, j = 1 \sim n)$ relative to o_C are given by Equation (21).

$$\left\{ \vec{r}^{\,la}_{Li} = (x^{la,C}_i, R_{la})^T_C, \ \vec{r}^{\,la}_{Rj} = (x^{la,C}_j, -R_{la})^T_C \ (i, j = 1 \sim n) \right. \tag{21}$$

In Figure 2, if the $i-\text{th}(i=1\sim n)$ elastic gasket on the left is in contact with the sub-vehicle, Q_i represents its contact point. If the elastic gasket is not in contact with the sub-vehicle, Q_i represents the intersection point of the extension line of the elastic gasket along its length direction and the left side (or its extension line) of the sub-vehicle. Obviously, the position of Q_i, as well as the distance between Q_i and L_i, are two factors that determine whether the $i-\text{th}$ elastic gasket contacts the sub-vehicle. If the contact conditions are met, the distance between Q_i and L_i also determines the compression amount of the $i-\text{th}$ elastic gasket, which is also the basis for calculating the elastic force. The meaning of point $\text{V}_j(j=1\sim n)$ in Figure 2 is similar and will not be repeated.

The position vector of point Q_i relative to the sub-vehicle in the D coordinate system is given by Equation (22).

$$\vec{r}^{\,\text{s}}_{\text{Q}i}=(x^{\text{s,D}}_{\text{Q}i},y^{\text{s,D}}_{\text{Q}i})^{\text{T}}_{\text{D}} \tag{22}$$

where

$$\begin{cases}x^{\text{s,D}}_{\text{Q}i}=(-x^{\text{la,C}}_{\text{s}}+x^{\text{la,C}}_{i})(\cos\eta_2+\sin\eta_2\tan\eta_2)+R_{\text{s}}\tan\eta_2\\ y^{\text{s,D}}_{\text{Q}i}=R_{\text{s}}\end{cases} \tag{23}$$

The position vector of L_i relative to Q_i in the C coordinate system is given by Equation (24).

$$\vec{r}^{\,\text{Q}i}_{\text{L}i}=(0,y^{\text{Q}i,\text{C}}_{\text{L}i})^{\text{T}}_{\text{C}} \tag{24}$$

where

$$y^{\text{Q}i,\text{C}}_{\text{L}i}=x^{\text{la,C}}_{\text{s}}\tan\eta_2-y^{\text{la,C}}_{\text{s}}-x^{\text{la,C}}_{i}\tan\eta_2+R_{\text{la}}-R_{\text{s}}\sec\eta_2 \tag{25}$$

The position vector of Q_i relative to the UUV can be obtained through comprehensive analysis, as given by Equation (26).

$$\vec{r}^{\,\text{u}}_{\text{Q}i}=\begin{pmatrix}y^{\text{u,B}}_{\text{la}}+x^{\text{la,C}}_{i}\\ -x^{\text{u,B}}_{\text{la}}+R_{\text{la}}-y^{\text{Q}i,\text{C}}_{\text{L}i}\end{pmatrix}_{\text{C}} \tag{26}$$

Next, the elastic constraints between the launch tube and the sub-vehicle will be analyzed.

It is assumed that the natural length of each elastic gasket is l_{e} and the stiffness coefficient is k_{e}. Then, the force and moment exerted on the sub-vehicle by elastic gaskets will be calculated.

The y-axis component of position vector $\vec{r}^{\,\text{Q}i}_{\text{L}i}$ in the C coordinate system is $y^{\text{Q}i,\text{C}}_{\text{L}i}$. When $y^{\text{Q}i,\text{C}}_{\text{L}i}>l_{\text{e}}$, the elastic gasket is not compressed, and the elastic force is zero. When $y^{\text{Q}i,\text{C}}_{\text{L}i}\le l_{\text{e}}$, the elastic gasket is compressed, elastic force is generated. In addition, when $x^{\text{s,D}}_{\text{Q}i}\in[-l_{\text{s}1},l_{\text{s}2}]$, the $i-\text{th}$ elastic gasket comes into contact with the left-side wall of the sub-vehicle, thus generating elastic force. Therefore, two switch functions are defined as given in Equations (27) and (28).

$$s^{\text{x}}_{\text{L}i}(x^{\text{s,D}}_{\text{Q}i})=\begin{cases}1, & -l_{\text{s}1}\le x^{\text{s,D}}_{\text{Q}i}\le l_{\text{s}2}\\ 0, & \text{otherwise}\end{cases} \tag{27}$$

$$s^{\text{y}}_{\text{L}i}(y^{\text{Q}i,\text{C}}_{\text{L}i})=\begin{cases}1, & y^{\text{Q}i,\text{C}}_{\text{L}i}\le l_{\text{e}}\\ 0, & \text{otherwise}\end{cases} \tag{28}$$

When both switch functions are equal to 1, the $i-\text{th}$ elastic gasket on the left side exerts an elastic force on the sub-vehicle. The method of calculating the elastic force and its moment is as follows.

After introducing the two switch functions of Equations (27) and (28), the elastic force vector (elastic constraint) exerted on the sub-vehicle by the i-th elastic gasket on the left side is given by Equation (29).

$$\vec{f}_{\mathrm{L}i} = [0, -s^{\mathrm{x}}_{\mathrm{L}i} s^{\mathrm{y}}_{\mathrm{L}i} k_{\mathrm{e}}(l_{\mathrm{e}} - y^{\mathrm{Q}i,\mathrm{C}}_{\mathrm{L}i})]^{\mathrm{T}}_{\mathrm{C}} \tag{29}$$

The combined force exerted on the sub-vehicle by all the elastic gaskets on the left side can be calculated by Equation (30).

$$\vec{f}_{\mathrm{Le}} \triangleq (0, f^{\mathrm{C}}_{\mathrm{Le},y})^{T} = \sum_{i=1}^{n} \vec{f}_{\mathrm{L}i} = [0, -\sum_{i=1}^{n} s^{\mathrm{x}}_{\mathrm{L}i} s^{\mathrm{y}}_{\mathrm{L}i} k_{\mathrm{e}}(l_{\mathrm{e}} - y^{\mathrm{Q}i,\mathrm{C}}_{\mathrm{L}i})]^{\mathrm{T}}_{\mathrm{C}} \tag{30}$$

The moment of $\vec{f}_{\mathrm{L}i}$ relative to the sub-vehicle is $\vec{M}^{\mathrm{L}i}_{\mathrm{s}}$, which can be calculated by Equation (31).

$$\vec{M}^{\mathrm{L}i}_{\mathrm{s}} = \vec{r}^{\mathrm{s}}_{\mathrm{Q}i} \times \vec{f}_{\mathrm{L}i} = \vec{b}_{3}[-s^{\mathrm{x}}_{\mathrm{L}i} s^{\mathrm{y}}_{\mathrm{L}i} x^{\mathrm{s,C}}_{\mathrm{Q}i} k_{\mathrm{e}}(l_{\mathrm{e}} - y^{\mathrm{Q}i,\mathrm{C}}_{\mathrm{L}i})] \tag{31}$$

The combined moment exerted on the sub-vehicle by all elastic gaskets on the left side can be calculated by Equation (32).

$$\vec{M}^{\mathrm{Le}}_{\mathrm{s}} = \sum_{i=1}^{n} \vec{M}^{\mathrm{L}i}_{\mathrm{s}} = \vec{b}_{3} \sum_{i=1}^{n} [-s^{\mathrm{x}}_{\mathrm{L}i} s^{\mathrm{y}}_{\mathrm{L}i} x^{\mathrm{s,C}}_{\mathrm{Q}i} k_{\mathrm{e}}(l_{\mathrm{e}} - y^{\mathrm{Q}i,\mathrm{C}}_{\mathrm{L}i})] \tag{32}$$

The reaction force of $\vec{f}_{\mathrm{L}i}$ exerts to the UUV, and its moment relative to the UUV is shown in Equation (33).

$$\vec{M}^{\mathrm{L}i}_{\mathrm{u}} = \vec{r}^{\mathrm{u}}_{\mathrm{Q}i} \times (-\vec{f}_{\mathrm{L}i}) = \vec{b}_{3} s^{\mathrm{x}}_{\mathrm{L}i} s^{\mathrm{y}}_{\mathrm{L}i} (y^{\mathrm{u,B}}_{\mathrm{la}} + x^{\mathrm{la,C}}_{i}) k_{\mathrm{e}}(l_{\mathrm{e}} - y^{\mathrm{Q}i,\mathrm{C}}_{\mathrm{L}i}) \tag{33}$$

Similarly, the combined moment exerted on the UUV by all elastic gaskets on the left side also can be calculated by Equation (34).

$$\vec{M}^{\mathrm{Le}}_{\mathrm{u}} = \sum_{i=1}^{n} \vec{M}^{\mathrm{L}i}_{\mathrm{u}} = \vec{b}_{3} \sum_{i=1}^{n} [s^{\mathrm{x}}_{\mathrm{L}i} s^{\mathrm{y}}_{\mathrm{L}i} (y^{\mathrm{u,B}}_{\mathrm{la}} + x^{\mathrm{la,C}}_{i}) k_{\mathrm{e}}(l_{\mathrm{e}} - y^{\mathrm{Q}i,\mathrm{C}}_{\mathrm{L}i})] \tag{34}$$

The conditions under which the elastic gaskets on the right side of the launch tube take effect, as well as the derivation process for the force and moment it exerts on the multi-vehicle system, are similar to those on the left side. Owing to space constraints, these details will not be discussed at length.

2.4. Dynamics Equations

Based on Newton's laws and theorem of moment of momentum, the system of dynamics equations for UUV and sub-vehicle can be given by Equation (35).

$$\begin{cases} m_{\mathrm{u}} \vec{a}_{\mathrm{u}} = \vec{G}_{\mathrm{u}} + \vec{F}^{\mathrm{w}}_{\mathrm{u}} + \vec{F}^{\mathrm{en}}_{\mathrm{u}} - \vec{f} - \vec{f}_{\mathrm{Le}} - \vec{f}_{\mathrm{Re}} \\ \vec{b}_{3} J_{\mathrm{u}} \ddot{\eta}_{1} = \vec{M}^{\delta_{\mathrm{e}}}_{\mathrm{u}} + \vec{M}^{\mathrm{w}}_{\mathrm{u}} + \vec{M}^{\mathrm{f}}_{\mathrm{u}} + \vec{M}^{\mathrm{Le}}_{\mathrm{u}} + \vec{M}^{\mathrm{Re}}_{\mathrm{u}} \\ m_{\mathrm{s}} \vec{a}_{\mathrm{s}} = \vec{G}_{\mathrm{s}} + \vec{F}^{\mathrm{w}}_{\mathrm{s}} + \vec{f} + \vec{f}_{\mathrm{Le}} + \vec{f}_{\mathrm{Re}} \\ \vec{b}_{3} J_{\mathrm{s}} (\ddot{\eta}_{1} + \ddot{\eta}_{2}) = \vec{M}^{\mathrm{w}}_{\mathrm{s}} + \vec{M}^{\mathrm{Le}}_{\mathrm{s}} + \vec{M}^{\mathrm{Re}}_{\mathrm{s}} \end{cases} \tag{35}$$

Substituting the relevant equations in Sections 2.2 and 2.3 into Equation (35), the multi-vehicle coupling dynamics equations can be obtained as Equation (36).

$$\begin{cases} m_{\mathrm{u}}\ddot{x}_{\mathrm{u}}^{\mathrm{A}}\cos\eta_1 + m_{\mathrm{u}}\ddot{y}_{\mathrm{u}}^{\mathrm{A}}\sin\eta_1 = -m_{\mathrm{u}}g\sin\eta_1 + F_{\mathrm{u},x}^{\mathrm{w,B}} + f\sin\eta_2 - \\ \sum\limits_{i=1}^{n} s_{\mathrm{L}i}^{\mathrm{x}}s_{\mathrm{L}i}^{\mathrm{y}}k_{\mathrm{e}}(l_{\mathrm{e}} - y_{\mathrm{L}i}^{\mathrm{Q}i,\mathrm{C}}) + \sum\limits_{j=1}^{n} s_{\mathrm{R}j}^{\mathrm{x}}s_{\mathrm{R}j}^{\mathrm{y}}k_{\mathrm{e}}(l_{\mathrm{e}} - y_{\mathrm{V}j}^{\mathrm{R}j,\mathrm{C}}) + T \\ \\ -m_{\mathrm{u}}\ddot{x}_{\mathrm{u}}^{\mathrm{A}}\sin\eta_1 + m_{\mathrm{u}}\ddot{y}_{\mathrm{u}}^{\mathrm{A}}\cos\eta_1 = -m_{\mathrm{u}}g\cos\eta_1 + F_{\mathrm{u},y}^{\mathrm{w,B}} - f\cos\eta_2 \\ \\ J_{\mathrm{u}}\ddot{\eta}_1 = M_{\mathrm{u}}^{\delta_{\mathrm{e}}} + M_{\mathrm{u}}^{\mathrm{w}} - f(x_{\mathrm{la}}^{\mathrm{u,B}}\cos\eta_2 + y_{\mathrm{la}}^{\mathrm{u,B}}\sin\eta_2 + x_{\mathrm{s}}^{\mathrm{la,C}}\sin\eta_2 - y_{\mathrm{s}}^{\mathrm{la,C}}\cos\eta_2) + \\ \sum\limits_{i=1}^{n} s_{\mathrm{L}i}^{\mathrm{x}}s_{\mathrm{L}i}^{\mathrm{y}}(y_{\mathrm{la}}^{\mathrm{u,B}} + x_i^{\mathrm{la,C}})k_{\mathrm{e}}(l_{\mathrm{e}} - y_{\mathrm{L}i}^{\mathrm{Q}i,\mathrm{C}}) + \sum\limits_{j=1}^{n}[-s_{\mathrm{R}j}^{\mathrm{x}}s_{\mathrm{R}j}^{\mathrm{y}}(y_{\mathrm{la}}^{\mathrm{u,B}} + x_i^{\mathrm{la,C}})k_{\mathrm{e}}(l_{\mathrm{e}} - y_{\mathrm{V}j}^{\mathrm{R}j,\mathrm{C}})] \\ \\ m_{\mathrm{s}}\ddot{x}_{\mathrm{u}}^{\mathrm{A}}\cos\eta_1 + m_{\mathrm{s}}\ddot{y}_{\mathrm{u}}^{\mathrm{A}}\sin\eta_1 - m_{\mathrm{s}}\ddot{\eta}_1(y_{\mathrm{la}}^{\mathrm{u,B}} + x_{\mathrm{s}}^{\mathrm{la,C}}) - m_{\mathrm{s}}\ddot{y}_{\mathrm{s}}^{\mathrm{la,C}} \\ = m_{\mathrm{s}}\dot{\eta}_1^{\,2}(x_{\mathrm{la}}^{\mathrm{u,B}} - y_{\mathrm{s}}^{\mathrm{la,C}}) + 2m_{\mathrm{s}}\dot{\eta}_1\dot{x}_{\mathrm{s}}^{\mathrm{la,C}} - m_{\mathrm{s}}g\sin\eta_1 + F_{\mathrm{s},x}^{\mathrm{w,B}} - f\sin\eta_2 + \\ \sum\limits_{i=1}^{n} s_{\mathrm{L}i}^{\mathrm{x}}s_{\mathrm{L}i}^{\mathrm{y}}k_{\mathrm{e}}(l_{\mathrm{e}} - y_{\mathrm{L}i}^{\mathrm{Q}i,\mathrm{C}}) - \sum\limits_{j=1}^{n} s_{\mathrm{R}j}^{\mathrm{x}}s_{\mathrm{R}j}^{\mathrm{y}}k_{\mathrm{e}}(l_{\mathrm{e}} - y_{\mathrm{V}j}^{\mathrm{R}j,\mathrm{C}}) \\ \\ -m_{\mathrm{s}}\ddot{x}_{\mathrm{u}}^{\mathrm{A}}\sin\eta_1 + m_{\mathrm{s}}\ddot{y}_{\mathrm{u}}^{\mathrm{A}}\cos\eta_1 + m_{\mathrm{s}}\ddot{\eta}_1(x_{\mathrm{la}}^{\mathrm{u,B}} - y_{\mathrm{s}}^{\mathrm{la,C}}) + m_{\mathrm{s}}\ddot{x}_{\mathrm{s}}^{\mathrm{la,C}} = \\ m_{\mathrm{s}}\dot{\eta}_1^{\,2}(y_{\mathrm{la}}^{\mathrm{u,B}} + x_{\mathrm{s}}^{\mathrm{la,C}}) + 2m_{\mathrm{s}}\dot{\eta}_1\dot{y}_{\mathrm{s}}^{\mathrm{la,C}} - m_{\mathrm{s}}g\cos\eta_1 + F_{\mathrm{s},y}^{\mathrm{w,B}} + f\cos\eta_2 \\ \\ J_{\mathrm{s}}\ddot{\eta}_1 + J_{\mathrm{s}}\ddot{\eta}_2 = M_{\mathrm{s}}^{\mathrm{w}} + \sum\limits_{i=1}^{n}[-s_{\mathrm{L}i}^{\mathrm{x}}s_{\mathrm{L}i}^{\mathrm{y}}x_{\mathrm{Q}i}^{\mathrm{s,C}}k_{\mathrm{e}}(l_{\mathrm{e}} - y_{\mathrm{L}i}^{\mathrm{Q}i,\mathrm{C}})] + \sum\limits_{j=1}^{n} s_{\mathrm{R}j}^{\mathrm{x}}s_{\mathrm{R}j}^{\mathrm{y}}x_{\mathrm{V}j}^{\mathrm{s,C}}k_{\mathrm{e}}(l_{\mathrm{e}} - y_{\mathrm{V}j}^{\mathrm{R}j,\mathrm{C}}) \end{cases} \tag{36}$$

where the relevant physical quantities of the right elastic gasket are given by Equations (37) to (39).

$$\begin{cases} x_{\mathrm{V}j}^{\mathrm{s,D}} = (-x_{\mathrm{s}}^{\mathrm{la,C}} + x_j^{\mathrm{la,C}})(\cos\eta_2 + \sin\eta_2\tan\eta_2) - R_{\mathrm{s}}\tan\eta_2 \\ y_{\mathrm{V}j}^{\mathrm{R}j,\mathrm{C}} = -x_{\mathrm{s}}^{\mathrm{la,C}}\tan\eta_2 + y_{\mathrm{s}}^{\mathrm{la,C}} + x_j^{\mathrm{la,C}}\tan\eta_2 + R_{\mathrm{la}} - R_{\mathrm{s}}\sec\eta_2 \end{cases} \tag{37}$$

$$\begin{cases} s_{\mathrm{R}j}^{\mathrm{x}}(x_{\mathrm{V}j}^{\mathrm{s,D}}) = \begin{cases} 1, & -l_{\mathrm{s}1} \le x_{\mathrm{V}j}^{\mathrm{s,D}} \le l_{\mathrm{s}2} \\ 0, & \text{otherwise} \end{cases} \\ s_{\mathrm{R}j}^{\mathrm{y}}(y_{\mathrm{V}j}^{\mathrm{R}j,\mathrm{C}}) = \begin{cases} 1, & y_{\mathrm{V}j}^{\mathrm{R}j,\mathrm{C}} \le l_{\mathrm{e}} \\ 0, & \text{otherwise} \end{cases} \end{cases} \tag{38}$$

$$\begin{cases} x_{\mathrm{Q}i}^{\mathrm{s,C}} = -x_{\mathrm{s}}^{\mathrm{la,C}} + x_i^{\mathrm{la,C}} \\ x_{\mathrm{V}j}^{\mathrm{s,C}} = -x_{\mathrm{s}}^{\mathrm{la,C}} + x_j^{\mathrm{la,C}} \end{cases} \tag{39}$$

Prior to the onset of separation, no relative motion exists between the UUV and the sub-vehicle. At this point, in Equation (36):

$$\begin{cases} x_{\mathrm{s}}^{\mathrm{la},C} = x_{\mathrm{s0}}^{\mathrm{la},C}, y_{\mathrm{s}}^{\mathrm{la},C} = 0, \eta_2 = 0 \\ \dot{x}_{\mathrm{s}}^{\mathrm{la},C} = 0, \dot{y}_{\mathrm{s}}^{\mathrm{la},C} = 0, \dot{\eta}_2 = 0 \\ \ddot{x}_{\mathrm{s}}^{\mathrm{la},C} = 0, \ddot{y}_{\mathrm{s}}^{\mathrm{la},C} = 0, \ddot{\eta}_2 = 0 \end{cases}, \begin{cases} F_{\mathrm{s},x}^{\mathrm{w,B}} = 0, F_{\mathrm{s},y}^{\mathrm{w,B}} = 0 \\ M_{\mathrm{s}}^{\mathrm{w}} = 0 \end{cases} \tag{40}$$

where $x_{\text{s0}}^{\text{la},C}$ is a known parameter, representing the distance from the centroid of the sub-vehicle to the bottom center of the launch tube. By substituting Equation (40) into (36), the dynamics equations for the two-body rigidly connected state can be derived.

$$\begin{cases} (m_{\text{u}}+m_{\text{s}})\ddot{x}_{\text{u}}^{\text{A}}\cos\eta_1+(m_{\text{u}}+m_{\text{s}})\ddot{y}_{\text{u}}^{\text{A}}\sin\eta_1-m_{\text{s}}\ddot{\eta}_1(y_{\text{la}}^{\text{u,B}}+x_{\text{s0}}^{\text{la},C}) \\ =m_{\text{s}}\dot{\eta}_1^{\,2}x_{\text{la}}^{\text{u,B}}+F_{\text{u},x}^{\text{w,B}}-(m_{\text{u}}+m_{\text{s}})g\sin\eta_1+T \\ \\ -(m_{\text{u}}+m_{\text{s}})\ddot{x}_{\text{u}}^{\text{A}}\sin\eta_1+(m_{\text{u}}+m_{\text{s}})\ddot{y}_{\text{u}}^{\text{A}}\cos\eta_1+m_{\text{s}}\ddot{\eta}_1x_{\text{la}}^{\text{u,B}} \\ =m_{\text{s}}\dot{\eta}_1^{\,2}(y_{\text{la}}^{\text{u,B}}+x_{\text{s0}}^{\text{la},C})+F_{\text{u},y}^{\text{w,B}}-(m_{\text{u}}+m_{\text{s}})g\cos\eta_1 \\ \\ -m_{\text{s}}\ddot{x}_{\text{u}}^{\text{A}}(x_{\text{la}}^{\text{u,B}}\sin\eta_1+y_{\text{la}}^{\text{u,B}}\cos\eta_1+x_{\text{s0}}^{\text{la},C}\cos\eta_1)+ \\ m_{\text{s}}\ddot{y}_{\text{u}}^{\text{A}}(x_{\text{la}}^{\text{u,B}}\cos\eta_1-y_{\text{la}}^{\text{u,B}}\sin\eta_1-x_{\text{s0}}^{\text{la},C}\sin\eta_1)+ \\ \left\{J_{\text{u}}+J_{\text{s}}+m_{\text{s}}[(x_{\text{la}}^{\text{u,B}})^2+(y_{\text{la}}^{\text{u,B}})^2+(x_{\text{s0}}^{\text{la},C})^2+2x_{\text{s0}}^{\text{la},C}y_{\text{sp}}^{\text{u,B}}]\right\}\ddot{\eta}_1 \\ =M_{\text{u}}^{\delta_{\text{e}}}+M_{\text{u}}^{\text{w}}-m_{\text{s}}g(x_{\text{la}}^{\text{u,B}}\cos\eta_1-y_{\text{la}}^{\text{u,B}}\sin\eta_1-x_{\text{s0}}^{\text{la},C}\sin\eta_1) \end{cases} \tag{41}$$

Upon complete separation of the sub-vehicle from the UUV, the dynamics Equations of the UUV reduce to Equation (42).

$$\begin{cases} m_{\text{u}}\ddot{x}_{\text{u}}^{\text{A}}\cos\eta_1+m_{\text{u}}\ddot{y}_{\text{u}}^{\text{A}}\sin\eta_1=F_{\text{u},x}^{\text{w,B}}-m_{\text{u}}g\sin\eta_1+T \\ -m_{\text{u}}\ddot{x}_{\text{u}}^{\text{A}}\sin\eta_1+m_{\text{u}}\ddot{y}_{\text{u}}^{\text{A}}\cos\eta_1=F_{\text{u},y}^{\text{w,B}}-m_{\text{u}}g\cos\eta_1 \\ J_{\text{u}}\ddot{\eta}_1=M_{\text{u}}^{\delta_{\text{e}}}+M_{\text{u}}^{\text{w}} \end{cases} \tag{42}$$

3. Hydrodynamic Modeling

3.1. Hydrodynamic Calculation Method of the Multi-Vehicle System

The hydrodynamic modeling method adopted in this paper is established based on Ref. [5], and the flow shape model of the UUV is appropriately improved to obtain better results. Therefore, this section only briefly describes the key equations and calculation results of the hydrodynamic modeling of the multi-vehicle.

Hydrodynamic calculation method of UUV:

The hydrodynamic calculation process for the UUV is as follows: First, a series of hydrodynamic data matrices under various angles of attack are obtained through CFD simulations. Subsequently, based on the least-squares method, approximate functional relationships between the angle of attack and the lift coefficient C_L, drag coefficient C_D, and pitch moment coefficient C_M are fitted.

Using the aforementioned relationships, the lift, drag and pitching moment coefficients of UUV are obtained by the real-time angle of attack of UUV. The relationship between these coefficients and the corresponding lift L_{u}, drag D_{u} and moment M_{u} is as shown in Equation (43) [22], where S_{u} and l_{u} represent hydrodynamic characteristic area and length, respectively.

$$\left\{L_{\text{u}}=C_L\cdot\frac{1}{2}\rho v^2S_{\text{u}},D_{\text{u}}=C_D\cdot\frac{1}{2}\rho v^2S_{\text{u}},M_{\text{u}}=C_M\cdot\frac{1}{2}\rho v^2S_{\text{u}}l_{\text{u}}\right. \tag{43}$$

The hydraulic force and moment of UUV defined by Equation (14) can be calculated according to Equation (44), where α_{u} is the attack angle of UUV, and V_{u} is the drainage volume of UUV.

$$\begin{cases} F_{\text{u},x}^{\text{w,B}}=D_{\text{u}}\cos\alpha_{\text{u}}+L_{\text{u}}\sin\alpha_{\text{u}}+\rho gV_{\text{u}}\sin\eta_1 \\ F_{\text{u},y}^{\text{w,B}}=-D_{\text{u}}\sin\alpha_{\text{u}}+L_{\text{u}}\cos\alpha_{\text{u}}+\rho gV_{\text{u}}\cos\eta_1 \\ M_{\text{u}}^{\text{w}}=M_{\text{u}} \end{cases} \tag{44}$$

Hydrodynamic calculation method of sub-vehicle:

The hydrodynamic calculation method for the sub-vehicle is not entirely identical to that used for the UUV. The key difference lies in the fact that during the separation process of the sub-vehicle, the range of hydrodynamic forces acting on it constantly changes. Therefore, it is not feasible to use a single hydrodynamic coefficient. Instead, it is necessary to use pressure distribution data at different angles of attack for interpolation and to determine the range of the sub-vehicle entering the water in order to calculate the hydrodynamic force and moment.

The hydraulic force and moment of the sub-vehicle defined in Equation (16) can be calculated according to Equation (45) [5].

$$\begin{cases} F_{s,x}^{w,B} = F_{s,x}^{v,B} + \rho g (V_2 - h_2 S_2) \sin \eta_1 \\ F_{s,y}^{w,B} = F_{s,y}^{v,B} + \rho g (V_2 - h_2 S_2) \cos \eta_1 \\ M_s^w = M_s^v - \rho g (V_2 - h_2 S_2) \delta r \sin(\eta_1 + \eta_2) \end{cases} \quad (45)$$

3.2. Improvement of UUV Geometry and CFD Simulation Results

The shape of the sub-vehicle utilized in this paper is consistent with that described in Ref. [5]. The geometric configuration of the UUV has been optimized for streamlining to minimize the likelihood of flow separation. The pressure distribution contour plots on the longitudinal plane of the UUV at various angles of attack are shown in Figure 3.

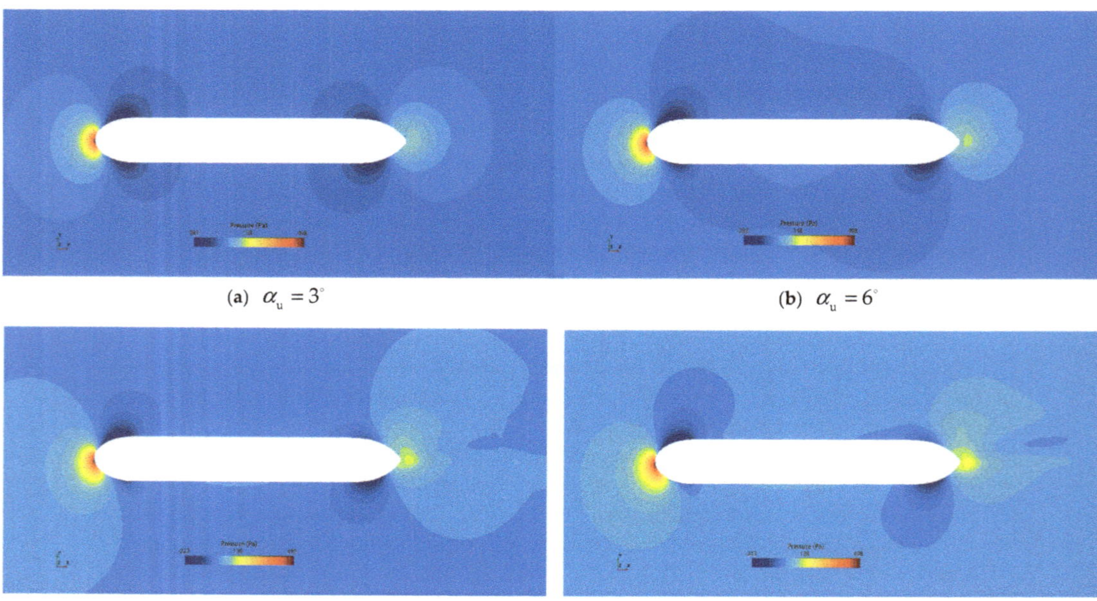

(a) $\alpha_u = 3^\circ$ (b) $\alpha_u = 6^\circ$ (c) $\alpha_u = 9^\circ$ (d) $\alpha_u = 12^\circ$

Figure 3. UUV pressure contours at various attack angles on the longitudinal plane.

The variation curves of the UUV lift and drag coefficient with angle of attack calculated by fitting CFD data are shown in Figure 4. The variation curves of sub-vehicle lift and drag with angle of attack calculated by CFD data are shown in Figure 5. As observed in Figure 4, the curves obtained through the fitting method exhibit strong consistency with CFD data. The trend of variation conforms to the physical principles governing streamlined vehicles at small angles of attack, thus confirming the effectiveness of the hydrodynamic modeling approach proposed in this paper.

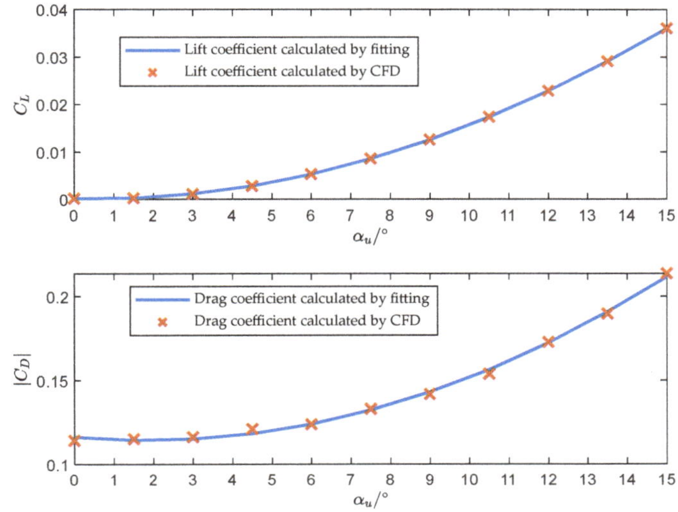

Figure 4. The hydrodynamic lift and drag coefficient curves of UUV.

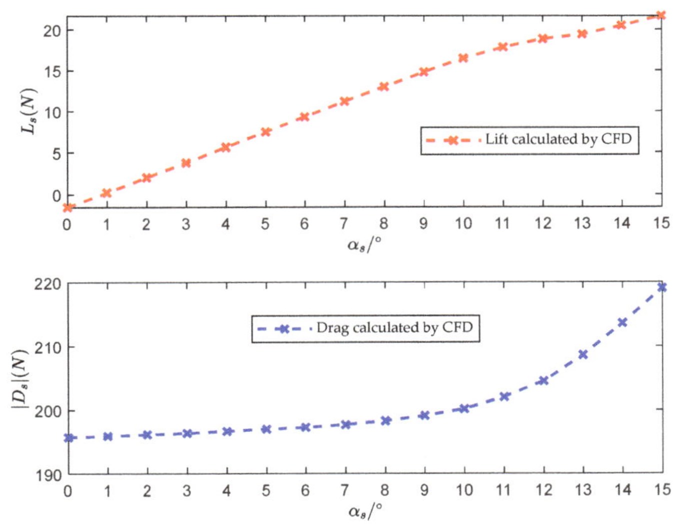

Figure 5. The hydrodynamic lift and drag curves of the sub-vehicle.

4. Simulation and Result Analysis of Multi-Vehicle Separation Process

4.1. Simulation Process Description

In this paper, the second-order differential equations of the multi-vehicle system dynamics, as given in Equation (36), are converted into a set of 12-dimensional first-order differential equations using the state space method and subsequently solved numerically with the fourth-order Runge–Kutta algorithm.

The primary purpose of installing elastic gaskets in the launch tube is to impose elastic constraints on the sub-vehicle, thereby mitigating the lateral loads encountered during separation while minimally impacting its pitch attitude. Therefore, it is particularly important to determine the appropriate stiffness and distribution for elastic gaskets. This study will focus on exploring the influence of the stiffness and distribution of the elastic gaskets installed in the launch tube on the motion and mechanical characteristics of the multi-vehicle system in the separation process. The product of the number of elastic gasket groups and the stiffness coefficient of the elastic gasket is defined as the total stiffness of the elastic gasket, expressed as K_{total}.

Two simulation cases are established below:

(1) The influence of elastic gasket stiffness variation on the motion and mechanical characteristics of the multi-vehicle system.

(2) The influence of elastic gasket distribution variation on the motion and mechanical characteristics of multi-vehicle systems.

The separation process of the UUV and its sub-vehicle is numerically simulated in accordance with the principle block diagram, as shown in Figure 6.

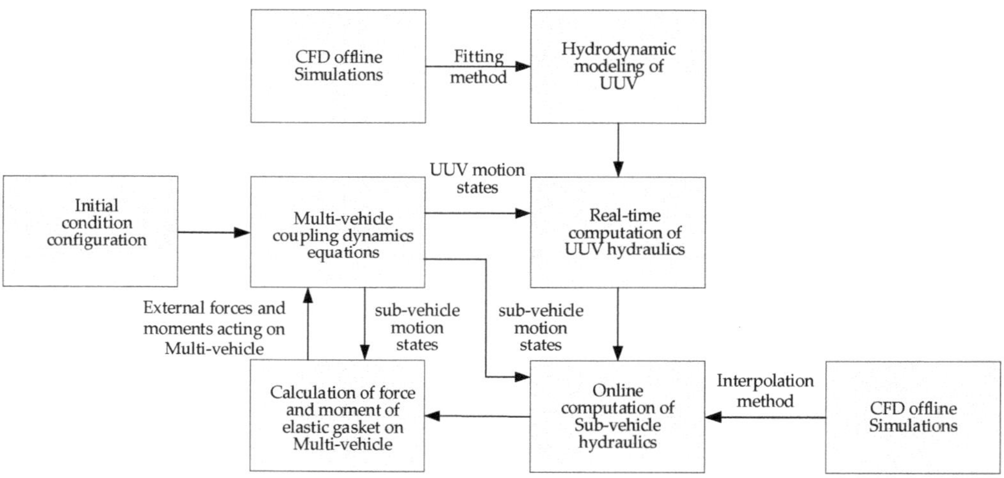

Figure 6. Simulation principle block diagram.

The simulation process can be divided into three distinct stages, each characterized by specific dynamic behaviors and interactions among the multi-vehicle system. These stages are as follows:

Stage1: Constant-Speed Sailing

At this stage, the sub-vehicle is fixed with the UUV, and the system's initial installation parameters are determined, providing initial conditions for the separation. The motion can be calculated using Equation (41).

Stage2: Two-Body Separation

The UUV provides launch thrust for a short time (t_h) to the sub-vehicle, which then relies on inertia to leave the launch tube. The coupling dynamics characterized by the multi-vehicle at this stage can be solved using Equation (36).

Stage3: Post-separation Sailing

The purpose of this stage is to analyze the effects of the separation process disturbance on the UUV attitude. The dynamics equation for this stage is presented in Equation (42).

The three stages mentioned above are illustrated in Figure 7.

The multi-vehicle system model and initial motion parameters are listed in Table 2.

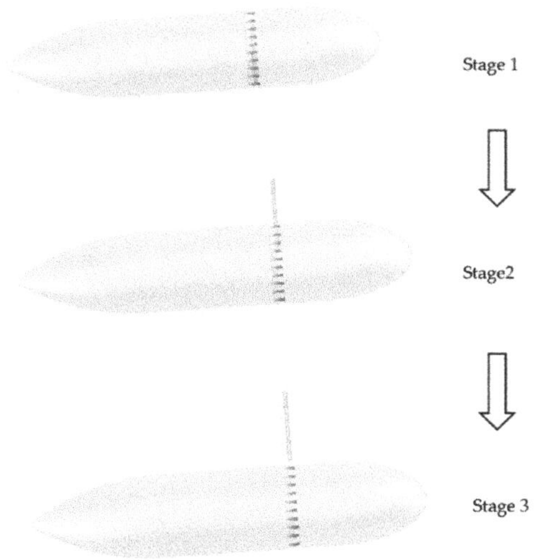

Figure 7. State diagram of the multi-vehicle in three stages.

Table 2. Model and initial motion parameters of the multi-vehicle.

Model Parameters	Value	Motion State Parameters	Value
$m_{\mathrm{u}}/\mathrm{kg}$	5975	$\eta_{10}/^{\circ}$	10
$m_{\mathrm{s}}/\mathrm{kg}$	1195	$x_{\mathrm{s0}}^{\mathrm{la},C}/\mathrm{m}$	0.8866
$J_{\mathrm{u}}/\mathrm{kg}\cdot\mathrm{m}^2$	9497.4	$y_{\mathrm{s0}}^{\mathrm{la},C}/\mathrm{m}$	0
$J_{\mathrm{s}}/\mathrm{kg}\cdot\mathrm{m}^2$	2050	$\eta_{20}/^{\circ}$	0
f/N	145,600	T_0/N	40.42
t_h/s	0.06	$M_{\mathrm{u}\,0}^{\delta_e}/\mathrm{N}\cdot\mathrm{m}$	4470.44

4.2. Influence of Elastic Gasket Stiffness on the Multi-Vehicle System

The first case examines the influence of elastic gasket stiffness on the motion and mechanical characteristics of the multi-vehicle system during the separation process. The number of elastic gaskets installed in the launch tube is set to 20, with their serial numbers increasing from bottom to top. The compression amounts of the left and right elastic gaskets are $\Delta_{\mathrm{L}i}, \Delta_{Rj}(i, j = 1 \sim 20)$. The initial compression amount for all the elastic gaskets is 0.5 mm. This simulation is divided into three groups. In each group, the stiffness coefficients of all elastic gaskets are set to the same value. The stiffness coefficient values of three groups of simulated elastic gaskets are set as follows.

$$\begin{cases} k_{e_1} = 2.5 \times 10^5\ \mathrm{N/m} \\ k_{e_2} = 5.0 \times 10^5\ \mathrm{N/m} \\ k_{e_3} = 1.0 \times 10^6\ \mathrm{N/m} \end{cases}$$

Simulation results and analysis:

Figure 8 shows the variation in the compression amount of the left and right elastic gaskets during the separation process. The horizontal axis (γ_t) indicates the relative displacement between the sub-vehicle and the launch tube. As shown in the figure, with the increase in relative displacement, the compression of both sides of the elastic gaskets exhibits a trend of first increasing and then decreasing. The difference lies in the fact that the compression amount variation of the left elastic gaskets is more continuous, and the maximum compression amount increases as the position approaches the top of the launch tube, while the compression amount curves of the right elastic gaskets change abruptly, with the maximum compression occurring in the middle. These differences are primarily determined by the force characteristics acting on the sub-vehicle during the process of leaving the launch tube.

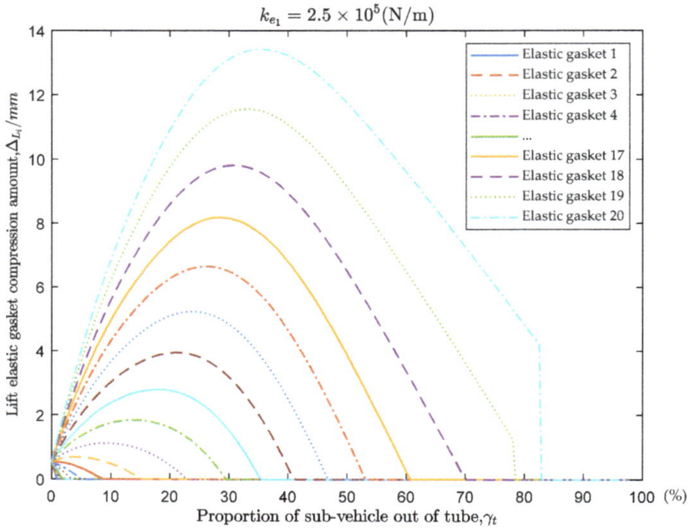

(a)

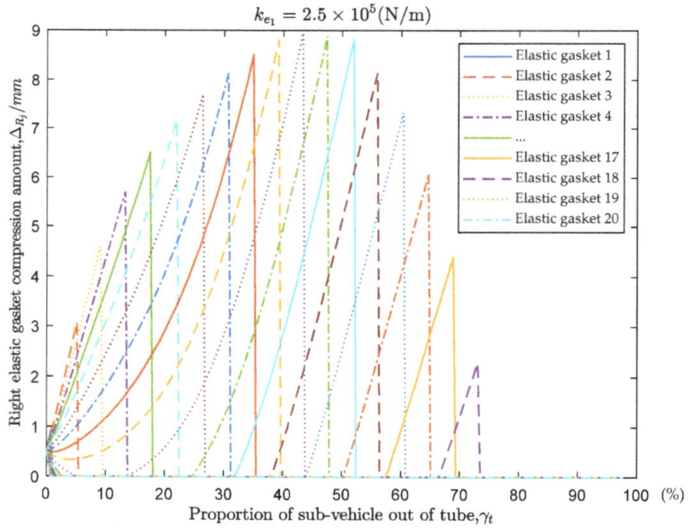

(b)

Figure 8. The variation curves of the compression amount of both sides of elastic gaskets. (Different elastic gasket stiffness coefficient) (**a**) Compression amount variation curve of the left elastic gasket. (**b**) Compression amount variation curve of the right elastic gasket.

Specifically, during the movement of the UUV to the right, the sub-vehicle experiences a hydrodynamic force to the left. The left elastic gaskets are continuously compressed due to the hydrodynamic force, with a greater compression amount near the top of the launch tube. Meanwhile, the right elastic gaskets provide a balancing moment only as the tail of the sub-vehicle passes by, resulting in a shorter compression amount. This leads to differences in the compression characteristics between the left and right elastic gaskets. As the length of the sub-vehicle exiting the launch tube increases, the elastic constraint gradually decreases, and the proportion of rigid-body motion due to hydrodynamic forces increases. Consequently, the proportion of the constraint force also decreases. Overall, the compression of the elastic gaskets initially increases and then decreases.

Additionally, it can be observed that for the elastic gaskets on the same side, the compression distribution characteristics are the same regardless of different stiffness levels. As the stiffness of the elastic gaskets increases, the compression amount decreases noticeably. This indicates that increased stiffness effectively reduces the lateral displacement and angular changes of the sub-vehicle, which is beneficial for controlling its attitude.

The constraint forces (elastic forces) provided by each elastic gasket on the left and right sides are summed individually, as shown in Figure 9. The curves of the constraint forces on both sides exhibited a characteristic of initially increasing and then decreasing, which is consistent with the variation in the compression amount of the elastic gaskets. The constraint forces on the right side show fluctuations, which corresponds to the sudden change in the compression amount of the right-side elastic gaskets.

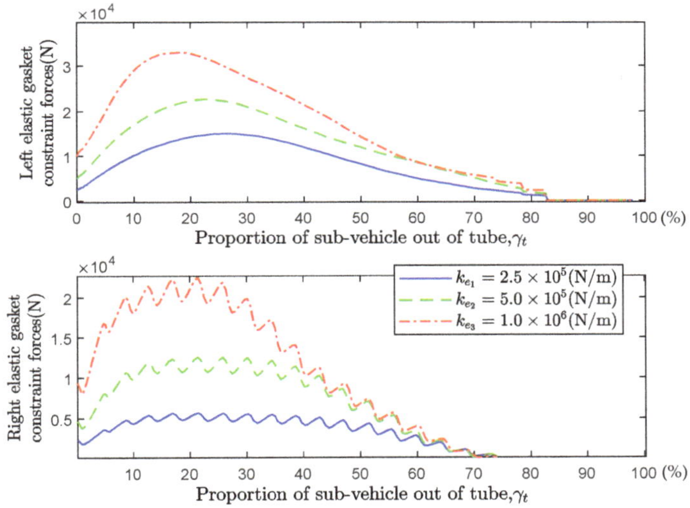

Figure 9. The combined elastic constraint force curves of the elastic gaskets on both sides (different elastic gasket stiffness coefficient).

A comparison of the constraint force curves for different stiffness values shows that as the stiffness of the elastic gaskets increases, the constraint forces acting on the surface of the sub-vehicle also increase significantly, which poses a potential threat to its structural safety. Conversely, selecting elastic gaskets with lower stiffness is found to significantly reduce the constraint forces, which proves advantageous for the structural design of the sub-vehicle.

Then, the influence of the stiffness variation on the pitching attitude of the sub-vehicle during the separation process is analyzed. As can be seen from Figure 10, an increase in the stiffness of the elastic gasket has a significant impact on the lateral and pitch motions of the sub-vehicle, which is manifested in the reduction of lateral displacement, pitch angle, lateral velocity and pitch angular velocity. However, the influence on the primary motion (axial motion) of the sub-vehicle is not obvious, as evidenced by the almost overlapping axial displacement and velocity parameters in Figure 10. It can be concluded that increasing the stiffness can effectively suppress the lateral motion of the sub-vehicle, preventing it from colliding with the UUV, which is beneficial for improving the safety of separation. Of course, the selection of the stiffness of the elastic gasket also needs to take into account the adverse effects of increased stiffness on the structural safety of the sub-vehicle.

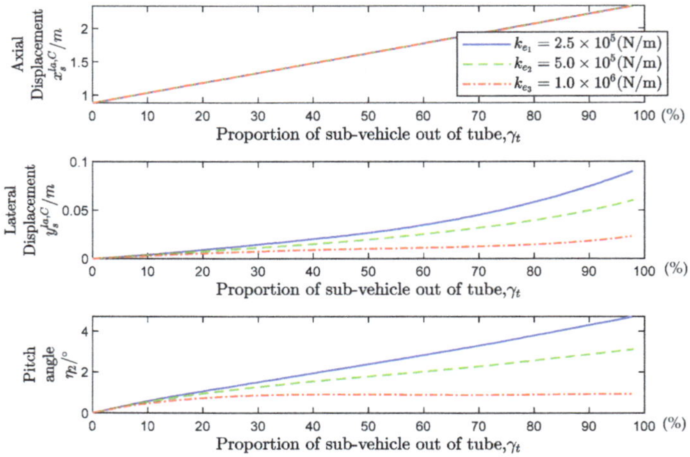

(**a**)

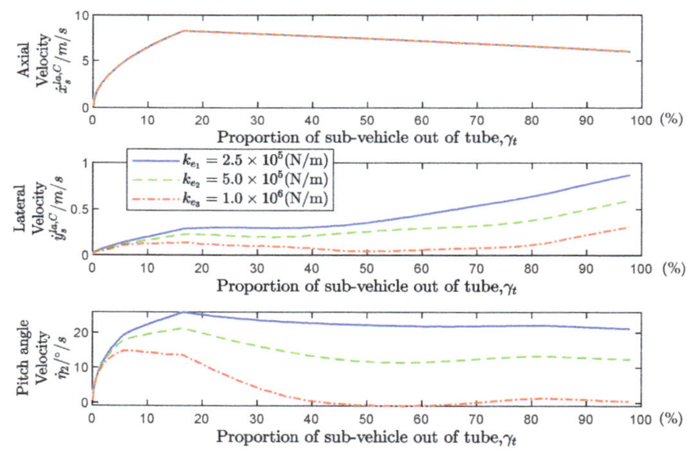

(**b**)

Figure 10. Motion parameters variation curves of the sub-vehicle (different elastic gasket stiffness coefficient). (**a**) Position motion parameter variation curves of sub-vehicle. (**b**) Velocity motion parameters variation curve of sub-vehicle.

Finally, the influence of the separation process and the variation in the stiffness of the elastic gaskets on the pitching attitude of the UUV is analyzed. Figure 11 shows the changes in the motion parameters of the UUV during three stages. It can be seen that the separation process has caused a significant disturbance to the motion of the UUV. Using elastic gaskets with higher stiffness can effectively suppress the pitching motion of the UUV. It is also found that, regardless of the stiffness of the elastic gaskets used, the UUV cannot spontaneously return to a Constant-Speed Sailing state after the separation process. Therefore, it is necessary to study the control of UUV after multi-vehicle system separation.

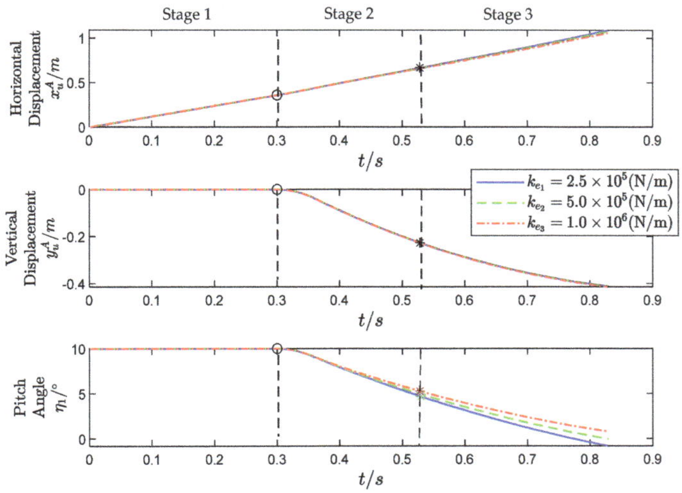

(a)

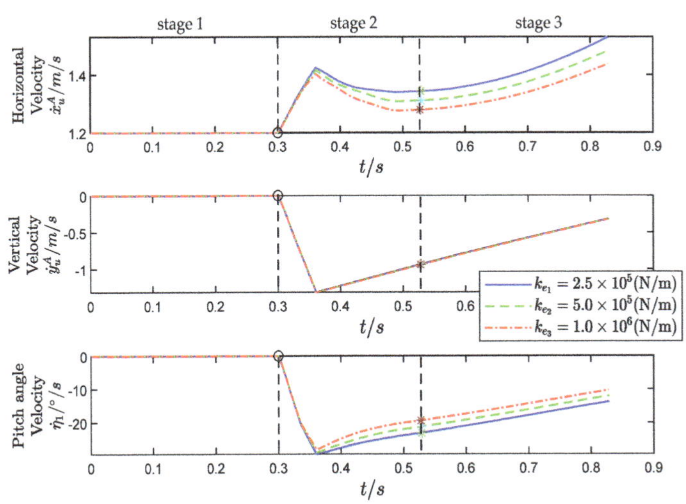

(b)

Figure 11. Motion parameter variation curves of the UUV (different elastic gasket stiffness coefficient). (**a**) Position motion parameters variation curves of UUV. (**b**) Velocity motion parameters variation curves of UUV.

4.3. Influence of Elastic Gasket Distribution on the Multi-Vehicle System

The second case examines the influence of elastic gasket distribution variation on the motion and mechanical characteristics of the multi-vehicle system during the separation process.

The number and stiffness coefficients of the elastic gaskets are adjusted as follows to ensure that the total stiffness remains equal ($K_{total} = 5 \times 10^6$ N/m); the elastic gaskets are evenly distributed in these three cases.

$$\begin{cases} n_1 = 10, K_e = 5 \times 10^5 \text{ N/m} \\ n_2 = 20, K_e = 2.5 \times 10^5 \text{ N/m} \\ n_3 = 40, K_e = 1.25 \times 10^5 \text{ N/m} \end{cases}$$

Simulation results and analysis:

Figure 12 shows the distribution of the maximum compression amount of the elastic gaskets under different installation schemes. The horizontal axis (γ_G) indicates the relative position of the elastic gaskets inside the launch tube (the larger the γ_G, the higher the installation position). As shown in this figure, the compression distribution patterns of the three schemes on the same side are identical. With the increase in the number of elastic gaskets, the peak compression on the left side slightly increases, while the peak compression on the right side decreases to some extent. However, the overall differences remain minimal. Table 3 presents the average values of the maximum compression of elastic gaskets in the bottom, middle and top regions of the launch tube. Based on the data, under the condition of identical total stiffness, the maximum average compression amount of elastic gaskets in the same region of the launch tube remains essentially consistent.

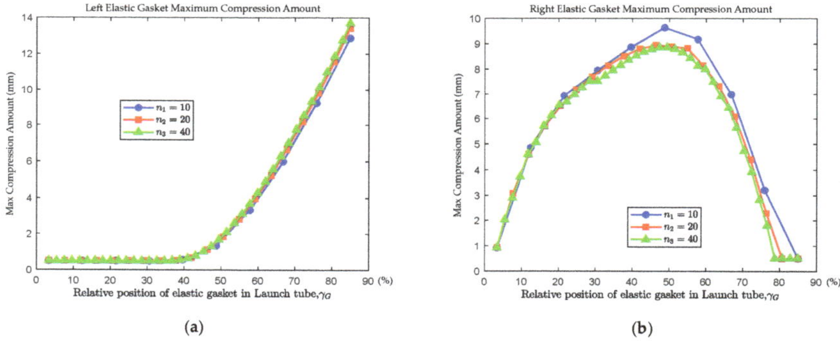

Figure 12. Max Compression amount curves of both sides' elastic gaskets (different installation schemes of elastic gasket). (**a**) Maximum compression amount curves of left-side elastic gaskets. (**b**) Maximum compression amount curves of right-side elastic gaskets.

Table 3. Maximum average amount compression of elastic gaskets at different positions in the launch tube (Different installation schemes of elastic gasket).

Location	Number of Elastic Gaskets	The Average Compression in the Bottom	The Average Compression in the Middle	The Average Compression in the Top
Left elastic gasket	$n_1 = 10$	0.5 mm	1.74 mm	9.37 mm
	$n_2 = 20$	0.5 mm	1.92 mm	9.46 mm
	$n_3 = 30$	0.5 mm	1.96 mm	9.58 mm
Right elastic gasket	$n_1 = 10$	4.23 mm	9.23 mm	3.56 mm
	$n_2 = 20$	4.21 mm	8.57 mm	3.44 mm
	$n_3 = 30$	4.21 mm	8.54 mm	3.42 mm

It can be observed that the distribution characteristics of the maximum compression amount of the elastic gaskets on different sides are distinct. The compression amount of the left-side gaskets increases as they approach the top of the tube, whereas the compression amount of the right-side gaskets initially increases and then decreases. These patterns are related to the force characteristics acting on the sub-vehicle. The maximum compression of each gasket does not occur at the same moment, but corresponds to the peak times shown in Figure 8.

The impact of the layout variation of the elastic gaskets on the motion of the sub-vehicle is also analyzed. Figure 13 shows the motion parameters with discernible changes. It is seen that with the increase in the number of elastic gaskets, the lateral displacement and pitch angle of the sub-vehicle, as well as the lateral velocity and pitch angular velocity, all increase slightly, but the increase is very small. Consistent with the conclusion analyzed above, when the total stiffness remained constant, the variation in the number of elastic gaskets had a small influence on the pitching attitude of the sub-vehicle.

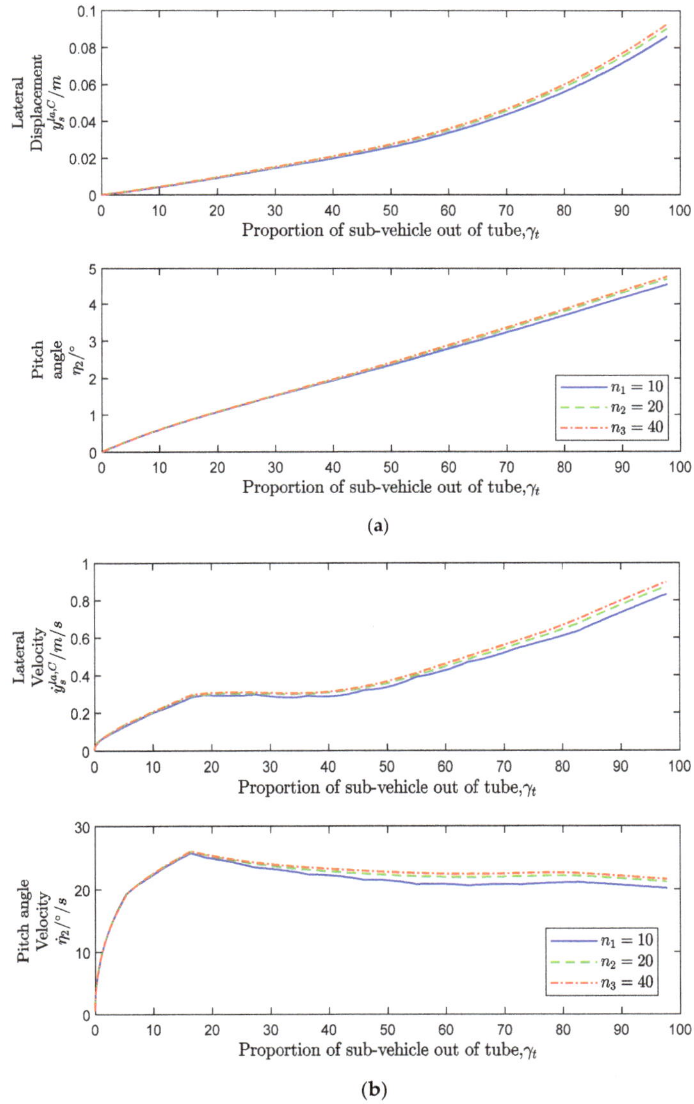

Figure 13. The lateral and pitching motion variation curves of the sub-vehicle (different installation schemes of elastic gasket). (**a**) The variation curves of sub-vehicle lateral displacement and pitch angle. (**b**) The variation curves of sub-vehicle lateral velocity and pitch angle velocity.

The influence of the distribution variation of elastic gaskets on the load is also an important factor to pay attention to. As shown in Figure 14, when the total stiffness of the elastic gaskets remains consistent, the trend and magnitude of the constraint force provided by the left-side elastic gaskets are relatively close, while the differences in the curves on the right side are more significant. When the number of elastic gaskets decreases, the curves on the right side show obvious fluctuations, which are caused by the contact and detachment process between the right-side elastic gaskets and the tail of the sub-vehicle. These fluctuations are the same as those shown in Figure 8b, and impose additional vibration loads on the sub-vehicle, affecting structural safety. When the number of elastic gaskets increases, the contact and separation process becomes more continuous, and the curve fluctuations are significantly reduced. Therefore, when designing the layout scheme of the elastic gaskets, increasing their number appropriately and distributing them evenly can significantly improve the load environment of the sub-vehicle.

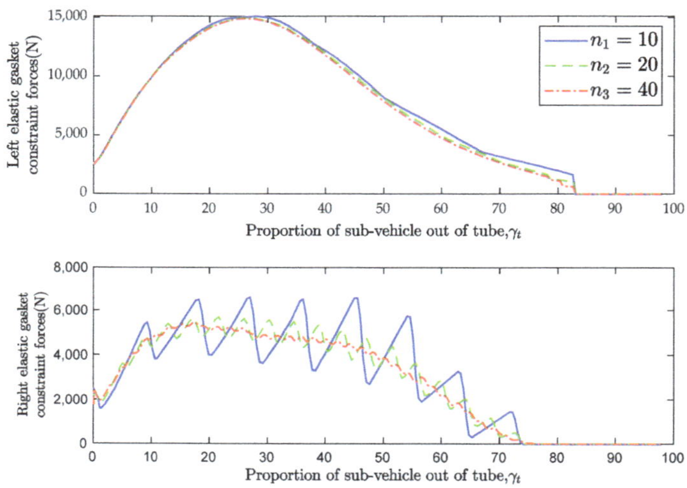

Figure 14. The combined elastic constraint force curves of the elastic gaskets on both sides (different installation schemes of elastic gasket).

5. Conclusions

This paper has studied the problem of the safety assessment of underwater separation of multi-body systems with elastic constraints. Based on the Newton–Euler method, a multi-vehicle coupled dynamics model has been established, with a particular focus on constructing the elastic gaskets constraint model. Utilizing CFD data, the hydrodynamic model of the UUV has been developed through a fitting method, and the hydrodynamic model of the sub-vehicle has been established through an interpolation method. Building on these models, an FSI simulation method for the multi-body separation process has been developed, and the effects of variations in elastic constraint parameters on the motion and mechanical properties of the multi-vehicle system have been systematically investigated.

The following conclusions are drawn:

1. During the separation process, the pitching attitude of the sub-vehicle is negatively correlated with the variation in elastic constraint stiffness, while the load is positively correlated with it. This contradictory correlation posed challenges in parameter design.
2. When the total stiffness of the elastic gaskets remained constant, changes in the number of elastic gaskets had a minimal impact on the sub-vehicle's motion state

during separation, but significantly affected the load fluctuations on the sub-vehicle, leading to structural vibration issues.

3. The analysis method established in this paper is capable of quickly assessing the safety impact of different elastic gasket schemes on the separation of underwater vehicles and reveals the influence patterns of parameter changes on motion and load characteristics, thereby facilitating the optimization of design parameters.

The simulation results demonstrate that investigating the coupling dynamics of multi-body systems with elastic constraints is essential to ensure the navigation safety and structural safety of the multi-vehicle system. The multi-body dynamics model of UUV and the sub-vehicle established in this paper, along with the simulation conclusions derived, serve as valuable references for parameter design in engineering practice.

Further research efforts include the following: (1) Integrating the CFD hydrodynamic models of the UUV and sub-vehicle with their coupling multi-body dynamics model to establish a closed-loop simulation model, thereby enhancing the accuracy and reliability of simulation results. (2) Conducting physical experiments and performing comparative analyses with numerical simulation outcomes to refine numerical simulation techniques. (3) Exploring novel approaches for modeling multi-body coupling dynamics [23]. (4) Implementing active control on the UUV during the sub-vehicle separation process to stabilize its motion posture and improve navigational safety.

Author Contributions: Conceptualization, J.C.; Methodology, Y.H.; Resources, Z.H.; Writing—original draft, Y.H. and R.L.; Writing—review & editing, J.C. and Y.H.; Project administration, J.C.; Funding acquisition, Y.Z. All authors have read and agreed to the published version of the manuscript.

Funding: This research was funded by the National Natural Science Foundation of China, grant number 52272369.

Data Availability Statement: The original contributions presented in the study are included in the article, further inquiries can be directed to the corresponding author.

Conflicts of Interest: The authors declare no conflict of interest.

References

1. Liu, Y.; Chen, L.; Su, Q.; Liu, C.; Lai, M. Research on the development and combat application of foreign underwater unmanned vehicle. *Ship Sci. Technol.* **2020**, *42*, 1–7.
2. Zhang, X.; Hua, J. Study on the development and application of foreign extra-large unmanned underwater vehicles. *Chin. J. Ship Res.* **2024**, *19*, 17–27.
3. Zhong, H. Review and Prospect of Equipment and Techniques for Unmanned Undersea Vehicle in Foreign Countries. *J. Unmanned Undersea Syst.* **2017**, *25*, 215–225.
4. Chen, X. Study on Automatic Navigation System of Unmanned Underwater Vehicles. Master's Thesis, Dalian Maritime University, Dalian, China, 2008.
5. Chen, J.; Han, Y.; Li, R.; Zhang, Y.; He, Z. Coupling Dynamics Study on Multi-Body Separation Process of Underwater Vehicles. *Drones* **2024**, *8*, 533. [CrossRef]
6. Han, Y.; Yin, W.; Zhang, Y. Aircraft-Rocket Coupling Dynamics for Gravity Air-Launch Without Launching Tube. *J. Nanjing Univ. Aeronaut. Astronaut.* **2022**, *54*, 311–320.
7. Han, Y.; Yin, W.; Zhang, Y. Aircraft-Rocket Coupling Dynamics for Internally Carried Gravity Air-Launch Method. *J. Nanjing Univ. Aeronaut. Astronaut.* **2020**, *52*, 963–971.
8. Wang, X.; Rui, X.; Yang, F.; Zhou, Q. Launch dynamics modeling and simulation of vehicular missile system. *J. Guid. Control Dyn.* **2018**, *41*, 1370–1379. [CrossRef]
9. Zhang, D.; Wang, C.; Shen, Y.; Wei, Y.; Xu, H. Dynamic modeling and motion prediction of two projectiles launched successively underwater. *Ocean Eng.* **2024**, *292*, 116551. [CrossRef]
10. Weiland, C.J.; Vlachos, P.P.; Yagla, J.J. Concept analysis and laboratory observations on a water piercing missile launcher. *Ocean Eng.* **2010**, *37*, 959–965. [CrossRef]

11. Shang, S.-C.; Sun, J.-Z. Research on the Affection of the Underwater Missile Launching Process. In Proceedings of the 3rd International Conference on Mechanical and Electronics Engineering (ICMEE 2011), Hefei, China, 23–25 September 2011, pp. 2594–2599.
12. Wang, Y.; Lin, T.; Jiang, H. Numerical analysis for water-exit trajectory of submarine-launched UUV. In Proceedings of the 2018 International Conference on Mathematics, Modelling, Simulation and Algorithms (MMSA 2018), Chengdu, China, 25–26 March 2018; pp. 276–279.
13. Tan, D. Modeling and Simulation for Underwater Trajectory of the Submarine Horizontal Launched Vehicle on the Condition of Ignition Failure. *J. Ordnance Equip. Eng.* **2018**, *39*, 16–20.
14. Cheng, Y.-S.; Liu, H. Mathematical modeling of fluid flows for underwater missile launch. *J. Hydrodyn.* **2006**, *18*, 481–486.
15. Zhang, H.; Lu, H.; Pei, Y.; Ye, J.; Zou, Z. Numerical investigation to vertical launching of submarine launching missile. *Chin. J. Hydrodyn.* **2010**, *25*, 406–415.
16. Wang, Z.; Gu, H.; Lang, J.; Xing, L. Safety Analysis of Initial Separation Phase for AUV Deployment of Mission Payloads. *J. Mar. Sci. Eng.* **2024**, *12*, 608. [CrossRef]
17. Li, W.; Zhang, Z.; Lu, J.; Li, Z.; Wang, C. Investigations on the flow characteristics and the structural response of the launch tube during the underwater launching process. *Ocean Eng.* **2023**, *279*, 114603. [CrossRef]
18. Lv, B.; Huang, B.; Peng, L. 21. Research on the uncertain factors to the control of submarine during missile launching process. *Ship Sci. Technol.* **2017**, *39*, 185–189, 193.
19. Brito, M.; Canelas, R.B.; García-Feal, O.; Domínguez, J.M.; Crespo, A.J.C.; Ferreira, R.M.L.; Neves, M.G.; Teixeira, L. A Numerical Tool for Modelling Oscillating Wave Surge Converter with Nonlinear Mechanical Constraints. *Renew. Energy* **2020**, *146*, 2024–2043.
20. Brito, M.; Bernardo, F.; Neves, M.G.; Neves, D.R.C.B.; Crespo, A.J.C.; Domínguez, J.M. Numerical Model of Constrained Wave Energy Hyperbaric Converter under Full-Scale Sea Wave Conditions. *J. Mar. Sci. Eng.* **2022**, *10*, 1489. [CrossRef]
21. Li, J. Navigation Safety Analysis of Submarine after Underwater Vehicle Launching. Master's Thesis, Harbin Engineering University, Harbin, China, 2022.
22. Wu, W. *Fluid Mechanics*, 2nd ed.; Peking University Press: Beijing, China, 2021.
23. Zhao, T.; Dai, J. Dynamics and coupling actuation of elastic underactuated manipulators. *J. Robot. Syst.* **2003**, *20*, 135–146.

Journal of
Marine Science
and Engineering

MDPI

Article

Research on the Impact of Deep Sea Offshore Wind Farms on Maritime Safety

Wenbo Yu [1], Jian Liu [1,*], Pengcheng Yan [2] and Xiaobin Jiang [1,2]

1 Shanghai Investigation, Design & Research Institute Co., Ltd., No. 388, Yixian Road, Hong Kou District, Shanghai 200434, China; ywb1225@126.com (W.Y.); dmu_jxb@163.com (X.J.)
2 Merchant Marine College, Shanghai Maritime University, 1550 Haigang Avenue, Shanghai 201306, China; yanpengcheng@stu.shmtu.edu.cn
* Correspondence: liujian@sidri.com

Abstract: With the rapid development of offshore wind farms, the construction of deep sea wind farms has increasingly significant impacts on the safety of maritime navigation. This paper conducts a cluster analysis of ship trajectories based on AIS data to analyze the characteristics of ship traffic flow in the waters near the Shanghai deep sea offshore wind farm. A fuzzy hierarchical analysis method is proposed. Combined with the layout of wind farms and the navigational environment, a risk assessment model for offshore wind farm navigation is established. This model quantifies the factors that affect the safety of ship navigation due to the wind farm and evaluates the navigation risks in the surrounding waters. The results of the research show that the construction of wind farms increases traffic density, interferes with traditional shipping routes, and consequently increases the risk of collisions. The fuzzy hierarchical analysis method has good operability and feasibility in the safety assessment of offshore wind farms, and can provide effective support for future safety assessment of offshore wind farms. The sections are arranged as follows: Firstly, the background and significance of the paper are introduced, as well as the current research status. Secondly, an overview of Shanghai offshore wind farms and their nearby shipping routes is introduced, and then the risk situation of existing wind farms is pointed out. Then the risk assessment method is carried out, and the navigational risk of offshore wind farms is evaluated. Finally, the paper proposes measures to reduce the navigational risk of ships in the vicinity of wind farms.

Keywords: fuzzy analytic hierarchy process; deep sea offshore wind farm; navigation safety; risk assessment; safety countermeasures

1. Introduction

With the transformation of the global energy structure, offshore wind power as a clean and renewable energy source has attracted widespread attention. In recent years, the construction of deep sea offshore wind farms has gradually become a new trend in the development of offshore wind energy. However, the construction of wind farms inevitably affects the safety of shipping in the surrounding waters, especially in areas with heavy maritime traffic. As an economic hub and a major energy-consuming city in China, the construction of deep sea offshore wind farms in Shanghai not only contributes to optimizing the energy structure, but also poses new challenges to the safety of ship navigation.

Currently, domestic and international scholars have conducted extensive research on the navigational safety of offshore wind farms. Krzysztof Naus et al. used historical AIS data to generate quantitative and qualitative characteristics, describing the vessel traffic conditions in and around the wind farm areas and assessing the impact of offshore wind farms on navigational safety and efficiency [1]. Andrew Rawson et al. compared and analyzed vessel traffic before and after the construction of offshore wind farms, using AIS data and GIS to evaluate the impact of wind farms on navigational safety in order to predict and manage potential risks [2].

Cao uses fuzzy comprehensive evaluation and a collision probability model to evaluate the navigation risk of offshore wind farms in Putian Port [3]. Marcjan et al. used the risk matrix method and AIS data to analyze the navigational risks of wind farms in the southern Baltic Sea [4]. Lv et al. assessed the navigational safety risks of offshore wind farms by establishing fuzzy inference rules on the impact of navigational risks in offshore wind farms [5] .

Yu et al. assessed the risk of collisions between ships and offshore wind turbines by combining Bayesian networks with evidence inference [6]. Yu et al. proposed a rule-based Bayesian inference method for assessing the risk of collision between ships and offshore facilities [7].

Yuh-Ming Tsai et al. use a fault tree analysis approach to perform a ship-to-ship and ship-to-turbine collision risk analysis [8]. Kang et al. carried out a risk assessment using a modified FMEA method to investigate the relationship between failure modes and their effect on the probability of failure of the whole system [9] .

Sinha uses FMECA to evaluate the risk and priority number of a failure to help prioritize maintenance work. He also illustrates the usefulness of RPN numbers in identifying failures which can assist in designing cost-effective maintenance plans [10]. Hong aims to identify and evaluate the economic risks of tropical cyclones to offshore wind farms within China's Economic Exclusive Zone and help improve decision-making for planners and investors [11].

Gatzert aims to comprehensively present current risks and risk management solutions for renewable energy projects and to identify critical gaps in risk transfer, thereby differentiating between onshore and offshore wind farms with a focus on the European market [12]. Junmin Mou et al. conducted a qualitative and quantitative analysis of potential accident types in offshore wind farms using fault tree analysis to identify key risk factors during their operation [13].Victor Ceder et al. used historical AIS data, ice condition data, and ship performance simulation to analyze the impact of offshore wind farms on shipping routes and winter navigation in the Gulf of Bosnia [14].

Regarding the interference of wind farms with navigation systems, Simbo A. Odunaiya argues that wind turbines may block or reflect radio signals, leading to attenuation or distortion of navigation signals from systems like VOR, thereby affecting the accuracy of aircraft positioning and navigation [15]. Similarly, Vandermolen, Jon et al. suggest that the rotating blades of wind turbines may intercept radar signals, impacting the radar system's ability to detect targets such as weather patterns and aircraft [16]. Additionally, T. Stupak et al. believe that the tall wind turbines and metal structures in offshore wind farms can generate multiple direct and sidelobe echoes on radar, making it difficult to detect vessels near or behind the wind farm [17].

Recent progress in the integration of renewable energy shows the great potential for the decarbonization of offshore operations, particularly through smart port infrastructure optimization. Notably, the pioneering study by Seyed behblood Issa Zadeh systematically divides carbon reduction measures for modern seaports into three broad categories: energy management systems, infrastructure and equipment upgrades, and policy regulatory interventions. By synthesizing the literature on carbon footprint reduction for smart seaports optimized for energy infrastructure, they further show that smart energy infrastructure optimization for smart ports can achieve substantial efficiency gains while maintaining operational reliability [18,19].

However, systematic research on the impact of deep sea offshore wind farms on ship navigation safety remains relatively scarce. To meet the requirements for the planning and sustainable development of wind farms in Shanghai, this study aims to establish a computational model for assessing the risks between wind farms and ship navigation. By analyzing AIS data and employing the fuzzy analytic hierarchy process (FAHP), combined with the layout of wind farms and the navigational environment, the model evaluates the impact of deep sea offshore wind farms on ship navigation safety. Furthermore, corresponding safety management strategies are proposed.

2. Overview of the Wind Farm and Its Adjacent Shipping Routes

2.1. Overview of the Wind Farm

The construction costs of an offshore wind farm are significantly higher than those of an onshore wind farm. Therefore, it is crucial to evaluate whether the location of an offshore wind farm is optimal. The Shanghai coastal region falls within the temperate and subtropical humid climatic zones, which are characterized by abundant wind energy resources. According to the "Shanghai 2024 Offshore Wind Power Project Competitive Allocation Work Program" [20], the competitive allocation project is divided into six bidding sections, with a total installed capacity of 5.8 million kW. The existing and planned sites for Shanghai offshore wind farms are shown in Figure 1. The offshore wind farm is located near the mouth of the Yangtze River, adjacent to waters with high vessel traffic density and complex traffic patterns, which will inevitably have some impact on the navigational environment of the surrounding waters.

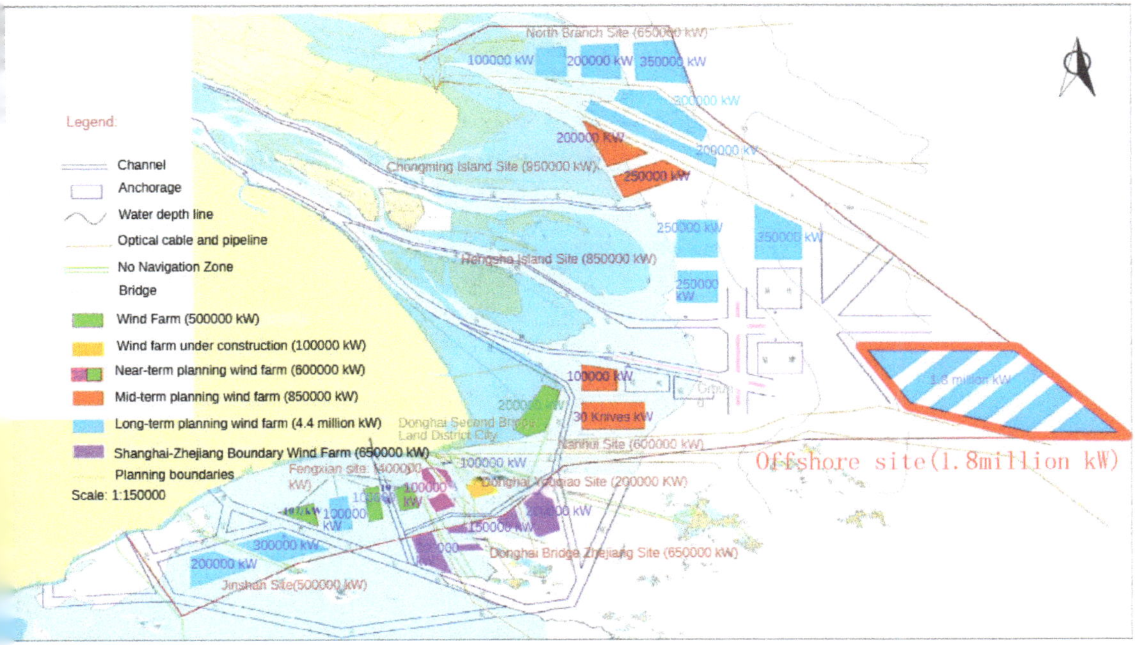

Figure 1. Schematic diagram of Shanghai offshore wind farm.

The proposed site for the Shanghai offshore wind farm is located to the north of the Yangtze Estuary Ship Routing System. The area of the offshore site is shown in Figure 1.

The interior of the offshore site includes areas of the navigation route that are not suitable for the installation of offshore wind turbines, so that part of the route area needs to be removed from the offshore site. The main navigation routes in the vicinity of the offshore site include the Inner Yangtze Estuary route, the divergence area, and the Outer Yangtze Estuary route. The relationship between the offshore site and the shipping route is shown in Figure 2.

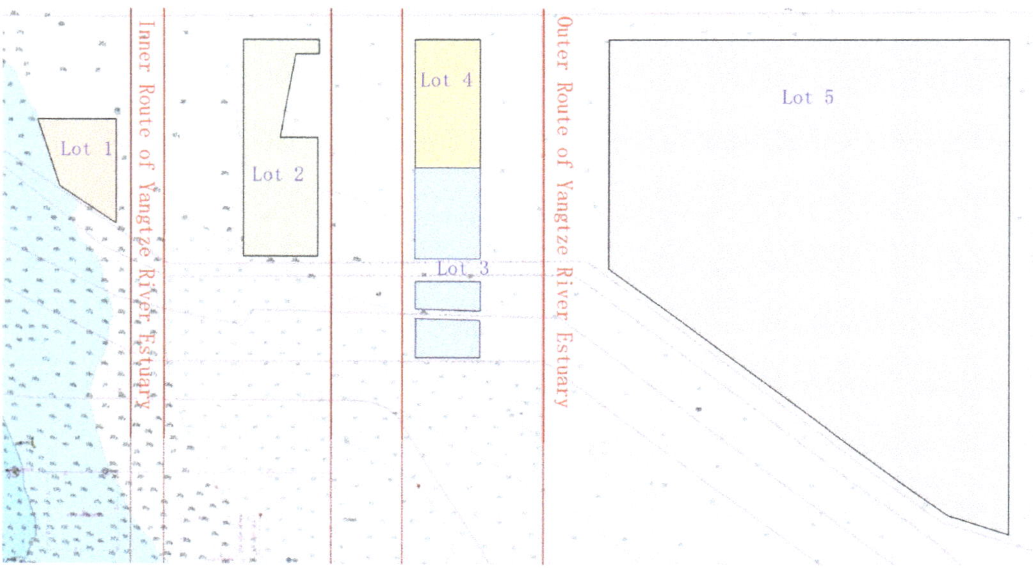

Figure 2. Schematic diagram of the relationship between the locations of Shanghai offshore wind farms and shipping routes.

2.2. Characteristics of Vessel Traffic Flow Based on AIS Data

In order to understand the ship traffic flow in the nearby waterways, the traffic volumes of several major routes in the vicinity of the offshore wind farm in 2023 were statistically analyzed. A schematic representation of the selected ship traffic flow cross-sections is shown in Figure 3. Among them, observation line 1 mainly records the vessel traffic flow in the Inner Yangtze Estuary route, observation line 2 focuses on the traffic flow in the divergence area, and observation line 3 records the traffic flow in the Outer Yangtze Estuary route. Observation line 4 is designed to monitor the traffic flow along the regular route from the Yangtze Estuary to Nantong and Lusi Port, while observation line 5 is used to measure the traffic flow along the regular route from the Yangtze Estuary to Lianyungang.

Further analysis was carried out on the flow of vessel traffic in representative months of each quarter in the area, as shown in Figure 4. Based on the navigational conditions in the waters where the offshore wind farm sites and their surrounding areas are located, it can be observed that the deep sea offshore wind farm site in Section 1 has a certain impact on ship navigation. Similarly, the location of the deep sea offshore wind farm in Section 2 also has an impact on vessel navigation. In contrast, the deep sea offshore wind farm sites in Sections 3 and 4 are located away from the divergence area and the outer Yangtze Estuary route, generally in areas with low traffic density. However, the traffic density on the western side of the wind farm sites in these two sections is higher than on the eastern side, so the potential impact of the western sites on navigational safety needs to be considered.

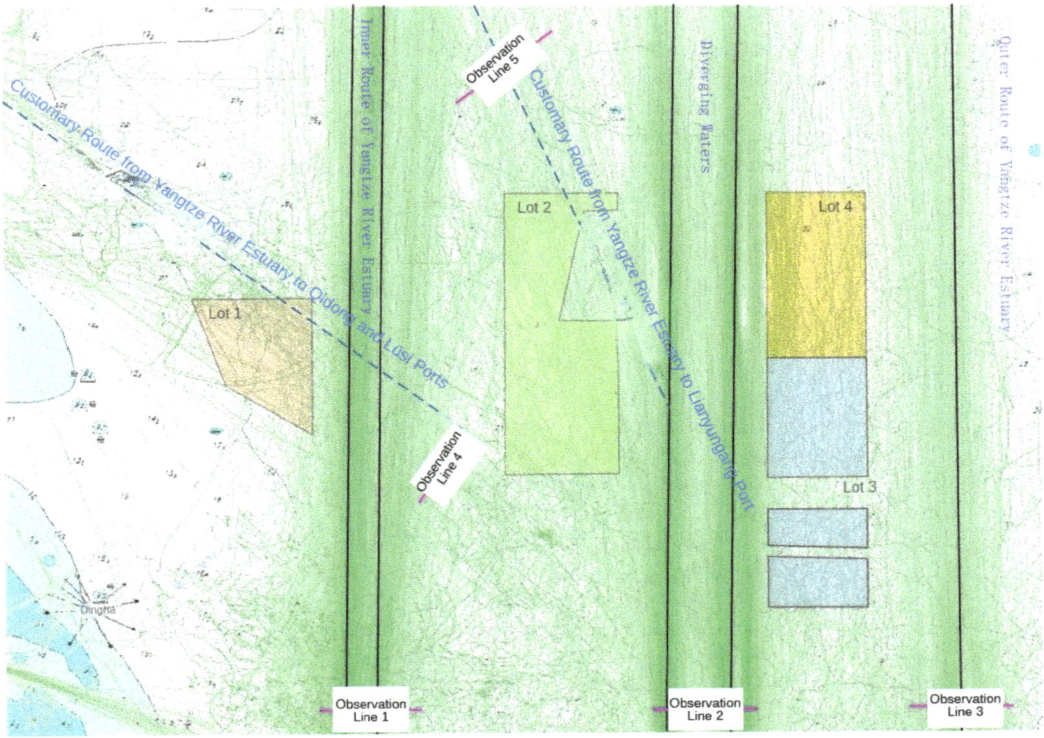

Figure 3. Schematic diagram of ship traffic flow cross-section selection.

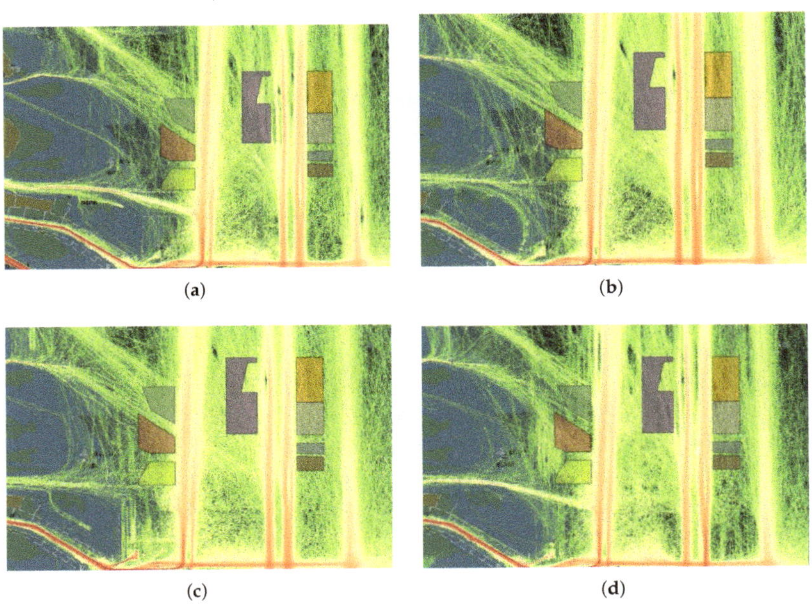

Figure 4. Vessel traffic flow density in representative months of each quarter in 2023: (**a**) Vessel traffic flow density in February. (**b**) Vessel traffic flow density in May. (**c**) Vessel traffic flow density in August. (**d**) Vessel traffic flow density in November.

3. Risk Assessment Indicator System

From the perspective of vessel traffic flow, the waters where the deep sea offshore wind farm is located experience relatively dense vessel traffic with a high volume of vessel movements. The traffic flow analysis shows that in addition to the officially published north–south routes within the Yangtze Estuary, the bifurcated waters, and the routes outside the Yangtze Estuary, there are several potential customary routes in the vicinity of the wind farm. Some of these routes intersect, contributing to a complex navigational environment.

In order to more accurately assess the impact of the offshore wind farm on navigational safety, it is essential to conduct an in-depth investigation of the existing risk factors and the magnitude of their influence. The fuzzy analytic hierarchy process is used to assess the safety of navigation in this context.

3.1. The Basic Principle of Fuzzy Analytic Hierarchy Process

The fuzzy analytic hierarchy process is a multi-criteria decision-making method that integrates the analytic hierarchy process with fuzzy mathematics. By constructing an evaluation matrix, FAHP transforms expert opinions into fuzzy numbers, thereby addressing the uncertainties and ambiguities inherent in expert judgments and ultimately deriving the weights of each criterion.

The basic steps of FAHP include, first, establishing an evaluation index system; second, constructing a hierarchical structure model; third, performing pairwise comparisons; fourth, calculating relative weights; and finally, performing consistency checks. FAHP makes evaluation conclusions intuitive and clear, with a streamlined and efficient process. It ensures that evaluators maintain clear thinking and consistent principles throughout the multi-index evaluation process. FAHP has been widely applied to complex decision-making and evaluation problems such as port management, transport, and supply chain management.

The impact of offshore wind farms on the navigational safety of vessels involves numerous complex and imprecisely quantifiable factors, such as the degree to which meteorological conditions affect vessel navigation and the relationship between wind farm size and navigational risk. These factors are characterized by their inherent fuzziness. Using the FAHP, these ambiguous and qualitative factors can be quantified. This is achieved through the construction of factor sets, rating sets, and fuzzy relationship matrices, ultimately leading to a comprehensive rating result. This approach scientifically reflects the level of navigation safety risks.

3.2. Establishment of the Evaluation Index System

At present, more than 1000 vessels pass through the waters around the Shanghai deep sea offshore wind farm on a daily basis. The vessels passing through the area are mainly those entering and leaving the north and south channels, as well as transit vessels on the north–south routes. These vessels are diverse in type, large in size, and include numerous anchored and transit vessels.

The Shanghai deep sea offshore wind farm will have multiple impacts on the surrounding navigable waters. The numerous wind turbines and associated facilities occupy a significant portion of the marine space, reducing the original expansive navigable area. As the navigable area decreases, the density of vessel traffic increases, leading to increased traffic flow and complexity within the port access channels. In addition, the towering structures of wind turbines obstruct the line of sight of vessel operators, potentially interfering with the navigation of other vessels in the channel and posing a risk to maritime safety.

In order to assess the impact of offshore wind farms on maritime safety, a hierarchical structure model was established, judgment matrices were constructed, and the weights of factors at each level were calculated. This process clarifies the relative importance of different risk assessment indicators to navigation safety risks and provides a reasonable basis for weighting in subsequent fuzzy comprehensive assessments. This approach ensures that the assessment results are more scientific and rational. Based on the traffic risk assessment model, risks in the areas surrounding the wind farm were identified, and a corresponding evaluation index system was designed.

Through a review of relevant literature and extensive consultation with frontline pilots and industry experts, including 20 captains, 15 offshore wind power engineers, and 15 maritime managers, initial indicators were selected based on the principles of systematicity, hierarchy, simplicity, and feasibility in constructing the indicator system. These initial indicators were then refined through questionnaire surveys and factor analysis to determine the final evaluation indicators. This study did not take into account the influence of subjective factors; therefore, the evaluation indicator system does not include any personnel-related metrics.

Based on the risks identified during the implementation of offshore wind projects, the target layer of the evaluation system is defined as "Navigation Risk Assessment for Offshore Wind Farms". This approach allows for a more comprehensive and accurate analysis of the relationships between factors and their impact on the target layer. The constructed evaluation indicator system for assessing the impact on the safety of navigation is presented in Table 1.

Table 1. Evaluation indicator system for navigation safety of offshore wind farms.

Target Layer A	Criterion Layer B_x	Indicator Layer C_{ij}
Navigation Risk Assessment of Offshore Wind Farm	Natural condition B_1	Visibility Wind Tidal Currents Waves
	Navigational condition B_2	Fairway Wind Farm Electromagnetic Interference Anchorage
	Surrounding Vessel B_3	Engineering Ships Fishing Ships
	Construction Conditions B_4	Construction Operations

3.3. Determination of Indicator Weights Using the Analytic Hierarchy Process

(1) Construction of the Judgment Matrix

Based on the evaluation indicator system for offshore wind farm navigation risk assessment established in Table 1, invite experts in related fields, including captains, offshore wind power engineering experts, and maritime management experts, etc. Based on their professional knowledge and practical experience, compare the relative importance of the factors in the guideline layer. Then, score them according to the 1–9 scale methodology so as to construct a judgment matrix.

Specifically, C_{ij} represents the ratio of the relative importance of two factors ai and aj under the same criterion B_x. The value of C_{ij} ranges from $[1/9, 9]$, where the values 1, 3, 5, 7, and 9 indicate that ai is equally important, slightly more important, significantly more important, strongly more important, and extremely more important than aj, respectively. The values 2, 4, 6, and 8 represent intermediate levels of importance. Note that $C_{ij} > 0$, $C_{ii} = 1$, $C_{ij} = 1/C_{ji}$ [21].

Based on this, the judgment matrices C, C_1, C_2, C_3, and C_4 for the navigation risk assessment of offshore wind farms can be constructed as follows:

$$C = \begin{bmatrix} 1 & 3 & 5 & \frac{1}{2} \\ \frac{1}{3} & 1 & \frac{1}{2} & \frac{1}{3} \\ \frac{1}{5} & 2 & 1 & \frac{1}{3} \\ 2 & 3 & 3 & 1 \end{bmatrix} \quad (1)$$

$$\begin{cases} C_1 = \begin{bmatrix} 1 & 2 & \frac{1}{3} & \frac{1}{5} \\ \frac{1}{2} & 1 & \frac{1}{5} & \frac{1}{7} \\ 3 & 5 & 1 & \frac{1}{2} \\ 5 & 7 & 2 & 1 \end{bmatrix} \\ C_2 = \begin{bmatrix} 1 & \frac{1}{3} & \frac{1}{5} & \frac{1}{2} \\ 3 & 1 & \frac{1}{3} & 2 \\ 5 & 3 & 1 & 3 \\ 2 & \frac{1}{2} & \frac{1}{3} & 1 \end{bmatrix} \\ C_3 = \begin{bmatrix} 1 & 3 \\ \frac{1}{3} & 1 \end{bmatrix} \\ C_4 = \begin{bmatrix} 1 \end{bmatrix} \end{cases} \quad (2)$$

(2) Calculation of the Weight Vector

After constructing the judgment matrix, it is necessary to calculate the weight vector A based on the judgment matrix to ensure that the evaluation conclusions are intuitive and operable. The constructed judgment matrix C_k is a positive matrix, which is unique and necessarily has a maximum eigenvalue λ_k.

The corresponding weight vector W_j satisfies the formula. By normalizing W_j, the weights of each factor in the indicator layer relative to their respective criteria layer and the weights of each factor in the criteria layer relative to the target layer can be obtained.

Through calculation using Matlab software R2018a, the maximum eigenvalues corresponding to the matrices C, C_1, C_2, C_3, and C_4 are $\lambda_0 = 4.2472$, $\lambda_1 = 4.0201$, $\lambda_2 = 4.0593$, $\lambda_3 = 2$, and $\lambda_4 = 1$, respectively. The fuzzy consistency matrices were normalized to calculate the fuzzy weights of each evaluation criterion. The corresponding weight vectors are as follows:

$$\begin{aligned} W &= (0.3926,\ 0.0895,\ 0.1460,\ 0.3719) \\ W_1 &= (0.1183,\ 0.0617,\ 0.3180,\ 0.5021) \\ W_2 &= (0.0840,\ 0.2617,\ 0.4959,\ 0.1584) \\ W_3 &= (0.7500,\ 0.2500) \\ W_4 &= (1.0000) \end{aligned} \quad (3)$$

(3) Consistency Check

To assess the reliability of the conclusions of the matrix analysis, in particular to determine whether there are significant discrepancies between the expert opinions collected during the evaluation of the pilotage support organization's capabilities, a consistency test is necessary. Let CI be the consistency index and CR the consistency ratio, calculated according to the following formula:

$$CI = \frac{\lambda_{\max} - n}{n - 1} \quad (4)$$

$$CR = \frac{CI}{RI} \quad (5)$$

If the consistency ratio $CR < 0.1$, the matrix A is considered to have passed the consistency check. However, if $CR \geq 0.1$, it indicates that the discrepancy in the consistency index is too large and an adjustment of the importance weights of the indicators is required. Here, RI refers to the average random consistency index corresponding to the order of the matrix, which is determined by the order n of the matrix A, as shown in Table 2.

Table 2. Average random consistency index RI of the judgment matrix.

The order of the matrix	1	2	3	4	5	6	7	8	9
RI	0	0	0.58	0.90	1.12	1.24	1.32	1.41	1.45

After calculation, the values of CR, CR_1, CR_2, CR_3, and CR_4 are all less than 0.1, indicating satisfactory consistency.

4. The Evaluation of Ship Navigation Risk

The fuzzy comprehensive evaluation method is an approach that transforms qualitative indicators into quantitative analysis. By calculating comprehensive scores for each indicator based on the evaluation results, it provides a relatively accurate and integrated assessment of outcomes that are influenced by multiple hierarchical factors.

4.1. The Standard Values of Risk Assessment Indicators

The assessment of navigation risks in waters with waterborne activities can be carried out using either qualitative or quantitative methods, depending primarily on the scale of the project and the complexity of the technology involved. For most projects, a qualitative risk assessment is appropriate. The assessment criteria are based on the subjective assessment of navigation risk levels by national and international scientists and the results of relevant national research. The risk assessment criteria are divided into five levels: low risk (L), relative low risk (RL), moderate risk (M), relative high risk (RH), high risk (H), denoted as $V = \{H, RH, M, RL, L\}$. Based on "Technical Guidelines for Navigational Safety Analysis of Offshore Wind Farm Siting" in China Sites", the risk matrix for different influencing factors is shown in Table 3 [22].

Table 3. Evaluation criteria for risk levels of influencing factors.

Risk Level / Influencing Factors	L	RL	M	RH	H
Visibility < 1000 m Days (d)	<15	15∼25	25∼40	40∼50	≥50
Standard wind days (d)	<30	30∼60	60∼100	100∼150	≥150
Tidal current velocity (m/s)	0.25	0.25∼0.75	0.75∼1.25	1.25∼2	≥2
Wave height (m)	<0.3	0.3∼0.5	0.5∼1	1∼1.5	≥1.5
Distance from nearby route (nautical miles)	≥5	2∼5	1∼2	0.5∼1	<0.5
Distance from other wind farms (km)	≥10	5∼10	2∼5	1∼2	<1
Distance from nearby anchorage (km)	≥10	5∼10	2∼5	1∼2	<1
Daily traffic volume of Engineering Ships in the water area (vessels/day)	<2	2∼3	3∼5	5∼10	≥10
Daily traffic volume of Fishing Ships in the water area (vessels/day)	<10	10∼15	15∼25	25∼70	≥70
Days of construction (d)	<3	3∼7	7∼15	15∼30	≥30

4.2. Fuzzy Comprehensive Evaluation Results

According to Table 1, the influencing factor sets for the criteria layer of navigation risk assessment for offshore wind farms are listed, where the primary indicator factor set is denoted as $A = \{B_1, B_2, B_3, B_4\}$, and the secondary indicator factor set is denoted as $B_1 = \{C_{11}, C_{12}, C_{13}, C_{14}\}$, $B_2 = \{C_{21}, C_{22}, C_{23}, C_{24}\}$, $B_3 = \{C_{31}, C_{32}\}$, $B_4 = \{C_4\}$.

By assigning the values $\{90, 75, 60, 45, 30\}$ to the risk evaluation criteria, the evaluation indicator factor set can be derived, as shown in Table 4.

Table 4. Set of navigational risk assessment indicators for offshore wind farms.

Primary Indicator	Weight Coefficient	Secondary Indicator	Weight Coefficient	Evaluation Conclusion
Natural conditions	W_1	Visibility	W_{11}	H, RH, M, RL, L
		Wind	W_{12}	H, RH, M, RL, L
		Tidal current	W_{13}	H, RH, M, RL, L
		Waves	W_{14}	H, RH, M, RL, L
Navigational conditions	W_2	Nearby route	W_{21}	H, RH, M, RL, L
		Wind farm	W_{22}	H, RH, M, RL, L
		Electromagnetic interference	W_{23}	H, RH, M, RL, L
		Anchor ground	W_{24}	H, RH, M, RL, L
Surrounding ships	W_3	Engineering ships	W_{31}	H, RH, M, RL, L
		Fishing Ships	W_{32}	H, RH, M, RL, L
Construction conditions	W_4	Construction operations	W_4	H, RH, M, RL, L

A single factor fuzzy evaluation matrix is constructed step by step in ascending order. Using the evaluation criteria of the conclusion set V, each factor B_i is evaluated. Let r_{ij} represent the ratio of the number of times that factor B_i is evaluated as v_j to the total number of experts. Thus, r_{ij} denotes the membership degree corresponding to this indicator, and the single-factor fuzzy relation matrix R_i can be constructed based on r_{ij}. Fifty experts were invited to evaluate the navigation risks of offshore wind farms in deep sea areas, and the results are presented in Table 5.

Table 5. Evaluation Results of Navigation Risks for Offshore Wind Farms in Deep Sea Areas.

r_{ij}	H	RH	M	RL	L
C_{11}	0.10	0.24	0.62	0.04	0
C_{12}	0.12	0.20	0.46	0.16	0.06
C_{13}	0.16	0.48	0.28	0.08	0
C_{14}	0.02	0.16	0.54	0.20	0.08
C_{21}	0.78	0.16	0.06	0	0
C_{22}	0	0	0	0.16	0.844
C_{23}	0.16	0.10	0.44	0.24	0.06
C_{24}	0	0	0.12	0.58	0.3
C_{31}	0.34	0.52	0.12	0.02	0
C_{32}	0.72	0.22	0.06	0	0
C_4	0.08	0.64	0.18	0.10	0

Based on a comprehensive analysis of the above table, the risk matrices for each risk assessment indicator are presented in Table 6. Integrating the above analyses, the primary risks posed by the wind farm site to the adjacent waters are mainly reflected in the impacts on the nearby shipping routes and navigational vessels.

Table 6. Risk Matrices for Risk Assessment Indicators

Level	Visibility	Wind	Tidal Current	Waves	Proximity to Shipping Routes	Other Wind Farms	Electromagnetic Interference	Nearby Anchorage	Nearby Engineering Ships	Nearby Fishing Ships	Construction Operation
V											
IV			■			■	■			■	■
III	■	■		■							
II					■			■			
I									■		

V—High, IV— Relatively High, III—Moderate, II—Relatively Low, I—Lower

From the table above, the fuzzy relation matrices for each factor can be obtained as follows:

$$R_1 = \begin{bmatrix} 0.10 & 0.24 & 0.62 & 0.04 & 0 \\ 0.12 & 0.20 & 0.46 & 0.16 & 0.06 \\ 0.16 & 0.48 & 0.28 & 0.08 & 0 \\ 0.02 & 0.16 & 0.54 & 0.20 & 0.08 \end{bmatrix}$$
$$R_2 = \begin{bmatrix} 0.78 & 0.16 & 0.06 & 0 & 0 \\ 0 & 0 & 0 & 0.16 & 0.84 \\ 0.16 & 0.10 & 0.44 & 0.24 & 0.06 \\ 0 & 0 & 0.12 & 0.58 & 0.3 \end{bmatrix} \quad (6)$$
$$R_3 = \begin{bmatrix} 0.34 & 0.52 & 0.12 & 0.02 & 0 \\ 0.72 & 0.22 & 0.06 & 0 & 0 \end{bmatrix}$$
$$R_4 = \begin{bmatrix} 0.08 & 0.64 & 0.18 & 0.10 & 0 \end{bmatrix}$$

Based on the weight vector Wi obtained through the analytic hierarchy process (AHP), the single-factor fuzzy evaluation vector for each indicator can be derived using the formula for the single-factor fuzzy evaluation vector:

$$\begin{aligned} A_1 &= W_1 \times R_1 = (0.0802,\ 0.2737,\ 0.4619,\ 0.1405,\ 0.0439) \\ A_2 &= W_2 \times R_2 = (0.1449,\ 0.0630,\ 0.2422,\ 0.2528,\ 0.2971) \\ A_3 &= W_3 \times R_3 = (0.4350,\ 0.4450,\ 0.1050,\ 0.0150,\ 0) \\ A_4 &= W_4 \times R_4 = (0.0800,\ 0.6400,\ 0.1800,\ 0.1000,\ 0) \end{aligned} \quad (7)$$

By conducting a comprehensive fuzzy evaluation based on the single-factor fuzzy evaluation, the comprehensive fuzzy evaluation matrix can be obtained:

$$R = \begin{bmatrix} 0.0802 & 0.2737 & 0.4619 & 0.1405 & 0.0439 \\ 0.1449 & 0.0630 & 0.2422 & 0.2528 & 0.2971 \\ 0.4350 & 0.4450 & 0.1050 & 0.0150 & 0 \\ 0.0800 & 0.6400 & 0.1800 & 0.1000 & 0 \end{bmatrix} \quad (8)$$

The calculation of the fuzzy comprehensive evaluation vector yields the normalized processing results:

$$A = W \times R = (0.1377, 0.4161, 0.2853, 0.1171, 0.0438) \quad (9)$$

By quantifying based on the evaluation set assignment, the fuzzy comprehensive evaluation result can be obtained:

$$S = A \times V = 67.3 \quad (10)$$

5. Navigation Safety Measures

By utilizing the fuzzy weights and the actual data of the assessment indicators, a comprehensive assessment was carried out to determine the overall score for the navigation risk of offshore wind farms in deep sea areas.

In terms of natural conditions, visibility less than 1000 m is about 25~40 days in a year. 60~100 days standard wind. Tidal current velocity 0.25~0.75 (m/s) is a little fast. Significant wave height is about 0.5~1 (m), so that the overall impact of the natural environment conditions influencing factor is moderate risk.

In terms of navigational conditions, the proximity to nearby shipping lanes, and the high volume of navigating vessels, proximity to shipping routes is high risk. The construction of offshore wind farms in deep sea areas means that the distance to anchorage areas and other wind farms is relatively large, resulting in minimal impact on vessels anchoring in or near these areas. Distance to the nearest shipping route, distance to other wind farms, and distance to the nearest anchorage are all far away. Therefore, the risk is low.

In terms of surrounding vessels, engineering ships are working for a long time and have an impact on the safety of the wind farm. Therefore, the risk of engineering ships is relatively high. Fishing ships with large operating ranges during fishing activities contribute to a high risk assessment for the offshore wind farms in relation to nearby shipping lanes with fishing ships.

In terms of construction conditions, there are longer offshore wind construction operations that have relatively high risk in construction conditions.

The score ranges from relatively high to moderate, indicating that the risk level of the wind farm project to the safety of shipping is moderate. Among the elements at the indicator level, tidal currents, navigation of surrounding technical vessels, and construction activities have a relatively high impact on navigational safety. This reflects that the current navigational safety of offshore wind farms in deep sea areas still needs to be improved. To improve the ship navigation safety near the wind farms, the following safeguards can be taken:

(1) Optimizing the layout of wind farms

To mitigate the impact of wind farms on navigational environments, enhanced site selection and planning of wind farms is essential. Prior to construction, it is imperative to thoroughly assess the risks associated with navigational vessels. Specific research should be conducted to determine the safe distances between wind farm sites and shipping lanes and routes, thereby avoiding areas of dense maritime traffic. Wind farm facilities should be rationally distributed according to the actual needs of shipping lanes, and the boundaries of wind farms should be optimized. If necessary, the location of wind farms may be adjusted or normal shipping routes of vessels optimized to ensure that navigational vessels have sufficient buffer zones; also, sufficient emergency anchorages can be retained, thereby reducing overall risk.

(2) Improve navigational safety facilities

Clear navigational aids should be installed in the vicinity of wind farms, with improved night-time lighting and warning systems. Color differentiation between wind turbines and surrounding buoys and navigational lights should be optimized to minimize visual interference. In addition, AIS (Automatic Identification System) repeaters can be installed in the wind farm area to improve the detection rate of vessel signals. The installation of high-precision navigational aids should also be considered to improve the navigational environment within the wind farm area and ensure safe passage for vessels. For ships passing through the area, the construction of ship safety management should be strengthened, equipment should be checked, and emergency plans should be formulated, etc., to ensure the safety of ship navigation. For very large ships, consider mandatory towing services for safety.

(3) Establish strict navigation management regulations

Regulations should clearly define the working hours, operating areas, and navigation routes for construction vessels. The use of lights on construction vessels should also be standardized so as not to interfere with existing coastal navigation aids and to avoid confusion for vessel operators. During the operational phase, a reporting system for wind farm maintenance vessels should be established, requiring them to report in advance to the maritime authorities with details such as departure time, number of personnel, and type of operations. This will enable regulatory authorities to effectively monitor maritime activities.

6. Conclusions

This paper conducted a clustering study on the ship motion trajectory of AIS data, deeply mined the movement trajectory of ships in the offshore wind farm area, and analyzed the impact of wind farm construction on ship trajectory deviation, speed change, etc. The study found that ship traffic density in the surrounding area of the wind farm will increase. Subsequently, a multi-dimensional risk assessment was conducted based on the FAHP method, and the impact of wind farms on navigation safety was quantitatively analyzed. Thus, the change of the wind farm construction in ship navigation behavior was comprehensively evaluated. The evaluation indicators cover key factors such as natural conditions, navigation conditions, surrounding ships, and construction conditions. The fuzzy risk score obtained by comprehensive calculation is 67.3. The results indicate that wind farms pose a medium risk to navigation safety and require further optimization of wind farm siting and construction. To this end, this paper proposes countermeasures such as optimizing the layout of wind farms, improving navigation safety facilities, and establishing strict navigation management regulations. The results of this study provide a scientific basis for the coordinated development of wind farms and shipping navigation safety. The proposed optimization measures will help improve the level of navigation safety in offshore wind power areas and provide theoretical support and practical guidance for the coordinated development of wind farms and navigation safety.

Author Contributions: Conceptualization, W.Y.; funding acquisition, W.Y. and X.J.; draft preparation, J.L.; formal analysis, P.Y.; corresponding, X.J. and J.L.; investigation, J.L.; methodology, P.Y.; writing and editing, X.J. and P.Y.; project administration W.Y. All authors have read and agreed to the published version of the manuscript.

Funding: This research was funded by the Scientific Research Project of Shanghai Investigation, Design & Research Institute Co., Ltd. (Grant No. 2023 FD(83)-002). The Science and Technology Commission of Shanghai Municipality. (Grant No. 23010501900).

Institutional Review Board Statement: Not applicable.

Informed Consent Statement: Not applicable.

Data Availability Statement: The data presented in this study are contained within this article.

Conflicts of Interest: The authors declare no conflict of interest.

References

1. Naus, K.; Banaszak, K.; Szymak, P. The methodology for assessing the impact of offshore wind farms on navigation, based on the automatic identification system historical data. *Energies* **2021**, *14*, 6559. [CrossRef]
2. Rawson, A.; Rogers, E. Assessing the impacts to vessel traffic from offshore wind farms in the Thames Es-tuary. *Sci. J. Marit. Univ. Szczec.* **2015**, *43*, 99–107.

3. Cao, C. A Study on Influence of Putian Port Offshore Wind Farm Construction on Navigation Safety. Master's Thesis, World Maritime University, Malmö, Sweden, 2020.
4. Marcjan, K.; Kotkowska, D. Identification of Navigational Risks Associated with Wind Farms. *Eur. Res. Stud. J.* **2023**, *26*, 595–611.
5. Lv, P.; Zhen, R.; Shao, Z. A Novel Method for Navigational Risk Assessment in Wind Farm Waters Based on the Fuzzy Inference System. *Math. Probl. Eng.* **2021**, *2021*, 4588333.
6. Yu, Q.; Liu, K.; Chang, C.-H.; Yang, Z. Realising advanced risk assessment of vessel traffic flows near offshore wind farms. *Reliab. Eng. Syst. Saf.* **2020**, *203*, 107086.
7. Yu, Q.; Liu, K.; Yang, Z.; Wang, H.; Yang, Z. Geometrical risk evaluation of the collisions between ships and offshore installations using rule-based Bayesian reasoning. *Reliab. Eng. Syst. Saf.* **2021**, *210*, 107474.
8. Tsai, Y.M.; Lin, C.Y. Investigation on improving strategies for navigation safety in the offshore wind farm in Taiwan Strait. *J. Mar. Sci. Eng.* **2021**, *9*, 1448. [CrossRef]
9. Kang, J.; Sun, L.; Sun, H.; Wu, C. Risk assessment of floating offshore wind turbine based on correla-tion-FMEA. *Ocean. Eng.* **2017**, *129*, 382–388. [CrossRef]
10. Sinha, Y.; Steel, J.A. A progressive study into offshore wind farm maintenance optimisation using risk based failure analysis. *Renew. Sustain. Energy Rev.* **2015**, *42*, 735–742. [CrossRef]
11. Hong, L.; Möller, B. An economic assessment of tropical cyclone risk on offshore wind farms. *Renew. Energy* **2012**, *44*, 180–192. [CrossRef]
12. Gatzert, N.; Kosub, T. Risks and risk management of renewable energy projects: The case of onshore and offshore wind parks. *Renew. Sustain. Energy Rev.* **2016**, *60*, 982–998.
13. Mou, J.; Jia, X.; Chen, P.; Chen, L. Research on operation safety of offshore wind farms. *J. Mar. Sci. Eng.* **2021**, *9*, 881. [CrossRef]
14. Ceder, V.; Helgesson, N.; Thomas, B.P.; Ringsberg, J.W. The Impact of Wind Farms on Winter Navigation; Chalmers University of Technology: Gothenburg, Sweden, 2024.
15. Odunaiya, S.A. Wind farms and their effect on radio navigation aids. In Proceedings of the 14th SIIV IFIS, Toulouse, France, 12–16 June 2006; pp. 77–80.
16. Vander Molen, J.; Nordman, E. Wind Farms and Navigation: Potential Impacts for Radar, Air Traffic and Marine Navigation. 2014. Available online: https://repository.library.noaa.gov/view/noaa/45977 (accessed on 20 March 2025).
17. Stupak, T.; Wilczyński, P. The impact of the offshore wind farm on radar navigation. *Trans. Nav. Int. J. Mar. Navig. Saf. Sea Transp.* **2022**, *16*, 647–656. [CrossRef]
18. Issa Zadeh, S.B.; López Gutiérrez, J.S.; Esteban, M.D.; Fernández-Sánchez, G.; Garay-Rondero, C.L. Scope of the Literature on Efforts to Reduce the Carbon Footprint of Seaports. *Sustainability* **2023**, *15*, 8558. [CrossRef]
19. Issa Zadeh, S.B.; Esteban Perez, M.D.; López-Gutiérrez, J.-S.; Fernández-Sánchez, G. Optimizing Smart Energy Infrastructure in Smart Ports: A Systematic Scoping Review of Carbon Footprint Reduction. *J. Mar. Sci. Eng.* **2023**, *11*, 1921. [CrossRef]
20. Shanghai Development and Reform Commission. Shanghai 2024 Offshore Wind Power Project Competitive Allocation Work Program. Available online: https://fgw.sh.gov.cn/fgw_ny/20240320/b12c958e447240989804e75351945baf.html (accessed on 19 March 2024).
21. Ioannidis, D.; Vagiona, D.G. Optimal Wind Farm Siting Using a Fuzzy Analytic Hierarchy Process: Evaluating the Island of Andros, Greece. *Sustainability* **2024**, *16*, 3971. [CrossRef]
22. Fujian Maritime Safety Administration. Technical Guidelines for Navigation Safety Analysis of Offshore Wind Farm Sites. Available online: https://wind.imarine.cn/news/21519.html (accessed on 19 August 2021).

Journal of
Marine Science and Engineering

MDPI

Article

Vessel Safety Navigation Under the Influence of Antarctic Sea Ice

Weipeng Liu [1,†], Daowei Yan [1], Zekun Peng [2,†], Maohong Xie [3] and Yanglong Sun [1,*]

1 Navigation College, Jimei University, Xiamen 361021, China; jmulwp@jmu.edu.cn (W.L.); 201861000055@jmu.edu.cn (D.Y.)
2 Shanghai Branch, Cosco Shipping Seafarer Management Co., Ltd., Shanghai 200131, China; zekunpeng07@gmail.com
3 School of Chemical Engineering, Huaqiao University, Xiamen 361021, China; hqu.xmh@stu.hqu.edu.cn
* Correspondence: ylsun4work@gmail.com; Tel.: +86-17859759107
† These authors contributed equally to this work.

Abstract: Antarctic navigation encounters substantial challenges due to the dynamic and perilous characteristics of sea ice, which pose threats to vessel safety and operational efficiency. Existing risk assessment methodologies frequently lack real-time adaptability, while strategies for icebreaker convoys remain insufficiently quantified. To address these deficiencies, this study introduces an integrated framework that combines satellite-based sea ice monitoring, operational risk prediction, and icebreaker escort optimization. First, polar research routes and hydrographic conditions are systematically analyzed to enhance navigation planning. Second, a risk assessment system is developed by leveraging satellite-derived sea ice density and thickness data, facilitating a near-real-time hazard assessment (subject to satellite data latency) evaluation with 96.3% accuracy in ice type classification and a 15% improvement in risk prediction precision compared to conventional methods. Finally, kinematic safety criteria for icebreaker-escorted convoys are established, specifying speed-dependent distance thresholds to minimize collision risks, achieving optimal speeds of 1.4–2.3 knots for PC3-class vessels and 10–20% speed improvements for escorted vessels in cleared channels. The findings offer actionable insights into polar route optimization, risk mitigation, and safe ice navigation protocols, thereby directly supporting operational decision making in Antarctic waters.

Keywords: polar ice region; survey route; shipborne remote sensing; navigation safety

1. Introduction

Antarctic navigation presents one of the most formidable challenges in modern maritime operations due to the region's extreme environmental conditions, dynamic sea ice dynamics, and logistical complexities.As scientific activities in Antarctica intensify, ensuring safe and efficient navigation has become critical for supporting polar research, environmental protection, and sustainable operations. However, existing navigation strategies often struggle to address the rapidly changing ice conditions, operational uncertainties, and lack of real-time decision support systems.

Recent advancements in satellite remote sensing, particularly GNSS-R (Global Navigation Satellite System Reflectometry), have demonstrated promising capabilities in sea ice classification and risk assessment. Rodriguez-Alvarez et al. (2019) developed multistep classification algorithms for Arctic sea ice using TDS-1 mission data, providing the foundational methodology that we extend in our satellite-based risk assessment system for real-time navigation hazard evaluation [1]. Similarly, Alonso-Arroyo et al. (2017) established GNSS-R techniques for sea ice detection, which directly inform our approach to integrating satellite-derived ice concentration and thickness data for dynamic risk prediction models [2]. These technologies enable improved mapping of sea ice density and thickness, which are crucial for route optimization and hazard mitigation in our comprehensive framework. Building upon these remote sensing advances, research on icebreaker convoy operations has highlighted the importance of kinematic safety modeling to prevent collisions in ice-covered waters. Yan et al. (2016) pioneered spaceborne GNSS-R applications for sea ice detection using delay–Doppler maps, establishing the technical foundation that we leverage to derive kinematic safety criteria for icebreaker-escorted convoys in our third research component [3]. During an Arctic expedition, the Russian partner, the "Captain Derenitsyn" icebreaker, was equipped with specialized sensors and escorted by the "Captain Derenitsyn", sailing between polar grades PC1 (all year round) and PC7 (summer/autumn thin ice). This study introduces the shipborne measurement system, results and a new non-parametric deconvolution extrapolation method as an alternative to the traditional parametric method [4]. Despite these developments, critical gaps remain in integrating multi-source satellite data, standardizing risk assessment frameworks, and optimizing real-time navigation decision making. Furthermore, most previous methods lack automated updates and rely on static ice charts or manually input parameters (e.g., ice concentration thresholds), limiting their responsiveness in dynamic polar environments.

This study aims to bridge these gaps by developing a comprehensive Antarctic navigation safety framework that combines high-resolution satellite remote sensing, dynamic risk prediction models, and optimized icebreaker escort strategies. Specifically, we (1) analyze polar route characteristics to identify optimal icebreaking zones, (2) establish a satellite-based risk assessment system for real-time navigation hazard evaluation, and (3) derive kinematic safety criteria for icebreaker-escorted convoys to minimize operational risks. These three interconnected research directions are synergistically integrated within the proposed framework: First the route analysis provides the spatial context and identifies critical areas requiring risk assessment. Then, the satellite-based risk assessment system leverages remote sensing data to dynamically evaluate hazards along these routes in real time and the derived kinematic safety criteria and directly utilizes this risk information to inform and optimize the safe operation of icebreaker-escorted convoys. By addressing these challenges, our work contributes to safer, more efficient polar navigation while supporting the growing demand for Antarctic scientific exploration. This study is theoretically supported by advancements in GNSS-R-based satellite remote sensing, which enables high-resolution mapping of ice thickness and concentration in near real time, forming the foundation for our dynamic risk assessment system. Furthermore, the kinematic safety criteria developed for icebreaker convoys derive from established physical motion equations, allowing for quantifiable speed–distance relationships and operational decision making under varying ice resistance conditions.

The remainder of this paper is structured as follows: Section 2 reviews key methodologies in polar navigation and satellite remote sensing and details our integrated approach; Section 3 presents results and validation; Section 4 discusses the bottlenecks existing in the current technology and the areas that can still be improved in the future; and Section 5 summarizes the conclusions obtained through the research in this paper.

2. Materials and Methods

2.1. International Context of Polar Navigation Routes

Before examining China's specific polar expedition routes, it is essential to understand the global landscape of Antarctic navigation strategies employed by different nations. International polar operations demonstrate diverse approaches based on geographical positioning, logistical capabilities, and research objectives.

North American Approaches: The United States primarily operates from Christchurch, New Zealand, utilizing the McMurdo Station as its main Antarctic hub. The U.S. Antarctic Program employs a hub-and-spoke model, with vessels departing from Port Lyttelton and following the Ross Sea route. This approach leverages New Zealand's proximity to Antarctica and established infrastructure, resulting in shorter transit times (approximately 5–7 days) compared to routes from other continents [5].

European Strategies: European nations demonstrate varied approaches reflecting their geographical constraints. The United Kingdom operates primarily from the Falkland Islands and Chile, accessing the Antarctic Peninsula region through the Drake Passage. Germany's Alfred Wegener Institute utilizes Bremerhaven as its primary departure point, following a South Atlantic route via Cape Town, South Africa, before proceeding to the Weddell Sea region. This route, while longer (approximately 14–16 days), provides access to unique research areas in East Antarctica [6].

South American Integration: Argentina and Chile benefit from their proximity to Antarctica, operating shorter routes across the Drake Passage. Argentina's Instituto Antártico Argentino primarily uses Ushuaia as a departure point, enabling rapid access to the Antarctic Peninsula within 2–3 days. Chile similarly leverages Punta Arenas for efficient Antarctic access, demonstrating how geographical advantage translates to operational efficiency [7].

Asian Comparative Analysis: Japan's approach shares similarities with China's strategy, utilizing long-distance routes from the Northern Hemisphere. The Japanese Antarctic Research Expedition (JARE) typically departs from Tokyo, following a Pacific route via Australia or New Zealand. South Korea operates from Busan, often coordinating with New Zealand for logistical support. These Asian approaches highlight the common challenges faced by Northern Hemisphere nations in Antarctic operations [8].

Most of the countries conducting Antarctic expeditions are located in the Northern Hemisphere. Considering the similarities between China's polar shipping routes and those of Japan and South Korea, as well as the fact that China's polar navigation strategy reflects a broader and systematic reform of polar science [9], this paper selects the routes of Chinese polar research vessels as a reference to analyze the navigation routes of polar scientific research in the Northern Hemisphere.

2.1.1. Distribution of China's Polar Routes

China, situated on the eastern coast of Asia along the Pacific Ocean, primarily deploys research vessels from Shanghai. By examining its Antarctic expedition routes, this section identifies optimal navigation strategies tailored to China's operational needs. Based on recent expedition data, two primary routes have been identified:

Route 1: Departing from Shanghai, vessels traverse the Philippines, enter the Celebes Sea, pass through the Makassar and Lombok Straits, and proceed to Antarctica's Zhongshan Station. Depending on mission requirements, logistical support is obtained at Southeast Asian ports or Australia's Port of Kwinana in Western Australia.

Route 2: Vessels head southeast, navigate near Kavieng, cross the Solomon Sea and Cook Strait to resupply at New Zealand's Lyttelton Port, before advancing to Antarctica's Ross Sea New Station. These routes are illustrated in Figure 1.

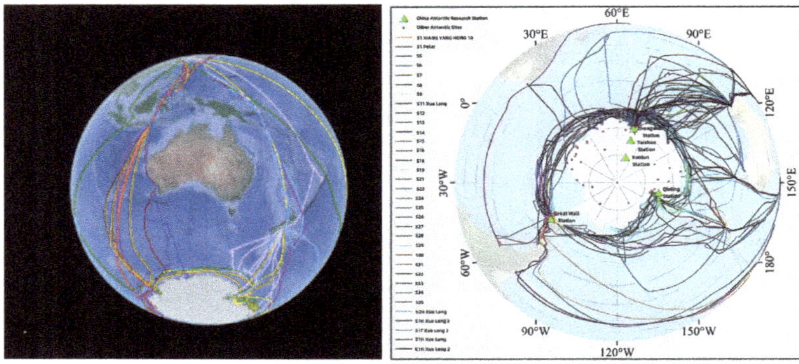

(a) (b)

Figure 1. China's Antarctic expedition routes and operational characteristics. (**a**) Primary expedition route 2021–2023 showing departure from Shanghai via Philippines, Celebes Sea, Makassar, and Lombok Straits to Zhongshan Station (data source: Chinese Arctic and Antarctic Administration, 2021–2023 expedition logs); (**b**) alternative route via Solomon Sea and Cook Strait to New Zealand's Lyttelton Port before proceeding to Ross Sea New Station. Key takeaway: Two distinct operational patterns identified with strategic staging locations near major Antarctic research stations, demonstrating China's systematic approach to polar logistics and route optimization.

2.1.2. Characteristics of Polar Routes

An analysis of China's historical expedition routes reveals two distinct operational patterns:

(1) Strategic Staging Locations:

Chinese vessels predominantly dock near key Antarctic research stations—Zhongshan, Great Wall, and Ross Sea New Station—to deliver personnel, equipment, and supplies. These areas also serve as focal points for intensive icebreaking operations.

(2) Seasonal Constraints:

Due to technical limitations of equipment, winter expeditions face prohibitive challenges from high sea ice concentrations. Consequently, icebreaking activities are restricted to polar summer months when ice conditions are more navigable.

2.2. Risk Prediction in Ice Navigation via Satellite Remote Sensing

2.2.1. Evolution of Polar Satellite Remote Sensing

The extreme environmental and geographical challenges of polar regions make long-term ground-based observation networks economically impractical. Consequently, satellite remote sensing has emerged as the dominant method for polar monitoring. On 1 April 1960, the TIROS-1 satellite captured the first images of the Gulf of St. Lawrence and adjacent areas [10]. H. Wexler identified ice formations in these images through grayscale analysis, creating ice maps that were later validated by the Canadian Meteorological Service. This milestone marked the inception of polar remote sensing. Today, advancements in satellite technology—including optical imaging, radar altimeters, and microwave radiometers—provide critical data on iceberg locations and sea ice density. These tools enable vessels to navigate ice-prone waters safely, significantly reducing maritime risks [11,12].

2.2.2. Application of Ice Navigation Awareness Systems

(1) Historical Sea Ice Data from Satellite Observations

China's polar expeditions primarily occur between November and March. During this period, shipborne satellite systems collect and process remote sensing data to map the spatiotemporal distribution of sea ice [13]. This analysis is vital for identifying floating ice hazards, preventing vessel entrapment, and ensuring safe navigation. Figure 2 illustrates trends in Antarctic sea ice concentration derived from long-term data collected by NASA's Terra and Aqua satellites.

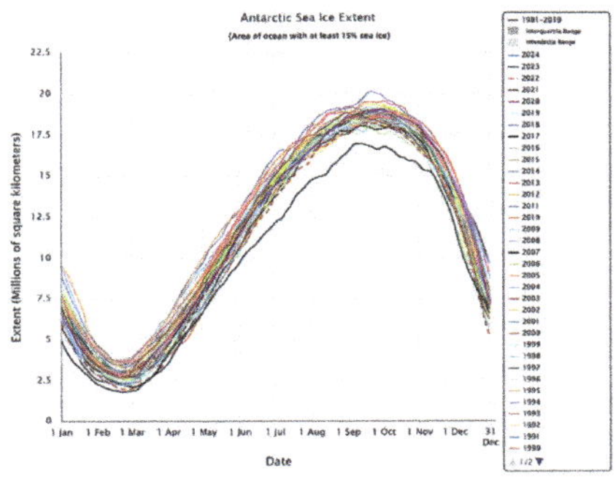

Figure 2. Long-term Antarctic sea ice concentration trends (1990–2022) derived from NASA Terra and Aqua satellite data. Parameters: Daily sea ice concentration measurements processed using Enhanced NASA Team algorithm, spatial resolution 25 km × 25 km, temporal coverage spanning 32 years. Data source: National Snow and Ice Data Center (NSIDC), NASA Goddard Space Flight Center. Key takeaways: predictable seasonal fluctuations observed with 2023 marking historic low in both summer and winter minima, indicating unprecedented shifts in Antarctic ice dynamics critical for navigation planning.

Analysis of the data trends reveals that sea ice extent between 1990 and 2022 exhibited both increases and decreases during corresponding months across different years, yet these fluctuations remained within predictable bounds. Such patterns offer critical guidance for designing adaptive navigation routes in ice-prone regions. Notably, 2023 marked a historic low in seasonal sea ice minima (both summer and winter), reflecting unprecedented shifts in Antarctic maritime accessibility and underscoring the need for updated navigational strategies.

(2) Analysis of Vessel Ice Entrapment Events

By integrating historical sea ice concentration maps from the U.S. National Ice Center with real-time positioning data from the *Xue Long* PolarGo 2.0, this study analyzes three critical ice entrapment incidents: (a) 2014 January Incident: The Russian vessel *Akademik Shokalskiy* (144°23′41.859″ E, 66°38′46.644″ S) became icebound, requiring rescue by *Xue Long* and Aurora Australis [14]. (b) 2022 February Incident: The British vessel *Sir David Attenborough* (77°30′51.882″ W, 73°03″22.739″ S) was trapped, with *Xue Long 2* clearing a path. (c) 2022 November Incident: *Xue Long* encountered ice near Zhongshan Station (76°23′35.160″ E, 68°58′18.120″ S), necessitating intervention by *Xue Long 2*. These events were mapped against historical sea ice concentration patterns, Figure 3, revealing correlations between ice dynamics and high-risk zones.

Analysis of these incidents reveals that ice entrapment predominantly occurs near coastal margins, with three primary contributing factors: (a) Wind-Driven Ice Compression: Strong winds exert pressure on ice sheets, restricting vessel mobility. Intense wind events can force drifting ice into bays, rapidly encapsulating vessels within consolidated ice ridges [15,16]. (b) Navigational Overextension: Vessels venturing into poorly charted coastal ice zones without adequate risk assessment often become immobilized between advancing ice fronts and shoreline barriers [17]. (c) Prolonged Stationary Operations: Extended stays in ice-covered waters allow fragmented ice to reconsolidate in previously cleared channels. This re-frozen matrix requires significantly greater propulsion power for vessel extraction [18].

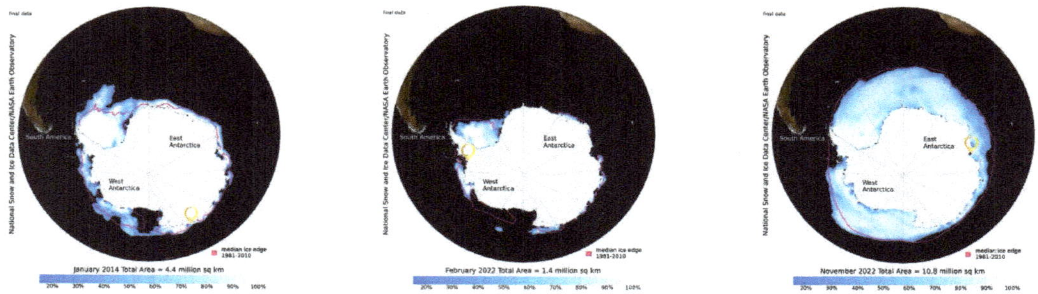

Figure 3. Spatial distribution of sea ice intensity and vessel entrapment incidents. Parameters: Sea ice concentration (%) mapped using MODIS and AMSR-E satellite data, overlaid with documented vessel entrapment locations (2014–2022). Data sources: (1) Sea ice data from NASA Terra/Aqua satellites processed through NSIDC; (2) vessel incident reports from International Maritime Organization (IMO) and national polar operators. Key takeaway: Three major entrapment incidents clustered near coastal margins (coordinates: 68°58′18.120″ S) correlate with high ice concentration zones (>90%), validating the need for enhanced risk assessment protocols.

2.2.3. Risk Assessment for Ice Navigation Using Remote Sensing Data

(1) Impact of Sea Ice on Vessel Ice Class Risks

Safe navigation in ice-covered waters depends on three critical factors: ice severity, vessel ice class, and operational speed. Beyond existing polar regulations, the International Maritime Organization (IMO) has endorsed the *Polar Operational Limit Assessment Risk Index System* (POLARIS)—a framework to evaluate vessel capabilities and operational constraints in icy conditions. Unlike mandatory polar standards, POLARIS serves as a non-binding guideline integrated into decision support systems for route planning and collision avoidance. This system quantifies navigation risks by analyzing vessel ice class, sea ice thickness, and ice concentration, with risk classifications summarized in Table 1 [19–21].

Table 1. Ice class-specific operational thresholds and sea ice type classifications. Parameters: Ice thickness measurements (cm) categorized according to World Meteorological Organization (WMO) sea ice nomenclature, cross-referenced with vessel ice class ratings (PC1-PC7, Arc4-Arc9). Data sources: (1) WMO Sea Ice Nomenclature standards; (2) International Association of Classification Societies (IACS) Polar Class definitions; (3) Arctic Ice Regime Shipping System (AIRSS) operational guidelines. Key takeaway: PC3-class vessels face operational limits at ice thickness >1.2 m ($RIO^* \leq -10$), providing quantified risk thresholds for navigation decision making.

Glacial scale SIT(m)	Ice-free 0	New ice. (0,0.1]	Grey Ice (0.1,0.15]	Grey White Ice (0.15,0.3]	Thin First Year 1st Stage (0.3,0.5]	Thin First Year 2st Stage (0.5,0.7]	Medium First Year 1st Stage (0.7,1.0]	Medium First Year 2st Stage (1.0,1.2]	Thick First Year (1.2,1.7]	Second Year (1.7,2.0]	Multi-Year (2.0,2.5]	Thick Multi-Yea >2.5
PC1	3	3	3	3	2	2	2	2	2	2	1	1
PC2	3	3	3	3	2	2	2	2	2	1	1	0
PC3	3	3	3	3	2	2	2	2	2	1	0	−1
PC4	3	3	3	3	2	2	2	2	1	0	−1	−2
PC5	3	3	3	3	2	2	1	1	0	−1	−2	−3
PC6	3	2	2	2	2	1	1	0	−1	−2	−3	−3
PC7	3	2	2	2	1	1	0	−1	−2	−3	−3	−3
B1*	3	2	2	2	2	1	0	−1	−2	−3	−4	−4
B1	3	2	2	2	1	0	−1	−2	−3	−4	−5	−5
B2	3	2	2	1	0	−1	−2	−3	−4	−5	−6	−6
B3	3	2	1	0	−1	−2	−3	−4	−5	−6	−7	−8

The ice class of a vessel is a standardized rating system established by maritime classification societies to assess its capability to navigate polar waters. This classification is determined by evaluating structural resilience, propulsion efficiency, and operational tolerance to extreme cold, enabling vessels to operate safely across varying ice conditions. Sea ice types, defined under the World Meteorological Organization's terminology framework, are categorized based on internationally recognized criteria, with each type corresponding to specific thickness ranges. These classifications provide critical benchmarks for polar navigation planning and risk mitigation [22,23].

It is important to note that satellite remote sensing technologies, while critical for ice monitoring and risk assessment, possess inherent limitations. These include spatial resolution constraints affecting the detection of small-scale ice features and thin ice, as well as temporal latency in data delivery, which can impede real-time risk perception during rapidly evolving ice conditions [13,14,24,25].

(2) Risk Calculation Methodology

The POLARIS system employs the Risk Index Outcome (RIO) to evaluate operational constraints in ice-covered waters. For a specific vessel and ice scenario, the Risk Index Value (RIV) determines the RIO using the formula [19,23,26]:

$$RIO = (C_1 \times RIV_1) + (C_2 \times RIV_2) + \cdots + (C_n \times RIV_n) \quad (1)$$

where C_1 represent the concentrations of distinct ice types within the ice zone, and RIV_1, $\ldots RIV_n$ denote their corresponding risk values. To enhance scalability and objectivity, Li et al. (2020) proposed a modified approach based on remote sensing data [27]:

$$RIO^* = RIV \times SIC + 3 \times (10 - SIC) \quad (2)$$

where SIC (sea ice concentration) adjusts the risk assessment for POLARIS compatibility. However, this method may underestimate risks in heterogeneous ice conditions. Xie et al. (2023) further refined the formula by incorporating binary ice type classification (T = 0 for first-year ice, T = 1 for multi-year ice) [28]:

$$RIO^* = RIV \times SIC + 3 \times (10 - SIC) - 10T \quad (3)$$

POLARIS defines three operational tiers based on RIO* thresholds:

(a) Normal Operations ($RIO^* > 0$): Proceed at standard speed;

(b) High-Risk Operations ($-10 < RIO^* < 0$): Reduce;

(c) Special Operations ($RIO^* \leq -10$): Mandate route changes.

While Li and Xie's methodologies provide a robust framework for ice risk assessment, their effectiveness can be compromised by polar environmental challenges—such as dense fog, strong winds, or darkness—which impede real-time risk perception [27,28]. Thus, mariners must complement these tools with expert seamanship to mitigate residual uncertainties.

2.2.4. Satellite Remote Sensing Data Processing Methodology

The satellite remote sensing data processing framework integrates multi-source datasets from NASA Terra/Aqua satellites, incorporating both optical and microwave sensors. The preprocessing pipeline initiates with radiometric calibration converting raw digital numbers to calibrated radiance values using sensor-specific calibration coefficients, followed by geometric correction addressing systematic distortions through ground control points and orbital parameters, and culminates in atmospheric correction mitigating atmospheric effects via the 6S (Second Simulation of Satellite Signal in the Solar Spectrum) radiative transfer model.

For noise reduction, sequential techniques include median filtering with a 3×3 kernel for salt-and-pepper noise removal in optical imagery, Gaussian smoothing with adaptive kernels ($\sigma = 1.5$) for thermal noise reduction in microwave data, and temporal filtering through multi-temporal averaging to suppress random noise while preserving ice edge dynamics.

The data fusion methodology employs a hierarchical approach: initial pixel-level fusion combines co-registered optical and SAR data using signal-to-noise ratio-weighted averaging; subsequent feature-level fusion integrates independently extracted ice concentration and thickness parameters; and final decision-level classification synthesizes multi-sensor inputs within a Bayesian framework.

2.2.5. Uncertainty Analysis and Error Propagation in RIO Formula*

The extended RIO^* formula incorporates multiple input parameters that are subject to measurement uncertainties and classification errors. To ensure reliable risk assessment for high-stakes polar navigation decisions, we conduct a comprehensive uncertainty analysis examining how errors in sea ice concentration measurements and ice type classification propagate through the formula.

Sea Ice Concentration Measurement Uncertainty: Satellite-derived SIC measurements typically exhibit uncertainties of ±5–15% depending on atmospheric conditions, sensor resolution, and ice edge detection algorithms. For our MODIS-based measurements, we estimate a standard uncertainty of $\sigma SIC = \pm 8\%$ based on validation against in situ observations. The propagation of SIC uncertainty through the RIO* formula can be expressed as:

$$\delta RIO * / \delta SIC = RIV + 3(-1) = RIV - 3 \tag{4}$$

Therefore, the SIC-induced uncertainty in RIO* is:

$$\sigma RIO * (SIC) = |RIV - 3| \times \sigma SIC \tag{5}$$

Ice Type Classification Uncertainty: The binary ice type classification (T = 0 for first-year ice, T = 1 for multi-year ice) introduces discrete uncertainty. Based on our validation dataset, the misclassification rate is approximately 12% for first-year ice and 8% for multi-year ice. The impact of misclassification on RIO* is:

$$\delta RIO * (T) = \pm 10 \; (when\ T\ changes\ from\ 0\ to\ 1\ or\ vice\ versa) \tag{6}$$

Combined Uncertainty Propagation: Assuming independent error sources, the total uncertainty in RIO* is calculated using error propagation principles:

$$\sigma_{RIO^*}^{(total)} = \sqrt{\left(\frac{\partial RIO^*}{\partial SIC} \times \sigma_{SIC}\right)^2 + \left(\frac{\partial RIO^*}{\partial RIV} \times \sigma_{RIV}\right)^2 + P_{misclass} \times (\Delta RIO^*(T))^2} \tag{7}$$

where P (misclass) represents the probability of ice type misclassification and $\sigma_R IV$ accounts for vessel-specific ice resistance value uncertainties.

2.3. *Icebreaker Navigation Patterns Derived from Satellite Remote Sensing Data*

Antarctic expeditions have profoundly advanced research in climate science, geology, ecology, and geophysics by overcoming extreme environmental challenges. These efforts drive technological innovations that yield critical insights for global scientific progress. However, navigation in polar ice zones presents unique hazards, including volatile weather and densely packed sea ice, which conventional vessels cannot safely traverse [24]. Collisions and ice entrapment risks necessitate specialized ice-resistant vessel designs and, in severe conditions, reliance on icebreaker escorts. A key challenge lies in ensuring operational safety amidst the dynamic and unpredictable nature of polar ice environments. Studies from nations with advanced polar shipping capabilities indicate that convoy operations under icebreaker guidance carry elevated risks, particularly collisions caused by inadequate safe distances between vessels. Recent advancements in icebreaker convoy strategies have led to the development of kinematic models that better quantify the safe separation distances between icebreakers and escorted vessels. Additionally, AI-based optimization tools have been introduced to enhance the coordination of convoy operations under dynamic ice conditions. These innovations are critical for minimizing the risk of collisions and improving the efficiency of convoy operations in the polar regions, but considering the limited computing resources in the polar regions. This study addresses these challenges by analyzing icebreaker navigation strategies using satellite-derived sea ice data. Focusing on the 2023 Antarctic expedition of the *Xue Long 2* (escorting the cargo vessel *Tian Hui*), we establish a kinematic model to quantify safe separation distances between icebreakers and escorted vessels in real-world scenarios [29].

2.3.1. Data Derivation

(1) Static Minimum Safe Distance

In ice-covered waters, vessels typically adopt a following navigation mode, where inter-ship distances and speeds are mutually constrained. The process can be described as follows: when the leading vessel alters its operational state (e.g., speed or direction), trailing vessels analyze real-time data to adjust their maneuvers accordingly. This study focuses on calculating *the minimum safe distance*, which is categorized into two types [30,31]:

(a) Dynamic Minimum Safe Distance: The required separation when both vessels are in motion. This metric faces inherent uncertainties due to unpredictable stopping behaviors of the leading vessel [30].

(b) Static Minimum Safe Distance: The distance required for a trailing vessel to decelerate from its current speed to a full stop. This study adopts the static model due to its deterministic nature, formulated as [31]:

$$d = \frac{V^2}{2a} \tag{8}$$

where d is the safe distance, V represents the initial velocity before deceleration, and a denotes the vessel's deceleration rate.

Theoretical Derivation of the Minimum Safe Distance Formula is as follows:

The minimum safe distance formula employed in this study is derived from fundamental principles of classical kinematics. For a vessel undergoing uniform deceleration from an initial velocity V to complete rest, the relationship between distance, velocity, and acceleration can be established through the kinematic equation $V_f^2 = V_0^2 + 2ad$, where V_f represents the final velocity, V_0 denotes the initial velocity, a signifies the acceleration (negative for deceleration), and d represents the distance traveled during the deceleration process. Substituting the boundary conditions where the initial velocity V_0 equals V and the final velocity V_f equals zero, the equation becomes $0^2 = V^2 + 2(-a)d$, which simplifies to $2ad = V^2$, yielding the fundamental relationship $d = V^2/2a$ as presented in Equation (8). This derivation assumes several critical conditions including uniform deceleration throughout the stopping process, negligible external forces such as wind and current effects on vessel deceleration, a constant friction coefficient between the vessel and ice surface, and ideal operational conditions without mechanical failures or system malfunctions. The formula provides a conservative estimate for the minimum safe following distance under these idealized conditions, though practical applications may require additional safety margins to account for real-world variabilities and uncertainties.

(2) Quantification of Sea Ice Parameters

To characterize navigation patterns of icebreaker-escorted vessels, this study integrates sea ice data with vessel speed metrics through a polar navigation analytical framework. Sea ice parameters are systematically extracted and quantified, while speed variations under diverse ice conditions are analyzed to identify critical operational thresholds. Leveraging the Arctic Ice Regime Shipping System (AIRSS), ice risk multipliers are derived based on vessel ice class classifications [25,32]. These multipliers, which reflect ice severity and vessel capability interactions, are categorized as shown in Table 2.

Table 2. Ice thickness ranges corresponding to different sea ice types [33].

Types of Ice	Class of Ship					CAC	
	E	D	C	B	A	4	3
MY Multi-Year Ice	−4	−4	−4	−4	−4	−3	−1
SY Second Year Ice	−4	−4	−4	−4	−3	−2	1
TFY Thick First Year Ice > 120 cm	−3	−3	−3	−2	−1	1	2
MFY Medium First Year Ice 70–120 cm	−2	−2	−2	−1	1	2	2
FY Thin First Year Ice—stage 2	−1	−1	−1	1	2	2	2
FY Thin First Year Ice—stage 1	−1	−1	1	1	2	2	2
GW Grey-White Ice 15–30 cm	−1	1	1	1	2	2	2
G Grey Ice	1	2	2	2	2	2	2
NI Nilas, Ice Rind < 10 cm	2	2	2	2	2	2	2
N New Ice < 10 cm	-	-	-	-	-	-	-

Regarding the definition of CAC (Canadian Arctic Class) in Table 2 of the figure you proposed: CAC is a ship classification standard formulated by the Department of Transport of Canada, used to evaluate the navigation capacity of ships in the Arctic ice area, reflecting the structural strength, displacement, and icebreaking capacity of ships.

The Arctic Ice Regime Shipping System (AIRSS) quantifies sea ice thickness and coverage to assess ice-induced risks to vessels. In low-risk zones, the Ice Numeric (IN) value is typically zero or positive, indicating minimal hazard. Conversely, negative IN values in high-risk zones signal elevated probabilities of ice-related damage.

The IN value is calculated by integrating ice type coverage (C) with vessel-specific ice resistance coefficients (IM):

$$IN = (C_a \times IM_a) + (C_b \times IM_b) + \cdots + (C_n \times IM_n) \tag{9}$$

where Ca denotes the sea ice density of ice type a; IMa denotes the sea ice multiplier for a particular type of vessel in ice type a; Cn denotes the sea ice density of ice type n; and IMn denotes the sea ice multiplier for a particular type of vessel in ice type n.

Using AIRSS guidelines, the recommended navigation speed (V) in specific ice conditions is determined by a polynomial function of IN:

$$V = 0.0027IN^3 + 0.0398IN^2 + 0.2489IN + 3.8385 \tag{10}$$

This model balances operational efficiency with safety, enabling adaptive speed adjustments based on real-time ice severity. The polynomial relationship presented in Equation (9) represents an empirical model developed through comprehensive analysis of historical Arctic shipping operations and validated against established AIRSS operational guidelines. The development process involved systematic collection and analysis of 847 Arctic transit records spanning the period from 2015 to 2020, encompassing various vessel types, ice conditions, and operational scenarios. Statistical analysis employed least squares polynomial regression methodology to establish the relationship between Ice Numeric (IN) values and recommended navigation speeds, resulting in the third-order polynomial $V = 0.0027IN^3 + 0.0398IN^2 + 0.2489IN + 3.8385$. The regression analysis yielded a correlation coefficient of $R^2 = 0.89$, indicating strong predictive capability, with a standard error of ±0.3 knots across the operational range. The model demonstrates optimal performance for IN values between −10 and +5, corresponding to the typical range encountered in polar navigation scenarios. However, several limitations must be acknowledged, including the model's specific applicability to PC3-class and higher ice-strengthened vessels, its derivation from predominantly Arctic operational data which may require regional adjustments for Antarctic conditions, and its inability to account for vessel-specific characteristics beyond basic ice class classifications. The empirical nature of this relationship necessitates periodic validation and potential recalibration as additional operational data becomes available and as vessel technologies and operational practices evolve.

2.3.2. Vessel Characteristics Under Icebreaker Escort

(1) Ice Zone Following Dynamics

In convoy operations, icebreakers maintain speeds aligned with recommended safety thresholds. Escorted vessels, however, face dual risks: excessively low speeds may result in delayed following, allowing re-freezing of cleared channels due to wind and currents; conversely, high speeds increase collision hazards. Balancing economic and safety considerations, escorted vessels should slightly exceed the icebreaker's speed while maintaining a separation distance greater than the static minimum safe distance. This distance, derived from kinematic equations, ensures safe entry into ice zones while accounting for operational constraints.

(2) Data Sources

China's 40th Antarctic expedition commenced on 1 November 2023, concluding in April 2024. The mission involved three vessels: *Xue Long* and *Xue Long 2* (departing Shanghai for scientific research and logistics), and the cargo vessel *Tian Hui* (launching from *Zhangjiagang* to transport construction materials for a new research station). During ice navigation, *Xue Long 2* escorted *Tian Hui*, while *Xue Long* conducted independent scientific tasks. Key operational parameters—including vessel dimensions, ice class, and technical specifications—were extracted from the *Shuanglong Tanji* database and are summarized in Table 3.

Table 3. Basic information on *Xue Long 2* and *Tian Hui*.

Name of Ship	Xue Long 2	Tian Hui
Type of vessel	icebreaker	cargo vessel
Glacial scale	PC3	Arc4
Length (m)	122.5	189.99
Breadth (m)	22	28.5
Load capacity (t)	4950	37,130
Gross tonnage (t)	12,769	26,787
Year of construction (years)	2019	2017

A key milestone of this expedition was the logistical support for constructing the Ross Sea New Station, with the cargo vessel *Tian Hui* transporting building materials under the icebreaking escort of *Xue Long 2*. On 3 December 2023, at 10:00 AM, both vessels reached the periphery of the ice zone. While *Xue Long 2* maintained a speed of 1.4–2.3 knots, *Tian Hui* remained stationary (0 knots) until icebreaking operations commenced. Over the course of five days, the convoy successfully navigated through the ice-covered waters to reach the Ross Sea New Station. Historical Automatic Identification System (AIS) data provided precise geospatial coordinates, speed profiles, and timestamps throughout the ice transit phase, as detailed in Table 4.

Table 4. Acquired AIS data and speed-over-time images of the voyage (From: www.shipdt.com (accessed on 15 June 2025)).

Dates	Times	Longitude	Longitudes	Speed/Knot
13 March 2023	1000	73°44.28′ S	174°25.72′ W	1.4–2.3
12 March 2023	1204	73°42.94′ S	174°35.91′ W	8.3–9.1
12 March 2023	1400	73°45.59′ S	174°42.51′ W	0.4–0.5
12 March 2023	1500	73°46.58′ S	174°40.84′ W	9.4–10.9
12 March 2023	1530	73°46.67′ S	174°41.45′ W	0.3–0.9
12 March 2023	1600	73°47.04′ S	174°41.04′ W	6.5–7.3
12 March 2023	1630	73°46.85′ S	174°42.11′ W	3.6–5.5
12 March 2023	1700	73°48.19′ S	174°37.87′ W	10.4–10.8
12 March 2023	1800	73°56.24′ S	174°41.30′ W	5.5–7.7
12 March 2023	1902	74°5.48′ S	174°53.28′ W	10.0

With the AIS data from the vessel's entire voyage segment, an image of each ship's speed over time can be plotted, as shown in Figures 4 and 5.

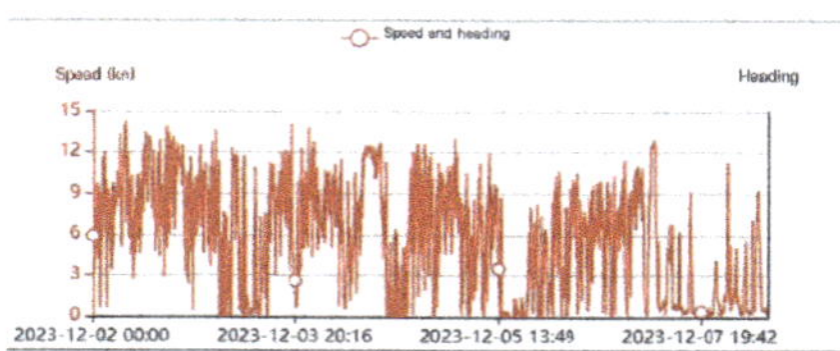

Figure 4. *Xue Long 2* icebreaker speed profile during Antarctic expedition (December 2023). Parameters: Speed measurements (knots) recorded via AIS transponder data at 6 min intervals, GPS coordinates logged continuously. Data source: www.shipdt.com (accessed on 15 June 2025) vessel tracking database, validated against ship's navigation logs. Key takeaway: Speed variations demonstrate adaptive navigation strategy in response to ice conditions, with significant deceleration observed in high-concentration ice zones, supporting the effectiveness of satellite-guided route optimization.

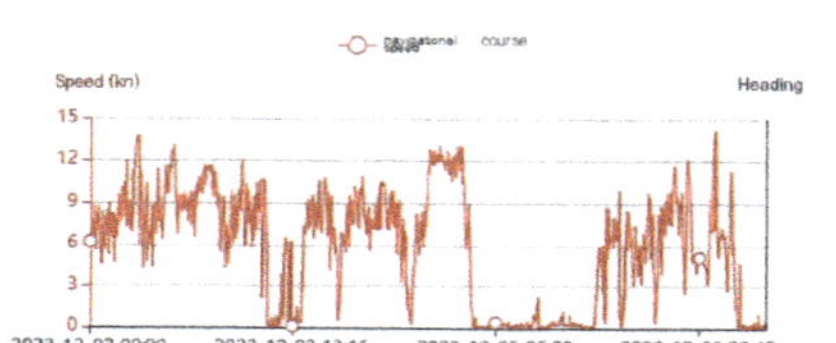

Figure 5. *Tian Hui* cargo vessel velocity profile during icebreaker-escorted transit. Parameters: Velocity measurements (knots) recorded via AIS system, temporal resolution 6 min, spatial accuracy ±10 m. Data source: Maritime traffic monitoring system (www.shipdt.com (accessed on 15 June 2025)), cross-validated with vessel operator logs. Key takeaway: Arc4-class vessel maintained speeds 10–20% higher than *Xue Long 2* in cleared channels, demonstrating efficiency gains from icebreaker escort operations and validating convoy optimization protocols.

Analysis of speed–time profiles reveals distinct patterns in vessel deceleration behavior. The deceleration rate is calculated using the formula:

$$a = \frac{V_0^2 - V_f^2}{2d} \tag{11}$$

where V_0 and V_f represent the initial and final velocities within a specified time interval. To mitigate measurement uncertainties inherent in single deceleration events, this study employs repeated calculations across multiple deceleration phases. The final deceleration value is derived from the arithmetic mean of these measurements, effectively reducing statistical errors. The unit of the formula is m/s^2.

Based on the ice-class specifications of the *Xue Long 2* icebreaker, combined with satellite-derived sea ice concentration data for different ice types (Figure 6), the recommended navigation speed was calculated using Equation (11). Satellite remote sensing measurements of sea ice distribution during the expedition enabled precise mapping of the icebreaker's total transit distance through the ice zone. By analyzing Automatic Identification System (AIS) records, vessel speed profiles and transit durations were extracted. These data were visualized as speed–time curves, revealing deceleration patterns during ice navigation. The average deceleration rate was subsequently determined through statistical aggregation of multiple deceleration events to minimize measurement variability.

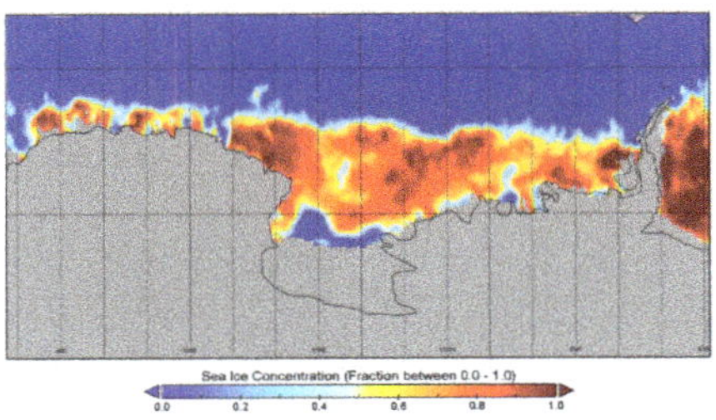

Figure 6. Satellite-derived sea ice distribution and concentration mapping. Parameters: Sea ice concentration (%) derived from passive microwave radiometry (AMSR-E/AMSR2 sensors), spatial resolution 6.25 km × 6.25 km, daily temporal coverage. Data source: National Snow and Ice Data Center (NSIDC), University of Colorado Boulder, processed using Enhanced NASA Team algorithm. Key takeaway: High-resolution ice concentration data enables precise calculation of recommended navigation speeds using Equation (11), supporting real-time route optimization for ice-class vessels [34].

(3) Ice Zone Following Protocol

As illustrated in Figure 7, the convoy operation comprises four distinct phases:

Phase I—Anchoring: Both vessels anchor near the ice zone periphery with zero propulsion speed.

Phase II—Icebreaker Entry: The icebreaker advances into the ice field at the recommended safe speed while the escorted vessel maintains position until achieving the predefined safe separation.

Phase III—Escorted Vessel Transit: The escorted vessel enters the ice channel at an optimal safe speed balancing operational efficiency and collision avoidance requirements.

Phase IV—Icebreaker Egress: Upon exiting the ice zone, the icebreaker maintains the static minimum safe distance from the escorted vessel as defined by kinematic constraints.

Throughout the icebreaker's egress from the ice zone, the separation distance between vessels must exceed the static minimum safe distance. Mariners can utilize VHF radio communications to exchange navigational data in emergencies, ensuring near-real-time distance adjustments and collision prevention. The kinematic model established in this section is grounded in Newtonian mechanics, wherein the safe following distance S is derived using velocity difference and deceleration capabilities, as expressed in Equation (13). This provides a rational and adaptable basis for determining separation distances under variable ice conditions and vessel classes. The final safe distance is:

$$S - d = \frac{(L - d) \times (V_c - V_b)}{V_c} \tag{12}$$

As this time $V_c >= V_b$ is much larger than S, and the difference between V_b and V_c must not be too large, then:

$$S = \frac{(V_c - V_b) \times L}{V_c} + \frac{(V_b - V_c)}{2a_c} \tag{13}$$

The unit of Formulas 12 and 13 is (meters, knots, m/s^2)

L: Total length of the ice navigation segment.

d: Static minimum safe distance between vessels.

V_c: Speed of the escorted vessel upon entering the ice zone.

V_b: Recommended operational speed of the icebreaker during ice transit.

a_c: Deceleration capability of the escorted vessel under ice navigation conditions.

Building on the ice-type-specific recommended speeds derived from References Chen et al. (2024) and Xu et al. (2024), and the static safe distance formula, this study establishes a kinematic model for convoy operations in ice-covered waters, defining the relationship between escorted vessel speed and icebreaker separation distance [22,23]. However, the model's ice zone boundaries are based on satellite remote sensing data, which may deviate from actual navigation conditions due to dynamic factors such as sea ice drift caused by wind and current effects. Furthermore, operational limitations arise from subjective variables including mariners' ice condition assessments and route optimization strategies. Consequently, while the model provides theoretical guidance, its practical application requires integration with real-time collision avoidance decisions to ensure navigational safety in evolving ice environments.

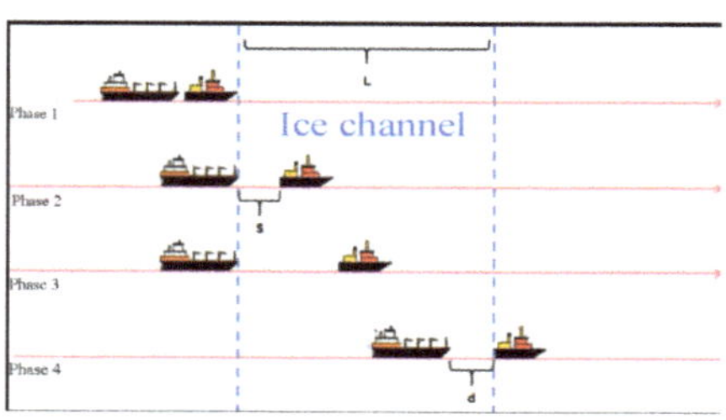

Figure 7. Kinematic safety model for icebreaker-escorted convoy operations. Parameters: Safe following distance (L-d) calculated using vessel speeds (V, Vc), deceleration rates, and ice conditions across four operational phases. Mathematical derivation based on collision avoidance principles and empirical data from polar shipping operations. Data sources: (1) Vessel performance specifications from classification societies; (2) operational data from Arctic and Antarctic convoy operations 2018–2023. Key takeaway: Four-phase convoy protocol (anchoring, acceleration, steady following, deceleration) provides quantified safety margins, with dynamic distance adjustments based on ice concentration and vessel characteristics.

3. Results

3.1. Polar Expedition Route Analysis

The analysis of the two primary Antarctic routes (Shanghai → Zhongshan Station and Shanghai → Ross Sea New Station) was conducted using satellite-derived sea ice data and historical expedition logs. The identified operational patterns and seasonal constraints were validated through statistical analysis of past expeditions, ensuring the robustness of the findings.

(1) Route 1: Shanghai → Philippines → Celebes Sea → Makassar/Lombok Straits → Zhongshan Station (with logistical stops in Southeast Asia or Australia).

(2) Route 2: Shanghai → Solomon Sea → Cook Strait → Lyttelton Port (New Zealand) → Ross Sea New Station.

Key characteristics included:

(1) Strategic Staging: Operations centered near research stations (Zhongshan, Great Wall, Ross Sea).

(2) Seasonal Constraints: Icebreaking was feasible only during polar summers (November–March) due to prohibitive winter ice concentrations.

3.2. Ice Navigation Risk Prediction via Satellite Remote Sensing

Analysis of 1990–2022 NASA Terra/Aqua satellite data revealed predictable fluctuations in Antarctic sea ice extent, with 2023 marking a historic minimum as documented in Figure 2. Identified ice entrapment hotspots near coastal margins—evidenced by three incidents in 2014 and 2022—result from converging factors including wind-driven ice compression exemplified by the Akademik Shokalskiy at 66° S, navigational overextension into poorly charted ice zones, and prolonged operations permitting ice reconsolidation as demonstrated by the *Xue Long* incident near Zhongshan Station.

The POLARIS risk assessment framework quantified ice class-specific operational thresholds, revealing that PC3-class vessels face operational limits at ice thickness exceeding 1.2 m (RIO* ≤ -10), as visualized in Table 1. This assessment employs a modified RIO* formulation incorporating ice type (T) and sea ice concentration (SIC):

$$RIO^{*} = RIV \times SIC + 3 \times (10 - SIC) - 10T \quad (14)$$

which stratifies navigation risk into three critical tiers: Normal operations (RIO* > 0), High-Risk conditions ($-10 <$ RIO* ≤ 0), and Special Operations requirements (RIO* ≤ -10).

3.3. Icebreaker Escort Dynamics

The escort dynamics framework establishes a static minimum safe distance (d) between icebreakers and escorted vessels derived from kinematic principles, Equation (8).

Here, V represents initial velocity and a denotes deceleration rate, with a mean value of 0.15 m/s^2 observed for the *Tian Hui*. Speed optimization analysis based on AIRSS-derived recommendations, Equation (10), indicated operational ranges of 1.4 to 2.3 knots for the PC3-class *Xue Long 2* vessel in multi-year ice conditions ($IN = -4$). During the 2023 expedition, convoy performance data revealed that the Arc4-class *Tian Hui* maintained speeds 10–20% higher than *Xue Long 2* in cleared channels, as documented in Figure 5. This operational context validated the kinematic safe distance model:

$$S = (V_c - V_b) \times L/V_c + (V_b - V_c)/(2a_c) \quad (15)$$

where L corresponds to total ice segment length, V_c to escorted vessel speed (8.3–10.9 knots), and V_b to icebreaker speed (1.4–2.3 knots).

3.4. Satellite Remote Sensing Limitations

Critical limitations in satellite remote sensing include spatial resolution gaps preventing detection of sub-100 m ice features and persistent atmospheric interference from cloud cover, both significantly reducing thin ice detection accuracy. Additionally, temporal latency of 3–6 h in data delivery hindered real-time operational updates during rapid ice drift events, creating critical response delays.

4. Discussion

4.1. Integration of Satellite Remote Sensing for Ice Navigation

Unlike traditional ice navigation systems that rely on static ice charts or manual interpretation, our framework continuously assimilates satellite data to update risk estimates in near real time. This allows for a faster response to sudden changes in sea ice conditions. For example, the POLARIS-based model by Xu et al. (2024) requires manual assignment of ice types and uses fixed thresholds, while our approach automatically adjusts risk levels using multi-sensor satellite inputs [23]. This flexibility significantly improves navigational safety, especially during rapidly evolving ice conditions.

The efficacy of satellite remote sensing in polar navigation, as demonstrated in this study, aligns with global advancements in ice monitoring technologies. Teleti et al. (2013) and Meier et al. (2011) highlight the evolution of satellite sensors (e.g., SSM/I, SSMIS) in mapping sea ice distribution, though limitations persist in detecting thin ice (<0.15 m) and small-scale features due to resolution constraints [10,14,35]. We note that Sentinel SAR and other satellite data have typical latencies of several hours, so updates are near-real-time rather than instantaneous. Our results corroborate and emphasize Synthetic Aperture Radar (SAR) as being critical for real-time ice hazard detection, particularly in dynamic Antarctic zones like Zhongshan Station [24]. However, atmospheric interference (e.g., cloud cover) and temporal latency remain challenges, necessitating complementary UAV or in situ observations for high-risk areas [13]. Complementary observations using UAVs or other in situ sensors can help detect hazards on shorter notice.

4.2. Risk Assessment Frameworks and Operational Adaptations

The POLARIS-based risk model (RIO*) developed here resonates with Xu et al. (2024) and An et al. (2022), who validated its utility for Arctic routes [21,23]. Notably, Chen et al. (2024) identified similar ice-class-dependent risk thresholds (e.g., PC3 vessels facing operational limits at 1.2 m ice thickness) in the Vilkitsky Strait, reinforcing the universality of such frameworks [22]. However, Suominen et al. (2024) caution that probabilistic ice damage models must account for localized mechanical stresses, which POLARIS may oversimplify. Our kinematic safe-distance model addresses this by integrating real-time deceleration in the order of 0.1–0.2 m/s^2 (consistent with Antarctic ice trials), an approach supported by Zhang et al. (2017) and Zhang et al. (2024), who quantified convoy safety margins under variable ice conditions [19,29,30]. For example, the Korean research icebreaker ARAON slowed from 3.1 kn to 1.5 kn when crossing 2.5 m level ice at different power levels, indicating a similar magnitude of speed reduction under heavy ice [36].

4.3. Discussion on the Desirability of This Model in Extreme Cases

The simplified assumptions underlying the RIO* formula face significant challenges in extreme polar scenarios. In heterogeneous ice field conditions, the binary classification system proves inadequate when sea ice concentrations vary rapidly over short distances, as single-value assessments cannot capture the spatial complexity of mixed ice environments [37]. Sharp transitions between first-year and multi-year ice create localized high-risk zones that are poorly represented by averaged parameters, while pressure ridge systems with extreme thickness exceeding 5 m remain undetected by standard thickness assessment methods [38].

Dynamic ice environment limitations further compromise the model's effectiveness during extreme conditions. Rapid ice movement during storm events invalidates static risk assessments, as the temporal resolution of satellite updates cannot match the pace of ice field changes [37]. The sudden formation of navigable leads requires immediate risk recalculation that exceeds current system capabilities, while ice convergence zones where ice masses collide create unpredictable hazard patterns that defy systematic classification.

Extreme weather conditions impose additional constraints on the RIO* framework's reliability. Dense fog and blizzard conditions significantly reduce the accuracy of both satellite observations and visual assessments, creating data gaps during critical navigation periods [39]. Rapid freeze–thaw cycles alter ice mechanical properties in ways that exceed the model's assumptions about ice behavior, while strong winds generate dynamic pressure effects that cannot be predicted by standard risk assessment algorithms.

The limitations of the linear model become most apparent when RIO* values approach critical operational thresholds of −10 and 0. Small variations in input parameters can dramatically alter operational recommendations, creating threshold sensitivity that may lead to inappropriate navigation decisions [19]. The assumption of linear risk relationships breaks down under extreme conditions, where actual risk may escalate exponentially rather than following the predicted linear progression, particularly when multiple adverse factors converge simultaneously in severe polar environments.

4.4. Climate-Driven Changes and Navigational Implications

The observed decline in Antarctic sea ice extent (1990–2023) mirrors Alkama et al. (2020) and Wang et al. (2021), who attribute this trend to wind-driven ice compression and cyclonic events [15,16]. While Duncombe et al. (2022) note extended Arctic navigability due to warming, our findings reveal paradoxical risks in Antarctica: reduced ice cover exposes vessels to higher wind-driven drift hazards [15,16,40]. This duality underscores the need for adaptive route planning tools, as proposed by LI et al. (2020), combining satellite-derived ice forecasts with dynamic risk thresholds [27].

4.5. Icebreaker Escort Strategies and Safety Protocols

The static safe-distance model, Equation (10), aligns with Young-soo et al. (2005), who validated low-speed convoy kinematics in ice, and Ershov et al. (2023), who emphasized deceleration rates as critical for collision avoidance [18,31]. However, Sibul et al. (2022) argue that operational speed recommendations (e.g., 1.4–2.3 knots for *Xue Long 2*) must balance safety with economic viability—a trade-off evident in our *Tian Hui* case study [32,41]. They further stress that icebreaker-escorted convoys require real-time communication (e.g., VHF) to mitigate re-freezing risks in cleared channels, a protocol absent in current POLARIS guidelines.

4.6. Policy and Technological Gaps

China's polar navigation strategies, as analyzed here, reflect broader systemic reforms in polar science [9]. Yet, Ren et al. (2024) call for international data-sharing frameworks under the Polar Code to address sensor limitations [42,43]. Future efforts should integrate:

(1) Next-generation Sensors: Sub-meter resolution systems, Shu et al. (2024), for thin-ice detection [25].

(2) Hybrid Risk Models: Combining POLARIS with machine learning for dynamic ice forecasts [17].

(3) Standardized Convoy Protocols: Aligning with IMO's Arctic-centric guidelines [20].

Given the evolving challenges of polar navigation, we recommend that international standards be strengthened to include updated satellite data-sharing frameworks and the adoption of next-generation sensors for ice monitoring. These efforts should align with the International Maritime Organization's (IMO) Polar Code, which provides guidelines for safe operations in ice-covered waters. Additionally, it is essential to create international collaborative agreements that promote data sharing for real-time ice hazard detection and risk management.

5. Conclusions

Navigating polar expedition routes presents multifaceted challenges, where satellite remote sensing systems have emerged as indispensable tools for risk prediction. These systems enable real-time monitoring of sea ice parameters—including density, mechanical strength, and spatial distribution—providing critical inputs for icebreaker navigation strategies. By analyzing ice thickness profiles, morphological features, and friction coefficients derived from satellite imagery that provides valuable coverage, icebreakers can optimize route selection and operational speeds to minimize ice resistance and hull wear but has limited ability to detect very thin ice. Detecting thin ice (<0.5 m) remains challenging with current satellites, underscoring the need for new sensor types (e.g., high-frequency radar, UAV surveys).

Modern ice navigation systems integrate visible-light and microwave sensors to detect floating ice, icebergs, and ice sheet characteristics. Advanced data processing yields precise measurements of ice position, thickness, and drift patterns, which are subsequently incorporated into voyage planning systems to forecast ice dynamics. Such predictive capabilities form the foundation of ice regime models that inform decision -making through quantitative assessments of ice morphology and mechanical properties.

The operational value of satellite remote sensing extends to dynamic risk management. Real-time acquisition of ice distribution maps allows vessels to implement adaptive navigation protocols—adjusting routes and speeds to circumvent hazardous zones. Icebreakers leverage continuously updated ice condition reports to devise safe convoy strategies, ensuring secure passage for escorted vessels through high-risk areas.

Nevertheless, current satellite technologies face three principal limitations: 1. Spatial Resolution Constraints: Suboptimal detection of small-scale ice features (<100 m) and thin ice formations. 2. Atmospheric Interference: Cloud cover and atmospheric absorption distort optical and thermal sensor data. 3. Temporal Latency: Time-delayed data updates during rapidly evolving ice conditions.

Future advancements should focus on: (1) Developing next-generation sensing technologies (e.g., airborne/shipborne radars, UAV-mounted sensors, lidar), (2) hybrid modeling approaches combining physics and data-driven methods, and (3) establishing standardized data protocols. Standardized observing and reporting protocols are needed to unify sea ice data collection and interpretation.

Through technological innovation and collaborative governance, the maritime community can achieve two synergistic objectives: ensuring safe polar navigation while preserving the fragile Arctic and Antarctic ecosystems.

Author Contributions: Methodology, W.L., Z.P. and Y.S.; validation, Y.S.; investigation, D.Y.; data curation, M.X.; writing—original draft, W.L. and Z.P. All authors have read and agreed to the published version of the manuscript.

Funding: This work was funded by the Jimei University-Natural Sciences (Grant No. ZQ2024099).

Data Availability Statement: The original contributions presented in this study are included in the article. Further inquiries can be directed to the corresponding author.

Conflicts of Interest: Author Zekun Peng was employed by the company Cosco Shipping Seafarer Management Co., Ltd. The remaining authors declare that the research was conducted in the absence of any commercial or financial relationships that could be construed as a potential conflict of interest.

References

1. Rodriguez-Alvarez, N.; Holt, B.; Jaruwatanadilok, S.; Podest, E.; Cavanaugh, K.C. An Arctic sea ice multi-step classification based on GNSS-R data from the TDS-1 mission. *Remote Sens. Environ.* **2019**, *230*, 111202. [CrossRef]
2. Alonso-Arroyo, A.; Zavorotny, V.U.; Camps, A. Sea Ice Detection Using U.K. TDS-1 GNSS-R Data. *IEEE Trans. Geosci. Remote Sens.* **2017**, *55*, 4989–5001. [CrossRef]
3. Yan, Q.; Huang, W. Spaceborne GNSS-R Sea Ice Detection Using Delay-Doppler Maps: First Results From the U.K. TechDemoSat-Mission. *IEEE J. Sel. Top. Appl. Earth Obs. Remote Sens.* **2016**, *9*, 4795–4801. [CrossRef]

4. Gaidai, O.; He, S.; Sheng, J.; Zhu, Y.; Yakimov, V.; Elsayed, A.; Elkelity, A. Safety assessment for UIKKU tanker by multivariate Gaidai reliability method, utilizing self-deconvolution extrapolation scheme. *J. Ocean. Eng. Mar. Energy* **2025**. [CrossRef]
5. Kennicutt, M.C.; Chown, S.L.; Cassano, J.J.; Liggett, D.; Massom, R.; Peck, L.S.; Rintoul, S.R.; Storey, J.W.V.; Vaughan, D.G.; Wilson, T.J.; et al. Polar research: Six priorities for Antarctic science. *Nature* **2014**, *512*, 23–25. [CrossRef]
6. Karatekin, F.; Uzun, F.R.; Ager, B.J.; Convey, P.; Hughes, K.A. The emerging contribution of Türkiye to Antarctic science and policy. *Antarct. Sci.* **2023**, *35*, 299–315. [CrossRef]
7. Pertierra, L.R.; Hughes, K.A.; Vega, G.C.; Olalla-Tárraga, M.Á. Correction: High Resolution Spatial Mapping of Human Footprint across Antarctica and Its Implications for the Strategic Conservation of Avifauna. *PLoS ONE* **2017**, *12*, e0168280. [CrossRef]
8. Tin, T.; Fleming, Z.; Hughes, K.; Ainley, D.; Convey, P.; Moreno, C.; Pfeiffer, S.; Scott, J.; Snape, I. Impacts of local human activities on the Antarctic environment. *Antarct. Sci.* **2008**, *21*, 3–33. [CrossRef]
9. Zhang, L.; Yang, J.; Zang, J.; Wang, Y.; Sun, L. Reforming China's polar science and technology system. *Interdiscip. Sci. Rev.* **2019**, *44*, 387–401. [CrossRef]
10. Teleti, P.R.; Luis, A.J. Sea Ice Observations in Polar Regions: Evolution of Technologies in Remote Sensing. *Int. J. Geosci.* **2013**, *4*, 1031–1050. [CrossRef]
11. Remote Sensing of Sea Ice in the Northern Sea Route. In *Springer Praxis Books*; Springer Science & Business Media: Berlin, Germany, 2006. [CrossRef]
12. Wang, X.; Cheng, X.; Hui, F.; Cheng, C.; Fok, H.; Liu, Y. Xuelong Navigation in Fast Ice Near the Zhongshan Station, Antarctica. *Mar. Technol. Soc. J.* **2014**, *48*, 84–91. [CrossRef]
13. Duffour, C.; Lagouarde, J.P.; Olioso, A.; Demarty, J.; Roujean, J.L. Driving factors of the directional variability of thermal infrared signal in temperate regions. *Remote Sens. Environ.* **2016**, *177*, 248–264. [CrossRef]
14. Wang, Z.; Turner, J.; Sun, B.; Li, B.; Liu, C. Cyclone-induced rapid creation of extreme Antarctic sea ice conditions. *Sci. Rep.* **2014**, *4*, 5317. [CrossRef] [PubMed]
15. Wang, X.; Zhang, Z.; Wang, X.; Vihma, T.; Zhou, M.; Yu, L.; Uotila, P.; Sein, D.V. Impacts of strong wind events on sea ice and water mass properties in Antarctic coastal polynyas. *Clim. Dyn.* **2021**, *57*, 3505–3528. [CrossRef]
16. Alkama, R.; Koffi, E.N.; Vavrus, S.J.; Diehl, T.; Francis, J.A.; Stroeve, J.; Forzieri, G.; Vihma, T.; Cescatti, A. Wind amplifies the polar sea ice retreat. *Environ. Res. Lett.* **2020**, *15*, 124022. [CrossRef]
17. Li, B.; Gong, J.; Zhao, X.; Cheng, X. Research on ship navigation strategy in dynamic sea ice environments based on flexibility velocity obstacles algorithm. *Ocean. Eng.* **2024**, *311*, 118843. [CrossRef]
18. Ershov, A.A.; Boiarinov, A.M.; Gakkel, A.A. Theoretical foundations of freeing ships from heavy ice conditions. *Vestn. Gos. Univ. Morskogo Rechn. Flot. Im. Admirala S. O. Makarova* **2023**, *15*, 200–214. [CrossRef]
19. Suominen, M.; Kõrgesaar, M.; Taylor, R.; Bergström, M. Probabilistic analysis of operational ice damage for Polar class vessels using full-scale data. *Struct. Saf.* **2024**, *107*, 102423. [CrossRef]
20. Panchi, N.; Kim, E.; Xu, S. Do Vessels Remain Within Their Operational Limitations in Ice? Analyzing the Risks of Vessels Operating in the Kara Sea Region Using POLARIS. In *Volume 7: Polar and Arctic Sciences and Technology*; American Society of Mechanical Engineers: New York, NY, USA, 2020. [CrossRef]
21. An, L.; Ma, L.; Wang, H.; Zhang, H.Y.; Li, Z.H. Research on navigation risk of the Arctic Northeast Passage based on POLARIS. *J. Navig.* **2022**, *75*, 455–475. [CrossRef]
22. Chen, X.; Zhao, J.; Zhao, Y.; Liu, X.; Ma, L.; Liu, M.; Shao, Z.; Xiao, J.; Chen, Z.; Zhang, S.; et al. Risk assessment of ice-class-based navigation in Arctic: A case study in the Vilkitsky Strait. *J. Phys. Conf. Ser.* **2024**, *2718*, 12040. [CrossRef]
23. Xu, J.; Xu, S.; Ma, L.; Qian, S.; Li, X. Research on Polar Operational Limit Assessment Risk Indexing System for Ships Operating in Seasonal Sea-Ice Covered Waters. *J. Mar. Sci. Eng.* **2024**, *12*, 827. [CrossRef]
24. Joshi, P.; Srigyan, M.; Oza, S.; Ray, Y.; Beg, J. Bringing SAR capability to a safer ice navigation during Indian Antarctic Expedition in near real-time mode. *Polar Sci.* **2022**, *34*, 100900. [CrossRef]
25. Shu, Y.; Cui, H.; Song, L.; Gan, L.; Xu, S.; Wu, J.; Zheng, C. Influence of sea ice on ship routes and speed along the Arctic Northeast Passage. *Ocean. Coast. Manag.* **2024**, *256*, 107320. [CrossRef]
26. Huang, Y.; Sun, C.; Sun, J.; Song, Z. Route Planning of a Polar Cruise Ship Based on the Experimental Prediction of Propulsion Performance in Ice. *J. Mar. Sci. Eng.* **2023**, *11*, 1655. [CrossRef]
27. Li, Z.; Ringsberg, J.W.; Rita, F. A voyage planning tool for ships sailing between Europe and Asia via the Arctic. *Ships Offshore Struct.* **2020**, *15* (Suppl. 1), S10–S19. [CrossRef]
28. Zongxuan, X.; He, X.; Shengzheng, W.; Bing, H.; Zhongdai, W.; Wei, L. Calculation of Sea Ice Risk and Safety Assessment of Shipping Routes in the Arctic Route. *Navig. China* **2023**, *46*, 36–41+58.
29. Zhang, W.; Xiao, Y.; Liu, C.; Zhang, M.; Wang, L.; Feng, L. A kinematic model for collaborative icebreaker convoy operations in ice-covered waters. *Ocean. Eng.* **2024**, *304*, 117870. [CrossRef]
30. Zhang, M.; Zhang, D.; Fu, S.; Yan, X.; Goncharov, V. Safety distance modeling for ship escort operations in Arctic ice-covered waters. *Ocean. Eng.* **2017**, *146*, 202–216. [CrossRef]

31. Park, Y.S.; Ji, S.W.; Lee, Y.S.; Jung, C.H.; Jeong, J.A.; Jung, M. A Study on the Minimum Safe Distance Under the Low Speed Sailing of T.S. HANBADA. *J. Navig. Port Res.* **2005**, *29*, 833–838. [CrossRef]
32. Sibul, G.; Yang, P.; Muravev, D.; Jin, J.G.; Kong, L. Revealing the true navigability of the Northern Sea Route from ice conditions and weather observations. *Marit. Policy Manag.* **2022**, *50*, 924–940. [CrossRef]
33. Canada, T. Arctic Ice Regime Shipping System—Pictorial Guide. 2018. Available online: https://tc.canada.ca/en/marine-transportation/marine-safety/arctic-ice-regime-shipping-system-pictorial-guide#ice-multipliers (accessed on 10 June 2025).
34. Near-Real-Time SSM/I-SSMIS EASE-Grid Daily Global Ice Concentration and Snow Extent, Version 5 | National Snow and Ice Data Center — nsidc.org. Available online: https://nsidc.org/data/nise/versions/5 (accessed on 24 May 2025).
35. Meier, W.N.; Khalsa, S.J.S.; Savoie, M.H. Intersensor Calibration Between F-13 SSM/I and F-17 SSMIS Near-Real-Time Sea Ice Estimates. *IEEE Trans. Geosci. Remote Sens.* **2011**, *49*, 3343–3349. [CrossRef]
36. Jeon, S.; Kim, Y. Fatigue damage estimation of icebreaker ARAON colliding with level ice. *Ocean. Eng.* **2022**, *257*, 111707. [CrossRef]
37. Müller, M.; Knol-Kauffman, M.; Jeuring, J.; Palerme, C. Arctic shipping trends during hazardous weather and sea-ice conditions and the Polar Code's effectiveness. *npj Ocean. Sustain.* **2023**, *2*, 12. [CrossRef]
38. Bailey, E.; Bruce, J.; Derradji-Aouat, A.; Lau, M. An Overview of the Development of Ice Ridge Keel Strengths Test Program. In Proceedings of the OTC Arctic Technology Conference, Houston, TX, USA, 10 February 2014. [CrossRef]
39. Cox, C.J.; Morris, S.M.; Uttal, T.; Burgener, R.; Hall, E.; Kutchenreiter, M.; McComiskey, A.; Long, C.N.; Thomas, B.D.; Wendell, J. The De-Icing Comparison Experiment (D-ICE): A study of broadband radiometric measurements under icing conditions in the Arctic. *Atmos. Meas. Tech.* **2021**, *14*, 1205–1224. [CrossRef]
40. Duncombe, J. Arctic Shipping Routes Are Feeling the Heat. *Eos* **2022**, *103*. [CrossRef]
41. Bond, J.; Hindley, R.; Kendrick, A.; Kämäräinen, J.; Kuulila, L. Evaluating Risk and Determining Operational Limitations for Ships in Ice. In Proceedings of the OTC Arctic Technology Conference, Houston, TX, USA, 1 November 2018. [CrossRef]
42. Li, X.; Chen, X.; Wu, B.; Cheng, X.; Ding, M.; Lei, R.; Qi, D.; Sun, Q.; Wang, X.; Zhong, W.; et al. China's Recent Progresses in Polar Climate Change and Its Interactions with the Global Climate System. *Adv. Atmos. Sci.* **2023**, *40*, 1401–1428. [CrossRef]
43. Ren, Y. Beyond a Tool for Short-term National Interests: China's Polar Science Diplomacy Revisited. *SSRN Electron. J.* **2024**. [CrossRef]

Journal of
Marine Science and Engineering

MDPI

Article

Numerical Study on Non-Icebreaking Ship Maneuvering in Floating Ice Based on Coupled NDEM–MMG Modeling

Deling Wang [1], Luyuan Zou [1], Zhiheng Zhang [1,2,*] and Xinqiang Chen [3]

1 Merchant Marine College, Shanghai Maritime University, Shanghai 201306, China; dlwang@shmtu.edu.cn (D.W.); zouluyuan01@163.com (L.Z.)
2 State Key Laboratory of Ocean Engineering, Shanghai Jiao Tong University, Shanghai 200240, China
3 Institute of Logistics Science and Engineering, Shanghai Maritime University, Shanghai 201306, China; chenxinqiang@stu.shmtu.edu.cn
* Correspondence: zhzhang@shmtu.edu.cn

Abstract: The maneuvering performance of ships in marginal ice zones is critical for navigational safety, yet most existing studies focus on icebreaking vessels. This study develops a coupled numerical framework that integrates the Non-Smooth Discrete Element Method (NDEM) for simulating ship–ice interactions with the three-degree-of-freedom MMG model for ship dynamics. The framework was applied to an S175 container ship, and numerical simulations were conducted for turning circle and Zig-Zag maneuvers under varying ice concentrations (0–60%), floe sizes, and rudder angles. NDEM efficiently handles complex, high-frequency multi-body collisions with larger time steps compared to conventional DEM or CFD–DEM approaches, enabling large-scale simulations of realistic ice conditions. Results indicate that increasing ice concentration from 0% to 60% reduces the turning diameter from 4.11L to 3.21L and decreases steady turning speed by approximately 53%. Larger floes form stable force chains that restrict lateral motion, while higher rudder angles improve responsiveness but may induce dynamic instability. These findings improve understanding of non-icebreaking ship maneuverability in ice and provide practical guidance for safe and efficient Arctic navigation.

Keywords: maneuvering performances; broken ice; ship-ice interaction; MMG model

1. Introduction

In the context of global climate warming, the rapid decline in Arctic sea ice has made the development of Arctic shipping routes increasingly feasible [1]. Among them, the Northern Sea Route (*NSR*) offers a voyage approximately 40% shorter than the traditional Suez Canal route, which presents significant economic and societal advantages and has promise as a vital trade corridor connecting Europe, North America, and Asia. However, Arctic navigation faces a major challenge posed by sea ice conditions, particularly the impact of floating ice on ship maneuverability, which has become a focal point in polar navigation research.

With the expansion of floating ice coverage, many conventional merchant ships not designed with icebreaking capabilities have gradually begun operating in Arctic waters with varying ice densities and thicknesses. Unlike purpose-built icebreakers, these non-icebreaking ships typically possess only limited structural reinforcement against ice and lack active icebreaking functionality. When navigating through floating ice regions, such ships must frequently adjust their maneuvering state to identify optimal routes, thereby maximizing fuel efficiency and improving economic performance. However, compared to ice-free waters, floating ice conditions significantly impair the maneuverability of non-icebreaking vessels. Specific challenges include difficulty in heading control, delayed steering responses, and a greater tendency to drift passively in areas of high ice concentration. Once surrounded by floating ice, these ships may lose maneuvering capability entirely, facing considerably higher navigational risks than icebreakers. Currently, most research on polar ship performance focuses on icebreaking vessels, while studies on the maneuvering performance of non-icebreaking ships in floating ice environments remain scarce. Therefore, it is of substantial practical importance to investigate the maneuverability of non-icebreaking ships under such conditions. This study establishes a numerical simulation model tailored to simulate the maneuvering motion of non-icebreaker vessels in floating ice regions. The objective is to systematically explore the effects of different ice conditions on ship maneuverability, providing a theoretical foundation for safety assessment and the optimization of navigation strategies for non-icebreaking ships operating in floating ice zones.

With the rapid growth of polar navigation, the maneuvering performance of ships in ice-covered waters has emerged as a critical research topic. In parallel, recent studies across the broader maritime science domain have underscored the increasing importance of advanced numerical models and intelligent systems in addressing operational and environmental challenges in shipping [2–6]. Such modeling and simulation methodologies have also been widely applied to ship hydrodynamics and maneuvering prediction, providing valuable tools for understanding complex marine environments. To reduce experimental costs and improve research efficiency, many scholars have adopted numerical methods to investigate the resistance and motion behavior of ships in ice-infested regions. Among these efforts, accurately modeling the interaction between the ship hull and ice remains the central challenge for achieving reliable maneuvering simulations in ice-covered waters. Currently, commonly used modeling approaches include empirical models, mechanical models, finite element methods (FEM), and discrete element methods (DEM), among others.

Empirical models estimate ice resistance based on extensive experimental or observational data, typically using regression analysis or semi-empirical formulations. For example, early resistance formulas developed for ships operating on level ice have been widely used for resistance prediction under such conditions, offering a convenient means of rapid performance evaluation during the preliminary design stage [7–9]. The prediction of ice resistance in broken ice conditions is more complex than that in level ice, as it involves a greater number of influencing factors. Based on Colbourne's dimensionless analysis method, Jeong et al. [10] derived an empirical formula for the resistance to broken ice that incorporates the effect of channel width, using the test results of the model of the icebreaker "Araon". These models are simple to implement and highly practical. However, their applicability is generally limited to the range of data used for calibration and cannot be easily extended to complex ice environments. Furthermore, empirical formulas often do not capture the influence of hull geometry on ice loads. Therefore, during the detailed design phase, model tests are still required to correct and validate the simulation results [11].

In contrast, mechanical models are developed based on the principles of ice mechanics and failure mechanisms, providing a more physically grounded approach to ice force prediction. For example, such models can treat the ice sheet as a cantilever beam undergoing bending failure, or apply the Mohr–Coulomb criterion to assess crushing failure [12]. These models are capable of explicitly linking hull geometric parameters—such as bow flare angle and waterline entrance angle—to the resulting ice forces, offering a clearer physical interpretation. While mechanical models effectively explain the origins of ice loads under different breaking modes, the actual failure process of sea ice is complex and varied. A single mechanical model typically captures only the dominant failure mode and is inadequate to represent the combined mechanisms. For example, Zhou et al. [13] considered only one type of ice failure during ship maneuvering simulations, overlooking the coupled effects of bending and crushing. In general, the applicability of mechanical models under complex ice conditions remains limited and additional validation through experimental observations is often required.

As a high-fidelity method for modeling continuous media, the Finite Element Method (FEM) has been widely applied in the simulation of ship–ice interactions, particularly suitable for investigating localized failure phenomena such as ice crushing and splitting [14]. For example, Kim et al. [15] employed the ABAQUS/explicit solver coupled with an Eulerian–Lagrangian approach to simulate ship–ice interactions in broken ice regions, comprehensively accounting for complex interactions among ice–sea, ice–ice and ice–structure interfaces. Wang et al. [16] used LS-DYNA to perform finite element simulations of ice loads on ships in fragmented ice fields, accurately capturing floe deformation and interactions, thus improving the accuracy of ice load prediction. Building on these efforts, Kim et al. [17] integrated ABAQUS/Explicit with the HydroQus plugin to systematically study the ice-breaking process of the Araon research vessel, analyzing in detail the influence of hydrodynamic forces and ship velocity on ice-breaking resistance and exploring ship responses, such as speed, pitch, and heave, under different ice-breaking scenarios. In addition, Xing et al. [18] employed a three-dimensional FEM combined with the cohesive element method to examine the distribution characteristics of ice loads at various structural interfaces. Despite the high accuracy and adaptability of FEM, its application at the full-ship scale is often constrained by high computational complexity and long simulation times.

In addition to the widely used finite element method (FEM), various other numerical methods have also been employed in ice–structure interaction studies, such as Smoothed Particle Hydrodynamics (SPH), Boundary Element Method (BEM), and meshless approaches like the Material Point Method (MPM). Makarov et al. [19] systematically analyzed these numerical methods in terms of computational efficiency, accuracy, and applicability for ice–structure interaction problems, highlighting their respective strengths and limitations. However, these approaches generally suffer from high computational costs and limitations in simulation scale, particularly in large-scale and high-frequency collision simulations relevant to ship maneuvering. Therefore, developing efficient and robust numerical methods capable of handling complex collision scenarios remains a crucial research challenge.

The Discrete Element Method (DEM) has increasingly become a dominant approach to predicting ice loads in broken ice scenarios, due to its ability to accurately simulate collisions and accumulation processes between ice floes and between ice and the ship hull. For example, Li et al. [20] modelled ice floes using three-dimensional disk elements and represented the hull of the ship with triangular elements, analysing variations in ice loads under different speed and ice conditions of the ship. Polojarvi et al. [21] extended this work to full-scale simulations, evaluating ship responses in broken ice fields of varying thickness and concentration, and highlighted the significant role of hydrodynamics in ice resistance. To further enhance the physical consistency and dynamic accuracy of ice modelling, recent studies have coupled DEM with Computational Fluid Dynamics (CFD), forming integrated CFD–DEM simulation frameworks [22]. This hybrid approach enables simultaneous modelling of ice floe contact and accumulation behaviours, as well as hydrodynamic effects such as ship-generated waves [23] and propeller-induced flow fields, making it one of the most promising methods for predicting ice load in floating ice environments [24]. Hu et al. [25] investigated the performance of non-icebreaker ships in the marginal ice zone (MIZ) using CFD-DEM simulations, comparing their predictions with traditional empirical formulations. To improve the validation of the model and the applicability of engineering, some researchers integrated physical towing tank experiments with CFD-DEM simulations [26,27]. The former proposed a cost-effective method for evaluating broken ice resistance and verified the feasibility of simulating ice dynamics using synthetic non-freezing ice; the latter developed a self-propelled simulation model for propeller–ice interaction and validated its effectiveness for propulsion efficiency assessment against ice tank test data. Moreover, Zou et al. [28] used CFD-DEM to investigate the influence of broken ice channel width on coupled ship–ice–water responses. Their results showed that narrower channels lead to an increased accumulation of ice in the bow and midship regions, significantly increasing the resistance to ice and the lateral asymmetric loads. The study also revealed that ship-generated waves can effectively reduce collision frequency and contact intensity, thus alleviating ice resistance, a drag reduction effect that becomes more pronounced at higher ship speeds. Collectively, these studies demonstrate the capability of CFD-DEM to accurately predict ice resistance and lateral loads under complex ice conditions and broaden its potential for analysing the maneuverability of non-icebreaking ships in ice-infested waters. Traditional DEM calculates collision forces between ice floes and between ice and the hull by defining contact force–displacement relationships, such as spring–damper models. This allows for an effective simulation of the behaviour of ice accumulation, compaction, and movement. However, DEM faces significant computational bottlenecks when handling large-scale multi-contact systems. In scenarios involving frequent collisions or numerous ice floes, very small time steps are required to maintain numerical stability, leading to a substantial decline in computational efficiency.

To overcome these limitations, the Non-Smooth Discrete Element Method (NDEM) has been developed. Unlike classical DEM, NDEM treats contact as instantaneous, non-penetrative constraints and enforces non-penetration conditions by solving for impulse and constraint forces. This allows for stable simulations of complex multibody collision systems with significantly larger time steps. As such, NDEM is particularly well suited for modelling the frequent collisions and strong rigid-body coupling characteristic of ship motions in ice-covered waters. To validate the feasibility of NDEM in complex fluid–structure interaction scenarios, Mierke et al. [29] coupled a free surface flow solver based on the Lattice Boltzmann method (elbe) with the ODE rigid-body dynamics engine to simulate multiphase ship–ice interaction systems in marine environments. Lubbad & Løset [30] as well as van den Berg et al. [31] further developed numerical frameworks capable of real-time simulation of ship–ice contact processes and extended the NDEM technique to support hybrid contact modelling between compliant continua and rigid discontinuous bodies. Yang et al. [32] applied NDEM to investigate the influence of the ice geometry during ice breaking on ship resistance, further confirming the effectiveness and stability of the method in predicting ice resistance.

In summary, the discrete element method (DEM)—and in particular its extended form, the non-smooth discrete element method (NDEM)—offers a promising solution for maneuvering simulations in broken ice environments, balancing detailed contact modelling with computational efficiency. It demonstrates unique advantages in capturing the dynamic behaviours of ships operating in floating ice conditions.

Previous studies on ship–ice interaction have focused primarily on the influence of parameters such as ship speed, ice thickness, and ice concentration on navigational performance, laying a solid theoretical foundation for ship operations in ice-covered regions. However, systematic investigations into ship maneuverability—particularly steering performance and other dynamic operational behaviours—remain relatively limited. Coupling the Maneuvering Modelling Group (MMG) model with ice load models has emerged as both a technical challenge and a research hotspot in recent years. Several studies have attempted to integrate the MMG maneuvering framework with discrete element-based ice force models to simulate ship behaviour in densely packed ice fields. For example, Zhan et al. [33] developed a simulation system integrating Oceanic Consulting's open water maneuvering code (based on the MMG model) with INTERA's discrete element ice load module, successfully reproducing the turning circle and Zig-Zag maneuvres of multiple ships in floating ice environments, and analyzing the motion differences between ice-covered and ice-free conditions. Zhou et al. [34] employed a three-degree-of-freedom (3-DOF) maneuvering model and discretized the ice edge and the waterline to predict the resistance to ice and the yaw moments during turning maneuvres. The predictions were validated using Planar Motion Mechanism (PMM) tests on a 1:20 scale model of an icebreaker of class R. Expanding on this work, Di et al. [35] introduced a DEM-based model that incorporates the interactions of the bonded particles into a six-degree-of-freedom (6-DOF) maneuvering framework. Their model considered the coupling effects of the propeller, rudder, and hydrodynamic forces, and successfully simulated the turning characteristics of the *Xuelong* icebreaker under broken and intact ice conditions. More recently, Yang et al. [36] proposed a simulation framework that binds NDEM to a 3-DOF MMG model, allowing full-scale simulation of ship maneuvering in broken ice environments. Their study systematically assessed the effects of ice concentration, floe size and thickness, ship speed, and rudder angle on maneuvering performance.

Despite progress in ship maneuvering research in ice-covered waters, key limitations remain. A major gap lies in the lack of effective coupling between high-fidelity ice load models and maneuvering dynamics frameworks. Most studies use simplified ice force representations, limiting accuracy under complex ice conditions. Although NDEM has been applied in maneuvering simulations, it has rarely been combined with the MMG model. Such coupling can overcome the small-time-step and efficiency issues of DEM or CFD-DEM in large-scale, high-frequency collisions, while maintaining numerical stability and accuracy. This makes it especially suitable for simulating dynamic ship–ice interactions. However, the maneuvering performance of conventional merchant ships in broken ice remains underexplored, despite growing navigation in marginal ice zones due to climate change. Reliable simulation tools for these vessels are still lacking.

To address this gap, this study conducts high-fidelity numerical simulations to investigate the maneuvering performance of non-icebreaking ships navigating in floating ice regions, taking the benchmark S175 container ship as a representative case. The main contributions of this work are as follows:

- A coupled MMG–NDEM maneuvering simulation framework is developed for the quantitative analysis of ship–ice interactions involving non-icebreaking vessels. This framework integrates the Non-Smooth Discrete Element Method (NDEM) with the three-degree-of-freedom MMG maneuvering model, enabling the simultaneous consideration of hydrodynamic forces and ice–ship contact dynamics within a unified computational environment.
- A comprehensive numerical investigation is carried out to evaluate the maneuvering performance of the S175 container ship, including standard turning circle and Zig-Zag maneuvers, under a range of representative ice conditions.
- A systematic parametric study is performed to quantify the effects of ice floe size, ice concentration, and ice incidence angle on turning capability and steering stability, thereby revealing the underlying physical mechanisms responsible for maneuvering performance degradation in ice-covered waters. The findings not only advance the understanding of non-icebreaking ship behaviour in such environments but also provide scientific support for navigational safety assessments, operational planning, and the development of Arctic shipping routes.

2. Numerical Method

2.1. 3 DOF Maneuvering Model

In this study, two coordinate systems are employed: the Earth-fixed coordinate system and the body-fixed coordinate system. The latter moves with the ship at the maneuvering speed, but does not follow the ship's oscillatory motions. In the body-fixed coordinate system, the x–y plane coincides with the surface of the still water, as illustrated in Figure 1. The positive x axis and the y axis point to the bow and starboard sides of the ship, respectively. The variables u and v denote the surge and sway velocities of the ship, δ denotes the rudder angle, β is the drift angle, and ψ is the heading angle of the ship.

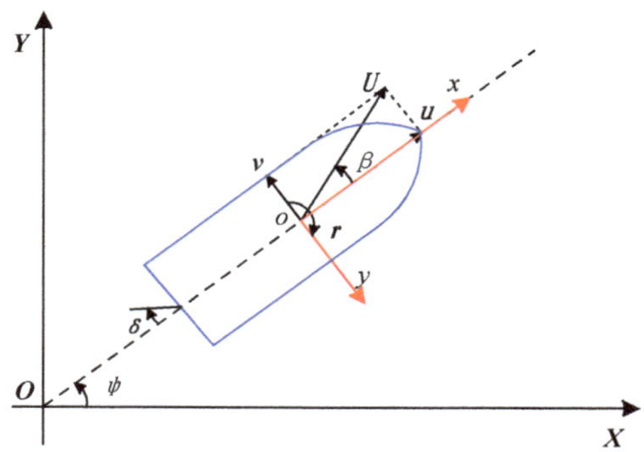

Figure 1. Earth-fixed and body-fixed coordinate systems used for maneuvering modeling.

The relationship between the earth-fixed coordinate system and the body-fixed coordinate system can be expressed as follows.

$$\begin{cases} X = x\cos\psi(t) - y\sin\psi(t) + X_0(t) \\ Y = x\sin\psi(t) + y\cos\psi(t) + Y_0(t) \\ Z = z \end{cases} \tag{1}$$

where $(X_0(t), Y_0(t))$ denotes the position coordinates of the ship in the Earth-fixed coordinate system and t represents time.

The MMG model with three degrees of freedom (3-DOF) is utilized. According to the conceptual framework of the MMG model, the external forces and moments (X, Y, N) that affect the movement of the ship are decomposed into fluid inertia forces, fluid viscous forces, propeller thrust, and rudder forces acting on the hull [37]. The basic structure of the MMG mathematical model is represented as shown in Equation (2).

$$\begin{cases} (m + m_x)\dot{u} - (m + m_y)vr = X_H + X_P + X_R \\ (m + m_y)\dot{v} + (m + m_x)ur = Y_H + Y_R \\ (I_{zz} + J_{zz})\dot{r} = N_H + N_R \end{cases} \tag{2}$$

where m represents the mass of the ship. The terms m_x and m_y represent the added masses along the x axes and the y axes, respectively. J_{zz} represents the added inertia moments on the z axes. The subscripts H, P, and R mean the hydrodynamic forces acting on the hull, propeller, and rudder, respectively.

The hydrodynamic force acting on the hull is expressed as follows.

$$\begin{cases} X_H = 0.5\rho LdV^2 X'_H(v',r') - \mathcal{R}(u_0) \\ Y_H = 0.5\rho LdV^2 Y'_H(v',r') \\ N_H = 0.5\rho L^2 dV^2 N'_H(v',r') \end{cases} \tag{3}$$

with

$$\begin{cases} X'_H(v',r') = X'_{vv}v'^2 + X'_{vr}v'r' + X'_{rr}r'^2 \\ Y'_H(v',r') = Y'_v v' + Y'_r r' + Y'_{vvv}v'^3 + Y'_{vvr}v'^2 r' + Y'_{vrr}v'r'^2 + Y'_{rrr}r'^3 \\ N'_H(v',r') = N'_v v' + N'_r r' + N'_{vvv}v'^3 + N'_{vvr}v'^2 r' + N'_{vrr}v'r'^2 + N'_{rrr}r'^3 \end{cases} \tag{4}$$

where $\mathcal{R}(u_0)$ represents the resistance coefficient of the ship. The components X_H, Y_H, and N_H correspond to the forces or moments in the surge, sway, and yaw directions, respectively. The total speed is calculated as $V = \sqrt{u^2+v^2}$. The nondimensional form of r is given by $r' = \frac{rL}{V}$.The coefficients X'_{vv}, Y'_r, N'_{rr}, etc., represent the hydrodynamic derivatives with respect to specific physical variables. These coefficients, which are indicative of the nonlinear hydrodynamic behaviour of the ship, are typically determined through Planar Motion Mechanism (PMM) tests or Circular Motion Tests (CMT). It is important to note that the specific form of the expressions of the hydrodynamic derivatives is not unique. Polynomial forms proposed by Yasukawa et al. [38,39] generally provide more accurate descriptions of the variation in the hydrodynamic coefficients, offering greater reliability for the precise prediction of the characteristics of the movement of the ship.

The rudder force provides the primary moment required for the maneuvering motion of the ship and is expressed as follows.

$$\begin{cases} X_R = -(1-t_R)F_N \sin\delta \\ Y_R = -(1+a_H)F_N \cos\delta \\ N_R = -(x_R + a_H x_H)F_N \cos\delta \end{cases} \tag{5}$$

where t_R represents the thrust deduction factor for the rudder and a_H denotes the increase factor in the rudder force. The variables x_R and x_H refer to the longitudinal coordinates of the center of the rudder and the additional lateral force acting point, respectively. F_N represents the normal rudder force [39], which is calculated as:

$$F_N = \frac{1}{2}\rho \frac{6.13\Lambda}{\Lambda + 2.25} A_d U_R^2 \sin\alpha_R \tag{6}$$

where ρ represents the density of water, and Λ and A_d denote the aspect ratio of the rudder and the area of the rudder, respectively. U_R and α_R represent the resultant inflow velocity to the rudder and the effective inflow angle, respectively. The estimation formulas for these parameters are as follows:

$$\begin{cases} \alpha_R = \delta - \tan^{-1}\left(\frac{v_R}{u_R}\right) \\ u_R = u_p \varepsilon \sqrt{1 + 8kK_T/(\pi J_P^2)} \\ u_p = u\left[(1-w_p) + \tau\beta_P^2\right] \\ v_R = \left(\gamma v' + C_{Rr}r' + C_{Rrrr}r'^3 + C_{Rrrv}r'^2 v'\right)U \\ U_R^2 = u_R^2 + v_R^2 \end{cases} \tag{7}$$

where ε, k, τ, and γ represent the interaction coefficients between the hull, propeller, and rudder. The term v_R denotes the inflow velocity in the direction x in the rudder, while

C_{Rr}, C_{Rrrr}, and C_{Rrrv} are experimental constants that accurately describe v_R [40]. The variables u_p and v_R refer to the inflow velocities in the propeller and rudder, respectively. Furthermore, K_T, w_p, and J_P correspond to the propeller thrust coefficient, wake coefficient, and propeller advance ratio, respectively.

The lateral forces and yaw moments generated by the propeller are typically minimal and difficult to measure. In the MMG model, these effects are typically considered in combination with the hydrodynamic maneuvering forces acting on the hull, so only the longitudinal hydrodynamic forces generated by the propeller require calculation.

The hydrodynamic forces generated by the propeller can be expressed as

$$X_P = (1 - t_p)\,\rho n_p^2 D_P^4 K_T(J_P) \tag{8}$$

$$K_T(J_P) = j_0 + j_1 J_P + j_2 J_P^2 \tag{9}$$

$$J_P = \frac{u(1 - w_p)}{n D_P} \tag{10}$$

where t_p and n_p represent the thrust reduction coefficient and the propeller revolution, respectively. D_p denotes the diameter of the propeller, while K_T represents the propeller thrust coefficient. K_T can be expressed as a quadratic polynomial in terms of J_p, where J_p is the advance coefficient, and w_p is the wake coefficient; J_0, J_1, and J_2 are regression parameters. More details of the maneuvering coefficients related to the propeller, the rudder, and the hull forces can be found in [41,42].

It is worth noting that the present study adopts a three-degree-of-freedom (3-DOF) maneuvering model, incorporating surge (u), sway (v), and yaw (r) motions. This simplification follows the classical MMG framework and is based on the assumption that, under most floating ice conditions, ice loads act predominantly near the waterline and primarily induce motions in the horizontal plane. The 3-DOF formulation also enables more efficient computations, facilitating extensive parametric investigations. However, in certain situations, such as concentrated bow impacts or heavy ice conditions, vertical-plane responses, including pitch and heave, as well as roll motions, may become non-negligible due to the distribution and magnitude of ice–ship contact forces. The present model does not explicitly account for such six-degree-of-freedom coupling effects, and therefore its applicability is most appropriate for moderate speed of ships and ice concentrations of approximately 20–60%. This limitation is further discussed in the Conclusion, where potential extensions to a full 6-DOF framework are outlined.

2.2. Ice Resistance Model

During navigation in broken ice regions, the hull of the ship frequently experiences collisions and frictional interactions with floating ice. Discrete ice floes introduce additional resistance and moments on the hull surface, significantly affecting ship maneuvering performance. In this study, the ship–ice interaction is modelled as a discontinuous contact process between multiple rigid ice floes and the ship hull. Each ice floe is simplified as a two-dimensional rigid body with defined mass, velocity, and moment of inertia, possessing independent translational and rotational degrees of freedom. This modelling assumption is a commonly adopted and effective simplification in studies of ship–ice interaction, providing a reasonable representation of the dynamic behaviour of floating ice during collision processes.

2.2.1. Collision Detection Method

In numerical simulations of ship–ice interactions, it is essential to resolve two primary types of collisions: those between the ship hull and ice floes, and those among ice floes themselves. The efficiency of the collision detection stage largely determines the overall computational performance of the simulation framework. To address this, a two-stage hybrid strategy is adopted, combining the Sweep and Prune (SAP) algorithm for broad-phase filtering and the Gilbert–Johnson–Keerthi (GJK) algorithm for narrow-phase contact resolution.

In the broad-phase, SAP rapidly excludes distant objects that cannot physically interact by constructing axis-aligned bounding boxes (AABBs) for each object, projecting them onto coordinate axes, and sorting the boundary coordinates. Overlaps are identified by traversing the sorted lists, reducing the number of potential collision pairs from $O(n^2)$ to near-linear complexity under sparse contact conditions (Figure 2). The remaining candidate pairs are passed to the GJK algorithm, which determines whether two convex bodies intersect by analyzing the Minkowski difference between them. If the origin lies within this difference, a collision is detected. GJK iteratively constructs a simplex toward the origin using support functions, providing not only the intersection status but also the minimum distance vector and penetration depth. Its geometric robustness and efficiency make it well-suited for frequent, high-precision contact checks in rigid-body simulations.

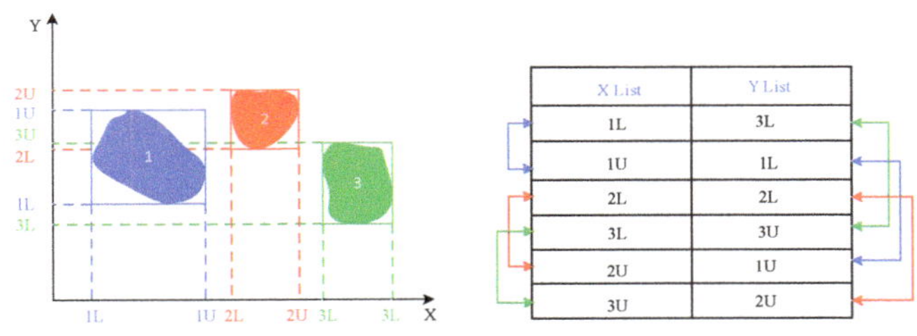

(a) AABB surrounding boxes

(b) Search for potential collision pairs

Figure 2. SAP algorithm diagram. (**a**) Axis-aligned bounding boxes (AABB) of three objects. (**b**) Search process for potential collision pairs. Blue, red, and green represent different objects.

While intelligent collision detection methods based on fuzzy logic and neural networks [43,44] have shown potential in pattern recognition and autonomous navigation, they require substantial labeled data and extensive training, and may lack deterministic guarantees. In contrast, the SAP–GJK combination is data-independent, interpretable, and fully compliant with Newtonian mechanics, making it particularly suitable for high-frequency multibody contact simulations in the NDEM–MMG framework.

2.2.2. Constraint Solving

Once contact bodies and contact point information are obtained, the contact force and normal penetration distance can be treated as complementary variables. A schematic illustration of the collision between body A and body B at the contact point is shown in Figure 3. The collision impulse is calculated based on the change in relative velocity at the contact point before and after impact, following the impulse–momentum relationship for rigid bodies in the Non-Smooth Discrete Element Method (NDEM) [45]. This approach decomposes the total contact impulse into normal and tangential components, where the normal component is associated with the contact normal direction, and the tangential component corresponds to the tangential direction. Both components incorporate the effects of translational and rotational inertia of the colliding bodies, as well as the moment arms from the centers of mass to the contact point. The discrete forms in Equations (11) and (12) are obtained by inverting the effective mass matrix in the local contact frame, ensuring that the calculated impulses satisfy the non-penetration constraint in the normal direction and the frictional constraint in the tangential direction.

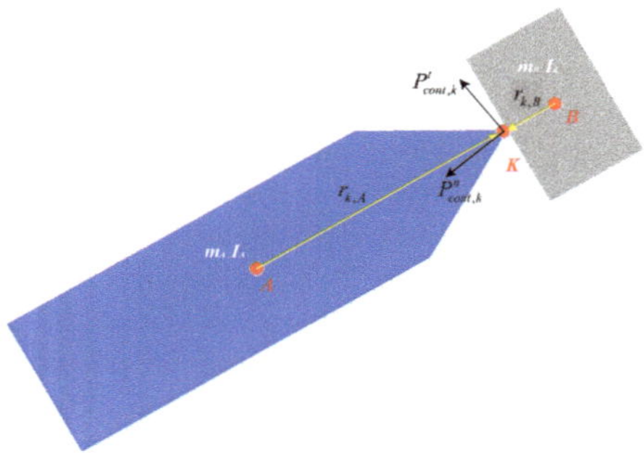

Figure 3. Illustration of the collision between object A and B.

$$P_{\text{cont},k} = P^{n}_{\text{cont},k} + P^{t}_{\text{cont},k} \tag{11}$$

$$\begin{cases} P^{n}_{\text{cont},k} = \dfrac{(\Delta V_{\text{rel}} \times n) \times n}{\frac{1}{m_A} + \frac{1}{m_B} + \left[\left(\frac{r_{k,A} \times n}{I_A}\right) \times r_{k,A}\right] \times n + \left[\left(\frac{r_{k,B} \times n}{I_B}\right) \times r_{k,B}\right] \times n} \\ P^{t}_{\text{cont},k} = \dfrac{(\Delta V_{\text{rel}} \times t) \times t}{\frac{1}{m_A} + \frac{1}{m_B} + \left[\left(\frac{r_{k,A} \times t}{I_A}\right) \times r_{k,A}\right] \times t + \left[\left(\frac{r_{k,B} \times t}{I_B}\right) \times r_{k,B}\right] \times t} \end{cases} \tag{12}$$

where $P^{n}_{\text{cont},k}$ and $P^{t}_{\text{cont},k}$ denote the normal and tangential collision impulses, respectively; m_A and m_B represent the masses of the collision bodies A and B; ΔV_{rel} is the change in relative velocity at the contact point k; and $r_{k,A}$ and $r_{k,B}$ are the position vectors from the center of mass of bodies A and B to the contact point. I_A and I_B denote the inertia tensors of bodies A and B, respectively; n and t represent the normal and tangential unit vectors. In addition, the tangential collision impulse must satisfy the Coulomb friction law, which is expressed as Equation (13):

$$-\mu \left\| P^{n}_{\text{cont},k} \right\| \leq P^{t}_{\text{cont},k} \leq \mu \left\| P^{n}_{\text{cont},k} \right\| \tag{13}$$

where μ is the friction coefficient.

It should be noted that impulse-based response models grounded in non-smooth dynamics theory do not directly compute contact forces. In this study, the contact force is estimated using the contact force conversion model proposed by Yulmetov et al. [46], which classifies contact events into collision contact or static contact. For static contact, the contact force is approximated based on the variation of the impulse during the simulation time step. For collision contact, the contact force is calculated using the collision duration T_{col}, which is determined by Equation (14):

$$T_{\text{col}} \approx \frac{\pi}{2}\sqrt{\frac{M^*}{K}} \tag{14}$$

where M^* is the reduced mass and K is the contact stiffness. Given that the mass of floating ice is relatively small compared to the mass of the ship, the reduced mass during ship–ice collisions can be approximated as the mass of the ice. When the ice approaches the hull, the effects of added mass become significant; hence, an added mass coefficient of 1.0 is introduced to estimate the reduced mass, as expressed in Equation (15).

$$M^* \approx (1+\alpha)M_{\text{ice}} \tag{15}$$

where α is the added mass coefficient and M_{ice} is the mass of the interacting ice floe. Contact stiffness K is a key parameter commonly used in Discrete Element Method (DEM) modelling. In the present study, a contact stiffness of 1.0×10^6 N/m is selected for the numerical simulations [47]. It is worth noting that the calculation of the duration of the collision here considers only the effect of body mass on the collision process and does not account for the influence of simultaneous multibody contact or eccentric collisions.

2.3. Ice Field Generation

In this study, the numerical ice field is made up of identical rectangular ice floes. Therefore, the generation of the ice field requires only the initialization of the floe positions and orientations. The coordinates of each floe vertex in the ice field are calculated using Equation (16) [48]:

$$\begin{cases} P'_{i,x} = P_{i,x}\cos\alpha - P_{i,y}\sin\alpha + P_{\text{loc},x} \\ P'_{i,y} = P_{i,x}\sin\alpha + P_{i,y}\cos\alpha + P_{\text{loc},y} \end{cases} \tag{16}$$

where $(P_{i,x}, P_{i,y})$ are the original vertex coordinates of the ice floe, α is a randomly assigned rotation angle, and $(P_{loc,x}, P_{loc,y})$ are the initialized centroid coordinates of the floe. The final floe vertex coordinates $(P'_{i,x}, P'_{i,y})$ are obtained through random rotation and translation, as illustrated in Figure 4. During the ice field generation process, the SAP and GJK algorithms are also used to perform preliminary screening and fine-level validation to ensure that the ice floes do not overlap.

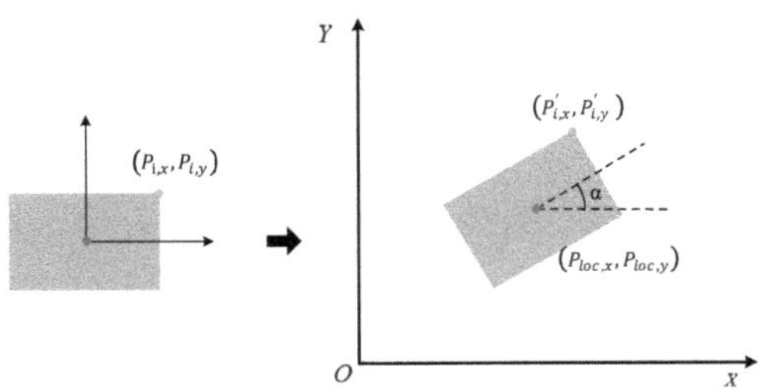

Figure 4. Determine the random distribution of ice floes.

2.4. Fluid Force Model

The motion of broken ice in water is influenced by buoyancy forces and hydrodynamic drag. In this study, the hydrodynamic forces that act on the ice floes are modelled using the Morison equation, as expressed in Equation (17):

$$\begin{cases} \mathbf{F}_{\text{drag}} = -0.5\, C_d\, \rho_w\, A_{\text{proj}}\, \mathbf{U}_{\text{rel}}\, |\mathbf{U}_{\text{rel}}| \\ \boldsymbol{\tau}_{\text{drag}} = -0.5\, C_a\, \rho_w\, l_{avg}^3\, A_{\text{sub}}\, \boldsymbol{\Omega}\, |\boldsymbol{\Omega}| \end{cases} \tag{17}$$

where C_d and C_a are the drag coefficient and the rotational damping coefficient, respectively; ρ_w is the water density; A_{proj} and A_{sub} denote the projected area and submerged area of the ice floe; and $\mathbf{U}_{\text{rel}}$ and $\boldsymbol{\Omega}$ represent the relative translational velocity and the angular velocity, respectively. This model effectively captures the hydrodynamic response of ice floes under fluid forces.

2.5. Ship–Ice Coupled Model

To simulate ship maneuvering behaviour in floating ice regions, this study establishes a dynamic simulation framework that couples a three-degree-of-freedom (3-DOF) ship maneuvering model (MMG) with the Non-Smooth Discrete Element Method (NDEM). The general flow diagram of numerical simulation is illustrated in Figure 5. Within this framework, the ship is subjected to hydrodynamic forces generated by the propeller and rudder, while simultaneously undergoing multiple-point collisions with ice floes. These collisions induce discontinuous impulsive forces and moments, which significantly affect the performance of the maneuvering of the ship. To complement the schematic in Figure 5, the algorithmic sequence of the coupled MMG–NDEM simulation is summarized in Algorithm 1. This pseudocode outlines the core steps taken in each simulation time step, including ship dynamics update, contact detection and response, and integration.

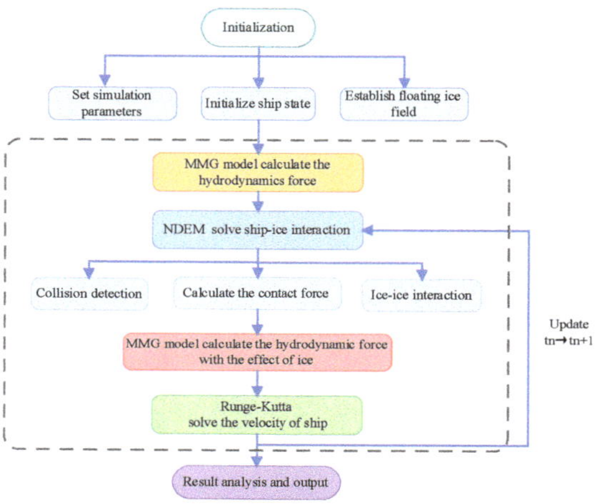

Figure 5. Coupled MMG-NDEM scheme for ship maneuvering simulation in broken ice area.

Algorithm 1: Coupled MMG–NDEM simulation loop

Input: Simulation parameters, initial ship state, initial ice field
Output: Time evolution of ship motion and ice responses
Initialization:
Set time step Δt, total duration T, and initialize $t \leftarrow 0$
Initialize ship position and velocity from MMG model
Generate floating ice field with randomized floe positions and orientations
while $t < T$ **do**
  Compute hydrodynamic forces on ship from MMG model;
  Predict rigid body motion of ship using MMG equations;
  `/* Broad-phase collision detection */`
  Apply SAP algorithm to identify potential contact pairs (ship-ice and ice-ice);
  `/* Narrow-phase collision detection */`
  Use GJK algorithm to test each pair and obtain contact points and normals;
  Compute contact forces and impulses via NDEM solver;
  Update ship velocity and angular rate using Runge–Kutta integration;
  Update ice floe positions and orientations;
  $t \leftarrow t + \Delta t$;
return *Final ship trajectory and ice distribution*

In the subsequent coupling process, the MMG model provides the velocity and position parameters of the ship required by the NDEM model to calculate ship–ice interactions. After updating the position and velocity of the ship, the NDEM collision solver is used to calculate the ice forces acting on the hull. The computed ice forces are then fed back into the MMG model. The governing equations follow the standard 3-DOF MMG maneuvering model [37], which describes the ship's horizontal-plane dynamics. In this study, the model is extended by introducing additional force terms—X_{ice}, Y_{ice}, and N_{ice}—to account for ice loads computed by the NDEM model. The resulting coupled equations are expressed as Equation (18):

$$\begin{cases} (m+m_x)\dot{u} - (m+m_y)vr = X_H + X_P + X_R + X_{ice} \\ (m+m_y)\dot{v} + (m+m_x)ur = Y_H + Y_R + Y_{ice} \\ (I_{zz}+J_{zz})\dot{r} = N_H + N_R + N_{ice} \end{cases} \quad (18)$$

The MMG model computes maneuvering forces and hydrodynamic responses based on the current motion state of the ship, which are then used to determine the acceleration and dynamic behaviour of the ship. To ensure high accuracy and numerical stability, the fourth-order Runge–Kutta method (RK4) is employed to solve the integral Equation (18).

Since the ice forces are calculated in the earth-fixed coordinate system, they must be transformed into the body-fixed coordinate system. The transformation is given by Equation (19):

$$\begin{cases} X_{\text{ice}} = F_{\text{ice},x}\cos\psi + F_{\text{ice},y}\sin\psi \\ Y_{\text{ice}} = -F_{\text{ice},x}\sin\psi + F_{\text{ice},y}\cos\psi \\ N_{\text{ice}} = M_{\text{ice},z} \end{cases} \quad (19)$$

where ψ is the angle of direction of the ship. The transformed forces X_{ice}, Y_{ice} and the moment N_{ice}, together with the propeller thrust and the rudder forces, are input into the 3-DOF MMG equations to update the velocity of the ship and the angular velocity.

3. Results and Discussion

3.1. MMG Model Validation in Open Water

Due to the lack of experimental data available on the turning performance of ships in fractured ice regions for comparative analysis, this study performs independent validation of the NDEM and MMG models. Previous research [32] has validated the numerical simulation results of ship–ice collision processes, providing methodological reference and theoretical support for the present study. In this study, the S175 container ship, a classical benchmark vessel widely used in maneuvering research and validated through extensive model tests and CFD simulations, was selected as a representative non-icebreaking merchant ship for hydrodynamic investigations. Figure 6 illustrates the three-dimensional hull form of the S175 model used in this study, which forms the basis for subsequent numerical simulations. Numerical simulations of turning circle and Zig-Zag maneuvers were performed under open-water conditions using the proposed MMG model, and the results were compared against available experimental data to validate its effectiveness. The principal dimensions and hull form coefficients of the S175 container ship are listed in Table 1. Furthermore, the relative coefficients used in the MMG model, which characterize the hydrodynamic contributions of the hull, propeller, and rudder to surge, sway, and yaw motions, are summarized in Table 2 [40].

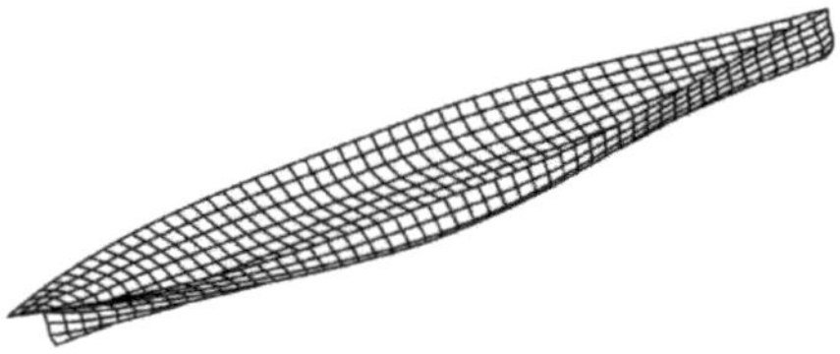

Figure 6. Three-dimensional geometry of the S175 container ship model used in this study. The data were from [49].

Table 1. Principal dimensions and parameters of the S175 container ship and its scaled model.

Category	Parameter	Full Scale	Model Scale
Hull	Length between perpendiculars, L (m)	175.0	3.0337
	Beam, B (m)	25.4	0.4403
	Draft, D (m)	9.5	0.1647
	Displacement, ∇ (m^3)	24742	0.127
	Coordinate of center of gravity	(−2.545, 0, 0)	(−0.042, 0, −0.01)
	Metacentric height	–	0.0173
	Radius of gyration in roll, k_{xx}	$0.33B$	$0.33B$
	Radius of gyration in pitch, k_{yy}	$0.25L$	$0.25L$
	Radius of gyration in yaw, k_{zz}	$0.269L$	$0.269L$
	Wetted surface area (m^2)	5396	1.6216
Propeller	Diameter, D_p (m)	6.5064	0.1128
	Pitch ratio	0.915	0.915
	Number of blades	5	5
Rudder	Area, A_d (m^2)	32.46	0.0098
	Height, H (m)	7.7	0.1335
	Aspect ratio, Λ	1.8268	1.8268

Table 2. Hydrodynamic derivatives and interaction coefficients for the 3-DOF MMG maneuvering model of the S175 container ship.

	Symbol	Value	Symbol	Value	Symbol	Value
Hull	m'_x	0.000238	Y'_v	−0.0116	N'_v	−0.00385
	m'_y	0.007049	Y'_r	0.00242	N'_r	−0.00222
	J'_{xx}	0.0000034	Y'_{vvv}	−0.109	N'_{vvv}	0.001492
	J'_{zz}	0.000419	Y'_{vvr}	0.0214	N'_{vvr}	−0.0424
	X'_{vv}	−0.00386	Y'_{vrr}	−0.0405	N'_{vrr}	0.00156
	X'_{vr}	−0.00311	Y'_{rrr}	0.00177	N'_{rrr}	−0.00229
	X'_{rr}	0.0002	Z_H/D	0.5	N_{10}	0.0082
	C_r	0.001	k_f	1.04		
Propeller	t_p	0.175	1-w_{p0}	0.816	x_P	−0.47
	j_0	0.5179	j_1	−0.1179	j_2	−0.3618
Rudder	t_R	0.29	x'_H	−0.48	x'_R	−0.5
	a_H	0.237	ε	0.921	γ	0.088 ($v' < 0$)
	K	0.631	Z_H/D	0.7		0.193 ($v' \geq 0$)
	C_{Rr}	−0.156	C_{Rrr}	−0.275	C_{Rrvv}	1.96

First, the numerical simulation results of the S175 container ship model are compared with the experimental turning trajectory, as shown in Figure 7. The experimental data were obtained from tests conducted in the Ocean Engineering Basin of Shanghai Jiao Tong University (50 m × 30 m × 5 m), using a ship model with a scale ratio of 1:57.689.

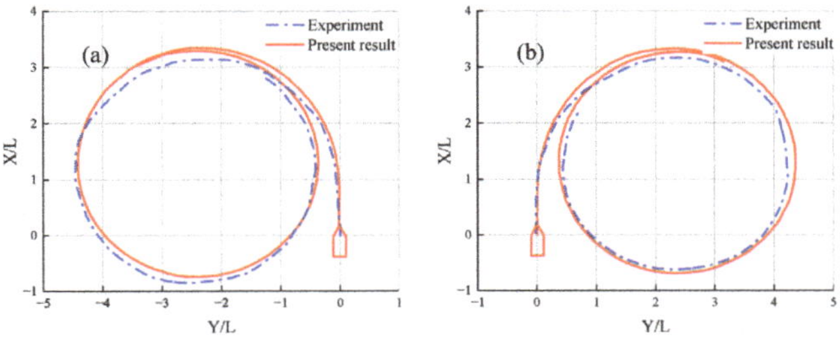

Figure 7. S175 container ship model turning trajectories: (**a**) port turning ($\delta = -35°$); (**b**) starboard turning ($\delta = 35°$).

By comparing the diameter of the turn and the advance, the errors of the port and starboard turning diameters were found to be 3% and 5%, respectively, while the errors of the port and starboard advances were both approximately 9%. The comparison results are summarized in Table 3. These results demonstrate that the MMG model can effectively simulate the turning motion of the ship.

Table 3. Relative errors of turning diameter and advance for port and starboard turning.

Turning Diameter	Relative Error	Advance	Relative Error
Port turning	3%	Port turning	9%
Starboard turning	5%	Starboard turning	9%

In addition, a comparative analysis was conducted between the simulated response to the heading angle of the S175 container ship during the Zig-Zag maneuver and the corresponding experimental data, as shown in Figure 8. The first and second overshoot angles computed in the numerical simulation agree well with the experimental results reported by [50]. This further validates the accuracy and reliability of the 3-DOF MMG model proposed in this study.

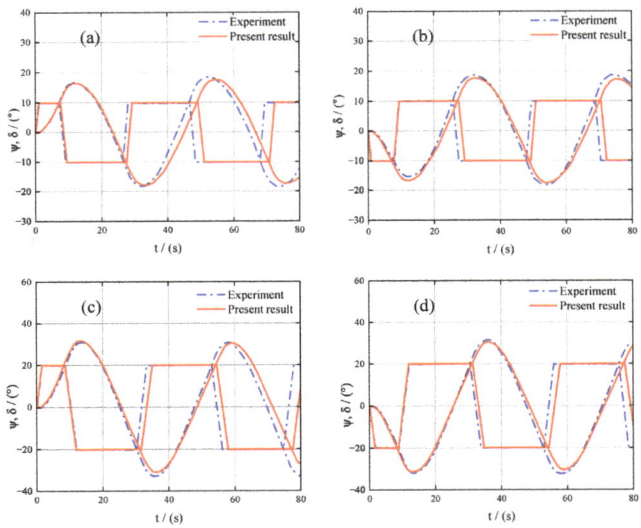

Figure 8. S175 container ship model Zig-Zag maneuver: heading and rudder angle time history curves in calm water—(**a**) 10°/10° (starboard rudder); (**b**) −10°/−10° (port rudder); (**c**) 20°/0° (starboard rudder); (**d**) −20°/−20° (port rudder).

3.2. Turning Maneuver of the Ship in Broken Ice Fields

3.2.1. Effect of Ice Concentration

Ice concentration is a key parameter for quantifying the extent of ice coverage, typically used to describe the proportion of a given water area that is covered by ice floes. In this study, following the WMO sea ice classification standards and recommended navigability guidelines for non-icebreaking ships, three typical ice fields with concentrations of 20%, 40%, and 60% were selected for simulation. Each ice field consists of rectangular ice floes with dimensions of 0.25 m × 0.20 m × 0.02 m, covering a total area of 20 m × 20 m. The three ice fields with different concentrations are illustrated in Figure 9.

A concentration of 20% represents a sparse ice region where non-icebreaking ships can navigate relatively freely, while concentrations of 40% to 60% represent typical medium-concentration broken ice fields, which are commonly encountered by such ships during navigation. When the ice concentration exceeds 70%, non-icebreaker ships generally cannot navigate independently; therefore, this condition was not considered in the present study. The simulation parameters are summarized in Table 4.

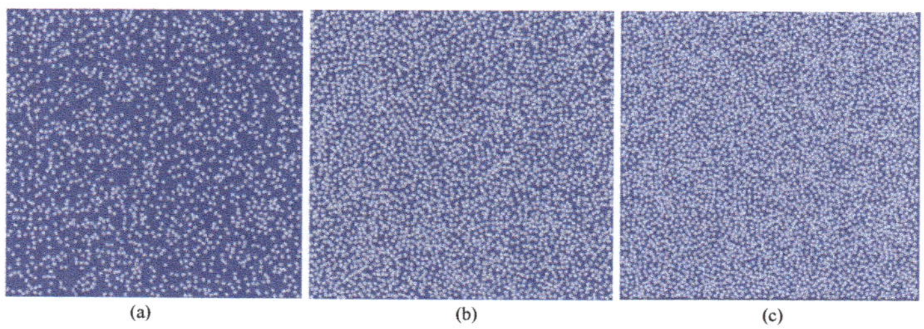

Figure 9. Floating ice fields with different ice concentrations: (**a**) 20%; (**b**) 40%; (**c**) 60%.

Table 4. Physical and numerical parameters used in the simulations.

Parameter	Value
Water density (kg/m^3)	1025
Ice density (kg/m^3)	917
Ship–ice friction coefficient	0.28
Ship–ice restitution coefficient	0.50
Ice–ice friction coefficient	0.44
Ice–ice restitution coefficient	0.25
Time step (s)	0.002
Form drag coefficient, C_d	1.0
Angular drag coefficient, C_a	0.05

Figure 10 presents the turning trajectories of the S175 container ship in floating ice fields with different ice concentrations (20%, 40%, and 60%). The corresponding numerical simulation results are summarized in Table 5. It can be clearly observed that as the ice concentration increases, the overall turning trajectory of the ship is more contracted and the turning diameter is significantly reduced. This indicates that floating ice has a considerable impact on the turning ability of the ship. However, this does not imply an improvement in maneuvering performance, as the time required for the ship to complete the same turning angle increases in high-concentration ice regions. In open water, the ship moves freely along its inertial path under the dominance of hydrodynamic forces, resulting in the largest turning radius. As the concentration of ice increases to 20% and 40%, the presence of floating ice introduces disturbances to the motion of the ship. In particular, an outer "barrier" effect emerges along the outer turning path, constraining the lateral motion of the ship and thus limiting the outward side slip, causing the turning trajectory to contract inward. In medium density (40%) and higher ice fields, frequent contact between the outer hull and stern of the ship with floating ice produces a passive constraint effect, leading to further contraction of the trajectory boundaries. These results demonstrate that ship maneuverability is substantially inhibited in high concentration floating ice regions, a trend that is consistent with findings from previous studies on ship maneuver performance in ice-covered waters [33,36].

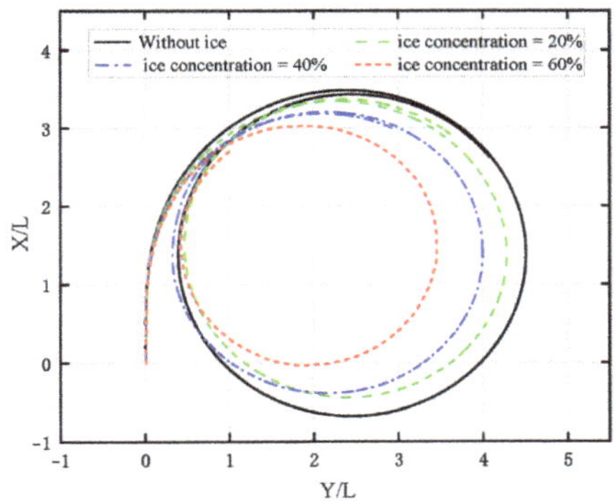

Figure 10. Turning trajectories of the S175 container ship under different ice concentrations: 20%; 40%; and 60%.

Table 5. Simulated turning performance of the S175 container ship under different ice concentrations.

Ice Concentration (%)	Tactical Diameter D_T (m)	Time to 180° Turning (s)	Turning Diameter D (m)	Steady Speed (m/s)	Angular Velocity (rad/s)
0	4.51L	35.27	4.11L	0.549	0.090
20	4.31L	35.98	3.81L	0.524	0.089
40	3.99L	37.12	3.78L	0.457	0.085
60	3.40L	38.16	3.21L	0.258	0.080

L is the ship length between perpendiculars.

According to the classical geometric relationship of turning motion, the turning diameter of a ship is determined by its forward velocity V and angular velocity r as expressed in Equation (20):

$$D = \frac{2V}{r} \tag{20}$$

Based on this, if the motion states of the ship in open water and in regions covered by ice are indicated as (V_0, r_0) and (V_1, r_1), respectively, the turning radius will increase when the following condition is met:

$$\frac{V_1}{r_1} > \frac{V_0}{r_0} \tag{21}$$

In addition to incorporating the effects of ice forces, changes in forward velocity and angular velocity under ice disturbance can be expressed as

$$\begin{cases} \Delta V = \left(\frac{F_{\text{ice}}}{m} + a_{v1} - a_{v0} \right) \Delta t \\ \Delta r = \left(\frac{T_{\text{ice}}}{I} - a_{r1} + a_{r0} \right) \Delta t \end{cases} \tag{22}$$

where ΔV and Δr represent the reductions in velocity and angular velocity caused by the combined effects of ice forces and hydrodynamic forces, while F_{ice} and T_{ice} denote the resistance to ice in direction and the ice-induced moment, respectively.

The simulation results indicate that as the ice concentration increases, the stable turning speed of the ship decreases from 0.549 m/s to 0.258 m/s—an over 50% reduction—whereas the angular velocity decreases from 0.090 rad/s to 0.080 rad/s, with a relatively smaller reduction. This suggests that in floating ice environments, the reduction in forward velocity is much greater than the reduction in angular velocity, meaning that the ship can maintain a certain turning tendency despite. According to Equation (20), when the reduction in angular velocity is less than the forward velocity, the turning radius will decrease, which is consistent with the results of the numerical simulation. According to the ice-induced disturbance criterion proposed by Yang et al. [36], the turning radius will increase when the inhibitory effect of ice moments on angular velocity exceeds the decelerating effect of ice resistance on forward velocity; otherwise, the turning radius will decrease. In this study, under 40% ice concentration, the reduction in angular velocity is less than that of forward velocity, consistent with the observed trajectory contraction. This indicates that in medium-concentration ice conditions, ice resistance dominates the turning characteristics of the ship, and maneuvering strategies should focus on enhancing propulsion efficiency and controlling side-slip motion.

The ship turning trajectory and the local ice interaction process in a field of 40% ice concentration are illustrated in Figure 11. As shown in Figure 11, the ship forms a continuous curved path through the floating ice field during the turning maneuver, indicating significant hull–ice interaction and accumulation along the outer turning edge. Figure 11 presents a magnified view of the local region of contact between the ship and the ice, where multiple discrete ice floes collide with the hull. These collisions generate concentrated resistance and ice moments, particularly around the bow and port-side area, and are responsible for the constrained lateral motion and reduced turning diameter observed in the simulations.

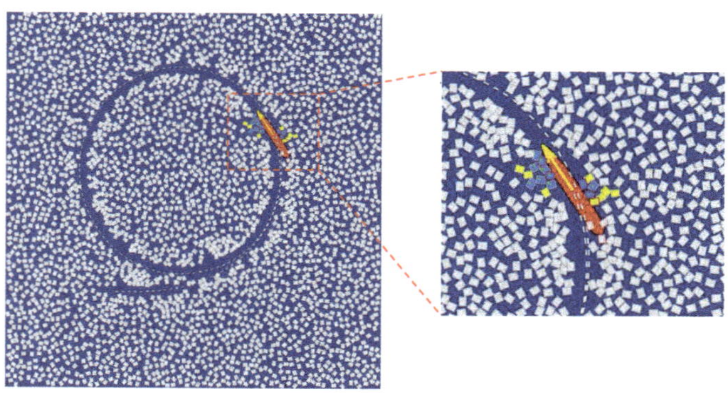

Figure 11. Simulated turning trajectory of the ship in a broken ice field with 40% ice concentration. The left panel shows the global maneuvering path; the right panel presents a magnified view of the local ship–ice interaction region. The yellow arrows indicate the ship's motion direction, and the red color represents the ship's hull.

To further elucidate the physical mechanisms underlying the contraction of the turning trajectory of the ship, the time histories of the dimensionless ice resistance and ice moment experienced by the ship during the turning maneuver in a field of ice concentration 40% are presented in Figure 12. As shown in Figure 12a, the ship experiences significant fluctuations in ice resistance during the initial phase of the turning maneuver, mainly due to large-scale unstable contacts between the bow and the outer hull with floating ice. As the ship gradually transitions into a steady motion state, these fluctuations in ice resistance diminish. This trend indicates that the resistance to ice is predominantly concentrated during the initial phase of the maneuvering process and is a key factor that contributes to the reduction in the turn speed and the contraction of the turning trajectory. Figure 12b depicts the corresponding time history of the dimensionless ice moment. Throughout the maneuver, the ship is predominantly subjected to a negative ice moment, corresponding to a clockwise acting direction. In the initial phase, this negative moment exhibits pronounced fluctuations, indicating that the ship encounters strong interfering thrusts from ice floes on the outer side, which inhibit the growth of angular velocity and directly affect the turning capability of the ship. As the ship completes its adjustment to the direction and gradually overcomes the ice-induced disturbances, the fluctuations in the ice moment decrease significantly and stabilize. These results suggest that the constraining effect of floating ice on the angular velocity of the ship tends to become sustained and stable in the later stages of the turning maneuver, highlighting the directional and persistent characteristics of the passive attitude disturbances induced by the ice field.

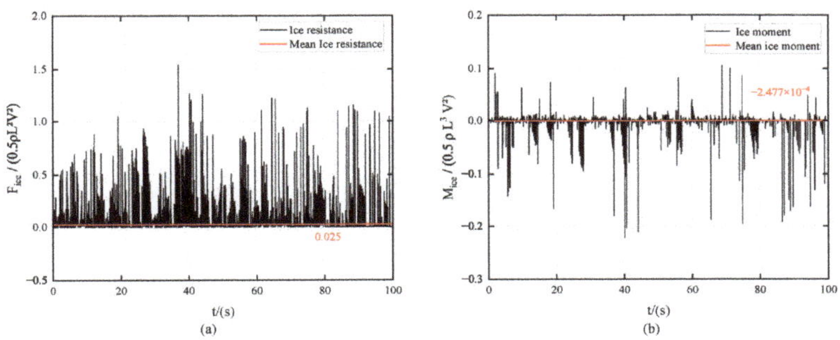

Figure 12. Time histories of the dimensionless ice resistance (**a**) and ice moment (**b**) during the turning maneuver of the ship in a 40% ice concentration field.

In summary, floating ice environments exert significant mechanical interference on the turning motion of non-icebreaking ships, which manifests itself in several key aspects. Firstly, outer ice floes create a boundary-limiting effect, leading to a contraction of the ship's turning trajectory. Secondly, substantial ice resistance and negative ice moments during the initial phase of the ship's motion reduce both the forward speed and angular velocity, thus delaying the transition to a stable turning state. Third, in high-concentration ice fields, the increased frequency of ship-s-ice contacts amplifies the disturbance effects, substantially increasing the complexity of the maneuvering process. Therefore, in the planning of navigation paths and the design of maneuvering strategies for non-icebreaking ships operating in ice-covered regions, it is essential to fully account for the combined influences of ice concentration and ice floe distribution to ensure navigational safety and controllability.

3.2.2. Effect of Ice Size

Existing studies on the prediction of ice resistance have consistently shown that the size of the ice floe has a significant impact on both the magnitude and fluctuation of ice resistance. This influence is particularly critical when considering the maneuvering performance of non-icebreaking ships, as excessively large ice floes can severely affect the ship's speed and attitude changes. To verify the rigid-body assumption for the selected floe sizes, we adopt the flexural characteristic length from thin-plate theory on an elastic foundation as a conservative upper bound [51–53]. Sea ice can also fail by crushing, splitting, or mixed modes depending on confinement and contact conditions; here, the flexural limit is used solely to bound the floe size so that the pre-broken floes in this study are expected to behave as rigid bodies during contact. Cases in which intra-floe deformation or crushing dominates are beyond the scope of the present model. The maximum characteristic size is therefore estimated as:

$$l = \sqrt[4]{\frac{D}{k}} = \sqrt[4]{\frac{Eh^3}{12(1-v^2)\rho_\omega g}} \tag{23}$$

where D is the stiffness of the ice plate, is the elastic modulus of the water foundation, h is the Young modulus, v is the thickness of the ice, ρ_ω is the Poisson ratio, g is the density of the water, E is the gravitational acceleration. The ice thickness is set to 0.02 m in the model scale, which corresponds to a full-scale thickness of 1.15 m. E and v are taken as 5 GPa and 0.3, respectively. According to Equation (23), the maximum characteristic size l is calculated to be 16.22 m, corresponding to a model scale size of 0.28 m. Consequently, three representative ice floe sizes are selected in this study: 0.15 × 0.10 m, 0.20 × 0.15 m, and 0.25 × 0.20 m. The ice concentration is fixed at 40%. The three ice fields with different floe sizes are shown in Figure 13.

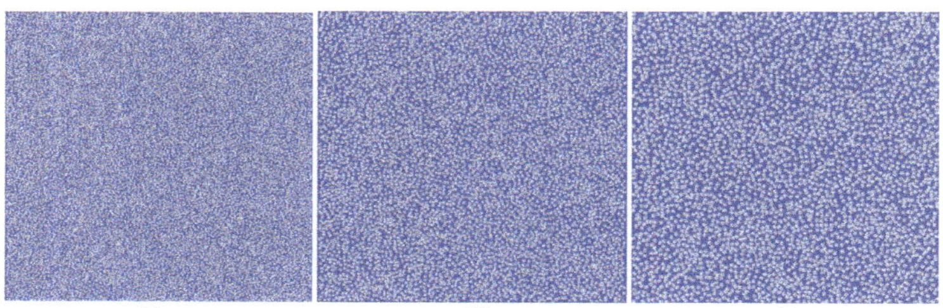

Figure 13. Ice fields with different floe sizes under a fixed ice concentration (40%). The selected floe sizes are (**a**) 0.15 × 0.10 m; (**b**) 0.20 × 0.15 m; and (**c**) 0.25 × 0.20 m.

The results shown in Figure 14 and Table 6 indicate that, under the condition of constant ice concentration, the size of the ice floe has a significant impact on the turning trajectory of the ship and the maneuvering performance. As the size of the ice floe increases, the wing of the ship noticeably contracts inwards, and the diameter of the wing gradually decreases. Small ice floes impose relatively weaker constraints on the motion of the ship, allowing the ship to maintain a higher speed, which results in a larger turning diameter. In contrast, large ice floes exert stronger decelerating and lateral constraint effects on the ship, leading to a noticeably shortened turning path.

This phenomenon can also be explained by the differences in force chain structures formed within the ice field. As illustrated in Figure 15, during ship–ice interactions, large ice floes tend to form stable and longer force chains. These stable force chains are predominantly distributed around the bow and outer regions of the ship, continuously imposing substantial resistance and lateral constraint on the hull. In contrast, although small ice floes interact with the ship at a higher contact frequency and form a greater number of force chains, the chains formed by these smaller ice floes are limited in length, stability, and duration and therefore cannot exert a sustained blocking effect. Instead, they mainly produce random and frequent disturbance effects. As a result, in ice fields with small floes, the ship experiences weaker lateral constraints and maintains a higher speed, leading to a larger turning radius. In contrast, in fields with large floes, the lateral constraints and decelerating effects are significantly enhanced, resulting in a markedly reduced turning radius.

From the perspective of the evolution of the velocity of the ship and the angular velocity, the influence of the size of the ice floe on the maneuver performance also exhibits significant differences. The force chains formed in the bow region primarily contribute to longitudinal deceleration, while those formed along the side of the ship directly affect variations in angular velocity. In small ice floe regions, frequent side contacts generate short and unstable force chains that tend to induce high-frequency disturbances in angular velocity, thereby reducing the stability of the turning motion and resulting in a larger overall turning radius. In contrast, in large ice floe regions, stable and persistent force chains not only enhance the longitudinal deceleration effect, but also effectively suppress fluctuations in angular velocity, leading to a noticeably contracted turning trajectory. In general, large ice floes dominate the characteristics of the turning motion by increasing resistance and lateral constraints, while in small ice floe regions, the ship exhibits greater dynamic freedom and a larger turning radius.

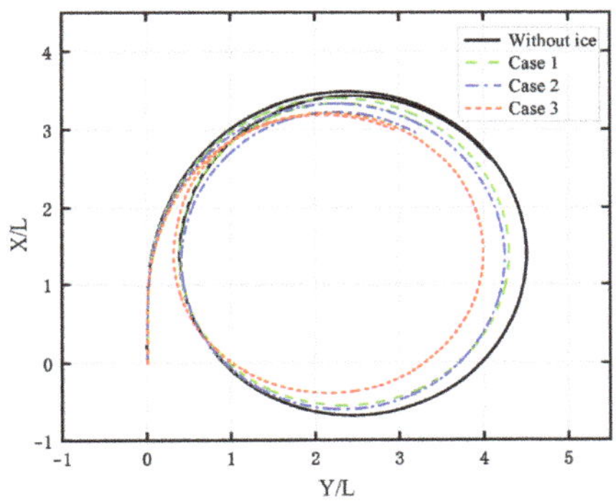

Figure 14. Comparison of ship turning trajectories under different ice floe sizes at a fixed ice concentration of 40%. The solid black line indicates the trajectory in open water (without ice), while Cases 1–3 correspond to floe sizes of (a) 0.15 × 0.10 m; (b) 0.20 × 0.15 m; and (c) 0.25 × 0.20 m, respectively.

Table 6. Maneuvering performance under different ice floe sizes at fixed 40% concentration.

Case	Ice Floe Size (m)	D_T (m)	180° Time (s)	D (m)
Without ice	–	4.51L	35.27	4.11L
1	0.15 × 0.10	4.24L	36.16	3.91L
2	0.20 × 0.15	4.19L	36.47	3.84L
3	0.25 × 0.20	3.99L	37.12	3.78L

L is the ship length between perpendiculars.

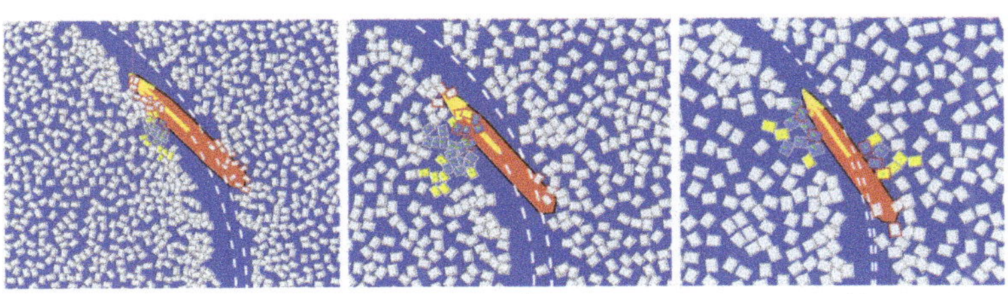

(a) (b) (c)

Figure 15. Force–chain structures in the ship–ice contact region for three representative floe sizes: (**a**) 0.15 × 0.10 m; (**b**) 0.20 × 0.15 m; and (**c**) 0.25 × 0.20 m. Larger floes form longer, more stable force chains concentrated near the bow, whereas smaller floes generate more dispersed, short-duration contacts. The yellow arrows indicate the ship's motion direction, and the red color represents the ship's hull. The floating ice is color–coded by velocity, with blue representing higher–speed floes and yellow representing lower–speed floes.

Finally, Figure 16 presents the average ice resistance and ice moment experienced by the ship during turning maneuvers in ice fields with different floe sizes. The data further confirm the above analytical conclusions. Compared to the ice moment, ice resistance is more sensitive to changes in the size of the ice floe, with larger floes resulting in a pronounced increase in ice resistance.

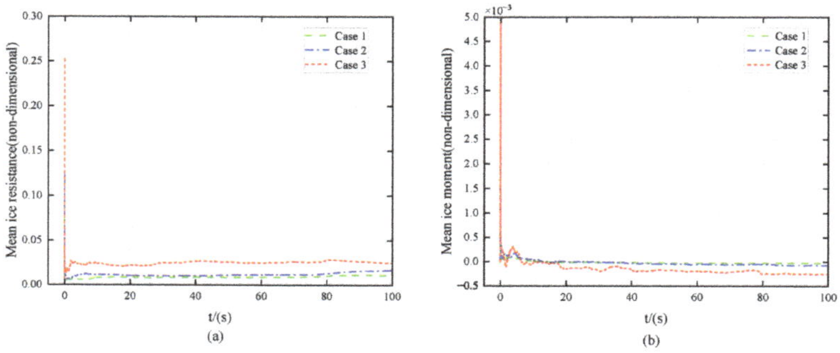

Figure 16. Time histories of the non-dimensional mean ice resistance (**a**) and mean ice moment (**b**) acting on the ship during turning maneuvers in ice fields with different floe sizes, under a constant ice concentration of 40%. Cases 1, 2, and 3 correspond to floe sizes of 0.15 × 0.10 m, 0.20 × 0.15 m, and 0.25 × 0.20 m, respectively.

From an operational standpoint, the simulation results provide useful guidance for navigating in broken ice regions. When sailing in high ice concentrations (e.g., >40%), the increased turning resistance and reduced turning radius suggest that vessels should reduce speed in advance and adopt wider initial turning angles to compensate for the restricted maneuverability. For example, in 60% concentration scenarios, the turning time increases noticeably, requiring earlier rudder input to avoid oversteering. Similarly, in environments with large floes, the stronger contact forces and sudden velocity drops indicate a need to limit abrupt heading changes. Maintaining a moderate and steady speed helps avoid excessive impact loads and enables better directional control. These findings suggest that ship operators navigating in marginal ice zones should dynamically adjust maneuvering strategies according to real-time ice concentration and floe size assessments, which can be integrated into intelligent decision-support systems.

3.3. *Zig-Zag Maneuvering of the Ship in Broken Ice Fields*

The preceding analysis of turning maneuvers indicates that floating ice not only generates forward resistance, thus reducing the ship's speed, but also significantly diminishes the ship's responsiveness to rudder angle changes and constrains its lateral motion freedom. Consequently, performing emergency evasive maneuvers in ice-covered waters is considerably more challenging for non-icebreaking ships than in open water. In this section, typical Zig-Zag maneuver simulations are conducted in floating ice regions to systematically analyze the combined effects of ice concentration and rudder angle amplitude on rudder effectiveness.

3.3.1. Effect of Ice Concentration Zig-Zag Maneuvering

In this section, numerical simulations of Zig-Zag maneuvers are carried out under different ice concentration conditions (0%, 20%, 40%, and 60%) to systematically evaluate the effects of ice concentration on response speed of maneuvering of the ship, response delay, and attitude stability. The results aim to provide theoretical insights into the mechanisms of degradation of the effectiveness of the rudder under complex ice conditions. To ensure fair comparisons and repeatability of the results, the size of the ice floe size (0.25 m × 0.20 m), propeller rotational speed (10.05 rps), and rudder turning rate (12.0°/s) are kept constant throughout the simulations. All tests are performed according to the standard 20°/20° Zig-Zag maneuver command, with the initial speed of the ship corresponding to a Froude number of $Fn = 0.15$.

Figure 17 shows the response curves of the heading angle of the ship performing 20°/20° Zig-Zag maneuvers under different conditions of ice concentration. The results clearly show that the concentration of ice has a significant impact on the maneuvering performance of the ship. Under ice-free conditions, the ship exhibits a rapid response to the heading angle with a pronounced overshoot angle and sharp rudder reversal behaviour, reflecting the high efficiency of the rudder and strong maneuvering sensitivity. As the ice concentration increases to 20%, 40%, and 60%, the response curves exhibit an increasing lag, and the maximum yaw angle progressively decreases. In particular, at 60% ice concentration, the response delay becomes substantial and the response amplitude is significantly attenuated. This phenomenon indicates that the ice environment weakens the effectiveness of the rudder, delays the build-up of angular velocity, and leads to a marked reduction in maneuvering sensitivity. In addition, the "damping" trend observed in the response curves suggests that the control of the attitude of the ship becomes more delayed and uncertain in high-concentration floating ice conditions.

To further quantify changes in maneuver performance, Table 7 summarizes key maneuver indicators under different conditions of ice concentration. The results show that the first overshoot angle ψ_1 slightly decreases with increasing ice concentration, from 31.41° to 30.04°, indicating a reduction in rudder effectiveness. The maximum yaw rate ($d\psi/dt$) exhibits a more pronounced decreasing trend, declining from 4.986°/s to 4.584°/s, which suggests a gradual weakening of the yaw capability of the ship. Variations in response time t_ψ and lag time T_L are relatively small; however, overall fluctuation trends indicate that increasing the concentration of ice introduces certain disturbances to the maneuvering rhythm of the ship.

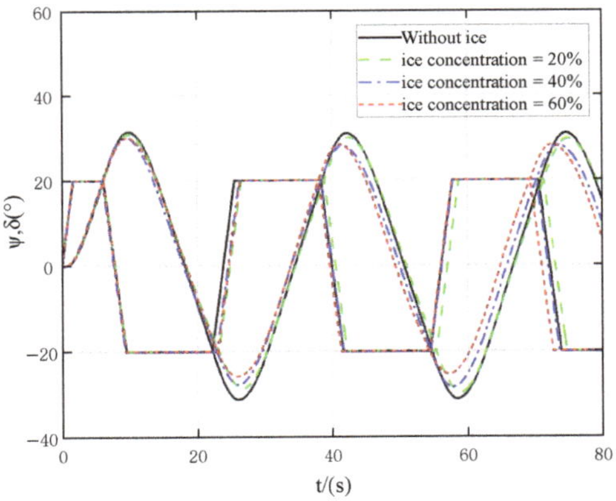

Figure 17. Heading angle response curves of the ship during 20°/20° Zig-Zag maneuvers under different ice concentration conditions. The figure illustrates how increasing ice concentration dampens the yaw response, resulting in reduced overshoot and increased time delay.

In addition, Figure 18 illustrates the planar motion trajectories of the ship during the Zig-Zag maneuvers under different ice concentration conditions. In ice-free water, the trajectory exhibits a well-defined symmetrical "Zig-Zag" pattern, characterized by large turning amplitudes and clear turning paths. As the concentration of ice increases to 20%,

40%, and 60%, the trajectories gradually narrow, the turning angles decrease, and the Zig-Zag path tends to straighten, indicating that the resistance to ice significantly weakens the responsiveness to turning of the ship. In high concentration ice fields, the trajectory exhibits pronounced "compression" and "drift lag" phenomena, with some paths even showing asymmetric yaw behaviour, reflecting the increasing influence of ice particle disturbances and non-uniform lateral loads on the ship.

Table 7. Key maneuvering indicators under different ice concentration conditions.

Ice Concentration (%)	Overshoot Angle ψ_1 (°)	Response Time t_ψ (s)	Lag Time T_L (s)	Max Yaw Rate $d\psi/dt$ (°/s)
0	31.412	6.140	4.520	4.986
20	30.985	6.200	4.540	4.871
40	30.194	6.020	4.340	4.756
60	30.044	6.140	4.450	4.584

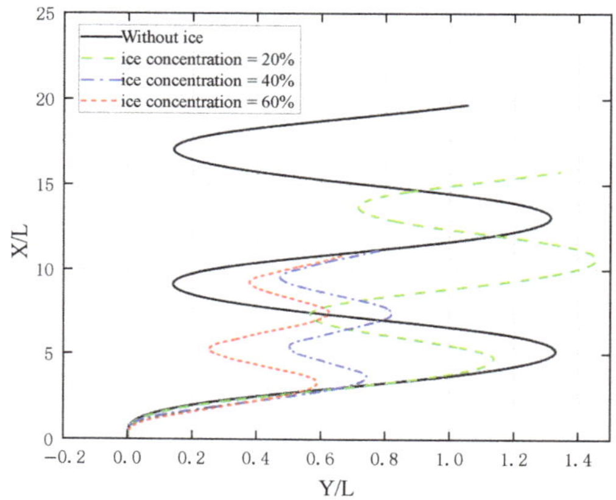

Figure 18. Planar motion trajectories of the ship during 20°/20° Zig-Zag maneuvers under different ice concentration conditions. The results show that higher ice concentrations lead to reduced lateral motion and tighter trajectory envelopes.

In summary, increasing ice concentration exerts a systematic impact on the ship's Zig-Zag maneuver performance, manifested by a slower rudder response, a reduced turning amplitude, and a diminished attitude control capability. Although the ship can still complete Zig-Zag maneuvers under low-to-moderate ice concentrations (20–40%), a clear trend of rudder effectiveness degradation is already evident. Under 60% ice concentration, maneuvering performance deteriorates significantly, which requires special attention to adapting rudder control timing and attitude stability control strategies.

3.3.2. Effect of Rudder Angle on Zig-Zag Maneuvering

The angle of the rudder is a key control parameter in ship maneuvering. To evaluate the influence of rudder angle on the ship's Zig-Zag maneuvering response in ice-covered waters, this section conducts numerical simulations under a fixed 40% ice concentration condition with three typical rudder angle settings: 10°/10°, 15°/15°, and 20°/20°. In all test cases, the size of the ice floe is maintained at (0.25 m × 0.20 m), the initial ship speed corresponds to a Froude number of $Fn = 0.15$, and the turning rate of the rudder is set at 12.0°/s, ensuring the consistency and reliability of the comparative results.

Figure 19 presents the response curves of the head angle of the ship in the three rudder angle settings, with the corresponding maneuver performance indicators summarized in

Table 8. The numerical simulation results show that increasing the angle of the rudder significantly improves the yawing capacity of the ship, as evidenced by the larger amplitude of the response curves and the improved sensitivity of the system. In addition, as the angle of the rudder increases, both the response time and the lag time show noticeable changes. Although a larger rudder angle slightly extends the time required to reach the target heading deviation, the lag time is clearly reduced, indicating that enhanced rudder effectiveness facilitates faster initiation of yaw motion and a more responsive system. Furthermore, the yaw rate response curves shown in Figure 20 provide additional information on the dynamic characteristics of the maneuver response. Under conditions of a high angle of rudder, the yaw rate of the ship increases significantly, resulting in a more pronounced response following the rudder commands, with higher turning acceleration and faster attitude adjustment rates. However, this also makes the ship more susceptible to disturbances induced by ice moments, leading to higher-frequency attitude oscillations.

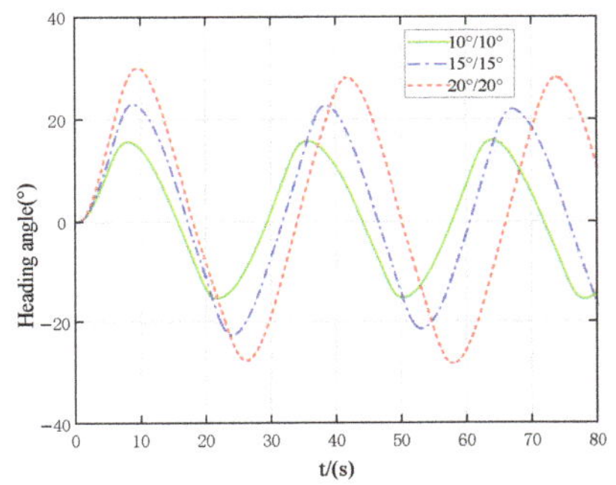

Figure 19. Heading angle response curves of the ship during Zig-Zag maneuvers under three different rudder angle settings: 10°/10°, 20°/20°, and 30°/30°. Larger rudder angles result in faster heading response and increased overshoot.

Table 8. Comparison of Zig-Zag maneuvering indicators under different rudder angle settings.

Rudder Angle (°)	Overshoot Angle ϕ_1 (°)	Response Time t_ϕ (s)	Lag Time T_L (s)
10/10	15.664	4.980	5.630
15/15	23.115	8.140	5.030
20/20	29.961	8.940	4.540

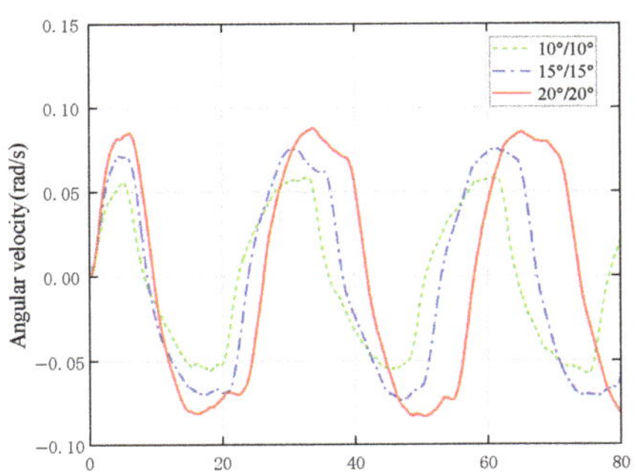

Figure 20. Yaw rate response curves of the ship under three rudder angle settings: 10°/10°, 15°/15°, and 20°/20°. Higher rudder angles result in a sharper and earlier peak yaw rate, indicating improved turning effectiveness and quicker maneuver initiation.

In general, larger rudder angles provide stronger rudder-induced excitation and significantly improve maneuvering sensitivity, but they may also introduce more intense dynamic responses and increased path uncertainty. In complex floating ice environments, maneuvering strategies should carefully balance "response speed" and "dynamic stability" to select an appropriate rudder angle amplitude, thereby ensuring safe and controllable course adjustments.

4. Conclusions

This study systematically investigated the maneuvering performance of non-icebreaking ships in floating ice regions. A numerical simulation framework was established by coupling the MMG ship maneuvering model with NDEM, enabling the simulation of ship maneuvering behaviour in floating ice environments. The effects of ice concentration, ice floe size, and rudder angle on the maneuvering performance of non-icebreaking ships were thoroughly analyzed. The main conclusions are as follows.

(1) An efficient and robust coupled MMG-NDEM model was developed that is capable of effectively simulating complex dynamic interactions between the ship and floating ice. The model incorporates efficient collision detection techniques and integrates NDEM to compute ice resistance and ice-induced moments in real time, accurately capturing the physical processes of collision and friction between the ship and the ice.

(2) Numerical simulations confirmed the significant influence of ice concentration on ship maneuvering performance. As the ice concentration increases from 0% to 60%, the turning diameter of the ship decreases from $4.11L$ to $3.21L$, and the steady turning speed drops by approximately 53%. Meanwhile, the time required to complete a 180° turning maneuver increases from 35.27 s to 38.16 s. These results demonstrate that higher ice concentration markedly impairs maneuvering sensitivity, leading to a substantial contraction of the turning path and increased resistance to heading changes.

(3) The study revealed that ice floe size significantly impacts ship maneuvering performance. As the floe size increases from 0.15 m× 0.10 m to 0.25 m× 0.20 m, the ship's turning diameter decreases from $3.91L$ to $3.78L$, and the time required for a 180° turn increases from 36.16 s to 37.12 s. Larger ice floes tend to form more stable and extended force chain structures, which impose greater longitudinal resistance and lateral constraints on the hull, resulting in reduced turning radius and maneuvering speed. In contrast, smaller floes generate more frequent but short-lived disturbances, offering weaker constraints and thus leading to a comparatively larger turning path.

(4) Zig-Zag maneuver simulations in floating ice regions were conducted to assess the influence of rudder angle variations on ship maneuverability. As the rudder angle increased from 10°/10° to 20°/20°, the first overshoot angle rose significantly from 15.664° to 29.961°, indicating enhanced yaw responsiveness and maneuvering sensitivity. Concurrently, the response time increased from 4.980 s to 8.940 s, and the system exhibited more pronounced dynamic fluctuations. Notably, the lag time T_L decreased from 5.630 s to 4.540 s, suggesting a faster onset of directional response but also highlighting increased instability associated with higher rudder amplitudes. These results underscore the necessity of optimizing rudder angle selection in complex ice conditions to achieve a trade-off between maneuvering effectiveness and directional stability.

This study provides valuable guidance for the navigation of non-icebreaking ships in floating ice regions. It is recommended that route planning prioritizes avoiding high ice concentration areas (>60%) to mitigate maneuvering risks, while favoring transit through low-to-moderate ice concentrations. Additionally, rudder angles should be dynamically adjusted according to ice conditions: larger angles can enhance maneuverability in low-to-moderate ice fields, whereas smaller angles can improve heading stability in high-density ice. In complex ice environments, maintaining heading stability should take precedence over frequent course adjustments, and a smooth, gradual maneuvering strategy is recommended to ensure safe and controllable navigation.

Although an efficient and robust coupled MMG-NDEM model was developed and used to systematically analyze the effects of floating ice on ship maneuvering performance, several limitations remain. The current model is based on two-dimensional, three-degree-of-freedom dynamics and does not account for six-degree-of-freedom motion coupling. The ice field was modelled using idealized rectangular floes, which do not fully represent the multiscale characteristics of natural ice fields. Some ice–ship contact parameters were empirically selected and require further optimisation. In addition, complex hydrodynamic effects and highly coupled propeller–ice interactions were not considered.

Future research will aim to extend the present model to full six-degree-of-freedom (6-DOF) simulations, thereby incorporating pitch, roll, and heave motions in addition to surge, sway, and yaw. Moreover, multiscale three-dimensional ice fields with realistic floe geometries and thickness distributions will be implemented, along with fully coupled hydrodynamic interactions among the propeller, rudder, and ice. To enhance engineering applicability, future developments will also include full-scale validation using sea trial data and systematic uncertainty quantification. Overall, this study provides a solid foundation for advancing the analysis of the maneuvering performance of non-icebreaking ships in floating-ice environments and offers concrete directions for achieving higher-fidelity and engineering-ready simulations.

Author Contributions: Conceptualization, D.W., L.Z., Z.Z. and X.C.; Data curation, D.W.; Formal analysis, L.Z.; Funding acquisition, D.W., Z.Z. and X.C.; Investigation, X.C.; Methodology, D.W.; Resources, Z.Z.; Software, L.Z.; Supervision, Z.Z.; Validation, D.W., L.Z. and Z.Z.; Visualization, L.Z.; Writing—original draft, D.W. and L.Z.; Writing—review & editing, L.Z. All authors have read and agreed to the published version of the manuscript.

Funding: This research was funded by the Special Project on Key Technologies and Equipment for the Deep Sea and Polar Regions (Grant No. 2024YFC2816600).

Institutional Review Board Statement: Not applicable.

Informed Consent Statement: Not applicable.

Data Availability Statement: Data are contained within the article.

Conflicts of Interest: The authors declare no conflicts of interest.

Abbreviations

The following abbreviations are used in this manuscript:

MMG	Maneuvering Modeling Group
NSR	Northern Sea Route
DEM	Discrete Element Method
FEM	Finite Element Method
SPH	Smoothed Particle Hydrodynamics
BEM	Boundary Element Method
MPM	Material Point Method
NDEM	Non-Smooth Discrete Element Method
CFD	Computational Fluid Dynamics
MIZ	Marginal Ice Zone
DOF	Degree of Freedom
PMM	Planar Motion Mechanism

CMT	Circular Motion Tests
GJK	Gilbert–Johnson–Keerthi (algorithm)
SAP	Sweep and Prune (algorithm)
AABB	Axis-Aligned Bounding Box
RK4	Fourth-Order Runge–Kutta Method

References

1. Kujala, P.; Goerlandt, F.; Way, B.; Smith, D.; Yang, M.; Khan, F.; Veitch, B. Review of risk-based design for ice-class ships. *Mar. Struct.* **2019**, *63*, 181–195. [CrossRef]
2. Chen, X.; Wei, C.; Xin, Z.; Zhao, J.; Xian, J. Ship detection under low-visibility weather interference via an ensemble generative adversarial network. *J. Mar. Sci. Eng.* **2023**, *11*, 2065. [CrossRef]
3. Chen, X.; Ma, F.; Wu, Y.; Han, B.; Luo, L.; Biancardo, S.A. MFMDepth: MetaFormer-based monocular metric depth estimation for distance measurement in ports. *Comput. Ind. Eng.* **2025**, *207*, 111325. [CrossRef]
4. Guo, R.; Xiao, G.; Zhang, C.; Li, Q. A study on influencing factors of port cargo throughput based on multi-scale geographically weighted regression. *Front. Mar. Sci.* **2025**, *12*, 1637660. [CrossRef]
5. Wang, T.; Xiao, G.; Li, Q.; Biancardo, S.A. The impact of the 21st-Century Maritime Silk Road on sulfur dioxide emissions in Chinese ports: Based on the difference-in-difference model. *Front. Mar. Sci.* **2025**, *12*, 1608803. [CrossRef]
6. Xiao, G.; Amamoo-Otoo, C.; Wang, T.; Li, Q.; Biancardo, S.A. Evaluating the impact of ECA policy on sulfur emissions from the five busiest ports in America based on difference in difference model. *Front. Mar. Sci.* **2025**, *12*, 1609261. [CrossRef]
7. Lewis, J.W.; Edwards, R.Y., Jr. *Methods for Predicting Icebreaking and Ice Resistance Characteristics of Icebreakers*; The National Academies of Sciences, Engineering, and Medicine: Washington, DC, USA, 1970.
8. Lindquist, A. Straightforward method for calculation of ice resistance of ships. In Proceedings of the POAC'89, Lulea, Sweden, 12–16 June 1989.
9. Riska, K.; Patey, M.; Kishi, S.; Kamesaki, K. Influence of ice conditions on ship transit times in ice. In Proceedings of the International Conference on Port and Ocean Engineering Under Arctic Conditions, Ottawa, ON, Canada, 12–17 August 2001.
10. Jeong, S.Y.; Choi, K.; Kim, H.S. Investigation of ship resistance characteristics under pack ice conditions. *Ocean Eng.* **2021**, *219*, 108264. [CrossRef]
11. Huang, L.; Li, Z.; Ryan, C.; Ringsberg, J.W.; Pena, B.; Li, M.; Ding, L.; Thomas, G. Ship resistance when operating in floating ice floes: Derivation, validation, and application of an empirical equation. *Mar. Struct.* **2021**, *79*, 103057. [CrossRef]
12. Han, K.; Zhang, Y.; Ye, L.; Guo, C.; Wang, C. Experimental research on propeller-ice contact process and prediction of extreme ice load. *Ocean Eng.* **2023**, *287*, 115912. [CrossRef]
13. Zhou, L.; Gu, Y.; Ding, S.; Liu, R. Prediction of ice-resistance distribution for R/V Xuelong using measured sea-ice parameters. *Water* **2022**, *14*, 517. [CrossRef]
14. Jeon, S.; Kim, Y. Numerical simulation of level ice–structure interaction using damage-based erosion model. *Ocean Eng.* **2021**, *220*, 108485. [CrossRef]
15. Kim, J.H.; Kim, Y.; Kim, H.S.; Jeong, S.Y. Numerical simulation of ice impacts on ship hulls in broken ice fields. *Ocean Eng.* **2019**, *182*, 211–221. [CrossRef]
16. Wang, C.; Hu, X.; Tian, T.; Guo, C.; Wang, C. Numerical simulation of ice loads on a ship in broken ice fields using an elastic ice model. *Int. J. Nav. Archit. Ocean Eng.* **2020**, *12*, 414–427. [CrossRef]
17. Kim, J.; Yoon, D.H.; Choung, J. Numerical study of ship hydrodynamics on ice resistance during ice sheet breaking. *Ocean Eng.* **2024**, *308*, 118285. [CrossRef]
18. Xing, W.; Cong, S.; Ling, X.; Li, X.; Cheng, Z.; Tang, L. Numerical study of ice loads on different interfaces based on cohesive element formulation. *Sci. Rep.* **2023**, *13*, 14434. [CrossRef]
19. Makarov, O.; Bekker, A.; Li, L. Comparative analysis of numerical methods for the modeling of ice–structure interaction problems. *Contin. Mech. Thermodyn.* **2022**, *34*, 1621–1639. [CrossRef]
20. Li, Z.; Liu, Y.; Sun, S.; Lu, Y.; Ji, S. Analysis of ship maneuvering performances and ice loads on ship hull with discrete element model in broken-ice fields. *Chin. J. Theor. Appl. Mech.* **2013**, *45*, 868–877.
21. Polojärvi, A.; Tuhkuri, J.; Gong, H. Comparison of full-scale and DEM simulation data on ice loads due to floe fields on a ship hull. In Proceedings of the International Conference on Port and Ocean Engineering Under Arctic Conditions, Moscow, Russia, 14–18 June 2021; Luleå Tekniska Universitet: Luleå, Sweden, 2021.
22. Mucha, P. Fully-coupled CFD-DEM for simulations of ships advancing through brash ice. In Proceedings of the SNAME Maritime Convention, Tacoma, WA, USA, 30 October–2 November 2019; SNAME: Alexandria, VA, USA, 2019; p. D023S004R005.

23. Huang, L.; Tuhkuri, J.; Igrec, B.; Li, M.; Stagonas, D.; Toffoli, A.; Cardiff, P.; Thomas, G. Ship resistance when operating in floating ice floes: A combined CFD&DEM approach. *Mar. Struct.* **2020**, *74*, 102817. [CrossRef]
24. Tang, X.; Zou, M.; Zou, Z.; Li, Z.; Zou, L. A parametric study on the ice resistance of a ship sailing in pack ice based on CFD-DEM method. *Ocean Eng.* **2022**, *265*, 112563. [CrossRef]
25. Hu, B.; Liu, L.; Wang, D.Y. Prediction of performance of a non-icebreaking ship in marginal ice zone. *J. Hydrodyn.* **2022**, *34*, 315–328. [CrossRef]
26. Xie, C.; Zhou, L.; Ding, S.; Liu, R.; Zheng, S. Experimental and numerical investigation on self-propulsion performance of polar merchant ship in brash ice channel. *Ocean Eng.* **2023**, *269*, 113424. [CrossRef]
27. Xue, Y.; Zhong, K.; Ni, B.Y.; Li, Z.; Bergström, M.; Ringsberg, J.W.; Huang, L. A combined experimental and numerical approach to predict ship resistance and power demand in broken ice. *Ocean Eng.* **2024**, *292*, 116476. [CrossRef]
28. Zou, M.; Tang, X.J.; Zou, L.; Zou, Z.J.; Zhang, X.S. Numerical investigations of the restriction effects on a ship navigating in pack-ice channel. *Ocean Eng.* **2024**, *305*, 117968. [CrossRef]
29. Mierke, D.; Janssen, D.; Rung, T. GPU-accelerated large-eddy simulation of ship-ice interactions. In Proceedings of the MARINE VI: VI International Conference on Computational Methods in Marine Engineering, Rome, Italy, 15–17 June 2015; CIMNE: Barcelona, Spain, 2015; pp. 850–861.
30. Lubbad, R.; Løset, S. A numerical model for real-time simulation of ship–ice interaction. *Cold Reg. Sci. Technol.* **2011**, *65*, 111–127. [CrossRef]
31. van den Berg, M.; Lubbad, R.; Løset, S. An implicit time-stepping scheme and an improved contact model for ice-structure interaction simulations. *Cold Reg. Sci. Technol.* **2018**, *155*, 193–213. [CrossRef]
32. Yang, B.; Sun, Z.; Zhang, G.; Wang, Q.; Zong, Z.; Li, Z. Numerical estimation of ship resistance in broken ice and investigation on the effect of floe geometry. *Mar. Struct.* **2021**, *75*, 102867. [CrossRef]
33. Zhan, D.; Molyneux, D. 3-dimensional numerical simulation of ship motion in pack ice. In Proceedings of the International Conference on Offshore Mechanics and Arctic Engineering, Rio de Janeiro, Brazil, 1–6 July 2012; American Society of Mechanical Engineers: New York, NY, USA, 2012; Volume 44939, pp. 407–414.
34. Zhou, Q.; Peng, H.; Qiu, W. Numerical investigations of ship–ice interaction and maneuvering performance in level ice. *Cold Reg. Sci. Technol.* **2016**, *122*, 36–49. [CrossRef]
35. Di, S.C.; Wang, Q.; Xue, Y.Z.; Li, J.L. Manoeuvrability Analysis of an Icebreaker Based on Discrete Element Metho. *Eng. Mech.* **2018**, *35*, 249–256.
36. Yang, B.; Zhang, G.; Rao, H.; Wang, S.; Yang, B.; Sun, Z. Numerical simulation of the maneuvering performance of ships in broken ice area. *Ocean Eng.* **2024**, *294*, 116783. [CrossRef]
37. Yasukawa, H.; Sakuno, R. Application of the MMG method for the prediction of steady sailing condition and course stability of a ship under external disturbances. *J. Mar. Sci. Technol.* **2020**, *25*, 196–220. [CrossRef]
38. Yasukawa, H. Simulations of ship maneuvering in waves (1 st report: Turning motion). *J. Jpn. Soc. Nav. Archit. Ocean Eng.* **2006**, *4*, 127–136.
39. Yasukawa, H.; Yoshimura, Y. Introduction of MMG standard method for ship maneuvering predictions. *J. Mar. Sci. Technol.* **2015**, *20*, 37–52. [CrossRef]
40. Zhang, W.; Zou, Z.J.; Deng, D.H. A study on prediction of ship maneuvering in regular waves. *Ocean Eng.* **2017**, *137*, 367–381. [CrossRef]
41. Lee, J.H.; Kim, Y. Study on steady flow approximation in turning simulation of ship in waves. *Ocean Eng.* **2020**, *195*, 106645. [CrossRef]
42. Zhang, Z.; Zhang, X.; Zhang, H.; Bu, S.; Zou, Z. Numerical evaluation of turning performance of ships in regular and long-crested irregular waves. *Ocean Eng.* **2024**, *308*, 118201. [CrossRef]
43. Sharkawy, A.N.; Koustoumpardis, P.N.; Aspragathos, N. Human–robot collisions detection for safe human–robot interaction using one multi-input–output neural network. *Soft Comput.* **2020**, *24*, 6687–6719. [CrossRef]
44. Mahmoud, K.H.; Sharkawy, A.N.; Abdel-Jaber, G. Development of safety method for a 3-DOF industrial robot based on recurrent neural network. *J. Eng. Appl. Sci.* **2023**, *70*, 44. [CrossRef]
45. Stewart, D.E.; Trinkle, J.C. An implicit time-stepping scheme for rigid body dynamics with inelastic collisions and coulomb friction. *Int. J. Numer. Methods Eng.* **1996**, *39*, 2673–2691. [CrossRef]
46. Yulmetov, R.; Lubbad, R.; Løset, S. Planar multi-body model of iceberg free drift and towing in broken ice. *Cold Reg. Sci. Technol.* **2016**, *121*, 154–166. [CrossRef]
47. Kim, H.; Daley, C.; Colbourne, B. A numerical model for ice crushing on concave surfaces. *Ocean Eng.* **2015**, *106*, 289–297. [CrossRef]
48. Metrikin, I. A software framework for simulating stationkeeping of a vessel in discontinuous ice. *Model. Identif. Control* **2014**, *35*, 211–246. [CrossRef]

49. Zhang, Z.; Li, Z.; Du, Y.; Jiang, X. A rapid motion forecast strategy for ships in waves using seakeeping and maneuvering modules. *Ocean Eng.* **2024**, *309*, 118539. [CrossRef]
50. Yasukawa, H. Simulations of ship maneuvering in waves: 2nd report: Zig-zag and stopping maneuvers. *J. Jpn. Soc. Nav. Archit. Ocean Eng.* **2008**, *7*, 163–170. [CrossRef]
51. Lu, W.; Lubbad, R.; Løset, S. In-plane fracture of an ice floe: A theoretical study on the splitting failure mode. *Cold Reg. Sci. Technol.* **2015**, *110*, 77–101. [CrossRef]
52. Lu, W.; Lubbad, R.; Løset, S. Out-of-plane failure of an ice floe: Radial-crack-initiation-controlled fracture. *Cold Reg. Sci. Technol.* **2015**, *119*, 183–203. [CrossRef]
53. Lu, W.; Lubbad, R.; Løset, S.; Kashafutdinov, M. Fracture of an ice floe: Local out-of-plane flexural failures versus global in-plane splitting failure. *Cold Reg. Sci. Technol.* **2016**, *123*, 1–13. [CrossRef]

MDPI AG
Grosspeteranlage 5
4052 Basel
Switzerland
Tel.: +41 61 683 77 34

Journal of Marine Science and Engineering Editorial Office
E-mail: jmse@mdpi.com
www.mdpi.com/journal/jmse

MDPI

www.ingramcontent.com/pod-product-compliance
Lightning Source LLC
Chambersburg PA
CBHW061618220926
51850CB00005B/542